Human

Relations

in

Management

TEXT AND READINGS

by

I. L. HECKMANN, JR., PH.D.
Department of Management
University of Illinois

S. G. HUNERYAGER, M.S.
Department of Management
University of Illinois

published by

SOUTH-WESTERN PUBLISHING CO.

Cincinnati 27   Chicago 5
Burlingame, Calif.   Dallas 2
New Rochelle, N. Y.

P15

Library of Congress Catalog Card No.: 60-8320

H260

Printed in the United States of America

PREFACE

An understanding of the basic nature of any function in a business organization, whatever that function may be, cannot be acquired simply by obtaining knowledge of the tools and techniques used to carry out that function. Nor can understanding be acquired by accumulating knowledge of only the theoretical and philosophical aspects of the activity concerned. Instead, a thorough understanding of the fundamental nature of any function requires an absolute integration of knowledge concerning what the function is, what it does, who is responsible for it, and so on.

It is therefore obvious that integrated knowledge of the human relations discipline is necessary to understand the inherent nature of this important managerial function. Unfortunately, when the student of human relations begins his quest for knowledge in this area, he soon finds himself handicapped by the absence of literature that would help him integrate the myriad facets of this subject. As a consequence, what he learns is a quantity of information concerning some parts of human relations, but little concerning the totality of the function itself. The net result, of course, is frequently a conceptual framework of human relations that is built on an extremely weak foundation.

The basic purpose of this book is to present to the reader an integrated view of the fundamental and foundational aspects of human relations. As such, the book is designed to explore in detail those areas that are most significant to this field. Beginning with a broad, general introduction to human relations as an emerging discipline, all-important subjects such as leadership, motivation, organization, communication, and so forth, are considered with the view not only that they are important areas in and of themselves, but also that they are mainly parts of a unified whole. It is hoped that this approach will facilitate the reader's understanding of the nature of the discipline of human relations. And since the practice of any function is correlated with one's knowledge and understanding of the function concerned, it is likewise hoped that this approach will contribute to an increase in the reader's effectiveness in practicing human relations at work and in his everyday life.

In order to facilitate its purpose, this book is designed so that it can be used in a number of ways in the academic and business worlds. It is constructed, for example, so that it can be efficiently used as a basic textbook in human relations in liberal arts colleges, colleges of commerce and business administration, and so on. On the other hand, its design makes it very convenient to use as a supplementary text in a case or problems course in human relations, personnel management, or related courses. Concerning this latter point, most of the articles that have been included in this book have been assigned as readings and have been subjected to intensive comment and analysis in a case course in human relations and a basic course in personnel management taught by the authors. In either case, it is hoped that the questions at the end of each article and at the end of each part will be used to strengthen the reader's understanding of human relations.

For the business world, this book is designed so that it can be effectively used as a basic text or reference book for industrial training courses and management development programs. In addition, it is hoped that the busy executive, who, like the student, does not have time to search out, obtain, and read the significant articles in the field, will find this book useful for increasing his knowledge and understanding of, and consequently the effectiveness of his practice of, human relations.

We should like to express our gratitude to the many authors and publishers who so cooperatively granted permission to reprint the articles used in this book. In particular, we should like to thank the American Management Association for its cooperation. Professor M. J. Mandeville, University of Illinois, also deserves our sincere thanks for his advice, assistance, and encouragement.

I. L. HECKMANN, JR.
S. G. HUNERYAGER

CONTENTS

PART 1. HUMAN RELATIONS

The concept of human relations

For the past fifteen years there have been few terms more frequently used, more badly twisted, and more misunderstood than the term "human relations." Indeed, these two words have been subjected to such a variety of uses by so many different people that one wonders whether the term has any common meaning whatsoever.

To illustrate, when attempting to define "human relations," writers will use such nebulous terminology as "the interrelationships among people," "group interaction," "the golden rule in action," "relations between employees and employers," "high-level personnel administration," and others. Replies will range here from one extreme to the other—from those who refuse to give any definition whatsoever to those who use the phrase all-inclusively to embrace all aspects of human behavior regardless of specific situations. Hence the student can readily see the semantical difficulties encountered when endeavoring to define, in a few words, a term as broad as "human relations." Definitions, as noted above, are certainly available to anyone who may want to utilize them; however, it is the opinion of the authors that to be able to define this term in a few simple (or confusing) words is of little importance. What is important is that the reader must have a basic understanding—a particular frame of reference—when approaching a subject with a range as comprehensive as is presented by the field of human relations.

As the years have progressed, people in industry and in the academic realm have developed a new orientation towards this subject matter. Now, instead of viewing human relations as a catch-all term—a label on a bottle—increasing emphasis has been accorded to it as a new "discipline" in and of itself. *In short, recognition is now being given to human relations as a systematic, developing body of knowledge devoted to explaining the behavior of industrial man,* be he company president or gatekeeper. Social scientists—men in the behavioral sciences—have been studying the worker and his work for many years. The majority of our knowledge in this area is certainly not new; but the attempt to synthesize it into a systematic whole is of recent vintage, albeit much still remains to be accomplished.

It is the intent of this book to draw together knowledge, research, and ideas of leading practitioners and students of the human relations field supplemented by viewpoints of the authors. Some of the material reaches far back into time to show that a great deal of our knowledge of the worker is far from being new or recent; some of it is highly critical of accepted ideas and stresses the necessity for even further research and experimentation in the laboratory and in the factory. All in all, it should provide much food for thought.

Historical background of the human relations movement in industry

A major difficulty in presenting historical facts is the period of time to choose as a starting point. This difficulty does not escape us here. To pinpoint an exact date, year, or even decade and say that this was when the human relations movement in industry was ordained and to trace its path from there on is impossible. Obviously, certain relationships have always existed between employer and employee.

It was not, however, until the latter part of the nineteenth century that much attention was given to the human element in business. Previous to this, the era of the corporate mogul held forth, with the principal approach to labor being that of the commodity concept of earlier economists, namely, that workers were something to be bought and sold in the market place with only isolated attention being given to them as human beings. Labor unions were struggling for survival, and the humble laborer had to face his pitiful lot of long hours, low wages, and miserable working conditions.

Then, around the turn of the century, Frederick Taylor, along with other lesser known but equally important figures, pioneered the "scientific management" movement. This movement, aimed at systematizing managerial practices and stressing research, standards, and controls in the operation of a business firm, seized industry with a fervor. Indeed, the mass production era had appeared.

Criticism has been levied at Taylor and his contemporaries on the basis that their preachments tended to exploit the worker more than they benefited him. Much was made of the fact that Taylor, in his original efforts, overlooked the social aspects of a man's job and the satisfactions that men must realize in their work. This is the major point of Georges Friedmann's article. His claim is that scientific management ignored the worker as an integrated personality and was more intent on discipline and control rather than morale. The worker was viewed solely as an individual; little if any recognition was given to the complex social network that comprises any organization of human beings.

But in all fairness to Taylor and his associates in the scientific management movement, it should be pointed out that they did not, as such, overlook the human element in industry. What they did overlook was the relationship of the individual working man to the work group of which he was a part, and it remained for later "pioneers" to demonstrate the tremendous influence these interpersonal relationships have upon industrial productivity and morale.

Not until the decade of the 1920's did the slowly evolving "humanistic" movement take a turn for the better. The major focal point here, as any student of management well knows, was the ever-famous Hawthorne Studies conducted by Elton Mayo and colleagues. From this study emerged the first truly objective proof of the positive correlation between productivity and employee participation in the decisions affecting him and his work. In short, Mayo and later colleagues concluded that the factory was a social system in and of itself, and that informal groupings in the work situation had a dramatic and vital part to play in the industrial picture. No more was the worker to be viewed solely as a "factor of production" —rather, he had now become a human being, with wants, desires, attitudes, and feelings vitally affecting his productive usefulness. Although much criticism has been levied at the methods used by Mayo and his associates, the conclusions of their study, nevertheless, stand out as a landmark in the ensuing human relations movement.

Other contributing factors in this same time period may be enumerated briefly. This was the era of paternalism and welfare management. Employment departments, later called personnel departments, had been instituted by many companies to cope with employee turnover, trade unionism, and problems of selection, and to research new frontiers in employee relations. Oliver Sheldon, writing early in that decade, stressed that the human element had been neglected in industry and that techniques had taken precedence over leadership, understanding, and cooperation. He emphasized the necessity for a professional approach to the human problems of the business environment. Thus there was a dawning awareness on the part of many businessmen of a growing body of thought and knowledge directed towards this human resource.

Interest waned somewhat during the 1930's because of the depression; but with the impetus of resurgent and militant unionism after passage of the Wagner Act, once again business attention was turned

towards workers and human resources. World War II and postwar
business expansion encouraged what was by that time an exploding
movement in industry. Countless numbers of studies were being
performed by psychologists, sociologists, anthropologists, and other
social scientists to aid the business world. Corporate management
had taken on an air of professionalization, and personnel management stood at unprecedented heights. Professional managers, both
by force and by choice, recognized the importance of the contributions of social scientists to the direction of men. Slowly but surely,
this movement has crystallized into a form now recognizable as a
definite body of knowledge. *Today management is explained as being
in part a social process—a process of combining techniques with men
for the mutual benefit of both.*

The interdisciplinary aspects of human relations

It is quite evident from what has preceded that the application
of the term "human relations" to describe a particular body of knowledge raises the question of just where this knowledge originates.
Brief attention should be given to this question, as it is important in
setting the framework for the entire book.

Whenever an attempt is made to explain human behavior in any
set of circumstances, one encounters a rather formidable task. Obviously there are many diverse phenomena affecting man's reactions
to individual situations. Our concern here, however, is the work
environment. The study of man, behavior, and the industrial environment overlaps into many of the social science fields. An attempt to
explain this behavior necessitates an examination of each of these
separate disciplines as a primary step, and then a drawing together
or an integration of knowledge must closely follow. This is the
interdisciplinary approach to human relations.

What fields of study are drawn upon? Indeed, they are varied
and diverse. Human relations is really the application of all the
social science disciplines to the management of men. The fields of
psychology and social psychology, for example, have given us multi-
tudinous amounts of extremely useful concepts concerning the relation
of the individual to his work environment. Testing, job placement,
job satisfaction, incentives, and many more subjects have been re-
searched intensively by psychologists, with resulting valuable contributions to the study of man's behavior and its causes.

Although somewhat overlapping with social psychology and
anthropology, sociologists have certainly made major contributions
with their study of groups, their interrelatedness, and their effects

upon group members. One of the newest yet most fruitful branches of sociology has been the work of the group dynamics people. Their concepts of role structures, status, and informal groupings are vital to the efficacy of industrial organizations. The Hawthorne Study was more of a sociological study than anything else. In retrospect, many of our most recent developments in human relations have stemmed from this area.

Political science is another field providing useful information with relation to organization, power struggles between groups and individuals, and the over-all administrative process. Semantics, one of our newer disciplines, is greatly aiding the field of communications. Industrial engineering virtually speaks for itself. Physiology is making giant contributions in studying monotony, fatigue, boredom, and job placement. Economics and its many branches, especially labor economics, naturally ranks as one of the foremost disciplines contributing to the theory of industrial human relations. All of these and still more have and will continue to make their special contributions to what will someday undoubtedly be a general theory of man and work. Even today, teams of researchers composed of scientists from several of these fields are combining in common efforts on a myriad of projects. Thus new frontiers are breached continuously, and efforts in all directions regarding human behavior and worker motivation are resulting in truly amazing discoveries.

The importance of industrial human relations

With the growth of the human relations movement, increasing emphasis has been given to the worker as a *whole man*. No longer is he viewed solely as an economic tool, but rather as a human being, driven and controlled by diverse elements of society, with fears and frustrations, expectations and desires—all a part of his total make-up. How he performs on his job—his efficiency and productivity—are dependent as much, if not more, on the external aspects surrounding his work place as on the tools and materials he uses.

Therefore, it must be recognized that man as a worker is unique compared to other productive factors. He alone must be *motivated*, not only to do his job, but to strive constantly to improve his performance. This, then, remains the cardinal objective of the human relations function: to discover newer and better ways of understanding man and his relation to his work, of motivating him to higher standards of workmanship, and of helping as many people as possible to realize their maximum potential.

Charles Malik, whose recent speech is reprinted later in this part, although applying the term "human relations" in a much broader sense than most other writers in this book, nevertheless stresses that the future of industrial man and, indeed, the entire world rests with what he terms a "reaffirmation" of human values and morale character. Both managements and workers should strive for individual excellence and satisfaction in work. And it is only by giving recognition to this excellence that companies can truly provide for the positive motivation of employees.

Glen Cleeton takes the same point of view. He advocates that the organization of work must be such that it provides the opportunity for "self-realization" and that work must be made challenging and stimulating to jobholders. He places primary emphasis on worker needs, showing how the causes of job dissatisfaction lead to breakdowns in morale and motivation.

Hence it should become apparent to both the observer and the participant in industrial relations of the necessity for providing proper leadership of people, for providing an organizational "climate" whereby people have the opportunity to find satisfaction and fulfillment in their daily work, for improving communications, for explaining and getting acceptance of necessary changes in policies and procedures, and for getting worker participation and involvement— all of which add up to a stronger and closer identification between worker, work, and manager.

Cognizance should also be given here to another very fundamental point: namely, that the application of effective human relations in an organization is not something that can be compartmentalized or departmentalized. This is not the exclusive job of the personnel department or the public relations function. Nor is it the duty of a select group of individuals somewhere in the company, which is discussed in Alan Filley's article at the end of this part. Quite to the contrary, effective human relations, and all the ramifications of the term, are the primary responsibility of each and every supervisor, manager, and/or executive in the organization. Anyone who directs and supervises others must, of necessity, apply the principles stressed throughout this book. To fail in this regard cannot help but contribute to the malfunctioning of the corporate entity. Perhaps the best summating statement is the oft-repeated phrase: "The end product of all business is people." The more this is accepted, the more promising will be the future of industrial man.

THE PHILOSOPHY OF MANAGEMENT *

Oliver Sheldon

Industry is not a machine; it is a complex form of human association. The true reading of its past and present is in terms of human beings—their thoughts, aims and ideals—not in terms of systems or of machinery. The true understanding of industry is to understand the thoughts of those engaged in it. The advance of science and the cult of efficiency have tended to obscure the fundamental humanity of industry. We have paid in largely to our account of applied industrial science, but we are almost bankrupt of human understanding. The material side of industry has its place, but it is a subordinate one. Indeed, if the fundamental problem of industry can be reduced to the limits of a single question, that question would be: How best can we achieve and maintain a fair balance between the *things* of production—the machines, the buildings, the materials, the systems—and the *humanity* of production—the workers, the foremen, the managers, the shareholders?

This is the problem which is at the root of all the problems facing industrial management. Industry cannot be rendered efficient while the basic fact remains unrecognized that it is primarily human. It is not a mass of machines and technical processes; it is a body of men. It is not a complex of matter, but a complex of humanity. It fulfills its function, not by virtue of some impersonal force, but by human energy. Its body is not an intricate maze of mechanical devices, but a magnified nervous system.

The present industrial "impasse" is due to the subordination of the human to the material element. Whilst our industries have grown increasingly scientific, we are denied the fruits of our efforts, because we have failed to keep pace in the art of human leadership, understanding and co-operation. Pursuing things, we have neglected men. Winning efficiency from our machines, we have forfeited efficiency in our workers. The need of industry is a stronger electrical thrill of common human understanding. "It would be a curious ending to our industrial leadership of the world if the successful conversion of our industries to the needs of the Great War proved to be our last great triumph. At present, it looks as if the reconver-

---

* From Oliver Sheldon, *The Philosophy of Management* (Englewood Cliffs, N. J.: Prentice-Hall, Inc., 1923), pp. 27-30. Reprinted with permission.

sion of our industry to the needs of our life might prove to be beyond our powers." [1]

An industry designed to meet the needs of our life—physical, mental, and moral—must be living. The aim of management must be to render industry more effectively human—more truly a corporate effort of human beings, united for a common object and moved by a common motive. To achieve that end we need, firstly, a motive and an ideal; secondly, leadership and co-ordination; thirdly, work and co-operation. All these factors are interdependent.

In the course of the succeeding chapters, it will appear that the ultimate motive of industry should be that of service to the community; that the art of leadership will develop with the growth of the science and social responsibility of management, and that co-operation will come when the motive, or the ideal, is real and when the leadership is compelling. Only efficient management can justly demand greater efficiency from Labour—and efficiency cannot grow if the partners in industry are trying to realize different ideals. On the other hand, the bond of a great ideal has ever led to the strongest forms of association and the finest achievements. But since to management is entrusted the guidance of industry, it must take the initiative in defining and pursuing that ideal. Management in itself has no axe to grind. Whether the motive of industry be primarily profit or service, and under whatever form it is conducted, management must persist. It is therefore the body from which the setting up of a new ideal may most naturally come. The future of industry rests in its hands.

The background of industry, however, is composed, not only of the thoughts and interests of those engaged in it, but also of the entire mentality of the community to which it stands related. The progress of any section of a community is governed by the progress of the whole. It is impossible to carry out a great scheme of industrial development, founded upon the common humanity of those engaged in industry, unless it is supported by a vivid public feeling, an informed public opinion, and a resolute public will. "It is not consistent with equity or wisdom," said Burke, "to set at defiance

---

[1] *Manchester Guardian.* 6th June, 1921.

Cf. also the address of Hon. James J. Davis, Secretary of Labour, U.S.A., to a convention of the National Hardwood Lumber Association at Philadelphia, 1921.

"This great volume of wealth, this rapid advance, we have been able to achieve in fifty short years by intense application of a genius for the *mechanics* of industry. Now I believe we are to work a new era in the world's progress by applying our national genius to the *humanics*, the human side of industry. . . . Greatly as we have been building, our material resources have still been only partly uncovered. Our *human* resources have hardly been touched at all."

the general feelings of great communities and of all the orders which compose them." The redirection of industry demands what Wells has finely described as "a renascence of thought about political and social things"—"a great deliberate renascence of will and understanding." Nothing short of this can ensure that the turmoil and oscillation of the present will develop into an ordered progress in the future. Without the application of concentrated thought, the unwavering pursuit of a common purpose, and the rigour of infinite and patient effort on the part of all grades and classes of the community, there seems little hope of lasting reconstruction. We may build our Jerusalem or create our Babel. We may discover our Utopia, or yield to Nemesis. The choice between progress and chaos lies before us. We shall achieve the one or fall into the other, according as the intellectual and moral capacities of the people are either brought to bear upon the great task of building a worthy industrial and social future or are allowed to be squandered in the nothingness of little things.

The background of industry is a medley of thought. Springing from a past across which the winds of diverse philosophies have blown, and swept hither and thither by the stormy blasts of war, this thought is left scattered and purposeless. The task of this generation, and of industrial management in particular, is to consolidate and redirect it, so that industry may set out upon the highway to a new era.

QUESTIONS

1. Explain the following statement by Sheldon: "Industry is not a machine; it is a complex form of human association."
2. How does Sheldon relate industrial efficiency to human relations?
3. List and explain the three basic requirements for better human relations in industry as they are presented in this reading.
4. How appropriate do you think Sheldon's writing is in our present industrial environment?
5. Do you agree with Sheldon that the material side of industry is a subordinate one? Subordinate to what? Has there been any significant development along these lines since his writing?

THE VALUE AND LIMITS OF HUMAN RELATIONS *

Georges Friedmann

When the expansion of the means of production through the second industrial revolution necessarily introduced into the factories the scientific management of labor at the end of the nineteenth century, Taylor and his collaborators, and his first imitators, considered the problems of output from the angle of the isolated worker, of the individual. Scientific Management elaborated a methodical group of innovations in the structure and organization of business concerned with the preparation and performance of work, and constantly tried to envelop the worker in an unbreakable network which would compel him to make better use of the machines and to produce more. When all is said and done, it cared very little for the worker's loyalty to its system, as Taylor himself explained to his colleagues of the American Society of Mechanical Engineers: what it required of the worker "is not to produce more by his own *initiative* but to execute punctually the *orders given* extending into the smallest details." More than that, as I have set forth elsewhere one of the chief psychological aspects of Taylorism is precisely the attempt, through the medium of strict individualization of tasks, always to consider the workers "as separate inividuals." Taylor rejected any sort of collective incentive such as co-operation or participation in profits. He affirmed and dogmatically repeated that the basis of human nature is personal interest, and refused to recognize in the worker anything but strictly individualistic motives. The guiding thread of Taylor's attitude was precisely the wish to isolate the worker and separate him from his comrades, and so it need hardly be said that Taylor (and the first generation of those who succeeded him) understood nothing—and wished to understand nothing—of the group forces which have repercussions in the worker's consciousness, especially the trade union influence.

When the social sciences, the physiology of work, and industrial psychology turned to the new field of studies constituted for them by the workshops of large-scale industry (though they very quickly assumed a critical attitude toward the *technicist* methods of Taylorism) they accepted for some time, as an implicit inheritance, the purely individualistic position adopted by the first pioneers of

---

* From Georges Friedmann, *Industrial Society* (Glencoe, Illinois: The Free Press, 1955), pp. 365-372. Reprinted with permission.

rationalization. This is the period I called that of the "human factor," discussed in the first part of this book. We have seen that it probably represented a necessary stage and that a scientific study from the point of view of the bio-psychological constitution of the individual at work, of the problems of fatigue, accidents, rest periods, and the adaptation of the machine to man, has been useful and profitable in many respects.

But even while conducting their experiments and studies, and while disregarding practical conclusions and advice, physiologists and psychologists were already realizing that the exclusive consideration of the individual was not enough. Or rather, as well as the individual considered as a whole, the man at work, the total man with his varied interwoven interests and bonds with his environment, invaded the bio-psychological problems of the workshops, enlarging them, strengthening them, and casting new light on them. From this point of view the studies of monotony, assembly-line work, automation, and skill formed a crossroads from which it was quite clear that the horizons of research had so far been remarkably limited. It was realized that the study of the human factor could not be successful if one confined oneself to considering only the individual's bio-psychological elements. There is no important human problem of the worker at grips with the machine whose examination has not increasingly led to the enrichment and surpassing of a narrowly individualistic bio-psychology, through collective influences.

The gradual shift of the psychologists' attention toward the social factor was especially stimulated by their studies of worker reactions to rationalization. At every step they were impressed, in the enterprise, by the importance of the collective psychology of the industrial group and the human interrelationships among workers, supervisors and management which create an "atmosphere." Seen from this angle, the different methods of control, the calculations of wages and times, the distribution of work periods and rest pauses, become so many important elements which condition the collective mentality of a workshop or firm and, through this, output. Their studies constantly face them with this fundamental fact: the degree of the worker's loyalty to the firm. This I have called integration, in order to indicate that it tends to bring into play the *integral* personality—intellectual, as well as emotional and social. To the investigators this appears more and more as the framework containing particular attitudes and concrete problems. Thus, hostility to rationalized work imposed from above immediately suggests the idea of the participation of worker delegates in the economic and technical management of the firm. Similarly, beneath the phenomenon of slowdowns, or restriction of output, appear causes of an economic and social nature. The psychologists, helping Scientific Management to become more flexible and self-critical, discovered the complexity of the human element. The technicist rationalizer supposed that he could still do without the worker's inner compliance and demanded only that he strictly obey given instructions. This attitude is definitely outmoded. The psychologist showed how important is the worker's psychological share in the methodical changes of his tasks for the practical success of Scientific Management. For this reason he interested himself in discovering what was the worker's inner reaction to measures of rationalization. He confirmed the necessity of effective cooperation and harmony among the various categories of the personnel.

So the human factor was no longer the special preserve of the sciences of man as an abstract individual. But there was still no clear understanding of this advance. It took the human relations movement to make manifest the interpenetration of social and individual factors in the life and organization of the firm.

The human relations movement had developed both on the empirical plane, through the initiative of managers in large corporations, and on the scientific plane, through methodical studies in which teams from the various social sciences collaborated. Both stressed, once and for all the importance of the collective mentality of the personnel, the industrial *esprit de corps*. Both confirmed the fact that the inability of Taylorism to master the difficulties in the application of rationalization was largely due to an underestimation of the psychological problems of the factory. What at first sight seemed to be an obstacle of a technological nature revealed itself, through thorough examination, as an inability to handle men. So from then on a conscious effort was made to introduce psychology into industrial organization; or, more exactly, to influence the worker's behavior by the expedient of carefully studied innovations all aiming at changing the collective state of mind of the firm.

Their common feature was to seek all effective means capable of strengthening the social group constituted by the firm in the face of the other collectivities surrounding it. The protagonists of this movement, less clouded in vision than their predecessors in rationalization, had an inkling (though without clearly recognizing the fact) that the worker belongs not only to the social group formed by the factory, but to other groups also, more or less intimately according to the individual concerned—family, skill group, union, class, political party, nation—and that, in the societies of our time, the different groups (especially the unions and parties) exert a centrifugal and often powerful influence with reference to that of the factory. If it is desired to reinforce the power, cohesion and unity of the firm as a collectivity, it will be a question of opposing and, if possible, neutralizing these centrifugal forces by other, centripetal forces. In each firm the success of human relations will depend on the skillfulness in strengthening the latter by selected means. The same concern is differently expressed by the psychologists when they demand that the worker, who in the original system of Taylorism is never anything but the object of measures of rationalization, should become their subject.

Without straining the point, it is interesting to notice here in passing that in its search for doctrinal foundations the human relations movement tried to find support in the *Gestalt* theory. We have seen psychologists and "personnel counsellors" appeal to the organic whole constituted, according to them, by the organized firm. The rationalizers should try to ensure reciprocal relations between different department and workshops, and a mutual adjustment of their activities to one another, so that they will not form a mere conglomerate but a functional whole, in which the collective spirit will by this very fact be disseminated into all the parts. Thus one would ensure the unity of the enterprise, would create for it an *esprit de corps* and obtain the co-operation of its members. Yet a philosophical theory (even so rich and deep a one as that of *Gestalt*), thus imposed from the outside upon industrial problems, can hardly do more than give rise to verbal developments and illusory solutions. This may be estimated by reading this extract from an author with such a viewpoint: "When employers and employees are willing to sit down together to try to solve their problems rather than to bargain on the basis of who possesses the greater economic power of the moment, then we shall be on the road to settling 'the labor question.'"

But other counsellors in industrial relations, without troubling to find ideological foundations for their efforts, aimed only at directly affecting the managerial state of mind through a whole range of practical measures: by spreading a new idea of the functions and attitude of the supervisory personnel; definining and educating a new type of industrial leader; seeking for the integration of the worker but also of the employer, engineer, and foreman; and making experiments with the role played by sport clubs, factory committees, methods of wage payment and profit-sharing, and the division of the firm into semi-autonomous workshops. The repercussion of all these elements of integration upon the liberation of the worker's physical and mental potential and, by this means, upon the quantity and quality of output, conscientiousness, and job satisfaction, has been recognized since then. Having begun with strictly technological methods which were content to bend the worker to their rigorous discipline, Scientific Management, thus renovated, tries to *conquer* him by methods based on social psychology. It tries to reinforce his participation in the firm and for this purpose to develop a "morale" within it, to unify it and reshape it through a spirit of community. Formerly, in Taylor's day, the watchword was *discipline*. Now it is *morale*. The change from one to the other is a measure of the trend toward social psychology which we have pointed out in the course of these pages. By the very tenacity of their efforts, the champions of the movement admit the setback to the technicist tendencies of Taylorism, and the inadequacy of the strictly bio-psychological tendencies of the human factor approach. They recognize that all the practical chances of rationalization are endangered if they do not solve the problems of collective psychology presented by rationalization's practical application.

Their effort has not been without results, as appears from the experiments of Western Electric, Bat'a and many others, both in America and Europe. The contrary would have been surprising. The human relations movement bears witness to a more complete and deeper consciousness of realities and problems on the part of managements and their advisors on organization. Above all, by trying to discover and develop collective counterforces capable of strengthening the worker's loyalty to the firm, it has put its finger on a sensitive point in industrial conflicts wtihin our civilization. It is incontestable that an intelligent and well-advised management, if it directs its attention and resources toward this goal, can succeed in strengthening the bonds of collective mentality within the firm and, by this means, succeed in affecting the workers' behavior. However, as has been said above, if it is to be successful the power of the other social groups to which the worker belongs (primarily class, party, and union) must not be so great under the given historical circumstances that it exceeds that of the business collectivity, even when reinforced, or in other words, so great that the centripetal influences would be incapable of counterbalancing the entire range of centrifugal influences.

Also, even assuming that the economic and social conditions are not too unfavorable, it is possible that the creation of this *esprit de corps* has certain factual limitations which the human relations movement has been unable to discern. This is Geiger's suggestion when he observes with great insight that if the modern firm, as an organizational and technical entity, penetrates positively into the worker's consciousness, it is always felt negatively as a typically capitalist milieu of production. And though Otto Lipmann recognizes the possibility of a certain degree of integration of the worker with the firm, he seems to agree with this clear-sighted opinion when he writes: "The worker does not believe in a community between himself, the employer and the supervisory personnel; he considers the idea a booby-trap." The practical limits of the effort of the human relations movement seem to emerge from these remarks. It may be admitted to have succeeded, in the best cases, in integrating the worker into the firm considered as a collectivity of organization, technology, and social services, but not as an association of men bound by common ends and sentiments, equal in dignity and rights. But when the movement claims to go further than this, when it undertakes the radical transformation of the structure of the firm through management committees, new methods in regard to wages, profit sharing and participation in management, does it not already represent a retreat on the part of the system of industrial production defined in terms of wages and capital, and its inner penetration by another system and other institutions which are in the process of formation? To say that the worker is becoming the *subject* of measures of rationalization, isn't this by the same token to say that he is no longer exclusively a *wage earner?*

In all my publications since *La Crise du Progrès* (Chapter II, "On ne nous demande pas de penser"), I have called attention to the doctrine of the separation of planning and execution of work which, since Taylorism, has characterized most of the systems of Scientific Management throughout the world, and I have emphasized its technical, psychological and moral dangers. Recent developments in mechanization have kept the problem alive up to now (1954) in all industrially developed countries. I shall merely quote the statement of Alexander R. Heron in his remarkable book, *Why Men Work,* especially significant since Mr. Heron is Vice-President of an important firm, the Crown Zellerbach Corporation, in which he directs the industrial relations department, which, under his influence, has created an excellent morale in the firm:

> We shall do a lasting injury to our business and industrial relations if we fail to distinguish between the right to think and the right to decide. Demagogues are confusing our views of this distinction. They are equally dangerous whether they are the demagogues in union management or in business management. When leaders of some of the large industrial unions laid down their demands of 1945 and 1946, those

demands contained the type of program which would have permitted several members of the football team to call the signals on the field. When leaders of management deny in action that they can accept the value of worker thinking without surrendering the responsibility for decisions, they are equally shortsighted.

If the organization of business and industry is to function effectively, the obligation to make decisions must be centralized within each operating unit, large and small. But if those decisions are to be effectively carried out, the decisions themselves must be made on the basis of all available thinking which is pertinent.

We cannot hope to have a healthy American business body, an effective industrial organism, composed of distinctly separate units distinguished as the *workers* and the *thinkers*. We cannot expect teamwork from 90 per cent of the team members if we insist on telling them that their function is to work, ours to think.[1]

---

[1] Without confusing situations and environments which are very different in character, it is important to observe here that similar problems arise within the present framework of Soviet industry. In the words of the journal of the Young Communists of the U.S.S.R. (*Komsomolskaia Pravda*, July 17, 1953): "There are in our country many students for whom there is a gulf separating the work of an engineer from that of an ordinary worker, and who have nothing but contempt for those who are engaged in production. In their opinion it is the exclusive task of the engineer to make plans and that of the worker to carry them out."

Among the many articles which have been published in France on the subject of "human relations" may be mentioned that of Michel Crozier, "Human Engineering," in *Les Temps Modernes*, July, 1951, and that of P. Fraisse and Y. Guibourg in *Esprit*, May, 1953.

QUESTIONS

1. How does Friedmann sum up Taylor's approach to the management of people?
2. What does Friedmann mean by the term "integration"? To what extent does this coincide with our current concepts of industrial morale?
3. What contributions have psychologists made to the advancement of human relations? What are some of the shortcomings of the psychologist in his study of man at work?
4. Friedmann talks extensively of the group and its influence on the worker. Explain how he links group membership with motivation.
5. Critically evaluate this article in terms of your own work experience. Do you feel that the goals of workers and management must always be at opposite ends? Why or why not?

THE HUMAN FACTOR IN INDUSTRY *

Glen U. Cleeton

THE BASIS OF SATISFACTION IN WORK

A generation ago leaders in industry began to give explicit attention to problems of production efficiency. Marked progress has been made in the determination of minimal time requirements in work performance and in the establishment of patterns for the simplification and standardization of motions made by the worker in performing job operations. However, the human factors in industry over and above the routines of job performance are frequently neglected. Consequently, the inherent challenge of work as a normal human activity is often dissipated to such an extent that many industrial jobs become dull and uninteresting, if not, indeed, frustrating.

Through methods study, involving time and motion analysis, mechanical efficiency of production has been greatly improved. Obviously, mechanical efficiency is an appropriate management objective because it leads to greater productivity and thereby benefits all consumers, including the workers who are the producers. But mere production efficiency as such is remote satisfaction to the worker because he responds to his work in terms of personalized desires and needs.

In addition to basic physical needs, every worker has certain desires which he, as a human being, seeks to satisfy to some degree in the activities of day-to-day living. Among these are: (1) the need to share thoughts and feelings with others; (2) the need for dominance—power in exercising control over persons and other elements in one's environment; (3) the need for self-determination—individuality and independence; (4) the need for achievement, acquisition, and possession; (5) the need for approbation—recognition and admiration by others; and (6) the need for ideation—realistic, autistic, projective.[1]

If opportunity to satisfy desires in addition to those relating to physical needs is not provided in work activities, and if the worker finds no supplementary means of giving expression to these motivating forces, feelings of frustration may develop which encourage

* From *The Annals of the American Academy of Political and Social Science*, Vol. 274 (March, 1951), pp. 17-24. Reprinted with permission.

[1] For a discussion of the nature of these desires and their relation to morale and motivation see Glen U. Cleeton, *Making Work Human* (Yellow Springs, Ohio: Antioch Press, 1949), pp. 15-100.

compensatory behavior inimical to good work performance. Through the effects of frustration the worker may become sufficiently maladjusted to be considered by management as a "chronic troublemaker." To prevent worker maladjustment, management must seek the attainment of its production objectives in ways which permit the worker to satisfy normal human desires through work activities.

Economic emphasis

Unfortunately, industrial organization is fundamentally economic and places emphasis on monetary rewards for work which supply only the means of satisfying physical wants and needs. Obviously, the primary purpose of the worker who seeks employment is to obtain purchasing power with which to satisfy physical needs. Furthermore, the frank purpose of the employer is to profit by the worker's efforts. Consideration of the monetary reward to the worker and the gain of the employer from such work is inescapable. However, through preoccupation with material motivation, both workers and employers frequently fail to grasp the significance of the spiritual values of work. Hence, there is often mutual failure to recognize that work should provide opportunity for individual self-realization which would contribute to the personal and social adjustment of the worker.[2]

General disregard for the spiritual values of work has produced numerous work relations situations in which greed is rampant, tensions are acute, and group conflicts are in daily evidence. In recent years because of disputes between employers and workers, strikes and lock-outs have been of such frequent occurrence as to indicate a distinctly unhealthy social situation—one which may explode into violence of an uncontrollable nature unless ways of producing greater satisfaction in work for its own sake are found and utilized. Furthermore, to reach the heart of the problem of human relations in industry, employers and workers must find a basis for developing mutual respect for the desires and needs of each other.[3]

Mental and emotional considerations

To understand problems of human relations in industry, employers must recognize that frequently tasks performed are not the most

---

[2] For a discussion of psychological satisfactions in work see "Self-Realization Through Work" in Cleeton, *op. cit.*, pp. 45-76.

[3] For a discussion of ways and means of making this principle explicit see Robert W. Johnson (Chairman, Board of Directors, Johnson & Johnson), *People Must Live and Work Together—or Forfeit Freedom* (Garden City: Doubleday & Company, Inc., 1947).

important element in work experience; that which transpires in the mind of the worker, both on and off the job, is often of greater significance than job operations in determining work satisfaction. Looking forward to promotion or advancement, considering ways of improving the work environment, overestimating the relative importance of what is being done, seeking acclaim and recognition by others for accomplishment, trying to please a boss who is admired or to be of service to loved ones, trying to achieve a sense of social contribution—mental configurations relating to these self-involved aspirations pass through every worker's mind in the daily performance of his job.

If these mental-emotional patterns are favorably toned, and if the capacity of the worker for ideation is directed into constructive channels, work can be made challenging and interesting to those who perform it. Work activities which, taken by themselves, seem dull and tiresome assume an air of liveliness and sparkle when enriched by hope and constructive thoughtfulness on the part of the worker.

As a human being, every worker consciously or unconsciously seeks a responsive social relationship with his employers and fellow employees. In this respect the worker is favorably motivated by:

   (1) Leadership which he can like, respect, and admire.
   (2) Surroundings which promote physical well-being.
   (3) Acceptance as a recognized member of a group.
   (4) Recognition as an individual, a partner, not a servant.
   (5) Fair treatment in relation to others.
   (6) Reasonable sense of permanency.
   (7) Knowledge of the results of his efforts.
   (8) Knowledge of company plans and policies.
   (9) Approval for special effort or good results.
 (10) Respect for his religious, political, moral, and social beliefs.
 (11) Evidence that other workers are doing their share of total production.
 (12) A friendly social atmosphere in which he is considered with respect by his fellow workers and his supervisors.[4]

OVERCOMING DISSATISFACTION IN WORK

When a person becomes a member of a group he is influenced by the attitudes and opinions of the group. He is affected by and contributes to the morale of the group. This emergence of morale in group relations merits careful recognition by management. From time to time and by various means, management should ascertain the attitudes of workers toward their work and should then try to deter-

---

[4] For a list of qualities of leadership in supervisors and managers to which the worker responds favorably see Cleeton, *op. cit.*, pp. 72-73.

mine the probable effect of these attitudes on productivity. When
determined, if unfavorable, probable causes should be sought and
corrective action taken. The causes most often found are poor
leadership, unpleasant or uncomfortable working conditions, and
opinions which conflict with management policy.

Sometimes, the sources of attitude conflict will be found to
generate from strongly held views by one or more individual members of the group. When such is the case, carefully planned handling
of the situation becomes necessary, particularly if the troublemakers
have organized support within the group or from labor leaders outside the group.

A certain amount of dissatisfaction may be expected in any group
because it is human nature to find fault. There will always be things
related to a worker's job, the place and conditions of work, the
worker's associates, supervision, method of wage payment, and special privileges about which there will be intermittent worker complaints. This is a normal phenomenon; in fact, a certain amount of
grousing is evidence of interest in work. Perhaps the grumbler wants
nothing more than an audience; perhaps he really wants nothing
done nor expects that it will be.

However, when feelings with reference to specific circumstances
reach the point of seeming injustice to the worker, or when it appears
to him that there is abuse of control over his life fostered by the
work situation in which he finds himself, he develops attitudes
which result in a sense of grievance. If his feelings thus aroused are
not resolved, the sense of dissatisfaction may become a controlling
factor in his work performance. In turn, he may sensitize negative
attitudes in other workers with whom he is associated, and, through
a sort of chain reaction, a situation may arise in which tensions are
greatly out of proportion to the inciting elements. Obviously, the
resolution of minor grievances tends to reduce the possibility of major
group conflicts.[5]

Establishing a Basis for Mutual Understanding

The maintenance of harmonious human relations in industry
requires that management and workers understand each other's
points of view. To achieve such understanding, methods of communication must exist up and down the line through the entire
hierarchy of authority in the social group which constitutes a

---

[5] This thesis is developed in greater detail in an article by the author entitled,
"Strikes Can be Prevented," *Personnel*, Vol. 27 (July 1950), pp. 80-82.

business firm. In any company where it is taken for granted that information about policies and practices will trickle through an organization simply by being announced at the top, or that understanding arises out of mere knowledge of the existence of such information, an examination of the thinking, attitudes, and behavior patterns of workers and supervisors would bring forth surprising evidence to the contrary.[6]

Differences of interpretation

Even where a written agreement between management and workers exists in the form of a labor contract, the parties to the agreement cannot assume that they understand each other or, for that matter, that they agree with each other simply because they have attempted to set forth their ideas in written form. An experiment in group dynamics conducted by one company clearly demonstrates this point. After long negotiations, compromises, and reconstruction of phrasing, a contract was formulated through collective bargaining in which a sincere effort was made by both sides to arrive at a workable agreement. However, since disputes had arisen during the life of the previous contract, the personnel officer of the company obtained permission to hold a meeting to discuss the application of the provisions of the new contract in terms of day-to-day operations.

Attending the meeting were representatives of top management, department heads, foremen, union officials, and union stewards. The contract was read and discussed paragraph by paragraph in relation to operations. The differences in interpretation brought to light were surprising and disturbing. In fact, the differences were so great that it appeared unlikely that mutually acceptable interpretations could be reached. However, through patient deliberations involving four sessions of several hours each, reasonable unanimity was achieved.

Results of intergroup discussions

Important conclusions may be drawn from the foregoing example and other instances of intergroup discussions:

(1) Without being aware of differences in understanding until a crisis arises, top management and its supervisory staff may differ with

---

[6] For an expository treatment of the concept of the business firm as a social organism and illustrations of the operation of intergroup communication see Burleigh B. Gardner and David G. Moore, *Human Relations in Industry* (Rev. ed., Chicago: Richard D. Irwin, 1950).

each other on the interpretation of labor contract provisions, management policy, and operating practices unless mutual understanding and agreement are reached through group discussion.

(2) Management and its representatives may differ with union officials
and their agents on the interpretation of matters already agreed
upon in substance unless these are discussed in the light of possible
application.

(3) Although the cleavage at the outset of intergroup discussions
usually places management and its representatives on one side and
workers and their representatives on the opposite side, continuation
of the discussions brings a realignment of groups, which paves the
way for mutual understanding.

(4) Through discussions by groups of nonhomogeneous interests, clearer
understanding can be attained and a basis for more harmonious
intergroup relationships can be established if such discussions are
conducted on a level of mutual respect.

(5) Intergroup discussions including different authority levels in a
company frequently become a sort of arbitration in advance of
dispute, thereby forestalling the development of conflict.

(6) Even though issues are not always settled through intergroup
discussions, the elements of difference are at least brought to light
in a manner which permits ameliorating action to be taken.

(7) Collective bargaining is usually more effectively engaged in where
intergroup discussions have been used as a means of solving work
relations problems of a noncontractual nature.

The virtues of intergroup discussion as a technique of attaining
mutual understanding suggest that it should be more widely used as
a tool of human relations in industry. However, if so used, management and its representatives must acquire skill in leadership.

Although opportunity should be given for all participants in a
conference to express views, a conference should not be permitted
to become a town meeting. Furthermore, both workers and management should agree in advance that intergroup conferences will not
be used as propaganda forums by any of the parties concerned.
Usually the chief task confronting the conference leader is that of
keeping discussions "on the beam" because the thinking of many
persons participating in conferences is of the free association, rather
than controlled association, type. The leader must also recognize
that initially many differences are simply conflicts of desire rather
than disagreement as to the facts or fundamental principles involved.
To overcome this limiting element in group discussions, the conference leader should search for a point of agreement in fact or
principle as a foundation on which to build a superstructure of
constructive group thinking.

Providing Adequate Reward for Work

It is fruitless to talk about capitalizing on the spiritual values of work, adjusting work conditions to provide psychological satisfactions, or promoting mutual understanding between management and workers if income from work does not provide adequately for the physical needs of the worker and his family. But the problem of assuring adequate rewards for work is broader than the provision of satisfactions in work; it is one of paramount social significance, because economic maladjustment of a large number of workers, if uncorrected, could wreck the enterprise system. Paradoxical as it may seem, the private enterprise system stands to suffer more from substandard wages for large masses of our population than from the allegedly high wages against which protest is frequently offered by those seeking to profit through the work of others.

Within recent years the share of the national income paid to workers in the form of wages has shown a gratifying increase. This increase is gratifying not only to recipients of the wages, but to all persons who wish to see the benefits of our industrial society widely distributed, because a reasonably good case can be made for the principle that economic stability depends on the provision of a fair standard of living for the majority of workers.

Minimum standards of adequacy

Definition of a socially acceptable standard of living for workers is extremely difficult. Furthermore, in a period of shifting wage rates and fluctuating price levels, it is even difficult to obtain reliable data on the distribution of wages on a nationwide basis. However, it is estimated that at least 25 per cent of workers have an average income of less than $25 to $30 per week, despite phenomenally high wages earned by members of the skilled crafts and extremely favorable rates currently being paid to workers in many mass production industries. Probably no one conversant with the economics of family living would argue that an average family (three persons) could meet more than subsistence standards on an income of less than $50 to $60 per week. If this assumption is a reasonable one, then at least one-third of American families are trying to live on substandard incomes.

In those private enterprises which pay substandard wages, it seems safe to assume that much could be done to provide a higher reward for the worker through the elimination of waste, and by more intelligent and resourceful management of production and marketing.

To assert, as some representatives of management do in these laggard industries, that wage increases above substandard levels would put them out of business is, of course, a debatable contention. Efforts of the past half century have proved conclusively that lifting wages did not destroy wholesale trade, coal mining, the steel industry, or other industries concerned with the production of electrical goods, automobiles, heavy machinery, printing, petroleum, rubber, and power and light.

Merit differentials

In many industries management has sought to apply the principle that merit in job performance should be rewarded in wage differentials, preferential employment, and upgrading of the individual worker. In applying this principle, it has become evident that there are fundamental differences in the capacities of human beings, as well as differences in the degree to which capacities will be exercised by the worker. Management has sought to measure capacities before employing the worker, has sought to instill in the worker methods of operation which fully utilize his capacities, and has established schemes of differential reward for productivity and general job proficiency.

The techniques employed by management for measuring capacity, training in job performance, and applying incentive rewards have frequently been opposed by workers and their labor organizations. Sometimes this opposition has been based on a difference in philosophy between management and labor leaders, but more often conflict on these issues arises out of misunderstanding primarily due to failure of management to communicate to the worker the reasons for, and the nature of, these techniques. Most workers are not opposed to efficiency of production and variation in individual reward. However, many conflicts arise out of inept attempts by production expediters to attain high production standards.[7]

Providing an adequate reward for work is a twofold problem. In the first place, it is one of general social responsibility for lifting the lower third of wage earners to a real income level which will permit living on a socially acceptable standard of human dignity and decency. In the second place, it is one of individual company

---

[7] For statements of labor's views on this question see: William Gomberg, *A Trade Union Analysis of Time Study* (Chicago: Science Research Associates, 1948); Clinton S. Golden and Harold J. Ruttenberg, *The Dynamics of Industrial Democracy* (New York: Harper & Brothers, 1942); Morris L. Cooke and Philip Murray, *Organized Labor and Production* (New York: Harper & Brothers, 1940).

responsibility for rewarding merit and encouraging individual initiative. These objectives cannot be achieved (1) if productivity is restricted by incompetence of workers, union policies, inadequate production engineering and research, or limitations of management; (2) if an excessively large share of the worker's income is absorbed by taxes; or (3) if national fiscal policy fosters price fluctuations which destroy the purchasing power of wages.

The Control of Tyranny in Human Relations

Despotism in industrial relations has existed in a variety of forms in the past, and continues in evidence in present-day work situations to some extent. The early history of industrial expansion is replete with examples of dominative exploitation of the worker by the employer for the purpose of accumulating capital. This exploitation brought about mutual co-operation by workers to resist domination through the formation of unions. However, in the development of worker organizations dominating personalities have emerged, and in some instances the worker finds himself and his actions controlled with a degree of absolutism considerably beyond that which would be endured if he were given freedom of choice.

To a considerable extent, social gains by workers as a group have been accompanied by insistent propaganda designating capitalistic tyranny as the foe of labor, and the philosophy of the worker-supreme has been offered as the antidote to capitalism. However, in those countries where this philosophy has been carried to its ultimate conclusions, despotism equally as destructive of individual freedom as any other form of political, social, or economic tyranny has been practiced by cliques using the worker as a symbol.

Despotism is abhorrent to the democratic philosophy, whether practiced by entrepreneurs, labor leaders, or government officials. Consequently, means of softening the effect of tyranny have been sought through restrictive and directive legislation. Doubtless mutual good will can accomplish more than legislation in establishing social patterns of democracy in industrial relations. However, public opinion appears to demand further experimentation with labor-management legislation in the hope that a socially acceptable formula for human relations in industry can be established.

Conclusions

From a human relations point of view, the true measure of good industrial relations is the extent to which the sense of human dignity

is preserved and individual initiative is promoted. To this end workers must find satisfaction in work, both physical and psychological;
but psychological satisfactions in work cannot be promoted unless
provision is made for the physical needs of workers through adequate
reward. Group conflict in human relations can be reduced through
cultivation of mutual understanding and elimination of tyranny in
industrial relations through social control.

The ultimate solution to functionally appropriate and reasonably
equitable industrial relations probably cannot be found in legislation.
However, it seems certain that we shall experiment further with
administrative law before abandoning hope for more effective implementation. Perhaps the solution to human relations problems lies in
a better understanding of social institutions on the part of the average
citizen, and clearer recognition by employers and workers of the
fact that each company is in itself an institution in which conflicting
social forces must be brought into harmonious adjustment.

From the standpoint of the scholar interested in human relations
in industry, there is need for (1) an extension of research on the
question of individual adjustment and the possibilities of establishing
work patterns which will bring satisfaction to the worker through
the impact of his total personality in the work situation, and (2)
an extension of research which will provide better understanding of
the group dynamics involved.[8]

---

[8] Cf. Frederick H. Harbison and Robert Dubin, *Patterns of Union-Manage-
ment Relations* (Chicago: Science Research Associates, 1947), and National
Planning Association, case studies on *Causes of Industrial Peace under Collective
Bargaining* (Washington, 1948 to date).

QUESTIONS

1. What are the major components of work satisfaction? Explain in detail.
2. Do you agree with Cleeton about the merits of intergroup discussion for
   attaining mutual understanding? Why or why not?
3. What does Cleeton feel the true test of industrial human relations to be?
4. Why do workers frequently oppose management procedures aimed at
   maximizing worker efficiency?
5. How can management best achieve a balance between the economic interests of workers and noneconomic motivations? Should one take precedence over the other?

HUMAN RELATIONS AND THE
INDUSTRIAL ORDER *

Charles H. Malik

The term "human relations" covers everything. However, in this discussion we are particularly interested in those relations that obtain in the industrial and business world. Critical human relations, sometimes issuing in revolution, have always existed in the economic realm—namely, in the production and distribution of material goods —and man has always had to consider them. We can abundantly find such critical conditions in ancient times among the Greeks and Romans, in the medieval period, in recent centuries, and certainly in the present century. But perhaps there are special conditions calling for special consideration today. The problem is always whether human reason can face a developing situation and adequately meet it; or whether, given man's limitations, including his rigidity, his greed, and his dullness, certain situations so get out of hand that a violent upheaval becomes inevitable. It is always a question of adequacy or bankruptcy of man with respect to his reason and to his powers of accommodation on the basis of justice.

The special conditions which the economic world faces today so far as human relations are concerned include:

a. The general enlightenment of the masses consequent upon the spread of democracy and its attendant processes of education and mass information, resulting in the revolutionary concept of human rights and, therefore, of the equality of all men;

b. The tremendous revolution in science and technology whereby economic productivity is multiplying a thousandfold and, therefore, the creation of wealth virtually knows no limits today;

c. The existence of a militant and successful movement preaching the doctrine of the eternal class struggle;

d. The rise of the underdeveloped peoples of Asia, Africa, and Latin America who can no longer passively acquiesce in their external exploitation and who therefore vigorously demand an equitable share in any economic association they may enter into with the more highly developed countries;

e. A general breakdown in morals and standards whereby people think that cleverness and force determine human existence and that what-

* An address by Dr. Charles H. Malik, President of the General Assembly of the United Nations, presented on February 18, 1959, at the Midwinter Personnel Conference of the American Management Association in Chicago. Copyright, 1959, by the American Management Association. Reprinted with permission.

ever you do, provided you can manage to get away with it, is all right; and

f. The haunting fear of war, leading to profound nervousness and anxiety.

Democracy, science, communism, the awakened underdeveloped peoples, the general breakdown in morals, and the fear of war—these are the six new factors which complicate the problem of human relations in the economic sphere, and indeed in any sphere, beyond anything known in the past.

Maze of fear, danger, and rebellion

Democracy makes people adamant about what they consider their minimum economic rights. Just being human makes a man feel that he is as good as the other fellow and therefore is as much entitled to material enjoyment as he is. An absolute economic law results which can be expressed in two propositions: (a) in a democracy, always, the standard of living of the masses necessarily rises; and (b) to avert trouble, the possibility of this constant rise must always be clearly present.

The phenomenal increase in productivity and therefore the well-nigh infinite multiplication of wealth as a result of science, technology, and rational organization give rise to two problems. The first is whether there is a rational law for the equitable distribution of this wealth, or whether the whole nation of "equitable distribution" has no meaning. This raises questions of prices, wages, relations between capital and labor, relations between the economic process and the government as the source and enforcer of law, and international economic relations. The second problem is simply the excitation of desire when people see this infinite variety of goods on display in shop windows, on radio and television commercials, and in the advertisement pages of magazines and newspapers. Man in his frailty is easily seduced by all this material beckoning and inviting, with the result that his conception of his minimum economic rights is constantly expanding. In modern civilization, then, the principle of desire is constantly stressed without a balancing principle of self-control.

Communism introduces three complications so far as human relations are concerned. Class war is viewed as something eternal, and therefore strain and tension must always exist until the classless society supervenes; a premium is placed on force, violence, and revolution and therefore on complete despair of reason and of concord and agreement between classes; and the civil government is viewed as the agency of justice which, by taking over all means of production, will itself insure the equitable distribution of wealth. If conflict and contradiction belong to the essence of things, and if there is nothing above—and therefore nothing governing and controlling—this limitless play of economic desire, then obviously it is hopeless for those who do not own the means of production to come to an agreement with those who do. There is left for them only the possibility of revolution whereby they will seize the reins of government and themselves avenge justice against those who have so obdurately wronged her—because, being slaves of desire, they could not have helped it! Since understanding and therefore peace between classes are impossible, we have here the acme of hopelessness.

The rise of Asia and Africa accentuates the color problem and to that extent further complicates human relations in modern civilization. Also, the Asians and Africans want either to industrialize themselves and thereby become economically independent of the West or, insofar as considerable economic interdependence must persist between them and the more highly developed countries for a long time to come, to have an equitable if not an equal share in the management of enterprises bearing upon their economies. The age of crude exploitation is completely gone, and there is open before us all today the prospect either of estrangement or of honest cooperation on the basis of equality and mutual respect.

The breakdown in morals manifests itself in the weakening of principle and standard. Conscious ideals of personal excellence are brushed aside in favor either of improvement of the material product (better and better automobiles, for example) or of social progress (longevity, community hygiene, the progress or glory of society or the nation). That a man should seek individual, personal, human excellence whereby he as a person, apart from his profession in life, the excellence of his product, or the glory or misery of the group or nation to which he belongs, may be said to be good or wise or a saint or in tune with something wonderful above this sorry show of endless change and imperfection—that is exceedingly rare.

The new dimensions of war entail new dimensions of anxiety. The Western Hemisphere has been practically insulated from the possibility of invasion for centuries. So were distant parts of the earth such, for example, as Australia, the heart of China, and the heart of Russia. In the past, wars have always occurred between contiguous states, and the Anglo-Saxon world has never been really in danger of being invaded, or at least has never actually been invaded, since 1066. But today all that is entirely swept away. There is no hamlet or back yard in the whole world that may not be the target of sudden devastating attack. The feeling of complete safety and security which the farmer in Nebraska or Siberia used to enjoy is replaced by the sense that he is as much exposed to sudden annihilation as the French or German farmer along the Rhine. One is no longer able to look forward to the future with peace of mind; the future reveals itself as the realm of dread, death, and judgment.

The result of these complicating factors is to create an entirely new situation in which modern man is jittery and unsure of himself, and human relations in the industrial order are plagued with tension, mistrust, and a spirit of defiance. There is the suspicion that somebody is all the time trying to get the better of someone else. Misunderstanding, strikes, and open rebellion abound. Goodwill is thus subverted and poisoned at its source, and there is a marked despair of reason.

Wanted: A reaffirmation of values

What is the way out of this maze of fear, danger, and rebellion? What can be done to help in restoring creative confidence, sanity, and obedience, to human relations?

People at every level are troubled about this problem, and the techniques they have elaborated to cope with it in its many aspects are worthy of respect and adoption. It is always possible to devise better methods of working and living together, of dealing with one another, of treating one another. But the thing is much deeper than method and experiment and technique; it reaches deep down into the spirit of man and the sources of his being.

Nothing need be accepted as impersonal and irresistible fate in human life. We are all absolutely responsible for our fate; and, no matter what and how conditions may develop, we can always do something about them. Not even cosmic changes are beyond the reach, the understanding, and even the control and manipulation of man.

Concerning the fear of war, I can say that the anxiety generated is well founded. But people are not oblivious to this danger; they are not sitting back and saying we can do nothing about it. The whole United Nations is working day and night on how to alleviate tension and promote understanding and peace, and I dread to think where we would be today if the United Nations did not exist. Statesmen all over the world—with American statesmen in the forefront—are devoting more time and energy to this problem than perhaps to any other. If there are terrible inventions aimed at destruction and death, there is also a feverish search for adequate instruments of defense. And we can be sure this search has not been without its rewards. While the so-called "balance of terror" is terrible enough, there is one saving grace about it: so long as it is a reality, neither side will dare strike, for sure and unspeakable retribution would immediately be wreaked upon its head. It is good, also, that those who have never known the fear and danger of invasion and conquest and destruction of home and hearth should now share this chastening emotion which some of us in the old world have known throughout all our history. The urban and industrial areas and the working classes have every reason to be anxious about the future, and it is understandable how human relations have become sour and unhappy as a result, but all these attenuating considerations should help to restore some perspective, some peace, to the human heart.

Concerning the underdeveloped countries, while it is happily true that exploitation now is out of the question, a much more wonderful prospect is opening up—namely, partnership. There is no reason to suppose that corporation laws and regulations are sacrosanct, and in their dealings with Asia, Africa, and Latin America the great Western concerns must henceforth modify their rigidity in favor of much greater flexibility and openness of mind. The concept of nationalization must be viewed as a norm, and whole new systems of partnership between governments and corporations must be sought. The underdeveloped cannot develop themselves without the agency of the developed, and the developed cannot creatively perform this function without the willing consent of the underdeveloped. In this mutuality of need and complementarity of function we have a natural given condition for the development of better human relations. Let people therefore be guided by their higher interests, their higher selves; let them see that the association of equals is far more glorious and stable than the association of superior and native; and let them rise to the joyous level of our common humanity beyond all distinction of race, color, and even culture. In short, let them be men and not mere economic exploiters, and the envy, distrust, and recalcitrance of the underdeveloped, as well as the overweening paternalism of the developed, will be overcome.

The poison introduced into human relations by the doctrine and practice of dialectical materialism is difficult to extirpate. The difficulty stems from the fact that the doctrine has behind it a superbly organized international revolutionary movement. There are only two ways of dealing peacefully with this problem: to prevent the international movement from spreading, and to invalidate Marxist theory and prediction by demonstrating that human nature is not so depraved and the class struggle not so eternal and hopeless as Marx thought them to be. If free society succeeds in developing abundance with justice and without revolution or the loss of the values of freedom, then Marxist prediction goes with the wind. Unless this takes place, Marx will be proved right. But, since Marx and his movement mean, in addition to economic doctrine, atheism and revolution and a radical repudiation of the tested values of the past, it is imperative that he be proved wrong. When wise leadership in the political, the economic, the intellectual, and the spiritual realms grasp all this, it should rise above its blind urges and make a conscious effort to show that Marx was mistaken. Not only is this possible, but it has actually been taking place; for free society has been demonstrating (and perhaps has room to demonstrate even more) its virile adaptability and flexibility; and even Communist society in its development clearly proves that, far from being a god, Marx was a very fallible man indeed.

It is vigorous free society, rediscovering its roots and reaffirming the sources of its life, that can develop healthy and creative human relations in the industrial order and that therefore can face and meet the challenge of war, communism, and the rising East.

In a fundamental sense, certainly all men are born equal and certainly they are entitled by nature to the enjoyment of inalienable rights. But there is such a thing as excellence in workmanship and excellence in moral character, and we are certainly not all equally excellent in these respects. Discontent, distrust, frustration, and rebellion—these will continue plaguing and poisoning human relations until the objective demands of excellence are recognized. If I rise to the challenge of excellence neither in what I do—namely, in my workmanship—nor in what I am—namely, in my character—I should be ashamed to ask for more and more benefits and more and more attention. Only the shame of our failure to measure up to objective standards of excellence can curb our endless demands, can put us in our place and restore sanity and reason to human relations. What is wanted is more shame and therefore more satisfaction, because we all fall so far short of what we should do and what we should be!

Sloppiness in workmanship is the curse of this age. People in the past slaved to produce perfect works of art much more than they do now. They are in a hurry today, they are practical, they have their minds much more on their rights and enjoyments than on their work, their hands shake, their eyes are moist, their minds are misty, and they do not love their work. Human relations in the industrial order will not improve until people, in place of worshiping themselves, worship the objective standard of excellence of their work. Again, what is wanted is pride in excellence and not in mere being!

Carelessness in character is another curse. Surely the clean, the honest, the faithful, the true, the loving, the considerate, the disciplined; the man who rises above the petty and unworthy, who gives himself to great causes, who willingly suffers in secret, who is touched with divine humor—surely this man, even if nobody knows about him and sings his praises, even if his character brings him suffering, is superior to the mean and clever individual who congratulates himself because he gets away with so many rotten things. How can human relations improve without an absolute premium's being placed upon quality of life and solidity of character? And how can this take place without a leaven of people who in the quality of their own life and love put to shame the rest of us who seek only our pleasure? "But if the salt hath lost its savor, wherewith shall it be salted?"

Beyond all techniques and methods, the excellence of human relations is grounded in the family, the university, and the Church. It is these that are at the base of free Western society, and it is their reaffirmation that is most needed today. The family supplies the foundations of character, the school and the university discipline the mind, and the Church provides the fear and love of God without which neither character nor mind can endure. For the family that is based only on natural love will soon degenerate, and the university that knows only human reason will end either in human pride and therefore despair or in subservience to the state.

Wanted, then, above everything else are the fear and love of God! Where these are present, man knows that there is an objective standard by which he is judged in secret. He will then develop a conscience; he will meditate upon the law of God. His greed and his selfishness will be effectively curbed; his cupidity and his desire will be turned to higher ends. He will denounce war but he will not be afraid of it, because he has overcome the fear of death; he will see clearly through the falsehoods and snares of communism. The underdeveloped are his brethren; he will help and serve them without any thought of superiority or exploitation. He will seek fellowship and sharing, and in giving he will find the deepest joy. His relations with his fellow men will not be stiff, formal, mechanical, mercenary; he will see reflected in them the very image of God—though with infinite imperfections. All differences and all frictions will dissolve in the crucible of the higher loyalty of God.

Secularism, atheism, anti-intellectualism, and the unhappy family —these are the causes of all deterioration in human relations. Therefore, support the Church, support the university, and let the splendor of the family shine for ever more.

Questions

1. List the special conditions now facing the economic world of today.
2. What is the principle of "self-control" to which Malik refers? Is this type of training and development the job of specific companies? If not, whose responsibility is it?
3. How does class conflict affect industrial relations in our own economy?
4. "The excellence of human relations is grounded in the family, the university, and the Church." Explain.
5. Does this article have any practical application in industry of today or do you think it is too theoretical?

WHAT IS HUMAN RELATIONS? *

Alan C. Filley

Dr. Brock Chisholm, at Indiana University, recently stated that the United States has become a leader in mechanization, in creating machines to do the work of many men, but has delayed in understanding the individual as a human being. Paying only lip service to human relations, as so many do with religion, motherhood and love, has become an accepted thing among us.

Business leaders are no exception. The lower levels of the management hierarchy are delegated the responsibility of making sure that the worker is "motivated," that his human dignity is respected. New titles of "counselor" and "V.P. of H.R." are given often merely because of the idea that such a thing is good publicity, indicating a progressive company rather than from any real desire to understand the problems of the worker.

Human relations in business has suffered the same problems that befell personnel administration in its early stages of business acceptance and has, in most cases, been understood to mean the same thing as personnel administration or, carried even further into obscurity, to mean a sort of *super*-personnel administration.

The approach to sound human relations application in the business organization would seem to be two-fold: First, there must be a clear definition of the function of human relations and of its place in the business environment; and secondly, the principles of sound human relations procedure must be understood and applied by all members at *all* levels in the business organization. Perhaps there has been too much impatience on the part of managers to give lip service, if not actual application, to the second point without the logical understanding of the first.

For this reason, this paper emphasizes *organization* for a human relations program rather than the principles of application of human relations, so the cart may be moved to its rightful place *behind* rather than *before* the horse. The objectives are: (1) To show the source of the human relations function in the business. (2) To show the place of "motivation" in the management function. (3) To show the relationship of personnel administration to human relations. (4) To indicate future trends of human relations in business.

* From *Advanced Management,* Vol. 23, No. 4 (April, 1958), pp. 17-20. Reprinted with permission.

The confusion between human relations and personnel administration

The distinction between motivation, human relations and personnel administration has been a sore spot with the students of such fields of study. Basic writings in personnel speak of something that is "practiced by everyone in the organization" yet are filled with policy and procedures for employment, training and the rest of the basic personnel functions. One might assume, then, that these authors advocate training *all* managers in the business in the procedures of personnel administration. For example, that all managers should be trained in employment techniques: in finding sources of possible job applicants, in gathering information about the applicant, in induc tion of the employee into the job or in acquainting the employee with the medical, financial and non-financial services available to him.

However, a further examination of the intent of these authors will show that what should be practiced by everyone in the organization is not personnel administration; instead, it is human relations.

The personnel function evolves quite logically from the line functions of the business as the organization increases in scope and complexity. It is not masterminded from the top with little relationship to the needs of the rest of the business, as was the case when many formal personnel staffs were hastily organized during and after World War II. At that time, personnel administration (as is now done with human relations) was *the* thing to which any modern business subscribed, needed or not. And in most cases the intent of that recognition of personnel was based on a human relations rather than on a personnel need, for most businesses had someone carrying on the functions of personnel whether the staff was labeled personnel or not.

Let us endeavor to find the root of our confusion by tracing the logical growth of the personnel staff in a growing company. At first, when the company was small, the employment, training and other personnel functions were easily carried out by the line manager. As the company grew, the line manager delegated the responsibility for the personnel functions to one of his men—the beginnings of a personnel staff. Next, as the business increased in scope and complexity, the formal staff was organized to aid the line in the special personnel capacity. Just as the finance function of the business was responsible for the finances of the business as they controlled the business organization, so the personnel staff become responsible for the *people* in the organization as they were related to the business. It is important to note that we are here concerned with the relationship of the person and the job, for we shall later examine another relationship, that of the person to other individuals in the organization.

Since the personnel staff dealt with personalities, it was quite natural that management should delegate to personnel the responsibility for recognizing and solving the myriad social problems that arose in the organization. To the personnel manager went the problem of dealing with the sentiments and morale factors concerning the employee and the job of giving the line management an insight into dealing with such problems. The personnel staff could try to place the right man, properly trained, into what seemed the right job, but it was the supervisor of the employee who felt the full brunt of the social problems within the area of his supervision. Thus, writings in the personnel field contained such statements as "The personnel manager is always endeavoring to work himself out of a job . . . he is continually influencing and training the line supervisors and executives to do a personnel job." [1]

A personnel job? No, it's a *human relations job.* In spite of the development of the customary tools of personnel administration, there remained the need for aiding individuals in the organization in the problems arising out of their relations with others in the business environment. As the organization grew, the personnel staff could handle the technical requirements of setting job standards, hiring, training and facilitating the work of the new employee. But what was to be done with the undefinable, intangible *social problems* that arose?

These social problems occurred in the relationships of the worker to his supervisor, his fellow workers and those under his control. Likewise, they occurred in the relationship of the workers' group and the management group. The worker brought to the job a certain set of wants and needs determined by his home, social and community situation. No staff could deal with these problems as they were reflected in the job. Rather, it became the supervisors' function to deal with these non-logical human problems.

The functions of personnel and human relations

In order to understand the functions of human relations it is essential that we see the distinction between these functions and those of personnel administration. The functions of personnel administration are concerned with the relationship of the individual to his job

[1] Paul Pigors and Charles A. Myers, *Readings in Personnel Administration* (New York: McGraw-Hill Book Co., 1952), p. 91.

while human relations is concerned with the relationship of the individual to other individuals in the organization. And what function of the business is likely to be in contact with a greater proportion of the individuals in the varied operations of the business? The personnel staff, of course. This staff, which is concerned with the relationship of the individual to his job, is of necessity the seat and the example of sound human relations procedures.

Let us examine the functions of personnel administration in greater detail:

1. *Research and Standards*—It is the job of the research and standards function to collect, analyze and interpret information through job analysis and job evaluation for the purpose of setting equitable wages and salaries in the organization. It is concerned with establishing the requirements of the job.

2. *Employment*—The requirements of the job having been determined, the employment function provides the right man to fill the job. Through proper selection, placement and promotion, this function endeavors to find the right man to fit the properly organized job rather than hastily changing the job to fit the man.

3. *Training*—This function is concerned with giving employees information and skills in order that maximum productivity may be achieved, that effectiveness in their present jobs may be improved and that employees may be prepared for further advancement in the organization.

4. *Health and Safety*—With careful selection and training of employees it is natural that their effectiveness on the job should not be impaired due to unsafe practices or due to poor health. This function is concerned with protecting and maintaining the health and safety of each employee for the mutual benefit of the employer, employee and fellow workers.

5. *Employee Services*—Since the employee wants or needs other benefits in the job situation besides mere pay, the employee services function of personnel provides and maintains the recreational facilities, the cafeteria, the insurance programs, the retirement program and other financial and non-financial benefits.

Notice that the personnel functions enumerated above call for specialized skills on the part of the personnel staff. Such skills would not pervade the management of the organization any more than would the shop foreman be expected to be highly skilled in accounting techniques.

The skill that *does* pervade the entire organization is that of dealing with the relationship of one individual with another or of the relationship of one group of individuals with another group. These, then, are the activities of the human relations function of the business:

1. *Management development*—Often top management expects supervisors to practice a considerate approach to employee problems while failing to practice sound human relationships themselves. For example, foremen fresh from a course in human relations become aware that the techniques which management expects them to use in dealing with the workers are the very things in which management itself often fails. Management attitudes must often be changed in order to prevent their merely acting a role of human understanding to which they themselves do not subscribe. Such role playing on the part of management promotes inconsistency of behavior—a prime factor in causing employee adjustment problems.

2. *Employee relations*—This function endeavors to provide the employee with the proper information in order to promote motivation, job-satisfaction and cooperation with fellow employees. While the promotion of sound employee relations is the concern of all levels of management, it is of particular importance at those levels which are likely to come into contact with employees at the operative level.

The employee relations function should take a positive approach to the morale problems of the employees. Through its attitude surveys in the organization, the employee relations people should be able to determine possible future problems in employee behavior which may be averted through the use of sound judgment and planning.

Still more effective in determining the individual wants and needs of the employees is the use of a sound program of employee counseling. Such counseling helps the workers with personal problems that are outside the work situation as well as helping employees to adjust to the work situation. Too often the difficulties of the employee in his external environment are reflected on the job. Such counseling also provides an excellent means of both upward and downward communication. Management policy and practice may be explained to the employees and employee attitudes may be sampled and communicated to top management. Since employee confidence in the counseling service is essential, it should be removed from the aura of management control in order that the worker will not feel that his frank statements to the counselor will reflect on his job.

3. *Labor relations*—This function is concerned with developing a labor contract that expresses the wishes of both labor and management and endeavors to promote sound labor-management relations. Collective bargaining and grievance procedure are important parts of labor relations and require sound application of human relations procedures. The union organization provides a useful channel of communication. It is important that the information which the union obtains is accurate and that it is accepted and distributed by the union with a feeling of genuine confidence and cooperation. It is also important that management get accurate descriptions of employee wants and needs from the union. If such two-way communication is maintained, many of the programs of dissemination of information are best worked out through the union organization.

4. *Public or community relations*—This function realizes that the employee brings to the job attitudes that have already been shaped by the environment in which he lives. An understanding of the individual's actions on the job may be derived through understanding the community in which he lives. Since an accurate picture of the business by the community is essential for community relations, the public relations program must be one of positive community action; i.e., the program must keep the community accurately informed of the actions of the business and of any changes that are likely to take place which will affect the community.

Examples of human relations problems

Perhaps the distinction between personnel and human relations may be more easily understood by stating several examples.

Example 1. Worker "A" has been properly screened, inducted and placed on a job in the inspection center of an appliance manufacturer. Job descriptions indicate that Worker "A" is fully capable of doing the work and adequate job instructions have been given. Several months after induction on the job, Worker "A" applies for a transfer to another department, stating that he is dissatisfied with his present job and would be more satisfied with the new position.

The personnel functions of employment and placement have been performed adequately and the activities of transferring the worker would seem to solve the worker's problem. The human relations factor would enter if it should be found that the reason for wanting a transfer is not because the worker feels better qualified to do the new job but, instead, because the worker has not been accepted in the

informal society of his present associates. Perhaps the fellow-workers
feel that Worker "A" is being primed to take one of their own jobs
or that, since he was not introduced by the foreman to the fellow-
workers, he is a spy from top management sent to report on their
efficiency.

Example 2. Mrs. Smith has been doing a satisfactory job in the
billing office of a service company for 20 years. Recently, her absenteeism has greatly increased and she is careless in the quality of her
work. Her supervisor is afraid that because she is due to retire soon,
she is looking forward to her retirement rather than sustaining any
effort to do her present work well.

It could reasonably be assumed that the payments for pensions
from the company were at such a comfortable level that they served
as an incentive for the worker to reduce output shortly before
retirement.

Human relations understanding may lead the supervisor to discuss the problem with Mrs. Smith and, instead of taking a hasty
move to penalize her, may find that a groundless rumor that she is to
be fired before her retirement age has caused Mrs. Smith to lose faith
in the company for which she has worked for many years.

Such examples are, of course, rather obvious but they do occur
frequently without even the simplest attempt being made to understand them.

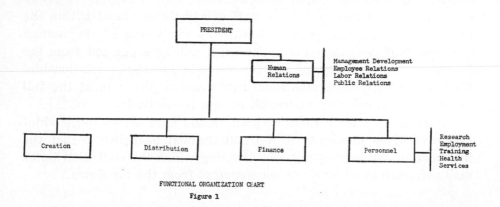

FUNCTIONAL ORGANIZATION CHART
Figure 1

As Figure No. 1 shows, the personnel department is one of the
four basic functions of the organization. Whether it is of a true staff
nature is a matter for discussion. A great deal of time and effort has
been expended in explaining or justifying why so much line authority has been delegated to the personnel department. It would seem
to this author that when the distinction between personnel adminis-

tration and human relations has been clearly defined, the position of the personnel department will be comparable to that of the finance function of the business.

The human relations staff is clearly a staff by definition. It exists to aid the line in dealing with the social problems of all employees, including management. Davis points out:

> "The nature of the leadership function (i.e., the fact that human relations is a part of nearly everything the leader does) requires that most human relations responsibilities remain with him but a small proportion can be delegated to a staff. . . . If (the staff) can get managers to practice good human relations, its big job is done. The staff human relations group, therefore, works through managers rather than for them." [2]

Several things must be emphasized. First, that human relations (dealing with human beings) is a function that must be practiced by everyone in the organization. The human relations staff will have failed should it either retain the sole authority for making decisions in this area, or should it fail to instill in everyone in the organization the best techniques for understanding and dealing with human problems as they arise.

Secondly, that of necessity the effective human relations staff must be a *small, fast moving* and *highly skilled* group. Because of the need for human relations in dealing with all personnel problems and because of the personnel department's contact with the employee group as a whole, the human relations staff will likely be placed within the personnel department. It is felt that as the worth of the human relations staff becomes more apparent, it will be separated from the personnel staff entirely, except for possible functional relationship. Until it is clearly separated from the personnel department the full value of its communicative wealth cannot be derived.

Thirdly, the human relations staff should have access to the chief executive. This proximity to top management is to insure that the information and human relations training which the staff distributes may permeate to *all levels of management* from the top down.

The filter function

The function of human relations in a business may be further clarified by explaining its relationship to the functions of management. The functions of management may be defined as planning,

---

[2] Keith Davis, *Human Relations in Business* (New York: McGraw-Hill Book Co., 1957).

organizing, applying and controlling. These are all tangible and easily understood, but there is the intangible to cope with. The intangible, non-logical human problems with which management must deal include all of the evasive conditions which have been termed motivation, morale, personnel administration, etc.

Job satisfaction, expressed in the numerous intangible terms mentioned above, is maintained by passing information from one individual to another. The act of passing information from a sender to a receiver we call communication. The information that is transmitted may be facts or it may be an expression of the attitudes or sentiments of the sender. It is important that management receive both facts and sentiments from the lower levels of the organization and it is essential *that management is able to separate the two.*

This distinction is necessary in order that management may evaluate the expressions of attitudes and sentiments among the employees of the organization to determine the true problems to be acted upon. By the same token, as information is directed downward through the communicative channels of the organization, management must insure that accurate and true information is filtered throughout the business.

The function of human relations now becomes one of sifting facts that are communicated throughout the business from expressions of opinion. This management function, which insures that facts are not clouded by expressions of opinion, we shall call the "filter function."

Unless the filter function is included in the functions of planning, organizing, applying and controlling work activities, management will fail. As an organization grows, its channels of communication are lengthened and the division of the work processes becomes more complex. Without adequate operation of the filter function, workers lose pride in their work and in themselves and live constantly in fear of further changes in the organization which may affect their jobs. As functionalization in the business increases economical efficiency, the filter function *must* maintain human relations efficiency.

Quite often, particularly in those areas of the business which are not likely to contribute immediately to the net profit, new staff functions put forth a great deal of effort in proving their value to the organization. At such times the hue and cry of the staff executive is that he "must report directly to the chief executive." With the separation of the functions of human relations and personnel, it should be evident that the personnel staff performs an obvious saving service to the business and that only the human relations people need access to top management.

Through activities of personnel, the right worker may be placed in the right job. It then becomes the job of line managers to manage, aided by an understanding gained through the filter function and advice and service from the human relations staff. The wants and needs of the work force change during the course of time. Those needs relating to the individual and his job may be properly filtered through the management organization or the human relations staff, and put into action by the personnel staff. The assumption that people do not want to work is unfounded and when it does occur, it is a sign of failure of the filter function, not the worker himself.

Questions

1. How does Filley distinguish between human relations and personnel administration?
2. Do you agree with what he lists as the major activities of the human relations function in a business?
3. Define what Filley terms "the filter function."
4. Can a firm truly organize for human relations as Filley proposes?
5. Contrast this with preceding articles. How does it enhance your understanding of human relations problems in industry?

General Questions on Part I

1. List and discuss five of the more important human relations functions that any manager faces in his job.
2. How does Charles H. Malik's article differ from those of Cleeton, Friedmann, and Sheldon? In what ways is it similar? Do you think that many of his points apply to the typical business firm?
3. Explain the principal limitations of the original scientific management movement as it related to the human element.
4. Just what is meant by the term "human relations?"
5. What is the most significant difference between Friedmann's article and Cleeton's? What do you think is the major idea of each?
6. Whose responsibility is it to practice good human relations in a business enterprise?
7. Do you agree with Alan Filley's point of view concerning human relations?
8. Present your own definition of the term "human relations." What major obstacles stand in the way of obtaining a common definition for this term?
9. Historically speaking, what have been some of the outstanding factors providing impetus towards recognizing the human element in industry?
10. In what ways has Part 1 enhanced your understanding of industrial human relations?

Bibliography for Part I

Articles

BARASH, MYER. "An Industrial Relations Philosophy," *Personnel Journal*, Vol. 36, No. 7 (December, 1957), pp. 257-258.

DIEBOLD, JOHN T. "Scientific Management Applied to the Field of Human Relations," *Advanced Management* (December, 1953), pp. 27-30.

JOHNSON, ROBERT WOOD. "Human Relations in Modern Business," *Harvard Business Review*, Vol. 27 (September, 1949), pp. 521-541.

MACRURY, KING. "Human Relations in Industry: Objectives and Instruments," *Industrial and Labor Relations Review*, Vol. 4, No. 4 (July, 1951), pp. 571-576.

MOORE, DAVID G. "Human Behavior and Industry," *Journal of Business*, Vol. 28, pp. 38-40.

ROETHLISBERGER, F. J. "A New Look for Management," *Worker Morale and Productivity*, General Management Series No. 141, American Management Association, 1948, pp. 11-19.

SPATES, THOMAS G. "Leadership and Human Relations at the Places Where People Work," *Advanced Management*, Vol. 13, No. 3 (September, 1948), pp. 98-102.

URWICK, L. F. "Human Factors in Top Management," *Industrial Welfare and Personnel Management* (January-February, 1955), pp. 4-6.

Books

BERRIEN, F. K. and W. H. BASH. *Human Relations*. New York: Harper and Brothers, 1951.

CORDINER, R. J. *New Frontiers for Professional Managers*. New York: McGraw-Hill Book Company, 1957.

DAVIS, K. *Human Relations in Business*. New York: McGraw-Hill Book Company, 1957.

DUBIN, R. *Human Relations in Administration*. Englewood Cliffs, New Jersey: Prentice-Hall, Inc., 1951.

GARDNER, B. B. and D. G. MOORE. *Human Relations in Industry*. Homewood, Illinois: Richard D. Irwin, Inc., 1945.

KNOWLES, W. *Personnel Management*. New York: American Book Company, 1955.

PART 2. LEADERSHIP

In a very real sense, the story of human relations in the context of the business environment is partly the story of leadership. The reason for this is basically simple. The leader's fundamental responsibility in any form of organization is to get work done through people. This requires him to collect and combine the efforts of individuals to achieve a common goal. To do this successfully, he must of necessity utilize the basic principles, concepts, and techniques of human relations. In other words, as the format of this book indicates, he must motivate his subordinates, communicate to them, prepare them for changes, counsel them, and so on. For unless he does these things, he cannot possibly hope to accomplish immediately and continually the goals of the organization efficiently. Consequently, the key to effective leadership is human relations.

Although human relations is an integral part of the leadership function, it is not, of course, the only responsibility a leader has. In fact, there are many things a leader must do and can do long before contact with human beings becomes necessary. These "things" include, generally speaking, the basic managerial functions involved in all leadership positions, namely, planning, organizing, coordinating, and controlling work. But to consider these functions here is beyond the scope of this book. The serious student of leadership must therefore direct his investigation toward additional fields of knowledge, particularly those of management, psychology, and sociology, if he wishes to perceive the totality of the leader's job. What is important to recognize here, however, is that managerial functions such as planning, organizing, coordinating, and controlling all lead to the determination of work that must be performed by human beings. If this were not true, there would be no need for leaders—managers. To be a leader, therefore, requires that one have people to lead. And the purpose of leading these people is to get done work that we have determined must be done. This, as we said before, requires the practice of human relations.

Unfortunately, leadership, like human relations, is a vast and complicated area. Although much research and writing have been done on this important function, it is surprising to discover how little we actually know about it. And it is even more surprising to discover that much of what we do know is subject to widespread disagreement. This is especially true of the current picture of research on leadership—that of extensive but unorganized activity. It is confusing, to say the least.

Approaches to Leadership

Traitist approach

Some organization and clarity of thought can be accomplished in the study of leadership by viewing it in the light of several of the approaches that have been used to investigate it and to explain its nature. One of the earliest of these approaches is frequently called the *traitist* theory. Utilizing an inductive procedure, researchers and writers in this area have attempted to explain leadership on the basis of traits and characteristics of successful leaders. Ordway Tead, for example, insists that there are ten qualities that are essential for effective leadership, namely, physical and nervous energy, a sense of purpose and direction, enthusiasm, friendliness and affection, integrity, technical mastery, decisiveness, intelligence, teaching skill, and faith.[1] Chester I. Barnard, on the other hand, lists such factors as physique, skill, technology, perception, knowledge, memory, imagination, determination, persistence, endurance, and courage.[2]

Examination of Tead's and Barnard's lists indicates immediately a basic difficulty with the traitist approach, namely, that seldom, if ever, do any two lists agree on the essential traits and characteristics of effective leadership. The net result is that of confusion, predicated on a foundation of generalities and semantical problems. Because of these difficulties and numerous other considerations, such as size of sample, period of time covered, and so on, it is not surprising to find many other researchers who vehemently disagree with the traitist theory.

Type approach

Another basic attempt to explain the nature of leadership is that of the *leadership-type* approach. Researchers following this route have concluded that there are essentially four types of leaders: (1)

---

[1] Ordway Tead, *The Art of Leadership* (New York: McGraw-Hill Book Company, Inc., 1935), p. 83.
[2] Chester I. Barnard, *The Functions of the Executive* (Cambridge, Mass.: Harvard University Press, 1938), p. 260.

the dictatorial leader; (2) the autocratic leader; (3) the democratic
leader; and (4) the laissez-faire leader.

Dictatorial leadership, according to this approach, is that type of
leadership which gets work done through fear. The dictatorial
leader—or negative leader as he is frequently called—holds over the
heads of his subordinates the threat of penalties and punishment,
such as discharge, demotion, poor ratings that may prevent promotions or wage increases, and so on. The theory is that the followers,
in order not to lose the means of satisfying some of their needs and
wants, are motivated to do what the leader tells them to do. Although
this type of leadership apparently gets results, there is serious doubt
that the quantity and the quality of the results achieved can remain
high over the long run, particularly in view of the fact that the
results obtained are frequently accompanied by the dissatisfaction of
those led.

Autocratic leadership is characterized by centralization of authority and decision-making in the leader. Although this type of leader
tends to emphasize neither negative nor positive leadership, he
motivates his subordinates by forcing them to rely upon him for need
satisfaction. As such, he takes full authority and responsibility for
the work to be done. He permits no participation in the decision-
making process and tolerates no deviations from what he has told his
followers to do. This type of leadership also gets results. But it
suffers from the serious disadvantage that it can be only as good as
the leader is. If the leader is weak and inefficient, the followers will
be weak and inefficient.

Democratic leadership, unlike autocratic leadership, is based on
decentralization of authority and decision-making. This type of leader
is characterized by the degree to which he consults with his subordinates on problems, goals, and tasks that face him and the group
as a whole. The theory behind this type of leadership is that it
encourages the followers to function as a social unit and that it
makes full use of the talents and abilities of the members of the
group. As a result, the subordinates achieve a greater measure of
belonging and recognition, which motivates them to higher levels of
efficiency. Although some people do not agree with this, there is,
nevertheless, general agreement that democratic leadership offers
more promise to industry than any other type of leadership. It
suffers, however, from the disadvantage of requiring a better quality
of leader.

Laissez-faire leadership, or *free-rein leadership* as it is popularly
called, exists when the leader allows the group to establish its own

goals and make its own decisions. Usually the only contact the leader has with the group occurs when he provides it with the information it needs to get a job done. As such, he makes little contribution to over-all effort. The net result is frequently disorganization or chaos, primarily because this type of leadership permits different individuals to proceed in different directions.

Situationist approach

A third approach to the study of leadership is that of the *situationists*. According to these advocates, leadership is specific and always relative to the particular situation in which it occurs. Therefore, who becomes the leader or who is the leader of a given group engaging in a particular activity is a function of the total situation, which includes not only the leader and the subordinates and other groups to which the leader is related, but also myriad other human, physical, organizational, and time variables as well. In essence, situationists are more concerned with finding new ways of identifying leaders than they are with developing a theory of leadership.

A basic conclusion of the situationist approach is that the successful leader must be adaptive and flexible. As the situation changes, whether it be from minute to minute or from day to day, so must the leader change his style of leadership. Consequently, at any one point in time he may display certain traits and characteristics and follow the format of a particular type of leadership, whereas at another point in time he may display an entirely different set of traits and follow another type of leadership. If this conclusion is accepted, it does offer some logical explanation for the confusion that exists in and between the traitist and the type approaches. However, much empirical work needs to be done before this conclusion can be validated. And therein lies a problem for the situationists, for in this approach even the measuring instruments that are employed become a part of the situation and thereby influence it.

Other approaches

Although space does not permit a detailed examination of them, there are several other approaches to the study of leadership that should be briefly mentioned here. One of these approaches is to analyze leadership from the viewpoint of the *group* involved. Advocates of this approach maintain that the success of the leader is determined in many ways by his subordinates. Accordingly, these researchers investigate the make-up of groups and the actions and interactions of the members within it. Another approach is that of *organization.* Followers of this approach view leadership as a functional relationship between leader, followers, and organization. Although closely akin to the situationist approach, it is usually concerned, however, only with the structure of leadership.

Even though much confusion and disagreement exists in our present state of knowledge of leadership, there are signs that some day the various approaches to this important function will be combined into highly organized, interdisciplinary research. When this occurs, our understanding of leadership will become clearer than ever before. As a result, industry in particular and mankind in general should benefit immeasurably.

In choosing the articles that follow, an attempt was made to pick those that will help the reader gain greater insight into the nature and the complexities of leadership *per se* and the approaches used to study and explain it. Stogdill's article was chosen, therefore, as an illustration of the organization approach. Knickerbocker's article was selected as a detailed example of the situationist viewpoint. McGregor's article was picked because, as its title indicates, it is an excellent commentary on conditions of effective leadership. And, last of all, McMurry's article was included because it is an excellent example of one man's opinion about a particular type of leadership, namely, the autocratic approach. If the reader will definitely study the contents of these articles and integrate, compare, and contrast the information they contain, his understanding of the nature of leadership should become clearer and more useful to him.

LEADERSHIP, MEMBERSHIP AND ORGANIZATION * [1]

Ralph M. Stogdill

The present paper is concerned with a point of view regarding the relation of leadership to group organization. It represents one attempt within the Ohio State Leadership Studies [2] staff to clarify and systematize certain aspects of the leadership problem. Such clarification appears to be necessary as a preliminary step toward the development of an integrated program of research on leadership problems in formal organizations.

The pioneering work of Lewin,[3] Moreno,[4] and their followers has resulted in marked progress in the development of methods for studying leadership as a phenomenon of *groups*. However, comparable progress remains to be made in the development of methods for the study of leadership as an aspect of *organization*. Several factors appear to have operated as barriers to the development of scientific theory and method in this area. One is the lack of an adequate definition of leadership. A second is the fact that in much of the literature on leadership, the terms "group" and "organization" are used interchangeably or are defined in exactly the same terms. A third derives from two opposed theoretical approaches represented, on the one hand, by those theories of organization in which the leader is conceived as a symbol of authority or as an embodiment of superior personal traits, and on the other hand, by a type of group-oriented theory in which leadership appears to be regarded as a manifestation of social pathology. A fourth, and related obstacle, results from a reaction of social scientists against the authoritarian principles ad-

* From the *Psychological Bulletin*, Vol. 47, No. 1 (January, 1950), pp. 1-14. Reprinted with permission.

[1] A cooperative contribution of the U. S. Navy, Office of Naval Research, and the Ohio State University Research Foundation. The opinions presented are those of the author, and should not be regarded as having the endorsement of the Department of the Navy. The paper was presented in part before the Midwestern Psychological Association, Chicago, Ill., April 29, 1949.

[2] The Ohio State Leadership Studies are designed as a ten-year program of research on leadership problems in military, business, industrial, educational and civilian governmental organizations. The staff includes C. L. Shartle, Director; Alvin E. Coons, Melvin Seeman and Ralph M. Stogdill, Associate Directors; John Hemphill, Research Associate; Donald T. Campbell, Research Consultant; Richard T. Morris and Charles M. Westie, Research Assistants.

[3] Kurt Lewin, Ronald Lippitt, and Sybille K. Escalona, *Studies in Topological and Vector Psychology I*, University of Iowa Studies in Child Welfare, Vol. 16, No. 3, 1940.

[4] J. L. Moreno, *Who Shall Survive?* (Washington: Nervous and Mental Diseases Publishing Co., 1934).

vanced in many discussions of organization. Some social theorists appear to reject all concepts of organization as authoritarian; and some researchers appear reluctant to deal experimentally with such concepts as responsibility, authority, stratification and similar phenomena related to organization. It is beyond the scope or purpose of this paper to portray the magnitude of the latter two difficulties. Nevertheless, it seems relevant to recognize the fact that they are present and act to the detriment of scientific work in the field.

The Ohio State Leadership Studies are being conducted on the basis of these assumptions: (1) that group organization is a recognizable social phenomenon in our culture, (2) that as such it is a legitimate subject for scientific study; and (3) that the variables of organization can be isolated and defined so as to permit their scientific study. It is the purpose of the present paper to examine various concepts relevant to leadership and organization, and to develop a formulation of the problem which will suggest hypotheses that can be subjected to experimental test.

Groups and organizations

Wilson [5] has reviewed the important sociological literature relating to concepts of the social group. He reports that in "current sociological literature one finds no consensus as to the meaning of the *group*," and concludes that much experimental work is yet to be done in order to delimit the group concept in any satisfactory manner. An important step in this direction has been made by Hemphill,[6] who has devised scales for the measurement of such group dimensions as size, permeability, stability, viscidity, homogeneity of membership, and the like.

The most satisfactory definition available at the present time appears to be that of Smith [7] who defines a *social group* as "a unit consisting of a plural number of organisms (agents) who have collective perception of their unity and who have the ability to act/or are acting in a unitary manner toward the environment." Krech and Crutchfield [8] present a similar view. They state that "the criteria for establishing whether or not a given set of individuals constitutes a

---

[5] Logan Wilson, "Sociography of Groups," in G. Gurvitch and W. E. Moore (eds.), *Twentieth Century Sociology* (New York: Philosophical Library, 1945), pp. 139-171.

[6] John K. Hemphill, *Situational Factors in Leadership* (Ohio State University, Bureau of Educational Research Monograph 31, 1949).

[7] Mapheus Smith, "Social Situation, Social Behavior, Social Group," *Psychological Review*, Vol. 52 (1945), pp. 224-229.

[8] David Krech and Richard S. Crutchfield, *Theory and Problems of Social Psychology* (New York: McGraw-Hill, 1948).

psychological group are mainly two: (1) all the members must exist as a group in the psychological field of each individual, i.e., be perceived and reacted to as a group; (2) the various members must be in dynamic interaction with one another."

A special kind of group is the *organization*. An organization may be defined as a social group in which the members are differentiated as to their responsibilities for the task of achieving a common goal.

Znaniecki[9] has reviewed the sociological literature relating to various concepts of organization. He stresses the fact that the terms *group* and *organization* are rather tenuous concepts, in that it is often difficult to determine whether a particular aggregate of persons constitutes a group, and that it may also be difficult at times to determine whether a particular group can be regarded as an organization. He points out that social organization

> ... can be realized only in a lasting "social group" or "association." Individuals belonging to such a group are aware that they will be regularly expected to perform certain actions, and some of them act as organizers, leaders, coordinators of the regular activities of others with reference to the common purpose. Not all of these individuals need be continuously active; indeed, in many groups a considerable proportion remain passive, acting only in reaction to the actions of others. The common purpose of the organized actions may be simple or complex.

Some of the consequences of distinguishing between the terms "group" and "organization" are the following: First, there is nothing in the term "group" which gives any clue as to the nature of leadership. Second, there is nothing in the group definition which provides any foundation for integrating leadership with group phenomena, except at a superficial level of social perception or interaction. Third, the group orientation can suggest research methods relating to leadership only in so far as the social group is defined in terms of organization. The concept of organization, however, with its implications for the differentiation of responsibility roles, does permit the study of leadership as an aspect of the relationships between members who are coordinating their efforts for the achievement of common goals.

A group may or may not have leaders. If it does have leaders, it is an organization, for at least some of the members are thereby differentiated from the others as to responsibility, or role expectation in relation to some common purpose. The members of a group may or may not have mutual responsibilities for a common task. If the

[9] Florian Znaniecki, "Social Organization and Institutions," in G. Gurvitch and W. E. Moore (eds.), *Twentieth Century Sociology* (New York: Philosophical Library, 1945), pp. 172-217.

members do have differentiated responsibilities in relation to common goals then the group is an organization—a particular kind of group. The continued presence of leaders and of responsibility differentiations in relation to group goals are indicative of organization. It may not always be easy to determine the exact point at which a group emerges into an organization.

Leadership as an aspect of organization

The following definition of leadership may serve as a starting point for discussion. Leadership may be considered as the process (act) of influencing the activities of an organized group in its efforts toward goal setting and goal achievement. The definition of leadership relates it directly to the organized group and its goal. It would appear that the minimal social conditions which permit the existence of leadership are the following:

1. A group (of two or more persons).
2. A common task (or goal oriented activities).
3. Differentiation of responsibility (some of the members have different duties).

There are innumerable other group and situational factors which may influence leadership in varying degrees, but these appear to be the minimal conditions which will permit the emergence of leadership. There must be a group with a common task or objective, and at least one member must have responsibilities which differ from those of the other members. If all members perform exactly the same duties in exactly the same way there is no leadership. A leader then is a person who becomes differentiated from other members in terms of the influence he exerts upon the goal setting and goal achievement activities of the organization.

The foregoing discussion suggests that leadership cannot emerge unless the members of a group assume different responsibilities. It has been suggested that group organization also is founded upon differentiation of responsibility. It would then appear that leadership and organization are derived from a common factor or, viewed from a different light, that leadership is an aspect of group organization. This view has been expressed in various forms by writers in the field of business organization. Davis,[10] for example, states that the

> . . . development of organization structure is largely a problem in the division of responsibility, and involves two important problems:

---

[10] Ralph C. Davis, *Industrial Organization and Management* (New York: Harper, 1940).

(1) the grouping of similar functions to form the various organization elements in a manner that will promote effective cooperation, and (2) the determination of the proper relationships between functional groups and organization elements, with a view to promoting both cooperation and effective executive leadership.

The definition of leadership does not specify how many leaders an organization shall have, nor whether the leadership influence of an individual is continuous or intermittent, nor whether the influence of the leader shall be for the welfare or detriment of the organization and its members. It merely specifies that leaders may be differentiated from other members in terms of the extent to which they influence the activities of the organization in its efforts toward the achievement of goals. The definition of effective and ineffective leadership is an additional problem.

Aspects of responsibility

Brown [11] in a challenging analysis of organization maintains that "An enterprise is a mosaic of its individual responsibilities. The sum of them must exactly equal the whole requirement of administration." He continues, "Responsibility is that part in administration which is assigned to a particular member of an enterprise. Its definition is an act of organization."

Responsibility cannot be regarded as a simple or uncomplicated variable. Jucius [12] writes,

> By responsibility is meant, first, the obligation to do an assigned task, and, second, the obligation to someone for the assignment. But what is meant by obligation and how far does it extend? This implies a willingness to accept, for whatever rewards one may see in the situation, the burden of a given task and the risks which attend in the event of failure. Because of the rewards and penalties involved, it is highly essential to specify the limits of responsibility.

Formal organization can seldom define all the possible variations of responsibility and personal interaction to be expected of all members in all situations. Nevertheless, organization appears to be founded upon a basic system of stable expectations regarding differential responsibilities and relationships among the members. This is not a one-way process. That is, it is not the organization alone which sets up role expectations for its members. The members set up expectations for each other and for the organization as a whole. It is assumed for purposes of the present discussion that this principle

[11] Alvin Brown, *Organization of Industry* (New York: Prentice-Hall, 1947).
[12] Michael J. Jucius, *Personnel Management* (New York: Irwin, 1947).

applies not only to stratified organizations, such as military and indus-trial establishments. It applies as well to membership in any organized group, whether it be a business, political, educational, religious, fraternal, or social organization and regardless of size, stratification, purpose, or member characteristics. The essential relationship which makes possible the conduct of organized group activities is a differentiation of responsibility roles among the mem-bers. Without this there is no possibility of coordination or of leadership toward goal achievement. The very process of organization defines the responsibilities of the members and thereby the formal leadership of the group. It is true that in some organized groups, such as recreational groups, the responsibilities of members may appear to be vaguely defined. However, this is not equivalent to saying that no responsibilities exist.

Responsibility, in its broadest scope, defines not only the duties for which a member is accountable; it defines also the persons to whom and for whom he is accountable in the discharge of his duties. In doing so, it also defines a member's formal status, or location in the organization hierarchy. Authority and formal status systems in organization are but aspects of the division of responsibility.

Responsibilities in a systematic organization are determined by the assignment of persons to particular positions, the duties of which are outlined in an organization manual or organization chart. In less systematic organizations the responsibilities of a particular job or position may be determined by on-the-spot instructions, by general hints or by unverbalized assumptions. In a systematic organization an individual's *work patterns* (the tasks he *actually* performs) will correspond fairly closely with his *responsibility patterns* (the tasks he *is supposed* to perform). However, as the mission and activities or the organization change there will be found in many instances an increasing discrepancy between the tasks being performed and the responsibilities originally outlined and defined.

Attributes of organization

The studies of Roethlisberger [13] and others have directed atten-tion to the factor of informal groups within formal organization. In-formal organization, as usually defined, refers to the friendship groups and cliques—based upon close association, mutual interests or an-tagonisms, and the like—which develop within formal organization.

----

[13] F. J. Roethlisberger and William J. Dickson, *Management and the Worker* (Cambridge: Harvard University Press, 1939).

It has been pointed out by Homans [14] that this conception is too narrow, since what is informal in a factory may be formal in a primitive society. Firey,[15] who defines informal organization in terms of schism, presents a more useful approach to the problem. He maintains that "if we regard behavioral conformity, in which interactional processes are highly repetitive and synchronized, as the overt counterpart of a social system, then behavioral nonconformity may be taken as the overt counterpart of schism within a system."

An organization in operation seldom corresponds exactly with the organizational model as charted. The intervention of human social factors and other influences result in the emergence of informal organization, that is, in the development of work patterns and interaction patterns which do not correspond with responsibility patterns.

It would appear then that there are two fundamental sets of variables which define the operations of an organized group. These are:

1. *Variables which define formal organization.* These are:
    a. Responsibility variables (the work one is expected to do).
    b. Formal interaction variables (the persons with whom one is expected to work).

2. *Variables which define informal organization.* These are:
    a. Work performance variables (the tasks one actually performs).
    b. Informal interaction variables (the persons with whom one actually works).

If we regard the variables listed above as basic variables of organization, we can also regard them as variables of membership and of leadership. In other words, an organization can be studied in terms of these four types of variables: responsibilities, work performances, formal interactions and informal interactions. Leadership can also be studied in terms of the same variables.

Responsibility variables define the duties that the members are expected to perform. The responsibilities of a given position may remain the same, whether A or B occupies the position. *Work performance* variables are defined by the tasks performed and by the methods of their performance. Individual A may accept a position previously occupied by B. The responsibilities as defined by organization charts and manuals may remain the same, but the tasks actually

[14] G. C. Homans, "A Conceptual Scheme for the Study of Social Organization," *American Sociological Review*, Vol. 12 (1947), pp. 13-26.
[15] Walter Firey, "Informal Organization and the Theory of Schism," *American Sociological Review*, Vol. 13 (1948), pp. 15-24.

performed by A may differ somewhat from those performed by B, and the methods of performance may vary markedly.

Formal interaction variables define the persons to whom and for whom the members are accountable, as well as others with whom they are expected to cooperate, in the discharge of their responsibilities. *Informal interaction* variables are defined by the persons with whom the members actually work and cooperate in the performance of their tasks.

Informal organization comes about as a result of the development of discrepancies (a) between work performance and responsibilities as defined and (b) between informal interactions and formally defined interactions. Thus leadership is ever confronted with the task of reconciling discrepancies—discrepancies between what ought to be done and what is being done, between goals and achievements, between organizational needs and available resources, between the needs of individual members and the requirements of organization, between formal lines of cooperation and informal patterns of cooperation.

An organization in action comprises a complex of many variables in interaction. In making a pictorial representation of a business organization, the usual procedure is to plot the division of formal responsibility on a two dimensional chart. The horizontal dimension of the chart shows the division of responsibility for various kinds of work. The vertical dimension of the chart shows the division of responsibility for different levels of decision-making, and indicates the persons to whom one is accountable and those for whose performance one is accountable in the discharge of duties. This dimension defines the formal authority and status systems of the organization. Level (position in the organization hierarchy) and function (kind of work performed) are not independent dimensions. Although functions tend to differ from level to level, there is considerable overlap. Results from the Ohio State Leadership Studies [16, 17] have shown that the functions of top leadership tend to be supported at each lower level in the leadership structure by increasingly more detailed and routine work in the same functions.

Personal interaction can also be conceived as varying in both horizontal and vertical directions. The horizontal dimension is defined by the range (number) of members with whom an individual inter-

[16] Carroll L. Shartle, "Leadership and Executive Performance," *Personnel*, Vol. 25 (1949), pp. 370-380.

[17] Ralph M. Stogdill and Carroll L. Shartle, "Methods for Determining Patterns of Leadership Behavior in Relation to Organization Structure and Objectives," *Journal of Applied Psychology*, Vol. 32 (1948), pp. 286-291.

acts. Some persons tend to work alone or with single individuals, while others are observed to work with large numbers of persons. The vertical aspect of personal interaction is defined by the number of strata (echelons) above and below his own in which a member works with others. Some persons may be observed to work only with others at the same level in the organization. Others tend to work only with subordinates, and still others tend to work only with superiors. These tendencies may or may not represent expression of individual differences in social interaction patterns. Results obtained thus far in the Ohio State Leadership Studies suggest that these patterns of interaction may be determined in part by the functions served by various types of positions. Technical consultants and staff aides tend to spend more time with superiors. Members in supervisory positions are observed, as would be expected, to spend more of their time with assistants, and subordinates. Members in coordinative positions tend to spend time with superiors and subordinates, as well as with associates at the same level in the organization. A member's function or duties may determine to a considerable degree which persons in the organization he may influence, as well as the nature of the influence that he can exert.

Group organization defines and delimits leadership

The very process of defining responsibility serves to structure and delimit the role that the leader may play in the organization. He cannot perform all the duties of all the members. His own accomplishment is therefore dependent upon the performance of others. His responsibilities are circumscribed by the outlined procedures and delegated responsibilities necessary for the achievement of stated goals.

Each member must work within the organizational framework which defines the limits of his participation (how far he ought to go and beyond which he ought not to go) in performance of duties. It also sets the requirements for his cooperation with others and defines his relationships with his superiors and subordinates. This organizational structuring is not viewed alike by all persons. To some it appears as a barrier to participation or recognition. To others it appears as a prod and stimulus to greater effort and participation. For still others it provides a secure and comfortable sphere of activities and working relationships. Organization, therefore, in defining the responsibilities and working relationships of its members, sets up barriers to participation, as well as facilitating it.

Even as the organization sets boundaries by providing a framework within which members discharge their responsibilities, so the individual presents various barriers to the influence of the organization upon his own behavior and reactions. Some members may be limited in capacity to discharge their responsibilities, while others who are highly skilled in the techniques of their responsibilities are limited in capacity to interact with others. Each member carries into the organization his past experiences, his needs, ideals, personal goals, and committments to other organizations, which may modify and determine his capacity for participation. It would appear that the extent to which the behavior of different members is determined by the characteristics of the group represent a continuum from little to great, and also, that the extent to which the behavior of the different individuals determines the behavior of groups may be conceived as representing a similar continuum.

It becomes apparent that a study in leadership represents a study of relationships, of variables in interaction. According to Pigors,[18] a study of leadership must consider: (1) the leader, (2) the members as individuals, (3) the group as a functioning organization, and (4) the situation.

All organizations operate within a larger cultural and environmental framework. No organization can escape entirely the influence of the external situation. The organization may be influenced by the availability of resources, by changes in the social order of which it is a part, by competition of other organizations for the participation, resources or loyalty of its members, and by innumerable other factors outside the control of the organization itself. These factors also influence the leadership of the group.

Leadership and effectiveness of organization

According to Barnard [19] the persistence of cooperation depends upon two conditions: (a) effectiveness, the accomplishment of cooperative purpose, and (b) efficiency, the satisfaction of individual motives. Thus, although in many situations it may appear desirable to effect a maximum of goal achievement with a minimum of organizational expenditure, such a procedure might jeopardize the welfare or morale of the members. It then becomes evident that there are many situations in which organization is confronted by a complex of con-

---

[18] Paul Pigors, *Leadership or Domination* (New York: Houghton Mifflin, 1935).
[19] Chester I. Barnard, *The Functions of the Executive* (Cambridge: Harvard University Press, 1938).

tradictory factors which must be considered in arriving at a decision. It also becomes apparent that the effectiveness of an organization cannot always be evaluated in terms of the degree to which it has attained its objectives. It may be necessary first to evaluate the goals and objectives themselves or the cost of their attainment. A carefully thought out discussion of factors to be considered in setting organizational goals, arriving at decisions, and evaluating the success of an organization has been presented by Simon.[20] He states "The accomplishment by an administrative program of its organizational goals can be measured in terms of *adequacy* (the degree to which its goals have been reached) or of *efficiency* (the degree to which the goals have been reached relative to the available resources)." Simon, in agreement with Barnard, maintains that the criterion of adequacy alone is not valid as a measure of group accomplishment. He observes that "the fundamental criterion of administrative decision must be a criterion of *efficiency* rather than a criterion of *adequacy*. The task of administration is to maximize social values relative to limited resources."

If organizational goals are employed as reference points in evaluating effectiveness, then the goals themselves must be subject to evaluation. In addition, the cost (human or material) of goal attainment must be considered as a factor in evaluation. Both Barnard and Simon imply that organization cannot be regarded as a unit in isolation—or as a law unto itself. The motive of organization is the creation of social value or goods for its members, and these values bear some significant relation to the values of society in general.

Since leadership is related to the determination of group goals, it becomes apparent that the leader is seldom a free agent. In influencing the activities of the organization in its striving toward goal achievement he must consider certain social values, not only in relation to the members, but in relation to society as well. If he ignores the welfare of the members he is likely to lose their following. If he ignores the welfare of society he is likely to lead his group into difficulty. Thus leadership is subject to determination by factors which are external to the organization, as well as by internal group factors.

The definition of leadership

The definition of leadership as a process of influencing the activities of an organized group in its task of goal setting and goal

---

[20] Herbert A. Simon, *Administrative Behavior* (New York: Macmillan, 1947).

achievement should perhaps be reexamined. Does it define leadership? What are its implications? Admittedly, it defines only at a high level of generality. Certainly it does not include all social acts and influences, but it is nevertheless, an inclusive rather than a restrictive definition of leadership. Even so, it is more restrictive than most of those attempted in the recent literature. The definition restricts leadership to influence within the organized group. It does not imply domination or direction of others, nor any technique of influence; nor does it specify any particular member who should be regarded as a leader. The definition permits the study of any member of an organization to determine the extent of his leadership influence, and permits consideration of the possibility that every member may contribute toward determining the leadership of the organization.

The definition carries the implication that leadership may be not so much an attribute of individuals as an aspect of organization. In this respect it parallels the concept of authority. It is generally recognized that an executive in a business concern has authority in relation to his employees only during the time they are working as members of the organization. His authority does not extend outward into the direction of their personal or social lives. Nor does his position as an executive give him authority over other persons who are not members of his organization. In other words, authority is a relationship that exists between persons who are mutually participating as members of an organized enterprise. Authority is not an attribute of one or a few persons. Authority is an interactional process by means of which the organization defines for each individual the scope for action he has in making decisions, carrying out responsibilities, and enlisting the cooperation of others. The authority of any single individual will be largely circumscribed and defined by the authority of others, and at the same time, his own degree of authority will in part determine the authority of others.

Leadership appears also to be determined by a system of interrelationships. As such it must be regarded as an aspect of organization, just as authority is a derivative of organization. If leadership is determined by a system of interacting variables, then each of the several dimensions of responsibility and personal interaction might be conceived as representing a gradient of influence. If so, then it should be possible to measure leadership influences in terms of these dimensions.

Some members may be regarded as rating higher than others in leadership by virtue of the fact that they have responsibility for making decisions which exert a marked influence upon the activities of the organization. Some members may influence the activities of the organization as a result of personal interaction with other members, even though they do not hold positions of high level responsibility. Some members may rate high in both types of influence. It would not be expected that any organization could be found in which all influence is exerted by a single member. It would rather be expected that all the members of the organization could be ordered or ranked to some degree in terms of the influence they exert in various dimensions. The proposal to measure leadership in terms of the influence exerted by individuals may appear to contradict the statement that leadership is an aspect of organization rather than an attribute of individuals. But this is not a necessary conclusion. It was pointed out that authority is generally understood to be an aspect of organization. However, it can be observed that some members exercise more authority than others. The judgment can also be made that some persons have "too much" or "too little" authority. Such observations indicate an evaluation of conditions relative to various factors in the organization. In the same way it can be observed that member A exerts more leadership influence in some situations; while members B, C, and D exert more influence in determining activities of the organization in other instances. It may be that the leadership of A is circumscribed by the leadership of B, C, and D who are in competition with him; or it may be that the leadership of A is dependent upon the supporting leadership of B, C and D. In either event, the leadership influence of any one member is determined in part by the leadership exerted by others, and the balance may change from time to time.

SUMMARY

An organization is composed of individuals. Its existence is dependent upon the cooperation and performance of individuals who play different roles. Measures of authority, leadership, and the like, are but measures of aspects of organization, even though the measurements are made in terms of members and the relationships among members. Leadership exists only in so far as individuals, as members of organization, are differentiated as to the influence they exert upon the organization; and the leadership influence of any one member will be determined to a large degree by the total leadership structure of the organization. It is for this reason that leadership has been here defined in terms of influence upon the activities of the organization, rather than in terms of influence upon persons.

The advantages of this formulation of the leadership problem are as follows: First, it removes leadership from the broad, vaguely defined realm of social interaction in general, and integrates it with the basic variables which describe an organized group. Second, and more important, is the fact that it suggests the development of methods for studying leadership as an aspect of work performance, work methods and working relationships.

> An attempt is being made to develop such methods for the Ohio State Leadership Studies. For example, the goals and structure of organization and the responsibility patterns of members are determined by examining organization charts and manuals and by interviews with members of the organization. Work patterns are determined by modified job analysis procedures. Sociometric methods are employed to determine working relationships between the members and to chart the informal organization. The social values and role concepts of leaders and members are studied by means of attitude scales. These methods are supplemented by various check lists and rating scales.

In conclusion, a word of caution may be in order. The present paper has been concerned with a search for the minimal factors which will permit a functional integration of the concepts: leader, member and organization. In attempting to isolate these minimal common elements, many other important factors associated with leadership and group functioning have been excluded as not contributing to this central purpose. The present formulation represents merely one segment of a set of hypotheses to be subjected to experimental test.

QUESTIONS

1. State and discuss the barriers to the development of a theory of leadership.
2. Distinguish the terms "group" and "organization."
3. Define the basic variables of organization.
4. Explain the effect of organization on the meaning and limits of leadership.
5. How does Stogdill define leadership? Do you agree with this definition?

LEADERSHIP: A CONCEPTION AND
SOME IMPLICATIONS *

Irving Knickerbocker

During several years of working with the problems of human relations which arise in organizations of people, my colleagues and I have sought a satisfactory conceptualization of the phenomena of leadership. We have gradually crystallized some ideas which have been helpful both theoretically and practically. However, a recent survey of the literature on leadership suggests that we have wandered from the paths customarily followed by students of the subject.

Motivated by the conviction that some systematic frame of reference, however rough, is better than none, we offer the following analysis of leadership for what it may suggest to those who are interested. While these are in part speculative considerations, they have been tested for usefulness through some years of practice.

Much of the literature on leadership represents an attempt to study the leader as an entity possessed of characteristic traits and occupying rather inertly a status position relative to other individuals who are not too clearly related to him.[1] Actually, the leader emerges as a consequence of the needs of a group of people and of the nature of the situation within which that group is attempting to operate. Stogdill,[2] after an exhaustive survey of the literature, concludes that "leadership is not a matter of passive status, or of the mere possession of some combination of traits. It appears rather to be a working relationship among members of a group, in which the leader acquires status through active participation and demonstration of his capacity for carrying cooperative tasks through to completion."

Jenkins,[3] reviewing the literature dealing with the problem of the selection of leaders in various fields, finds that "The situation does not appear to be a particularly happy one with regard to the deriving of general principles or of setting up a systematic theory of leadership from the available information. A few statements may be set forth, however, that appear to hold for the findings of a number of the

---

* From the *Journal of Social Issues*, Vol. 47, No. 4 (Summer, 1948), pp. 1-34. Reprinted with permission.

[1] A notable exception is "Functions of the Executive" by Chester Barnard (Cambridge, Mass.: Harvard University Press, 1938).

[2] Ralph M. Stogdill, "Personal Factors Associated with Leadership: A Survey of the Literature," *Journal of Psychology*, Vol. 25, 1948, 35-71.

[3] William O. Jenkins, "A Review of Leadership Studies with Particular Reference to Military Problems." *Psychological Bulletin*, Vol. 44, 1947, No. 1, 75.

investigations reviewed; this list should be thought of as a series of hypotheses for further investigation." His first statement is as follows: "1 Leadership is specific to the particular situation under investigation. Who becomes the leader of a given group engaging in a particular activity and what leadership characteristics are, in a given case are a function of the specific situation including the measuring instruments employed. Related to this conclusion is the general finding of wide variations in the characteristics of individuals who become leaders in similar situations, and even greater divergence in leadership behavior in different situations."

These authors, and a few others, have apparently recognized some of the inadequacies of the literature of leadership and of traditional research approaches to the subject. However, we are left standing on the threshold of a house which has not yet been erected. It is the purpose of this article to draw a tentative architect's sketch of the house which is so badly needed.

Although the evidence does not support the romantic conception of the leader endowed with magic attributes, this conception is widely held. One wonders why it persists with such vitality. Perhaps the fact that each of us commenced his life under the guidance of a leader —a big man, of tremendous endowment, with almost limitless power —would help to explain the prevalence and tenacity with which this Leader concept is held.

Each of us had a father, a prestige figure, magically endowed. Many of us found security in that figure. Since we continue to need security, perhaps we continue to carry with us out of childhood the father symbol, the Leader. If such an assumption may be accepted, then we can readily see that the leader, or the man whom we conceptualize as a leader, should be larger, more intelligent, more mature, more cultured, more impressive than we.[4]

Individuals so endowed relative to the group with which they are associated would statistically be seen more often as potential leaders and statistically be placed more often in a position where they might practice leadership, and finally, might statistically more often become leaders. All this could happen frequently enough to give us the feeling that leaders somehow are different and permit us to make the misleading research finding that the leader is an entity who can be considered apart from his functional relationship to his followers.

Following our assumptions further, we should not be surprised to find that men who have achieved through function a position of

4 Stogdill, op. cit.

leadership have usually possessed many of the mythical attributes of the leader. They serve as ink blots onto which people project their desires for security and dependence. To be sure, the degree of such endowment may be expected to vary with the closeness of the association between leader and followers. It is more difficult for their immediate associates to see them as leaders magically endowed. A consideration of Hitler and Roosevelt as seen by remote followers and immediate associates may lend some reality to this hypothesis.

It is interesting to speculate upon the possibility of the leader created by concerted action through various media of publicity in the absence of any true functional relationship between leader and followers. It doesn't seem impossible that such a leader might exist as an entity devoid of functional followers, but becoming for people the symbol, Leader. Certainly for most people the great leaders of history have been ony a symbol. Any functional relationship between the people and the leader has been remote, if it existed at all. *Yet the leader in each case has arisen through performing certain functions relative to some group somewhere, sometime.* It would be interesting to compare the attitudes toward the leader of individuals from two groups, one composed of those functionally related to him as leader, the other composed of those for whom he existed as the symbol, Leader. From the historical literature there would appear to be sharp differences between the man and leader to his functional followers and the same Leader to those people who were not functionally related to him.

There is no reason to assume that the two concepts, Leader and functional leadership, may not be fused in many cases. Certainly the former would appear to grow out of the latter. If people are in search of the former, some of them at least may try to see in each functional leader, a Leader. It would appear that those leaders with sufficient sense of the dramatic to lend themselves readily to conforming to the outward appearance of being a Leader may more readily become one. Lincoln was rather a disappointment to many people in this respect. Hitler and Mussolini took to the role more readily. The functional leader always earns respect and prestige to the extent that he fulfils his function, but immediate contact is apt to inhibit the growth of the extremes of the Leader concept. Hence the many cynical proverbs concerning the prophet in his own country.

It would appear then that the usual notion of the leader serves to cover two quite separate concepts.[5] The first is an emotionally held

---

[5] A. C. Van Dusen, "Measuring Leadership Ability," *Personnel Psychology*, Vol. 1, No. 1, 1948, p. 68.

conviction that some men are Leaders and as such are set apart from
the common horde. These Leaders do not owe their position to their
functional relationship to followers, but to an almost magical aura
which surrounds them. They have god-like attributes which they
have not earned but rather with which they have been endowed.

Our hypothesis is that this concept arises in our culture out of the
relationship of the very young child with his father. An examination
of the leader concept in other cultures or an analysis of differences
between leader concepts among male and female in our own culture
should help test this hypothesis. If the hypothesis be granted, then
the statistical appearance of certain traits ascribed to the Leader, and
the statistical appearance of leaders with these traits is not surprising. Nor is it surprising that experimentally devised but functional tests of leaders do not bear out the coincidence of the specific
traits and the function of leadership.

The other concept—functional leadership—places emphasis not on
a fixed set of personal characteristics nor on particular kinds of leadership behavior, but upon the circumstances under which groups of
people integrate and organize their activities toward objectives, and
upon the way in which that integration and organization is achieved.
Thus the leadership function is analyzed and understood in terms of
a dynamic relationship. A leader may acquire followers, or a group
of people may create a leader, but the significant aspects of the
process can only be understood in dynamic, relationship terms. Evidence and speculation to date make it appear that this functional or
operation conception of leadership provides the more useful approach.[6]

We need some schema which will emphasize this relationship
between leader and led as a dynamic pattern. As an aid to thinking
about such relationships, we have developed the following simple
schema: [7]

------

[6] Ordway Tead, *The Art of Leadership* (New York: McGraw-Hill Book
Company, Inc., 1935), p. 20, p. 61.
Jenkins, *op. cit.*
Stogdill, *op. cit.*
T. N. Whitehead, *Leadership in a Free Society* (Cambridge, Mass.: Harvard
University Press, 1936), p. 68.
R. M. Stogdill, and C. L. Shartle, "Methods for Determining Patterns of
Leadership Behavior in Relation to Organization Structure and Objectives,"
Journal of Applied Psychology, Vol. 32, No. 3, 1948, pp. 286-291.
[7] In the interests of brevity, only three of a half dozen or more interrelated
generalizations are here mentioned. The reader will discover that they are closely
integrated with others outlined by McGregor in the preceding article.

1. *Existence for each individual may be seen as a continual struggle to satisfy needs, relieve tensions, maintain an equilibrium.*

Each of us uses many different *means* for the satisfaction of his needs. We use muscular skills, personal appearance, intelligence, knowledge. We use tools, food, money. The means we habitually use may become needs themselves. In each specific case, however, some *means* is used for the satisfaction of a need or of a pattern of needs.

2. *Most needs in our culture are satisfied through relationships with other individuals or groups of individuals.*

This assumption points up the fact that people and our relationship with people constitute the *means* upon which we rely most heavily for the satisfaction of our needs. Other people as it were possess the means which we would use to satisfy our needs. We do not grow our own food, make our own clothes, provide our own transportation, educate ourselves, or even provide our own recreation. We satisfy such needs, and many others, through means controlled and provided by others. When we are lonely, another person appears to us as means and controls in a sense the means we would like to use. When we are insecure, a closer relationship with someone is the means we seek and that someone controls the means. Often another person may possess the means in the form of money, skill, knowledge, or tools which we need as means for the satisfaction of our needs. We attempt then to establish a relationship which will be a means to gain the use of something which in turn will be a means to need satisfaction. To the manager the worker possesses the means of skill or hands. Through relationship with the worker as means, the manager hopes to obtain the further means he requires to satisfy his needs. To the worker, the manager controls the means of job and pay. So all of us seek through relationships with others the means, or the means to the means, for satisfying needs.

3. *For any individual the process of employing his relationship with other individuals as means for the satisfaction of his needs is an active rather than a passive process.*

He does not wait passively for the occurrence of such relationships as will provide means for need satisfactions. He institutes appropriate relationships or utilizes those which already exist toward the end of satisfying his needs. The relationship is thus an active, striving one, through which each party is operating to augment his means for need satisfaction (or to protect the means already at hand). Since each individual possesses some quantum of means small or large which some other individual might utilize for need satisfaction, each individual through his control of those means has some bargaining power relative to others. The control of means ("scarce means," the economists call them), which others desire for the satisfaction of needs, constitutes what we ordinarily call power. The use of power (or "means control") to gain the means for need satisfaction from others appears to be the essential aspect of all human relationships. The individual who controls many or scarce means which other people seek to utilize for need satisfaction is in a position of power. Such power may be used by an individual either to reduce the means of other individuals (punishment), or to augment their means (reward) toward the ultimate end of inducing these other individuals to provide him with means for the satisfaction of his own needs.

———

This approach furnishes us with the bare essentials of a schema for considering the dynamic aspect of the relationship between people. That relationship appears to consist essentially in an active striving to procure through other people the means for need satisfaction. The relationship is of course bilateral, each party seeking means through the other. We should expect an individual to attempt to establish a relationship only when it appears to promise means and to maintain it only so long as it continues to do so. We might also predict that the greatest number of individuals would attempt to establish a relationship with that individual who in their perceptual field gave greatest promise of providing means.[8] Finally, we might predict that individuals would attempt to break off relationships with and avoid those individuals who threaten to reduce their means, and if they could not do so would react protectively and possibly aggressively.

Let us consider a group of people including one who would be designated by the others as the leader if we asked. Let us make a general application of our schema to such a situation. We have a leader attempting to find a means through the activities of the group members for the satisfaction of *his* needs. At the same time the group members are in the relationship with him simply because he appears to them the best means available for the satisfaction of such of *their* needs as can be satisfied through this group.

Let us ask some questions concerning the individuals in the group.

———

[8] H. H. Jennings, in *Readings in Social Psychology*, ed. Newcomb & Hartley (New York: Henry Holt and Company, 1947), p. 412.

Question 1

Why are the individuals in the group?

Because through it or through the leader they anticipate finding means for satisfying needs (or means for protecting themselves against a threatened loss of need satisfaction). If we run over groups that we know well; such as a labor union, a church, a business association, a social club, etc., we seem to find that we joined such groups because they appeared to offer means. We leave them when they no longer seem to do so.

Question 2

Why do the individuals accept direction of their activities?

Because this behavior appears to them to provide means for the satisfaction of their needs. The leader is seen as a means; through the relationship with him, needs are satisfied (or a reduction in need satisfaction is prevented). The leader may promise a chicken in every pot, a glorious future, or more money for less work. If the group member sees satisfaction of needs in the direction the leader indicates, if he believes the leader will serve as a means for getting those satisfactions, the group member follows. On the other hand, the leader may say "follow me, or disaster may befall you," "follow me, or I'll see to it that you rue the day you refuse," "follow me or else. . . ." Again, if the group member believes that the leader controls the relevant means, if the group member sees a threat to his available means in failing to go in the directions the leader indicates, the group member follows. The individual then is related to the leader as a means to need satisfaction or as a means to protect available means from reduction. He follows and permits his activities to be directed because he believes that to do so will get him what he wants.

Question 3

Why does the leader arise?

Even in the simplest situation, such as when a group embarks on discussion which will eventuate in a decision of some sort, a leader seems to be essential. Operationally, it is difficult for a group to speak or act except through an individual member. If everyone talks at once, no one can hear or attend. If everyone plans at once, or acts at once without a plan, there is no group but rather a collection of individuals planning or acting. For the group to act as a unit or to show organization, it is necessary that individual members speak for

it. The necessity for an ordering of discussion is readily apparent
as a means to a group. Such ordering must come through the action
of an individual. Someone must verbalize the necessity for order, the
methods of ordering, the final agreement on methods, and, the agent.
Some individual must order and in doing so he provides simple but
necessary means for the group. Even at this very simple level, the
necessity for a leader is real and apparent to most groups. To the
extent that the objectives of the group require greater diversity of
effort and greater coordination, the need for a leader will increase.

Now let us look at the leader and ask some questions about his
behavior. Let us again answer the question in terms of our frame of
reference and examine the answers for the sense they make.

Question 4

How is the leader to be characterized?

The leader is not a disembodied entity endowed with unique
characteristics. He is the leader of a group and is the leader only in
terms of his functional relationship to the group. Therefore the part
he plays in the total dynamic pattern of the behavior of the group
defines him as leader. He is a leader not because he is intelligent,
skillful or original, but because his intelligence, skill or originality is
seen as a means by the group members. He is a leader not because
he is relatively imposing of stature, well-dressed, fluent of speech, or
from a higher socio-economic background, but because these factors
tend to predispose group members to expect better means from their
possessor.

The leader is followed because he promises to get, or actually gets
his followers more nearly what they want than anyone else. If he
does so, he will be followed be he small, insignificant looking and
relatively speechless. In our culture we have some predisposition to
expect people with certain characteristics to provide better means.
Also certain characteristics such as intelligence may by and large in
fact enable certain individuals to provide better means. However,
the leader is a product not of his characteristics, but of his functional
relationship to specific individuals in a specific situation. As a result,
the variability of leaders' characteristics upsets all but the broadest
statistical efforts at analysis.

Question 5

How does the leader arise?

The leader appears to arise in one of two ways. First, as a result
of agreement among members of a group that some individual serves

as better means than any other. Such agreement may be wholly predictive, a matter of guess-work, or may be the result of experience among various members. The agreement of the members of a group may be verbalized or tacit. The member of a group who suggests "let's go get a cup of coffee" may collect a following and for a minute or so be a leader simply because he has voiced at an instant an operation which appears as a means to other members. The member of a group who is known to possess some special skill which is at the moment a necessity may be turned to and be expected to function as a leader because of his possession. In our culture it is not unusual for any group to make it first a business to choose a leader.

The second way in which a leader may arise is as a result of objectives which require a group of people for their achievement. An individual, for example, wants to accomplish something which can only be accomplished if he can direct the activities of a number of other people. He seeks then to find a group, or an assortment of individuals, who will accept his direction of their activities. If our basic assumptions above are correct, he will acquire "followers" only if, *in their eyes*, following him promises to result in increased need satisfaction (or in avoidance of reduction of need satisfaction).

Question 6

Why does the leader lead?

Through leading, the leader obtains means of satisfying his needs. Perhaps he finds satisfaction in the operation of leading, in manipulating people or in helping them. Perhaps the prestige and recognition accorded the leader are important sources of satisfaction. Or, to take the most obvious aspect, perhaps the result of the activities he directs is itself the means he seeks.

Consider, for example, the industrial manager. He may obtain satisfaction from his leadership role in a variety of ways. He may obtain satisfaction simply from being "the boss," from being able to tell people what to do, to control their activities and their satisfactions. He may find satisfaction, in being regarded as their benefactor, in their gratitude for his favors, or their fear of his punishments. He may enjoy the way he is treated by those outside the organization who are impressed with his title and position. Finally, he may obtain a higher salary, promotion, and recognition from the achievements of the group whose activities he directs.

The motivation of the individual certainly plays a part in the likelihood of his leading. Many adults seem to dislike to lead. Others lead occasionally when, by reason of some special skill or knowledge they possess, it seems to them or to the group reasonable that they should do so. Some lead when only through the concerted activities of a group of people can they find a means to some need satisfaction. Still others enjoy leading. The actual operation of leading is a means to need satisfaction for them. Such individuals are apt to seek situations in which whatever means they have will be in demand. They attempt to acquire the skills which will be means, and a manner which will indicate their possession of means. If there are "born leaders," they arise from this group. Due to the many objectives in our culture which can only be achieved through group effort, many organizations arise. A great many people find leading—that is the job of a superior in an organization—to be the means through which they satisfy important needs.

Question 7

What is the function of the leader?

The function of the leader is to organize the activities of the members of the group toward the accomplishment of some end through controlling means for the satisfaction of the relevant needs of the members of the group. When the leader has been chosen by a group of people who have decided upon an objective to be attained, the leader's function is obvious and his job is relatively simple. When the leader, however, is not chosen by the group, but appointed and given means control by someone outside the group, or appoints himself because he requires a group to achieve his purposes (as in business or military organizations), his job is considerably more difficult. In such circumstances the objective to be attained through the activities of the group is the objective of those who appointed him leader. This may not be the objective of the group he is to lead. Nevertheless, he must appear to the people he is to lead as a means for *their* need satisfaction or they will not accept his direction.

Sometimes, as a consequence, the appointed leader is an individual who would never have been chosen by the group he leads, but one who cannot be rejected because he controls important means for need satisfaction. He is "accepted" as the lesser evil. He appears to the group as a means only in the negative sense. Nevertheless, even in such extreme cases, the leadership function remains the same.

Question 8

Can all of the various kinds of leaders be accounted for by this same frame of reference?

The term leader is certainly used to designate many different positions and functions. It may be used to indicate a figurehead, a position in an organization, a self-appointed dictator possessed of sufficient "or else" power to force a following, or an individual who has been designated as leader by voluntary action of the group. To cut through the diverse usage which has been made of the term leader, we might say that to the extent that any individual succeeds in collecting an actual following, he does so because he controls means. The dictator may be followed because he has created or made use of a situation in which all alternatives to following him are less desirable as means. The superior in the formal organization, for instance in industry, may often occupy a position similar to that of dictator without being particularly aware of it. The man who can control means available to other people can use his control to force that alternative behavior which appears a better means within the restricted choice although a worser one within a larger but forbidden frame of reference. To the extent that the means controlled are scarce means, to that extent the possibility of limiting alternatives as a means of control is possible. The leader chosen by voluntary action of a group is seen as the best means rather than the lesser evil. But all leaders, whatever their personal objectives, must serve as means for their followers, or they will not be leaders (i.e., they will have no followers).

Our conclusions from the above discussion of the nature of leadership may be summarized as follows:

1. The symbolic or romantic conception of the Leader, although widely prevalent, does not explain the phenomena of leadership. It exists, I have suggested, as a consequence of the nature of the individual's relationship with his father in early childhood. It represents a magical, perhaps wishful, attempt to find security through surrogate relationships resembling that early one. The leader, realistically and factually, is not a person endowed with a list of characteristics which make him what he is.

2. When conceived in terms of the dynamics of human social behavior, leadership is a function of needs existing in a given situation, and consists of a relationship between an individual and a group.

3. The functional relationship which is leadership exists when a leader is perceived by a group as controlling means for the satisfaction of their needs. Following him may be seen either as a means

to increased need satisfaction or as a means to prevent decreased
need satisfaction.

----

4. The leader may "emerge" as a means to the achievement of
objectives desired by a group. He may be selected, elected, or spontaneously accepted by the group because he possesses or controls
means (skill, knowledge, money, associations, property, etc.) which
the group desires to utilize to attain their objectives—to obtain
increased need satisfaction.

5. On the other hand, the leader may appoint himself or be
appointed by someone outside the group to be led. In this instance
leadership is a means to the achievement of the leader's objectives
(or the objectives of those who appoint him). However, there will
be no relationship with the group—no followers—except in terms of
the leader's control of means for the satisfaction of the needs of the
followers. Either the leader's objections must also be those of the
group (and he himself be seen by the group as a means to their
attainment), or else accepting the leader's direction must be seen by
the group members as the best available means to prevent reduced
need satisfaction.

In business and industry, the leader is of the "appointed" (sometimes "self-appointed") kind. The members of management are not
selected by the group they are to lead, but are appointed by those
higher in management (or by owners) to achieve the objectives for
which the business was created. There are some very special problems faced by the leader in such a situation, as will be apparent from
the discussion above. It is my purpose to examine this kind of
leadership in industry in more detail in the following pages.

The group of people comprising an industrial organization is not
a group which has arisen to achieve an objective common to all its
members. The owners, or the managers, have recruited a number of
isolated individuals—created a group—because the combined efforts
of many people are required to achieve the *owner's* objectives.

People become members of an industrial organization, and accept
direction of their activities by the manager-leader, because to do so
offers the best of the alternative means for need satisfaction. In our
culture it is necessary for most people to have a job in order to live
satisfactorily.

We usually feel that the individual is free to work or not, and
free to choose his employer. Under any but extremely unusual conditions, however, these choices are not "free." The alternative to

working is a serious curtailment of need satisfaction for most people —so serious usually that it is not even perceived as an alternative.

Moreover, alternative possibilities of employment are extremely limited for most people most of the time. Jobs are seldom easy to get, and the prerequisites which one obtains through seniority built up with one employer represent important potentialities of need satisfaction which must be sacrificed if one seeks other employment. The "labor market" which exists in the perception of the average worker or clerk includes a narrow list of feasible alternatives indeed.

As a consequence, the relationship of the manager-leader in industry to his employees is frequently one in which: (1) his objectives are not their objectives, and (2) the relationship is maintained and the employees accept his direction of their activities only because to do otherwise would in their eyes represent a serious reduction in need satisfaction.

Within this context, let us examine the alternative methods which the manager-leader may utilize to organize the activities of people and direct them toward organizational objectives. Briefly, there appear to be four. We break them down for purposes of description; in actuality they are seldom, if ever, seen in such purity.

1. The leader may direct the activities of people through his control of scarce means by forcing a choice of means the alternative to which is lesser means or none at all.

The manager in industry is clearly in such a position when jobless men are plentiful, when jobs are scarce and jobs are the only means to survival. He is also in such a position when an employee knows that to be fired is to be blacklisted by other employers. As we have seen, even under ordinary labor market conditions he is still in this position to some degree because the worker is seldom in a position to know that he can find another equally satisfactory job immediately. In all three cases the manager controls scarce means which may be better means only because the alternative means are restricted.

The manager utilizing this method directs the activities of his subordinates chiefly by holding over their heads the threat of dismissal if they do not accept his direction. It is an interesting fact that "insubordination" is one of the cardinal sins of industry. Under most labor agreements, the worker can be fired summarily for insubordinate behavior. Reinstatements in cases of this kind, even when the most militant labor unions are involved, are rare today.

The formula for leadership of this kind is: "Do what I say, or else. . . ." To be sure, it is seldom stated as baldly as this, but it is implicit in the relationship, and clearly recognized by both leader and "followers." Successful use of this method obviously requires a situation in which the manager controls many important means, and his subordinates control few.[9] Even then, of course, the leader faces the indirect protective and aggressive consequences of the frustration he engenders. Restriction of output, subtle forms of "sabotage," or militant unionism are frequent consequences.

2. The leader may attempt to provide adequate means for the need satisfaction of his subordinates, in the hope that they will accept his direction of their activities out of gratitude and loyalty.

This is commonly termed "paternalism." The leader attempts to use his means control in a positive rather than a negative manner. His own objectives (which include organizational objectives) are not those of his subordinates, but he attempts to win their support by aiding them in achieving their objectives.

Historically, this method has been more successful than the first, "or else" method. There are two inherent difficulties, however. One is that the paternalistic approach is by its very nature limited in the kinds of means it can provide. The follower is necessarily put in the position of being the recipient of the leader's benevolences. He cannot achieve independence; he is always in the leader's debt.

At times this type of relationship becomes intolerable to people. They resent being the "children" of a paternalistic leader. There have been several particularly violent "revolts" in paternalistic industrial organizations, stemming apparently from exactly this kind of resentment.[10]

The other difficulty is that paternalism operates in violation of the psychological law of effect. Instead of arranging so that efforts directed toward organizational goals *result* in increased means for need satisfaction, the paternalistic leader provides the means, and expects the efforts to follow. Minimum "get-by" performance, minimum acceptance of direction, plus an expectation of constantly increasing means are the natural psychological consequences of this Santa Claus-like method of leadership.

The formula for leadership of this kind is: "Do what I say because I am good to you." Implied is the further element: "If you don't do what I say, I will not be good to you."

---

[9] The frustration of managers who, during the lush war years, found their means control drastically reduced pointed up rather sharply their reliance on this method of leadership. By 1945 many of them were wishfully talking about the return of normalcy when there would be more people than jobs and they would be "in the saddle" once more.

[10] An interesting example is cited in *Dynamics of Industrial Democracy* by Clinton Golden and Harold Ruttenberg (New York: Harpers, 1942), pp. 13-17.

3. The leader may direct the activities of people as a result of a bargain, in which he agrees to provide them with certain means in return for which they agree to permit the direction of their activities within certain specified limits.

This is a common situation in industry today. Management bargains with the Union. Each controls means and each enters into an agreement providing for exchange of means. Through such an agreement the manager-leader obtains the right to direct within limits the activities of people who to that extent become his followers.

The difference between this and the first two methods is chiefly characterized by the freedom of choice possible to the follower. Such freedom is relative, of course, and a matter of the perceptual field of the individual. When bargaining is carried on in good faith in a relationship of mutual confidence, the followers' dependence upon the manager-leader is much less than in either the "or else" situation or the paternalistic situation. Of course, this is just another way of saying that the leader's power (means control) is relatively reduced.

The formula for this type of leadership is: "Let us agree that you will do as I say in certain respects, in return for which I will do what you want in certain other respects." Implied by each party is: "If you don't agree, I will prevent you from attaining your objectives."

4. The leader may create conditions such that the objectives he seeks and the objectives his subordinates seek have something in common. Then the direction of their activities becomes to both a "mutual means" for the achievement of his objectives and theirs as well. The activities of the people in achieving their objectives are at the same time the activities the leader desires from them so he can achieve his objectives.

This method of leadership in industry is often talked about but seldom approached in practice. The usual attempt by management is to convince workers by words—by propaganda—that they and management have common objectives. The real problem, however, is at the level of action and not of words. The leader must create conditions such that the people discover through actual experience the mutuality of objectives. Then, and then only, will the leader be encouraged by his followers to direct their activities.

Some of the situations described by Golden and Ruttenberg [11] involve leadership of this fourth kind. Joseph Scanlon, a former associate of Golden and now on the M. I. T. staff, has been experi-

---

[11] Golden and Ruttenberg, *op. cit.*

menting with the development of "cost reduction sharing" plans which are based on this method.[12] In certain respects, James F. Lincoln has successfully created these conditions in the Lincoln Electric Company at Cleveland. A few other daring industrialists are exploring this frontier of human relations in industry.

As applied so far in industry, this method seems to require implementation along two lines. First, there must be a plan which enables the group of workers, *as a group*, to obtain increased means for need satisfaction from efforts directed toward organizational goals. The monetary means thus obtainable must be clearly, simply, and directly related to achievement, and they must represent a *common* objective.[13] Equally important to the monetary return are means for the satisfaction of less tangible needs such as those for knowledge, development, participation, recognition, achievement, status.

The second requirement is to provide the opportunity for satisfaction of these social and egoistic needs. Some formal machinery is necessary by which workers, through representative committees, can meet with management to find solutions to all the problems of more efficient operation of the enterprise. It is through this device, also, that the mutuality of objectives can become a reality.

Leadership of this fourth kind is frequently perceived by managers as involving a tremendous loss of power and control. They feel they would sacrifice their "rights" to direct the activities of their subordinates. Because of the emotional nature of this reliance on personal power in many instances, it is difficult to convince such managers of the incorrectness of their belief. To be sure, they would lose their personal illusion of control in the narrow sense. Moreover, they would be forced to take realistic account of the needs of their subordinates.[14]

However, this method has two positive consequences of tremendous importance. First, because it substitutes the possibility of increased need satisfaction, *of many kinds,* for the negative fear of reduced need satisfaction, it results in genuine motivation toward organizational objectives. The negative consequences of the first two methods, and of many examples of the third—restriction of output,

---

[12] Joseph N. Scanlon, "Adamson and His Profit-Sharing Plan," A.M.A. Production Series No. 172, 1947.

[13] It is in this respect that most "profit sharing" plans fail, since the group's achievement often has little directly to do with the amount of profit earned by the company.

[14] It is perhaps this which lies behind the currently fashionable exhortation to industrial management to acquire a greater sense of "social responsibility."

sabotage, hostility, resistance to change, etc.—vanish into thin air because their causes are removed. Second, this method taps the resources of the whole group. The successful leader of this kind soon discovers the tremendous potentialities for problem solving, for cost reduction, for improved methods, which remain largely latent in the group under other methods of leadership.

Actually, because this method most closely approximates the "natural" relationship of functional leadership, it gives the leader in the end, more rather than less control. His followers perceive him as a positive means to increased need satisfaction; instead of resenting his direction of their activities or accepting it passively, they seek it and encourage it. Reliance on personal power seldom if ever yields this result.

Certainly the phenomenal results obtained by those industrial leaders who have honestly attempted to use this method provide some evidence that the apparent "loss of control" is more than offset by the increased means obtained by leader and followers alike. Our belief is that explorations along this frontier will ultimately demonstrate that past conceptions of leadership have led to a considerable underestimation of the potentialities of organized group effort.

———

Now let us consider one further aspect of the problem faced by the appointed leader, the leader who by reason of his position in an organization has control of means, whose job it is to direct the activities of his subordinates toward the goals of the organization. In industry he earns his living by leading. He is supposed to be a leader. He is exhorted and implored to lead. He takes training courses in leading. Yet in far too many cases he does not appear to be very successful. His followers don't like him and he does not like to be a leader. He commonly regrets that he must accomplish his objectives through people and longs for a mechanical set-up which will not depend on people for its success. Lacking security in his ability as a leader, he tends to depend to an ever greater degree on power, means control, management "rights," and he prays for economic conditions which will give him the whip hand, which will limit alternate choice of means for employees. What is the dilemma of such appointed leaders?

In terms of our frame of reference, there are four methods which a leader may use for diverting the activities of people:

1. *Force*—the leader uses his control of means to *force* the choice of certain activities which he desires as means. The alternative to following him is reduction of need satisfaction.

2. *Paternalism*—the leader provides means, and hopes for acceptance of his leadership out of loyalty and gratitude.

3. *Bargain*—the leader may arrive at a *bargain,* a more or less voluntary choice, made by each party to furnish certain means in return for certain means.

4. *Mutual means*—the leader creates the situation in which certain activities of his and of the group; if performed together, will serve as *mutual means,* means for each to satisfy their own (perhaps different) needs.

The appointed leader, however, is not free to choose among these methods. To a greater or less extent the method is prescribed by the policy of the organization in which he leads. In general today in industrial organizations the method lies somewhere in the region between force and bargaining. The initial concept of leadership in industry seems to have been that of force. Paternalism enjoyed popularity for many years among some managers; it is generally frowned upon but widely practiced today. The rise of unions made possible the opposition of force to force and created the necessity for bargaining.

Today bargaining is the common method used by management to obtain direction of those activities necessary to management's objectives. The appointed leader, endowed with such management "prerogatives"—means control—as management has been able to salvage at the bargaining table, is expected to lead. What leading means will depend on the attitude of his top management and its policy. The frame of reference within which he must lead has been established over a considerable period and is fixed in the attitudes of his subordinates as well as his superiors. Yet he is exhorted to be a good leader; he is trained to use this or that technique; his effectiveness is examined through morale surveys. He is prompted to be tough, to be fair, to use consultative supervision but to retain management rights. The dilemma of the appointed leader is simply that he must succeed as a leader despite the fact that he cannot control the conditions in terms of which he leads.

The essence of leadership lies in the functional relationship between leader and followers. When the conditions of the relationship are established not by the leader but by the policy of the organization, and when that policy favors the "or else" method, or paternalism, or a grudging and hostile bargaining method, the leader is on the spot. He appears to be on the spot in many cases today in industry. In fact, the methods of force and bargaining seem to be somewhat on the spot also. Although force can be used to control the activities of people, it engenders opposing force, and it often defeats its own purpose.

The method of bargaining backed by force is beginning to seem inadequate even to those who cannot conceive of an alternative. Where bargaining rests on mutual respect and force has dropped out, the situation is not too bad. In such cases the mutuality of means which exists, although tenuous, becomes more apparent. "The greater the profits of the company, the larger the cut to labor" idea.

From there to the fourth method is not too impossible a step, although it requires skill, understanding and imagination of a very high order. When management successfully creates the necessary conditions, the organization and its objective become a means not only to management but also to labor. Through this mutual means each satisfies needs. A leader in this situation is a man whose direction of activities is an effective aid for all concerned to attain their objectives. Under such circumstances, the dilemma of the appointed leader disappears.

Questions

1. Explain what Knickerbocker means by the term "functional leadership."
2. How does "functional leadership" differ from the concept "leader"?
3. Discuss the relationship of leadership to need satisfaction.
4. How does the leader emerge according to Knickerbocker? Do you agree?
5. What methods can a leader use to direct the activities of people? Which method do you recommend? Why?

CONDITIONS OF EFFECTIVE LEADERSHIP
IN THE INDUSTRIAL ORGANIZATION *

Douglas McGregor

This discussion of relationships among people at work is written from the point of view of dynamic psychology which, because of its origin in the clinic, directs attention to the whole individual living and interacting within a world of other individuals. Life, from the point of view of dynamic psychology, is a continuous striving to satisfy ever-changing needs in the face of obstacles. The work life is but a segment—although a large one—of the whole.

THE SETTING

Within this framework we shall examine some of the important forces and events in the work situation which aid or hinder the individual as he strives to satisfy his needs. First of all, we must recognize a fundamental fact: the direct impact of almost all these forces upon the individual is through the behavior of other people. This is obvious when we speak of an order from the boss, or pressures exerted by fellow workers to get the individual to join a union. It is perhaps less obvious when we speak of the impact of the business cycle, or the consequences of a fundamental technological change. Nevertheless, the direct influence of these forces on the individual— whether he is a worker or a plant manager—occurs through the medium of the actions of other people. We must include not only the easily observed actions of others, but subtle, fleeting manifestations of attitude and emotion to which the individual reacts almost unconsciously.

For purposes of discussion we may arbitrarily divide the actions of other people which influence the individual in the work situation into three classes: actions of superiors, of subordinates, and of associates. We shall limit our attention mainly to the actions of superiors as they affect the subordinate in his striving to satisfy his needs. This relationship is logically prior to the others, and it is in many ways the most important human relationship in industry.

The fundamental characteristics of the subordinate-superior relationship are identical whether one talks of the worker and the supervisor, the assistant superintendent and the superintendent, or the

* From the *Journal of Consulting Psychology*, Vol. 8 (March-April, 1944), pp. 55-63. Reprinted with permission.

vice-president and the president. There are, to be sure, differences in the content of the relationship, and in the relative importance of its characteristics, at different levels of the industrial organization. The underlying aspects, however, are common to all levels.

THE DEPENDENCE OF THE SUBORDINATE

The outstanding characteristic of the relationship between the subordinate and his superiors is his dependence upon them for the satisfaction of his needs. Industry in our civilization is organized along authoritative lines. In a fundamental and pervasive sense, the subordinate is dependent upon his superiors for his job, for the continuity of his employment, for promotion with its accompanying satisfactions in the form of increased pay, responsibility, and prestige, and for a host of other personal and social satisfactions to be obtained in the work situation.

This dependence is not adequately recognized in our culture. For one thing, it is not consistent with some of our basic social values. The emphasis is usually placed upon the importance of the subordinate's own efforts in achieving the satisfaction of his needs. Nevertheless, the dependence is real, and subordinates are not unaware of it. Among workers, surveys of attitudes invariably place "fair treatment by superiors" toward the top of the list of factors influencing job satisfaction.[1, 2] And the extent to which unions have attempted to place restrictions upon management's authority reflects not only a desire for power but a conscious attempt to reduce the dependence of workers upon their bosses.[3, 4]

Psychologically the dependence of the subordinate upon his superiors is a fact of extraordinary significance, in part because of its emotional similarity to the dependence characteristic of another earlier relationship: that between the child and his parents. The similarity is more than an analogy. The adult subordinate's dependence upon his superiors actually reawakens certain emotions and attitudes which were part of his childhood relationship with his parents, and which apparently have long since been outgrown. The adult is usually unaware of the similarity because most of this complex of childhood emotions has been repressed. Although the emotions influ-

[1] Harold B. Bergen, "Measuring Attitudes and Morale in Wartime," *The Conference Board Management Record*, Vol. 4, No. 4 (April, 1942), pp. 101-104.
[2] Robert N. McMurry, "Management Mentalities and Worker Reactions," *Advanced Management*, Vol. 7, No. 4 (Oct.-Dec., 1942), pp. 165-172.
[3] Robert R. R. Brooks, *When Labor Organizes* (New Haven: Yale University Press, 1938).
[4] Twentieth Century Fund, *How Collective Bargaining Works: A Survey of Experience in Leading American Industries* (New York: The Fund, 1942).

ence his behavior, they are not accessible to consciousness under ordinary circumstances.

Superficially it may seem absurd to compare these two relationships, but one cannot observe human behavior in industry without being struck by the fundamental similarity between them. Space limitations prevent elaboration of this point here, in spite of its great importance.[5]

There are certain inevitable consequences of the dependence of the subordinate upon his superiors. The success or failure of the relationship depends on the way in which these consequences are handled. An understanding of them provides a more useful basis than the usual "rules of thumb" for a consideration of problems of industrial relations. These consequences of the dependence of the subordinate will be discussed under two main headings: (1) the necessity for security in the work situation, and (2) the necessity for self-realization.

THE NECESSITY FOR SECURITY

Subordinates will struggle to protect themselves against real or imagined threats to the satisfaction of their needs in the work situation. Analysis of this protective behavior suggests that the actions of superiors are frequently perceived as the source of the threats.[6] Before subordinates can believe that it is possible to satisfy their wants in the work situation, they must acquire a convincing sense of security in their dependent relationship to their superiors.

Management has recognized the financial aspects of this need for security, and has attempted to provide for it by means of employee retirement plans, health and accident insurance, the encouragement of employee credit unions, and even guaranteed annual wages.[7] How-

---

[5] The relevant literature is vast. A fair introduction to it may be obtained through the following: Walter C. Langer, *Psychology and Human Living* (New York: D. Appleton-Century Co., 1943); A. H. Maslow and Bela Mittelmann, *Principles of Abnormal Psychology* (New York: Harper and Brothers, 1941); John Dollard, Leonard W. Doob, *et al.*, *Frustration and Aggression* (New Haven: Yale University Press, 1939); John Levy and Ruth Monroe, *The Happy Family* (New York: Alfred A. Knopf, 1941).

[6] Cf., for example, the detailed observation of the "bank-wiring" group at the Hawthorne Plant of Western Electric, reported in Chaps. XVII to XXIII of F. J. Roethlisberger and W. J. Dickson, *Management and the Worker* (Cambridge, Mass.: Harvard University Press, 1939). For evidence at another level of the industrial organization, see Conrad M. Arensberg and Douglas McGregor, "Determination of Morale in an Industrial Company," *Applied Anthropology*, Vol. 1, No. 2 (January-March, 1942), pp. 12-34.

[7] Discussion of plans for financial security will be found in the research reports of the National Industrial Conference Board and the Personnel Division of the American Management Association, and in the publications of the Policyholders' Service Bureau of the Metropolitan Life Insurance Company.

ever, this recognition does not get at the heart of the problem: the personal dependence of the subordinate upon the judgments and decisions of his superior.

Labor unions have attacked the problem more directly in their attempts to obtain rules governing promotions and layoffs, grievance procedures, arbitration provisions, and protection against arbitrary changes in work-loads and rates.[8, 9] One important purpose of such "protective" features in union contracts is to restrict superiors in the making of decisions which, from the *worker's point of view*, are arbitrary and threatening. They help to provide the subordinate with a measure of security despite his dependence on his superiors.

The conditions of security: An atmosphere of approval

There are three major aspects of the subordinate-superior relationship—*at any level of the organization*—which affect the security of the subordinate. The most important of these is what we may term the "atmosphere" created by the superior.[10] This atmosphere is revealed not by what the superior does but by the manner in which he does it, and by his underlying attitude toward his subordinates. It is relatively independent of the strictness of the superior's discipline, or the standards of performance which he demands.

A foreman who had unwittingly created such an atmosphere attempted to establish a rule that union officials should obtain his permission when they left the job to meet with higher management, and report to him when they returned. This entirely reasonable action aroused intense resentment, although the same rule was readily accepted by union officials in another part of the plant. The specific actions were unimportant except in terms of the background against which the subordinates pereceived them: an atmosphere of disapproval in the one case and of approval in the other.

Security for subordinates is possible only when they know they have the genuine approval of their superior. If the atmosphere is equivocal, or one of disapproval, they can have no assurance that their needs will be satisfied, *regardless of what they do*. In the absence of a genuine attitude of approval subordinates are threatened, fearful, insecure. Even neutral and innocuous actions of the superiors

---

[8] Cf. *Union Agreement Provisions* (U. S. Department of Labor, Bureau of Labor Statistics, Bulletin No. 686 [Washington: GPO., 1942]).

[9] Sumner H. Slichter, *Union Policies and Industrial Management* (Washington: The Brookings Institution, 1941).

[10] The vital importance of this attitude in familiar superior-subordinate relationships is stressed everywhere in the literature of dynamic psychology. See, for example, J. McV. Hunt, *Personality and the Behavior Disorders* (New York: The Ronald Press Company, 1944), Vol. II.

are regarded with suspicion. Effective discipline is impossible, high standards of performance cannot be maintained, "sabotage" of the superior's efforts is almost inevitable. Resistance, antagonism, and ultimately open rebellion are the consequences.

The conditions of security: knowledge

The second requirement for the subordinate's security is knowledge. *He must know what is expected of him.* Otherwise he may, through errors of commission or omission, interfere with the satisfaction of his own needs. There are several kinds of knowledge which the subordinate requires:

1. *Knowledge of over-all company policy and management philosophy.* Security is impossible in a world of shifting foundations. This fact was convincingly demonstrated—to management in particular—during the first few months of the existence of the War Labor Board. The cry for a national labor policy was frequently heard. "Without it we don't know how to act." Likewise, subordinates in the individual company require a knowledge of the broad policy and philosophy of top management.[11]

2. *Knowledge of procedures, rules and regulations.* Without this knowledge, the subordinate can only learn by trial and error, and the threat of punishment because of innocent infractions hangs always over his head.[12]

3. *Knowledge of the requirements of the subordinate's own job; his duties, responsibilities, and place in the organization.* It is surprising how often subordinates (particularly within the management organization) are unable to obtain this essential knowledge. Lacking it, one can never be sure when to make a decision, or when to refer the matter to someone else; when to act or when to "pass the buck." [13] The potential dangers in this kind of insecurity are apparent upon the most casual consideration.

4. *Knowledge of the personal peculiarities of the subordinate's immediate superior.* The good salesman never approaches a new prospect without learning all he can about his interests, habits, prejudices, and opinions. The subordinate must sell *himself* to his superior, and consequently such knowledge is indispensable to him. Does the

---

[11] A few employee "handbooks" demonstrate an awareness of this point. See for example, *Employee Relations in General Foods* (2nd ed., New York: General Foods Corporation, May 19, 1941).

[12] This is the usually recognized reason for the publication of employee handbooks. Cf. Alexander R. Heron, *Sharing Information with Employees* (Stanford, Cal.: Stanford University Press, 1942).

[13] Donaldson Brown, "Industrial Management as a National Resource," *The Conference Board Management Record*, Vol. V, No. 4 (April, 1943), pp. 142-148.

boss demand initiative and originality, or does he want to make all the decisions himself? What are the unpardonable sins, the things this superior never forgives or forgets? What are his soft spots, and what are his blind spots? There can be no security for the subordinate until he has discovered the answers to these questions.

5. *Knowledge by the subordinate of the superior's opinion of his performance.* Where do I stand? How am I doing? To know where you stand in the eyes of your superiors is to know what you must do in order to satisfy your needs.[14] Lacking this knowledge, the subordinate can have, at best, only a false sense of security.

6. *Advance knowledge of changes that may affect the subordinate.* Resistance to change is a common phenomenon among employees in industry.[15, 16, 17] One of the fundamental reasons is the effect of unpredictable changes upon security. If the subordinate knows that he will always be given adequate warning of changes, and an understanding of the reasons for them, he does not fear them half so much. Conversely, the normal inertia of human habits is tremendously reinforced when one must be forever prepared against unforeseen changes in policy, rules, methods of work, or even in the continuity of employment and wages.

It is not necessary to turn to industry for evidence in support of the principles outlined above. Everywhere in our world today we see the consequences of the insecurity caused by our inability to know what we need to know in order to insure even partially the satisfaction of our needs. Knowledge is power, primarily because it decreases dependence upon the unknown and unpredictable.

The conditions of security: Consistent discipline

The third requirement for the subordinate's security in his relationship of dependence on his superiors is that of consistent discipline. It is a fact often unrecognized that discipline may take the form of positive support for "right" actions as well as criticism and punishment for "wrong" ones. The subordinate, in order to be secure, requires consistent discipline in both senses.[18]

---

[14] This, of course, is the reason for merit rating plans. Cf. National Industrial Conference Board, Inc., *Employee Rating: Methods of Appraising Ability, Efficiency and Potentialities* (Studies in Personnel Policy No. 39, [New York: N.I.C.B., 1941]).

[15] F. J. Roethlisberger and W. J. Dickson, *loc. cit.*

[16] Douglas McGregor and Irving Knickerbocker, "Industrial Relations and National Defense: A Challenge to Management," *Personnel*, Vol. 18, No. 1 (July, 1941), pp. 49-63.

[17] Sumner H. Slichter, *loc. cit.*, Ch. VII-IX.

[18] This, of course, is simply the well-known principle underlying all theories of learning. We need not discuss here its many complicated features.

He requires first of all the strong and willing backing of his superiors for those actions which are in accord with what is expected of him. There is much talk among some managements about superiors who fail to "back up" their subordinates. The insecurity that arises when a subordinate does not know under what conditions he will be backed up leads him to "keep his neck pulled in" at all times. Buck-passing and its consequent frictions and resentment are inevitable under such circumstances.

Given a clear knowledge of what is expected of him, the subordinate requires in addition the definite assurance that he will have the unqualified support of his superiors so long as his actions are consistent with those policies and are taken within the limits of his responsibility. Only then can he have the security and confidence that will enable him to do his job well.

At the same time the subordinate must know that failure to live up to his responsibilities, or to observe the rules which are established, will result in punishment. Every individual has many wants which conflict with the demands of his job. If he knows that breaking the rules to satisfy these wants will *almost inevitably* result in the frustration of his vital long-range needs, self-discipline will be less difficult. If, on the other hand, discipline is inconsistent and uncertain, he may be unnecessarily denying himself satisfaction by obeying the rules. The insecurity, born of uncertainty and of guilt, which is inevitably a consequence of lax discipline, is unpleasant and painful for the subordinate.

What frequently happens is this. The superior, in trying to be a "good fellow," fails to maintain discipline and to obtain the standards of performance which are necessary. His subordinates—human beings striving to satisfy their needs—"take advantage of the situation." The superior then begins to disapprove of his subordinates (in spite of the fact that he is to blame for their behavior.) Perhaps he "cracks down" on them, perhaps he simply grows more and more critical and disapproving. In either event, because he has failed to establish consistent discipline *in an atmosphere of genuine approval,* they are threatened. The combination of guilt and insecurity on the part of the subordinates leads easily to antagonism, and therefore to further actions of which the superior disapproves. Thus a vicious circle of disapproval—antagonistic acts—more disapproval—more antagonistic acts are set up. In the end it becomes extremely difficult to remedy a situation of this kind because both superior and subordinates have a chip-on-the-shoulder attitude which must be abolished before the relationship can improve.

Every subordinate, then, requires the security of knowing that he can count on the firm support of his superiors for doing what is "right," and firm pressure (even punishment) to prevent his doing what is "wrong." *But this discipline must be established and maintained in an atmosphere of approval.* Otherwise, the subordinate's suspicion and resentment of his superiors will lead to the opposite reaction from the desired one. A mild degree of discipline is sufficient in an atmosphere of approval; even the most severe discipline will in the end be unsuccessful in an atmosphere of disapproval. The behavior of the people in the occupied countries of Europe today provides a convincing demonstration of this psychological principle.

THE NECESSITY FOR INDEPENDENCE

When the subordinate has achieved a reasonable degree of genuine security in his relationship to his superiors, he will begin to seek ways of utilizing more fully his capacities and skills, of achieving through his own efforts a larger degree of satisfaction from his work. Given security, the subordinate seeks to develop himself. This *active* search for independence is constructive and healthy. It is collaborative and friendly, yet genuinely self-assertive.

If, on the other hand, the subordinate feels that his dependence on his superiors is extreme, and if he lacks security,[19] he will fight blindly for freedom. This *reactive* struggle for independence is founded on fear and hatred. It leads to friction and strife, and it tends to perpetuate itself because it interferes with the development of an atmosphere of approval which is essential to security.

These two fundamentally opposite ways in which subordinates seek to acquire independence have entirely different consequences. Since we are concerned with the conditions of the successful subordinate-superior relationship, we shall emphasize the active rather than the reactive striving for independence.[20]

The conditions of active independence: Participation

One of the most important conditions of the subordinate's growth and development centers around his opportunities to express his ideas and to contribute his suggestions before his superiors take action on

[19] It is the subordinate's own feelings and not the "objective" facts which are vital in this connection.

[20] A. H. Maslow, "The Authoritarian Character Structure," *The Journal of Social Psychology*, Vol. 18, 1943, pp. 401-411.

matters which involve him.[21, 22] Through participation of this kind he becomes more and more aware of his superior's problems, and he obtains a genuine satisfaction in knowing that his opinions and ideas are given consideration in the search for solutions.[23]

Participation of this kind is fairly prevalent in the upper levels of industrial organizations. It is often entirely lacking further down the line. Some people insist that the proponents of participation at the lower levels of industry are unrealistic idealists. However, there are highly successful instances in existence of "consultative supervision," [24] "multiple management," [25] and "union-management cooperation." [26] The important point is that participation cannot be successful unless the conditions of security are adequately met. Many failures among the currently popular Labor-Management Production Drive Committees can be traced directly to this fundamental fact that active independence cannot be achieved in the absence of adequate security.[27, 28]

There is a real challenge and a deep satisfaction for the subordinate who is given the opportunity to aid in the solution of the difficult but fascinating problems that arise daily in any industrial organization. The superior who, having provided security for his subordinates, encourages them to accept this challenge and to strive *with him* to obtain this satisfaction, is almost invariably surprised at the fruitfulness of the results. The president of one company remarked, after a few management conferences designed to encourage this kind of participation, that he had never before realized in considering his problems how many alternative possibilities were available, nor how inadequate had been the knowledge upon which he based his decisions. Contrary to the usual opinion, this discovery is

[21] The work of Kurt Lewin and his students at the University of Iowa on group dynamics is relevant to this whole discussion, but it is especially pertinent to this matter of participation. Cf. K. Lewin, R. Lippitt, and S. K. Escalona, *Studies in Topological and Vector Psychology I*, University of Iowa Studies in Child Welfare, Vol. 16, No. 3, 1940.

[22] Alex Bavelas, "Morale and the Training of Leaders," in Goodwin Watson, (ed.), *Civilian Morale*, Second Yearbook of the Society for the Psychological Study of Social Issues (New York: Houghton Mifflin Co., 1942).

[23] The fear is often expressed that subordinates, given the slightest opportunity, will seek to usurp their superiors' "prerogatives." Actually, such attempts are symptomatic of the reactive struggle for independence. These fears are groundless when subordinates are given adequate security.

[24] H. H. Carey, "Consultative Supervision and Management," *Personnel*, Vol. 18, No. 5 (March, 1942), pp. 286-295.

[25] Charles P. McCormick, *Multiple Management* (New York: Harper and Brothers, 1938).

[26] Clinton S. Golden and Harold J. Ruttenberg, *The Dynamics of Industrial Democracy* (New York: Harper and Brothers, 1942).

[27] "Mill and Factory's Survey of the Labor-Management Production Drive," *Mill and Factory*, Vol. 30, No. 6 (June, 1942), pp. 57-60.

[28] "Are War Production Drives Worth While?" *Factory Management and Maintenance*, Vol. 100, No. 10 (October, 1942), pp. 74-80.

as likely at the bottom of an organization as at the top, once the initial feelings of inadequacy and hesitancy among workers are overcome.[29]

The genuine collaboration among all the members of an industrial organization which is eulogized by "impractical idealists" is actually quite possible. But it can only begin to emerge when the mechanisms of genuine participation become an established part of the organization routines.

The conditions of active independence: Responsibility

A corollary of the desire for participation is a desire for responsibility. It is another manifestation of the active search for independence. Insecure or rebellious subordinates—seeking independence in the reactive sense—do not accept responsibility. They are seeking freedom, not the opportunity for self-realization and development.

The willingness to assume responsibility is a genuine maturational phenomenon. Just as children cannot grasp the meaning of the algebraic use of symbols until their intellectual development has reached a certain level, so subordinates cannot accept responsibility until they have achieved a certain degree of emotional security in their relationship to their superiors. Then they want it. They accept it with obvious pleasure and pride. And if it is given to them gradually, so that they are not suddenly made insecure again by too great a load of it, they will continue to accept more and more.

The process of granting responsibility to subordinates is a delicate one. There are vast individual differences in tolerance for the inevitable pressures and insecurities attendant upon the acceptance of responsibility. Some subordinates seem to be content to achieve a high degree of security without independence. Others thrive on the risks and the dangers of being "on their own." However, there are few subordinates whose capabilities in this direction are fully realized. It is unwise to attribute the absence of a desire for responsibility to the individual's personality alone until one has made certain that his relationship to his superiors is genuinely secure.

Many superiors are themselves so insecure that they cannot run the risk of being responsible for their subordinates' mistakes. Often they are unconsciously afraid to have capable and developing subordinates. The delegation of responsibility, as well as its acceptance, requires a confident and secure relationship with one's superiors.[30]

---

[29] Clinton S. Golden and Harold J. Ruttenberg, *loc. cit.*, Chap. IX.

[30] Irving Knickerbocker and Douglas McGregor, "Union-Management Cooperation: A Psychological Analysis," *Personnel*, Vol. 19, No. 3 (November, 1942), pp. 530-533.

The conditions of active independence: The right of appeal

There are occasions when subordinates differ radically but sincerely with their superiors on important questions. Unless the superior follows an "appeasement" policy (which in the end will cost him his subordinates' respect), there exists in such disagreement the possibility of an exaggerated feeling of dependence and helplessness in the minds of the subordinates. They disagree for reasons which seem *to them* sound; yet they must defer to the judgment of one person whom they know to be fallible.

If these occasions are too frequent, the subordinates will be blocked in their search for independence, and they may readily revert to a reactive struggle. The way out of the dilemma is to provide the subordinate with a mechanism for appealing his superior's decisions to a higher level of the organization. The subordinate can then have at hand a check upon the correctness and fairness of his superior's actions. His feeling of independence is thereby increased.

This is one of the justifications for an adequate grievance procedure for workers.[31, 32] All too often, however, there is no similar mechanism provided for members of management. To be sure, in the absence of a union it is difficult to safeguard the individual against retaliative measures by his immediate superior, but it is possible to guarantee a reasonable degree of protection.

If the relationship between subordinate and superior is a successful one, the right of appeal may rarely be exercised. Nevertheless, the awareness that it is there to be used when needed provides the subordinate with a feeling of independence which is not otherwise possible.

SUMMARY

The subordinate in the industrial organization is dependent for the satisfaction of many of his vital needs upon the behavior and attitudes of his superiors. He requires, therefore, a feeling of confidence that he can satisfy his needs if he does what is expected of him. Given this security, he requires opportunities for self-realization and development.

Among the conditions influencing the subordinate's feelings of security are: (1) an "atmosphere" of approval, (2) knowledge of

---

[31] Solomon Barkin, "Unions and Grievances," *Personnel Journal*, Vol. 22, No. 2 (June, 1943), pp. 38-48.

[32] United States Department of Labor, Division of Labor Standards. *Settling Plant Grievances* (Bulletin No. 60) Washington: Government Publications Office, 1943.

what is expected of him, and of how well he is measuring up to these expectations, (3) forewarning of changes that may affect him, and (4) consistent discipline both in the form of backing when he is "right" and in the form of punishment when he is "wrong."

The conditions under which the subordinate can realize his own potentialities include: (1) an adequate sense of security in relation to his superiors, (2) opportunities to participate in the solution of problems and in the discussion of actions which may affect him, (3) the opportunity to assume responsibilities as he becomes ready for it, and (4) the right of appeal over the head of his immediate superior.

These conditions are minimal. Upon their fulfillment in some degree rests the success or failure of the subordinate-superior relationship at every level of the industrial organization from that of the vice-president to that of the worker.

QUESTIONS

1. What is the outstanding characteristic of the superior-subordinate relationship? Why?
2. State the basic conditions of effective leadership.
3. What are the consequences of the dependence of the subordinate upon his superior?
4. Discuss the aspects of the superior-subordinate relationship that affect the security of the subordinate.
5. Explain how responsibility and participation affect a subordinate's growth and development.

THE CASE FOR
BENEVOLENT AUTOCRACY *

Robert N. McMurry

"Humanation," according to Harold J. Ruttenberg, "is the full release of the human creativeness of the working and managing forces voluntarily cooperating with each other to apply their creative energies to their daily work through organized programs of joint participation in the production process. Its goal is to bring everyone, irrespective of his point of authority or responsibility, into full participation in the productive process." [1]

This philosophy of the roles and relationships of management and worker, and many like it—for example, the democratic-participative, consultative, and "bottom-up" schools of management, to name only a few—appear to constitute the wave of the future in the minds of many personnel experts. Everywhere the goal is becoming "groupness"; the watchword, "management must democratize."

Such a philosophy is a welcome swing of the pendulum away from the brutality of the ill-famed Pennsylvania Coal and Iron Police and the "company store." And it is a fine ideal—an ultimate goal to shoot for. But it is as one-sided as the pessimistic view of human nature it replaces. Some day it may work in many companies, but today, human nature being what it is, democratic management is practical in only a small minority of companies.

COLD REALITIES

I shall be candid about the reasons why I think democratic management will not work.

Not only are many employees unwilling or unable to make a positive effort to contribute to the productive process, but there is nearly always a group of workers and supervisors of indeterminate size who either dislike their work, have come without the expectation of producing (the "gold bricks"), or are chronically dissatisfied. Such employees may be actively destructive and disruptive. Typical are the employees in the automotive plants who weld pop bottles in the gasoline tanks they assemble "just for kicks"; typical also are

* From the *Harvard Business Review*, Vol. 36, No. 1 (January-February, 1958), pp. 82-90. Reprinted with permission.

[1] "Humanation," *Management Record*, November, 1956, p. 389.

the foremen who look the other way when such antics are taking place. To expect such persons, of whom each business has its quota, to give their creative energy and thought to the firm is downright silly.

But even if many employees are genuinely desirous of participating actively in promoting the success of the enterprise, various obstacles may keep a wholly humanistic or democratic plan of administration from working.

Inclement climate

In the first place, democratic management cannot flourish in an unfavorable climate; its principles must be accepted throughout the organization from top to bottom, especially at the top. And the character of this climate is determined almost entirely by the management philosophies of the one or two executives who hold the actual power in the organization.

Very few members of top management are by nature sympathetic to the "bottom-up" philosophy of management. They are more likely to be hard-driving, egocentric entrepreneurs who have come up outside the business in careers where they have had to keep the power in their own hands; or they may be veterans and victors in the give-and-take, no-quarter in-fighting for positions of power within the business; or they may be the fortunate bureaucrats who managed to outlive and outlast their competitors for power or had sponsors on whose coattails they rode to a position of eminence in the organization.

Such men cannot ordinarily bring themselves to use any concept of management other than a purely authoritarian one. They may give lip-service to humanistic or democratic-participative philosophy of leadership, but they are never able, somehow, to implement it in their own companies. I suspect that not more than 10 per cent of the business enterprises in the United States today have top policy-formulating managements which can accept, implement, and use a genuinely humanistic or "bottom-up" philosophy of management.

Centralized decisions

In the second place, most commercial enterprises are very delicately balanced. One minor act—for example, a small price concession in some remote corner of the territory the company serves—can have tremendous and often costly repercussions. It can establish a chain reaction which will affect sales elsewhere. It can have implications for purchasing policies, manufacturing activities, relations with the government, public relations, and eventually profits.

It is easy to see, therefore, why so many managers feel that little true decision making may safely be delegated "down the line." Furthermore, there must be uniformity of policies and practices throughout the organization. One area cannot operate by one set of rules and another by a different set. Likewise, any deviation from policy that is permitted must be approved by those high enough in the management hierarchy to be able to see the action in proper perspective and estimate the probable consequences. This means that in practice *every* position below the one or two at the top must be almost totally structured—must be devoid of real decision-making responsibility. There may be room for some freedom of action *within* the structure, but even this is often more apparent than real.

The bureaucratic man

In the third place, the democratic-participative philosophy of management is completely incompatible with the bureaucratic traditions of most corporations. Business enterprises—especially large, secure, prestigeful ones—have a great attraction for those who have strong needs for security and status. Such people often make excellent subordinates. In their search for security, they do their best to meet their superiors' expectations as completely as they can, thus earning the latters' approbation and support. They are the "good soldiers," the loyal "organization men." But they cannot administer, direct, or inspire others. They belong in staff rather than in line positions.

Unfortunately, partly because management does not know how to recognize qualified candidates for leadership positions and partly because of a dearth of prospects, many of those chosen for leadership positions are taken from this pool of congenital nonleaders. Over the years, middle management comes to be composed almost exclusively of these bureaucrats who "live by the book." So strong are the pressures toward bureaucratization that any group of 100 or more employees, if not carefully controlled, will almost certainly turn into a bureaucracy within five years.

Once the organization has begun to become bureaucratized, the bureaucrats begin to perpetuate themselves. This is easy for them to do because most supervisors select their subordinates, and nearly everyone selects his subordinates in his own image. Moreover, a weak department or division head invariably tends to select as his subordinate *someone who is weaker than he* and hence no threat to him. When this selection of weaker subordinates has been repeated several times—particularly in a "tall" organization with many supervisory echelons—the low man in the hierarchy is often weak indeed.

It requires only one bureaucrat in the hierarchy to insure that everyone below him will be as inadequate as he is himself, or more so.

Actual trial

When democratic-participative management is subjected to actual trial, further weaknesses sometimes manifest themselves. While decision making stoutly refuses to remain at a low level, dissatisfaction with top management's decisions is found at every level, including the very lowest. Furthermore, to a substantial number of employees, participative or "bottom-up" management is interpreted to mean that the employees have the right to veto management's decisions. Hence, while employees have few positive contributions to make, many are not at all reluctant to demand their "rights." Others interpret democratic supervision to mean lax handling by their superiors. They become resentful of any attempt to impose discipline.

BOTTOM-UP RESISTANCE

When allowance is made for the fact that a great many people *prefer* regimentation, that most of those in top entrepreneurial positions tend to be autocrats, that most decision making must be centralized and structured, and that many companies drive their potential humanistic leaders out of the organization altogether (sometimes into the union), it is not surprising to find that most businesses today are autocratically administered from top to bottom, largely by bureaucrats. And the sample of companies with which I am familiar and on which I base this statement is a large one, including many firms that not only are leaders in their industries but would strenuously object to being called autocracies—even benevolent autocracies. To separate fact from fiction, here is an illustration:

> One of our leading corporations is glowingly pictured in the press as a democratic-participative organization in which the president has only one vote, the same as each member of the executive committee. And although he has the right to veto, he never uses it. Journalists have considered this firm a splendid example of democracy in action.
>
> But if you will attend the executive committee meetings, you will find that there is rarely any disagreement. This is because the president always states his position clearly in advance. In consequence, the vote is almost always unanimous. Still, management prides itself on its public image.

Even in groups where decision making is pushed far down in the organization by management fiat, it is resented—and this resentment can be kept at a low level only by the continued application of pressure from above. The minute that decision making is permitted to find its natural level, it will rise at once to the highest permissible echelon in the organization. As Harry S. Truman said of the presidency: "Only at my level did the 'buck' really stop."

Illusion of group decisions

The inadequacies of the democratic-participative philosophy of management in action are especially evident where group decision making is encouraged, as in many so-called "consultative" management programs. In a number of these programs, it is obligatory not only that everyone in the group participate in making the decision, but also that all of the group's decisions be unanimous.

Those who advocate group decision-making programs advance the following reasons:

(1) Several minds are usually better than one in problem solving.
(2) Having shared in its making, the members of a group will accept more readily the decision which has been reached.
(3) Participation in decision making is a stimulating, educational, and unifying experience for members of the group.
(4) Group decision making improves intragroup communication.
(5) When decisions have been made by the group, each member feels that he has the group's support in carrying them out.
(6) If the group has actual decision-making (not simply advisory) responsibility, its members' contributions will be more carefully considered, less frivolous, and hence sounder.

While the foregoing arguments in favor of group decision making are cogent, they overlook several of the more pressing reasons for questioning its merits. Chief among these are:

(1) Group decisions stimulate individual dependence on the group (which may well account for the growing popularity of this philosophy).
(2) Some members always fear to oppose the group. It is significant that in a recent study, one-fourth of a group, who had been given certain facts, were induced by the majority, which had *not* been given the facts, to agree to a decision that these facts proved clearly to be wrong.[2]
(3) When the group's members vary in status and power, subordinates are reluctant to disagree with their superiors.
(4) Some members, occasionally the more brilliant and nonconformist, are so unacceptable to others in the group that their contributions are not even seriously considered; they become "isolates."

Moreover, from a purely practical point of view group decisions ordinarily require more time to make; they are ill-adapted to emergencies or to situations requiring speed of decision, for one recalci-

---

[2] E. Paul Torrance, "Group Decision-Making and Disagreement," *Social Forces*, May, 1957, p. 314.

trant can delay decision making interminably. Also, unanimous group decisions *tend* to be conservative and opposed to innovations, hence less progressive—a fact that stockholders should be interested in.

Probably the greatest weakness of group decision making, especially where the decisions must be unanimous, lies in the spuriousness of the apparent high degree of agreement reached. Those members of the group who may not be in agreement with the majority may also be reluctant for any of the reasons enumerated above to express their disagreement openly. In consequence, they voice little, or at best minor, opposition to the group's decision. Only later do they begin actively to sabotage it. The danger is that management, assuming the decision taken is representative of the group's sentiments and that its members will support the conclusions which have been reached, may make its plans accordingly—only to discover later, with a shock, that many of the members are actually in disagreement and that the plan is either being openly resisted or more subtly and insidiously sabotaged by "passive resistance."

In many organizations, especially large, bureaucratic ones, individual autocracy has tended because of the emphasis on "groupness" to be replaced by *group* autocracy. Here strategic decisions are not made by the individual leader, particularly where he is a "weak" autocrat, because he lacks the courage. Instead, he takes refuge in the principle of unanimity; he calls together a group of his subordinates and lets them decide for him. In this way, he is able to maintain a bureaucratic autocracy without leadership, imagination, or drive, functioning under the guise of democratic management.

Lights of the future

I do not want to paint the picture of the humanistic or democratic-participative philosophy of management all black. I do not doubt, for instance, that it is superior to blind autocracy, especially when the latter leads to the development of a great inchoate and bumbling bureaucracy. Democratic leadership is obviously more productive. It stimulates and builds men; it invariably enhances morale. It has everything to recommend it except for the one fact that only in a relatively few small, socially well-integrated, and homogeneous groups —for example, the New England town meeting, the British Foreign Office, or some types of family-run firms—can it really be made to work.

A few companies, one of the most notable of which is General Mills, are making a sincere effort to introduce the humanistic philosophy of management into their organizations. At General Mills, the program has the active support of the president, Charles H. Bell. Consequently, the climate is not only extremely favorable, but an active campaign is being waged from the top down to make everyone in management conscious of the nature and advantages of this type of supervisory leadership. It will be interesting to observe the amount of impact this campaign has over the years on the overt behavior (not statements) of those in middle management, toward whom it is primarily aimed. It will also be instructive to note what will happen to the program should the pressure from the president to support it ever be relaxed.

LEADERS & FOLLOWERS

If democratic management runs counter to human nature and is only rarely practical, is there any way in which conventional auto-cratic-bureaucratic approaches can be modified and adapted in such a manner that pressure for production can be maintained without creating low levels of morale?

The answer appears to lie in a modification of prevailing autocratic-bureaucratic practices. We must recognize their causes and limitations but endeavor to minimize their ill effects by eliminating their worst features, introducing certain "cushioning" practices, and adapting the methods utilized more specifically to the needs of the employees. We might call the result *"benevolent* autocracy."

Under such an approach we would accept the fact that top management is by nature autocratic and that much of lower and middle management is composed of insecure bureaucrats. Where natural leaders are found, they will be utilized. Moreover, since competence as a leader is far from an all-or-none matter, we will often find that much can be done to help marginal supervisors become more effective through careful job placement and job structuring. We will not assume, however, that there will be many supervisors with great potential, and we will recognize that leaders cannot be developed from scratch by training.

Autocrat at the conference table

Benevolent autocracy is also based upon the premise that the autocrat is not necessarily an ineffective leader or a serious source of employee ill will. This is because two types of autocrats may be distinguished, the *strong* autocrat and the *weak* one:

(1) The strong autocrat is usually the very aggressive (often hypo-maniac), hard-driving, and self-reliant entrepreneur who is so preoccupied with his other interests and problems that he forgets to give much

thought to his employees. He is not a tyrant or a martinet. He does not exploit his employees or willfully mistreat them. He simply forgets at times that they are human beings with their own needs and problems. He is autocratic in his relations with others because he has learned by trial and error that this is the best way to get things done.

(2) The weak autocrat, by contrast, is the typical bureaucrat. He is often intelligent, loyal, conscientious, and technically well qualified for his position. His major weakness is his overwhelming need for *security*. He is basically a very dependent, fearful, and anxious person who is compensating for his insecurities by assuming an arbitrary, authoritarian exterior, often marked by great emphasis on his status and its symbols. He needs power. He adheres compulsively to prevailing practices, procedures, and policies. He *must* have a "book" to go by. His tyrannical manner serves as a defense mechanism to conceal his inner doubts and uncertainties; it also insures that no one will dare to question him and ask him to defend his judgments and actions. Typically, while he is a martinet to his subordinates, he is obsequious to his superiors—a veritable Uriah Heep.

It is obviously the weak autocrat who causes most of the trouble. If a system of benevolent autocracy is to be instituted, it is assumed that at least the top executives will be strong autocrats. Otherwise, little can be accomplished.

The philosophy of benevolent autocracy attempts to view the business scene realistically. In a nutshell, it assumes that most employees, regardless of their positions in the enterprise, have very real needs for security, for a well-defined structure in which to work, for opportunities to make contributions within this structure, for supervision which is permissive and supportive, and for an opportunity to feel that they have some voice in their own destinies. They must have confidence that the holder of ultimate power in top management, the "father figure" in the enterprise, while powerful and prestigeful, is also personally interested in them and in their problems. It is especially important for them to believe that he is prepared to take prompt remedial action on all valid complaints which are brought to his attention.

The benevolent autocrat structures his subordinates' activities for them; he makes the policy decisions which affect them; he keeps them in line and enforces discipline. He is like a good quarterback, who does not *ask* the line to decide what plays to attempt or what formations to use, but who *tells* them—and woe betide the hapless player who fails to follow his orders. He may encourage participation in the planning of a course of action, but much less frequently does he do so in its execution. In effect, he differs from the weak autocrat only in that he encourages participation by his subordinates prior to reaching *his* decision.

I believe that a proper utilization of these insights and a proper application of the principles which grow out of them will result in the maintenance of nearly as high a level of morale, even under continued pressure for production, as is possible where the democratic-participative type of leadership is available.

Not-too-great expectations

Before any steps can be taken to institute a program of benevolent autocracy, the ineffectiveness of exposition, admonition, and threats in influencing employee attitudes and behavior (the usual tactics of the autocrat) must be recognized and accepted by management, even where they seem essential and logically defensible. It is a long-established attribute of the American value system to assume that everyone has both the desire and the capacity to overcome his weaknesses and that he is inherently ambitious, seeking tirelessly to achieve a higher position both socially and economically. Consonant with this, it is believed that all that is necessary to insure that he will institute an immediate campaign of self-improvement is to have his limitations pointed out to him—and that then he will spring into action to change himself for the better.

However, as every psychiatrist has learned, logic alone is not enough. Even when it has been possible in therapy to give an individual insight into his limitations (not a mean task in itself), it is frequently next to impossible to get the patient to translate his insights into corrective action, even though he is paying for therapy and this means relief from distressing symptons. So, often his self-improvement campaign "withers on the vine"; for everyone is to some degree a prisoner of his past.

Even appeals to self-interest, including salaries and bonuses, are often fruitless. One of my greatest disillusionments in the course of 25 years of work for many different firms has been the discovery that at least three-fourths of those whom I have encountered in business have showed a pathetically small desire or capacity either for genuine self-improvement or for self-direction. They do not really want to improve themselves if this requires effort. They do not want responsibility. They simply want a safe, secure job and someone to tell them what to do. This conviction is one of the important reasons why I have come to look more sympathetically at the case for benevolent autocracy.

Introducing the Program

Introducing a program of benevolent autocracy does not involve management in the kinds of tortuous dilemmas that usually encumber an attempt to put a democratic-participative philosophy. in action. Of course, strong leadership is required, but the steps to take can be clearly defined, and they are well suited to the practical abilities of a good top-management team.

Proclaim the ideal

The first step in introducing the program is, paradoxically, to stress the desirability of the humanistic, democratic philosophy of management. The purpose of this first step is to create an organization-wide *climate* unfavorable to absolute-autocracy and bureaucracy. Even though top executives recognize that a complete democratic philosophy is basically unworkable, they can establish at least a consciousness of the *desirability* of using more participative management methods. The impact of such a pronouncement (which should be repeated at least quarterly) will not be revolutionary, but it still will serve several worthwhile purposes:

(1) It will make everyone conscious that absolute autocracy or bureaucracy is not the *only* philosophy of management.

(2) It will convey the impression that the holders of supreme power in the company are in favor of the new avant garde philosophy of participation in management decision making—as indeed they are; only they also recognize its limitations.

(3) It will provide a new and more precise definition of the *ideal* qualities and duties of supervision; in most companies such a statement has never before existed. The supervisors can then check their own administrative practices against this standard. While they will not be able to accept it emotionally, or to practice it, they will have an intellectual awareness of the need for mature administrators.[3]

Inventory & placement

The second step in the introduction of a program of benevolent autocracy is to take an executive and supervisory inventory. Its purpose is to evaluate the competence of the present supervisory force and particularly to determine the leadership qualifications of everyone in management. The methods to be employed have already been described in this magazine,[4] and an interesting application of them has been made at General Mills:

"The General Mills supervisory appraisals take the form of periodic reports by managers, analyzing the abilities of those whose work they

[3] See Hrand Saxenian, "Criterion for Emotional Maturity," *Harvard Business Review*, January-February, 1958, p. 56.

[4] See Robert E. Shaeffer, "Merit Rating as a Management Tool," *Harvard Business Review*, November, 1949, p. 693, and Robert N. McMurry, "War and Peace in Labor Relations," *Harvard Business Review*, November-December, 1955, p. 48.

supervise. The field review method was selected as best for their use. A trained interviewer questions each appraiser individually concerning each man and records the appraiser's opinions. The interviewers frequently are personnel men, but some of the most successful have been operating men who were trained and used for short periods. The interviewers help overcome semantic difficulties because they can explain what is sought and can probe to find out what a man thinks on any given point and his reasons for so thinking. They ask for illustrations and examples, call attention to inconsistencies, and suggest alternatives for the appraiser's consideration. In doing this, the interviewers also train the appraisers, focus their thinking, and help them to control their prejudice and biases." [5]

This technique, which requires interviews of approximately one hour with each of two raters, provides a surprisingly accurate measure of each supervisor's strong and weak points without provoking an undue amount of anxiety among those appraised since they themselves are not directly tested or interviewed. It makes it possible to place supervisors in one of three categories: (1) the natural leader who is already providing effective leadership; (2) the potential leader who can be developed; and (3) those bureaucrats whose inadequacies make them marginally qualified or clearly unsuited for supervisory work.

It is this latter category which contains the "problem" supervisors. They are often quite numerous and, to make matters worse, they cannot always be replaced, immediately at least, because no replacements are available. Since few of these marginal supervisors will be amenable to training, nothing remains but to reconstitute the leadership aspects of their positions. In most instances this means providing a strong subordinate to furnish needed leadership or establishing closer supervision from above. Needless to say, such supervisors must be replaced as rapidly as substitutes can be obtained.

This kind of inventory is the crucial step of the program. If it fails, nothing will be accomplished. Therefore, it is imperative that in this respect management be vigorous and, if necessary, ruthlessly authoritarian. Supervisors *must* have their leadership responsibilities absolutely structured for them.

Job definition

The third step in establishing a program of benevolent autocracy is to eliminate ambiguity on the job whenever and wherever it may occur. Nothing creates poor morale and anxiety in employees as much as does uncertainty with respect to company plans and prospects,

[5] D. E. Balch, *Executive Selection and Inventory*, American Management Association (1957), pp. 12-13.

their supervision, their duties, their authority, or their future with the company.

Business decisions fall into two roughly discrete classes: those which involve risk and those which do not. These two types have been defined by Drucker as "strategic" (involving risk) and "tactical" (the more routine problem-solving decisions) :

> The *strategic* decisions are those which involve futurity, have simultaneous impact on many aspects of the business, or involve substantial sums or unknowns. Decisions of this risk-taking type are reserved almost exclusively to top management. *Tactical* or problem-solving decisions are made every day by everyone.
>
> The machinist who sets the speed and feed of his machine is making a problem-solving decision; the accountant who allocates a charge to a particular account is making such a decision; so is the buyer in the purchasing department who decides to give an order to a particular supplier. Even a purchasing agent in charge of an annual procurement of $450,000,000 worth of materials may operate in an almost totally structured, risk-free environment, partly because the bulk of his activities follow well-established patterns and partly because, whenever he is faced with an unusual situation or one which involves risk, he must clear it with his superiors.
>
> The characteristic element in all such tactical decisions is that they involve a minimum of risk; they are totally structured.[6]

Nearly all the decisions at the working level and in middle and lower management are highly structured. This is absolutely necessary in the development and maintenance of good morale. It provides the guidance and the support which most people need and insures uniformity of policies and practices throughout the organization, which is an absolute necessity for efficient operation. This rigid structuring is not inconsistent with the principles of a benevolent autocracy. It exists not because of the whim of some autocrat in management but because a majority of the people in the enterprise need and ask for it.

There is nothing to prevent the astute supervisor from giving his subordinates a reasonably high degree of latitude of action *within the structure.* The machinist may set his speeds and feeds to suit himself within a fairly wide range; the clerk may have a voice in recommending the make of calculating machine the company is to buy; and the salesman may modify his presentation to suit himself as long as he conforms to policy on price, delivery dates, and so forth.

This is the key to the use of so-called consultative, participative management principles, even in an autocracy. The employees share in the problem solving, either individually or in a group, and each is

---

[6] See Peter F. Drucker, *The Practice of Management* (New York: Harper & Brothers, 1954), pp. 351-353.

encouraged to contribute his opinions and preferences—*but always within the structure.* No one takes any real risks; the superior always has the final say.

Performance reviews

The fourth step to insure good morale under substantial pressure for production is to make certain that everyone "knows where he stands" with his superior.

However, this should *not* be done, in my opinion, by having a superior confer periodically with a subordinate, using merit ratings or appraisal findings as a basis for his advice and judgments. In most instances the immediate superior, often a bureaucrat, is the poorest qualified person in the organization to provide counseling, at least in the conventional manner. This is partly because he usually lacks professional skill and partly because, due to his senior position, he often appears to be a threat to the employee's security.

I advocate, instead, discussions between boss and subordinate based on a statement of supervisory expectations. This statement is a composite of three elements:

(1) A position analysis prepared on the basis of the company's formal job description which spells out the place of the incumbent in the organization as a whole, that is, the nature and scope of his duties, responsibilities, authority, to whom he reports and who reports to him, and so forth.

(2) The employee's statement of his goals and objectives for the ensuing period (usually one year or less).

(3) The superior's statement of what he expects in terms of performance and self-improvement from the employee during the period.

These three elements are then collated, reviewed by the superior, and discussed by the superior and subordinate in conference; and in the process a mutually acceptable program of objectives for the employee is developed.

The tone of the conference is neither critical nor admonitory; the mission is purely constructive. If the man is not meeting expectations, the purpose of the discussion is to discover why and to explore what he and/or the supervisor can do to improve his performance. If he is surpassing expectations, he is commended. In either event, he is helped to know how well he is doing, not in abstract, general terms, but in concrete characteristics of his job. This procedure, if properly policed, will force even an autocrat or bureaucrat to show some constructive interest in his subordinates.

Opinion polls

The fifth and final phase in a program of benevolent autocracy is the conduct of periodic (preferably biennial) employee opinion polls. The primary purpose of such a poll is to "take the temperature" of the different employee groups, and more specifically to ascertain the state of their morale and to discern legitimate causes for such poor morale as may be evident. It enables management on its own initiative, without union pressure or prodding by employee petitions, to take or at least to consider such corrective action as may be indicated.[7] A poll does not commit the company to correct *every* condition which is causing or appears to be ground for dissatisfaction. Many dissatisfactions will be quite trivial; some will require no more than "talking out," while others will be of a nature that defies correction.

The results of the poll are then presented to the polling agency and through it to top management. The process has a sobering effect on those autocratic supervisors who are prone to become drunk with power and to tyrannize over their subordinates. While they resent bitterly this intrusion by management into the sanctity of their private, personal empires, most of them see the handwriting on the wall and will govern themselves accordingly.

The correction by management of *one* legitimate source of dissatisfaction is more valuable in building good employee morale than are a thousand speeches, bulletins, house organs, and letters to the employees' homes.

This phase of the program is of critical importance if morale is to be maintained at a high level in spite of continued pressure for production. It provides the safety valve by means of which accumulated resentments and aggressions can be vented before they are channeled into such anti-employer activities as limitation of output, slowdowns, excessive absenteeism, or various acts of minor or serious sabotage. At the same time, it also permits the discovery and elimination of many of the *causes* of poor morale, few of which are directly the result of pressure for production.

CONCLUSION

Benevolent autocracy gets its results because it rigidly structures, routinizes, and controls the relation of the supervisor to his subordinates in such a manner that, in spite of his frequent inherent tendencies to the contrary, he will employ the sound methods which come more naturally to the humanistic or democratic leader. The

---

[7] For a fuller explanation, see Robert N. McMurry, *op. cit.*, especially p. 57.

typical bureaucrat is incapable of conceiving or applying sound leadership principles on his own initiative. However, if he is told precisely what to do, and if his conformity to policy is enforced by periodic employee opinion polls, he will not only be happy to follow instructions but will probably turn in a surprisingly creditable performance. After all, his security is largely dependent on how faithfully he conforms to company policies and practices.

There is little doubt that if the humanistic or "bottom-up" concept of leadership could be introduced and accepted on a company-wide basis and sponsored by the company's president, it would make possible increased productivity, even under pressure, without an adverse effect on morale. But since it cannot, benevolent autocracy is the most promising alternative. While perhaps not as effective at the person-to-person level, it aims at the same over-all objectives. It is designed to permit the employer to keep the pressure on his people for production without affecting their morale too adversely, using the supervisors that are available.

Productivity

But *can* pressure be applied without affecting morale too adversely? In studies conducted by the Institute for Social Research at the University of Michigan, as reported by Rensis Likert,[8] it was found, as might be expected, that humanistic or democratic-participative management led to increased productivity without deterioration of morale. But it was also consistently found that the greater the pressure applied to the workers (regardless of the philosophy of management used), the higher the production.

Furthermore, the differences in productivity induced by additional pressure, while not great, were nevertheless large enough to be important in any highly competitive industry. While morale did fall as a result of pressure, this did not affect production, which continued to increase. Likert states:

> "On the basis of a study I did in 1937 I believed that morale and productivity were positively related; that the higher the morale, the higher the production. Substantial research findings since then have shown this relationship is much too simple. Some groups have low morale and low production. Other groups have fairly good morale and low production. Still others have fairly good production but low morale, while others have both high morale and high production.
>
> "Units with low morale and low production tend to have laissez-faire supervision. Where morale is fairly good but production is poor, the

---

[8] "Developing Patterns in Management," *Strengthening Management for the New Technology*, American Management Association (New York, 1955), pp. 10-11.

supervisors tend to try to keep people 'happy.' Such supervisors are often found in companies in which 'human relations' training programs have been introduced and emphasized. The morale of these less productive workers is essentially complacent in character. The result is a nice 'country club' atmosphere. Thus there is no clear evidence that the 'happy' employee is consistently the productive employee." [9]

SUMMARY

Since so many members of lower, middle, and even top management in the typical large business enterprises of today are dependent, insecure, and ineffective—productive only because they are bossed by one or two hard-driving strong autocrats—the outlook for the widespread introduction of a genuine humanistic, democratic-participative philosophy of leadership in the near future looks dim indeed.

But benevolent autocracy, while it is neither idealistic nor inspiring, is practical. It accepts people as they are and recognizes particularly that most people prefer to be led. It also faces the fact that there is a dearth of leaders in industry now and in the foreseeable future. It is, in the final analysis, simply a technique for "making the best of the worst."

What benevolent autocracy offers is not a beautiful vision of a world to come. Instead, it simply accepts reality with all of its limitations. While hardly a noble philosophy of management, it does have one invaluable attribute: *where it has been tried, it works.*

---

[9] *Ibid.,* p. 19.

QUESTIONS

1. Explain what McMurry means by "benevolent autocracy."
2. Why does McMurry believe that democratic management is practical in only a small minority of companies? Do you agree?
3. Discuss the reasons for questioning the merits of group decision making. Do you agree?
4. What are the premises that benevolent autocracy is based upon?
5. Discuss the steps necessary to introduce a program of benevolent autocracy.

GENERAL QUESTIONS ON PART 2

1. Distinguish the basic approaches to the study of leadership. Which approach do you think is best? Why?
2. Compare Knickerbocker's concept of leadership with that of Stogdill.
3. Explain the relationship of leadership to human relations.
4. Discuss the basic problems we face in studying leadership.
5. Prepare a list of five textbook definitions of leadership. Which do you think is most meaningful? Why?
6. State your own definition of leadership and explain it.
7. How important are personality traits to leadership?
8. Why are all managers, whether they be first-line foremen or company presidents, leaders?
9. What type of leadership accounts for the greatest productivity of groups? Why?
10. What effect does our culture have on our concept of leadership?

BIBLIOGRAPHY FOR PART 2

Articles

ALLEN, L. A. "Match Leaders to Followers," *Nation's Business*, Vol. 47, No. 5 (May, 1959), pp. 90-93.

ARGYRIS, CHRIS. "Leadership Pattern in the Plant," *Harvard Business Review*, Vol. 32, No. 1 (January-February, 1954), pp. 64-75.

BAILEY, J. H. "The Essential Qualities of Good Supervision: A Case Study," *Personnel*, 1956, pp. 311-326.

DAVIS, LOUIS E. "The Supervisor and Productivity," *Journal of Personnel Administration and Industrial Relations*, Summer, 1955, pp. 56-74.

DYER, W. G. "Cultural Barriers to Leadership," *Adult Leadership*, Vol. 7, No. 7 (January, 1959), pp. 189-192.

EMERY, D. A. "Managerial Leadership Through Motivation by Objectives," *Personnel Psychology*, Vol. 12, No. 1 (Spring, 1959), pp. 65-79.

HAYES, JOHN J. "Results of Training Supervisors in Democratic Concepts of Leadership," *Journal of American Society of Training Directors*, January-February, 1956, pp. 24-27.

JENNINGS, E. E. "Elements of Democratic Supervision," *Advanced Management*, October, 1954, pp. 19-22.

————. "When Democracy in Management Excels," *Nation's Business*, Vol. 47, No. 6 (June, 1959), pp. 35, 44-50.

KATZ, ROBERT L. "Skills of an Effective Administrator," *Harvard Business Review*, Vol. 33, No. 1 (January-February, 1955), pp. 33-41.

McGREGOR, DOUGLAS. "Leadership and the Conditions of Organizational Effectiveness," *Public Health Reports*, Vol. 47, No. 1 (January, 1952), pp. 42-46.

PELZ, DONALD. "Leadership Within a Hierarchical Organization," *Journal of Social Issues*, Vol. 7, No. 3 (1951), pp. 49-55.

STOWELL, LEON C. "Paths to Leadership," *Dun's Review and Modern Industry*, October, 1955, pp. 37-38, 116-117.

TARNAPOL, LESTER and JULIA. "How Top-Rated Supervisors Differ from the Low-Rated," *Personnel Journal*, February, 1956, pp. 331-335.

Books

APPLEY, L. A. *Management in Action*. New York: American Management Association, 1956.

ARGYRIS, C. *Executive Leadership*. New York: Harper and Brothers, Inc., 1953.

SHARTLE, C. L. *Executive Performance and Leadership*. Englewood Cliffs, N. J.: Prentice-Hall, Inc., 1956.

PFIFFNER, J. M. *The Supervision of Personnel*. Englewood Cliffs, N. J.: Prentice-Hall, Inc., 1951.

LINDGREN, H. C. *Effective Leadership in Human Relations*. New York: Hermitage House, Inc., 1954.

PART 3. MOTIVATION AND BEHAVIOR

In the introduction to leadership it was stated that the leader's fundamental responsibility in any form of organization is to get work done through people. This statement, it should be noted, makes explicit the fact that the basic objective of all leaders is the effective accomplishment of the duties and the responsibilities necessary for the successful operation of an organization. All activities of people who are in leadership positions must therefore be directed toward this end, for it is this goal that justifies the existence of—in fact, establishes the necessity for—a leader.

Implicit in this statement of leadership is the fact that getting the work of an organization done is immediately and finally dependent upon the behavior of the employees of that organization. The reason for this is obvious. Nothing that must be done in a firm can be done until some person assumes the obligation of and carries out the duties and responsibilities inherent in or delegated to his position. Consequently, whether the employee accomplishes his responsibilties through the use of inanimate and inarticulate tools, such as brooms, lathes, or electronic computers, or solely via cogitative and intellectual powers, all facets of work done in an organization are ultimate manifestations of some manner or form of human behavior. It seems logical to conclude, therefore, that the most immediate objective of leadership is the achievement of that type of employee behavior which will result in the effective accomplishment of the duties and responsibilities required to operate a firm successfully. To understand completely, then, the fundamental nature of human relations and leadership requires some comprehension of the basic aspects of employee behavior, for, in the final analysis, the leader's main task is to influence the behavior of people toward predetermined goals.

WHY PEOPLE BEHAVE AS THEY DO

Although human behavior is a vast and complicated subject composed of and influenced by many variables, it can be simply described as the total response of an individual to various motivating forces. In other words, we behave as we do because we are responding to forces that have the power to prompt—motivate—us to some manner or form of action. In a sense, therefore, behavior *per se* can be considered to be an end result—a response to basic forces. From a more fundamental viewpoint, however, it can be seen that behavior is actually only an intermediate step in a chain of events. Motivating forces lead to some manner or form of behavior, and that behavior must be directed toward some end. That is to say, there must be some reason why we are responding to the motivating force. And that reason could only be to satisfy the force which in the first place motivated us to behave. Consequently, all human beings, whether they do so rationally or irrationally, consciously or subconsciously, behave as they do to satisfy various motivating forces. In diagram form this sequence of human behavior may be summarized as follows:

MOTIVATING FORCES $\longrightarrow$ MOTIVATE $\longrightarrow$ BEHAVIOR $\longrightarrow$ END $\Big\langle$ SATISFACTION OF THE MOTIVATING FORCES

Basic motivating forces

The forces that motivate people, that is, the forces that lead to some manner or form of human behavior, are legion in number and vary considerably in degree, not only from individual to individual, but also from time to time within the same person. They range in nature from extremely ethereal and psychological motives, such as truth, love, and beauty, to concrete physical, instinctive, and basic physiological forces, such as hunger, thirst, and avoidance of pain. Because several of the articles that follow explore in detail the nature of some of the specific forces that motivate people, we shall briefly consider here only the major classes or types of forces that can be distinguished. But it should be noted that in this book we shall consider only those motivating stimuli that are inherent in and internal to the human being. These particular forces are commonly called *needs*. We shall purposefully exclude from our analysis consideration of forces such as fire, electricity, and so on. Although such stimuli quite obviously have the power to influence and determine human behavior, they are to a great extent outside the influence of management and hence leadership.

Although there have been many descriptions of the types or classes of needs that motivate human behavior, it is possible to classify most internal human motives under at least three general headings, namely, physiological, sociological, and psychological needs. Whether or not this is a complete classification of all human needs is impossible to say at this time. Our present state of knowledge of the things that motivate human beings is simply not complete enough to give a more definite classification. But the three categories stated here do allow a grouping of the known motives in a manner that makes it convenient to study them and to understand how they influence human behavior.

Physiological needs. Physiological needs are the most primitive and fundamental of all motivating forces. They are identified in both animals and men and are primarily instinctive in nature. They are the most obvious and the most easily observed of all human motives. Included in this class are our needs for food, water, shelter, air, sleep, and so on. In a sense, they are the most powerful of motivating stimuli, for we must satisfy most of them in order to exist. Consequently, they are the needs that we take care of first. They quite obviously exert a tremendous influence on behavior, especially in the world of work, because many of them, like food and shelter, are most easily satisfied with money earned from gainful employment.

Sociological needs. The second basic classification of human needs is that of sociological needs. Motives in this category stem primarily from man's relationship with other people. Unlike physiological needs, which are primitive and instinctive in nature, sociological needs exist on a more refined level and are acquired in the course of everyday existence. They include motives such as the need to belong, the need for love and affection, and the need for acceptance. Although considerably more difficult to observe than physiological motives, sufficient evidence of the operation of these needs is not difficult to find. In particular, as Part 4 indicates, one need only to witness the pleasure an individual obtains from acceptance by a group or the potent impact upon a person when members of a group refuse to converse with him.

Psychological needs. The third general group of human motives is classified as psychological needs. Needs in this category are influenced by and are, to a great extent, dependent upon relationships with other people, but they differ from sociological needs because they are concerned only with man's view of himself. Included in this classification are motives such as the need for recognition, achievement, and status, plus many, many others. Unlike physiological and sociological needs, these motivating forces are very difficult to satisfy. But their influence on human behavior is just as important—if not more so in the context of an organization—as the other two basic groups of needs. One has only to examine his own psychological motives to verify this.

Hierarchy of needs

As several of the following articles indicate, one of the most fundamental facets of needs as motivational forces is their hierarchical relationship. Although it is difficult to perceive this character of needs between the sociological and the psychological groups, primarily because of the extent to which these two classifications depend upon relationships with fellow men, it is apparent that physiological needs take precedence over all other needs. In fact, it is only when behavior has satisfied these instinctive motives that satisfaction of other needs becomes important. Consider, for example, the worker faced with continued unemployment. Certainly the loss of earning power is a more important determinant of his behavior than any concern he may have for belonging or recognition. However, when these primitive needs are satisfied—and as long as they are satisfied—sociological and psychological forces take precedence and exert the greatest influence on man's behavior. This point is particularly important in times of full employment, for it is the basic reason why employees are dissatisfied even though their wages, working conditions, and hours are extremely good.

Needs and frustration

Another important aspect of needs as basic motivational forces is the fact that they rarely influence behavior individually. Indeed, there is considerable evidence to prove that most of the time they operate in combination with each other. Consequently, at times the individual may be faced with a situation where his behavior to satisfy one need will frustrate or prevent him from satisfying another need. When such conflicts arise, the person must make a decision as to which need he will satisfy. Depending on the nature of the motives in conflict, he may quickly satisfy one need and forget the other, compromise to some extent, or choose the lessor of two evils. In any case, some degree of frustration will result.

Because frustration occurs whenever needs go unsatisfied, it should be noted that in addition to conflict between motives there are other ways in which an individual can become frustrated. Generally speaking, these obstacles to goal satisfaction are classified under the headings of environmental and personal factors. *Environmental factors* are external to the individual and exist in the situation in which he finds himself. An example of this type of barrier would be a supervisor who so ill-fits his job that he is unable to perceive the true ability of a subordinate and consequently impedes the employee's progress in promotions and wage increases. *Personal factors,* on the other hand, are internal to the individual. They usually result from the individual's overestimation of his capabilities. An example of this type of obstacle would be the employee who wants to become a foreman or a manager, but who simply does not—and never will—possess the abilities for such work. Until such an individual recognizes his limitations and sets different goals for himself, he will remain disappointed and frustrated. This has, of course, drastic implications in the practice of human relations and leadership, for quite frequently the leader will find himself in situations where he must help an employee recognize, understand, and accept the true nature of the employee's capability and potential.

How people react to frustration

Although reaction to frustration varies from individual to individual, there are definite patterns of behavior that can be observed. One common reaction occurs when the individual *compensates* or substitutes one need for another. This means, in essence, that a person simply directs his behavior away from a goal that he finds difficult or impossible to satisfy toward another goal from which he can obtain greater satisfaction. An example of this type of behavior would be the employee who, finding his need for belonging is not satisfied as a member of the organization that employs him, turns his energies toward the satisfaction of his motive by joining and becoming active in a union. It should be noted that this type of reaction can be either advantageous or detrimental to the interest of management, depending upon the nature of the substituted goal. Which behavior pattern the employee selects, however, is frequently a function of how rewarding such a reaction has been in his previous experience. If a particular response has in the past alleviated his frustration, he will more than likely repeat his action when he encounters similar frustrating situations in the future. The main point here, of course, is that if the employee's original motivating force was valid, he should have been able to satisfy it without having to turn his behavior toward a goal that might be contrary to the interest of his employer.

Another common reaction to frustration is *rationalization.* This type of behavior is evidenced by the individual who blames someone else for his failure to satisfy his need or who simply talks himself out of a goal. An example of this response is the worker who, failing to get a promotion, blames his supervisor for having it "in for him" or who maintains he did not want the job anyway. Although rationalization is frequently considered to be a harmless reaction to frustration, it can, unfortunately, lead to more serious responses, such as apathy, indifference, or disinterest, all of which are detrimental to an organization's efficiency.

One of the most serious responses to frustration is that of *aggression,* either in the form of opposition and antagonism or open conflict and physical violence. Whatever form this particular type of response takes, it always involves action against the barriers and obstacles that prevent satisfaction of a motivating force. It is most easily seen in children, who usually vent their frustration directly against the obstacle that deprives them of satisfaction, such as the child who hits his friend with the toy they are arguing about. Adults, on the other hand, most frequently vent their aggression against a barrier in an indirect manner, especially in an employment situation. Thus the foreman who has been reprimanded by his superior may in turn abuse his subordinates. Or the worker whose grievance has gone unnoticed or been improperly handled may resort to petty thievery or sabotage.

Perhaps the most extreme forms of reaction to frustration are regression and withdrawal. In *regression,* the individual is said to regress from adult levels of behavior to childish levels of behavior. Apparently such a response allows the person to escape the frustrations of adulthood and thereby to gain greater security and satisfaction. In *withdrawal,* the individual withdraws from reality to the extent that he is completely out of contact with the situation in which he exists. Both types of behavior are, of course, indicative of serious mental disorders.

MOTIVATION, ATTITUDES, AND MORALE

There is much evidence today that employers and managers are greatly concerned with employee morale. They tend to believe that, if morale is high, employees are satisfied and happy about their jobs, working conditions, pay, and other aspects of the employment situation and are consequently producing efficiently and effectively. On the other hand, if they believe morale is low, they assume that employees are dissatisfied with things in general and that quality and quantity of production are accordingly lower. Unfortunately, empirical data to support this assumed correlation between morale and productivity are difficult to obtain, primarily because of difficulties in defining morale and establishing benchmarks to measure it.

Although the term *morale* is used very loosely, there is general agreement that it refers to a combination of employee attitudes toward employment. That is to say, morale is a synthesis of how employees think and feel about their jobs, their working conditions, their superiors, their firm, their fellow workers, their pay, and so on. Defined in this way, the term includes both individual and group aspects of morale, *individual morale* being the structure of an employee's attitudes toward employment, whereas *group morale* is the general tone of employee attitudes in the organization as a whole or in a particular office or department.

Whatever are the difficulties in defining and measuring morale, it is possible to conclude, deductively speaking, that it plays an important role in motivation and behavior, albeit a complex one. The reason for this is obvious. If it is true that employee behavior is directed toward satiation of needs, the result of that behavior must directly influence the attitude of the individual. In other words, if a particular response results in satisfaction of one or more needs, it could be deduced that the individual's attitude with respect to his need, his action, and the result of his action is good. As long as such behavior results in satisfaction, consequent attitudes should remain good. If, on the other hand, behavior does not result in satisfaction, frustration and its consequences will occur and a negative (poor) attitude will result. From a management viewpoint this assumes, of course, that in both cases the employee's need and response are, in the first place, oriented toward the interests of the organization.

The implication of the relationship between morale and behavior is clear: significant attention must be given to morale as an indicator of need satisfaction, both of the individual employee and of the group as a whole. The leader must therefore make every effort possible and use every means at his disposal to determine and be cognizant of employee attitudes. If he will direct his energy toward this task, he should be able to motivate his subordinates more efficiently and consequently to improve his effectiveness as a leader.

Motivation and Performance

Although motives are the primary energizers of behavior, they are not the sole determinants of employee performance. In fact, human performance *per se* is largely dependent upon habits and skills that have been acquired through the process of learning and training. To expect effective performance from an employee with high motivation but no skill or potential for the job in question is therefore not only wishful thinking but also downright inefficient management. This quite obviously means that proper motivation of employees presupposes that they have been properly recruited, selected, placed, inducted, and trained.

Assuming, however, that employees possess at least the minimum degree or level of skill required for job performance, there is considerable evidence to prove that increased motivation can improve employee performance of almost any kind. In our everyday experience almost all of us have witnessed this interaction of motivation and skill when we saw the effect of the coach's pep talk or the highly motivated semi-skilled person "beat" the performance of the highly skilled but poorly motivated person. In short, if the level of skill is sufficient for the job, the absence or presence of motivation can make a prodigious difference in employee performance.

MOTIVATION, HUMAN RELATIONS, AND MANAGEMENT

In previous sections of this book emphasis was placed on two important points; namely, (1) that all members of management, whether they be first-line supervisors or chief executives, hold positions of leadership because of the very nature of their jobs, and (2) that human relations, as it is considered in this text, is manifested in the actions and practices of leaders, especially in the environment of the business unit. In this section, heavy emphasis is given to the concept of motivation because, in the final analysis, the leader will get work done efficiently and effectively only if he properly motivates the behavior of his subordinates.

Because the leadership function of motivating people requires a definitive and comprehensive understanding of the causes and effects of human behavior, effort was made to choose a selection of articles that would provide a sound foundation for the practice of human relations, a subject to be considered in detail in Part 9. Accordingly, Maslow's article was chosen because it is a classic and fundamental analysis of why people behave as they do. McGregor's article was picked because it is an excellent treatment of employee motivation and behavior in the context of an enterprise. The article by Stagner was selected because of its effective treatment of the relationship of motivation to industrial conflict, a subject of much concern and interest to management and society. And, lastly, Likert's article was included because it offers concrete proof that proper motivation of employees can increase productivity.

A THEORY OF HUMAN MOTIVATION *

A. H. Maslow

I. INTRODUCTION

In a previous paper [1] various propositions were presented which would have to be included in any theory of human motivation that could lay claim to being definitive. These conclusions may be briefly summarized as follows:

1. The integrated wholeness of the organism must be one of the foundation stones of motivation theory.

2. The hunger drive (or any other physiological drive) was rejected as a centering point or model for a definitive theory of motivation. Any drive that is somatically based and localizable was shown to be atypical rather than typical in human motivation.

3. Such a theory should stress and center itself upon ultimate or basic goals rather than partial or superficial ones, upon ends rather than means to these ends. Such a stress would imply a more central place for unconscious than for conscious motivations.

4. There are usually available various cultural paths to the same goal. Therefore conscious, specific local-cultural desires are not as fundamental in motivation theory as the more basic, unconscious goals.

5. Any motivated behavior, either preparatory or consummatory, must be understood to be a channel through which many basic needs may be simultaneously expressed or satisfied. Typically an act has *more* than one motivation.

6. Practically all organismic states are to be understood as motivated and as motivating.

7. Human needs arrange themselves in hierarchies of prepotency. That is to say, the appearance of one need usually rests on the prior satisfaction of another, more pre-potent need. Man is a perpetually wanting animal. Also no need or drive can be treated as if it were isolated or discrete; every drive is related to the state of satisfaction or dissatisfaction of other drives.

8. *Lists* of drives will get us nowhere for various theoretical and practical reasons. Furthermore any classification of motivations must deal with the problem of levels of specificity or generalization of the motives to be classified.

9. Classifications of motivations must be based upon goals rather than upon instigating drives or motivated behavior.

10. Motivation theory should be human-centered rather than animal-centered.

11. The situation or the field in which the organism reacts must be taken into account but the field alone can rarely serve as an exclusive explanation for behavior. Furthermore the field itself must be

---

* From the *Psychological Review*, Vol. 50, 1943, pp. 370-396. Reprinted with permission.

[1] A. H. Maslow, "A Preface to Motivation Theory," *Psychosomatic Medicine*, Vol. 5, 1943, pp. 85-92.

interpreted in terms of the organism. Field theory cannot be a substitute for motivation theory.

12. Not only the integration of the organism must be taken into account, but also the possibility of isolated, specific, partial or segmental reactions.

It has since become necessary to add to these another affirmation.

13. Motivation theory is not synonymous with behavior theory. The motivations are only one class of determinants of behavior. While behavior is almost always motivated, it is also almost always biologically, culturally and situationally determined as well.

The present paper is an attempt to formulate a positive theory of motivation which will satisfy these theoretical demands and at the same time conform to the known facts, clinical and observational as well as experimental. It derives most directly, however, from clinical experience. This theory is, I think, in the functionalist tradition of James and Dewey, and is fused with the holism of Wertheimer,[2] Goldstein,[3] and Gestalt Psychology, and with the dynamicism of Freud,[4] and Adler.[5] This fusion or synthesis may arbitrarily be called a "general-dynamic" theory.

It is far easier to perceive and to criticize the aspects in motivation theory than to remedy them. Mostly this is because of the very serious lack of sound data in this area. I conceive this lack of sound facts to be due primarily to the absence of a valid theory of motivation. The present theory then must be considered to be a suggested program or framework for future research and must stand or fall, not so much on facts available or evidence presented, as upon researches yet to be done, researches suggested perhaps, by the questions raised in this paper.

II. THE BASIC NEEDS

The *"physiological"* needs.—The needs that are usually taken as the starting point for motivation theory are the so-called physiological drives. Two recent lines of research make it necessary to revise our customary notions about these needs, first, the development of the concept of homeostasis, and second, the finding that appetites (preferential choices among foods) are a fairly efficient indication of actual needs or lacks in the body.

Homeostasis refers to the body's automatic efforts to maintain a constant, normal state of the blood stream. Cannon [6] has described

---

[2] M. Wertheimer, unpublished lectures at the New School for Social Research.
[3] K. Goldstein, *The Organism* (New York: American Book Co., 1939).
[4] S. Freud, *New Introductory Lectures on Psychoanalysis* (New York: Norton, 1933).
[5] A. Adler, *Social Interest* (London: Faber & Faber, 1938).
[6] W. B. Cannon, *Wisdom of the Body* (New York: Norton, 1932).

this process for (1) the water content of the blood, (2) salt content, (3) sugar content, (4) protein content, (5) fat content, (6) calcium content, (7) oxygen content, (8) constant hydrogen-ion level (acid-base balance) and (9) constant temperature of the blood. Obviously this list can be extended to include other minerals, the hormones, vitamins, etc.

Young in a recent article [7] has summarized the work on appetite in its relation to body needs. If the body lacks some chemical, the individual will tend to develop a specific appetite or partial hunger for that food element.

Thus it seems impossible as well as useless to make any list of fundamental physiological needs for they can come to almost any number one might wish, depending on the degree of specificity of description. We can not identify all pyhsiological needs as homeostatic. That sexual desire, sleepiness, sheer activity and maternal behavior in animals, are homeostatic, has not yet been demonstrated. Furthermore, this list would not include the various sensory pleasures (tastes, smells, tickling, stroking) which are probably physiological and which may become the goals of motivated behavior.

In a previous paper [8] it has been pointed out that these physiological drives or needs are to be considered unusual rather than typical because they are isolable, and because they are localized somatically. That is to say, they are relatively independent of each other, or other motivations and of the organism as a whole, and secondly, in many cases, it is possible to demonstrate a localized, underlying somatic base for the drive. This is true less generally than has been thought (exceptions are fatigue, sleepiness, maternal responses) but it is still true in the classic instances of hunger, sex, and thirst.

It should be pointed out again that any of the physiological needs and the consummatory behavior involved with them serve as channels for all sorts of other needs as well. That is to say, the person who thinks he is hungry may actually be seeking more for comfort, or dependence, than for vitamins or proteins. Conversely, it is possible to satisfy the hunger need in part by other activities such as drinking water or smoking cigarettes. In other words, relatively isolable as these physiological needs are, they are not completely so.

Undoubtedly these physiological needs are the most prepotent of all needs. What this means specifically is, that in the human being who is missing everything in life in an extreme fashion, it is most

    [7] P. T. Young, "The Experimental Analysis of Appetite," *Psychological Bulletin*, Vol. 38, 1941, pp. 129-164.
    [8] Maslow, *loc. cit*

likely that the major motivation would be the physiological needs rather than any others. A person who is lacking food, safety, love, and esteem would most probably hunger for food more strongly than for anything else.

If all the needs are unsatisfied, and the organism is then dominated by the physiological needs, all other needs may become simply non-existent or be pushed into the background. It is then fair to characterize the whole organism by saying simply that it is hungry, for consciousness is almost completely preempted by hunger. All capacities are put into the service of hunger-satisfaction, and the organization of these capacities is almost entirely determined by the one purpose of satisfying hunger. The receptors and effectors, the intelligence, memory, habits, all may now be defined simply as hunger-gratifying tools. Capacities that are not useful for this purpose lie dormant, or are pushed into the background. The urge to write poetry, the desire to acquire an automobile, the interest in American history, the desire for a new pair of shoes are, in the extreme case, forgotten or become of secondary importance. For the man who is extremely and dangerously hungry, no other interests exist but food. He dreams food, he remembers food, he thinks about food, he emotes only about food, he perceives only food and he wants only food. The more subtle determinants that ordinarily fuse with the physiological drives in organizing even feeding, drinking or sexual behavior, may now be so completely overwhelmed as to allow us to speak at this time (but *only* at this time) of pure hunger drive and behavior, with the one unqualified aim of relief.

Another peculiar characteristic of the human organism when it is dominated by a certain need is that the whole philosophy of the future tends also to change. For our chronically and extremely hungry man, Utopia can be defined very simply as a place where there is plenty of food. He tends to think that, if only he is guaranteed food for the rest of his life, he will be perfectly happy and will never want anything more. Life itself tends to be defined in terms of eating. Anything else will be defined as unimportant. Freedom, love, community feeling, respect, philosophy, may all be waved aside as fripperies which are useless since they fail to fill the stomach. Such a man may fairly be said to live by bread alone.

It cannot possibly be denied that such things are true but their *generality* can be denied. Emergency conditions are, almost by definition, rare in the normally functioning peaceful society. That this truism can be forgotten is due mainly to two reasons. First, rats have few motivations other than physiological ones, and since so much of the research upon motivation has been made with these animals, it is easy to carry the rat-picture over to the human being. Secondly, it is too often not realized that culture itself is an adaptive tool, one of whose main functions is to make the physiological emergencies come less and less often. In most of the known societies, chronic extreme hunger of the emergency type is rare, rather than common. In any case, this is still true in the United States. The average American citizen is experiencing appetite rather than hunger when he says "I am hungry." He is apt to experience sheer life-and-death hunger only by accident and then only a few times through his entire life.

Obviously a good way to obscure the "higher" motivations, and to get a lopsided view of human capacities and human nature, is to make the organism extremely and chronically hungry or thirsty. Anyone who attempts to make an emergency picture into a typical one, and who will measure all of man's goals and desires by his behavior during extreme physiological deprivation is certainly being blind to many things. It is quite true that man lives by bread alone—when there is no bread. But what happens to man's desires when there *is* plenty of bread and when his belly is chronically filled?

At once other (and "higher") needs emerge and these, rather than physiological hungers, dominate the organism. And when these in turn are satisfied, again new (and still "higher") needs emerge and so on. This is what we mean by saying that the basic human needs are organized into a hierarchy of relative prepotency.

One main implication of this phrasing is that gratification becomes as important a concept as deprivation in motivation theory, for it releases the organism from the domination of a relatively more physiological need, permitting thereby the emergence of other more social goals. The physiological needs, along with their partial goals, when chronically gratified cease to exist as active determinants or organizers of behavior. They now exist only in a potential fashion in the sense that they may emerge again to dominate the organism if they are thwarted. But a want that is satisfied is no longer a want. The organism is dominated and its behavior organized only by unsatisfied needs. If hunger is satisfied, it becomes unimportant in the current dynamics of the individual.

This statement is somewhat qualified by a hypothesis to be discussed more fully later, namely that it is precisely those individuals in whom a certain need has always been satisfied who are best equipped to tolerate deprivation of that need in the future, and that furthermore, those who have been deprived in the past will react differently to current satisfactions than the one who has never been deprived.

The safety needs.—If the physiological needs are relatively well gratified, there then emerges a new set of needs, which we may categorize roughly as the safety needs. All that has been said of the physiological needs is equally true, although in lesser degree, of these desires. The organism may equally well be wholly dominated by them. They may serve as the almost exclusive organizers of behavior, recruiting all the capacities of the organism in their service, and we may then fairly describe the whole organism as a safety-seeking mechanism. Again we may say of the receptors, the effectors, of the intellect and the other capacities that they are primarily safety-seeking tools. Again, as in the hungry man, we find that the dominating goal is a strong determinant not only of his current world-outlook and philosophy but also of his philosophy of the future. Practically everything looks less important than safety, (even sometimes the physiological needs which being satisfied, are now underestimated). A man, in this state, if it is extreme enough and chronic enough, may be characterized as living almost for safety alone.

Although in this paper we are interested primarily in the needs of the adult, we can approach an understanding of his safety needs perhaps more efficiently by observation of infants and children, in whom these needs are much more simple and obvious. One reason for the clearer appearance of the threat or danger reaction in infants, is that they do not inhibit this reaction at all, whereas adults in our society have been taught to inhibit it at all costs. Thus even when adults do feel their safety to be threatened we may not be able to see this on the surface. Infants will react in a total fashion and as if they were endangered, if they are disturbed or dropped suddenly, startled by loud noises, flashing light, or other unusual sensory stimulation, by rough handling, by general loss of support in the mother's arms, or by inadequate support.[9]

In infants we can also see a much more direct reaction to bodily illnesses of various kinds. Sometimes these illnesses seem to be immediately and *per se* threatening and seem to make the child feel unsafe. For instance, vomiting, colic or other sharp pains seem to make the child look at the whole world in a different way. At such

---

[9] As the child grows up, sheer knowledge and familiarity as well as better motor development make these "dangers" less and less dangerous and more and more manageable. Throughout life it may be said that one of the main conative functions of education is this neutralizing of apparent dangers through knowledge, *e.g.*, I am not afraid of thunder because I know something about it.

a moment of pain, it may be postulated that, for the child, the appearance of the whole world suddenly changes from sunniness to darkness, so to speak, and becomes a place in which anything at all might happen, in which previously stable things have suddenly become unstable. Thus a child who because of some bad food is taken ill may, for a day or two, develop fear, nightmares, and a need for protection and reassurance never seen in him before his illness.

Another indication of the child's need for safety is his preference for some kind of undisrupted routine or rhythm. He seems to want a predictable, orderly world. For instance, injustice, unfairness, or inconsistency in the parents seems to make a child feel anxious and unsafe. This attitude may be not so much because of the injustice *per se* or any particular pains involved, but rather because this treatment threatens to make the world look unreliable, or unsafe, or unpredictable. Young children seem to thrive better under a system which has at least a skeletal outline of rigidity, in which there is a schedule of a kind, some sort of routine, something that can be counted upon, not only for the present but also far into the future. Perhaps one could express this more accurately by saying that the child needs an organized world rather than an unorganized or unstructured one.

The central role of the parents and the normal family setup are indisputable. Quarreling, physical assault, separation, divorce or death within the family may be particularly terrifying. Also parental outbursts of rage or threats of punishment directed to the child, calling him names, speaking to him harshly, shaking him, handling him roughly, or actual physical punishment sometimes elicit such total panic and terror in the child that we must assume more is involved than the physical pain alone. While it is true that in some children this terror may represent also a fear of loss of parental love, it can also occur in completely rejected children, who seem to cling to the hating parents more for sheer safety and protection than because of hope of love.

Confronting the average child with new, unfamiliar, strange, unmanageable stimuli or situations will too frequently elicit the danger or terror reaction, as for example, getting lost or even being separated from the parents for a short time, being confronted with new faces, new situations or new tasks, the sight of strange, unfamiliar or uncontrollable objects, illness or death. Particularly at such times, the child's frantic clinging to his parents is eloquent testimony to their role as protectors (quite apart from their roles as food-givers and love-givers).

From these and similar observations, we may generalize and say that the average child in our society generally prefers a safe, orderly, predictable, organized world, which he can count on, and in which unexpected, unmanageable or other dangerous things do not happen, and in which, in any case, he has all-powerful parents who protect and shield him from harm.

That these reactions may so easily be observed in chldren is in a way a proof of the fact that children in our society, feel too unsafe (or, in a word, are badly brought up). Children who are reared in an unthreatening, loving family do *not* ordinarily react as we have described above.[10] In such children the danger reactions are apt to come mostly to objects or situations that adults too would consider dangerous.[11]

The healthy, normal, fortunate adult in our culture is largely satisfied in his safety needs. The peaceful, smoothly running, "good" society ordinarily makes its members feel safe enough from wild animals, extremes of temperature, criminals, assault and murder, tyranny, etc. Therefore, in a very real sense, he no longer has any safety needs as active motivators. Just as a sated man no longer feels hungry, a safe man no longer feels endangered. If we wish to see these needs directly and clearly we must turn to neurotic or near-neurotic individuals, and to the economic and social underdogs. In between these extremes, we can perceive the expressions of safety needs only in such phenomena as, for instance, the common preference for a job with tenure and protection, the desire for a savings account, and for insurance of various kinds (medical, dental, unemployment, disability, old age).

Other broader aspects of the attempt to seek safety and stability in the world are seen in the very common preference for familiar rather than unfamiliar things, or for the known rather than the unknown. The tendency to have some religion or world-philosophy that organizes the universe and the men in it into some sort of satisfactory coherent, meaningful whole is also in part motivated by safety-seeking. Here too we may list science and philosophy in general as partially motivated by the safety needs (we shall see later

---

[10] M. Shirley, "Children's Adjustments to a Strange Situation," *Journal of Abnormal (Soc.) Psychology*, Vol. 37, 1942, pp. 201-217.

[11] A "test battery" for safety might be confronting the child with a small exploding firecracker, or with a bewhiskered face, having the mother leave the room, putting him upon a high ladder, a hypodermic injection, having a mouse crawl up to him, etc. Of course I cannot seriously recommend the deliberate us of such "tests" for they might very well harm the child being tested. But these and similar situations come up by the score in the child's ordinary day-to-day living and may be observed. There is no reason why these stimuli should not be used with, for example, young chimpanzees.

that there are also other motivations to scientific, philosophical or religious endeavor).

Otherwise the need for safety is seen as an active and dominant mobilizer of the organism's resources only in emergencies, *e.g.*, war, disease, natural catastrophies, crime waves, societal disorganization, neurosis, brain injury, chronically bad situation.

Some neurotic adults in our society are, in many ways, like the unsafe child in their desire for safety, although in the former it takes on a somewhat special appearance. Their reaction is often to unknown, psychological dangers in a world that is perceived to be hostile, overwhelming and threatening. Such a person behaves as if a great catastrophe were almost always impending, *i.e.*, he is usually responding as if to an emergency. His safety needs often find specific expression in a search for a protector, or a stronger person on whom he may depend, or perhaps, a Fuehrer.

The neurotic individual may be described in a slightly different way with some usefulness as a grown-up person who retains his childish attitudes toward the world. That is to say, a neurotic adult may be said to behave "as if" he were actually afraid of a spanking, or of his mother's disapproval, or of being abandoned by his parents, or having his food taken away from him. It is as if his childish attitudes of fear and threat reaction to a dangerous world had gone underground, and untouched by the growing up and learning processes, were now ready to be called out by any stimulus that would make a child feel endangered and threatened.[12]

The neurosis in which the search for safety takes its clearest form is in the compulsive-obsessive neurosis. Compulsive-obsessives try frantically to order and stabilize the world so that no unmanageable, unexpected or unfamiliar dangers will ever appear.[13] They hedge themselves about with all sorts of ceremonials, rules and formulas so that every possible contingency may be provided for and so that no new contingencies may appear. They are much like the brain injured cases, described by Goldstein,[14] who manage to maintain their equilibrium by avoiding everything unfamiliar and strange and by ordering their restricted world in such a neat, disciplined, orderly fashion that everything in the world can be counted upon. They try to arrange the world so that anything unexpected (dangers) cannot possibly

[12] Not all neurotic individuals feel unsafe. Neurosis may have at its core a thwarting of the affection and esteem needs in a person who is generally safe.
[13] A. H. Maslow and B. Mittelmann, *Principles of Abnormal Psychology* (New York: Harper & Bros., 1941).
[14] Goldstein, *loc. cit.*

occur. If, through no fault of their own, something unexpected does occur, they go into a panic reaction as if this unexpected occurrence constituted a grave danger. What we can see only as a none-too-strong preference in the healthy person, *e.g.*, preference for the familiar, becomes a life-and-death necessity in abnormal cases.

The love needs.—If both the physiological and the safety needs are fairly well gratified, then there will emerge the love and affection and belongingness needs, and the whole cycle already described will repeat itself with this new center. Now the person will feel keenly, as never before, the absence of friends, or a sweetheart, or a wife, or children. He will hunger for affectionate relations with people in general, namely, for a place in his group, and he will strive with great intensity to achieve this goal. He will want to attain such a place more than anything else in the world and may even forget that once, when he was hungry, he sneered at love.

In our society the thwarting of these needs is the most commonly found core in cases of maladjustment and more severe psychopathology. Love and affection, as well as their possible expression in sexuality, are generally looked upon with ambivalence and are customarily hedged about with many restrictions and inhibitions. Practically all theorists of psychopathology have stressed thwarting of the love needs as basic in the picture of maladjustment. Many clinical studies have therefore been made of this need and we know more about it perhaps than any of the other needs except the physiological ones.[15]

One thing that must be stressed at this point is that love is not synonymous with sex. Sex may be studied as a purely physiological need. Ordinarily sexual behavior is multi-determined, that is to say, determined not only by sexual but also by other needs, chief among which are the love and affection needs. Also not to be overlooked is the fact that the love needs involve both giving *and* receiving love.[16]

The esteem needs.—All people in our society (with a few pathological exceptions) have a need or desire for a stable, firmly based, (usually) high evaluation of themselves, for self-respect, or self-esteem, and for the esteem of others. By firmly based self-esteem, we mean that which is soundly based upon real capacity, achievement and respect from others. These needs may be classified into two

[15] Maslow and Mittelmann, *loc. cit.*

[16] For further details see A. H. Maslow, "The Dynamics of Psychological Security-Insecurity," *Character and Personality*, Vol. 10, 1942, pp. 331-344, and J. Plant, *Personality and the Cultural Pattern* (New York: Commonwealth Fund, 1937), Ch. 5.

subsidiary sets. These are, first, the desire for strength, for achievement, for adequacy, for confidence in the face of the world, and for independence and freedom.[17] Secondly, we have what we may call the desire for reputation or prestige (defining it as respect or esteem from other people), recognition, attention, importance or appreciation.[18] These needs have been relatively stressed by Alfred Adler and his followers, and have been relatively neglected by Freud and the psychoanalysts. More and more today however there is appearing widespread appreciation of their central importance.

Satisfaction of the self-esteem need leads to feelings of self-confidence, worth, strength, capability and adequacy of being useful and necessary in the world. But thwarting of these needs produces feelings of inferiority, of weakness and of helplessness. These feelings in turn give rise to either basic discouragement or else compensatory or neurotic trends. An appreciation of the necessity of basic self-confidence and an understanding of how helpless people are without it, can be easily gained from a study of severe traumatic neurosis.[19, 20]

The need for self-actualization.—Even if all these needs are satisfied, we may still often (if not always) expect that a new discontent and restlessness will soon develop, unless the individual is doing what he is fitted for. A musician must make music, an artist must paint, a poet must write, if he is to be ultimately happy. What a man *can* be, he *must* be. This need we may call self-actualization.

This term, first coined by Kurt Goldstein, is being used in this paper in a much more specific and limited fashion. It refers to the desire for self-fulfillment, namely, to the tendency for him to become actualized in what he is potentially. This tendency might be phrased as the desire to become more and more what one is, to become everything that one is capable of becoming.

---

[17] Whether or not this particular desire is universal we do not know. The crucial question, especially important today, is "Will men who are enslaved and dominated, inevitably feel dissatisfied and rebellious?" We may assume on the basis of commonly known clinical data that a man who has known true freedom (not paid for by giving up safety and security but rather built on the basis of adequate safety and security) will not willingly or easily allow his freedom to be taken away from him. But we do not know that this is true for the person born into slavery. The events of the next decade should give us our answer. See discussion of this problem in E. Fromm, *Escape from Freedom* (New York: Farrar and Rinehart, 1941).

[18] Perhaps the desire for prestige and respect from others is subsidiary to the desire for self-esteem or confidence in oneself. Observation of children seems to indicate that this is so, but clinical data give no clear support for such a conclusion.

[19] A. Kardiner, *The Traumatic Neuroses of War* (New York: Hoeber, 1941).

[20] For more extensive discussion of normal self-esteem, as well as for reports of various researches, see A. S. Maslow, "Dominance, Personality and Social Behavior in Women," *Journal (Soc.) of Psychology*, Vol. 10, 1939, pp. 3-39.

The specific form that these needs will take will of course vary greatly from person to person. In one individual it may take the form of the desire to be an ideal mother, in another it may be expressed athletically, and in still another it may be expressed in painting pictures or in inventions. It is not necessarily a creative urge although in people who have any capacities for creation it will take this form.

The clear emergence of these needs rests upon prior satisfaction of the physiological, safety, love and esteem needs. We shall call people who are satisfied in these needs, basically satisfied people, and it is from these that we may expect the fullest (and healthiest) creativeness.[21] Since, in our society, basically satisfied people are the exception, we do not know much about self-actualization, either experimentally or clinically. It remains a challenging problem for research.

The preconditions for the basic need satisfactions.—There are certain conditions which are immediate prerequisites for the basic need satisfactions. Danger to these is reacted to almost as if it were a direct danger to the basic needs themselves. Such conditions as freedom to speak, freedom to do what one wishes so long as no harm is done to others, freedom to express one's self, freedom to investigate and seek for information, freedom to defend one's self, justice, fairness, honesty, orderliness in the group are examples of such preconditions for basic need satisfactions. Thwarting in these freedoms will be reacted to with a threat or emergency response. These conditions are not ends in themselves but they are *almost* so since they are so closely related to the basic needs, which are apparently the only ends in themselves. These conditions are defended because without them the basic satisfactions are quite impossible, or at least, very severely endangered.

If we remember that the cognitive capacities (perceptual, intellectual, learning) are a set of adjustive tools, which have, among other functions, that of satisfaction of our basic needs, then it is clear that any danger to them, any deprivation or blocking of their free use, must also be indirectly threatening to the basic needs them-

---

[21] Clearly creative behavior, like painting, is like any other behavior in having multiple determinants. It may be seen in "innately creative" people whether they are satisfied or not, happy or unhappy, hungry or sated. Also it is clear that creative activity may be compensatory, ameliorative or purely economic. It is my impression (as yet unconfirmed) that it is possible to distinguish the artistic and intellectual products of basically satisfied people from those of basically unsatisfied people by inspection alone. In any case, here too we must distinguish, in a dynamic fashion, the overt behavior itself from its various motivations or purposes.

selves. Such a statement is a partial solution of the general problems of curiosity, the search for knowledge, truth and wisdom, and the ever-persistent urge to solve the cosmic mysteries.

We must therefore introduce another hypothesis and speak of degrees of closeness to the basic needs, for we have already pointed out that *any* conscious desires (partial goals) are more or less important as they are more or less close to the basic needs. The same statement may be made for various behavior acts. An act is psychologically important if it contributes directly to satisfaction of basic needs. The less directly it so contributes, or the weaker this contribution is, the less important this act must be conceived to be from the point of view of dynamic psychology. A similar statement may be made for the various defense or coping mechanisms. Some are very directly related to the protection or attainment of the basic needs, others are only weakly and distantly related. Indeed if we wished, we could speak of more basic and less basic defense mechanisms, and then affirm that danger to the more basic defenses is more threatening than danger to less basic defenses (always remembering that this is so only because of their relationship to the basic needs).

The desires to know and to understand.—So far, we have mentioned the cognitive needs only in passing. Acquiring knowledge and systematizing the universe have been considered as, in part, techniques for the achievement of basic safety in the world, or, for the intelligent man, expressions of self-actualization. Also freedom of inquiry and expression have been discussed as preconditions of satisfactions of the basic needs. True though these formulations may be, they do not constitute definitive answers to the question as to the motivation role of curiosity, learning, philosophizing, experimenting, etc. They are, at best, no more than partial answers.

This question is especially difficult because we know so little about the facts. Curiosity, exploration, desire for the facts, desire to know may certainly be observed easily enough. The fact that they often are pursued even at great cost to the individual's safety is an earnest of the partial character of our previous discussion. In addition, the writer must admit that, though he has sufficient clinical evidence to postulate the desire to know as a very strong drive in intelligent people, no data are available for unintelligent people. It may then be largely a function of relatively high intelligence. Rather tentatively, then, and largely in the hope of stimulating discussion and research, we shall postulate a basic desire to know, to be aware of reality, to get the facts, to satisfy curiosity, or as Wertheimer phrases it, to see rather than to be blind.

This postulation, however, is not enough. Even after we know, we are impelled to know more and more minutely and microscopically on the one hand, and on the other, more and more extensively in the direction of a world philosophy, religion, etc. The facts that we acquire, if they are isolated or atomistic, inevitably get theorized about, and either analyzed or organized or both. This process has been phrased by some as the search for "meaning." We shall then postulate a desire to understand, to systematize, to organize, to analyze, to look for relations and meanings.

Once these desires are accepted for discussion, we see that they too form themselves into a small hierarchy in which the desire to know is prepotent over the desire to understand. All the characteristics of a hierarchy of prepotency that we have described above, seem to hold for this one as well.

We must guard ourselves against the too easy tendency to separate these desires from the basic needs we have discussed above, *i.e.*, to make a sharp dichotomy between "cognitive" and "conative" needs. The desire to know and to understand are themselves conative, *i.e.*, have a striving character, and are as much personality needs as the "basic needs" we have already discussed.[22]

III. Further Characteristics of the Basic Needs

The degree of fixity of the hierarchy of basic needs.—We have spoken so far as if this hierarchy were a fixed order but actually it is not nearly as rigid as we may have implied. It is true that most of the people with whom we have worked have seemed to have these basic needs in about the order that has been indicated. However, there have been a number of exceptions.

(1) There are some people in whom, for instance, self-esteem seems to be more important than love. This most common reversal in the hierarchy is usually due to the development of the notion that the person who is most likely to be loved is a strong or powerful person, one who inspires respect or fear, and who is self confident or aggressive. Therefore such people who lack love and seek it, may try hard to put on a front of aggressive, confident behavior. But essentially they seek high self-esteem and its behavior expressions more as a means-to-an-end than for its own sake; they seek self-assertion for the sake of love rather than for self-esteem itself.

(2) There are other, apparently innately creative people in whom the drive to creativeness seems to be more important than any other

---

[22] M. Wertheimer, unpublished lectures at the New School for Social Research.

counter-determinant. Their creativeness might appear not as self-actualization released by basic satisfaction, but in spite of lack of basic satisfaction.

(3) In certain people the level of aspiration may be permanently deadened or lowered. That is to say, the less prepotent goals may simply be lost, and may disappear forever, so that the person who has experienced life at a very low level, *i.e.*, chronic unemployment, may continue to be satisfied for the rest of his life if only he can get enough food.

(4) The so-called "psychopathic personality" is another example of permanent loss of the love needs. These are people who, according to the best data available [23] have been starved for love in the earliest months of their lives and have simply lost forever the desire and the ability to give and to receive affection (as animals lose sucking or pecking reflexes that are not exercised soon enough after birth).

(5) Another cause of reversal of the hierarchy is that when a need has been satisfied for a long time, this need may be under-evaluated. People who have never experienced chronic hunger are apt to underestimate its effects and to look upon food as a rather unimportant thing. If they are dominated by a higher need, this higher need will seem to be the most important of all. It then becomes possible, and indeed does actually happen, that they may, for the sake of this higher need, put themselves into the position of being deprived in a more basic need. We may expect that after a long-time deprivation of the more basic need there will be a tendency to reevaluate both needs so that the more prepotent need will actually become consciously prepotent for the individual who may have given it up very lightly. Thus, a man who has given up his job rather than lose his self-respect, and who then starves for six months or so, may be willing to take his job back even at the price of losing his self-respect.

(6) Another partial explanation of *apparent* reversals is seen in the fact that we have been talking about the hierarchy of prepotency in terms of consciously felt wants or desires rather than of behavior. Looking at behavior itself may give us the wrong impression. What we have claimed is that the person will *want* the more basic of two needs when deprived in both. There is no necessary implication here that he will act upon his desires. Let us say again that there are many determinants of behavior other than the needs and desires.

(7) Perhaps more important than all these exceptions are the ones that involve ideals, high social standards, high values and the

---

[23] D. M. Levy, "Primary Affect Hunger," *American Journal of Psychiatry*, Vol. 94, 1937, pp. 643-652.

like. With such values people become martyrs; they will give up everything for the sake of a particular ideal, or value. These people may be understood, at least in part, by reference to one basic concept (or hypothesis) which may be called "increased frustration-tolerance through early gratification." People who have been satisfied in their basic needs throughout their lives, particularly in their earlier years, seem to develop exceptional power to withstand present or future thwarting of these needs simply because they have strong, healthy character structure as a result of basic satisfaction. They are the "strong" people who can easily weather disagreement or opposition, who can swim against the stream of public opinion and who can stand up for the truth at great personal cost. It is just the ones who have loved and been well loved, and who have had many deep friendships who can hold out against hatred, rejection or presecution.

I say all this in spite of the fact that there is a certain amount of sheer habituation which is also involved in any full discussion of frustration tolerance. For instance, it is likely that those persons who have been accustomed to relative starvation for a long time, are partially enabled thereby to withstand food deprivation. What sort of balance must be made between these two tendencies, of habituation on the one hand, and of past satisfaction breeding present frustration-tolerance on the other hand, remains to be worked out by further research. Meanwhile we may assume that they are both operative, side by side, since they do not contradict each other. In respect to this phenomenon of increased frustration tolerance, it seems probable that the most important gratifications come in the first two years of life. That is to say, people who have been made secure and strong in the earliest years, tend to remain secure and strong thereafter in the face of whatever threatens.

Degrees of relative satisfaction.—So far, our theoretical discussion may have given the impression that these five sets of needs are somehow in a step-wise, all-or-none relationship to each other. We have spoken in such terms as the following: "If one need is satisfied, then another emerges." This statement might give the false impression that a need must be satisfied 100 per cent before the next need emerges. In actual fact, most members of our society who are normal, are partially satisfied in all their basic needs and partially unsatisfied in all their basic needs at the same time. A more realistic description of the hierarchy would be in terms of decreasing percentages of satisfaction as we go up the hierarchy of prepotency. For instance, if I may assign arbitrarily figures for the sake of illustration, it is as if the average citizen is satisfied 85 per cent in his physiological needs, 70 per cent in his safety needs, 50 per cent in his love needs, 40 per cent in his self-esteem needs, and 10 per cent in his self-actualization needs.

As for the concept of emergence of a new need after satisfaction of the propotent need, this emergence is not a sudden, saltatory phenomenon but rather a gradual emergence by slow degrees from nothingness. For instance, if preponent need A is satisfied only 10 per cent then need B may not be visible at all. However, as this need A becomes satisfied 25 per cent, need B may emerge 5 per cent, as need A becomes satisfied 75 per cent need B may emerge 90 per cent, and so on.

Unconscious character of needs.—These needs are neither necessarily conscious nor unconscious. On the whole, however, in the average person, they are more often unconscious rather than conscious. It is not necessary at this point to overhaul the tremendous mass of evidence which indicates the crucial importance of unconcious motivation. It would by now be expected, on a priori grounds alone, that unconscious motivations would on the whole be rather more important than the conscious motivations. What we have called the basic needs are very often largely unconscious although they may, with suitable techniques, and with sophisticated people become conscious.

Cultural specificity and generality of needs.—This classification of basic needs makes some attempt to take account of the relative unity behind the superficial differences in specific desires from one culture to another. Certainly in any particular culture an individual's conscious motivational content will usually be extremely different from the conscious motivational content of an idividual in another society. However, it is the common experience of anthropologists that people, even in different societies, are much more alike than we would think from our first contact with them, and that as we know them better we seem to find more and more of this commonness. We then recognize the most startling differences to be superficial rather than basic, *e.g.*, differences in style of hairdress, clothes, tastes in food, etc. Our classification of basic needs is in part an attempt to account for this unity behind the apparent diversity from culture to culture. No claim is made that it is ultimate or universal for all cultures. The claim is made only that it is relatively *more* ultimate, more universal, more basic, than the superficial conscious desires from culture to culture, and makes a somewhat closer approach to common-human characteristics. Basic needs are *more* common-human than superficial desires or behaviors.

Multiple motivations of behavior.—These needs must be understood *not* to be *exclusive* or single determiners of certain kinds of behavior. An example may be found in any behavior that seems to be physiologically motivated, such as eating, or sexual play or the like. The clinical phychologists have long since found that any behavior may be a channel through which flow various determinants. Or to say it in another way, most behavior is multi-motivated. Within the sphere of motivational determinants any behavior tends to be determined by several or *all* of the basic needs simultaneously rather than by only one of them. The latter would be more an exception than the former. Eating may be partially for the sake of filling the stomach, and partially for the sake of comfort and amelioration of other needs. One may make love not only for pure sexual release, but also to convince one's self of one's masculinity, or to make a conquest, to feel powerful, or to win more basic affection. As an illustration, I may point out that it would be possible (theoretically if not practically) to analyze a single act of an individual and see in it the expression of his physiological needs, his safety needs, his love needs, his esteem needs and self-actualization. This contrasts sharply with the more naive brand of trait psychology in which one trait or one motive accounts for a certain kind of act, *i.e.*, an aggressive act is traced solely to a trait of aggressiveness.

Multiple determinants of behavior.—Not all behavior is determined by the basic needs. We might even say that not all behavior is motivated. There are many determinants of behavior other than motives.[24] For instance, one other important class of determinants is the so-called "field" determinants. Theoretically, at least, behavior may be determined completely by the field, or even by specific isolated external stimuli, as in association of ideas, or certain conditioned reflexes. If in response to the stimulus word "table," I immediately perceive a memory image of a table, this response certainly has nothing to do with my basic needs.

Secondly, we may call attention again to the concept of "degree of closeness to the basic needs" or "degree of motivation." Some behavior is highly motivated, other behavior is only weakly motivated. Some is not motivated at all (but all behavior is determined).

---

[24] I am aware that many psychologists and psychoanalysts use the term "motivated" and "determined" synonymously, *e.g.*, Freud. But I consider this an obfuscating usage. Sharp distinctions are necessary for clarity of thought, and precision in experimentation.

Another important point [25] is that there is a basic difference between expressive behavior and coping behavior (functional striving, purposive goal seeking). An expressive behavior does not try to do anything; it is simply a reflection of the personality. A stupid man behaves stupidly, not because he wants to, or tries to, or is motivated to, but simply because he *is* what he is. The same is true when I speak in a bass voice rather than tenor or soprano. The random movements of a healthy child, the smile on the face of a happy man even when he is alone, the springiness of the healthy man's walk, and the erectness of his carriage are other examples of expressive, non-functional behavior. Also the *style* in which a man carries out almost all his behavior, motivated as well as unmotivated, is often expressive.

We may then ask, is *all* behavior expressive or reflective of the character structure? The answer is "No." Rote, habitual, automatized, or conventional behavior may or may not be expressive. The same is true for most "stimulus-bound" behaviors.

It is finally necessary to stress that expressiveness of behavior, and goal-directedness of behavior are not mutually exclusive categories. Average behavior is usually both.

Goals as centering principle in motivation theory.—It will be observed that the basic principle in our classification has been neither the instigation nor the motivated behavior but rather the functions, effects, purposes, or goals of the behavior. It has been proven sufficiently by various people that this is the most suitable point for centering in any motivation theory.[26]

Animal- and human-centering.—This theory starts with the human being rather than any lower and presumably "simpler" animal. Too many of the findings that have been made in animals have been proven to be true for animals but not for the human being. There is no reason whatsoever why we should start with animals in order to study human motivation. The logic or rather illogic behind this general fallacy of "pseudo-simplicity" has been exposed often enough by philosophers and logicians as well as by scientists in each of the various fields. It is no more necessary to study animals before one can study man than it is to study mathematics before one can study geology or psychology or biology.

---

[25] To be discussed fully in a subsequent publication.
[26] The interested reader is referred to the very excellent discussion of this point in H. A. Murray, *et al.*, *Explorations in Personality* (New York: Oxford University Press, 1938).

We may also reject the old, naive, behaviorism which assumed that it was somehow necessary, or at least more "scientific" to judge human beings by animal standards. One consequence of this belief was that the whole notion of purpose and goal was excluded from motivational psychology simply because one could not ask a white rat about his purposes. Tolman [27] has long since proven in animal studies themselves that this exclusion was not necessary.

Motivation and the theory of psychopathogenesis.—The conscious motivational content of everyday life has, according to the foregoing, been conceived to be relatively important or unimportant accordingly as it is more or less closely related to the basic goals. A desire for an ice cream cone might actually be an indirect expression of a desire for love. If it is, then this desire for the ice cream cone becomes extremely important motivation. If however the ice cream is simply something to cool the mouth with, or a casual appetitive reaction, then the desire is relatively unimportant. Everyday conscious desires are to be regarded as symptoms, as *surface indicators of more basic needs.* If we were to take these superficial desires at their face value we would find ourselves in a state of complete confusion which could never be resolved, since we would be dealing seriously with symptoms rather than with what lay behind the symptoms.

Thwarting of unimportant desires produces no psychopathological results; thwarting of a basically important need does produce such results. Any theory of psychopathogenesis must then be based on a sound theory of motivation. A conflict or a frustration is not necessarily pathogenic. It becomes so only when it threatens or thwarts the basic needs, or partial needs that are closely related to the basic needs. [28]

The role of gratified needs.—It has been pointed out above several times that our needs usually emerge only when more prepotent needs have been gratified. Thus gratification has an important role in motivation theory. Apart from this, however, needs cease to play an active determining or organizing role as soon as they are gratified.

What this means is that, *e.g.*, a basically satisfied person no longer has the needs for esteem, love, safety, etc. The only sense in which he might be said to have them is in the almost metaphysical sense that a sated man has hunger, or a filled bottle has emptiness. If we

[27] E. C. Tolman, *Purposive Behavior in Animals and Men* (New York: Century, 1932).
[28] A. H. Maslow, "Conflict, Frustration, and the Theory of Threat," *Journal of Abnormal (Soc.) Psychology*, Vol. 38, 1943, pp. 81-86.

are interested in what *actually* motivates us, and not in what has, will, or might motivate us, then a satisfied need is not a motivator. It must be considered for all practical purposes simply not to exist, to have disappeared. This point should be emphasized because it has been either overlooked or contradicted in every theory of motivation I know.[29] The perfectly healthy, normal, fortunate man has no sex needs or hunger needs, or needs for safety, or for love, or for prestige, or self-esteem, except in stray moments of quickly passing threat. If we were to say otherwise, we should also have to aver that every man had all the pathological reflexes, *e.g.*, Babinski, etc., because if his nervous system were damaged, these would appear.

It is such considerations as these that suggest the bold postulation that a man who is thwarted in any of his basic needs may fairly be envisaged simply as a sick man. This is a fair parallel to our designation as "sick" of the man who lacks vitamins or minerals. Who is to say that a lack of love is less important than a lack of vitamins? Since we know the pathogenic effects of love starvation, who is to say that we are invoking value-questions in an unscientific or illegitimate way, any more than the physician does who diagnoses and treats pellagra or scurvy? If I were permitted this usage, I should then say simply that a healthy man is primarily motivated by his needs to develop and actualize his fullest potentialities and capacities. If a man has any other basic needs in any active, chronic sense, then he is simply an unhealthy man. He is as surely sick as if he had suddenly developed a strong salt-hunger or calcium hunger.[30]

If this statement seems unusual or paradoxical the reader may be assured that this is only one among many such paradoxes that will appear as we revise our ways of looking at man's deeper motivations. When we ask what man wants of life, we deal with his very essence.

IV. Summary

(1) There are at least five sets of goals, which we may call basic needs. These are briefly physiological, safety, love, esteem, and self-actualization. In addition, we are motivated by the desire to achieve

---

[29] Note that acceptance of this theory necessitates basic revision of the Freudian theory.

[30] If we were to use the word "sick" in this way, we should then also have to face squarely the relations of man to his society. One clear implication of our definition would be that (1) since a man is to be called sick who is basically thwarted, and (2) since such basic thwarting is made possible ultimately only by forces outside the individual, then (3) sickness in the individual must come ultimately from a sickness in the society. The "good" or healthy society would then be defined as one that permitted man's highest purposes to emerge by satisfying all his prepotent basic needs.

or maintain the various conditions upon which these basic satisfactions rest and by certain more intellectual desires.

(2) These basic goals are related to each other, being arranged in a hierarchy of prepotency. This means that the most prepotent goal will monopolize consciousness and will tend of itself to organize the recruitment of the various capacities of the organism. The less prepotent needs are minimized, even forgotten or denied. But when a need is fairly well satisfied, the next prepotent ("higher") need emerges, in turn to dominate the conscious life and to serve as the center of organization of behavior, since gratified needs are not active motivators.

Thus man is a perpetually wanting animal. Ordinarily the satisfaction of these wants is not altogether mutually exclusive, but only tends to be. The average member of our society is most often partially satisfied and partially unsatisfied in all of his wants. The hierarchy principle is usually empirically observed in terms of increasing percentages of non-satisfaction as we go up the hierarchy. Reversals of the average order of the hierarchy are sometimes observed. Also it has been observed that an individual may permanently lose the higher wants in the hierarchy under special conditions. There are not only ordinarily multiple motivations for usual behavior, but in addition many determinants other than motives.

(3) Any thwarting or possibility of thwarting of these basic human goals, or danger to the defenses which protect them, or to the conditions upon which they rest, is considered to be a psychological threat. With a few exceptions, all psychopathology may be partially traced to such threats. A basically thwarted man may actually be defined as a "sick" man, if we wish.

(4) It is such basic threats which bring about the general emergency reactions.

(5) Certain other basic problems have not been dealt with because of limitations of space. Among these are (a) the problem of values in any definitive motivation theory, (b) the relation between appetites, desires, needs and what is "good" for the organism, (c) the etiology of the basic needs and their possible derivation in early childhood, (d) redefinition of motivational concepts, *i.e.*, drive, desire, wish, need, goal, (e) implication of our theory for hedonistic theory, (f) the nature of the uncompleted act, of success and failure, and of aspiration-level (g) the role of association, habit and conditioning, (h) relation to the theory of inter-personal relations, (i) implications for psychotherapy, (j) implication for theory of society, (k) the theory of selfishness, (l) the relation between needs and cultural pat-

terns, (m) the relation between this theory and Allport's theory of functional autonomy. These as well as certain other less important questions must be considered as motivation theory attempts to become definitive.

QUESTIONS

1. Compare the classes of basic needs stated by Maslow with those discussed in the introduction section. Explain any differences you see.
2. Explain what is meant by the "hierarchical" nature of needs. Is this hierarchy "rigid"?
3. What conditions are prerequisites for need satisfaction?
4. Is all human behavior determined by basic needs? Why?
5. Discuss the fundamental characteristics of basic needs.

THE HUMAN SIDE OF ENTERPRISE *

Douglas M. McGregor

It has become true to say that industry has the fundamental know-how to utilize physical science and technology for the material benefit of mankind, and that we must now learn how to utilize the social sciences to make our human organizations truly effective.

To a degree, the social sciences today are in a position like that of the physical sciences with respect to atomic energy in the thirties. We know that past conceptions of the nature of man are inadequate and, in many ways, incorrect. We are becoming quite certain that, under proper conditions, unimagined resources of creative human energy could become available within the organizational setting.

We cannot tell industrial management how to apply this new knowledge in simple, economic ways. We know it will require years of exploration, much costly development research, and a substantial amount of creative imagination on the part of management to discover how to apply this growing knowledge to the organization of human effort in industry.

MANAGEMENT'S TASK: THE CONVENTIONAL VIEW

The conventional conception of management's task in harnessing human energy to organizational requirements can be stated broadly in terms of three propositions. In order to avoid the complications introduced by a label, let us call this set of propositions "Theory X":

1. Management is responsible for organizing the elements of productive enterprise—money, materials, equipment, people—in the interest of economic ends.

2. With respect to people, this is a process of directing their efforts, motivating them, controlling their actions, modifying their behavior to fit the needs of the organization.

3. Without this active intervention by management, people would be passive—even resistant—to organizational needs. They must therefore be persuaded, rewarded, punished, controlled—their activities must be directed. This is management's task. We often sum it up by saying that management consists of getting things done through other people.

* From the *Management Review*, Vol. 46, No. 11 (November, 1957), pp. 22-28, 88-92. Copyright, 1957, by the American Management Association. Reprinted by permission of the American Management Association.

Behind this conventional theory there are several additional beliefs —less explicit, but widespread:

4. The average man is by nature indolent—he works as little as possible.

5. He lacks ambition, dislikes responsibility, prefers to be led.

6. He is inherently self-centered, indifferent to organizational needs.

7. He is by nature resistant to change.

8. He is gullible, not very bright, the ready dupe of the charlatan and the demagogue.

The human side of economic enterprise today is fashioned from propositions and beliefs such as these. Conventional organization structures and managerial policies, practices, and programs reflect these assumptions.

In accomplishing its task—with these assumptions as guides—management has conceived of a range of possibilities.

At one extreme, management can be "hard" or "strong." The methods for directing behavior involve coercion and threat (usually disguised), close supervision, tight controls over behavior. At the other extreme, management can be "soft" or "weak." The methods for directing behavior involve being permissive, satisfying people's demands, achieving harmony. Then they will be tractable, accept direction.

This range has been fairly completely explored during the past half century, and management has learned some things from the exploration. There are difficulties in the "hard" approach. Force breeds counter-forces: restriction of output, antagonism, militant unionism, subtle but effective sabotage of management objectives. This "hard" approach is especially difficult during times of full employment.

There are also difficulties in the "soft" approach. It leads frequently to the abdication of management—to harmony, perhaps, but to indifferent performance. People take advantage of the soft approach. They continually expect more, but they give less and less.

Currently, the popular theme is "firm but fair." This is an attempt to gain the advantages of both the hard and the soft approaches. It is reminiscent of Teddy Roosevelt's "speak softly and carry a big stick."

IS THE CONVENTIONAL VIEW CORRECT?

The findings which are beginning to emerge from the social sciences challenge this whole set of beliefs about man and human nature and about the task of management. The evidence is far from conclusive, certainly, but it is suggestive. It comes from the laboratory, the clinic, the schoolroom, the home, and even to a limited extent from industry itself.

The social scientist does not deny that human behavior in industrial organization today is approximately what management perceives it to be. He has, in fact, observed it and studied it fairly extensively. But he is pretty sure that this behavior is *not* a consequence of man's inherent nature. It is a consequence rather of the nature of industrial organizations, of management philosophy, policy, and practice. The conventional approach to Theory X is based on mistaken notions of what is cause and what is effect.

Perhaps the best way to indicate why the conventional approach of management is inadequate is to consider the subject of motivation.

PHYSIOLOGICAL NEEDS

Man is a wanting animal—as soon as one of his needs is satisfied, another appears in its place. This process is unending. It continues from birth to death.

Man's needs are organized in a series of levels—a hierarchy of importance. At the lowest level, but pre-eminent in importance when they are thwarted, are his *physiological needs*. Man lives for bread alone, when there is no bread. Unless the circumstances are unusual, his needs for love, for status, for recognition are inoperative when his stomach has been empty for a while. But when he eats regularly and adequately, hunger ceases to be an important motivation. The same is true of the other physiological needs of man— for rest, exercise, shelter, protection from the elements.

A satisfied need is not a motivator of behavior! This is a fact of profound significance that is regularly ignored in the conventional approach to the management of people. Consider your own need for air: Except as you are deprived of it, it has no appreciable motivating effect upon your behavior.

SAFETY NEEDS

When the physiological needs are reasonably satisfied, needs at the next higher level begin to dominate man's behavior—to motivate him. These are called *safety needs*. They are needs for protection against danger, threat, deprivation. Some people mistakenly refer to these as needs for security. However, unless man is in a dependent relationship where he fears arbitrary deprivation, he does not demand security. The need is for the "fairest possible break."

When he is confident of this, he is more than willing to take risks. But when he feels threatened or dependent, his greatest need is for guarantees, for protection, for security.

The fact needs little emphasis that, since every industrial employee is in a dependent relationship, safety needs may assume considerable importance. Arbitrary management actions, behavior which arouses uncertainty with respect to continued employment or which reflects favoritism or discrimination, unpredictable administration of policy —these can be powerful motivators of the safety needs in the employment relationship *at every level*, from worker to vice president.

SOCIAL NEEDS

When man's physiological needs are satisfied and he is no longer fearful about his physical welfare, his *social needs* become important motivators of his behavior—needs for belonging, for association, for acceptance by his fellows, for giving and receiving friendship and love.

Management knows today of the existence of these needs, but it often assumes quite wrongly that they represent a threat to the organization. Many studies have demonstrated that the tightly knit, cohesive work group may, under proper conditions, be far more effective than an equal number of separate individuals in achieving organizational goals.

Yet management, fearing group hostility to its own objectives, often goes to considerable lengths to control and direct human efforts in ways that are inimical to the natural "groupiness" of human beings. When man's social needs—and perhaps his safety needs, too—are thus thwarted, he behaves in ways which tend to defeat organizational objectives. He becomes resistant, antagonistic, uncooperative. But this behavior is a consequence, not a cause.

EGO NEEDS

Above the social needs—in the sense that they do not become motivators until lower needs are reasonably satisfied—are the needs of greatest significance to management and to man himself. They are the *egoistic needs*, and they are of two kinds:

1. Those needs that relate to one's self-esteem—needs for self-confidence, for independence, for achievement, for competence, for knowledge.

2. Those needs that relate to one's reputation—needs for status, for recognition, for appreciation, for the deserved respect of one's fellows.

Unlike the lower needs, these are rarely satisfied; man seeks indefinitely for more satisfaction of these needs once they have become important to him. But they do not appear in any significant way until physiological, safety, and social needs are all reasonably satisfied.

The typical industrial organization offers few opportunities for the satisfaction of these egoistic needs to people at lower levels in the hierarchy. The conventional methods of organizing work, particularly in mass-production industries, give little heed to these aspects of human motivation. If the practices of scientific management were deliberately calculated to thwart these needs, they could hardly accomplish this purpose better than they do.

Self-fulfillment Needs

Finally—a capstone, as it were, on the hierarchy of man's needs —there are what we may call the *needs for self-fulfillment*. These are the needs for realizing one's own potentialities, for continued self-development, for being creative in the broadest sense of that term.

It is clear that the conditions of modern life give only limited opportunity for these relatively weak needs to obtain expression. The deprivation most people experience with respect to other lower-level needs diverts their energies into the struggle to satisfy *those* needs, and the needs for self-fulfillment remain dormant.

Management and Motivation

We recognize readily enough that a man suffering from a severe dietary deficiency is sick. The deprivation of physiological needs has behavioral consequences. The same is true—although less well recognized—of deprivation of higher-level needs. The man whose needs for safety, association, independence, or status are thwarted is sick just as surely as the man who has rickets. And his sickness will have behavioral consequences. We will be mistaken if we attribute his resultant passivity, his hostility, his refusal to accept responsibility to his inherent "human nature." These forms of behavior are *symptoms* of illness—of deprivation of his social and egoistic needs.

The man whose lower-level needs are satisfied is not motivated to satisfy those needs any longer. For practical purposes they exist no longer. Management often asks, "Why aren't people more productive? We pay good wages, provide good working conditions, have excellent fringe benefits and steady employment. Yet people do not seem to be willing to put forth more than minimum effort."

The fact that management has provided for these physiological and safety needs has shifted the motivational emphasis to the social and perhaps to the egoistic needs. Unless there are opportunities *at work* to satisfy these higher-level needs, people will be deprived; and their behavior will reflect this deprivation. Under such conditions, if management continues to focus its attention on physiological needs, its efforts are bound to be ineffective.

People *will* make insistent demands for more money under these conditions. It becomes more important than ever to buy the material goods and services which can provide limited satisfaction of the thwarted needs. Although money has only limited value in satisfying many higher-level needs, it can become the focus of interest if it is the *only* means available.

THE CARROT-AND-STICK APPROACH

The carrot-and-stick theory of motivation (like Newtonian physical theory) works reasonably well under certain circumstances. The *means* for satisfying man's physiological and (within limits) his safety needs can be provided or withheld by management. Employment itself is such a means, and so are wages, working conditions, and benefits. By these means the individual can be controlled so long as he is struggling for subsistence.

But the carrot-and-stick theory does not work at all once man has reached an adequate subsistence level and is motivated primarily by higher needs. Management cannot provide a man with self-respect, or with the respect of his fellows, or with the satisfaction of needs for self-fulfillment. It can create such conditions that he is encouraged and enabled to seek such satisfactions for *himself,* or it can thwart him by failing to create those conditions.

But this creation of conditions is not "control." It is not a good device for directing behavior. And so management finds itself in an odd position. The high standard of living created by our modern technological know-how provides quite adequately for the satisfaction of physiological and safety needs. The only significant exception is where management practices have not created confidence in a "fair break"—and thus where safety needs are thwarted. But by making possible the satisfaction of low-level needs, management has deprived itself of the ability to use as motivators the devices on which conventional theory has taught it to rely—rewards, promises, incentives, or threats and other coercive devices.

The philosophy of management by direction and control—*regardless of whether it is hard or soft*—is inadequate to motivate because the human needs on which this approach relies are today unimportant motivators of behavior. Direction and control are essentially useless in motivating people whose important needs are social and egoistic. Both the hard and the soft approach fail today because they are simply irrelevant to the situation.

People, deprived of opportunities to satisfy at work the needs which are now important to them, behave exactly as we might predict—with indolence, passivity, resistance to change, lack of responsibility, willingness to follow the demagogue, unreasonable demands for economic benefits. It would seem that we are caught in a web of our own weaving.

A New Theory of Management

For these and many other reasons, we require a different theory of the task of managing people based on more adequate assumptions about human nature and human motivation. I am going to be so bold as to suggest the broad dimensions of such a theory. Call it "Theory Y," if you will.

1. Management is responsible for organizing the elements of productive enterprise—money, materials, equipment, people—in the interest of economic ends.

2. People are *not* by nature passive or resistant to organizational needs. They have become so as a result of experience in organizations.

3. The motivation, the potential for development, the capacity for assuming responsibility, the readiness to direct behavior toward organizational goals are all present in people. Management does not put them there. It is a responsibility of management to make it possible for people to recognize and develop these human characteristics for themselves.

4. The essential task of management is to arrange organizational conditions and methods of operation so that people can achieve their own goals *best* by directing *their own* efforts toward organizational objectives.

This is a process primarily of creating opportunities, releasing potential, removing obstacles, encouraging growth, providing guidance. It is what Peter Drucker has called "management by objectives" in contrast to "management by control." It does *not* involve the abdication of management, the absence of leadership, the lowering of standards, or the other characteristics usually associated with the "soft" approach under Theory X.

SOME DIFFICULTIES

It is no more possible to create an organization today which will be a full, effective application of this theory than it was to build an atomic power plant in 1945. There are many formidable obstacles to overcome.

The conditions imposed by conventional organization theory and by the approach of scientific management for the past half century have tied men to limited jobs which do not utilize their capabilities, have discouraged the acceptance of responsibility, have encouraged passivity, have eliminated meaning from work. Man's habits, attitudes, expectations—his whole conception of membership in an industrial organization—have been conditioned by his experience under these circumstances.

People today are accustomed to being directed, manipulated, controlled in industrial organizations and to finding satisfaction for their social, egoistic, and self-fulfillment needs away from the job. This is true of much of management as well as of workers. Genuine "industrial citizenship"—to borrow again a term from Drucker—is a remote and unrealistic idea, the meaning of which has not even been considered by most members of industrial organizations.

Another way of saying this is that Theory X places exclusive reliance upon external control of human behavior, while Theory Y relies heavily on self-control and self-direction. It is worth noting that this difference is the difference between treating people as children and treating them as mature adults. After generations of the former, we cannot expect to shift to the latter overnight.

STEPS IN THE RIGHT DIRECTION

Before we are overwhelmed by the obstacles, let us remember that the application of theory is always slow. Progress is usually achieved in small steps. Some innovative ideas which are entirely consistent with Theory Y are today being applied with some success.

Decentralization and delegation

These are ways of freeing people from the too-close control of conventional organization, giving them a degree of freedom to direct their own activities, to assume responsibility, and, importantly, to satisfy their egoistic needs. In this connection, the flat organization of Sears, Roebuck and Company provides an interesting example.

It forces "management by objectives," since it enlarges the number of people reporting to a manager until he cannot direct and control them in the conventional manner.

Job enlargement

This concept, pioneered by I.B.M. and Detroit Edison, is quite consistent with Theory Y. It encourages the acceptance of responsibility at the bottom of the organization; it provides opportunities for satisfying social and egoistic needs. In fact, the reorganization of work at the factory level offers one of the more challenging opportunities for innovation consistent with Theory Y.

Participation and consultative management

Under proper conditions, participation and consultative management provide encouragement to people to direct their creative energies toward organizational objectives, give them some voice in decisions that affect them, provide significant opportunities for the satisfaction of social and egoistic needs. The Scanlon Plan is the outstanding embodiment of these ideas in practice.

Performance appraisal

Even a cursory examination of conventional programs of performance appraisal within the ranks of management will reveal how completely consistent they are with Theory X. In fact, most such programs tend to treat the individual as though he were a product under inspection on the assembly line.

A few companies—among them General Mills, Ansul Chemical, and General Electric—have been experimenting with approaches which involve the individual in setting "targets" or objectives *for himself* and in a *self*-evaluation of performance semiannually or annually. Of course, the superior plays an important leadership role in this process—one, in fact, which demands substantially more competence than the conventional approach. The role is, however, considerably more congenial to many managers than the role of "judge" or "inspector" which is usually forced upon them. Above all, the individual is encouraged to take a greater responsibility for planning and appraising his own contribution to organizational objectives; and the accompanying effects on egoistic and self-fulfillment needs are substantial.

APPLYING THE IDEAS

The not infrequent failure of such ideas as these to work as well as expected is often attributable to the fact that a management has "bought the idea" but applied it within the framework of Theory X and its assumptions.

Delegation is not an effective way of exercising management by control. Participation becomes a farce when it is applied as a sales gimmick or a device for kidding people into thinking they are important. Only the management that has confidence in human capacities and is itself directed toward organizational objectives rather than toward the preservation of personal power can grasp the implications of this emerging theory. Such management will find and apply successfully other innovative ideas as we move slowly toward the full implementation of a theory like Y.

The Human Side of Enterprise

It is quite possible for us to realize substantial improvements in the effectiveness of industrial organizations during the next decade or two. The social sciences can contribute much to such developments; we are only beginning to grasp the implications of the growing body of knowledge in these fields. But if this conviction is to become a reality instead of a pious hope, we will need to view the process much as we view the process of releasing the energy of the atom for constructive human ends—as a slow, costly, sometimes discouraging approach towards a goal which would seem to many to be quite unrealistic.

The ingenuity and the perseverance of industrial management in the pursuit of economic ends have changed many scientific and technological dreams into commonplace realities. It is now becoming clear that the application of these same talents to the human side of enterprise will not only enhance substantially these materialistic achievements, but will bring us one step closer to "the good society."

Questions

1. What does McGregor mean by the "conventional view" of the organization of human effort in industry?
2. What are the beliefs behind this "conventional view"? Do you agree with these beliefs? Why?
3. Compare McGregor's classes of needs with those in Maslow's article and the introductory section. What differences exist?
4. What does McGregor mean by the "carrot-and-stick approach" of motivation?
5. What is management's responsibility and task in managing people? What difficulties does it face in applying the "new theory" of management?

PSYCHOLOGICAL ASPECTS OF INDUSTRIAL CONFLICT
II. MOTIVATION *

Ross Stagner

The problem of industrial conflict is the problem of what people want and the methods by which they try to get it. This is the psychological problem of motivation. It must be analyzed in terms of specific human beings: managers, and workers, and union leaders. It cannot be analyzed effectively in terms of industry and labor as collective groups, nor even in terms of a specific corporation and its local union.

It is completely fallacious to say that "The union wants this" or "The company demands that." A set of union demands will generally include the desires of various specific individuals. It is a political document calculated to obtain support from the people who are the union members. It must take account of people with vested interests in seniority, in skill, in job rates; it must consider the problems of men faced by old age, layoffs, irritating foremen, rising prices, and other frustrations. What the union wants is ultimately determined by what certain individuals want.

In the same way the company as an abstraction does not want anything. Anyone who has ever participated in planning for contract negotiations knows that production supervisors want different provisions, the personnel staff may have its own proposals, public relations may introduce some ideas, and so on. While there is likely to be greater unanimity in the management group, this is partly a result of company discipline, not uniformity of motives.

The problem of motivation is the problem of energy-mobilization. Under what circumstances do men exert great effort, endure hardship, overcome obstacles? Such behavior is seen only when strong motives impel the men concerned toward a goal they desire. Motives provide the dynamic basis for strikes, slowdowns and sabotage on the part of workers; lockouts, espionage and union-breaking on the part of employers. To understand such occurrences, we must get a clearer understanding of the motives on both sides.

There are many misconceptions regarding the causes of industrial conflict. Many newspaper columnists in the vein of Westbrook Pegler seem to believe that workers strike for fun or for no reason at all.

* From *Personnel Psychology*, Vol. 3, No. 1 (Spring, 1950), pp. 1-15. Reprinted with permission.

During the war many wildcat strikes were reported as being based on trifles such as running out of soap in the locker room or dislike of the foreman's neckties. A personal investigation of one of these, which could probably be duplicated many times, indicated that the apparently sudden, aimless wildcat strike had been brewing for months. The foreman in this particular instance had been playing favorites, giving some men dirty assignments and others soft jobs, granting or denying wage increases and so on with little regard for the merit of the individual worker, but rather on the basis of personal friendship. The personnel manager in charge admitted (after he learned the facts) that it was surprising that the men waited so long before exploding into an open strike.

Some union leaders also tend to foster a mythology of employers as being ready to precipitate a strike or a lockout at the drop of a monkey wrench. According to this view, managers are dominated by a desire to smash the union which is so strong that any pretext will be seized upon if conditions seem favorable to weaken the union. Actually, of course, most businesses lose a lot of money in a strike. The average manager does not blindly enter upon a course of action which is certain to lead to work stoppage. Overhead costs go on. Competitors pick up accounts, orders are cancelled. The Board of Directors may decide to fire the manager and hire one who can get worker cooperation.

The "dollar fallacy"

A second common error in the field of the psychology of motivation as applied to industry may be called the "dollar fallacy." According to this view employers are motivated only by a concern for dollars and cents, and workers likewise are motivated only by what is in the pay envelope.

The statistics of the Department of Labor are often referred to as evidence of the dominance of economic motivation in strikes. Thus, in 1948, it is reported 73.9% of all strikes in the U. S. A. involved higher wages or shorter hours, as an issue.[1]

No one knows better than the average personnel manager how fallacious these figures are. In many cases the workers first get angry and go on strike, then look around for something to demand. Higher wages and shorter hours are simple, neat and easy to formulate. It is thus likely that in many cases they are secondary demands,

---

[1] *Monthly Labor Review*, Vol. 68 (May, 1949), pp. 505-513.

made up to rationalize the fact that the workers are unable to state exactly what it is that they want. It is a truism of modern psychology that both employers and workers frequently are not conscious of their real motives. Thus, the workers who may be unaware of what they want, or whose real motives may be such that satisfaction is impossible, are likely to make economic demands in an attempt to get some balm for their frustrated egos.

The fallacy of the view that only money counts can be seen rather promptly if we consider even a single strike which lasts for any considerable period of time. Thus the Hinde and Dauch Paper Company has reported on the cost to their employees of a strike which lasted 103 days in 1946. The strike was eventually settled on the basis of an 18½¢ per hour wage increase—as compared with 13½¢ offered by the company before the strike was called. On this basis it has been computed that it would require the workers five years and most of a sixth year to recoup the wages lost during this one strike. The total loss to the employees was estimated at $684,000. The cost to the company in terms of profits is not reported, but it must have been considerable. Under the special conditions existing in 1946 there may not have been any net loss in sales accounts as a result of competition, but in ordinary times this would also constitute a serious threat to a company indulging in anti-labor activities. It seems extremely unlikely, therefore, that any oversimplified view which rests entirely upon an economic approach to motivation can ever give us an adequate picture of the dynamics of industrial conflict.

The limited possibilities of the purely economic approach to motivation have become obvious in many studies of union-management relations. In their excellent analysis of the S. Buchsbaum & Company situation, Whiteford, Whyte and Gardner have commented that "While economic factors must receive careful attention in any union-management study, it is very clear that in this case, as in many others, these factors formed only a small part of the motivation of the people in both camps."

Despite the fact that most operating personnel men are acquainted with this situation, the thinking of industry has until recently tended to focus on pay as the dominant employee motive. This may well be due to the fact that our economy is dominated by profit as a sign of competitive success. Since the success of a manager can be measured in terms of dollars of profit, he tends to generalize and assume that the success and satisfaction to the worker can be directly related to wages.

This is in actual fact no more correct for the worker than it is for the manager. If the executive had a dreary, monotonous job with little chance for planning, for individual self-expression, and so on, he probably would not be happy and satisfied even with a high profit rate. Common observation will confirm this statement. When the worker feels that work is dull, orders arbitrary, the job insecure and prospects for advancement dim, high wages have little soothing value for him. We have recently had strikes by "workers" receiving an average pay of $10,000 or more per year (airline pilots, Hollywood script writers). To imply that these are economically motivated, merely because pay increases were demanded, is to be very naive about human nature.

Psychologists are prone to emphasize the fact that each of man's activities tends to express various motives. For instance, one works to get money for food and shelter, but also wants an interesting job, a fair supervisor, friendly coworkers, security and so on. Having taken a job for purely economic reasons, the worker immediately begins trying to satisfy, on and through the job, his social and egoistic motives. A man may start a business and hope for profit, but he will start getting satisfactions out of planning, supervising others, meeting competition and so forth, in ways that are non-economic and even in ways that cost him money in terms of profit.

It is only if we keep this view uppermost in our minds that we can resolve the apparent conflict between the official statistics, which show workers striking for higher wages and employers striving always for higher profits; and the knowledge of operating executives that many strikes arise over issues of security, favoritism, power, recognition and similar non-economic goals.

We must therefore raise the question: What does modern psychology have to say with regard to human motives? What do executives want? What do workers want? How strong are these drives, and which will take priority over others? When we get satisfactory answers to such questions, we will have the facts with which to solve the knotty problem of industrial conflict.

Several different methods have been employed in attempts to estimate the potency of different motives to affect workers. We shall illustrate these by sample data and indicate briefly their strong and weak points.

First of all, we may directly ask the worker to indicate how important he considers specific items to be. Thus, a corporation with nation-wide operations asked its employees in 1947 to indicate which of a list of factors was most important to them on their jobs.

The question read as follows: "On the enclosed sheet you will find a list of factors which affect your job and the way you feel about the company. Read every item on the list. Mark with a number '1' the item that is *most important of all to you.* Then check over the list again and mark with a '2' the item which is second in importance. Continue this way until you have marked five (5) items." A total of 19 items was listed.

Table 1 shows the results for over 7,000 employees who answered (almost a 50% return, incidentally). If these results are taken at face value, the desire for *security* (for a *steady* job) was most powerful among these workers at this time. Although one may well question whether the average man can really decide what is most important about his job, we are impressed with the extent to which this table foreshadows the union drive for security, expressed, however in a demand for pensions and welfare funds. (It is interesting to note that pensions represent the only issue in which practically all its votes were in first position. These were no doubt from workers nearing retirement age, at which point the pension would look very important indeed.)

TABLE 1

Ratings of Importance by Workers on Various Job Factors

	% OF 7,000 WORKERS INCLUDING THIS ITEM IN THE FIRST FIVE	FIRST CHOICES ONLY
A steady job	61.9%	36.1%
Pay rate	52.6	7.2
A chance to get ahead	41.9	6.9
A square boss	39.6	4.8
Working on the job you prefer	35.3	15.2
Credit for the job you do	29.6	2.2
Vacations and holidays	21.5	0.4
Friendly working companions	21.3	0.7
Medical and health facilities	20.8	0.6
Pension	9.7	7.1

Psychologists have grave doubts as to the validity of such a direct question. Motives are subtle, and situations complex. Many experts in this area prefer an indirect method of assaying the significance of motives.

One such method is as follows: employees answer a considerable list of questions, such as "Are you told when you do a good job?" "Is your pay fair as compared with other jobs in the plant?" Satisfaction scores are determined by giving one point for each "Yes" answer. On this basis a group of highly satisfied workers is selected, and compared with a markedly dissatisfied group. We then determine how well a specific item predicts whether a man will fall in the high or the low group. Items which predict overall satisfaction seem to be valid evidences of factors important to the worker—evidences of strong motivation.

Actual use in plants has shown that this method does pick out "sore spots" in the organization. J. D. Houser, in his unfortunately little-read book, *What People Want From Business*, gives some excellent illustrations of its use. Table 2 is modified from one of his. Rank is determined by success with which the item distinguishes high and low morale cases within the group: executives, sales, non-sales employees. Percent dissatisfied is the percent of each group indicating an unsatisfactory feeling on this point.

TABLE 2

Degree of Dissatisfaction with Various Conditions, Among Workers and Executives

| | EXECUTIVES | | EMPLOYEES | | | |
| | | | Selling | | Non-Selling | |
	Rank	Percent Dissat.	Rank	Percent Dissat.	Rank	Percent Dissat.
Knowing whether work is improving or not	1	39	1	13	1	36
Opportunity for fair treatment and square deal	2	24	5	27	3	33
Opportunity for offering suggestions in work	3	63	3	66	2	76
Conflicting orders	4	44	12	52	10	62
Freedom to seek advice	5	43	6	54	5	61
Promotion for best qualified person	8	73	2	76	4	80
Reasons given for changes ordered in work	13	33	8	51	7	60
Assurance of pay increase when deserved	18	70	9	59	13	76
Pay—compared with same work in other stores	20	37	17	39	21	66

Modified from Houser, (4), p. 83.

This table suggests that both workers and executives in this company were especially concerned about *recognition*—about their standing with superiors, or praise for work well-done. Houser believes, on the basis of his wide experience in industrial consultation, that this is *the* fundamental human motive—the desire to be recognized as an individual. As he puts it, "What the worker wants is a minimum essential of life, and the word is consideration—regard for his simple dignity as a man. It is the least he can ask."

As has been noted above, psychologists are skeptical of attempts to overgeneralize about motives. Table 3 summarizes some data collected by a method similar to Houser's, but at the time of the upswing in the economic cycle in 1940. In this case concern over pay, which ranks low in most of Houser's surveys, hits first rank. This may, however, be due to the fact that price inflation was already under way, and pay may well have been the real "sore spot" with these workers.

TABLE 3

Factors Influencing Worker Satisfaction in 1940

	% SATISFIED (OF TOTAL GROUP)	CRITICAL RATIO *
Do you feel the factory could afford to pay more?	12	6.92
Do you like the kind of work you do on your job?	84	5.86
Are you told when you are doing a good job?..	47	4.47
Do you feel allowed to offer suggestions as to methods of improvement?	76	3.83
Do you believe that the bosses and supervisors are always fair to you?	91	3.76
Should the mill where you work be fixed up in light, heat, ventilation, etc.?	74	2.22
Are you friendly with the men who work alongside of you?	97	0.57

* The "Critical Ratio" is a measure of the difference between the 30 most satisfied and 30 most dissatisfied workers. Total group = 150 machine tool workers.

Another source of evidence is in the published reports of the intensive, clinical-type interviews conducted in the Western Electric Plant at Hawthorne, Illinois, which have provided so much data for modern industrial psychology. While these cannot be reduced to a simple table, it is clear from the detailed information published by Roethlisberger and Dickson that "social conditions on the job" (supervision, etc.) are considerably more important than physical working conditions or pay. This may be buttressed by the experimental studies in this same plant, which indicated that recognition and other ego-centered motives could speed up production as much as a very substantial increase in pay.

Finally, it is important to note that actual field studies of supervision and productivity emphasize the importance of ego-motivation. Katz, reporting on the Survey Research Center studies, comments that supervisors who get high productivity from their workers are characterized by: placing *less* emphasis on production as a goal;

encouraging *more* employee participation; and using positive methods of personal recognition of the individual employee.

All of this seems somehow reminiscent of the anecdote told of Samuel Gompers, longtime head of the American Federation of Labor. When someone asked him, "What does labor really want?," he is said to have replied succinctly, "More!" Workers want more of whatever is needed for complete *ego-satisfaction* at any given time: pay, security, praise, recognition, self-expression. No single specific kind of satisfaction can be cited as the key to worker motivation.

There are two lessons to be learned from these data. One is that we must not rely on past experience, but must ascertain now, in this situation, what the workers want. The second is that workers want more of whatever is needed to maintain status at the time. When old age looms, they crave security; when prices are soaring, they want higher pay; when conditions are stable, they want praise, recognition and fair treatment. Thus it seems safe to say that *ego-motivation,* in its various forms, is the key to understanding the desires of employees.

———

The psychology of executives has been studied less intensively than that of the workers, for various reasons. We have, however, two good investigations of executive motivation—one by J. D. Houser, the other by B. B. Gardner and his associates at the University of Chicago. It will be instructive to review these.

Houser interviewed top executives—only presidents or board chairmen. He asked a variety of questions about personnel policy; but his real focus was on the motives behind these policies. While his report does not present many details, his broad generalizations are stated firmly and backed by numerous illustrations. His main conclusion is that executives desire self-expression, power and recognition. They resist any forces which cramp their freedom of action; they want to carry out their ideas unhampered by opposition.

"The sheer love for power so typical of autocratic attitudes everywhere is undoubtedly one of the greatest forces producing individual and group frictions . . . with a great many executives, this love of power is a blind but strong impulse. The degree of its expression is the measure of their most vital satisfaction. This was revealed time and again in the interviews. Sometimes this motive was conscious; more often it was not . . . it was apparent that men leading enterprises were often more eager to assert themselves in a manner personally satisfying than they were to achieve large returns for the organization."

Indirect testing of motives

B. B. Gardner and his group of social scientists have been experimenting with the Thematic Apperception Test, a "projective" test for uncovering deeper motivation. A feature of the method is comparison of "successful" and "unsuccessful" executives to see what kinds of motives predict whether a man belongs in one group or the other. Their characterization of the "successful" executive stresses the following needs: need for achievement: not glory as such; need for prestige, but not as much as some of the unsuccessful executives; need to move upward; to accumulate property, to reap rewards for achieving, to acquire status in the eyes of associates; aggression, channeled into work or struggle for prestige, not into personal feuds; lack of an end-point (the needs were not focused on a final goal, but there was always a more distant ambition when the current one was satisfied).

If we look at these two studies, and compare the findings with the data reported by Houser for executives on his questionnaire technique (Table 2), we see a startling resemblance. In all cases ego-motivation rather than economic motivation is predominant.

We are thus led to the interesting conclusion that popular psychology is wrong about both executives and workers. Neither group is primarily concerned about pay as such, except when economically pinched. At other times they prefer ego-satisfactions such as prestige, power, recognition, security, treatment as an individual.

———————

To some extent we must go beyond the motivations of managers and workers and consider the dynamic aspects of the individual who is in the position of being an official of the union. Inasmuch as these are normally plant workers, they are likely to resemble the rank and file employee in most respects. In addition, however, they are likely to be ego-identified with the union and to be much concerned to make it a success. Just as the manager wants to keep his business above water, to make a profit, to out-distance competition, to increase sales, so the union officer wants to enlarge his union, build its treasury, make it bigger than competing unions and assert its bargaining power.

It seems pretty clear that in most cases, the union official cannot motivate strike activity if the workers are fundamentally satisfied. Strikes are supported by individual workers for quite varied reasons, but there must be some personal dissatisfaction which can be focused on the situation or he will not want to strike. Officials who precipitate many unpopular strikes lose their jobs. Thus, while the union officer may have personal motives for striking which do not affect the rank and file, he must attempt to relate the strike issues to the needs of the workers. This accounts for the mushrooming of demands in many strike situations. Each new demand may be needed to hold the support of some important group in the union.

The limitations set upon the union organizer or official by the emotional needs of the workers can well be illustrated by the following case:

"Company X is a small metal-fabricating plant in a medium-sized midwestern city. The workers felt very close to the president of the company, who was very friendly, paternalistic and careful of their problems. They turned deaf ears to both AFL and CIO organizers.

"Recently the president died and was replaced by another man —similar in personality but not well-acquainted with the local people. Because he did not know much about the technical side, he delegated much responsibility to a production man who was rather gruff and distant with the workers.

"Within two months the workers had signed to a man to join one of the unions they had earlier rejected." [2]

What has happened here might be stated psychologically as follows: The workers got a great deal of security and ego-satisfaction from their relationship to the president. His death caused them to feel insecure, and the poor human relations tactics of the production man increased this threat to them. They now see the union as a source of security, whereas before they saw it as a threat to their pleasant situation. The motive has not changed, but the situation now is seen in a different light.

From the organizer's point of view, the motivations and satisfactions may be quite different. He gets ego-expansion out of forming a new local; he feels proud when he wins a victory over a company official in grievance handling or contract negotiation. He has the same need for achievement, and often the same need for power and prestige, that we noted as characteristic of the company executive. His motives are very much the same as those of the executive; he is simply operating through a different organization to gain his satisfactions.

---

[2] Description by a participant.

A complete picture of industrial conflict therefore requires a consideration of two factors: what the people involved really want; and how they see the facts of the situation.[3] The same motives may in one instance be seen as demanding union action, slowdown or strike, and in another instance they lead to cooperation with management. From a practical viewpoint, management and union alike cannot change their motives; but it is possible to try to convince the workers that the facts are such as to call for certain action in pursuit of satisfaction. In either case, close knowledge of what the workers really want, right now, is important.

Ego as basic motivation

The evidence we have presented from industrial studies favors the modern theory of motivation now widely accepted by American psychologists. While this can be stated in different ways, the essential idea is this: man is concerned about his status. He wants enough food, clothing and the like to protect him from hardship, but beyond this, he will be trying to keep or improve his standing in the community. How he compares with others, and how he compares with his own ambition, are the crucial questions. Economic motives, then, may in some cases be significant and not in others. Surprisingly often, they are not. Ego-satisfactions frequently have more attraction power for the worker and the executive alike.

It is the power of injured egos to motivate persistent, stubborn defense and revenge which underlies a great many strikes and even more conflicts which do not flare into open hostility. It is the demand for more power by workers and their unions, the fight to protect status and power by company officials, which is crucial to modern industrial relations.

In the 1946 General Motors strike the union bolstered its plea for wage boosts without price increases by challenging management's right to keep information concealed, with the slogan "A look at the books." General Motors countered with the apt phrase, "A finger in the pie" to show what was implicit in the union demand. Psychologists will suspect that General Motors was right. The basic conflict is over self-assertion, over the right of the executive to independent decision versus the right of workers to challenge that decision or

---

[3] The "facts" are not the same to workers and managers. For further discussion of this, see the preceding article in this series, *Personnel Psychology*, Vol. 1, No. 2, pp. 131-145.

change it. "A finger in the pie" is an inevitable goal of union policy, however much union spokesmen may disclaim any such idea.

Capitalism strengthens ego motives

We may be pardoned for asking if any other result could be expected. Ours is a competitive, ego-centered culture. Our philosophy and our advertising alike stress achievement, prestige and power. "Superman" is no accidental hero; his adventures canalize the desires of American youngsters in a pattern that fits our society. We cannot expect executives to be the only persons craving free self-expression, enhanced status, a sense of planning and doing worth-while things. Workers imbibe these influences and crave these goals—less intensely, less unanimously, but regularly.

The problem of industrial conflict is the problem of democratic self-assertion versus self-assertion without democratic controls. Executives want ego-satisfaction; so do workers. The problem of industrial harmony will not be solved until we develop techniques for sharing these ego-goals.

Perhaps as good a way as any to sum up this idea is to quote a union organizer on the subject of a recent strike in a small Illinois factory. Asked what the real issue was, he replied: "The real issue wasn't the 15¢ an hour we asked for or the 5¢ we got. The real cause of the strike was that we had to convince that guy he couldn't be a little dictator any longer."

QUESTIONS

1. Why does Stagner say it is fallacious to say that "the union wants this"?
2. What are some of the popular misconceptions regarding the causes of industrial conflict?
3. Explain what is meant by ego-motivation.
4. What is the basic problem of industrial conflict?
5. How, according to Stagner, will industrial harmony be achieved? Do you agree?

MOTIVATION AND INCREASED PRODUCTIVITY *

Rensis Likert

Human relations research has great potential value for modern management. Many of its findings can serve as the basis for sound principles of management and good leadership. It is my purpose at this time to talk to you about some of the major conclusions that are emerging from this research.

As a background for stating these conclusions, it will be useful to consider the problem historically by examining two important trends.

The first of these two trends began almost a century ago, and has had by far the greater influence upon both management practices and industrial productivity. I refer to the whole movement in which Frederick W. Taylor and his colleagues provided pioneering leadership. For purposes of brevity, I shall use the term "scientific management" to refer to this whole movement.

Generally speaking, scientific management has brought about a very great improvement in productivity. But associated with these gains have been some serious problems and adverse effects.

Setting production goals through the use of time standards has often been accompanied by an expectation of higher levels of productivity. And, therefore, there has been increased pressure on the workers to produce more. Workers resented and resisted this; and the "speed-up" was and still is a major source of conflict and bitterness. Another aspect of this method of managing which caused resentment was the attitude that workers could contribute nothing of value to the organization of their jobs and to the methods of work to be used. As Henry Ford expressed it, "all that we ask of the men is that they do the work which is set before them."

These and similar adverse effects of scientific management were recognized more and more clearly during the second, third, and fourth decades of this century. The speed-up and "efficiency engineering" were sources of much hostility between workers and their supervisors. And these hostilities manifested themselves in a variety of ways, such as widespread restriction of output (even under incentive pay) and a demand for protection through unions, which eventually led to the Wagner Act.

*From the *Management Record*, Vol. 18, No. 4 (April, 1956), pp. 128-131. Reprinted with permission.

The second trend which I wish to examine started at the end of the First World War when a few business leaders and social scientists began to appreciate some of the problems that were the consequence of scientific management. More general recognition of these problems, however, was brought about dramatically by the famous Western Electric studies. These studies showed conclusively and quantitatively that workers were responding to the methods of scientific management by restricting their production to levels which they felt were appropriate. Moreover, neither group nor individual incentive methods of payment prevented this restriction.

These studies also revealed that the workers had developed an "informal organization" which differed from the "formal." And it was found that this informal organization exercised an important influence on the behavior of the workers, often effectively countermanding the official orders of the formal organization. The Western Electric studies also showed that when the hostilities, resentments, suspicions and fears of the workers were replaced by favorable attitudes, a substantial increase in production occurred, just as it was clear that unfavorable attitudes exerted an appreciable restraining influence upon productivity.

Mathewson, Houser, and others, in a modest number of studies during the Thirties, showed that conditions existing in the Western Electric Company were relatively widespread in American industry. Morale and motivational factors were generally found to influence production. Restriction of output was common, and "informal organizations" were found to exist in most of the companies studied.

During the past decade this second trend, which might be called the human relations trend, has gained greater impetus. The volume of research is still small but it is growing. The findings are consistent with the earlier studies and have important implications for the future trend of management theories and practices.

Some of the results of this more recent research can be shown by briefly presenting a few findings from studies conducted by the Institute for Social Research.

Orientation of Supervision: When foremen are asked what they have found to be the best pattern of supervision to get results, a substantial proportion—usually a majority—will place primary emphasis on getting out production. By this, they mean placing primary emphasis on seeing that workers are using the proper methods, are sticking to their work, and are getting a satisfactory volume of work done.

But other supervisors, whom we have called employee-centered, report that they get the best results when they place primary emphasis on the human problems of their workers. The employee-centered supervisor endeavors to build a team, whose members cooperate and work well together. He tries to have people work together who are congenial. And he not only trains people to do their present jobs well, but tends to train them for the next higher jobs. In other words, he is interested in helping them with their problems, both on and off the job. He is friendly and supportive, rather than unitive and threatening.

Higher levels of management, however, tend to place greater emphasis than do foremen on the production-centered approach as the best way to get results.

But which orientation actually yields the best results? A variety of studies in widely different industries show that supervisors who are getting the best production, the best motivation, and the highest level of worker satisfaction are employee-centered rather than production-centered.

However, there is an important point to be added to this finding. Those employee-centered supervisors who get the best results tend to recognize that high production is also one of their major responsibilities.

Closeness of Supervision: Related to orientation of supervision is closeness of supervision. Close supervision tends to be associated with lower productivity, while more general supervision seems to be related to higher productivity.

Low productivity, no doubt, at times leads to closer supervision, but it is also clear that close supervision causes low productivity. In one of the companies involved in this research program it has been found that when managers of high- and low-production divisions are switched, the high-production manager raises the productivity of the low-production division faster than the former high-production division slips under the low-production manager. Supervisors, as they are shifted from job to job, tend to maintain their habitual attitudes toward the supervisory process and their subordinates.

Both general supervision and close supervision are also related to how workers feel about their supervisors. Workers under foremen who supervise closely, or are production-centered, have a less favorable attitude toward the boss than do workers who are under foremen who supervise more generally or are employee-centered.

As we have seen, the research findings indicate that close supervision results in lower productivity, less favorable attitudes, and less

satisfaction on the part of the workers, while more general supervision achieves higher productivity, more favorable attitudes, and
greater employee satisfaction. These results suggest that it should
be possible to increase productivity in a particular situation by
shifting the pattern of supervision so as to make it more general.
To test this, we conducted an experiment involving 500 clerical
employees in a large company. The work these employees did was
something like a billing operation; there was just so much of it, but
it had to be processed as it came along.

Briefly, the experimental procedure was as follows. Four parallel
divisions were used, each of which was organized in the same way,
used the same technology and did exactly the same kind of work,
with employees of comparable aptitude. For the purpose of our
experiment, certain changes were initiated. In two of the divisions,
decision-making was introduced at lower levels; general supervision
of the clerks and their supervisors replaced close supervision; workers were given more information about matters that affected them;
and their ideas and suggestions were sought before decisions were
made. In addition, the managers, assistant managers, supervisors,
and assistant supervisors of these two divisions were trained in
group methods of leadership. The experimental changes in these
two divisions will be called Program I.

We faced many problems in attaining the desired changes. Pushing downward the level at which decisions were made proved difficult. Managers and supervisors seemed to feel that such action was
an admission that they were not essential. Therefore, they made
virtually no changes. However, when the general manager asked the
managers under him if they would help him with some of his work,
they responded favorably. He then asked them if there was work
that they could turn over to their subordinates in order to free them
to assist in his work. The managers then readily found work which
their subordinates could handle. A similar process was used all down
the line to get supervisors to turn over work to subordinates, and
thereby push decision levels down.

In order to provide an effective experimental control for Program
I, in the other two divisions the closeness of supervision was increased
and decision-making was pushed upward. This will be called Program
II. These changes were accomplished by a further extension of
scientific management. One of the first steps was to have the jobs
timed by the methods department, and standard times computed.
This showed that these divisions were overstaffed by about 30%. The

general manager then ordered the managers of these two divisions to cut staff by 25%. This was to be done by transfers and by not replacing persons who left. No one was to be dismissed.

The four divisions participating in the experiment were assigned on the basis of one high- and one low-productivity division to Program I, and one high and one low to Program II.

The experiment at the clerical level lasted for one year. Several months were devoted to planning before the exprimental year, and there was also a training period of approximately six months just before the experiment began. Throughout the period of the experiment, productivity was measured continuously and computed weekly. Employee and supervisory attitudes and related variables were measured just before and after the experimental year.

Productivity Reflected in Salary Costs: In Program II, where there was an increase in the closeness of supervision, productivity increased by about 25%. In this group, it will be recalled, the general manager had ordered a 25% cut in staff.

But a significant increase in productivity was also achieved in Program I, where supervision was modified so as to be less close and no reduction in work force was ordered. Although the increase in productivity in Program I was not so great as in Program II, it was nevertheless a little more than 20%. And one of the divisions in Program I increased its productivity by about the same amount as each of the two divisions in Program II. The other division in Program I, which historically had been the poorest of all the divisions, did not do so well.

Productivity and Workers' Responsibility: Although both programs were alike in increasing productivity, they were significantly different in the other changes which occurred. The productivity increases in Program II, where decision levels were moved up, were accompanied by adverse shifts in attitudes, interest, involvement in the work, turnover, and related matters. The opposite was true in Program I. Here it was found that when more general supervision was provided, the employees' feeling of responsibility to see that the work got done increased. In Program II, however, this work responsibility decreased. In Program I, when the supervisor was away, the employees kept on working. When the supervisor was absent in Program II, the work tended to stop.

Effect of Employee Attitudes: The experiment changed the workers' attitudes toward their supervisors. In Program I all the shifts were favorable; in Program II all the shifts were unfavorable.

This very brief description of the experiment, I hope, has made clear the pattern of results. Both experimental changes increased productivity substantially. In Program I this increase in productivity was accompanied by favorable shifts in attitudes, interests, and perceptions. The girls became more interested and involved in their work. They accepted more responsibility for getting the work done. Their attitudes toward the company and their superiors became more favorable. And they accepted direction more willingly. In Program II, however, all these attitudes and related variables shifted in an unfavorable direction. All the hostilities, resentments, and unfavorable reactions which have been observed again and again to accompany extensive use of scientific management manifested themselves.

This experiment with clerical workers is important because it shows that increases in productivity can be obtained with either favorable or unfavorable shifts in attitudes, perceptions, and similar variables. Further application of classical methods of scientific management did substantially increase productivity, but it was accompanied by adverse reactions upon the part of the workers involved. With the other approach used in the experiment, a substantial increase in productivity was also obtained, but here it was accompanied by favorable shifts in attitudes and similar variables. A fundamental conclusion from this experiment and other similar research is that direct pressure from one's superior for greater production tends to be resented, while group pressure from one's colleagues is not.

———

Thus, though scientific management has clearly demonstrated its capacity to get high production, this productivity is obtained at a cost which tends to have serious consequences in the long run.

People will produce at relatively high levels when the techniques of production are efficient, the pressure for production is great, the controls and inspections are relatively tight, and the economic rewards and penalties are sufficiently large. But such production is accompanied by attitudes which tend to result in high scrap loss, lowered safety, higher absences and turnover, increased grievances and work stoppages, and the like. It also is accompanied by communication blocks and restrictions. All these developments tend to adversely affect the operation of any organization.

The critical weaknesses in the scientific management approach, of course, are the resentments, hostilities, and adverse motivational and attitudinal reactions which it tends to evoke. In my judgment, these hostilities and unfavorable attitudes stem from powerful motives which scientific management has ignored in its theoretical basis as well as in the day-to-day operating procedures it has developed. But although scientific management has ignored these powerful motives, it has not been able to avoid the substantial impact of their influence in daily operations.

The fundamental cause, therefore, of the adverse reactions produced by scientific management is the assumption that all persons are simple economic men; that it is only necessary to buy a man's time and he will then willingly and effectively do everything which he is ordered to do. Management textbooks emphasize authority and control as the foundation of administration. They either take for granted the power to control or they hold that the relationship of employer and employee in an enterprise is a contractual obligation entailing the right to command and the duty to obey. The critical weakness of scientific management occurs at precisely the point where the human relations research approach has its greatest strength: motivation.

The power of human relations research findings lies in the understanding and insight which they provide into:

1. The character and magnitude of the powerful forces which control human behavior in working situations;
2. And the manner in which these forces can be used so that they reinforce rather than conflict with one another.

The fundamental problem, therefore, is to develop a management theory, as well as the supervisory and managerial practices needed for operating under this theory, which will make use of the concepts of scientific management while fully utilizing in a positive manner the major forces which influence human behavior in work situations. And, I believe, we are developing just such a theory which effectively combines the resources of scientific management and the findings of human relations research. There is not time here to examine it fully, but one or two aspects can be considered.

———

A basic condition of the theory is that all attempts to influence the behavior of subordinates in an organization should be of such a nature that there is a maximum probability that the subordinates will react favorably. When all of the influence attempts are reacted to favorably by a subordinate, the motivational forces acting upon him will be reinforcing, cumulative and maximized, rather than being minimized by being in conflict.

Two conditions appear to be necessary for a subordinate to react favorably to his superior's attempts to influence his behavior. First the influence attempts should be ones which he has reacted favorably to in the past—that is, they need to be familiar. Second, the influence attempts, as seen by the subordinate, should be supportive rather than threatening. And he will see them this way when they contribute to his sense of importance and personal worth; he will see them as threatening when they decrease his sense of personal worth.

From these conditions it is possible to derive a modified theory of management and the day-to-day operating procedures required to implement it.

Thus, for example, it is possible to state the following principle based on this theory: Any attempt to produce a change in an organization will work best when the people whose behavior needs changing want themselves to change. An attempted change, therefore, will work better when management creates a situation in which people can see the possibility and desirability of change and even initiate the change, rather than merely being ordered to change.

Research findings show that supervisors improve in their handling of human relations much more when provided with objective measurements about their operation and then stimulated to discuss these measurements with their subordinates as a group, than when they are merely given a supervisory training program. A supervisory training program is, after all, just another way of ordering a foreman to change his behavior.

Another operating principle based on this modified theory is also related to the best way to bring about changes and improvements. This principle indicates that an organization will perform more effectively when it functions as a network of integrated and coordinated teams, each of which has a high team spirit, high performance goals related to its part of the total job, favorable attitudes toward its supervision and management, and confidence and trust in them. These teams are knit into an integrated and coordinated organization by supervisors, managers and staff, who hold overlapping memberships in two or more teams or groups.

It is possible to demonstrate theoretically and in actual operation that an organization made up of integrated teams with high team spirit and high performance goals functions better than an organization operating under present managerial systems. The reason for this better performance is that such an organization will have appreciably superior motivation, greater acceptance of influence attempts, more confidence and trust on the part of all its members in one another, better two-way communication, and better decisions at all levels, based on the more accurate and adequate facts provided by the better communication.

The available research findings indicate that high group loyalty has an important influence upon performance at all levels in an organization. The data show that high group loyalty, coupled with high production goals in the work group, result in high productivity, accompanied by high job satisfaction and a feeling of working under little pressure.

Questions

1. Distinguish the two "trends" that Likert discusses. Show the weaknesses and the strengths of these trends.
2. Briefly explain the experimental procedure used to measure the effect of supervision on productivity.
3. Explain what is meant by "orientation of supervision" and discuss its effect on productivity.
4. What conditions are necessary for supervisors to influence the behavior of subordinates?
5. What are the benefits of human relations research?

General Questions on Part 3

1. Explain how motivation is related to leadership and human relations.
2. Define the following words:

   a. homeostasis
   b. somatically
   c. pre-empted
   d. receptors
   e. effectors

3. Distinguish sociological and psychological motives.
4. How is motivation related to industrial conflict?
5. Prepare a list of as many basic human needs as you can discover.
6. What is frustration? How do people react to it?
7. Explain how motivation is related to employee performance and behavior.
8. How is morale related to motivation?
9. Is motivation related to productivity? If so, how can this be proved?
10. Why do people behave as they do?

BIBLIOGRAPHY FOR PART 3

Articles

BRADFORD, L. P. "Building Employee Security," *Personnel*, Vol. 22, No. 4 (January, 1946), pp. 215-221.

BRIGHT, WILLIAM E., JR. "Motive Power: Put It to Work," *Supervisory Management*, February, 1956, pp. 16-19.

BURNS, ROBERT K. "Management and Employee Motivation," *Public Personnel Review*, Vol. 20, No. 2 (April, 1959), pp. 122-127.

BUSSE, F. A. "Making the Most of Your Manpower: Motivation," *Supervisory Management*, Vol. 4, No. 7 (July, 1959), pp. 32-36.

GORDON, O. J. "A Factor Analysis of Human Needs and Industrial Morale," *Personnel Psychology*, Spring, 1955, pp. 1-18.

KAHN, R. L. "Morale, Motivation, and Related Areas," *Personnel Psychology*, Vol. 12, No. 1 (Spring, 1959), pp. 37-40.

KRUMBOLTZ, J. D. "Measuring Achievement Motivation—A Review," *Journal of Counseling Psychology*, Vol. 4, No. 3 (Fall, 1957), pp. 191-198.

LIKERT, RENSIS. "Motivation: The Core of Management," *Personnel Series No. 155*, American Management Association, 1953, p. 20 ff.

ROSS, I. C. and ALVIN ZANDER. "Need Satisfactions and Employee Turnover," *Personnel Psychology*, Vol. 10, No. 3 (Autumn, 1957), pp. 327-338.

SALTONSTALL, ROBERT. "What Employees Want From Their Work," *Harvard Business Review* (November-December, 1953), p. 73 ff.

SUOJANEN, W. W. and G. C. HOYT. "Differences in Motivation Among White-Collar Workers," *Personnel*, Vol. 34, No. 2 (September-October, 1957), pp. 26-31.

THOMPSON, A. S. and J. A. DAVIS. "What Workers Mean by Security," *Personnel Psychology*, Summer, 1956, pp. 229-241.

TROXELL, J. P. "Elements in Job Satisfaction," *Personnel*, November, 1954, pp. 199-205.

VANNAH, W. E. "Automation: Some Human Problems," *Personnel*, September, 1955, pp. 100-106.

Books

HAIRE, M. *Psychology In Management.* New York: McGraw-Hill Book Company, Inc., 1956.

DAVIS, K., and W. G. SCOTT. *Readings In Human Relations.* New York: McGraw-Hill Book Company, Inc., 1959.

DRUCKER, P. *The Practice of Management.* New York: Harper and Brothers, 1954.

FRIEDMANN, G. *Industrial Society.* Glencoe, Ill.: The Free Press Publishers, 1954.

KNOWLES, W. *Personnel Management.* New York: The American Book Company, 1955.

PART 4. ORGANIZATION

The process of management inevitably revolves around some type of organization, for by its very nature management is that which deals primarily with the organization of *people* and, to a somewhat lesser degree, physical resources. It follows, therefore, that in industry a large part of the typical manager's job is the *integration* of human and physical resources. To accomplish this integration and to achieve basic business objectives, a company will design a formal organizational structure that sets forth desired job relationships between people and that provides for over-all coordination of effort.

Unfortunately, people do not always react or respond properly to formal lines of authority and responsibility. Instead, they tend to form smaller groups of their own, sometimes to overcome restrictions of the formal structure, and at other times to complement and strengthen the formal structure. These groups are most frequently referred to as *informal groups*. We shall see later that they can have a most pronounced effect on the formal structure devised by management and hence on organizational efficiency.

Human beings, since the very beginning of recorded history, have always tended towards "groupism." Psychologists and sociologists teach us that this gregariousness, or the desire for group association, is the ultimate of man's social needs. As such, this phenomenon of group response has probably been a major factor underlying the success of the American business economy. It is important that each and every business organization and the managerial personnel involved give due recognition to this tendency, although a great deal of research is still needed to discover how informal groups can best be blended into the formal structure to achieve optimum productivity and morale. At the same time, it must also be recognized that individuals can become overdependent upon particular groups, thus encouraging manipulation by a select few. Consequently, research effort must also be directed toward discovering "equilibrium points" whereby necessary employee identification can be achieved without making people overdependent on their employer to their own and the company's detriment.

The Formal Structure

Any successful business enterprise goes through certain stages of growth. As a company's size increases, more and more people are put on the payroll, new jobs are created, and additional departments are established. The result of this is that authority and responsibility relationships become increasingly complex, necessitating a more effective type of coordination than can normally be exerted by one person. At this point in time, it becomes necessary for management to determine just exactly what the formal, planned structure of the business should be to best accomplish its objectives. This is typically shown in an organization chart of some type along with job descriptions and man specifications.

Organization and authority

Alan Filley, in his article, "Human Relations in the Growing Company," clearly illustrates certain stages that a growing company goes through. At each of these stages, he shows that authority must be delegated farther and farther down the chain of command to secure maximum efficiency and performance.

Although it becomes mandatory to delegate authority in the large organization, this delegation does create human relations problems, oftentimes very serious ones. For example, some employees resent the control their boss exerts over them, so they join a union and do their best to oppose him and to make him look bad in his job. And if they do not resort to such direct action, more subtle and indirect means may be employed, such as restriction of output, willful damage to machinery, and disobeying of orders. This should indicate that the supervisor-leader, to get work done through others, must understand that he cannot abuse the authority bestowed upon him.

We are all undoubtedly aware that certain people have strong inner drives that motivate them to obtain positions of authority over others. Some researchers even claim this tendency to be a necessary prerequisite for executive success. Not debating this in any way, it nevertheless becomes imperative that management sets limits to a man's authority to prevent him from abusing it to the extent that he creates opposition on the part of employees. People will accept only so much control; beyond a certain point they will rebel against it by quitting their jobs or resorting to other means noted above. Obviously many unhealthy situations can result if authority is abused.

Authority limits can be set by a proper organizational structure and by clearly defined job responsibilities. Many human relations problems will be prevented if management observes this fact.

Specialization

Frequently referred to as "division of labor," specialization is a manifestation of the formal organization. Any organized effort of a group of people requires direction and coordination. To accomplish this, employees are grouped according to specific tasks and type of work to be done. This is frequently referred to as horizontal and vertical specialization. *Horizontal specialization* refers to specialization according to different kinds of duties and skills. Typical here are the areas of personnel, purchasing, operating, finance, accounting, and so on. All of these are grouped in terms of a particular type of work. On the other hand, *vertical specialization* refers to a division of authority into levels that are vertically scaled depending upon the degree or amount of authority held by persons in the chain of command. In the ordinary business, authority flows downward from the chairman of the board (assuming a corporate structure), through the president, then to the vice-presidents, and so on down the line until it culminates with the lowest supervisor.

Specialization, therefore, becomes mandatory in a business of any size. Unfortunately, it brings with it many human relations problems. Empire building on the part of various departments, professional jealousy and competition, and group conflicts are but a few. One of the real challenges of the industrial future and this emerging discipline of human relations is somehow to reconcile these problems so that specialization is made compatible with efficient organizational behavior.

Delegation and decentralization

Delegation and decentralization are too often confusedly interpreted to mean the same thing, namely, the extension of authority and responsibility to various individuals and segments of the company. Many firms also use the word "decentralization" to denote a multiplant operation. Be that as it may, the semantical overtones of these terms have created a great deal of misunderstanding in the minds of students.

Delegation is a term best used to describe specific job assignments. To a personnel man, for example, may be delegated the responsibility to recommend people for employment, to train supervisory personnel, to maintain employment records, and to perform many other tasks. How much authority to grant to him for carrying out these responsibilities will depend upon the individual company and its policy along these lines. Clearly, as the number and scope of duties and responsibilities increase in an organization, delegation becomes imperative.

Decentralization, however, is a much broader and more comprehensive term, although its difference is of degree rather than of kind. It is best used to describe a particular type or philosophy of management. When an executive delegates a job to be done, he normally tells his subordinates not only what to do but how to do it as well, often assigning responsibility but not the full authority to carry out this responsibility. But in a truly decentralized company, when a manager is given a job to do, how he does it, and subsequently the results attained, are left to his own discretion. Above all, he is given appropriate authority to carry out his responsibility. He is held accountable primarily for his results and not the procedural aspects of achieving them. Perhaps the success of well-known companies like General Motors, General Electric, Johnson and Johnson, and Sears, Roebuck and Company can be traced directly to this concept of management.

James Worthy, in a classic article, points directly to the importance of a decentralized organization structure to overcome what he terms "social disorganization." It is his thesis that the smaller the work group, the higher the morale of the group. His conclusions, derived from an extensive case study of Sears, Roebuck and Company, show that morale and operating efficiency are closely related to the degree the organization is "integrated." Such integration is best achieved through decentralized operations where the number of organizational levels is kept to a minimum and is relatively small in terms of numbers of employees. Hence, by so designing its formal structure, Sears, Roebuck has taken giant strides toward eliminating many of the human relations problems that arise in firms where one finds a great number of managerial levels with highly centralized control of authority.

Line and staff

As organizational theory has developed since the turn of the century, numerous variations in business structures have been introduced, with some having permanent applicability while others have only been passing fancies. One of these variations, the concept of line and staff, originated to allow more specialization within the structure as business units grew in size. It has become an indispensable part of both theory and practice.

The underlying idea behind the line-and-staff principle was simple. Operating men needed help and assistance in those aspects of their jobs that were not directly related to production and for which they had neither the necessary skill nor time. Line-and-staff type of organization, it was argued, would bring needed specialization and professional competence into the industrial picture. The staff man's job and authority relationship to the line would be one of counsel, advice, and assistance. His authority would be absolute only in his own limited sphere of concentration.

Thus the concept of line and staff, previously utilized in the military, the church, and other organizations, was incorporated into the industrial sphere. And with it came a myriad of human relations problems. Line personnel began to guard their authority as a jealous prerogative. The staff man, they felt, was trying to usurp their authority, to extend his influence into matters that did not concern him. Departmental frictions, empire building, overemphasis on professionalism, and countless other human problems have been attributed to line-and-staff organization. But in all fairness, the student should clearly understand that this principle in and of itself is not responsible for these many human problems. Rather, it is the lack of proper application of it to specific organizational needs. The task facing business today is to implement this principle into the formal structure so as properly to insure its adaptability to individual situations and needs.

Policy

One might legitimately ask: "What does policy have to do with the formal structure of a company?" The answer here is funda-mental to understanding just how the formal organization operates.

Policy is the lifeblood of any organization. It is an expression of management's intentions for directing and controlling the operations of the company. Policies serve as guides in making decisions and as aids in the accomplishment of objectives. They are set forth to allow many diverse individuals in a firm to make uniform and consistent decisions while acting in virtually complete independence of each other.

It is through formal policy statements that top management gives the necessary directions to people in the company. These statements take many diverse forms, such as policy handbooks, memos, operating letters, and so on. But regardless of form, they all have one thing in common, namely, that they serve as guides for handling recurring situations that arise in day-to-day operations.

Policies also have pronounced effects on people. They cause definite patterns of behavior to occur as individuals respond in different ways to different policies. Occasionally certain persons will disagree with a policy and will either openly or subtly oppose it. It is generally agreed that policies are as effective as supervisors and managers want them to be. Consequently, we can see that serious human relations problems can occur if top management does not give serious attention to how certain policies may affect people.

INFORMAL ORGANIZATION

The formal structure of a business enterprise illustrated in organization charts and manuals does not really tell us a great deal about the day-to-day relations between employees. Although it is true that this structure does set forth job relations and a limited span of personnel relationships, it is equally true that employees, as time progresses, frequently do not adhere to formal lines of authority and communications and ultimately set up their own network of interpersonal relations. They do this for various reasons, but primarily to satisfy the social aspirations and needs discussed in Part 3. Hence, management might designate in detail what it wants the relationships between people and jobs to be, but what management wants and what relationships actually do exist may be two different things.

The company as a social institution

It has taken many years for management to realize that, besides being an economic institution, the business firm is equally as much a *social institution*. People work together, develop friendships on the job, and spend the majority of their lives living and associating with others within the confines of a corporation. Roethlisberger, in a following article, stresses that this social climate of a business will produce ". . . customary, traditional, or routine ways of doing things. . . . And in so doing behavior to a great extent will be influenced by the expectations and hopes of others." Routines and patterns of interaction are developed between and by people and thereby act as sort of a "social cement" for ensuring collaboration and common effort, thus stimulating individual and group security. Friendships will develop, people will begin to share common interests, until finally a man's job and company become an integral part of his life.

This concept of viewing the corporation or any business enterprise as a social institution can be illustrated by the following "culture model" that social scientists use to explain what they feel to be the five basic dimensions of any given group culture:

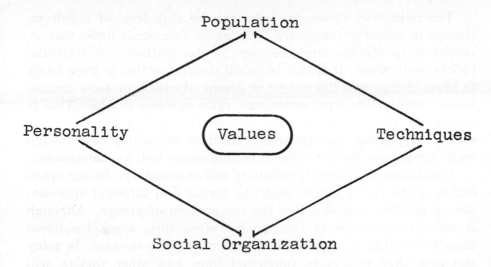

The value dimension in this model is really the core of any culture, regardless of group size, background, or location. These values are shared beliefs—shared by a majority of group members—and although subject to some change over time, they nevertheless remain the pivotal point of any culture. We shall see later that it is principally because of these values that informal groups in industry arise.

Social organization refers to traditional or patterned relations between various types of people. For our purposes, the principal point here is that people at work tend to form or become a member of small groups of their own that are not spelled out by the formal structure. This is usually referred to as *informal organization*, as was noted earlier. Such groups arise because of common beliefs, sentiments, values, attitudes, fears, interests, and so on. In time they develop small cultures of their own, which center around group values as illustrated in the above diagram. Any company, therefore, becomes one large social organization or culture made up of many small, diverse informal groups, each with a culture of its own. Sometimes these groups operate in opposition to the formal organization, but quite often they serve to reinforce and strengthen it.

Personality in a cultural sense refers to how a particular culture trains or shapes an individual to respond in certain ways, especially in terms of the values or beliefs of the culture group. Because our personality largely controls our behavior, our behavior is oriented to group norms or values. In relation to the work situation we can see how our behavior on the job is vitally influenced by associations with fellow workers.

The technology dimension indicates the skill level of a culture. Groups in industry frequently form along functional lines, that is, people doing similar work develop similar patterns of interests, beliefs, and values. It is this technical dimension that is most likely to bring change into the society or group. As skills or tools change, so also may group composition and value systems change. This is one reason why employees often vehemently resist technical or personnel changes that management is desirous of making even though such changes are likely to benefit employees as well as management.

Population, of course, is relatively self-explanatory. In our application of the above culture model to formal and informal organization, population best describes the composition of groups. Although it was stated previously that groups often form along functional lines, it should be recognized that this is not always the case. In many instances they will cross functional lines and other factors will determine their composition, among them being similar attitudes, interests, nationalities, friendships, likes and dislikes, fears, and religious preferences.

Thus the student of business must be cognizant that every company is a vast social network as well as an economic organization. To overlook this fact in the world of today would create serious human relations problems. Perhaps a better understanding of this social structure and its importance could be attained by taking a more detailed look at these informal groups.

The informal group

When we say that a company is a complex social network, we mean that employees interact with each other constantly, not always in a random sense, but rather in habitual, patterned routines. A brief observation of the daily routines of a randomly selected group of individuals would show the same people going to lunch together day in and day out, another group meeting by the coffee machine three times daily to joke and gossip, still another group that always take their breaks together, and so on until just about every employee has one select circle of people with whom he associates.

As to why these groups arise, a multiplicity of answers might be offered. Basically, there does not appear to be any planned reason behind these associations other than that they evidently seem to satisfy social motivations. Most of us have rather strong desires to associate with particular groups, especially if membership will bring with it a psychological feeling of status achievement. We realize, through these informal groups, feelings of prestige and social distinction. We can now exert some influence on the thoughts and actions of others and vice versa. Because the formal structure does not confer this upon us, we achieve it through our informal associations. We will go to great lengths to protect this status, sometimes even to the extent of endangering our position with the company. This is true not only of rank-and-file employees but of those at executive levels as well. Group solidarity becomes all important, and we will do all within our power to protect it. We become very touchy about changes of any kind and either subtly or directly resist them if necessary. Hence, we do all in our power to protect and promote our status and group.

All individuals, however, do not become part of an informal group for status alone. To others, belonging to an informal group is something of an emotionally satisfying experience. They develop certain traditions and customs, which become of paramount importance. Particular ways of doing things develop to which rigid adherence is paid. Maybe they are of Swedish descent and only want to associate with others who are Swedish; perhaps they will affiliate principally with people of their own religion; or possibly a certain class of employees is held in special esteem by the boss and they also want such a position. Sex, age, type of job, and special interests are other reasons why individual and group relationships occur. Education, office location, and personality are likewise important.

Whatever the reasons are, cliques and informal groupings are common in any firm whenever individuals are grouped together. Habits and customs develop along with group norms and standards of conduct. Value systems are originated to guide, direct, and control the behavior of members; unwritten laws are laid down, quite often in direct contrast to company rules. These values and beliefs will serve to bind people together, strengthen group lines, and, above all, give people a sense of belonging, security, and support.

The relationship of these groups to the effective functioning of the formal organization is of critical importance. Although this will be treated in a following section, attention should be directed to two salient points. First, the attitudes formed and the social satisfactions realized by group associations have a positive correlation with productivity and morale and are as directly related to efficiency as are the money wages a man receives.

Secondly, and also of the utmost importance to managements of today, is the fact that informal leaders arise to give direction and control to most informal groups and cliques. People look up to and respect these leaders *of their own choice*. Generally, informal leaders do not hold appointed leadership positions in the formal structure; yet they exert a profound and distinct influence on the operation of the organization. It therefore becomes necessary for supervisors, managers, and executives to recognize these leaders, to encourage their participation in the management process, and to find ways and means to direct their leadership activities and abilities along positive lines for enhancing departmental and organizational effectiveness.

Types of informal groups

To enhance understanding of informal organizations, researchers have identified and given diverse labels to various groups that can be found in a typical business firm. One of the more useful classifications of such groups is found in a subsequent article by Leonard R. Sayles.

Sayles begins by pointing to the most commonly found informal group—*the command group*. This group appears at all levels of the organization wherever individuals exert authority over others. In turn, the leaders of these groups are subordinate to other leaders and command groups in the level immediately above them. With these groups, ways and means have to be found to reconcile and integrate superior-subordinate relationships and to develop mutual understanding on the part of both sides.

A second common group type is the *friendship clique*. In Sayles's words:

"The friendship clique has emerged as the agency which welds the individual to the organization. Loyalty, even attachment, to the total organization with its impersonality, extended hierarchy, and social distance becomes ambiguous. However, attachment to the immediate and easily perceived face-to-face group is the predominant reality of organizational experience. For the individual it provides a source of personal security in an impersonal environment."

The third group he identifies is the *task group*. Here job assignments place different people together who form a group structure such as discussed previously. This particular group exerts a profound influence on work methods, output standards, and prestige relationships. Group values come into existence that resist the pressures of the formal organization if jobs are not properly structured and designed or if workers feel that management objectives and methods are contrary to their own.

The fourth and last group is called the *interest group*. These are formed not only for protection of members—as are task groups—but also for improving job and working conditions. Here groups may compete against each other, each seeking to advance its own position relative to other groups and becoming more or less a distinct unit functioning to enhance its own welfare. In so doing, it may generate instability and conflict throughout the larger organization.

THE DYNAMICS OF INFORMAL ORGANIZATION

Recognizing that informal groups do exist in business organizations, the question arises as to whether they are of value or hindrance to management. The answer here can be either negative or affirmative, depending upon what approach management decides to take towards the whole social system of the company and upon whether or not management is willing to attempt to utilize social groups to mutual advantage. If management chooses the latter course, informal groups have much to contribute to organizational cohesiveness. If, however, management refuses to recognize their importance, a great deal of internal friction can be generated in the company to the disadvantage of all concerned.

A major function of informal groups is to serve as a means of communications for members. They are a fine example of how a grapevine works and how it influences both upward and downward communications. Good management should therefore see to it that groups are properly and timely informed to prevent the distortion of important information. Too often worker resistance to managerial directives results from the latter's failure to foresee how quickly false rumors can circulate and virtually destroy the true meaning and intent of information.

Another important aspect of informal groups is the relation of these groups to supervisory effectiveness. A supervisor's successful performance on his job can hinge greatly on the degree to which he accepts and utilizes the informal organization existing within his department. A wise supervisor will carefully study and appraise his people to determine which type of group they seem to belong to and will then attempt to motivate employees within this particular context. Worker restriction of output and other resistance to management changes are prevalent in industry and frequently occur because some supervisor failed to perceive how to best integrate company objectives with employee objectives. Management, in selecting supervisors, can do much to overcome this problem by giving serious consideration to matching supervisory type with group type. Many studies on leadership show that better superior-subordinate relationships are attained if similar interests, ideas, and objectives exist between the two.

Research into group activities, supervision, and morale also has directed attention to some interesting evidence that indicates that high employee morale is positively related to the *role expectations of individuals*. Effort along these lines has attempted to relate different types of behavior to the different roles an individual assumes in his job. Jasinski has an interesting analysis of these phenomena in his article. It is his contention that an individual assumes different types of roles because of the many relationships thrust upon him and that his behavior will vary with the role being assumed. Internal conflict can arise within the employee, however, in trying to decide between various roles expected of him and the benefits to be derived from each. Management's job is to recognize how the different demands made upon people will affect their role expectations and, in turn, how these role expectations will influence behavior and adjustment.

Informal group membership, therefore, creates definite roles for people to carry out. In so doing, attitudes and values are created and changed that exert a profound influence on productivity and morale. Although the subject of morale and its determinates is a highly nebulous one, as was pointed out in Part 3, general agreement is usually reached when it is stated that group morale has a strong impact on individual morale, because as people identify themselves with certain groups, group values begin to shape and influence the attitudes and the beliefs of these individuals. In short, we too frequently let the majority will serve as our guides for thinking, and what is good for the group we come to feel is also good for us. So proper recognition and encouragement of group membership, along with policies and procedures designed to foster positive group feelings toward jobs and the company, can go a long way towards raising and maintaining employee morale.

Thus we can readily see that the organization is a living, dynamic organism—a social organism exerting all types of pressures on people, creating conflicts and frustration as well as positive feelings. The task facing managements of today is skillfully to blend together the formal organization with the informal in order to minimize conflict and to encourage healthy adjustment and coordination. This can be achieved by managerial recognition of the importance that informal groups have upon individual attitudes and morale. The supervisor should encourage groups to form; he should recognize their leaders and assign them jobs that reflect their group position; he should see that they are properly informed about policies and procedures. All in all, if proper encouragement is given to informal groups, they will respond in positive rather than negative ways.

THE SOCIAL STRUCTURE OF INDUSTRY *

F. Roethlisberger

Too frequently the human activities of industry are conceived of as essentially economic. An industrial organization is assumed to be composed of a number of individuals entering into relations of contract for the promotion of their own individual economic interests. It is not easy to explain why this conception, which runs counter to everyday experience, should be so firmly entrenched in the minds of men and why it should be so difficult to eradicate. In many of the written decisions of management it lies as an implicit premise, unchallenged and absolute. Fortunately, many executives in action are wiser than their theories and often make decisions in terms of factors not strictly economic. Yet few of them when challenged can resist the temptation to rationalize their practices in terms of this oversimplified theory of human motivation.

SOCIAL BEHAVIOR

To say that a more adequate way of conceiving of the human activities of industry is to view them as essentially social brings up the question of what is meant by "social." There are few words more overworked or more shot through with different meanings. For some people the word "social" applies only to those activities enjoyed after work in the company of one's friends. It calls forth ideas of social clubs, social sets, or social circles, of people who seek diversion through association with others, and of activities pertaining essentially to the pleasure-seeking world. For others, it may bring to mind people who are sociable by nature and in habit and who have a disposition for cooperative relations with their fellow men. Those who are more serious or "socially minded" may immediately think of social problems, such as crime, suicide, and divorce, or the conditions and welfare of different groups within the community—the poor, the alien, the neglected, the maladjusted. Their thoughts then may run to social legislation, social work, social diseases, social hygiene, and social security. Another group of serious students may think of social theories or social questions pertaining to the fundamental relation between capital and labor.

---

* From F. J. Roethlisberger, *Management and Morale* (Cambridge, Mass.: Harvard University Press, 1941), pp. 46-66. Reprinted with permission.

But in speaking of social or socialized behavior I shall not be referring to any of these high abstractions in particular, but to far more simple matters. From experience we know that individuals interact and that the expression of that interaction is commonly recognized as social behavior. *Whenever a person is acting in accordance with the expectations and sentiments of some other person, or groups of persons, his behavior is social or socialized.* Such behavior, it is easy to see, can occur in a bread line just as well as at a fox hunt. It is manifested by the millionaire socialite owner of a factory as well as by his most lowly skilled worker. It occurs just as much at work as it does outside of working hours. In fact, there are few acts of men that are not social in the way in which I have defined the word.

CUSTOMARY OR ROUTINE WAYS OF BEHAVIOR

One can hardly speak of socialized behavior without understanding customary, traditional, or routine ways of doing things. Strangely enough, custom has never been considered a subject of great scientific importance. For any one scientific book describing the folkways and customs of any locality there can be found at least ten books about what behavior in general is or should be. Compared with the dignity of exploring the inner workings of the brain, the study of customary behavior is likely to be thought of as undignified and commonplace. The reader would be bored if I should describe that mass of detailed behavior which goes to make up my daily existence. The facts about my shaving and washing before dressing in the morning, the articles of clothing I put on and the order in which I put them on, the kinds of foods I eat and when and how I eat them, the way in which the different objects on the table are arranged, the order in which the different members of my family sit—all this would probably soon elicit the comment, "So what? Roughly, everyone does the same things. These patterns of behavior which you so minutely describe are well-understood and recognized responses to rational or biological needs. Is there anything more to be said about them?"

In my opinion, there is. In the first place, it is a well-known fact that these routine patterns of behavior vary with different localities. We would all agree that coffee for breakfast and three meals a day are not universal routines of behavior. Yet, many of these routines are so close and fundamental to us that they lie outside the field of our conscious attention. As a result, we tend to identify our own particular local ways of behaving and thinking with behavior and thought in general. Our attention is directed to them only when we are brought into contact with groups whose customary ways of doing things are different from our own.

In the second place, these customary ways of doing things are frequently the occasion for the affirmation of our solidarity with groups. The family meal is more than an occasion for the satisfaction of biological needs. It also satisfies certain emotional needs of men. It is, for example, the occasion when the members of the family come together and when the father has an opportunity to see his children.

Now it can be seen that these customary ways of doing things constitute the framework within which the social life of groups is carried on. This framework is seldom completely coincident with biological needs. On biological grounds alone, a cup of hot water would be as good for me in the morning as a cup of coffee. A good case, in the name of science, could be made to the effect that some number other than three meals a day would be more appropriate to my sedentary way of living. Yet, were I to insist on such changes in family routines, it is probable that my wife would assume that something was wrong with me. I would be badgered with questions: "Aren't you feeling well? Don't you think you should see the doctor?" And, curiously enough, in spite of the fact that I should have science on my side, more often than not my wife would be right, not in sending me to the doctor but in feeling intuitively that my total disregard for the customary routines of behavior was symptomatic of a morbid preoccupation about my health. It is not entirely fortuitous that most neurotic ailments appear in connection with the breakdown of customary ways of doing things.

Socialized behavior, I have said, is behavior in accordance with the expectations and sentiment of others. Such behavior is expressed most often in terms of customary routines. These routines act as a sort of social cement. They bind men together in collaborative effort. Moreover, they change slowly and provide security for the individuals who perform them together.

MODERN INDUSTRIAL ORGANIZATION

Now in stating this formulation I have oversimplified matters. There are, of course, certain individuals throughout the field of modern business who are giving attention to problems of human collaboration. It might even be argued that there are distinct groups of people—personnel organizations—who give their entire time to this problem. And yet if one looks carefully at these individuals or personnel organizations one is apt to find a strong tendency to separate the strictly technical problems of production and distribution from the human problems connected with work association. It would not be an exaggeration to say that the activities of most personnel organizations are largely based upon this very sharp separation of technical or economic matters from matters of human concern. Very seldom do such organizations act in an advisory capacity regarding technical practices of the company. From the economic viewpoint most personnel people are considered supernumeraries. Most of their duties are concerned with the routine carrying out of policies that have been settled by other groups or with settling as best they can human problems that have already been created. There is a tendency in modern industrial organization to separate the economic function from all the social interrelations and to believe that in the settlement of economic problems it is not necessary to consider any other aspect of human organization. The following are concrete examples from factory situations.

Example No. 1

A company in the process of reorganization found that it had on its hands approximately 200 people whose jobs had been so greatly simplified that their highly developed skill was no longer required. Fortunately, the company was then enjoying renewed business activity so that it was possible to reabsorb these people in other parts of the plant. The executives of the company felt that this problem could be solved by transferring these employees to new jobs whenever vacancies occurred in other types of work. At the same time management insisted that there should be no diminution in the "take-home." Workers should be transferred only to jobs on which they could earn as much money as they had been able to earn on their old jobs.

Now it can be seen that the logic of management was very simple. It assumed that inasmuch as the worker was primarily interested in the "take-home," any transference to another job, regardless of its nature, in which the weekly pay was not affected would be satisfactory to the employee. This logic holds in many instances primarily because two jobs whose earnings are more or less the same carry with them more or less the same social status in the company. In this particular case, however, this assumption did not hold. It happened that many of the jobs which had been affected by the reorganization were, in terms of the attitudes of the employees toward them, "superior" to those to which they were being asked to transfer. The reorganization meant transferring stock assemblers and storeroom keepers to simple machine operations or assembly work. The results were not satisfactory. Many employees who were given a choice of new jobs did not care to accept. Instead they preferred to stay on their existing jobs until conditions made it imperative to transfer, even though staying involved the risk of diminished earnings.

Example No. 2

Many times management makes certain changes based upon logical and economic considerations and then finds that the human interrelations which were also affected by the change create new and difficult problems. Let me take, for example, a company in which the primary manufacturing activities were divided into six functional units such as operation, inspection, production, etc. Each of these functional units had its own hierarchy of authority and interacted with the other functional units only at certain specified points in the manufacturing process. Although this type of organization secured excellent vertical control within each function, there still existed the difficulty of coordinating the activities of the various functions. This lack of coordination, particularly at the lower levels, resulted in manufacturing inefficiency. To obviate this difficulty, it became necessary to reorganize the company on new lines. A number of different shops were set up, the activities of each centering around a particular product which it manufactured from start to finish. Under this new plan each shop had its own inspection and production people, who were now expected to report to supervisors in the operating line organization. Logically, this new setup should produce the desired effect of coordination of functions and probably in time will do so. But at present the company is finding that it is much easier to coordinate these logical functions on paper than to coordinate the people carrying them out. It is easier to change the logical basis of organization than to change the routine human sentiments that are being violated by the reorganization.

Immediately following this reorganization, the production and inspection people, the former in particular, began to register many complaints. They found the lighting conditions in their new surroundings faulty; they did not like the common washrooms. They found fault with the lockers. Some of them went to extreme lengths in registering their dissatisfaction. One employee, for instance, refused to use the washroom on the floor where he worked and laboriously climbed several stories to use a washroom for office employees. But far more serious were the organizational difficulties that developed. There was a tendency for production clerks to short-circuit the new formal lines of authority. Instead of reporting directly to their immediate superiors—the operating supervisors—they were likely to go to production supervisors up the line.

An explanation of this situation may be found in the fact that the new organization had broken down the sharp distinction between office people and shop people that had existed under the old arrangement. In the old organization, production clerks had regarded themselves as office people. Their feeling of superiority to shop people was not merely a fanciful whim, for, although there were no written statements by the company to this effect, in all the minor distinctions and privileges which differentiated office people from shop people—lockers and washroom facilities, for example—production people were socially identified with office people. Under the new organization they felt that their status had been jeopardized; in terms of the customary interhuman relations they felt they had been demoted. Their complaints were an expression of this disruption in the social equilibrium to which they had become accustomed.

Example No. 3

The foundry department of a manufacturing concern employed some fifty men who were almost all highly skilled craftsmen and long-service employees. These workers prided themselves on their traditions and clung to certain privileges, such as smoking on the job, which were denied to other employees in the factory. According to the nature of their work, the foundry workers were differentiated into four groups. These job groups, according to the foundrymen themselves, were not of equal importance. Each had its own social values and its own rank in the social scale. One of these groups was dominant, and in this group three or four members rigidly controlled the rest.

About three or four years ago, in line with its general policy, the company put all the foundry employees on group piecework. Up to this time they had been on straight piecework. Management felt that, under group piecework, earnings could be distributed more equitably and that such an arrangement would divide among all the employees the responsibility for turning out a satisfactory product and for reducing the amount of scrap due to defective castings. Such was the logic of what should happen. What actually happened was something quite different. Total output, instead of increasing, went down. The problem of scrap, instead of being solved, tended to reappear and complicate other issues. The iron molders felt they were not getting what they earned. Those operators with high outputs felt they were carrying the less efficient men. Molders did not see why they should be penalized for parts that were broken by the chippers and grinders. Some of the men who had previously earned about $1.00 an hour now earned about $.75 an hour; this in spite of the fact that the new rates under the group payment plan were not in any way "tighter" than the old rates under straight piecework.

So management was faced with the problem of disentangling itself from the human complications of its own logic. The situation was far more complex than my oversimplified account has suggested. In essence, however, it was a situation of extreme resistance to a change introduced by management which failed to take into account the social sentiments of the foundrymen. To the foundry employees there were four different social groups—four different ways of life— which, under the new wage payment system, were no longer recognized. The foundry employees never ceased to petition management to put them back on straight piecework or, failing this, to divide them, at least for the purpose of payment, into the four natural job groups. However, for technical reasons, management found it impossible to make either of these two moves. As a result, the employees tried to force the hand of management by restricting output even at the expense of lowered individual earnings.

Example No. 4

Suggestion plans, according to the general logic of management, are intended to promote constructive thinking and cooperation of employees. In one company such a system was introduced. The method of administration was very simple. Suggestions handed in by the employees were considered by a committee, and suitable awards were made for accepted suggestions. Management believed that notice of these awards should be posted publicly on the bulletin boards in order to stimulate submission of suggestions and give the suggesters full recognition. However, the public posting of awards met with increasing dissatisfaction on the part of the workers. If a worker submitted a suggestion that either eliminated an operation, or so simplified or changed a work routine that rate revision was necessary, a great deal of social pressure was put on this operator by his fellow workers. Often a foreman discriminated against a worker who turned in a suggestion that improved a process for which the foreman himself was responsible. He tended to interpret such a suggestion as criticism of his work and either penalized the worker or tried to rearrange the process in such a way that the suggestion was no longer of value. Many disputes arose as to the distribution of the "windfall" when an award was made public. If the suggester owed money, claimants would appear and ask the company to effect a settlement. For these reasons, management finally had to publish awards by code number only, thereby nullifying in part the original intention of the plan. Management's logical method of promoting collaboration had failed to take into account other important aspects of this human organization.

THE SOCIAL ORGANIZATION OF INDUSTRY

These examples show that industry has a social organization which cannot be treated independently from the technical problems of economic organization. An industrial organization is more than a plurality of individuals acting only with regard to their own economic interests. These individuals also have feelings and sentiments toward one another, and in their daily associations together they tend to build up routine patterns of interaction. Most of the individuals who live among these patterns come to accept them as obvious and necessary truths and to react as they dictate.

If one looks at a factory situation, for example, one finds individuals and groups of people associated together at work, acting in certain accepted and prescribed ways toward one another. There is not complete homogeneity of behavior between individuals or between one group of individuals and another, but rather there are differences of behavior expressing differences in social relationship. Individuals conscious of their membership in certain groups are reacting in certain accepted ways to other individuals representing another group. Behavior varies according to these stereotyped conceptions of relationship. The worker, for example, behaves toward his foreman in one way, toward his first-line supervisor in another way, and toward his fellow worker in still another. People holding the rank of inspectors expect a certain kind of behavior from the operators; the operators from the inspectors. Now these relationships, as we all know from everyday experience, are finely shaded and sometimes become very complicated. When a person is in the presence of his boss alone, he acts quite differently from the way he acts when his boss's boss is also present. Likewise his boss acts toward him alone quite differently from the way he behaves when his own boss is also there. These subtle nuances of relationship are so much a part of our everyday life that they are common place. We take them for granted. We hardly realize the vast amount of social conditioning

that has taken place in order that we can maneuver ourselves gracefully through the intricacies of these finely shaded social distinctions.
We only pay attention to them when we blunder into new social
situations where our past social training prevents us from making
the necessary delicate interpretation of a given social signal and
hence brings forth the socially wrong response.

In the factory, as in any social milieu, a process of social evaluation is constantly at work. From this process distinctions of good,
bad, inferior, superior, etc., arise. This process of evaluation is
carried on with simple and ready generalizations by means of which
values become attached to individuals and to groups performing
certain tasks and operations. It assigns to a group of individuals
performing such and such a task a particular rank in the established
prestige scale. Each work group becomes a carrier of social value.
In industry, with its extreme diversity of occupations, there are a
number of such groupings. Any noticable similarity or difference,
not only in occupation but also in age, sex, and nationality, can
serve as a basis of social classification, as for example the married
woman, the old-timer, the white-collared or clerical worker, the
foreign element. Each of these groups too has its own value system.

Now the patterns of interaction that arise between individuals
or between different groups can be graded according to the degree of
intimacy involved in a relationship. Grades of intimacy or understanding can be arranged on a scale and expressed in terms of social
distance. Social distance measures differences of sentiment and interest which separate individuals or groups from one another. Between
the president of a company and the elevator operator, there is considerable social distance; more, for example, than between the foreman and the bench worker. Social distance is to social organization
what physical distance is to physical space. However, physical and
social distance do not necessarily coincide. Two people may be
physically near but socially distant.

Just as each employee has a particular physical location, so he
has a particular social place in the total social organization. But
this place is not so rigidly fixed as in a caste system. In any factory
there is considerable social mobility or movement. Movement can
occur in two ways: The individual may pass from one occupation
to another occupation higher up in the prestige scale. Or the prestige
scale itself may change. It is obvious that these scales of value are
never completely accepted by all the groups in the social environment.
The shop worker does not quite see why the office worker, for example,

should have shorter hours of work than he has. Or the newcomer whose efficiency on a particular job is about the same but whose hourly rate is less than that of some old-timer wonders why service should count so much. The management group, in turn, from the security of its social elevation, does not understand what all the fuss is about. Advocates of a different social scale, therefore, are constantly trying to upset the existing social equilibrium and establish the supremacy of their own scale.

Any person who has achieved a certain rank in the prestige scale regards anything, real or imaginary, which tends to alter his status adversely as something unfair or unjust. It can be seen that any move on the part of the company may alter the existing social equilibrium to which the employee has grown accustomed and by means of which his status is defined. Immediately this disruption will be expressed in sentiments of resistance to the real or imagined alterations in the social equilibrium. In the case of the complaints of the production people previously given we have a good example of this phenomenon.

THE PROBLEM OF COMMUNICATION

In the technical organization of most companies there is very little explicit recognition given to these social distinctions. The blueprint organization plans of a company show the functional relations between working units, but they do not express these distinctions of social distance, movement, or equilibrium. This hierarchy of prestige values, which tends to make the work of men more important than the work of women, the work of clerks more important than the work at the bench, has no meaning for the technical organization. Nor does a blueprint plan show the primary groups, that is, those groups enjoying daily face-to-face relations. Logical lines of vertical and horizontal coordination of functions replace the actually existing patterns of interaction between people of different social places. From a technical standpoint, social place has no existence; only physical space exists. In place of all the sentiments of value residing in the social organization by means of which individuals and groups of individuals are differentiated, ordered, and integrated, there is substituted the logic of efficiency. Now it can be seen that this failure to recognize explicitly these human interrelations has certain consequences.

For example, the problem of communication is very important in the effective integration of any group or of a group of groups, of which industry is composed. Successful communication between individuals depends upon something more than a common language, a common set of words. People and groups with different experiences and social places, although having in common many of the same words, may vary widely in mental attitudes. These differences in modes of thought and ways of viewing things may make communication in some instances almost impossible. The trained expert with his precise and logical vocabulary has difficulty in communicating with the layman. The customary ways of thinking of the skilled toolmaker, for example, are quite different from those of the non-machine minded unskilled worker. They differ also from those of the engineer, the accountant, the marketing expert, the executive, or the administrator. As it is commonly expressed, people with different ways of thinking do not "get" each other.

If there is to be successful communication between the top and bottom of an industrial organization, these differences in modes of thought must be more clearly recognized. The same symbol does not necessarily have the same referent for different groups. Most symbols not only point out something, they also convey certain emotions. There is no better example than the case of the language of efficiency. The top of the organization is trying to communicate with the bottom in terms of the logical jargon and cold discriminations of the technical specialist, the engineer, the accountant, etc. The bottom of the orgnaization, in turn, is trying to communicate with the top through its own peculiar language of social sentiments and feelings. Neither side understands the other very well. To the bottom the precise language of efficiency, instead of transmitting understanding, sometimes conveys feelings of dismay and insecurity. The bottom, in turn, instead of transmitting successfully its fears of social dislocation, conveys to the top emotional expressions of petty grievances and excessive demands.

The following situation is an example of what I mean. A company found it advisable to reduce the hourly rates of a number of long-service employees. This move was made not with the idea of reducing labor costs, but primarily with motives of "fairness and justice" in mind. It happened that the company had been left after the depression with a number of long-service people whose hourly rates were "out of line" with the grades of work they were doing. When business picked up and new employees were hired at hourly rates comparable to the grades of work to which they were assigned, and put into work groups with these longer-service people under the group payment plan, a situation to the disadvantage of the younger and newer men was created. In fairness to these new men, management felt something should be done. Clearly, the executives of the company had human values in mind when making this change. The purpose of their plan was to redistribute more equitably the total earnings of a group piecework department among its individual members. But here is the curious part of the story. When the company put in this change, it explained the move to the employees concerned in terms of the language of efficiency. The employees' response to this move was bitter and voluble. The more management tried to explain its reasons for making this change, the more resistance it met. Finally, one executive in conference with the employee roprosontativos saw what had happened. The company had always had a policy favorable to its long-service employees. With this move, the long-service employees felt that the company had changed its policy with regard to them. It seemed to them that efficiency only, not service, now counted in the company. When the executive was able to reassure the employees that this move in no way had changed the basic company policy toward seniority, that long service was still valued and would be rewarded by certain considerations and privileges, the disturbance died down. The employees affected were satisfied to accept the change as long as the social values attaching to long service, which the company had upheld, had not been changed.

CONCLUSION

In conclusion, let me review briefly the points that I have made:

(1) Without misunderstanding, no particular economic activity can be torn apart from its surrounding social fabric and treated as a thing in itself. . . .

(2) Modern management tends to subsume the problems of group collaboration under the technical problems of production and efficiency. As a result, collaboration is conceived of as a logical contrivance for getting people to work together by appealing primarily to their individual economic interests.

(3) However, modern industry is built up of a number of small working groups. Between the individuals within these groups and between individuals of different groups, there exist patterns of behavior which are expressing differences in social relationship. Each job has its own social values and its rank in the social scale.

(4) Each industrial concern has a social as well as a physical structure. Each employee not only has a physical place but he also has a social place in the factory. Any technical change on the part of management may therefore affect not only the physical but also

the social location of an individual or group of employees. This fear of social dislocation is likely to be a constant threat to the social security of different individuals and groups of individuals within the industry.

(5) The failure on the part of management to understand explicitly its social structure means that it often mistakes logical coordination for social integration. This confusion interferes with successful communication up and down the line as well as between different groups within the industry.

As I have said before, primitive man attaches primary importance to the social organization of the group; his economic life is completely subservient to it. Primitive belief assumes that by strict upholding of the tribal customs expressing social organization it can meet the exigencies of nature—a food shortage or drought, for example. Modern belief, on the other hand, assumes that by the efficient production and distribution of goods, it can fulfill the demands of human nature. As a result we have the goods but the natives have the morale.

It is needless to point out that neither position is tenable. However, it is much easier to see the absurdity of primitive belief than to see the absurdity of our own. It seems obvious to our logical ways of thinking that no ritualistic performance of certain ceremonials can bring forth the rain that is necessary for the successful growing of crops. It is less obvious that the application of science to agriculture does not in itself provide the basis for meaningful human association at work.

QUESTIONS

1. To what does this social structure of industry refer?
2. What is Roethlisberger's concept of "socialized behavior"?
3. How does the process of communication influence informal organization?
4. Summarize the conclusions of this article.
5. Just how important is the social structure found within a business firm?

ORGANIZATIONAL STRUCTURE AND EMPLOYE MORALE *

James C. Worthy

1. INTRODUCTION

This discussion will review some of the findings of the research conducted by Sears, Roebuck and Co. in the field of employe attitudes and morale. This research is an integral part of our company's personnel program; its primary purpose is to assist executives in their efforts to maintain sound and mutually satisfactory employe relationships. Such relationships are conceived by our management not only as a positive good in themselves but as an essential condition for the continued economic success of the enterprise.

We have had 12 years of experience in the formal study of employe morale. During that period our surveys have covered over 100,000 employees, working in several hundred different company units both in Sears, Roebuck proper and in a number of other organizations as well. Types of employes covered include sales and clerical personnel, manual and professional workers, supervisory employes, and executives. The size of units surveyed has ranged from fewer than 25 employes to more than 10,000. Many different types of units have been surveyed, including retail stores, mail order plants, factories, warehouses, and offices. The geographical distribution of employes covered would correspond rather well with the geographical distribution of the U. S. population. By the same token, the communities in which units surveyed have been located cover practically the full range of sociological and cultural categories to be found in this country, except the small town and the rural.

2. METHODS OF STUDY

Time does not permit any detailed account of our survey methods; however, some brief explanation is necessary if only to indicate the extent to which confidence can be reposed in our findings.

Our original surveys were based solely on questionnaires, which were answered anonymously by employes. The questions covered a great variety of subjects—practically every subject, in fact, which we thought likely to have any influence on employe attitudes. In other words, the questionnaires had the simple, straightforward purpose of finding out how well employes liked their jobs, what their attitudes

* From the *American Sociological Review*, Vol. 15 (April, 1950), pp. 169-179. Reprinted with permission.

were toward supervision and management, and what factors in their employment situation might be contributing to dissatisfaction or poor working relationships. We assumed that when we had learned these things we would be able to take specific action to correct specific problems and thus restore peace and harmony where any lack thereof was found to exist.

We did find certain things that were susceptible of direct management action, but we also found many things that were difficult to take hold of. It soon became apparent that we were dealing with an infinitely complex system of influences and relationships, and not with a simple system of logical cause and effect. We began to question the adequacy of questionnaires and found, as we analyzed thousands of employe responses, that we could not even be sure we were asking the right questions or asking them in the right way.

Finally, there were real difficulties in attempting to analyze the significance of questionnaire responses. What was a "good" score on a certain point? Was a 65% "favorable" response to a question about employe discount policy equivalent to a 65% "favorable" response to a question about wage rates? Beyond certain relatively superficial points, there was often great uncertainty as to just what the tabulation of responses meant and what, if anything, could or should be done about it.

We have handled this problem by developing quite a different type of questionnaire and by supplementing it with other techniques (notably interviewing). Instead of covering a great many specific points, the questionnaire we now use seeks only to determine the general "feeling tone" of employes with respect to six key aspects of their working environment: (1) the company in general, (2) the local organization, (3) the local management, (4) immediate supervision, (5) fellow employes, and (6) job and working conditions. Ten items are included under each of these headings on which employes can express varying degrees of satisfaction or dissatisfaction. In scoring, we are not concerned with responses to each particular item in the questionnaire, but rather with the *general tendency* of responses in each of the six areas. In this respect, the questionnaire is patterned after the familiar "interest" or "personality" schedules used in psychological testing. As with such schedules, our questionnaire results can be expressed in "profiles." Furthermore, we have enough "cases" (i.e., units surveyed) to be able to translate raw scores into percentiles, thus greatly facilitating the process of interpretation and comparative analysis. As our survey people gain more experience in relating different types of profiles to concrete situations, they are developing real skill in using questionnaire results as a diagnostic tool.

The function of the questionnaire is not, however, to secure detailed information, but rather to "take the temperature" of an organization and its various subdivisions, to determine whether the general level of morale is high or low, and to point out areas of stress and strain which may be tending to undermine cooperative working relationships. In other words, by means of the questionnaire, we are able to locate problem departments and to identify the general nature of employe dissatisfactions. Only within broad limits, however, does the questionnaire tell *why* morale may be low. The real task of determining the "why" falls to a team of carefully trained interviewers. Because the questionnaire has already indicated the general nature and location of problems, the interviewing team is able to concentrate its time and energies on those departments and employe groups most requiring attention.

Surveys are conducted by members of the company's regional personnel staffs, with technical direction and coordination from the national personnel office in Chicago. (Administrative control of survey activities is strictly a regional responsibility.) People conducting the surveys receive special training in non-directive interviewing and in certain aspects of sociological and anthropological theory which we have found to contribute meaningfully to understanding the problems of organizations. In large part, they are trained by the case method, not only through studying reports dealing with "classic" situations (of which by this time we have a fair variety) but also through participating directly in survey work under the tutelage of experienced survey personnel.

In this connection, it should be noted that the entire survey program makes extensive use of clinical methods, not only for training younger practitioners, but for analyzing the significance of survey results and for working out necessary corrective measures with the executives responsible for the operating units involved. The participation of line executives, with their intimate and long-standing knowledge of their organizations, in these "clinical sessions" has contributed greatly to both the pragmatic value of the survey program and the growth of knowledge and understanding on the part of survey personnel. Valuable as our extensive statistical data has been and is, most of the insights and hypotheses which the program has produced have been an outgrowth of this clinical approach.

Thus, the scope of our survey program has broadened significantly since its inception 12 years ago. We have found that there is more to good morale than high wages and pleasant working conditions (although these are of unquestioned importance). We have learned that effective leadership involves more than "winning friends and influencing people" (although social skill is an essential ingredient of executive capacity). It has gradually become clear that to understand what might be taking place within any particular working group we must have some knowledge of a variety of factors both internal and external to the group itself, and that, above all, we must have some dynamic conception of the manner in which these factors relate themselves one to the other and to the total situation of which each is an influencing and influenced part.

The scope of the surveys has thus been broadened to include the functioning of the organization as a whole and the entire pattern of technical processes and formal and informal relationships which comprise it. To the extent permitted by practical operating considerations, community and regional factors are likewise taken into account. In recognition of this broader scope, our surveys are no longer known as *"morale* surveys" but as *"organization* surveys." Determining the level of morale has ceased to be an end in itself and is now useful chiefly as a means for diagnosing the problems of an organization. Above all, our survey teams seeks to deal not merely with the superficial manifestations of problems, but with the basic influences which have created the problems.

Surveys are concerned not merely with discovering the nature and origin of difficulties; their primary purpose is problem-solving. To this end, the survey team attempts to give the local manager a more complete picture of his organization and the way it is functioning, and to help him understand the various factors operative in his particular situation and their effects, not only on the attitudes and behavior of his people, but on the efficiency with which his organization is functioning. With this clearer picture of his organization, the manager is in a better position to take constructive action directed at the root of his problem rather than its superficial symptoms. However, the long-range objective of the survey program is not so much to correct immediate situations as to assist in developing the kind of organizations that can solve their own problems. A survey has failed in this essential purpose unless it leaves the particular store, plant, or department stronger and more self-reliant than it was before.

Our survey program is thus primarily an administrative device: its chief function is to assist local executives in doing a better job of handling the problems of their organizations. However, the surveys have also provided highly useful information about certain fundamental problems of human relations. One of the responsibilities of the research and planning staff of the national personnel office is the constant analysis and evaluation of survey data and the development of working hypotheses based on these data. Time will not permit any general review of our findings to date, but I would like to indicate some of the general directions of our current thinking.

3. A Problem of Integration

One line of thought on which we are working is the possibility of developing a typology of the malfunctioning of organization which can be useful in studying social groups as the typologies used by psychiatrists are useful in studying the malfunctioning of personality. This possibility was first suggested by the frequency with which the questionnaire "profiles" tended to form themselves into patterns with which we began to grow familiar. Our interviewing, likewise, attested that certain types of problems tended to occur in fairly well organized syndromes. For instance, we have found that certain kinds of difficulties typically follow changes in key management staff. We can usually predict not only what difficulties are likely to occur but the exact sequence in which they are likely to appear.

A typology of the malfunctioning of organization would be useful not only for scientific purposes but for administrative purposes as well, for with it could be developed a symptomatology by which problem situations could be diagnosed and acted upon more rapidly and more accurately. As already pointed out, our survey program is primarily an administrative device. Useful as it has been for this purpose, it has certain unwieldly features because sometimes it has to go a rather long way around to reach a fairly simple conclusion. For administrative purposes, we would be far better off if we had a group of people (preferably our administrators themselves) skilled at recognizing and diagnosing symptoms and dealing with the problem thus defined according to whatever therapy had been found useful for that particular type of difficulty.

It would be even more useful to be able to predict with reasonable accuracy the probable consequences of a given event or a given set of circumstances and to set in motion early a series of moves designed to minimize any adverse possibilities. We are able to do precisely this on a number of counts (for instance, cases of key executive changes) and our success here encourages us in our efforts to broaden the area in which we can predict with confidence.

As to our survey program as a whole, we are, as things stand now, somewhat in the position the medical profession would be in if the physician had to give a basic metabolism to determine whether a patient had a cold in the head. To continue the analogy, if we had a workable symptomatology (no matter how tentative), we could recognize the head cold and treat it accordingly. On the other hand, if the symptoms in the case indicated a more dangerous or more complicated disability, we could always apply our equivalent of the basic metabolism or such other procedure as the circumstances might require.

Any typology of malfunctioning must relate, of course, to the underlying dynamic system and not merely to the symptoms. All of our research testifies to the frequency with which the identical symptom can arise from entirely different factors. In one context, complaints over wages can be a danger signal; in another, merely an indication of the normal desire of everyone to be making a little bit more than he is. Sometimes, complaints over wages can really be complaints over wages; at other times, they can be merely a convenient target against which to direct verbalizations of resentment that arise out of situations that have little to do with wages. Because of the unreliability of symptoms taken in isolation we have found it more and more useful to think in terms of syndromes. The fact that our questionnaire is so constructed as to yield results in the form of profiles has greatly aided this purpose.

The psychiatrists have found the concept of *integration* a useful one around which to organize their ideas about personality and its disorders. We think a similar concept, related to group phenomena, could form the basis of a useful typology of the malfunctioning of organization. Certainly, the degree of integration (internal and external) of any organization relates very directly to the underlying dynamic factors in operation. One type of failure of integration leads to one type of difficulty which is different from that likely to arise from another type of failure of integration. Moreover, the methods for dealing with the two sets of circumstances are likely to differ, although often many of the superficial symptoms may be identical.

The scope of this paper does not permit a systematic exposition of the concept of integration. One of its aspects, however, is suggested by consideration of the problem of size of the organizational unit. Our researches demonstrate that mere size is unquestionably one of the most important factors in determining the quality of employe relationships: the smaller the unit the higher the morale, and vice versa. It is clear that the closer contact between executives and rank and file prevailing in smaller organizations tends to result in friendlier, easier relationships. To employes in such units the "big boss" is not some remote, little-known, semi-mythical personage but an actual, flesh and blood individual to be liked or disliked on a basis of personal acquaintance.

In broader terms, the smaller organization represents a simpler social system than does the larger unit. There are fewer people, fewer levels in the organizational hierarchy, and a less minute subdivision of labor. It is easier for the employe to adapt himself to such a simpler system and to win a place in it. His work becomes more meaningful, both to him and to his associates, because he and they can readily see its relation and importance to other functions and to the organization as a whole. The organization operates primarily through the face-to-face relationships of its members and only secondarily through impersonal, institutionalized relationships. The closer relations between the individual employe and the top executive in such a situation are only one aspect—but an important one—of the relatively simple and better-integrated social system of the smaller organization.

The importance of both external and internal integration is emphasized by other findings of our surveys. One of the most suggestive of these is that morale tends to be substantially lower in the large, industrialized metropolitan centers and higher in the smaller and less complex communities. For closely related reasons, morale tends to be lower in the Eastern sections of the country and higher in the West and South. Likewise, the simpler the industrial base of the community and the more homogeneous its population, the higher the level of employe morale.

These factors obviously relate, by various means, to the social characteristics of employe groups, and these social characteristics have an important bearing on the problem of integration. In certain cities of the south, a high percentage of employes grew up in small towns or in the country. Often their first job, after migrating to the "big city," is with our company. A great many of these young people have had religious upbringing which, together with parental admonitions, emphasizes the rightness of hard work for its own sake and the moral obligation of the employe to give his employer a full day's work for a fair day's pay.

Employes of units in large metropolitan centers, particularly those located in the East, are likely to have somewhat different social characteristics. Instead of coming from smaller towns and rural communities, most of them are likely to have originated within the metropolitan area itself. Likewise, many of them are likely to be the children or grandchildren of foreign-born stock whose personalities have been strongly molded by the special circumstances and influences of growing up within ethnic communities. The marked tendency toward lower morale among employes drawn from such groups seems, in part at least, to reflect the high degree of social disorganization characteristic of the great metropolitan agglomerations.

An important element of this disorganization is the tendency for sharp cleavages to develop between different groups comprising the community, and one of the most significant of these cleavages is that between workers and management. Where the rank and file members of an organization have been drawn largely from working class homes in which factory employment has been the chief means of family support for two or three generations, their patterns of thinking and systems of value will be those of the urban working class. One characteristic of their way of life, growing out of their family and neighborhood experiences and traditions, is often a latent or overt distrust of the employer and a strong tendency to identify their security and well-being with their fellow-workers and not with the employer. The management of an organization employing large numbers of people with this type of background is thus likely to involve complications seldom encountered in what is sometimes described as the "less mature" regions of the country.

The problem, however, is by no means an insuperable one. No better testimony is needed than the survey showings of many of our own company units. Despite the fact that in some locations employes may be drawn from backgrounds representing all that is worst in social disorganization, morale in many such units is unusually high. A thoroughgoing urban working class background on the part of the rank and file is significant chiefly because it tends to create attitudes and values which do not correspond fully with those usually characteristic of management and executive groups, and because this difference in outlook frequently leads to *mutual* misunderstanding and lack of confidence. Under these circumstances, not only are management's action and motives frequently misinterpreted by the rank and file, but management itself is often at a loss as to ways and means by which it can effectively mobilize the interest and cooperation of employes in achieving the aims of the enterprise.

This gap can be bridged—and our surveys provide striking proof of that fact—by *skillful and understanding leadership operating in an organizational structure which facilitates rather than inhibits effective integration.* Both leadership and structure are of crucial importance. The structural aspect, however, has received relatively less attention. Moreover, there are a number of curious and significant interrelations between type of structure and character of leadership that will bear close investigation.

4. Organizational Structure

The results of our research suggest that over-complexity of organizational structure is one of the most important and fundamental causes of poor management-employe relationships in our modern economic system, and that until this problem is faced and corrected no substantial improvement in those relationships is likely to be possible.

In viewing many business enterprises, one cannot but be impressed by the number of different departments and sub-departments into which they are divided, and the extent to which the activities of both individuals and groups have been highly specialized. In a very large number of cases, employes perform only elementary, routine functions because jobs have been broken down "scientifically" into their most elementary components. The resulting specialization undoubtedly has certain advantages, such as requiring less skilled people, shorter training time, etc. In many cases, however, the process has been carried to such extremes that jobs have little inherent interest or challenge; operations have been reduced to the simplest possible repetitive level and the worker makes nothing he can identify as a product of his own skill.

One has the feeling of division of labor having gone wild, far beyond any degree necessary for efficient production. Peter F. Drucker, in a penetrating analysis, has pointed out that over-specialization is not an inevitable consequence of mass production and that, "The traditional assembly line is simply a piece of poor engineering judged by the standards of human relations, as well as those of productive efficiency and output." [1]

The evidence of the studies conducted in our own company strongly support this conclusion, for we have found that where jobs are broken down too finely we are more likely to have both low output and low morale. Conversely, the most sustained efforts are exerted by those groups of employes who perform the more complete sets of tasks (e.g., salesmen, supervisors, master mechanics, etc.), and they likewise exhibit the highest levels of morale and esprit de corps.

---

[1] Peter F. Drucker, "The Way to Industrial Peace," *Harper's Magazine*, November, 1946.

The sharp trend toward over-specialization in our economy has not been limited, of course, to individual jobs. Just as particular activities have been broken down into their simplest possible components and each component assigned to a different person, so many *operations* (often after having been highly "simplified") have been separated out of the broader complex of activities of which they are a part and set up as specialized and semi-independent organizational entities. While over-specialization of individual jobs is serious enough, this over-specialization of the functions of entire departments and sub-departments has even more far-reaching consequences.

For one thing, it brings together in one place large numbers of employes on the same job level (and that level is likely to be fairly low where there has been any considerable over-specialization of individual jobs). This is another way of saying that the size of the administrative unit has been greatly expanded. Let us suppose an organization which performs three essential functions, A, B, and C. Let us suppose further that the volume of output requires three units of each function. Under these circumstances the organization could be set up in either of two ways:

1. It could be set up in three divisions, each function (A, B, and C) being represented in each division and each division, therefore, being a relatively independent administrative entity.

2. On the other hand, the organization could be set up in three *functional* divisions, one division having all three A units, another all three B units, and the third all three C units. In this case, none of the three divisions has any independence; each can operate only in closest coordination with the other two. Under the first alternative, there are really three administrative units; under the second only one, and that, by definition, three times as large.

This second type of arrangement is typical of much modern organization practice, both in industry and government. It is assumed this this separation and specialization of activities will permit better supervision, make possible smoother scheduling, and generally improve efficiency. There may be a certain spurious efficiency in this kind of organization but it is likely to have many off-setting liabilities.

One of the most serious of these liabilities is the fact that it so greatly expands the size of the administrative unit. Much of industry's present vast scale of operation is required not so much by economic or technical factors as by an unhappy and unnecessary principle of organization. The experience of many companies, of which my own is one, demonstrates that it is entirely possible to have many of the economic and technical advantages of large size without sacrificing too many of the essential human advantages of small size.

A further liability of over-functionalization is the fact that, from the standpoint of the individual employe, it tends to destroy the meaning of the job. He and those around him are working at highly specialized tasks which have meaning to management because they are a necessary part of a total process. But the worker cannot see that total process; he sees only the small and uninteresting part to which he and his fellows are assigned. In a real sense, the job loses its meaning for the worker—the meaning, that is, in all terms except the pay envelope.

Thus a very large number of employes in American industry today have been deprived of the sense of performing interesting, significant work. In consequence, they have little feeling of responsibility for the tasks to which they are assigned. Management in its efforts to maintain production in face of the resulting apathy is likely to resort to increasing supervisory pressure, but this procedure only creates more resistance on the part of employes. Sometimes the resistance is only passive, in the sense that employes fail to respond to the pressure or find means of avoiding it. Under certain circumstances, however, it can take more active form and lead to the creation of resistance groups in which employes band together (commonly through union organization) to exert a corresponding pressure against supervision and management.

Over-functionalization thus requires close and constant supervision at the work level to maintain production. Furthermore, the supervisors themselves must be closely supervised and controlled to assure the necessary degree of coordination between the many different units into which the organization has been sub-divided. In a simpler type of organization structure, coordination can usually be achieved on a fairly informal basis because there are fewer artificial barriers in the form of departmental separations and lines of authority.

Where the work of the organization is broken down into so many functional divisions, however, cooperation can no longer be achieved spontaneously. After all, each functional unit was set up as a distinct entity in order that it might achieve a more efficient system. Each unit, therefore, tends to operate primarily in terms of its own systems rather than in terms of the needs of the other departments with which it must cooperate. Each unit becomes jealous of its own prerogatives and finds ways to protect itself against the pressure or encroachments of others. Conflict develops on the employe as well as the supervisory level, thus forcing an extra load on higher levels of management who must be constantly reconciling differences.

In order to achieve the necessary degree of coordination and cooperation between administratively separated functions, management is thus forced not only to build up an elaborate hierarchy of many supervisory levels, but to institute a wide variety of formal controls. Unfortunately, these controls are themselves often a source of conflict, because the individual supervisor or manager is under strong compulsion to operate in such a manner as to make a good showing in terms of the particular set of controls to which he is subject, and often he can do so only at the expense of impairing the service he is expected to render to other departments. This conflict is particularly acute when two closely related functions report up two different administrative lines and operate under two different systems of standards and controls.

The management of organizations which have been over-functionalized to the extent characteristic of much of modern business imposes a severe burden on the top administrative staff. Functions and activities have been so subdivided and specialized that no individual unit can operate except in closest coordination with others, and the system is often so complex that this coordination cannot take place spontaneously. If it is to occur at all, it must occur on the basis of specific administrative action from the top, which requires the development of a specialized staff to assist the top administrator.

This growth of staff complicates the situation still further, because an evitable consequence is the elaboration of formal controls of various kinds to permit the staff to perform the functions and exercise the responsibilities which have been delegated to it or which it gradually assumes in an effort to strengthen its own position or extend its own authority. The result is a gradual undermining of the line organization for the benefit of the staff, an impairment of flexibility and adaptability, and a weakening of the effectiveness of the entire organization.

An objective appraisal suggests that to too large an extent work processes have been analyzed from a strictly "rational" or mechanical point of view with too little attention to the human factors involved. As a result, functions have been separated out of their context and set up as semi-independent activities. Necessary collaboration and cooperation between the units thus artificially separated becomes possible only through an elaborate system of controls and a complicated administrative hierarchy. Under these circumstances, management necessarily becomes strongly centralized, despite the frequently expressed concern of business leaders over the need for greater delegation of authority and responsibility. Too often, this is simply impossible because the nature of the organization structure makes effective decentralization impossible. For much the same reason, such organizations often require from their top administrators a high degree of driving pressure to hold the system together and make it operate with a reasonable degree of efficiency.

Where this is the case, executives and supervisors down the line quite understandably tend to pattern their own methods after those of their superiors. In many cases the copying may be done unskillfully and in such a way as to exaggerate the worst features of the pressure methods. As a result, supervisory methods at the middle and lower levels of over-functionalized organizations are often crude and inept.

Furthermore, the degree of pressure often required from the top is likely to create an atmosphere of anxiety and apprehension within the executive and supervisory group. This atmosphere tends to amplify the severity of pressure as it moves downward in the organization, so that even a moderate amount of pressure at the top is often greatly magnified by the time it reaches the lower levels. Attitudes of mind characterized by fear and apprehension are not particularly conducive to real skill in managing and leading subordinates. Above all, poor supervisory techniques at the lower levels of an organization generally reflect the experience and type of supervision to which the supervisors themselves have been subjected over the years and which they have come to accept as normal and expected behavior.

The significant point in all this, however, is that the over-complex, over-functionalized organization structure is likely to require the driver type of leader; the over-use of pressure as a tool of supervision is thus related primarily to the character of the structure and only secondarily to the character of the individual at the head of it. (On the other hand, it is recognized that the personality of the top man may have a great deal to do with the kind of organization structure he sets up. This entire problem of the reciprocal relationships between structure and personality should be studied carefully.)

5. SYSTEMS COMPARED

The most striking feature of the over-elaborate type of organization structure is its lack of integration, a deficiency which can be only partially and very unsatisfactorily overcome by driving pressure from the top. Our studies suggest that this type of structure is not only bad human relations but equally unsound from a standpoint of productive efficiency. Our studies also suggest that alternative systems of organization are conceivable and eminently practical.

For one thing, we seriously question the necessity for much of our present high degree of over-specialization and over-functionalization. The so-called "scientific management movement" which has given such impetus in this direction is based to a considerable extent on an extremely inadequate conception of human motivation and social organization. It has tended to approach the problems of management from an almost purely mechanistic point of view and has tried to organize human efforts in much the same way an engineer might design a machine. Much of our present over-specialization is based on this type of thinking.

However, the experience of a number of companies indicates that individual jobs and departmental functions need not be broken down to this degree in order to achieve productive efficiency. Quite the contrary; their experience has been that both efficiency and morale are best served by keeping specialization to a minimum. The experience of these companies likewise indicates that organization structures and administrative hierarchies can be vastly simplified, thus making possible a far higher degree of decentralization of authority and responsibility.

In the course of our survey work we have had an opportunity to study a fairly wide variety of organization structures. We have been struck by the sharp contrasts between otherwise comparable units which differ mainly in the complexity of their organizational structure and in the degree to which authority and responsibility are effectively decentralized to those farther down the line. A review of some of these contracts may be instructive.

In the more elaborate and complex organizations, the individual supervisor or executive is subject to constant control and direction and has little opportunity to develop the qualities of initiative and self-reliance. In systems characterized by extensive management decentralization, primary reliance is placed on the personal initiative and capacity of the people in the organization. There is usually a conspicuous lack of detailed supervision and of formal controls, and executives and supervisors (and to a large extent rank and file employes) enjoy considerable freedom in the way they accomplish their jobs.

They are judged primarily by their results, not on the details of the way they get those results. This concentration on end-results rather than on system and controls, together with management's alertness to recognize and reward good results, develops initiative and self-reliance and generates a far more powerful driving force than could ever be imposed from the top down. This pattern of administration not only gets today's job done better but permits the individual to grow and develop in a way that is impossible in more centralized systems. Furthermore, it contributes strongly to morale because employes work in an atmosphere of relative freedom from oppressive supervision and have a sense of individual importance and personal responsibility which other types of arrangements often deny them.

A number of highly successful organizations have not only paid little heed but have gone directly counter to one of the favorite tenets of modern management theory, the so-called "span of control," which holds that the number of subordinate executives or supervisors reporting to a single individual should be severely limited to enable that individual to exercise the detailed direction and control which is generally considered necessary. On the contrary, these organizations often deliberately give each key executive so many subordinates that it is impossible for him to exercise too close supervision over their activities.

In this type of organization structure, the individual executive is thrown largely on his own to sink or swim on the basis of his own ability and capacity. He cannot rely to more than a limited extent on those above him, and these superiors, by the same token, cannot too severely restrict, through detailed supervision and control their subordinates' growth and development.

Not all individuals can function effectively in this type of set-up. It requires a very large measure of self-confidence and personal capacity. The system tends to weed out those who lack these qualities in adequate degree. Those who are able to adapt to this type of organization, however, are likely to be not only better executives but also the type of people who can build and maintain teamwork and cooperation and a high level of employe morale, not so much because they consciously attempt to do so but because these results are a natural by-product of their ways of operating and a reflection of their own personalities.

On the other hand, in organizations characterized by many levels of supervision and elaborate systems of controls, the individual not only has little opportunity to develop the capacities of self-reliance and initiative but the system frequently weeds out those who do. Furthermore, those who survive in this type of organization are often likely, by virtue of the very qualities which enabled them to survive, to have personalities and ways of operating which do not make for greatest skill in building employe teamwork and cooperation.

An organization with few layers of supervision and a minimum of formal controls places a premium on ability to stimulate and lead. The driver type of executive, who functions through maintaining constant pressure and whose chief sanction is fear cannot operate as effectively in such an organization. In the more simple types of organization structures, where management has been effectively decentralized, an executive accomplishes results and moves to higher levels of responsibility chiefly to the extent that he is able to secure the willing, enthusiastic support of his colleagues and subordinates; he does not have the "tools" (with which a more centralized system would to some extent provide him) to accomplish the result in any other manner. The outcome is not only a higher level of accomplishment but, at the same time, a more satisfying type of supervision and a higher level of employe morale.

6. Conclusion

Our studies have shown that employe morale and operating efficiency are closely related to the degree the organization is integrated. Integration is not necessarily achieved, however, when the organization meets the requirements of machine-logic. As a matter of fact, what may appear to be logical from a purely technical standpoint may run directly counter to the personal and social demands of employes. We have seen a number of organizations which have a logical technology, division of labor, and hierarchy of control but which are badly disorganized from the standpoint of the actual working relationships of the people involved. Such organizations are well-integrated only on paper. In actual fact, they are irritating and frustrating from the standpoint of employes and inefficient, troublesome, and costly from the standpoint of management.

Our research indicates that two trends in particular are making effective integration difficult and contributing to the progressive deterioration of management-employe relations. One is the trend toward increasing size of the administrative unit; the other, the trend toward increasing complexity of organizational structure. Both trends appear logical in terms of widely held theories of business organization, but in both cases improvements in mechanical efficiency are at some point over-balanced by losses in the willingness and ability of employes to cooperate in the system. Moreover, the larger, more complex organizations are likely to become unadaptive and rigid, and to find it difficult to meet the requirements of economic and social change.

Intelligent planning on the part of management in setting up the formal structure of organizations can do much to improve the quality of human relations in industry. Flatter, less complex structures, with a maximum of administrative decentralization, tend to create a potential for improved attitudes, more effective supervision, and greater individual responsibility and initiative among employes. Moreover, arrangements of this type encourage the development of individual self-expression and creativity which are so necessary to the personal satisfaction of employes and which are an essential ingredient of the democratic way of life.

QUESTIONS

1. What is the problem of integration that Worthy refers to?
2. In the study summarized in this article, what were the major influences on employee morale?
3. What are the two basic approaches toward organizational structure?
4. How does organizational structure influence employee morale?
5. Does this article substantiate or refute Roethlisberger's? In what ways?

HUMAN RELATIONS IN THE GROWING COMPANY *

Alan C. Filley

Skill in managing its human relations creates a competitive advantage for any company, large or small. The deep personal interest of employees in the success of the small business is often the most important single factor in its survival and growth. In the larger organization, good human relations can mean the difference between conflict or cooperation with labor, high output or low—in fact, between continued profitable operations or actual failure.

The purpose of this article is to evaluate the human relations problems that are likely to occur in the growing business and to indicate ways of anticipating them before they can do serious damage to the organization. Although attention will be focused here on the simplest organization unit—the small business—a study of its growth processes should be illuminating for management in general.

From one point of view, the large organization may be regarded as a grouping of small business units. The growth picture in any unit of a large organization is similar to that in a small independent business, and the problems which face department heads or middle management are not unlike those of the owner-manager of the small firm.

The current emphasis on decentralized decision making is a direct result of the desire to improve human relations in the large organization. In effect, a small business atmosphere is created by dividing the company into a number of smaller units. The concept, as General Motors has expressed it, is:

> ... to divide the business into as many parts as consistently as can be done, place in charge of each part the most capable executive that can be found, and develop a system of coordination so that each part may strengthen and support each other part; thus not only welding all parts together in the common interests of a joint enterprise, but importantly developing ability and initiative through the instrumentalities of responsibility and ambition—developing men and giving them an opportunity to exercise their talents, both in their own interests as well as in that of the business.[1]

* From *Personnel*, Vol. 34, No. 2 (September-October, 1957), pp. 8-17. Copyright, 1957, by the American Management Association. Reprinted by permission of the American Management Association.

[1] Harlow H. Curtice, *The Development and Growth of General Motors*, Statement before Subcommittee on Antitrust and Monopoly of the U. S. Senate Committee on the Judiciary, December 2, 1955.

In considering the human relations aspects of growth, it is necessary first of all to draw a distinction between human relations and personnel administration. Human relations is concerned with social relationships in the organization, between employees and between groups. Personnel administration, on the other hand, is concerned with the relationship of the individual to his job and includes such things as job standards, employment, training, safety, health, and employee services. It requires specialized skills that are as important to the business as those required in production, sales, or finance.

In most companies, the personnel function is the job of certain individuals, just as the production function is the job of the plant manager and his foremen. The human relations function, however, *is the responsibility of everyone in the organization.* Hence the personnel staff, however skilled it may be, should not assume the task that is vested in *every* manager. Its services will be most effective if they are directed toward developing the human relations skills of management.

To illustrate the human relations problems that arise in a growing company, we have chosen a small business of the retail rather than the production type. In the manufacturing organization, functionalization usually takes place early in its growth and this tends to delay the development of certain social problems. In the retail store, on the other hand, these problems are apparent from the outset.

The pattern of growth

The pattern of growth outlined below must be taken as a rule-of-thumb guide, not as a body of fixed principles. In the first place, since the problems of human relations are *nonlogical,*[2] it is not only foolish but dangerous to learn a pat solution for them. Secondly, the timing of the conditions described here will vary with the type of business and the prevailing local economic conditions. And finally, the yardstick used to measure growth—number of employees—may not fit all situations. Other measures, such as delegation of responsibility, might be a better guide to the growth process in certain cases.

Phase One. In this opening phase of the growth of the small retail store, the owner-manager takes an active part in the business together with, say, from one to seven employees. The situation is similar to that in a large company where a newly organized depart-

---

[2] For a further discussion of the nonlogical aspects of human problems, see Keith Davis, *Human Relations in Business,* McGraw-Hill Book Company, 1957, p. 141.

ment operates under the close scrutiny of top management and is eager to prove its worth to the business.

The first employees in the new business are often friends, relatives, or former business associates of the owner-manager. As such, they have close personal ties with the owner that may compensate for small earnings or the lack of immediate possibilities for promotion. They are willing to put forth extra effort to help the business succeed and they can readily see the results in increased sales and new customers.

Jobs are loosely defined at first. For example, the person responsible for clerical work may also keep the books and help with sales. Everyone in the organization feels a responsibility for the *total* operation.

As yet, communication is no problem. Employees are well informed about the business and do not hesitate to discuss business affairs with the owner. There is little need to hide difficulties, since all are working for the success of the enterprise, and opportunities for communication are provided by the personal relationships that exist both within and outside the business.

The owner retains most of the authority and responsibility in the business, and all employees report directly to him. Since conditions change rapidly, he is likely to feel that he is the only one equipped to give final answers and to handle everything at the same time.

At some point in this phase, the employer will begin to think of himself as the "boss" rather than as "one of the bunch." As the business prospers, he demands personal recognition and assumes certain symbols of his newly acquired status. A corresponding adjustment is required of the work group. While some employees may continue to derive personal satisfaction from contributing to the well-being of the owner, others are likely to be jealous when the boss shows up with a new car or sits behind an expensive desk in a private office, especially if they feel that much of the success of the business is due to their own efforts, for which they have received no similar reward.

Up to this point, the owner has always thought of his employees in terms of personnel loyalty; now he begins to sort them out as "good" workers or "poor" workers. This rating is not quite fair, however, since it depends upon the employee's ability to search out new tasks rather than upon his willingness to put forth effort for the company. And if an employee does take the initiative, the owner is likely to be irked because he was not consulted.

Beginnings of functionalization

Eventually, some effort will be made, either by the owner or by the employees themselves, to arrive at a loose functionalization of the business. Work areas are designated informally, with the best ones going to the senior employees. The secretary becomes busy with her correspondence and records and no longer helps on the selling floor. Perhaps the most important step is hiring an accountant, to keep the financial records in order. Inventory records are tightened up, cost systems are installed, and the employees find that someone other than the boss takes a hand in finances.

To summarize this first phase:

1. Employees have close personal ties with the owner, participate actively in all areas of the business, and communicate freely.
2. Jobs are loosely defined.
3. The owner retains responsibility and authority.

These conditions are much the same as in a newly formed department in a large company where the entire staff works as a team.

The second phase

Phase Two. Until more than six or eight people are employed, few human relations problems are encountered. With the continued growth of the business, however, the owner finds that "there is too much work to be done" and decides to employ more people. Since jobs are not clearly defined, the new people are hired merely to meet the demand for more help. Even in larger organizations which ordinarily have adequate job descriptions, similar situations may occur in new departments where only preliminary standards can be set.

As the staff grows and more persons report to the owner, he finds that he is increasingly occupied with "putting out fires" and has less time for setting objectives and planning the future of the young company. With no one on hand to coordinate the activities of employees, work procedures are disorganized, inventories misplaced, purchase orders confused, and so on. The boss is annoyed when some employees seem to have nothing to do while others are hard at work; he fails to realize that no one really knows what his job is supposed to be.

At the same time, a loose social organization begins to take shape. Employees seek advice or information from certain members of the work group who have become informal leaders. These may be employees with longer experience or persons who are "close to the boss" and whose opinion is still valued by him. Some of the original employees who, for one reason or another, lose the opportunity to communicate with the boss may develop a certain amount of resistance to any new ideas which they have not helped to plan.

Employees become increasingly concerned about pay and advancement. Since the newer employees may have no personal or family ties with the owner, they are inclined to have less interest in the success of the business than in their own well-being and advancement.

As for the older employees, they may begin to feel that they are not receiving sufficient compensation for their efforts in getting the business started. Since there are no middle management levels to which they can advance so long as everyone still reports to the owner, they express their insecurity in complaints about wages. They would feel foolish asking for a pat on the back now and then, or a private office of their own, or even a bigger desk to indicate their status—they can only ask for more money.

To summarize Phase Two:

1. Work becomes functionalized, but informally, and jobs are loosely defined.
2. Employees still report to the owner, but they are not as well-informed as in the first phase and have come to rely upon informal leaders for communication.
3. The owner begins to judge his employees on a different basis.

Again, the situation is much the same as in a larger organization when the department head comes to associate less with his subordinates and more with managers at his own level. This change in orientation may result in resentment among employees, failures in communication, and the beginnings of informal organization.

Phase Three. The third phase appears when the staff increases to 15 or more. By this time the owner is harassed by a number of operating problems which he tries to solve by setting up a formal organization structure. This is likely to create a multitude of new problems, however. Even before the change is initiated, employees will begin to speculate about its possible effects. Most of them will feel that, while others may lose the privilege of reporting to the boss, they themselves will continue to report to him directly.

Serious difficulties arise, therefore, when the owner attempts to delegate authority and responsibility to his new middle managers. Many employees will not take the action seriously; they will bypass the new man and continue to go directly to the owner. As a result, the middle managers are out of touch with events and may come

to feel that this "short circuiting" of their authority is a sign of
failure on their part.

Enter the middle manager

The creation of new middle management levels may arouse resentment among older employees who have not been promoted. They
may feel that their job has been downgraded and that the only reward
for their loyal service is the loss of status and prestige. Even in a
large organization, upgrading often has the effect of a demotion on
the rest of the group.

The owner himself in many cases does not seriously intend to
delegate full responsibility to his subordinates. If he retains the right
to approve all decisions and thus negates the authority of the middle
managers, he will soon find himself making *all* the decisions again.

Rather than promote men from within the organization, the boss
often hires middle managers from outside. It does not occur to him
that his own employees might be capable of handling the new positions. Since he has been making all their decisions, it is difficult for
him to recognize their management potential.

This policy can have unfortunate consequences. The older employees feel that the new man does not understand their problems
or those of the company and they see their own chances for advancement diminishing. It takes time for the new manager to become
accustomed to the company and this adds impetus to the employees'
belief that he is not capable of handling the job.

Problems will arise in communications as well. Upward communication is restricted inasmuch as the new managers, eager to
prove their competence, pass on to the boss only the information that
is favorable. And, as mentioned earlier, any attempts by employees
to "short-circuit" the line cause hard feelings and meet with
resistance.

When difficulties at lower levels do reach the ears of the boss, he
wonders why he was not informed earlier. He vacillates between
encouraging independent decision making by his managers and being
concerned over his lack of information and his apparently diminished
authority.

Downward communication may be limited also. The owner may
feel that it is foolish or unnecessary to provide written communication in a small business since he himself is readily available and sees
all his employees frequently. But if he is too busy to talk to them,
employees are forced to turn to the "grapevine." They have a "left

out" feeling which may be expressed in critical remarks about the business to customers and outsiders. These statements are particularly damaging to a small business where good customer relations are at a premium.

If, then, employees come to feel that their loyalty has been rewarded only by loss of status, it is not unnatural that they should develop a resistance to change. Feeling that any change merely makes their job less important and reduces their participation, they counter by resisting the growth of the business. Older employees, particularly, hesitate to pass on the fruits of their experience to newer members for fear of being replaced altogether. Small "empires" are built throughout the business as employees take over the responsibility of others in order to make themselves irreplaceable.

Employees begin to feel their efforts have been unrewarded

Cliques will develop in the once unified team. Old employees line up against new ones, pro- against anti-boss, or pro- against anti-supervisor. These cliques take their tolls, of course, in grievances, lower morale, and ultimately, in customer dissatisfaction. Because these human feelings are *nonlogical* employees' complaints often center on something totally unrelated to the real source of the grievance. Those who believe that their efforts have been unrewarded begin to ask for pay increases or are absent more frequently from their jobs; once they gave little thought to earnings or hours or work, but now they work their "eight hours, and no more!"

To summarize Phase Three:

1. The first attempts at formal organization are made.
2. Employees become concerned with pay, status, and the obstacles to upward mobility.
3. A strong resistance to change develops among employees as middle management comes into being.
4. Both upward and downward communication are limited.

These conditions are similar to those in a department of a large business when growth forces formal organization and assistants to the department head are brought in.

The small business pictured here will continue to grow in much the same way until a point is reached, depending upon the factors outlined earlier, where it will be divided into smaller units.

The division may be according to the type of goods sold—men's clothing, women's clothing, shoes, and so on—or according to the functions performed—for example, sales, purchasing, and finance. In any case, each of these smaller units will resemble the original business, and many of the problems which arise within the units will be the same as in the company's early period of growth.

Certainly not all the problems indicated above will be found in the growth picture of every business. Needless to say, many managers are more adept at human relations than our prototype. On the other hand, the mere fact that a business grows is no proof of management's skill in human relations; many profitable enterprises could show greater earnings if they paid more attention to this factor.

Some generalizations can be made, therefore, which may be helpful to any company in dealing with the human relations problems associated with growth. These problems will be outlined below under four major heads:

1. Formal and informal organization.
2. Delegating authority.
3. Communication.
4. Problems of change.

Formal and informal organization

There are two types of organization in any business: the formal and the informal. The formal organization is based on the lines of delegation of responsibility and authority from the top to the bottom of the company. The informal organization arises from the social interaction of people in the work environment with no relationship to the formal hierarchy.

Little attention is usually given to formal organization by the owner-manager or department head until he finds himself flooded with day-to-day problems that could be handled as easily by some subordinate. It would be far more satisfactory, however, to anticipate this situation and plan the organizational structure in advance.

Jobs, too, should be clearly defined at the beginning. In the early stages of growth, employees may be expected or, in fact, encouraged, to participate in more than one job area, but each person must know the formal limits of his job.

If employees are aware of the standards for promotion and are able to judge their individual qualifications in this light, there will be little objection to the promotion of fellow workers. A simple form of merit rating should suffice to show each employee his weak and strong points. Even if seniority is not important in determining promotions, it is wise to give some sort of status recognition to all employees who have remained loyal to the company for a considerable length of time since their opinion carries considerable weight with their fellow workers.

It should be unnecessary to recruit managers outside the company to any great extent if job standards have been set up and employees have been encouraged to develop the skills required for promotion. Should a new man be brought in from outside, however, it is imperative that he be carefully briefed about his subordinates. He must seek their cooperation, avoid making changes too quickly, and try to win acceptance by the informal leaders in the organization.

Informal organization is a critical factor in the growing company. A small retail business, for example, can compete successfully with a large merchandising organization only on the basis of personalized service; and such service is a reflection of sound employer-employee relationships. A high degree of morale can be maintained throughout the growth pattern only so long as the manager takes pains to retain employee loyalty and cooperates with the leaders of the informal organization. By keeping them informed, for example, or delegating to them certain preferred tasks, management can retain some of the personal loyalty that existed when every one reported directly to the boss.

Delegating authority

One of the keys to business success is the delegation of the decision-making power, as Harlow H. Curtice has pointed out.[3] The failure to delegate decision making nearly cost Henry Ford his business.[4]

As we have seen, the owner-manager shuns the idea of delegating his powers and will do so only haltingly. It is natural for him to feel that a major part of the success of his business is due to his own efforts; nevertheless, he must eventually show his faith in the ability of others if the business is to continue to grow. By showing his willingness to delegate decision making early in the growth of the organization, the manager will lay the groundwork for the time when he must be concerned with planning long-range goals and policies rather than with immediate decisions.

It is also of primary importance that the manager allow his subordinates to make mistakes; only in this way will they be willing to make their own decisions. In large organizations, top management should tell middle managers only *what* to do, not *how* to do it. Adequate decision making by middle-managers may be accomplished satisfactorily, however, *only* if top management has provided the framework of policy and objectives within which to act.

---

[3] *Op. cit.*, p. 2.
[4] See Peter F. Drucker, *The Practice of Management*, Harper and Brothers, 1954, Chapter 10.

As a business grows, the simple spoken communication from the boss to his employees is eventually replaced by other channels: informal leaders or the grapevine. Once this shift has taken place, it will be difficult for employees to place much confidence in formal communications. They may feel that only the informal leaders are able to provide accurate information and that any sudden rush of formal communication from top management is merely a prelude to some unpleasant change.

Formal and informal communication

Formal communication should therefore be started early and maintained throughout the period of growth so that employees become accustomed to it. A sincere effort by management to keep its employees well informed can help to preserve the personal interest in the company that is so often lost as a business gets larger.

Informal channels should also be used, of course. Anyone who has ever been associated with a small business realizes that information cannot be kept secret for long. If management tries to do so, employees will take this as a personal affront; later, when the restricted information does leak out, it is likely to be twisted by the grapevine and thoroughly misunderstood. A more satisfactory approach is to feed the grapevine with reliable facts and thus take advantage of this highly effective channel of communication.

In the course of a company's growth, change inevitably creates problems. Employees come to fear both *potential* changes of which they have not been informed, and the *consequences* of changes which they do not understand.

Problems of change

One of the factors that enables a young company to compete effectively with a larger competitor is the manager's creative ability. Paradoxically, however, creativity precipitates change, and change, if poorly planned, may result in so much resistance from employees that its advantages are voided. Evidences of this may be seen even in some of our largest corporations where labor-management relations have been adversely affected by changes made in the early period of growth.

Employee attitudes toward change are affected by conditions both within and outside the organization.[5] As a result of internal changes

---

[5] For a full description of this concept, see F. J. Roethlisberger, *Management and Morale*, Harvard University Press, 1941, p. 21.

in the social structure of a growing company, employees become further removed from the decision-making process. Whereas formerly they felt free to express an opinion to the boss, now they are not consulted and feel resentful about decisions in which they have no part.

This situation can be avoided by developing a *substitute for direct participation*. Employees should be encouraged to share the administrative function by participating in committees and group meetings, and by being consulted either formally or informally through various channels before new plans are initiated. If care is taken to include employees in the decision-making process in this manner, much of the original loyalty and *esprit de corps* may be retained as the organization grows. And certainly if the employee participates in making changes, he will accept these changes more readily.

Outside influences

Attitudes toward changes are also influenced by conditions *outside* the work environment. It is not unusual for employees from a department or a small business to associate off the job. They may come from the same social class, attend the same church, or belong to the same club or union. Their wives often know one another and exchange gossip about their husbands' jobs. The local community, too, will have certain views about the company.

Where such a closely knit group exists, any change in the status of its members has a decided impact. For example, the men may feel that they can no longer act in the same way with the fellow employee who is promoted to middle management. Their wives may feel that they cannot share gossip with the wife of the new manager, and often feel snubbed by her. People being what they are, some resentment to the increased status of another is to be expected. Serious resistance may be averted, however, if the employees know why a particular person is chosen for promotion. They do not always realize that the only alternative to promotion from within is to bring in someone from outside the organization. When this is made clear, employees will usually prefer someone from their own group rather than an outsider who might represent an even greater threat.

Conclusion

Often the only thing which enables the small business to compete with a large organization is the motivation of its employees. The personal interest and loyalty of the employees of the small business often compensate for the efficiency and skill of the large organization. It would seem reasonable, then, for the small company to maintain its good human relations as it grows, and for the large organization to create through decentralization the small business atmosphere that nurtures good morale.

QUESTIONS

1. What distinction does Filley draw between human relations and personnel administration? Do you agree or disagree? Explain.
2. What does "functionalization" mean? In what phase of the growing company does it appear?
3. In what phase do human relations problems really start to manifest themselves?
4. How does the problem of change affect an organization?
5. Of what practical value would this article be to an executive?

WORK GROUP BEHAVIOR AND THE LARGER ORGANIZATION *

Leonard R. Sayles

The individual's most immediate and meaningful experiences of work are obtained in the context of the work group and his work associates. The larger organization is experienced by indirection, but membership in the small group contributes directly to the shaping of attitudes and behavior toward the entire world of work. For this reason of potency, therefore, the contribution of the small group to the total organization has been a subject of substantial research by those interested in human relations in industry.

CONCEPTIONS OF THE WORK GROUP

As Whyte observes, the individual is *not* a member of a single group within a larger structure.[1] Rather, he typically interacts in a variety of settings within the organization. It is the task of the researcher to identify those interaction patterns which are focused and concentrated so that it is reasonable to speak of a "group."

If we follow all the members of the organization through their hours on the job, or find some "high" vantage point and observe the total of all interactions, we are likely to be impressed with this proliferation of memberships. Most apparent is membership, except for that unique individual, the president, in some *command group;* that is, the employee shares a common supervisor with a number of colleagues. Distinguishable from this group, but closely related, is a *functional* or *task group*—those employees who must collaborate in some fashion if the work task defined by the organization is to be accomplished. In fact, both of these groups are rather well defined by the larger organization, and the group typically retains those boundaries.

However, there are two other kinds of clusterings that tend to overlap and penetrate the organization in unexpected ways. They are not defined by the formal organization and are often included under the general term, informal organization. One has received much attention from researchers: the *friendship clique.* The other is less

* From *Research in Industrial Human Relations*, Industrial Relations Research Association (New York: Harper, 1957), pp. 131-145. Reprinted with permission.
[1] William F. Whyte, "Small Groups in Large Organizations," in *Social Psychology at the Crossroads*, John Rohrer and Muzafer Sherif, eds. (New York: Harper, 1951), pp. 303-304.

well studied, but equally important. That is the *interest group*. This is comprised of employees who share a common economic interest and seek to gain some objective relating to the larger organization.

Memberships in these groups are not exclusive; often they will overlap considerably. However, the motivations of the members, and, more important, their behavior, are distinctive; and we have no reason to believe that the boundaries will be perfectly coincident.

The command group

Perhaps the most obvious kind of small group in the large organization is composed of tho supervisor and his immediate subordinates. As Jacques observes, the entire organization is composed of interconnected *command groups*, the subordinates in one group being the superiors in their own command group, with the exception of the first level.[2] While we might expect that research would have emphasized this unit of the organization, if we exclude the manifold studies of leadership styles dealt with elsewhere in this volume, there are relatively few systematic explorations of the relationship between the leader and his subordinates as a group, as individuals, and among the subordinates themselves. Jacques' volume is a notable exception.[3] His examination of the command group has a strong psychiatric flavor. He stresses the leader's ambivalence: his *authority* over his subordinates and *dependence* upon them, his sense of isolation, the problem of integrating pair relationships (leader and individual subordinates) with cohesiveness among subordinates, and the mixed feelings of the subordinates as a group who find the leader both expendable and indispensable (one to be protected or exposed?).

The friendship clique

This has been conceived as the elementary building block of human organization. As Mayo writes, "Man's desire to be continuously associated with his fellows is a strong, if not the strongest human characteristic." [4]

---

[2] Elliot Jacques, *The Changing Culture of a Factory* (New York: Dryden Press, 1952), pp. 273-297.

[3] There are two other noteworthy recent exceptions. Argyris devotes a small volume to the relationship between a plant manager in a medium-sized factory and his immediate subordinates. (Chris Argyris, *Executive Leadership* [New York: Harper, 1954]). Two researchers at the Harvard Business School provide us with a very revealing study of the day-to-day changes in the relationship between a first-line supervisor and assembly-line girls during a period of technological changes—Harriet Ronken and Paul Lawrence, *Administering Changes* (Boston: Graduate School of Business Administration, Harvard University, 1952).

[4] Elton Mayo, *Social Problems of an Industrial Civilization* (Boston: Graduate School of Business Administration, Harvard University, 1945), p. 111.

At the workplace we find a multitude of friendship groups representing the diverse interests of the workers placed there by the organization. The boundaries of these clusterings appear to reflect the employees' off-the-job interests and associations or previous work experience. Age, ethnic background, outside activities, sex, marital status, and so on, comprise the mortar that binds the clique together.

The friendship group has emerged as the agency which welds the individual to the organization. Loyalty, even attachment, to the total organization with its impersonality, extended hierarchy, and social distance becomes ambiguous. However, attachment to the immediate and easily perceived face-to-face group is the predominant reality of organization experience. For the individual it provides a source of personal security in an impersonal environment.

Where cliques are largely nonexistent, as in the rapidly expanding aircraft plants of California, turnover can be enormous. The presumption is that stable social groups take time to crystallize; during the period of formation many potential members will leave voluntarily because they do not find an established unit with which they can affiliate. This in turn inhibits the formation of permanent groups; the process is self-defeating.

Thus Lombard and Mayo conclude that the naive administrator who seeks to break up these cliques because of the inefficiency and wasted motion of the purely social activities involved is actually doing a disservice to the orgnaization.[5] In fact, they find that it takes skillful leadership to encourage their formation, at least in organizations undergoing rapid expansion. A recent well-received text [6] in the field of public administration comes out strongly on the side of encouraging on-the-job social life, concluding that production increased when social conversation was allowed. However, a study employing methods of precise interaction observation is unique in casting some doubts as to the positive correlation between social interaction and productivity.[7]

More serious criticism of the universal efficacy of friendship cliques, however, involves considerations of personality and work

---

[5] Elton Mayo and George F. Lombard, *Teamwork and Labor Turnover in the Aircraft Industry of Southern California* (Boston: Graduate School of Business Administration, Harvard University, 1940).

[6] Herbert Simon, Donald Smithburg, and Victor Thompson, *Public Administration* (New York: Knopf, 1950), pp. 113-114.

[7] A. B. Horsfall and Conrad Arensberg, "Teamwork and Productivity in a Shoe Factory," *Human Organization*, VIII (Winter, 1949), pp. 21 ff.

structure differences. A study of "rate busters" disclosed a significant majority who were indifferent to, if not hostile to, the social groupings they found on the job.[8]

A recent examination of British longshoremen finds that approximately half of the longshoremen on the docks studied have consciously avoided social entanglements of work group membership. Given an opportunity to join semipermanent gangs, they prefer random work assignments that leave them free to come and go at will, with no group responsibility.[9]

Formation of social groups also appears to be a function of the structure of the work situation itself. Argyris, in his Bank study, finds that incidence of informal social groupings among tellers is less than for bank employees who have less interaction with customers.[10] This conclusion would confirm a basic hypothesis of Chapple, that individuals seek some equilibrium in their rate and range of interaction.[11]

From this theoretical approach, we would expect that the whole range of group activities, not just social life, would be influenced by the interaction pattern fostered by the job. The previously cited study by the University of Liverpool researchers, for example, notes that dockworkers who were members of semipermanent crews were rarely found among the informal leaders of the longshoremen or among the active participants in the union.[12] Moving in the other direction, Lipset concludes that because some jobs handicap workers in maintaining adequate off-the-job relations with other friends (e.g., unusual working hours as among printers, actors, and policemen), they tend to form more closely knit "fellow worker" groups, as evidenced by their record of high participation in local union activities.[13]

Similarly, George Strauss has observed an unusually high degree of membership participation in certain occupational groups involv-

[8] These men tended to have a rural background emphasizing individualism. Orvis Collins and Donald Roy, "Restriction of Output and Social Cleavage in Industry," *Applied Anthropology*, V (Summer, 1946), pp. 1-14.

[9] University of Liverpool, *The Dock Worker* (Liverpool: University Press of Liverpool, 1954), pp. 61 ff.

[10] Chris Argyris, *Organizatoin of a Bank* (New Haven: Labor and Management Center, Yale University, 1954), p. 129.

[11] Eliot D. Chapple, "Applied Anthropology in Industry," in *Anthropology Today*, A. L. Kroeber, ed. (Chicago: University of Chicago Press, 1953), pp. 819-831. Many of the observations in this section are based on the theoretical work of Chapple.

[12] University of Liverpool, *op. cit.*, p. 72.

[13] Seymour M. Lipset, "The Political Process in Trade Unions: A Theoretical Statement," in *Freedom and Control in Modern Society*, Monroe Berger, Theodore Abel, and Charles Page, eds. (New York: Van Nostrand, 1954), pp. 101-102.

ing relative isolation from fellow workers, like insurance salesmen, utility meter readers and substation operators.[14]

Such studies add to the trend toward considering the *need for social relations* as a variable worth studying in itself. It would be interesting to know, for example, whether industrial occupations in which there is high inter-worker dependence in the work process, such that almost constant interaction is required, show less social life than groups characterized by relatively independent operations.

The task group

Perhaps one of the most important aspects of small group behavior in large organizations in their relation to the work process itself. The formally designated task builds a group structure, just as do individual social needs and the organizational authority structure.

More specifically, the work process stimulates group controls of (a) work method, (b) output standards or productivity, and (c) relative compensation and prestige relationships.

(a) *Impact on work method.* The experience of working in close proximity on a day-to-day basis induces methods that may depart from the organization's original conception of the job, or at least "fills in" the specific details of the operation not specified in the formal work plan. Thus, employees may exchange repetitive jobs, although such trading is illegal; one worker may do two jobs while a colleague rests; or, as Whyte[15] found, they may change the sequence of the operations to reduce tensions and provide short cuts. Roy observed similar "adjustments" in relations among toolroom clerks, job setters, and machinists where the objective was maximizing piece rate earnings.[16]

Some of these informal, or unplanned for, work methods may decrease worker output. For example, workers' machinations in Roy's machine shop tended to overstate make-ready time during job changes. However, other worker innovations, such as those described by Whyte, undoubtedly increase the total output. Gross found that radar teams, through communication circuits set up during off-the-job social periods, were compensating for deficiencies in the information provided by the formal organization.[17]

---

[14] Personal correspondence, Professor Strauss, University of Buffalo.

[15] William F. Whyte, "The Social Structure of the Restaurant," *The American Journal of Sociology*, LIV (January, 1949), pp. 306-307.

[16] Donald Roy, "Quota Restriction and Goldbricking in a Machine Shop," *The American Journal of Sociology*, LVII (March, 1952), pp. 427-442.

[17] Edward Gross, "Some Functional Consequences of Primary Controls in Formal Work Organizations," *American Sociological Review*, XVIII (August, 1953), pp. 370-371.

Similarly researchers have analyzed the initiative exhibited by a group of department store salesmen in evolving a new work pattern that solved a serious internal morale problem created by a new incentive system.[18]

However, the work structure can be designed so that elaborations of the informal group necessarily work in opposition to the major objectives of the organization. Recent studies of changes in the method of mining coal, conducted by the Tavistock Institute in Great Britain, illustrate such organization.[19] The change from jobs completed by small groups of miners in one shift to successive operations carried out by three shifts resulted in reduction of interaction and communication and a consequent decrease in the miners' recognition of their total responsibility for the operation.[20]

Thus the Tavistock studies suggest that the goal of the engineer in designing the technological organization is to provide the work group with a relatively autonomous task so that responsible *internal* leadership can develop. This kind of organizational structure is, in fact, the very essence of decentralization:

> A primary work organization of this type has the advantage of placing responsibility for the complete . . . task squarely on the shoulders of a single, small, face-to-face group which experiences the entire cycle of operations within the compass of its membership. For each participant the task has total significance and dynamic closure.[21]

The development of mutually convenient methods of conducting the work process can extend to the "job" of collective bargaining. We have ample evidence that union-management relationships at the work group level often depart radically from established practices and attitudes prevailing at higher levels, and may in fact contradict these other, more "formal" relationships.[22]

Aside from evolving methods which seem most convenient to work group members, the pattern of doing the job is fitted to the status system of the group. Those members with most prestige, if at all possible, receive the best jobs. Where possible, working loca-

---

[18] Nicholas Babchuck and William Goode, "Work Incentives in a Self-Determined Group," *American Sociological Review*, XVI (October, 1951), p. 686.

[19] E. Trist and K. Bamforth, "Some Social and Psychological Consequences of the Long Wall Method of Coal-Getting," *Human Relations*, IV, No. 1 (1951).

[20] The same problem can arise even though the employees are not separated into different time shifts. A study of a textile mill provides us with an example of the impact of worker-machine allocations. Cf. A. K. Rice, "Productivity and Social Organization in an Indian Weaving Shed," *Human Relations*, VI, No. 4 (1953).

[21] Trist and Bamforth, *op. cit.*, p. 6.

[22] Cf. Melville Dalton, "Unofficial Union-Management Relations," *American Sociological Review*, XV (October, 1950), pp. 611-619.

tion and equipment are similarly "assigned." And where these are not under group control, helping and trading can be adjusted to the status system. The exchange-of-favors system readily responds to the prestige hierarchy. Of course, the evaluation placed on jobs is itself a product of group interaction.

The methods evolved within the group for task completion become firmly established. Where outside forces (e.g., technological change) threaten to induce changes, the ranks close and resistance is applied. In part, of course, this may be the natural reaction of the culprit fearing punishment for rule infractions. A more reasonable explanation of the informal group's resistance to change, however, is the intimate relationship between the task group as an entity and the work methods they have evolved. A threat to one is a real threat to the other.

(b) *Impact on output standards.* Probably more attention has been given to this aspect of task group behavior than to any other. Starting with the work of Mathewson, and extending through the Western Electric studies, a long and distinguished line of studies indicate that work groups often formulate quite specific output standards and obtain close conformity from their members in *maintaining* these standards. Productivity itself is increasingly conceived as a group phenomenon.

Several reasons have been advanced as to why output control occupies a place of such importance in the life of the group. Work standards are one of the most important aspects of the job, which can in some fashion be influenced by worker action. The energy expenditure required by the job is largely determined by the number of units required, rather than by the nature of the job itself. Presumably without group control management would be able to utilize individual differences, and competition for promotion and greater earnings, to obtain higher and higher standards. This would penalize particularly the slower worker and the older employee. It might, however, penalize all workers by cutting piece rates, where such exist, and/or reducing the number of employees required by the operation. "Run away" output might have internal ramifications. We have observed situations where group controls were weak, and younger, low-prestige employees exceeded the production and earnings records of their "betters." The results were calamitous for the status hierarchy of the department and ultimately for the effectiveness of the formal organization.

Output control is a basic objective of group action as well as an essential element in maintaining group stability. Not only the relationship of the members to one another, but the durability of the worker relationship to his job depends on the efficacy of this process. Again we need to note that the resultant is not always unfavorable to management. We have many instances on record where the group has sanctioned increasingly high productivity,[23] rejected fellow workers who could not maintain high output, and resisted threats to existing high quality standards.

Evidently a great deal of the interest in "informal group relations" is the result of this presumed relationship between output standards evolving within the group and actual worker productivity. Wilensky in an earlier chapter reviews some of the efforts to find the magic formula to convert group norms from "low" to "high."

Some of the earliest research on productivity was based on the assumption that internal harmony in the work group would produce higher performance records. Increasingly researchers have become disillusioned with the relationship between social satisfaction and worker effort. Perhaps one of the most telling blows to the impetus to devote substantial energies to building work groups that are "sociometrically sound" is the provocative study by Goode and Fowler in a low morale plant. They found "the informal relationships which developed were such as to maintain pressures toward high production in the face of considerable *animosity* toward the owners and *among the workers themselves.*" [24] While their findings are severely limited by the somewhat unique environment they chose, it has become recognized that the relationship between friendship and output is a complex one.

More recently, Seashore finds in a study in a large "heavy equipment manufacturing company" that highly "cohesive" work groups are more likely to have output records that diverge *in either direction* from plant averages.[25] By implication, then, tightly knit work groups are almost as likely to have notably *poor* production records as outstandingly *good* ones.

The present author is inclined to believe that these inconsistencies in research results are due to an overemphasis on output as a part of informal group equilibrium. Control over output is also a major weapon in the arsenal of the group engaging in conflict with man-

---

[23] Cf. George Strauss, "Group Dynamics and Intergroup Relations," in William F. Whyte and others, *Money and Motivation* (New York: Harper, 1955), pp. 90-96.

[24] William Goode and Irving Fowler, "Incentive Factors in a Low Morale Plant," *American Sociological Review*, XIV (October, 1949), p. 624; italics added by author.

[25] Stanley Seashore, *Group Cohesiveness in the Industrial Work Group* (Ann Arbor: Institute for Social Research, University of Michigan, 1954), p. 98.

agement, other work groups, and even the local union. We need to know more about the *total situation* facing a given work group, including these external factors, before predicting its work performance.

The evolution of the method of *group decision* for gaining acceptance for changes in production methods and output standards is recognition of the potency of group standards. The theory presumes that leadership methods that involve the entire work group in the change process have two major advantages:

1. They can eliminate the major barrier of existing group standards which militate against any change, per se.

2. More positively, they commit the individual to new efforts in the context of his group membership. In a sense, the individual "promises" his fellows to accomplish some change in his behavior. Valuing the opinions of his associates, he feels bound to maintain his agreement.

Ideally the "decision" itself becomes the new standard or norm of conduct for the task group. Similarly efforts to develop plant-wide incentive systems are premised on the assumption that output and effort are dependent on the relation of the work group to the total social system of the plant.[26]

(c) *Impact on relative compensation and prestige relationships.* The fact that jobs take on a significant social meaning can be seen in the importance attached to wage differentials within the group itself. For example, we have many instances on record when management assigned an equal value to each job and the group found significant distinguishing characteristics. Jobs ranked by employees as *more important or desirable* are expected to have higher earnings than jobs ranked below. The established hierarchy is reinforced over time by the gradual perfection of the correlation between esteem accorded particular workers and prestige accorded to their jobs. The "more important" workers have moved to the "more important" jobs. (The importance attached to the job is not only a function of the earning capacity but also the quality of the surroundings, equipment, the tempo of the work required, etc.) Problems occur only when changes are introduced which violate the established hierarchy.

A persistent problem has been that jobs which the group evaluates as relatively undesirable may need to be compensated at a higher rate than the "desirable" jobs, in order to attract adequate personnel.

---

[26] Cf. William F. Whyte and others, *Money and Motivation, op. cit.,* p. 225.

However, this differential may be contrary to the status system of the work group. Similarly, jobs evaluated (by the group) as desirable may lack characteristics which would bring them a high rating under the organization's formal ranking plan. These contradictions between the group and the organization's ranking system become more important during periods of relative labor shortage, when new recruits are difficult to obtain and when the group undergoes aging.

While these several concepts of the "informal group" are not identical, and in some cases not even complementary in their basic dimensions, they do have one common feature. All stress equilibrium, the development of a system of interpersonal relations which stabilizes the work situation (among subordinates and between superior and subordinates), an interconnected series of friendship linkages, work flow relationships, output levels, and status-income relations. The objectives are the maintenance of individual and group stability by insuring a predictability of day-to-day events and effecting a *modus vivendi* as between individual on-the-job needs and the requirements of the formal organization.

As such, the *informal group* in any and all of its meanings is serving well-recognized and accepted human needs. Its existence and continued preservation are hardly matters for surprise. The building up of routines, of established methods of accomplishing tasks, of predictable social relationships, of group roles—these are all elements of structuring which social scientists have found typical of the human group. In fact, the elements define the group.

Particularly through the setting and maintenance of group standards, informal groups have protected their memberships from possible indiscretions that might reflect adversely on them all; also they have provided support for the individual, by acting as a buffer to outside organizations and by sustaining him through the provision of *known and acceptable* routines of behaving within the face-to-face work group.

Thus the informal group, as perceived in such studies, *reacts to* the initiations of other organizations, particularly management. Being defined in equilibrium terms, the reaction is always an attempt to *regain* the previous undisturbed state—to protect work methods, social relationships, and output levels incorporated in the norms of the group.

Concerted interest as the focus

Workers also band together into *interest groups*. These are formed not only to protect their members but also to exploit *oppor-*

tunities to improve their relative position. Improvements can take the form of "looser standards," a preferred seniority position, more overtime, more sympathetic supervision, correction of "inequities," better equipment, and countless other less tangible goals that make the job a better one and that often serve to substitute for the more traditional kinds of promotions and mobility.

Distribution of these benefits may be much influenced by pressures of united and determined informal groups. What management feels is "equitable," just as what the union determines is in the "members' interest," is determined to a large extent by attitudes expressed by those individuals who can support their demands by group reinforcements. Those work groups which for one reason or another are unable to exercise similar power in the market place of the plant are penalized.

This is not the traditional concept of the informal group seeking conformity with established norms of conduct. These are much more "free enterprise" units, interacting in a struggle for maximization of utility. All are not equally aggressive in the struggle for self-improvement or equally well equipped with the wherewithal to do battle via the grievance procedure and the more direct pressure tactics on union and management. Some lack the spirit of combat, others the means, while only a restricted few are endowed with the characteristics associated with sustained "activity" and progress toward the goals they seek.

Much of what we say implies a degree of dual or even treble *disloyalty*. Other groups, management, the union, and fellow workers, are perceived as either barriers or sources of assistance. From the point of view of the interest group, it is not high identification or loyalty that counts, but rather the right tactics in using or ignoring these other aggregations.

Thus, management is neither "good" nor "bad," liked or disliked as such. In fact, this approach suggests that it may not always be fruitful to think in pro-management and pro-union terms. It may well be that a group which is satisfied with *itself*, with its ability to protect and improve its own interests, is more favorable to *both* union and management.[27]

The results for the larger plant may not be a system tending toward equilibrium at all. We might expect that certain combinations of pressure groups actually involve the organization in increas-

---

[27] These areas will be further elaborated in the author's forthcoming study, *Technology and Work Group Behavior* (Ann Arbor: Bureau of Industrial Relations, University of Michigan, 1956).

ing instability—a trend toward disequilibrium. We have observed plants where the interaction of these groups involves increasingly greater discontent, turmoil, and nonadaptive behavior. That is, their behavior tends to reinforce the very problems it was designed to solve.

Similarly, the internal structure of these groups is much more responsive to changes in its external environment than is often implied in the concept of the informal work group as a relatively durable, impervious entity. Literally overnight, technical changes introduced by management can convert a cohesive task force into a disunited, apathetic "rabble," squabbling over internal differences. Similarly, we have observed a group of weakly-united employees become a force of some magnitude in the social system of the plant within a brief period, with no changes in personnel.

The existence of these *interest group* types suggests that greater attention should be given to matching supervisory "types" with group "types." We have tended to think of effective supervision as being the product of a relationship between a good leader and his group, on the assumption that the group of subordinates was a constant. In fact, variations in the effectiveness of supervision may be as much due to inherent differences in the group itself as to the leadership practices exhibited by the supervisor.

THE INTERNAL DYNAMICS OF THE WORK GROUP

We have concentrated primarily on the relationship of the small group to the larger organization, the functions served, the "compatibilities" and "incompatibilities." Therefore, we have failed to explore much of the research that stresses the intriguing inner processes of these groups, as semiautonomous organizations. This means neglecting the processes of self-selection and exclusion developed in the work of Moreno and his colleagues in the field of sociometry. We have also omitted the prolific findings of the "group dynamics school" with its emphasis on leadership patterns and role differentiation, factors contributing to cohesiveness, and the impact of the group itself on membership perceptions and attitudes. Bales and his associates at Harvard have probed deeply into the "ebb and flow" of the problem-solving process within the group. The sequential member roles have been analyzed effectively.

For our purposes it would seem appropriate at least to make specific reference to the work of George Homans. His work places substantial emphasis on the relationship of the internal life of the group to the outside environment (primarily the attitudes, organizational structure, and work method induced by management).[28] "Elaborations" of behavior and sentiment induced in the small group in turn modify the larger organization. While we believe an overemphasis on the concept of *equilibrium* may be misleading, Homans' theorizing does provide a framework within which to relate the small group to the larger organization of which it is a part.

CONCLUSION

Clusterings of workers-on-the-job all have these characteristics: They stem from the uniqueness of individual personality, which refuses to combine into larger "wholes" without changing those entities. The sum of a group of individuals is something more than the total of the constituents; it is a new organization, because most of the members (there are significant exceptions as we have noted) obtain satisfaction in gaining acceptance as a part of the group, and the group itself yields an influence over its members. Put in another way, there are pressures toward *conformity* within the group. These pressures result in the establishment of accepted ways of living together. The way of life of the group includes a complex system of customs and rules, vested interests, and interaction patterns which govern the relationship of members of the group to one another and to the larger environment of which it is a part.

This observance of group-sanctioned behavior and attitudes "fills out" the rationally conceived organization. What is on paper an organization becomes a "living, breathing" social organism, with all the intricacies, emotions, and contradictions we associate with human relations. While no organization would long persist which did not provide its members with this opportunity for spontaneous "human relations," a major problem of the larger organization becomes one of successfully incorporating the small group.

---

[28] George Homans, *The Human Group* (New York: Harcourt Brace, 1950).

QUESTIONS

1. How does a man's immediate work group influence his productivity?
2. What is the principal difference between the friendship clique and the task group?
3. Of all the different types of informal groups noted by Sayles, which do you feel is the most important?
4. Do you agree with Sayles in his classification of informal groups? Why or why not? What others might you add to his listing?
5. What are the major characteristics of all informal groups?

THE DYNAMICS OF
ORGANIZATIONAL BEHAVIOR *

Frank J. Jasinski

It seems reasonable to assume that most personnel men have been fairly well indoctrinated by now with the principles of sound human relations and that many line managers are equally aware of the benefits to be derived from greater consideration of the needs and motivations of the individual employee. Yet, as everyone knows, these splendid ideals exemplify what *should be* rather than what *is*. Life in the average industrial undertaking is still a far cry indeed from—in O. A. Ohmann's words—"[that] sociologists' heaven where everybody does what he *has to* because he *wants to*." [1]

Why is there this gulf between theory and practice? Why is it so difficult for enlightened managers to remold the organization in accordance with the doctrines endlessly being promulgated by the social scientists? Why do so many earnest efforts to institute a more desirable way of industrial life wither away at the root?

In an attempt to answer these questions, this article will take a look at organizational behavior from the anthropologist's viewpoint. It will discuss the various and often conflicting demands on the members of the organization to behave in a certain way and show how their responses to these expectations are further modified by the organization's own particular technology and climate. Possibly this analysis may help to underscore the fact that efforts to bring about a "change of heart" go awry, not so much from lack of good intentions on the part of all concerned, as from the failure to take into account all the influences that shape the interpersonal relations of people in a common work setting.

Roles and expectations

Most industrial undertakings have to rely on the joint efforts of many people to accomplish their purpose. Accordingly, the over-all task is divided into various "bits" each of which can be handled by one person. A bit can be the only one of its kind, or one of many other identical bits. These bits are traditionally labelled, "Turret Lathe Operator C," "Clerk-Typist A," "Junior Project Engineer,"

---

* From *Personnel*, Vol. 36, No. 2 (March-April, 1959), pp. 60-67. Copyright, 1959, by the American Management Association. Reprinted by permission of the American Management Association.

[1] O. A. Ohmann, "The Leader and the Led," *Personnel*, (Nov./Dec., 1958), p. 8.

and the like. The tasks they encompass are set forth in job descriptions or position guides which outline, in varying detail, what the organization expects from anyone who accepts responsibility for that segment of the total work of the organization.

To get someone to accept that responsibility, the organization must offer adequate recompense in the way of rights and privileges. In addition to pay, these inducements may include a variety of fringe benefits, from hospitalization insurance to stock options.

The sum total of all the duties and obligations as well as all the rights and privileges of a given position in the organization can be called its *institutional role*.[2] If an employee carries out his specified duties and obligations he can expect in return to receive the specified benefits accruing to his particular role.

Now a modern industrial organization does not specify precisely how its workers should behave in every aspect. Its interest in their behavior is confined to those acts which contribute to the over-all purpose of the enterprise—the manufacture of a product or the provision of a service. The individual members, on the other hand, expect more of one another than the organization specifies; and, having a fairly clear idea of the kind of behavior they desire and expect of their colleagues, they will reward, in various ways, those who behave as is expected of them and punish those who do not. The duties and obligations and rights and privileges devolving upon a worker in his relationships with other members of the organization can be called his *ideal-social role*. The behavior expected of him in these relationships may be quite distinct from the behavior stipulated or expected in his institutional role; sometimes as in the case of rate restriction, it can even run contrary to organizational expectations.

Because each member of the organization participates in a variety of relationships, he is subject to a number of ideal-social expectations. Thus, a foreman, for example, may have several ideal-social roles to fulfill. His general foreman may expect him as a subordinate to behave in a manner that goes beyond the specifications laid down in his job description. His work group will have their own ideas of how their superior should behave—another ideal-social role. The foreman's relationships with other foremen, personnel men, inspectors, time study engineers, and so on, will make other behavioral

[2] This term can be roughly equated with Ralph Linton's definition of "Status" in *Study of Man* (New York: Appleton-Century-Crofts, Inc., 1936). This formulation of rules draws upon several ideas presented by Ruth (Hudson) Rosen in her unpublished doctoral dissertation, *The Role of the Shop Steward*, submitted to the Department of Sociology, Yale University, 1951.

demands on him. It is here that various ideal-social roles may have certain expectations in common. Nevertheless, many may be unique and even in conflict with the others.

Each person's set of ideal-social roles also includes his own idea of what his behavior ought to be—his self-concept, or answer to the question: "Who am I?" Each of us has a picture of the kind of person we want to be and we all try, as far as possible, to behave in such a way as to live up to our picture of ourselves.

Which role to choose?

Confronted by these varying sets of expectations of the way he should behave, the individual may decide to live up to one particular set only, ignoring all the others, or he may vacillate among them, behaving the way he is expected to depending on the immediate pressures of the situation. Alternatively, he can make compromises, trying to meet each set of expectations at least minimally over a period of time.

However he decides to comport himself, his resultant behavior may be called his personal or *actual role*. This is what he actually does, from day to day, as a member of the organization.

How does an individual decide which role he should play?

A highly important factor in that decision is his self-concept. If he perceives his work situation as a place where he can fulfill his self-concept he will hehave in a manner that enables him to do so. But if the work situation does not seem to him to offer any means of achieving such satisfaction, he will probably merely put in his time without getting psychologically involved.[3]

In some cases, the individual's self-concept is in harmony with his defined institutional role. Thus, the rate-busters in the machine shop described by Melville Dalton accepted the economic rewards offered by management and produced as much as they could in order to get as many financial rewards as they could; they saw themselves as hard-working, independent people and rejected the informal social group and the rewards it offered.

On the other hand, an individual's self-concept may be contrary to the institutional role yet in keeping with the ideal-social roles imposed by his work group. Thus, the rate restrictors in the Dalton study saw themselves as "good Joes" and responsible members of the social group; they met management's expectations only minimally in

---

[3] C. Argyris, "The Organization: What Makes It Healthy?" *Harvard Business Review*, Vol. 36, No. 6 (Nov.-Dec., 1958), pp. 107-116.

fulfilling their institutional role, but accepted and fulfilled the informal ideal-social roles, as defined by their work group, to the hilt.

Between these two extremes is "the man in the middle." The Dalton study uncovered a number of these workers who had difficulty in resolving the conflict between management's expectations as expressed in their institutional role and the group expectations that shaped their ideal-social role. This conflict was further complicated by the fact that being "good Joes," conscientious workers, and "good providers" were all part of their self-concept. Dalton reports that these particular workers were constantly bumping up against the informally set ceiling rate and that nine of the 50 had had ulcers. None of the rate-busters, who accepted and fulfilled their institutional role, nor any of the "true" restrictors who for the most part rejected their institutional roles had ulcers.[4]

It must not be supposed, however, that actual behavior is determined simply by the response the individual chooses to make to the various roles expected of him. Though he may have a clear idea of how he should behave, other factors may combine to force him into a totally different behavior pattern. Perhaps the best way to illustrate how these other factors affect both expectations and actual behavior is to examine the foreman-worker relationship. The following case material is drawn, for the most part, from the automobile assembly industry, but is no less applicable to other work situations.

The foremen in this particular study[5] were well aware what kind of behavior their workers expected of them. A foreman should, the workers said:

> Know the work in his section and the jobs of his workers from a technical standpoint.
> Avoid using pressure on his men.
> Stick up for his men in dealing with higher management.
> Be helpful.
> Be friendly and avoid playing favorites.
> Understand his men, listen to them, and ask their advice.

On their part, the foremen, in describing how they "should" behave toward their men, seemed to accept much of what their workers expected of them. They described a good foreman's behavior toward his men as follows:[6]

---

[4] W. F. Whyte, *Money and Motivation* (New York: Harper & Brothers, Inc., 1955), pp. 39-49.

[5] C. R. Walker and R. H. Guest, *The Man on the Assembly Line* (Cambridge, Mass.: Harvard University Press, 1952); and A. N. Turner, "What Makes a Good Foreman," *Personnel*, March, 1955, pp. 382-392.

[6] C. R. Walker, R. H. Guest, and A. N. Turner, *The Foreman on the Assembly Line* (Cambridge, Mass.: Harvard University Press, 1956), p. 17.

> Treat your men as individuals on the job, since each one is different.
> Establish a personal relationship with your men, apart from the job relationship.
> Teach and promote your own men as far as possible.
> Be a shock absorber.
> Stand up for your men and interpret their needs and wishes to upper management.
> Consult your workers and delegate responsibility to them.

Apart from what was taught in the way of "good" human relations in the foreman training programs, the "ideal" foreman behavior described by both these workers and their foremen themselves went beyond what was formally expected and defined by management—at least it did not appear in the foreman's institutional role. Here, then, was a pattern of behavior which was verbally accepted at both ends of the foreman-worker relationship. Ostensibly, no conflict need have occurred.

Yes, the foremen's actual behavior, especially at one of the plants studied, generally bore no resemblance whatever to the ideal behavior set forth and "accepted" by both groups. Further, far removed though this behavior was from the mutually accepted ideal-social role of the foreman, it was almost impossible to change. As one foreman commented: [7]

> You can't treat the men as equals. They take advantage of good treatment. When I used to be a man on the line, I knew the way I'd like to be treated if I were to be happy on the job. When I got to be foreman, I started to treat my men in the same way—in other words, the way I'd like to be treated—but you just can't do it. *You can't change overnight what's been going on for 15 years,* and these men have been just spoiled by not having too good supervision in the past. . . . They can always quit if they don't like the job.

What are the causes of this deviation?

On the assembly line, at all events, a pervasive factor is the technological environment. As a rule, the men work independently of each other; the technologically interdependent work group is a rarity. For the most part, the work pace is controlled by the moving conveyor; a worker can leave his station only when replaced by a relief man.

Conversation among the workers is minimal not only because of their geographical immobility but also because of the nature of the job. Even workers at adjoining stations interact irregularly and for only a few seconds at a time.

---

[7] F. J. Jasinski, "Human Relations Training: The Missing Link," *Personnel,* May, 1956, p. 514.

An observation study by the Yale Technology Project showed the average exchange between a foreman and one of his workers lasted about 40 seconds—and the foreman did not speak to each of his workers every day.[8] There hasn't been a training course devised yet that can teach a foreman to cram understanding, friendliness, and fairness toward his employees within the space of 40 seconds.

While admittedly foremen and workers may not be so pressed for time in other work environments, the assembly line furnishes an extreme demonstration of the influence technology can have on this relationship. Although both these foremen and workers wanted better interpersonal relations, they had learned, realistically, to expect and even accept less. This did not, however, increase the social and personal satisfactions of either the workers *or* the foremen. (In a subsequent study, I found that assembly line workers who liked to talk thought that the company did nothing for its employees, and considered their jobs uninteresting even after working 12 or 14 years on the line.[9])

It would seem, therefore, that before embarking on a program to improve "human relations," management would be well advised to look to its technology and the behavior it actually *demands*.

The organizational framework

Another factor influencing the foreman-worker relationship is the organizational environment. The continuous assembly of the automobile on an "uninterrupted" conveyor makes the various foremen's sections unusually dependent on one another. In the automobile plants studied, the average foreman had more contacts with people outside his section than with his own workers—another limiting influence on his relationship with his men. And this relationship was further influenced organizationally by the fact that the foreman reported to a general foreman who rated his performance against the requirements of his institutional role. How much weight was attached, organizationally, to the foreman-worker relationship? Analysis of the general foremen's ratings of their foremen's performance showed that only 9 per cent of the comments were concerned with this relationship at all—and of this small percentage almost all emphasized its disciplinary aspects. Actually, only one foreman was specifically criticized for his "uncompromising attitude in dealing with his employees"—a fact that, incidentally, did not prevent him

---

[8] R. H. Guest, "Of Time and the Foreman," *Personnel*, May, 1956, pp. 478-486.
[9] F. J. Jasinski, "Technological Delimitation of Reciprocal Relationships," *Human Organization*, Summer, 1956.

from being given the highest possible rating. Some typical comments which presumably guided the foremen in their behavior toward their employees were these:

> Very aggressive and controls employees well.
> More forcefulness required to increase the efficiency of the operators.
> He is lax in controlling his people.[10]

Obviously, if the organization is set up in such a way that a
foreman is required to spend the greater portion of his time with
people outside his own work group, it is difficult for him, in any
event, to improve his relations with his men. It is even harder for
him to do so when he has a boss who regards consideration for the
feelings of employees as so much "coddling" and is likely to give him
an adverse performance rating on that very account.

Here again, management would do well to precede any program
for improving its human relations by a study of the organizational
influences presently affecting them.

The influence of ethos

A third set of factors affecting interpersonal relations can be
classified as ethological. Ethos—an anthropological concept—is the
sum total of the varying values placed by members of an organization
on the respective satisfactions or dissatisfactions to be derived from
the organization.[11] It is akin to "organizational climate" but goes
beyond this more common term in that it is shared by most members
of an organization and cannot be readily altered by individuals or a
management group.

Thus, the newly appointed foreman cited above, who tried to
behave the way he and the workers *said* he should behave discovered,
to his dismay, that the workers would not really accept this "ideal"
behavior. The workers had "adjusted" over time to "poor supervision" and sought to maintain that adjustment. The workers and
supervisors who could not accept the values that made up this plant's
ethos had left; those who remained had learned to live with it.

(Ethos can be changed, however. My colleague at the Yale
Technology Project, Robert H. Guest, is currently writing an analysis
of some drastic changes that have taken place in this same plant
with essentially the same people. It should be added that the changes
required nearly two-and-one-half years of determined but sincere

---

[10] F. J. Jasinski, "Human Relations Training: The Missing Link," *loc. cit.*
[11] cf. J. J. Horigmann, *Culture and Ethos of Kaska Society* (New Haven,
Conn.: Yale University Press, 1949), pp. 9-27.

managerial action, and that this action succeeded only because it included improvements in the technological and organizational environment as well as in the ethological. Certainly, it took a lot more than getting foremen to walk around smiling and saying a cheery "Hello" to their workers.)

Management, of course, does much initially to establish the organization's ethos. The very way individual jobs are designed and the organization is set up shows the worker how much value management attaches to the varying satisfactions he might derive from his participation in the enterprise. The automobile assembly worker who has been tightening the same series of nuts for 15 years and is aware that he is no more than a cipher in management's calculations is not likely to be taken in by a glad-handing foreman who has just finished a human relations booster course. The behavior of one foreman cannot be expected to alter a worker's perception of the values which he sees overwhelmingly reinforced and maintained by management's actions in the technological and organizational spheres.

Some implications for management

In sum, then, we see that organizational behavior is by no means a simple, straightforward matter. It is the outcome of a number of influences, all of them playing their part in the development and maintenance of behavioral patterns, whether "good" or "bad."

Though the organization's demands on the individual, as defined by his institutional role, are limited to the job to be done, the rights and privileges he receives from the organization in return are similarly limited—and if there is no formal provision for the satisfaction of his social and egoistic needs, he tends to seek this in his interactions with other members of the organization. Since these people are, in turn, seeking to satisfy their social and egoistic needs, they expect the individual to behave toward them in a certain way. These expectations, which go beyond the formal, organizational stipulations of behavior, and may vary with different relationships are defined in ideal-social roles.

Nevertheless, actual behavior is limited by technological, organizational, and ethological factors. Technological requirements may circumscribe the degree and nature of the worker's interactions with others, or of the intrinsic satisfaction he derives from his work. Organizational practices, though they may not directly involve the individual employee, may have an effect on the behavior of others and eventually on his own. Finally, the value system or ethos of the organization may be such that the employee sooner or later learns which satisfactions he can realistically expect in his interactions with others and which ones he must forego.

Since these three factors are interrelated in varying degrees, changes in one will have corresponding effects on the others. Yet management, seemingly unaware of this network of dependent variables, often tries to change behavior by concentrating on one side of a reciprocal relationship. Attempts are made to improve foreman-worker relationships, for example, by training foremen to behave differently. The more the other factors in the situation are ignored the more difficult the task of changing behavior becomes.

It seems imperative that more attention be paid to actual behavior —the adjustment made by the members of the organization to the several, and often contradictory demands made upon them and the factors circumscribing their actions. This, in turn, raises the fundamental question, why the particular adjustment has occurred and what sustains it.

To what degree have the institutional and ideal-social roles affected actual ones? What technological, organizational, and ethological factors have influenced employee's present expectations and behavior? What is the organization's ethos—how did it develop and how is it reinforced?

Recognizing and understanding what behavior *is* and why it got that way should bring management considerably nearer to the goal of what organizational behavior *should* be.

In conclusion, it may be said that changes can be made in certain interpersonal relationships without remaking the entire organization or revolutionizing its technology. Some attempts that have been and are being made along these lines may be all the more successful because of management's understanding of the other deterrents to change. Certainly, something may be gained, in light of such understanding, by realistically re-adjusting sights and intermediate goals slightly downward instead of always "going for broke"—and repeatedly going broke.

Ideally, of course, an effective, overall program of change should involve the organization's technology, administrative framework, and ethos. If such a program is impracticable today, who knows but that it may yet be attempted tomorrow?

QUESTIONS

1. What does Jasinski mean by role expectations?
2. What is an organization's institutional role?
3. How does an individual choose which role he will assume?
4. In what ways is the foreman-worker relationship influenced by organizational environment?
5. List and explain the three factors that affect interpersonal relations within an organization.

GENERAL QUESTIONS ON PART 4

1. How does the formal organization structure influence the formation of informal groups?
2. How does the informal organization, in turn, affect the formal structure of a company?
3. Should managements act to eliminate informal groupings that are not ordained by the formal organization structure? Why or why not?
4. How do you think Roethlisberger would answer the previous question?
5. How does the delegation of authority create complex human relations problems?
6. Contrast Worthy's article and Filley's. Do they concur regarding their conclusions?
7. Identify the types of informal groups that are commonly found in a business firm.
8. What is the link between employee morale and membership in informal groups?
9. In what ways can supervisors make effective use of informal groups?
10. How can managements go about reconciling informal and formal organizations?

BIBLIOGRAPHY FOR PART 4

Articles

CHAPPLE, ELIOT D. "The Natural Group in Industry," *Journal of Educational Sociology*, Vol. 19, No. 9 (May, 1946), pp. 534-539.

DAVIS, KEITH. "Learning to Live With the Informal Groups," *Advanced Management*, Vol. 16, No. 10 (October, 1951), pp. 17-19.

DOUTT, JOHN T. "Management Must Manage the Informal Groups, Too," *Advanced Management*, Vol. 24, No. 5 (May, 1959), pp. 26-28.

DRUCKER, PETER. "Integration of People and Planning," *Harvard Business Review* (November-December, 1955), pp. 35-40.

GARDNER, B. B. "The Industrial Structure and the Adjustment of the Individual," *American Journal of Orthopsychiatry*, Vol. 15 (April, 1945), pp. 350-351.

JENNINGS, E. E. "Principles of Group Decision," *Journal of Personnel Administration and Industrial Relations*, Spring, 1955, pp. 17-22.

LEAVITT, H. J. "Small Groups in Large Organizations," *Journal of Business*, January, 1955, p. 16.

ODIORNE, GEORGE S. "The Clique—A Frontier in Personnel Management," *Personnel*, Vol. 34, No. 2 (September-October, 1957), pp. 38-44.

RICHARDSON, F. L. W. JR. and CHARLES R. WALKER, "Work Flow and Human Relations," *Harvard Business Review*, Vol. 27 (January, 1949), pp. 107-122.

SAYLES, LEONARD R. "Human Relations and the Organization of Work," *Michigan Business Review*, November, 1954, pp. 21-25.

SEINIGER, W. B. "Charting the Informal Organization," *Advanced Management*, November, 1951, pp. 24-27.

STOCKFORD, LEE. "Morale and Group Behavior," *Office Executive*, August, 1956, pp. 39-41.

URWICK, LYNDALL F. "How the Organization Affects the Man," *Management Review*, Vol. 46, No. 7 (July, 1957), pp. 54-61.

Books

BARNARD, C. *The Functions of the Executive*. Cambridge, Mass.: Harvard University Press, 1938.

ROETHLISBERGER, F. *Management and Morale*. Cambridge, Mass.: Harvard University Press, 1941.

GARDNER, B. B., and D. G. MOORE. *Human Relations in Industry*. Homewood, Ill.: Richard D. Irwin, Inc., 1945.

DUBIN, R. *Human Relations in Administration*. Englewood Cliffs, N. J.: Prentice-Hall, Inc., 1951.

MARCH, J. G., and H. A. SIMON. *Organizations*. New York: John Wiley and Sons, Inc., 1958.

PART 5. COMMUNICATION

Communication, the process of transmitting and receiving information, is so fundamental to the practice of management that without it an organization could not exist. The reason for this is very apparent. If we could not communicate with employees, we could not inform them of the work we want done, how we want it done, when we want it done, who we want to do it, and so on. We could not in any way possible practice human relations, motivate people, or exercise the functions of leadership. In short, we could get nothing— absolutely nothing—done.

From a very basic viewpoint the absence of communication would also result in the denial of existence to the human being, for every aspect of human behavior is related in some manner or form to the process of sending and receiving information. Our physiological needs, for example, have the ability to motivate our behavior because they possess the power to send to us, primarily via neurological pathways, the information we need to satisfy our primitive motives. Thus we know we are hungry when we experience pangs of hunger in the stomach. Or we know we are thirsty or need warmth and shelter when we "feel" the dryness in our mouth or the coldness of our skin. On a considerably more complex and emotional level, the same concept is true of our reaction to sociological and psychological needs. We know we "belong," for example, when something has communicated to us that we have been accepted as a member of a group or organization. Or our desire for recognition is satisfied when our responses lead someone or something to convey to us in some manner or form that we have performed our work well. Whatever our needs be, therefore, our reaction to their motivational force is completely dependent upon the transmission and reception of some type or kind of information. In the employment situation, consequently, employee performance is directly correlated with the efficiency of the communication process.

Evidence to prove the importance of communication to the existence of an organization or a human being is not difficult to find. In almost any firm there can be found examples of inefficiency, waste and spoilage, misunderstandings, and so forth, all of which can be traced to some form of communication. One then need only to extrapolate these particular incidents to "see" their effect on the organization as a whole. And as far as the impact of communication on the human being is concerned, almost every hospital in the world contains an abundance of evidence. Perhaps the reader has seen or heard of the effect of a damaged or destroyed neurological system, or the result of the loss of hearing, sight, and speech. In fact, recent research has proved that man, when denied (to the extent that he can be denied in a controlled laboratory experiment) use of his communicative faculties (sight, touch, hearing, and so on) at the same time, can tolerate this condition for only a short length of time. Beyond a certain point, continued deprivation of his senses will result in psychological damage or even death.

Because the process of communication is so important to human relations and motivation, it is unfortunate that many managers, that is, people in leadership positions, are extremely poor communicators. In fact, of all the abilities required for successful management and leadership, the ability to communicate is undoubtedly the one ability that most managers are commonly deficient in. It is not surprising to find, therefore, so many subordinates in business today who do not clearly understand what they are doing, why they are doing it, how they should do it, and so on. Nor is it surprising to find, as a consequence, so many people who are dissatisfied with their work environment in general because they have not found the means to satisfy their basic motivational forces, especially their sociological and psychological needs. This situation is all the more unfortunate because many managers quite frequently think they are properly communicating to their subordinates when in reality they are not. Communication, as we shall see in the following paragraphs and articles, consists of far more than merely telling people things. Until managers learn this—in fact, until they learn, understand, and become skilled in the basic process of transmitting and receiving information—they cannot possibly lead and motivate people in the manner required to get work done efficiently.

WHY WE COMMUNICATE

The basic reason for any kind or type of communication, whether it be in the form of a nerve sending impulses to the brain or a foreman instructing a subordinate on how to do a job, is to get some manner or form of action (behavior). In the context of a business enterprise, the action desired is usually related, either directly or indirectly, to the efficient performance of duties and responsibilities.

This does not mean, incidentally, that the action wanted must necessarily be only in the form of concrete physical behavior, such as a worker operating a machine after receiving instruction on how to do so. On the contrary, action resulting from communication frequently can be and is in the form of an attitudinal response, the accepting of an idea, or a willingness not to behave in a particular way. This latter point, it should be noted, is especially true in counseling, particularly when it is disciplinary in nature.

Because some form of behavioral response will ultimately result from communication, it should not be inferred that overt or covert action will take place immediately or that it will always be observable to the eyes of men. Quite frequently behavior resulting from the receiving of information may not take place for many years. This is particularly true of formal education, of course. What the student learns in college may not actually influence his behavior until years later. The same is also true of present-day management development programs and other forms of executive development. Anything the young executive may learn about the subjects communicated to him during the course of such programs may not become manifested in his actions until considerably later in his career. And even then we may notice no apparent change in his behavior, especially if only an attitudinal response has occurred.

Although some manner or form of response is the basic objective of communication, especially in the context of a business organization, it must also be recognized that the type or kind of response desired by management of its subordinates, whether they be vice-presidents or operative employees, may not always materialize. Undoubtedly, one of the fundamental reasons why people sometimes fail to respond properly is because of various barriers to effective communication, a subject that will be considered in detail later in this part. Whatever the reasons why people fail to respond properly to communication, however, it should always be remembered that some manner or form of behavior (response) is going to result whenever we communicate. It is imperative, therefore, that every effort be made to prevent the various barriers to effective communication from operating. Unless this is done, it is very possible that employee response to communication may be unacceptable to management.

How We Communicate
How we transmit information

Perhaps the two most frequently used methods of communicating to people are the spoken and the written word. Oral communication, of course, takes place primarily in a face-to-face situation. It is, generally speaking, the most preferred method of transmitting information, principally because it is more personal in nature and because it more conveniently allows the transmitter to determine if the receiver understands and accepts what has been communicated to him. In addition, it possesses the advantages of being the fastest form of communication and of allowing both parties to participate in the situation and to share their opinions and feelings, advantages which are most important to motivation and the practice of human relations.

Written communication, although considerably less personal and participative in nature than oral transmission, is an essential part of any organization. Whenever information concerns many people, is very complex and extremely important, or has long-term significance, written media must almost always be used. However, because writing lacks the advantages of oral communication, skill is required to design properly the various forms used to convey the written word. But even when forms such as letters, manuals, handbooks, posters, and other media have been properly constructed, it is frequently necessary to explain orally and to clarify written information.

Other ways of communicating information to people include signs and symbols, pictures, facial expressions, gestures, what people do (the actions of others), silence, and so on. Although almost all of us utilize these means of communication every day of our lives, few of us recognize how powerful and significant these media are. And yet evidence of their impact and motivational force is not difficult to find. One need only to recall his reaction to a friend's facial expression or gesture, or how he was influenced by someone's action, or the purposeful silence of an acquaintance to understand the inherent nature of these forms of information transmission. Inanimate and inarticulate as they are, they most certainly speak "louder than words." As such, they play, along with oral and written communication, an extremely important part in the process of transmitting information.

How we receive information

Because we tend to use oral and written communication more than other forms of transmitting information in the business enterprise, we must of necessity receive information more by listening and seeing than by any other means of reception. This does not mean that other ways of receiving information are less important or useful to the communication process. On the contrary, if the transmitting media discussed in the preceding paragraph are important to communication, then the receptors required to receive the information transmitted by them are equally important. Accordingly, our senses of touch, smell, and taste also play important roles in the process of receiving information. But it should be emphasized that hearing and seeing, especially the hearing of spoken words and the seeing of written words, actions, gestures, and facial expressions, are by far our most relied upon means of receiving communication.

THE DIMENSIONS OF COMMUNICATION

Downward communication

In every business organization the most frequently used and relied upon dimension of communication is the downward direction. This refers, of course, to the process of transmitting information from the top of the organization (management) down through various levels to the bottom of the organization (workers). It is an essential dimension of transmission because without it a firm would cease to function. Accordingly, it is the direction used by management to communicate to employees information on company objectives, policy, procedure, and so on.

Upward communication

A second but equally important dimension of information transmission is that of upward communication. This direction of communication is predicated on the fact that employees not only possess the ability to receive communication, but also possess and must be allowed to use the capacity to transmit information. It is the only dimension of communication via which employees can convey to their superiors their actions, attitudes, and opinions about a multitude of subjects of vital concern to the efficient operation of a business enterprise. As such, it is the only means by which management can determine if the information it has transmitted has been received, understood, and accepted and if proper action has been taken or is being taken to accomplish the objectives of the company. Most important of all is the fact that this direction of information flow is the only way management can discover if the needs of subordinates are being satisfied. In other words, whether it be evidenced through records, reports, grievances, attitude surveys, interviews, suggestion systems, and so on, it is the only dimension that can communicate to superiors whether or not employees are being properly motivated. It is therefore unfortunate that it has only been in the past decade or so that management has recognized the inherent importance of facilitating the flow of information from the bottom to the top of the organization. But even today there are many managers who believe that the process of transmitting and receiving information means that they, the managers, transmit and that their subordinates, the employees, receive. What makes this situation all the more worse is, as we said before, the fact that many of the managers who think this way are, in the first place, extremely poor transmitters. Until such people recognize that, no matter what direction it takes, communication is inherently two-way in nature, they cannot possibly hope to practice human relations effectively.

Evidence that proves the importance of upward communication can be found in any efficiently managed firm. Successful suggestion systems, for example, have long been demonstrating their effectiveness as an upward communication medium by saving numerous organizations millions of dollars as a result of employees contributing their ideas. Encouraging workers to bring their grievances out into the open has resulted in the prevention of many major problems. And so on. But it should be emphasized that these examples materialize only when management, first, recognizes the importance of employees' communicating information to them and, second, facilitates the flow of such information. Unless recognition and facilitation exist, along with proper action by management with respect to the nature of the information transmitted, the inherent desire of people to communicate will be thwarted, and frustration, with all its dire implications to a firm, will result. In this respect it should be noted that some people believe that a basic reason for the formation of unions and the willingness of employees to join them is the lack of an effective upward communication system in the organization concerned. The theory here is that the union becomes the medium by which employees can convey their attitudes, opinions, wants, and needs to management.

Horizontal communication

A third dimension of communication necessary for the efficient operation of any business is called horizontal communication. This term refers to the flow—transmitting and receiving—of information between departments or people on the same level in an organization. It is a direction of communication that is absolutely essential to the success of any firm, for without it the activities of various functions, such as production, sales, personnel, purchasing, and finance, could not possibly be coordinated. An example that effectively illustrates this point occurred in a large manufacturing organization several years ago. The vice-president of sales of the company concerned, being disappointed over the sales volume of his organization, encouraged his sales personnel to do everything they could to improve conditions. He so thoroughly motivated his subordinates that within days orders began to flow in. Unfortunately, because this vice-president had not informed—horizontally communicated to—the manufacturing department of the nature of his plans, production quickly became bogged down by a load it was not geared to carry. The net result was that buyers, who had geared their own production to receipt of their orders within a certain period of time, canceled their orders and switched their business to other firms. This fiasco, it was recently estimated, has to date cost this company approximately three hundred thousand dollars in business—sales lost to competitors. And all because of an absence of horizontal communication.

FORMAL AND INFORMAL COMMUNICATION

Formal communication

The directions of information transmission that were discussed above, particularly downward and upward communication, represent what is frequently termed formal communication within an organization. The reason for this is because they are directions of communication that result from the delegation of authority and responsibility in the creation of a formal organization structure. In other words, when an individual has been given the authority and the responsibility to get work done, there is immediately created an upward line of communication that he should use to transmit information to and receive information from his superiors, and a downward line of communication that he should use to transmit information to and receive information from his subordinates. In many cases, especially in well-run organizations, these transmitting and receiving "lines" are clearly indicated on organization charts and in job descriptions. This is particularly true of horizontal communication, primarily because this dimension of information flow does not follow normal lines of authority and responsibility; consequently, because of its importance to over-all organizational efficiency, many managers formally determine its path.

Although there are inherent disadvantages in all forms of formal communication, primarily because of the authoritarian and superior-subordinate relationships established by them, there are several advantages of this type of communication that deserve mention. For example, horizontal communication, as was mentioned earlier, allows management to coordinate the various functions necessary to the organization. Formal downward communication allows management directly and immediately to send to or give employees information important to the operation of a company. And formal upward communication possesses the advantage of allowing management to establish lines that subordinates can use to convey information, such as suggestions and grievances, to superiors who have been delegated the authority and the responsibility to act upon it. This latter point illustrates, incidentally, a common misunderstanding of what is frequently called an open-door policy. If the chief executive of an organization, especially a large organization, literally left his door open to every conceivable type and kind of upward communication, he would have little time to devote to the top management aspects of running the business. What the term "open-door" really means is that communication from employees, if exceptional enough in nature to prohibit lower level managers and supervisors from acting on it, will be received personally by the chief executive. To allow otherwise would mean inefficient utilization of the executive's time and under-utilization of the time of lower-level managers. This does not mean to imply, however, that there should be no exceptions to this rule. On the contrary, in every organization there will occur times when employees, because of the personal nature of their information, should be allowed to see the "big boss." Unfortunately, it is always difficult to determine whether or not the nature of the information is personal enough to warrant consideration by the top man, especially when the employee, because of personality or other reasons, refuses to reveal what he wants to communicate. In addition, psychological and sociological barriers quite frequently make people reluctant just to "walk in."

Informal communication

As the section on organization pointed out, there also exists in every company a system of informal communication. This type of communication is a result of the natural desire of people to communicate with each other and arises from the social interaction of individuals. It is multidimensional in nature and is as flexible, dynamic, and varied as are the people who communicate along its paths. As a system of communication it is limited in direction and degree only to the extent that limits are self-imposed by members of an organization. As such, it contrasts sharply with the formal communication system because it frequently ignores or trespasses upon formally delegated lines of authority and responsibility. It is usually, but sometimes mistakenly, called the grapevine.

Although some people consider informal communication undesirable, undoubtedly because they do not understand it and utilize it properly, this system of transmitting and receiving information has several important characteristics that should be mentioned here. Perhaps one of its most important functions, if it is properly utilized, is to help disseminate and clarify management's formal communication. In this way it helps to improve over-all communication or, more frequently, to overcome management's failure to transmit information properly in the first place. Another important quality is that it allows employees to express their emotions orally to other people without fear of repercussion. This safety-valve feature plays an important role in human relations, because the cathartic value of "blowing-off steam" frequently alleviates employee problems or prevents them from growing larger.

One of the most important disadvantages of informal communication is that it frequently spreads rumor, untruth, and distorted information with an alarming rate of speed. Perhaps the basic reason for this is lack of proper formal communication. Consequently when employees do not understand or are "left-in-the-dark" about something, they immediately interpret actions and procedures as they want to see them. The net result is rumor and untruth. It should be noted, however, that many times the transmitter is unaware that he is transmitting such items of information. As a receiver he frequently assumes that the information he sees or hears is reliable and truthful and that he is passing it on exactly as he received it. Unfortunately there are also people who purposefully concoct misinformation. Perhaps the best way to deal with such individuals—in fact, the best way to deal with all rumors and untruths—is to establish a rumor board or some similar medium of communication. The basic purpose of such a device is to answer the rumor or untruth immediately and thereby to stop it before it becomes serious. This means that management must constantly listen to the grapevine and act immediately when necessary.

Another undesirable characteristic of informal communication, so some managers think and fear, is that unlike formal communication it is very difficult to control. In other words, it is believed that management has little to say about what will be commnuicated, when it will be transmitted, who will receive it, and so forth. Although this quality exists to some degree, its manifestation actually depends upon the ability of the managers involved. If people ignore the grapevine and make no attempt to listen to it and combat the misinformation being transmitted, then, of course, it cannot be controlled. If, on the other hand, managers study the grapevine by listening to it and by determining who its leaders are and what information it transmits, they can take intelligent actions that will ultimately lead to an integration of informal communication with the formal communication system.

BARRIERS TO EFFECTIVE COMMUNICATION

In a previous part of this section it was pointed out that some manner or form of action is the basic objective of all communication. It was also stated that the type or kind of response desired by management may not alway result, primarily because of various barriers that thwart proper behavior. The purpose of this section is to consider briefly the nature of some of the more important obstacles to efficient communication.

Semantics

The meaning of words is undoubtedly one of the more important barriers to effective communication. Altogether too frequently we feel that because we undertand the meaning of the terms we use, our subordinates will likewise understand them. Unfortunately, what we fail to recognize is that words mean different things to different people. The level of our education, the part of the country we come from, the ethnic group to which we belong—these and many other factors determine what words mean to us. Managers must consequently take this fact into consideration when they communicate. In other words, they must in the first place carefully choose the words—frequently simple, single-syllable words—that they wish to transmit to people. When the nature of the communication is such that it is impossible to use universally understandable terms, then every effort must be made to interpret the meaning of the message to the various individuals or groups concerned. If this is not done, people will automatically interpret the communication in accordance with their understanding of the words used. The net result is usually misinterpretation and undesired action.

Too many words

In addition to using complex and difficult-to-understand words and terms, many managers also clutter up their communications with too many words. Consider, for example, the following illustration. In a well-known organization, the office manager recently sent this memo to employees:

Employees of the XYZ Company who are desirous of receiving additional copies of the form which accompanies this memo should inform the receptionist of this office of the nature of their request in order to obtain without delay the extra copies they should like to have.

Although the nature of this communication may not be too difficult to understand, think how much simpler it would have been had the office manager simply written:

If you want additional copies of this form, ask the receptionist.

When we fail to condense our communication, we leave the door wide open to time-consuming misunderstanding and improper response. This is especially true of communication requiring immediate action of employees.

Physical distance

Another important barrier to effective communication, particularly in the larger organization, is physical distance between people. When we are far away from the persons to whom we wish to communicate, it becomes very difficult for us to determine if they receive, understand, accept, and properly react to what we have transmitted. We must also rely more and more on written media, which means that we encounter additional problems of construction and interpretation. To overcome the disadvantage of distance, we must utilize, where possible, physical devices such as telephones and intercommunication systems, and we must make sure that the people on the various levels through which our information is sent understand, accept, and pass on our message up or down the line. In particular we must make sure that the people on these levels communicate intact the nature of our information. That is to say, we must make sure that our information is not misinterpreted, distorted, or stopped by the people who are responsible for passing it on to and interpreting it for other people. As difficult as this is to do, we must do it if we want proper employee behavior.

People

In addition to being the basic cause of many of the barriers to effective communication, it should be noted that people *per se* are an important obstacle to information transmission. This type of barrier occurs when information that must be transmitted through other people is stopped before it reaches its final objective. Included among reasons why people hinder the flow of communication are factors such as misunderstanding of the original message (poor communication in the first place) and fear of passing on information because it might indicate inefficiency or inability to handle certain situations. This latter point is extremely relevant to upward communication. Altogether too frequently foremen and supervisors hestitate or fail completely to pass important information, such as employee attitudes, opinions, grievances, and suggestions, on to their superiors because they believe such information will impair their status or prestige or reflect on their supervisory ability. When such stoppages occur, problems that could have been prevented usually develop into situations that ultimately require drastic remedial action. It is important, therefore, for people to recognize that the stopping of information, rather than the content of the message stopped, is an indication of poor leadership ability.

Another very common way people serve as barriers to effective communication, that is, communication designed to elicit proper response from employees, concerns the way some people behave on the job. A frequently occurring illustration of this is the supervisor who consistently breaks many rules and regulations that have been established for safety or other reasons. When employees see such a person smoking in a no-smoking area or being frequently late to or absent from work, it is extremely difficult to obtain proper response from them no matter how well we communicate the rules themselves and the reasons for them. When such actions occur on the supervisory level, they are, of course, indicative of extremely poor leadership ability. But they serve as very effective barriers to communication.

Interest

As several of the following articles point out, one of the most fundamental obstacles to communication is that we do not pay as much attention as we should to the interests of the people to whom we communicate. This concept is based on the fact that we listen (or look) more attentively to communications that are geared to our interests and our basic needs. When we listen in this manner, we facilitate understanding and acceptance of the information transmitted and usually respond with the proper type of behavior. Until management recognizes this important aspect of communication and keys its information transmission to it, it will seldom achieve the benefits desired from training, cost reduction programs, quality improvement programs, suggestion systems, and so forth. It is fortunate, therefore, that the simple explanation of the "why" of a particular communication is frequently sufficient to relate the response desired to employee interests.

COMMUNICATION: THE BASIC PROCESS

Although the achievement of some manner or form of human behavior is the basic objective of all communication, especially in the context of a business enterprise, it should be apparent by now that the accomplishment of this goal requires more than telling, writing, or indicating something to people. In fact, it should be obvious that the basic process of communication, if it is to achieve proper employee response, must of necessity give attention to three important and sequentially related concepts. In the first place, it must begin with the proper transmission of information. In the second place, the receiver must understand this information. And in the third place, the receiver must accept the information transmitted to him. Unless these three conditions exist in the order stated, the fourth part of the process of communication, namely, action, will be seriously thwarted or left completely to chance. Let us briefly consider the nature of these facets of communication.

Transmitting information

The transmitting of information to people, particularly if it is done with written media, requires considerable planning on the part of the transmitter. Detailed attention must be given to the nature of the communication *per se*, the best medium to use, the people who should receive it, the interests and the needs of the people who will receive it, and the various barriers that could impede its effectiveness. In other words, every effort should be made to insure that what people are to receive is receivable. If this is not done—and it frequently .isn't—it is senseless to expect understanding, acceptance, and proper action.

Understanding information

It is obvious that the understanding of communication is dependent to an infinite degree on how well the communication was planned and transmitted in the first place. Not so obvious, however, is the fact that we frequently assume that the receiver understands what has been communicated to him. Because sound communication does not rest upon a structure of assumptions, primarily because even the best communication is sometimes misunderstood, it is therefore necessary that the transmitter determine whether or not the receiver comprehends his message. In essence, this requires the transmitter now to become the receiver and the receiver to become the transmitter. In other words, after communicating information to an employee, we must do everything possible to encourage that person

to indicate to us the degree of his understanding. We must facilitate
the transmission of this information and, most important of all,
listen attentively to it. This is why most people prefer oral communication. In a face-to-face situation it is considerably easier to
determine whether or not the receiver understands us. It is also
easier, of course, for the receiver to transmit to us. No matter what
dimension or medium of communication is used, however, it is imperative that we recognize that understanding can be determined
only if we utilize the inherent two-way nature of the process of communication. That is to say, we must be both transmitters and
receivers. Unless we accept this dual role, it is impossible to communicate effectively with and hence to motivate people.

Accepting information

Many people fail to recognize that in addition to proper transmission and understanding of communication, action is also dependent
to a great degree upon acceptance of the information received. Perhaps the basic reason for this is the assumption that people accept
what they understand. Unfortunately for the manager, however, this
assumption is not always true, especially when consideration is given
to the nature and the degree of the understanding involved. Consider,
for example, the case of the older worker who was given detailed
and explicit instructions on how to operate a new machine. According
to tests and demonstrations there was no doubt that this individual
understood how to run the machine and had the ability to do so. Yet
the quality and the quantity of his production were disappointingly
low. Why? Although he understood how to operate the new machine,
he did not understand why the machine was necessary, how it would
affect his status, or what influence the potential increase in productivity would have on his pay. As a consequence, he covertly refused
to accept the machine and accordingly produced at a lower level than
his ability warranted. In this case and thousands similar to it the
only answer is to explore thoroughly via two-way communication the
nature and the degree of the employee's understanding. Where voids
in his information exist, he must have communicated to him the
information he needs to satisfy his interests. Difficult as this is to
do, it must be done if action based on acceptance, rather than behavior based on rejection, is to result.

The articles that follow were purposefully selected to help the
reader gain greater understanding of the nature and the facets of
the basic process of communication. Roethlisberger's article was
chosen because it is an excellent interpretation of communication

within an administrative setting. Higham's article was included because, as its title suggests, it gives consideration to some important basic psychological factors that are deeply involved in communication. The article by Rogers and Roethlisberger was selected because it is a classic analysis of several of the things that impede and aid the communication process. Because the well-informed reader should be acquainted with experimental approaches to organizational communication, the article by Bavelas and Barrett was picked. The article by Planty and Machaver was included because it is an extremely good analysis of the benefits of upward communication and because it offers concrete suggestions on how to improve the effectiveness of this important dimension of information transmission. And, last of all, Davis' article was chosen because of its treatment of informal communication.

THE ADMINISTRATOR'S SKILL:
COMMUNICATION *

F. J. Roethlisberger

For some time I have been deeply interested in the process of interpersonal communication within the administrative setting. What is taking place when two people engaged in a common task interact? What do the actors involved perceive is taking place? What is a useful way for the executive to think about these interpersonal proceedings in which he is engaged, and what skills can he practice which will make him more effective as an administrator of people?

In this article I want to discuss these questions in terms of a specific, down-to-earth case in an industrial plant [1]—a case of misunderstanding between two people, a worker and a foreman. (It is not important that they happen to be foreman and worker; to all intents and purposes they might as well be superintendent and foreman or, for that matter, controller and accountant.) A brief review of the case should be useful in providing us with a point of departure as well as a point of return for our questions. And it should make it possible for us to discuss the practical application of some of the recent findings of general semantics and human relations.

A CASE OF MISUNDERSTANDING

In a department of a large industrial organization there were seven workers (four men and three women) engaged in testing and inspecting panels of electronic equipment. In this department one of the workers, Bing, was having trouble with his immediate supervisor, Hart, who had formerly been a worker in the department.

Had we been observers in this department we would have seen Bing carrying two or three panels at a time from the racks where they were stored to the bench where he inspected them together. For this activity we would have seen him charging double or triple setup time. We would have heard him occasionally singing at work. Also we would have seen him usually leaving his work position a few minutes early to go to lunch, and noticed that other employees

---

* From the *Harvard Business Review*, Vol. 31, No. 6 (November, 1953), pp. 55-62. Reprinted with permission.
[1] This case (names and places disguised) is adapted from a case in the files of the Harvard Graduate School of Business Administration.

sometimes accompanied him. And had we been present at one specific occasion, we would have heard Hart telling Bing that he disapproved of these activities and that he wanted Bing to stop doing them.

However, not being present to hear the actual verbal exchange that took place in this interaction, let us note what Bing and Hart each said to a personnel representative.

What Bing said

In talking about his practice of charging double or triple setup time for panels which he inspected all at one time, Bing said:

"This is a perfectly legal thing to do. We've always been doing it. Mr. Hart, the supervisor, has other ideas about it, though; he claims it's cheating the company. He came over to the bench a day or two ago and let me know just how he felt about the matter. Boy, did we go at it! It wasn't so much the fact that he called me down on it, but more the way in which he did it. . . . I've never seen anyone like him. He's not content just to say in a manlike way what's on his mind, but he prefers to do it in a way that makes you want to crawl inside a crack on the floor. What a guy! I don't mind being called down by a supervisor, but I like to be treated like a man, and not humiliated like a school teacher does a naughty kid. He's been pulling this stuff ever since he's been a supervisor. I knew him when he was just one of us, but since he's been promoted, he's lost his friendly way and seems to be having some difficulty in knowing how to manage us employees. He's a changed man over what he used to be like when he was a worker on the bench with us several years ago.

"When he pulled this kind of stuff on me the other day, I got so damn mad I called in the union representative. I knew that the thing I was doing was permitted by the contract, but I was intent on making some trouble for Mr. Hart, just because he persists in this sarcastic way of handling me. I am about fed up with the whole damn situation. I'm trying every means I can to get myself transferred out of his group. . . . He's not going to pull this kind of kid stuff any longer on me. When the union representative questioned him on the case, he finally had to back down, because according to the contract an employee can use any time-saving method or device in order to speed up the process as long as the quality standards of the job are met.

"You see, he knows that I do professional singing on the outside. He hears me singing here on the job, and he hears the people talking about my career in music. I guess he figures I can be so cocky because I have another means of earning some money. Actually, the employees here enjoy having me sing while we work, but he thinks I'm disturbing them and causing them to 'goof off' from their work. Occasionally, I leave the job a few minutes early and go down to the washroom to wash up before lunch. Sometimes several others in the group will accompany me, and so Mr. Hart automatically thinks I'm the leader and usually bawls me out for the whole thing.

"So, you can see, I'm a marked man around here. He keeps watching me like a hawk. Naturally, this makes me very uncomfortable. That's why I'm sure a transfer would be the best thing. I've asked him for it, but he didn't give me any satisfaction at the time. While I remain here, I'm going to keep my nose clean, but whenever I get the chance, I'm going to slip it to him, but good."

What Hart said

Here, on the other hand, is what Hart told the personnel representative:

"Say, I think you should be in on this. My dear little friend Bing is heading himself into a showdown with me. Recently it was brought to my attention that Bing has been taking double and triple setup time for panels which he is actually inspecting at one time. In effect, that's cheating, and I've called him down on it several times before. A few days ago it was brought to my attention again, and so this time I really let him have it in no uncertain terms. He's been getting away with this for too long and I'm going to put an end to it once and for all. I know he didn't like my calling him on it because a few hours later he had the union representative breathing down my back. Well, anyway, I let them both know I'll not tolerate the practice any longer, and I let Bing know that if he continues to do this kind of thing, I'm going to take official action with my boss to have the guy fired or penalized somehow. This kind of thing has to be curbed. Actually, I'm inclined to think the guy's mentally deficient, because talking to him has actually no meaning to him whatsoever. I've tried just about every approach to jar some sense into that guy's head, and I've just about given it up as a bad deal.

"I don't know what it is about the guy, but I think he's harboring some deep feelings against me. For what, I don't know, because I've tried to handle that bird with kid gloves. But his whole attitude around here on the job is one of indifference, and he certainly isn't a good influence on the rest of my group. Frankly, I think he purposely tries to agitate them against me at times, too. It seems to me he may be suffering from illusions of grandeur, because all he does all day long is sit over there and croon his fool head off. Thinks he's a Frank Sinatra! No kidding! I understand he takes singing lessons and he's working with some of the local bands in the city. All of which is o. k. by me; but when his outside interests start interfering with his efficiency on the job, then I've got to start paying closer attention to the situation. For this reason I've been keeping my eye on that bird and if he steps out of line any more, he and I are going to part ways.

"You know there's an old saying, 'You can't make a purse out of a sow's ear.' The guy is simply unscrupulous. He feels no obligation to do a real day's work. Yet I know the guy can do a good job, because for a long time he did. But in recent months he's slipped, for some reason, and his whole attitude on the job has changed. Why, it's even getting to the point now where I think he's inducing other employees to 'goof off' a few minutes before the lunch whistle and go down to the washroom and clean up on company time. I've called him on it several times, but words just don't seem to make any lasting impression on him. Well, if he keeps it up much longer, he's going to find himself on the way out. He's asked me for a transfer, so I know he wants to go. But I didn't give him an answer when he asked me, because I was steaming mad at the time, and I may have told him to go somewhere else."

VIEWS OF MISUNDERSTANDING

So much for the case. Let me start with the simplest but the toughest question first: "What is going on here?" I think most of us would agree that what seems to be going on is some misunderstanding between Hart and Bing. But no sooner do we try to represent to ourselves the nature of this misunderstanding than a flood of different theories appear. Let me discuss briefly five very common ways of representing this misunderstanding: (1) as a difference of opinion resolvable by common sense, by simply referring to the facts; (2) as a clash of personalities; (3) as a conflict of social roles; (4) as a struggle for power; and (5) as a breakdown in communication. There are, of course, other theories too—for example, those of the interactionists, the field theory of Kurt Lewin, and even the widely held views of Adam Smith or Karl Marx. But for our purposes here the five I have mentioned will suffice.

Common sense

For the advocates of common sense—the first theory, though most of them would not call it that—the situation resolves itself quickly:

> Either Hart is right or Bing is right. Since both parties cannot be right, it follows that if Hart is right, then Bing is wrong; or if Bing is right, then Hart is wrong. Either Bing should or should not be singing on the job, carrying two or three panels at a time and charging double or triple setup time, and so on.

"Let us get these facts settled first," say the common-sense advocates. "Once ascertained, the problem is easily settled. Once we know who is doing what he should not be doing, then all we have to do is to get this person to do what he should be doing. It's as simple as that."

But is it? Let us look again at our case. Let us note that there are no differences of opinion between Hart and Bing about some matters. For example both would agree that Bing is taking double or triple setup time when he carries his panels two or three at a time to his bench for inspection. Both would agree that Bing sings on the job and occasionally leaves his work place a bit early for lunch.

Where they differ is in the way each *perceives* these activities. Hart perceives Bing's activities as "cheating," "suffering from illusions of grandeur," "thinking he is Frank Sinatra," "interfering with Bing's efficiency as well as the efficiency of other workers," "disturbing the other workers," "inducing them to goof off," and "influencing them against [Hart]." To Bing, on the other hand, these activities are "perfectly legal," "something we've always been doing," "something that is not disturbing the other workers," and so forth.

Among these many different conflicting claims and different perceptions, what are the facts? Many of these evaluations refer to personal and social standards of conduct for which the company has no explicit rules. Even in the case of taking double and triple setup time, there are probably no clear rules, because when the industrial engineer set the standards for the job, he did not envisage the possibility of a worker doing what Bing is now doing and which, according to Bing, is a time-saving device.

But we can waste effort on this question. For, even if it were clear that Hart is not exploring the situation, that he is not getting these important facts or rules which would settle who is right and who is wrong, it would still be true that, so far as Hart is concerned, he *knows* who is right and who is wrong. And because he *knows*, he has no reason to question the assumptions he is making about Bing's behavior.

Now this is very likely to happen in the case of advocates of the common-sense theory. Significantly, Hart himself is a good advocate of it. Does this have anything to do with the fact that he is not being very successful in getting Bing to do what he should be doing? Let us postpone this question for future consideration.

Clash of personalities

For the second school of thought, what is going on between Hart and Bing can be viewed essentially as a clash of personalities—an interaction between two particular personality structures. According to this view, what is going on cannot be known in detail until much more information about these different personality structures is secured. Hence we can only speculate that what is going on may be something of this order:

> Neither Hart nor Bing feels too sure of himself, and each seems to be suffering from feelings of inadequacy or inferiority. Being unable to recognize, admit, or accept these feelings, however, each one perceives the behavior of the other as a personal attack upon himself. When a person feels he is being attacked, he feels strongly the need to defend himself. This, then, is essentially what is taking place between Hart and Bing. Because of his feelings of inferiority, each one is defending himself against what he perceives to be an attack upon himself as a person. In psychology, the feelings of each man are conceived as being rooted somehow in his "personality."

That this theory is pointing to some very important phenomena can hardly be questioned. Certainly I will not argue its validity. I am only concerned with what it is telling us and what follows from it. As I understand it, this theory says that neither Hart nor Bing is aware of his own feelings of inadequacy and defense mechanisms. These are the important facts that each is ignoring. From this it follows that there is little hope of correcting the misunderstanding without helping Bing and Hart to become aware of these feelings and of their need to defend against them. Short of this, the solution lies in transferring Bing to a supervisor whose personality will be more compatible with Bing's and in giving Hart a worker whose personality will be more compatible with Hart's.

Conflict of social roles

Let us look at the third explanation. Instead of viewing the misunderstanding as an interaction between two individual personality units, it can also be viewed as an interaction between two social roles:

> With the promotion of Hart to the position of a supervisor of a group in which he had been formerly a worker, a system of reciprocal expectancies has been disturbed. Bing is expecting Hart to behave toward him in the same way Hart did when Hart was a worker; but by telling Bing to stop "crooning his fool head off," for example, Hart is not behaving in accordance with the role of a friend. Similarly, Hart, as the newly appointed supervisor, is expecting that Bing should do what he tells Bing to do, but by singing Bing is not behaving in accordance with the customary role of the worker.

According to this theory, as any recent textbook on sociology will explain, when two actors in a relationship reach differing definitions of the situation, misunderstanding is likely to arise. Presumably this is what is happening between Hart and Bing. The role-expectation pattern has been disturbed. Bing views his singing as variant but permissive; Hart views it as deviant. From these differing definitions of what each other's role should be misunderstanding results. According to this view, it will take time for their new relationship to work out. In time Bing will learn what to expect from Hart now that Hart is his supervisor. Also in time Hart will define better his role vis-à-vis Bing.

Struggle for power

The fourth way of representing what is going on between Hart and Bing would be in terms of such abstractions as "authority" and "power":

> When Bing refuses to stop singing on the job when Hart tells him to, Bing is being disobedient to the commands or orders of a holder of power. When this occurs, Hart, who according to this theory is a

"power holder," has the right to exercise or apply sanctions, such as dismissal or transfer. But the threat to exercise these sanctions does not seem to be too effective in getting Bing to stop, because Bing is a member of the union, which also has power and the right to apply sanctions. By going to his union representative, Bing can bring this power structure into play.

In other words, what is going on in the case is not merely an interaction between two individual or social personalities; it is also struggle between two kinds of institutionalized power. It is an issue between the management and the union which may even precipitate a strike. Management will charge that it cannot have workers in the plant who are disobedient to the orders of their foremen. The union will charge that Bing is merely introducing a labor-saving device which the foreman has not enough sense to recognize. To avoid things getting to this stage, the struggle-for-power theory would recommend that if Hart and Bing between them cannot settle their differences, they should refer them to the grievance machinery set up for this purpose by union and management.

According to this theory, Hart got into trouble not because he had authority but because when he tried to exercise it and was unsuccessful, he lost it. Authority ceases to exist when it cannot be exercised successfully.[2]

Breakdown in communication

The fifth way of stating what is going on would be to say that Hart and Bing think they are talking about the same things when in fact they are not:

> Hart assumes he understands what Bing is doing and saying; Bing assumes he understands what Hart is doing and saying. In fact, neither assumption holds. From this "uncritical assumption of understanding," misunderstanding arises.
>
> Thus, when Hart tells Bing to stop "crooning his fool head off," Bing assumes that Hart is talking about Bing's singing when Hart may in fact be talking about his difficulties in maintaining his position as formal leader of the group. Hart assumes that Bing is singing deliberately to flaunt his authority, whereas in Bing's mind singing may be a way of relating himself to people and of maintaining his conceptions of himself.[3]

According to this theory, Hart and Bing are not on the same wave length, and as a result communication bypassing occurs. Each is

---

[2] For an elaboration of this view see Robert Bierstedt, "An Analysis of Social Power," *The American Sociological Review* (December, 1950), p. 730.

[3] For an analysis of this theory see Wendell Johnson, "The Fateful Process of Mr. A Talking to Mr. B," *Harvard Business Review* (January-February, 1953), p. 49.

behaving in accordance with the reality as he perceives it to be, but neither is aware of the assumptions that underlie his perceptions. Their misunderstandings arise as a result.

This theory strikes a new note that I should like to explore further.

Roots of Misunderstanding

So far our theories have explained well why there is misunderstanding and conflict; they have not shown so clearly how any new behavior patterns on the part of Hart or Bing or both can emerge or be encouraged to emerge from the present ones. In them we have found no responsible actor, no learner, and no practitioner of a skill.

Could it be that what is going on between Hart and Bing results also in part from the fact that nobody is taking any responsibility for what is going on? May we not assume that people can learn through experience how to determine their relationships with each other as well as be determined by them? Let us therefore look at these interpersonal proceedings from the point of view of a person who is responsibly involved in them and who may be capable of learning something from them. I shall start with Hart and raise the questions: (1) "What is Hart doing to contribute to misunderstanding?" (2) "What, if anything, might he learn to do differently to minimize this effect?"

From now on I shall be chiefly concerned with Hart, not because I think Hart is any more or less guilty than Bing of creating misunderstanding, but because I wish to develop a useful way of thinking for persons in a position of responsibility like Hart. This way of thinking, I hope, will not be in conflict with our other theories. It will merely spell out what a supervisor must learn if he is to take into account the significant processes which these other theories say have been going on.

So, instead of viewing Hart in his dealings with Bing as a supervisor expressing his personality, playing a social role, or exercising power, let us view him as a practitioner of a skill of communication. Let us see what skills, if any, he is using. And if we find, as I fear we may, that he has not been too skillful, let us see if he can learn to become a more skillful practitioner, and how this can be done.

Hart's trouble

When we ask ourselves what Hart is doing to facilitate misunderstanding, we meet again a number of different theories. Although I am not sure that these theories are pointing to different things, each uses a slightly different terminology, so I shall state them separately:

1. *Hart is making value judgments*—According to one view, the biggest block to personal communication arises from the fact that Hart is making value judgments of Bing from Hart's point of view. Hart's tendency to evaluate is what gets him into trouble. Not only is he evaluating Bing, but he is trying to get Bing to accept his evaluation as the only and proper one. It is this orientation that angers Bing and makes him feel misunderstood.[4]

2. *Hart is not listening*—According to another and not too different view, Hart gets into trouble because he is not listening to Bing's feelings. Because he is not paying attention to Bing's feelings, he is not responding to them as such. Instead, we find him responding to the effect of Bing's feelings upon his own. Not only is he ignoring Bing's feelings, but also he is ignoring the effect of what he is saying upon them. This kind of behavior also leads to Bing's feelings of being misunderstood.[5]

3. *Hart is assuming things that may not be so*—Still another point of view says that Hart is getting into trouble because he is making assumptions about Bing's behavior that may not be so. Hart is confusing what he sees with what he assumes and feels.

When Hart sees Bing leaving early for lunch, for example, he assumes that Bing is doing this deliberately, intentionally, and personally to discredit him and to test his authority. Because of this assumption he feels angry and his feelings of anger reinforce his assumption. Now if Bing's going to lunch a few minutes early is such an attempt to discredit him, then Hart's anger and his attempt to retaliate make sense. But if he starts with this assumption and makes no attempt to check it, then his anger makes less sense. Hart may be assuming something that is not so.

Again, Hart shows he may be making assumptions that are not so by the way he talks in trying to get Bing to stop singing at work or to stop inspecting panels two or three at a time. When he uses phrases like "crooning your fool head off" and "cheating the company," is he not assuming that Bing should feel about these activities in the same way that he himself does? And if Bing does not feel this way, then obviously, in Hart's view, Bing must be a "fool," "defective," or a "sow's ear." To Hart, Bing *is* a sow's ear. And how does one feel toward a sow's ear? Toward such an entity one must feel (by definition) helpless and hopeless. Note that Hart's assumptions, perceptions, and feelings are of a piece; each re-inforces the other to make one total evaluation.

In short, all of Hart's evaluations are suspect because he confuses what he sees with what he assumes and feels. As a result, there is no way for Hart to take another look at the situation. How can Hart check his evaluations when he is not aware that he is making them? By treating inferences as facts, there is no way for him to explore the assumptions, feelings, and perceptions that underlie his evaluations.[6] For Hart, Bing *is* the way he perceives Bing to be. There is no way for

---

[4] See Carl R. Rogers and F. J. Roethlisberger, "Barriers and Gateways to Communication," *Harvard Business Review* (July-August, 1952), pp. 46-50.

[5] Ibid., pp. 50-52.

[6] For a fuller explanation see Irving Lee, *How to Talk with People* (New York: Harper & Brothers, 1953).

him to say that "because of the assumptions I make and because of the way I feel, I perceive Bing in this way."

4. *Hart is making his false assumptions come true*—A fourth theory emphasizes still another point. This theory says that the very kind of misevaluations which our last theory says Hart is guilty of must provoke *ipso facto* the very kind of behavior on the part of Bing of which Hart disapproves.[7] In other words, Hart is getting into trouble because, by his behavior, he is making his assumptive world come true.

Let us examine this theory first by looking at the effect of Hart's behavior on Bing. Very clearly Bing does not like it. Bing tells us that when Hart behaves in the way Hart does, he feels misunderstood, humiliated, and treated like a child. These feelings give grounds to his perception of Hart as . . . , "a school teacher" pulling "kid stuff" on him. These perceptions in turn will tend to make Bing behave in the way that will coincide more and more with Hart's original untested assumptions about Bing's behavior. Feeling like a "marked man," Bing will behave more and more like a "sow's ear." Although he will try to "keep his nose clean," he will "slip it to [Hart], but good" whenever he gets the chance.

That this kind of misevaluation on the part of Hart will tend to produce this kind of behavior on the part of Bing is, according to this view, a fact of common experience. To explain it one does not have to assume any peculiar personality structure on the part of Bing—an undue sensitivity to criticism, defensiveness, or feeling of inferiority. All one has to assume is an individual personality with a need to maintain its individuality. Therefore, any attempts on the part of Hart which will be perceived by Bing as an attempt to deny his individual differences will be resisted. What Hart says about Bing is, from Bing's point of view, exactly what is *not*. Bing *is* what he is from his own frame of reference and from the point of view of his own feelings, background, and situation. Bing *is* what he assumes, feels, and perceives himself to be. And this is just what Hart's behavior is denying.

In spite of the different terminology and emphasis of these theories, they all seem to point to certain uniformities in the interpersonal proceedings of Hart and Bing which should be taken into account regardless of the actors' particular personalities or social roles. For the misunderstandings that arise, Hart and Bing are not to blame; the trouble resides in the process of interpersonal communication itself.

ADMINISTRATIVE SKILLS

Let us turn now to the second question: What might Hart learn to do differently in order to minimize the misunderstandings between him and Bing? I also want to consider briefly the question of what difference to Bing a slight difference in the behavior of Hart might make.

---

[7] For example, see Hadley Cantril, *The Why of Man's Experience* (New York: The Macmillan Company, 1950).

Problem of involvement

So far it would seem as if we had made Hart the villain in the piece. But let us remember that although Hart has been intellectually and emotionally involved in what has been going on, he has not been aware of this involvement. All of our theories have implied this. Hart's ego has been involved; his actual group memberships have been involved; his reference groups have been involved; his feelings, assumptions, and perceptions have been involved—but Hart is not aware of it. If any new behavior on the part of Hart is to emerge —and *all* our theories would agree to this—Hart must in some sense become aware of and recognize this involvement. Without such an awareness there can be no re-evaluation or no change in perception. And without such a change no learning can take place.

How can this change be accomplished? Some theories would seem to imply that misunderstanding will be minimized only when Hart *logically understands* the nature of his involvement with Bing. Hart will learn to evaluate Bing more properly only when he understands better the personality structures of himself and Bing and the social system of which they are a part. Only by the logical understanding and critical probing of his and Bing's feelings of inadequacy and defense mechanisms can he make a proper evaluation and bring about any real change in his behavior.

But there is another view. It holds that logical understanding is not of the first importance. Rather, misunderstanding will be minimized when Hart learns to *recognize and accept* responsibility for his involvement. Better understanding will be achieved when Hart learns to recognize and accept his own and Bing's individual differences, when he learns to recognize and accept Bing's feelings as being different from his own, and when as a result he can allow Bing to express his feelings and differences and listen to them.[8]

Let me explore this second theory further, for it suggests that Hart might possibly learn to do a better job without having to become a professional social scientist or be psychoanalyzed. Moreover, it coincides with some facts of common experience.

How can Hart be helped?

Some administrators have achieved the insights of the second theory through the school of "hard knocks" rather than through the help of books or by being psychoanalyzed. So should there not be simple skills which Hart can be taught, which he can learn and

---

[8] For a fuller explanation see Carl R. Rogers, *Client-Centered Therapy* (Boston: Houghton Mifflin Company, 1953).

practice, and which would help him to recognize and accept his involvement and to deal with it better?

Now it may be that Hart, because of certain personal deficiencies, is not able to recognize or accept his own feelings—let alone Bing's. That this holds for some supervisors goes without question. But does it apply to all? I do not think so, nor do I think it applies to Hart. Is it not possible that some supervisors may not be able to do these things because they have never learned how to do them?

The fact is, if our analysis up to this point is sound, that Hart does not get into trouble because he feels hopeless and helpless in the face of a worker who sings on the job, leaves early for lunch, and so on, and who refuses to stop doing these things when Hart tells him to. Any one of us who has had to deal with a worker behaving like Bing will recognize and remember feelings of inadequacy like Hart's only too well. We do not need to have very peculiar or special personality structures to have such feelings. Rather, Hart's trouble is that he assumes, and no doubt has been told too often, that he should *not* have feelings of inadequacy. It resides in the fact that he has not developed or been given a method or skill for dealing with them. As a result, these feelings are denied and appear in the form of an attribute of Bing—"a sow's ear."

In other words, I am suggesting that Hart gets into trouble partly because no one has assured him that it is normal and natural—in fact, inevitable—that he should have some feelings of inadequacy; that he cannot and *should* not try to escape from them. No one has helped him to develop a method of dealing with his own feelings and the feelings of Bing. No one has listened to him or helped him to learn to listen to others. No one has helped him to recognize the effect of his behavior on others. No one has helped him to become aware of his assumptions and feelings and how they affect the evaluations he makes.

Instead, too many training courses have told Hart what an ideal supervisor should be and how an ideal supervisor should behave. Both explicit and implicit in most of the instruction he receives is the assumption that an ideal supervisor should not become emotionally involved in his dealings with people. He should remain aloof, be objective, and deny or get rid of his feelings. But this goes against the facts of his immediate experience; it goes against everything upon which, according to our theories, his growth and development depend. Indeed, to "behave responsibly" and be "mature" in the way he is instructed to, without becoming emotionally committed, would be, to use the *New Yorker's* phrase, "the trick of the week!"

Is it any wonder, therefore, that Hart remains immature—socially, intellectually, and emotionally? He gets no understanding of how these frustrations and misunderstandings must inevitably arise from his dealings with others; he gets no help on how to deal with them when they do arise. He probably has had many training courses which told him how to recognize and deal with workers who are sow's ears. He probably has had no training course which helped him to see how his assumptions and feelings would tend to produce sow's ears by the bushel. He has not been helped to see how this surplus of sow's ears in modern industry might be diminished through the conscious practice of a skill. Thus he has not even been allowed to become intellectually involved and intrigued in the most important problem of his job. Yet there *are* training courses designed for just such a purpose, and they have worked successfully.[9]

Conclusion

Am I indulging in wishful thinking when I believe that there are some simple skills of communication that can be taught, learned, and practiced which might help to diminish misunderstanding? To me it is this possibility which the recent findings of general semantics and human relations are suggesting. They suggest that although man is determined by the complex relationships of which he is a part, nevertheless he is also in some small part a determiner of these relationships. Once he learns what he cannot do, he is ready to learn what little he can do. And what a tremendous difference to himself and to others the little that he can do—listening with understanding, for example—can make!

Once he can accept his limitations and the limitations of others, he can begin to learn to behave more skillfully with regard to the milieu in which he finds himself. He can begin to learn that misunderstanding can be diminished—not banished—by the slow, patient, laborious practice of a skill.

But we can expect too much from this possibility, so let me conclude by sounding two notes of caution:

(1) Although these skills of communication of which I am speaking deal in part with words, they are not in themselves words, nor is the territory to which they apply made up of words. It follows, then, that no verbal statement about these skills, however accurate, can act as a substitute for them. They are not truly articulate and never can be.

---

[9] See Kenneth R. Andrews, "Executive Training by the Case Method," and F. J. Roethlisberger, "Training Supervisors in Human Relations," *Harvard Business Review*, September, 1951, p. 58 and p. 47.

Although transmissible to other persons, they are but slowly so and, even then, only with practice.

(2) Let us remember that these interpersonal proceedings between Hart and Bing, or A and B whoever they may be, are extremely complex. So far as I know, there exists no single body of concepts which as yet describes systematically and completely all the important processes that our separate theories have said are taking place and how they relate to each other. Let us therefore accept gracefully and not contentiously that these interpersonal proceedings, unlike the atom, have not been as yet "cracked" by social science. Only then can we as students of human behavior live up to our responsibility for making our knowledge fruitful in practice.

QUESTIONS

1. Explain each of the common ways of representing misunderstanding between people.
2. What is Hart doing to facilitate misunderstanding?
3. According to Roethlisberger, Hart and Bing are not to blame for the misunderstandings that arise. Why? Do you agree?
4. What might Hart learn to do differently to minimize the misunderstanding between him and Bing?
5. What cautions must be observed in developing administrative skill in communication?

BASIC PSYCHOLOGICAL FACTORS
IN COMMUNICATION *

T. M. Higham

A celebrated authority on Canon law and mediaeval Universities, Dr. Hastings Rashdall, was one of those who could ride, but not understand a bicycle. One day, for example, having had a puncture in his front tyre, he was found vigorously pumping up the back one; when a passer-by pointed this out to him, he remarked, "What? Do they not communicate?" I sometimes wonder whether, in our present-day eagerness to "put people in the picture," we do not behave rather like Dr. Rashdall, strenuously pumping in information at one end of a firm, in the hopeful expectation that it will somehow find its way to the other. Perhaps we too ride, but cannot understand.

In the last few years, a great deal has been written on this topic of "communications," mainly to the effect that communication must be "two-way," a comment of unstartling originality, as anyone familiar with the derivation of the word must realise. Today you can hardly open one of the many journals, English or American, in the personnel field, without finding some article on the subject, or some review of the latest authoritative work on it; there is even a "Communications Training Centre" in existence, and one firm, at any rate, now has its "Communications Manager"; Technical Colleges, Evening Institutes and other organisations run courses in clear expression, and the art of speaking or writing; you can be trained in running a meeting or leading a conference. Training Officers and others make increased use of visual and other aids, as a help in putting their teaching across; industries make use of suggestion schemes, joint consultative committees, broadcast address systems and similar devices to try to ensure that information reaches to all levels in the business and is fed back again to the top. But, as P. H. Cook [1] (1951) has said:

> "There is as yet no firmly-established theory of communication which can provide guiding principles guaranteeing that effective communications will be achieved. As a result, much communication practice is dependent on unconfirmed hypotheses, personal hunches and techniques and tricks of doubtful merit."

* From *Occupational Psychology*, Vol. 31, No. 1 (January, 1957), pp. 1-10. Reprinted with permission.
[1] P. H. Cook, *The Productivity Team Technique* (London: Tavistock Institute of Human Relations, 1951).

The nearest approach to a theory of communications has probably come from students of cybernetics and information theory. The new science of "Communication Engineering," as Professor Meredith [2] (1955) pointed out recently, is so highly developed that "we are strongly tempted to use it as a ready-made frame of reference, and to fit all our ideas about communication into this frame." That I believe to be a mistake—not so much because it is difficult to see what relevance a man-made machine has in considering the problems of a God-made man, but rather because, in everyday life, at home, in industry, in social life generally, the problems of communication (that is, of the transmission of ideas and attitudes) between people and groups are not those which can be solved, or even greatly understood, by means of a knowledge of information theory. Until such time as a machine is developed which can not only interpret information, but also convey its like or dislike of its informant, I believe we should do well to stick to our knowledge of human and animal psychology in trying to understand the problems and workings of communication between individuals and groups.

In most of the studies of communication between individuals and groups which I have come across, scant recognition is given to what is, perhaps, the one fact which we do know from experience about it— that if a person dislikes or mistrusts us, he is not likely to be receptive to what we have to say, and his version of our words is likely to be distorted by his personal opinions of us, or his preconceived notions about our motives. For that reason a study of communication could well begin with an examination of the problems of the reception of information—that process by which we perceive what is said against a background of who says it. It is there that the work of animal psychologists, and the many experimental studies of perception, can help us.

The experiments of Schelderup-Ebbe [3] (1935) with hens, Maslow [4] (1936) with apes, and Lorenz [5] with dogs have shown clearly that a sizing-up process goes on when two animals meet, which subsequently merges into a dominance-submission relationship. Of these, the most vivid is probably Lorenz's description of the encounter of two adult male dogs.

---

[2] G. P. Meredith, "The Flow of Information," *Occupational Psychology*, Vol. 29, 1955, pp. 99-103.

[3] T. Schelderup-Ebbe, "The Social Behaviour of Birds," in C. Murchison, *A Handbook of Social Psychology* (Worcester: Clark University Press, 1935).

[4] A. H. Maslow, "The Dominance Drive as a Determiner of the Social and Sexual Behaviour of Infra Human Primates I-IV," *Journal of Genetic Psychology*, Vols. 48 and 49, 1936.

[5] K. Lorenz, *Man Meets Dog* (London: Methuen, 1954).

"Two adult male dogs meet in the street. Stiff-legged, with tails erect and hair on end, they pace toward each other. The nearer they approach, the stiffer, higher and more ruffled they appear, their advance becomes slower and slower. . . . They do not make their encounter head to head, front against front, but make as though to pass each other, only stopping when they stand at last flank to flank, head to tail, in close juxtaposition. Then a strict ceremonial demands that each should sniff the hind regions of the other. Should one of the dogs be overcome with fear at this juncture, down goes his tail between his legs and he jumps with a quick, flexible twist, wheeling at an angle of 180 degrees, thus modestly retracting his former offer to be smelt. Should the two dogs remain in an attitude of self-display, carrying their tails as rigid as standards, then the sniffing process may be of a long protracted nature. All may be solved amicably and there is still the chance that first one tail and then another may begin to wag with small but rapidly increasing beats and then this nerve-racking situation may develop into nothing worse than a cheerful canine romp."

Apart from the fact that such encounters take place primarily on a symbolic level, is the encounter between two humans so very different? When two individuals meet for the first time, there is usually a rather more refined process of 'sniffing over'—an interchange of neutral information (the weather, for example, or a search for mutual acquaintances) which serves the same purpose. An attempt to set up a dominance-submission relationship also emerges on some occasions, as Maslow [6] (1937) has shown. Pear [7] (1955) has explored with skill the part played by voice and social differences in the same situation. The fact that this process may be going on below the level of consciousness is a further factor: there are still, for example, some managers who sit with their backs to the light, in a chair just a little higher than that of their visitors, and continue to write after someone enters their office; but luckily their numbers are dwindling. But these, unlike the Admiral's gold braid and the peacock's tail, are more often than not unconscious ways of conveying an impression of importance. None the less, their effect on recipients is much the same.

What has not yet been satisfactorily demonstrated is the opposite of that—the approach or manner which makes for confidence and an easy reception. If there are mannerisms which tend to put the recipients of information in a subordinate position, by conveying an attitude of superiority, are there other ways in which an atmosphere of trust and confidence can be built up without loss of status by either party?

---

[6] A. H. Maslow, "Dominance-feeling, Behavior and Status," *Psychological Review*, Vol. 44, 1937, pp. 404-429.
[7] T. H. Pear, *English Social Differences* (London: Allen and Unwin, 1955).

If we recall the two dogs sniffing each other over, I believe we can say that such a situation is possible—and in fact many well-trained interviewers and counsellors are creating such a situation every day. Every interviewer is taught to "put the candidate at his ease"—in other words to make him receptive, whether it be to questions about himself or to advice and guidance. The exact ways in which this is done vary, but the essential part has been well put by Oldfield [8] (1941):

> "The adoption of an appropriate *general attitude* at the outset of the interview is a matter of greater importance than the maintenance of an effort to *behave* appropriately throughout its course. As an eminent psychologist remarked apropos this question, 'each interview is a world to itself. One hour I am a schoolmaster, the next a parson'."

It seems clear that to ensure good reception, you must create the right atmosphere. This is, perhaps, the one pre-requisite for effective communication. Where it does not exist, communication will be difficult, and all that is said is likely to be distorted. A further complication is that two people, or two groups, rarely if ever meet with what is called an "open mind." Each comes together, instead, with pre-conceived ideas about the other, and about the other's preconceived ideas about them.

During the preliminary "sniffing over," any small clues that can be fitted into the pre-existing picture will be readily grasped. The ingenious experiments of Asch [9] (1946) demonstrate this point neatly. It will be remembered that he read two lists of personality traits to two different groups of people. The first group's list was "Kind, Wise, Honest, Calm, Strong." The second group's list was "Cruel, Shrewd, Unscrupulous, Calm, Strong." The last two epithets in both lists were the same. After hearing the lists, separately, the two groups were told, "Suppose you had to describe this person in the same manner, but without using the terms you heard, what other terms would you use?" The first group, who heard the list "Kind, Wise, Honest, Calm, Strong," gave the following synonyms for "calm"—soothing, peaceful, gentle, tolerant, mild-mannered. But the second group, who heard "Cruel, Shrewd, Unscrupulous, Calm, Strong," produce synonyms for "calm" like cold, frigid, calculating. Similar results were got from the two groups with synonyms for "strong"—the first group listing such terms as fearless, helpful, just, forceful; the second group giving ruthless, overbearing, hard, inflexible, dominant. Both groups on

---

[8] R. C. Oldfield, *The Psychology of the Interview* (London: Methuen, 1941).
[9] S. E. Asch, "Forming Impressions of Personality," *Journal of Abnormal and Social Psychology*, Vol. 41, 1946, pp. 258-290.

hearing the first few epithets, got a fixed idea about the sort of person described; the later terms were merely fitted into the existing pattern.

This is not merely an academic point, illustrated by carefully controlled laboratory experiments; it is a very real factor in communication, simply because "the past in the worker's mind," as Zweig [10] (1952) calls it, is so strong and potent a factor in his reactions. The truth of that is seen in the study made recently by the Acton Society Trust [11] (1952) of communications in the coal mining industry. In an attempt to raise the output of coal, many attempts were made to tell the miners why a higher output was necessary, pamphlets, magazines, even a personal letter from the then Prime Minister, Mr. Attlee, were employed. But, as the report makes clear:

> "The mere provision of information . . . does not reduce proneness to prejudice . . . it does not succeed in modifying the underlying attitude of mistrust upon which credulity seems to be based."

In a later report, *Management under Nationalisation*, the Trust [12] (1953) quoted the comment of an Area Manager in the Coal Industry, pointing out that he:

> "can never forget that the (Coal) Board's biggest headache is the attitude of the miners and their misconceptions about the work the Board and its staff perform, and, perhaps most important, about the need for economic efficiency."

Then follows the comment of the Area General Manager:

> "We have issued booklets, but nobody bothered to read them. We had a few questions when we started joint consultative committees, but even these have now petered out. We have tried to put explanations into the minutes and put them up on the notice-board, but nobody bothered to read them. It is no use trying to put it over at the lodge meetings of the union, for only a few miners attend them. This is really our major difficulty, how to put this information across and how to rid the minds of the men of misconceptions."

The pathetic notion that you can improve communications by giving more and better information should surely be allowed to die a natural death; you will not get any reception if you are not trusted; but if relations are good, then there is a good chance that what you say will be received, and that you will get co-operation in return.

---

[10] F. Zweig, *The British Worker* (London: Penguin Books, 1952).
[11] Acton Society Trust, *The Worker's Point of View* (London: Acton Society Trust, 1952).
[12] Acton Society Trust, *Management under Nationalisation* (London: Acton Society Trust, 1953).

But even where trust and mutual confidence do exist, that tendency to come to an interview, meeting or conference with preconceived notions is still found, and we cannot afford to forget that the same situation is almost always seen in different ways by different people, depending on their personal capacities, inclinations and background. Zangwill's [13] (1937) experiment on "Aufgabe" showed the importance of that. Two groups of subjects were shown, separately, a vague, ill-determined ink-blot. They were not told what it represented, but one group was told that it might be like an animal; and the second group was told that it might resemble a landscape. Both groups drew and described what they had seen. The first group all drew cats, rabbits, or similar animals, while the second group drew mountains and hills. The same stimulus confronted both groups, but their preconceived ideas about it determined their reactions to it.

I believe, therefore, that in trying to understand human communication, we would be well advised to study the basic mental processes that underlie so much of everyday human behaviour—the study of perception in particular, and the many experiments on "Aufgabe" and attitude formation.

But further problems arise. Suppose that a person to whom we wish to communicate something has sniffed us over, asking unconsciously, "Is he friendly, can I trust him?", and decided that he is disposed to listen to us, we still need to know whether what we say will be understood, and if so, whether, at a later date, it will be recalled or repeated accurately. So I would suggest that comprehension and recall are legitimate subjects for research and study when considering human communications.

Both of these, as it happens, have been studied fully in recent years. I should like, therefore, only to point out a few of the researches or experiments which seem to me to throw light on how we succeed or fail in comprehending information and recalling it accurately.

Bartlett [14] (1951) has suggested that one of the chief functions of the mind, when it is active, is "filling up gaps"; that is, it is constantly trying to link new material into the pattern of older material, in order to make it meaningful. Our minds seem to prefer the simple and regular to the complex and irregular, and to organise what is received into tidy, meaningful bundles. That is why it is so difficult

[13] O. L. Zangwill, "A Study of the Significance of Attitude in Recognition," *British Journal of Psychology*, Vol. 28, 1937, pp. 12-17.
[14] F. C. Bartlett, *The Mind at Work and Play* (London: Allen and Unwin, 1951).

to get a new idea across; for a new idea has to be fitted into the existing structure in the mind, and it is often quite a struggle to do so. A simple demonstration of that difficulty was given by Wertheimer; to give you an example of it, suppose you look at these four words:

MAN   TABLE   KNIFE   CLOTH

You can, without much difficulty, form some kind of mental picture out of them. If I add the word TROLLEY, you can probably fit that in quite easily to your already established picture. But if I now add the words:

SURGEON   BLOOD   ANAESTHETIC

you will probably have a few puzzled moments before you are able to reorganise the picture in your mind. The meaning of the isolated words changes as the pattern alters, so that the table, once laid for a meal, with a knife handy for cutting a cake, becomes an operating table, with the knife poised over the man who a few moments earlier was sitting down to his tea.

Our mental habits persist and may help or hinder us; they will only do the former if we can link what we have to say on to what our listeners already know; for in that way, the new can be assimilated to the old.

But there is more to comprehension than mental habits; the interest of the subject matter and our own intelligence are also involved. Some idea of the extent of these factors can be seen in two very detailed and careful experiments carried out by the BBC Audience Research Department [15] (1950, 1951, 1952).

The first of these researches was an attempt to assess the intelligibility of a series of Forces Educational Broadcasts; the second was concerned with the comprehensibility of the five minute programme "Topic for Tonight" which follows the 10 o'clock news. What was particularly striking about both these researches was that they demonstrated that understanding was largely based on intellectual capacity—not perhaps a very new finding, but an interesting one because it showed the extent to which comprehension relies on intelligence. To quote from the report:

---

[15] P. E. Vernon, *An Investigation into the Intelligibility of Broadcast Talks*, Audience Research Department Report (London: British Broadcasting Corporation, 1950); R. Silvey, "The Intelligibilty of Broadcast Talks," *Public Opinion Quarterly* (Summer, 1951); W. A. Belson, *An Inquiry into the Comprehensibility of "Topic for Tonight,"* Audience Research Department Report (London: British Broadcasting Corporation, 1952).

"It would seem that the talk which is couched at a level of difficulty appropriate to the top third of the population can rarely convey much to people of even average intelligence and little or nothing to the backward quarter (of the population)."

But something else came out of the first research too; that was the finding that, apart from intellectual capacity, comprehension was "profoundly influenced by the extent to which (people) are interested in the subject, or have their interest in it aroused. The greater the listeners' interest, the greater their understanding is likely to be, and vice versa." This factor of interestingness was more important for intelligibility than any factor of style, language, and delivery. Certainly, such factors as limiting the number of main points, providing clear summaries, a lucid and lively style, concrete treatment, and the illustration of abstract points all *make for* intelligibility—the research proved that—but they do not *guarantee* intelligibility; they only come into play if the talk is interesting in the first place.

Although these studies are of great value in showing just how complicated a matter it is to get information across that will be remembered with any accuracy, a broadcast talk is not the same as face-to-face contact; there are, unfortunately, to my knowledge, no scientific studies of the intelligibility of personal talks to an audience as compared with broadcast talks. The nearest approach to such an investigation is the series of experiments conducted by Lewin [16] (1947) on the respective values of lectures and group discussions in changing food habits. It will be remembered that the latter proved far more effective because the audience participated in a decision. They were, in fact, "ego-involved." I should like to suggest that it is that factor of ego-involvement which lies behind the importance of interest in the subject matter of a talk, which was so well shown in the BBC researches.

Some years ago, I carried out some experiments on the transmission of rumour (Higham,[17] 1951). The method I used was to get someone to recount a short tale to a second person, who repeated it to a third, and so on; each version of the story was recorded on a recording machine, so that a permanent record was available; by those means the successive reproductions could be anaylsed to see what changes had taken place in the narrative. I used different types of story and different groups of subjects; one day, quite by accident

[16] K. Lewin, "Frontiers in Group Dynamics (II)," *Human Relations*, Vol. 1 1947, pp. 143-153.
[17] T. M. Higham, "The Experimental Study of the Transmission of Rumour," *British Journal of Psychology (General Section)*, Vol. 42, 1951, pp. 42-55.

(as I must admit), I made up a short tale about a professor discussing the prospects of his students in their forthcoming examinations; I tried this out on just such a group of his students as might be involved in this sort of discussion. To my surprise, I found that reproduction of the story showed few changes and comparatively small loss of detail, whereas all the other stories produced many changes and a great loss of content with successive reproductions. Applying an appropriate statistical technique, I found that such a result was unlikely to have happened by chance. The explanation was that the students were personally involved in the story; it was about something that affected their interests; and for all they knew it might have been true, or a prophetic warning! Because of this personal interest they remembered it better.

Joint Consultation, particularly through Works' Councils, shows this sort of thing well: matters which management thinks of burning interest are passed by almost without comment; but if an announcement is made that the price of tea in the canteen is going up, discussion is animated and prolonged. People will show most interest in things which concern them personally, or which are linked to their basic needs; that is perhaps why discussion methods seem to be more successful in bringing about change than are formal lectures, for if you take part in a discussion you become involved in it, and it means more to you.

None the less, I think we would be unwise to neglect the importance of the personal factor even in the comprehension of information. For, as many will testify, a good speaker can arouse interest in his audience, even if he breaks every known rule of lecturing. Professor Meredith [18] (1950) has given an excellent example of this in a talk he gave some time ago:

"I am not a theologian, but I was once privileged to attend, at a weekend conference, a lecture by a professor of theology. It was twenty-five years ago and it is still vivid to me today. The subject was Amos, of whom I previously knew precisely nothing. By the end of the lecture I had not only a dynamic impression of the character and message of the prophet but also a clear and colourful picture of the contemporary economic, political, and social structure of the people of Israel. The professor used no notes. He padded round the room, with his hands behind his back, and wearing felt slippers. From time to time he raised one foot to scratch the calf of the other leg. Now and then he looked at one or other of us directly in the eyes, with a kind of challenging glare. At other times he gazed through the window into the extreme

[18] G. P. Meredith, "The Art of Lecturing," *British Medical Journal*, 26 August, 1950.

distance, as if looking at Palestine, and describing what he saw, taking our gaze with him. I recall that he pronounced Jahweh with the sort of sound one makes in clearing one's throat."

Later Professor Meredith gives his views on why the professor of theology, and other lecturers he had heard, succeeded in communicating to their listeners. He says:

> "You can wander about, you can indulge in irritating mannerisms, you can hum and haw, you can remain glued to a desk, you can twiddle your fingers, you can commit all the crimes on the statute book (the latter would make entertaining reading if someone would write it: 'The Deadly Sins of the Lecture Theatre'), and you can get away with all of them if only you have the one supreme virtue. What is that virtue? The name I would give it is *vitality*. This was the common factor in all my remembered lectures."

I suggested earlier that the recall of information was a part of the process of communication which could well be studied. Indeed it has been thoroughly explored, notably and perhaps primarily by Sir Frederic Bartlett [19] (1932) whose book *Remembering* is still the classic on that subject. Later work by Allport and Postman [20] (1948) and others on rumour has supported these earlier findings. The factors of interest and personal involvement, which I mentioned earlier, are important in recall, because we tend to remember better and more accurately those things in which we have been personally interested; but with matters less personal, or less interesting, our minds tend to transform what we have heard, until our final recollection may be quite different from what actually took place. This is an important factor in two way information, because if, for example, a Works' Council holds a meeting, it is attended by delegates from different sections of the organisation, who have to report back to their constituents; and it is in this reporting back that mistakes and falsifications—albeit involuntary ones—are apt to occur.

Another BBC experiment has shown the importance of some other factors in recall as well. This experiment [21] (1954) was about the immediate memory of a feature programme, one of the "This is the Law" series, in which the script was enlivened by dramatisation, and by being cast in the form of a continuous story. In addition the subjects were all personally invited to the BBC to take part in the

---

[19] F. C. Bartlett, *Remembering* (London: Cambridge University Press, 1932).

[20] G. W. Allport and L. Postman, *The Psychology of Rumour* (New York: Holt, 1948).

[21] A. H. W. Nias and H. Kay, "Immediate Memory of a Broadcast Feature Programme, *British Journal of Educational Psychology*, Vol. 24, 1954, pp. 154-160.

experiment. Under such conditions about 80 per cent of the story was recalled accurately, with the same variations according to intelligence, occupation, etc. as had been found previously. What is interesting, though, is that the material—a connected story, dealing with everyday people and incidents in everyday language—"lent itself to quick and easy assimilation." But illustrations and dramatisations cannot just be left to make their point; as Vernon [22] has pointed out (1946) they must be related to the subject matter as a whole, otherwise the point is apt to be forgotten.

Here, as in the other aspects of communication which I have touched on, much work remains to be done. So much of what passes for "communication theory" (in the non-engineering sense) is based on hunches and prejudices that further careful experiments are needed. It is the importance of the personal factor in communication that particularly needs to be examined. Simply because we almost all have to live and work among other human beings, we all tend at times to be like the character in Shaw's "Fanny's First Play," who was asked to comment on a production. "You don't expect me to know what to say about a play," she said, "when I don't know who the author is, do you?"

If subjective evidence is acceptable, we have the testimony of teachers, sages and others over the centuries, that people tend to weigh up who we are before listening to what we have to say.

St. Thomas Aquinas warned his pupils "Non respicias a quo sed quod sane dicetur memoriae recommenda." Dr. Johnson said of someone, "What have you to say about Aristotle tells me very little about Aristotle, but a great deal about you." Emerson puts it more forcefully, "What you are sounds so loudly in my ears that I cannot hear what you say." In many speeches, talks, and other forms of communication, it is often the character of the man that shows through the words he uses, as for example in Sir Winston Churchill's war-time speeches. What is said, and how it is said, often matter less than who says it. As Lord Rosebery said of William Pitt the Elder:

> "It is not merely the thing that is said, but the man who says it that counts, the character which breathes through the sentences."

There needs to be some degree of warmth in a personal relationship for real communication to exist. When people in conference or consultation have built up stable and firm relationships, then com-

[22] P. E. Vernon, "An Experiment on the Value of the Filmstrip in the Instruction of Adults," *British Journal of Educational Psychology*, Vol. 16, 1946, pp. 149-162.

munication is not only easier, but, usually, better. As Sir Geoffrey Vickers [23] (1954) has put it:

> "Consider how much easier it is to communicate on a standing committee, the members of which are used to deliberating together, than on an ad hoc committee which has never met before. Consider also, how, if the atmosphere of a conference begins to deteriorate, all the experienced members will set to work to put it right again, that is, to recreate the mutual attitudes without which it is a waste of time to confer."

So I should like to suggest to you that successful communication will come about by careful placement of key-men—men, that is, who command trust and respect, who are sympathetic and intelligent; they are your eyes and ears, the people through whom information will flow to you and from you. As to most operatives, the foreman, not the Board of Directors, *is* the firm, it means careful selection and training of your supervisors. On a higher level, it means equally careful selection and training of junior staff. But a fundamental attitude of "consistent and fair treatment of employees, pursued in good times and bad, and humour and common sense in day to day relationships," as John Marsh of the Industrial Welfare Society put it recently, is not something you can just lay on; it is not a technique; it springs from qualities of character and personality, which is why selection is so important. As March [24] (1954) says:

> "The fully fashioned personnel or welfare service cannot be effective unless the foreman—who is 'the firm' to most employees—is efficient, just and consistently humane in his leadership. One knows of instances where the results of years of patient endeavour in building up morale have been dissolved within a few hours of a manager losing his temper. All this goes to show that there are no final answers to human relations questions."

And if at times we tend to forget that last sentence, and to think that we really have at last found the means to cure the human ills of industry once and for all—and judging by the rise and fall in the popularity of such means to that end as welfare schemes, joint consultations, communications and co-partnerships, at times we all do think that—then we would do well to remember the warning of Sir Thomas More:

> "It is not possible for all things to be well unless all men are good, which I think will not be for these many years."

---

[23] C. G. Vickers, "Human Communication," *British Management Review*, Vol. 12, 1954, pp. 71-79.
[24] J. Marsh, "Human Relationships in Industry," *Financial Times*, 30 September, 1954.

QUESTIONS

1. What are some of the basic reasons why people are not receptive to what we have to say?
2. How can the receptivity of people be improved?
3. What are some of the basic subjects that should be studied when considering human communications?
4. What does Higham recommend for successful communication?
5. Illustrate Higham's psychological factors with examples from your own experience.

BARRIERS AND GATEWAYS
TO COMMUNICATION*

Carl R. Rogers and F. J. Roethlisberger

Communication among human beings has always been a problem. But it is only fairly recently that management and management advisers have become so concerned about it and the way it works or does not work in industry. Now, as the result of endless discussion, speculation, and plans of action, a whole cloud of catchwords and catchthoughts has sprung up and surrounded it.

The Editors of the *Review* therefore welcome the opportunity to present the following two descriptions of barriers and gateways to communication, in the thought that they may help to bring the problem down to earth and show what it means in terms of simple fundamentals. First Carl R. Rogers analyzes it from the standpoint of human behavior generally (Part I); then F. J. Roethlisberger illustrates it in an industrial context (Part II).

—The Editors

PART I

It may seem curious that a person like myself, whose whole professional effort is devoted to psychotherapy, should be interested in problems of communication. What relationship is there between obstacles to communication and providing therapeutic help to individuals with emotional maladjustments?

Actually the relationship is very close indeed. The whole task of psychotheraphy is the task of dealing with a failure in communication. The emotionally maladjusted person, the "neurotic," is in difficulty, first, because communication within himself has broken down and, secondly, because as a result of this his communication with others has been damaged. To put it another way, in the "neurotic" individual parts of himself which have been termed unconscious, or repressed, or denied to awareness, become blocked off so that they no longer communicate themselves to the conscious or managing part of himself; as long as this is true, there are distortions in the way he communicates himself to others, and so he suffers both within himself and in his interpersonal relations.

---

* From the *Harvard Business Review*, Vol. 30, No. 4 (July, 1952), pp. 46-52. Reprinted with permission.

The task of psychotherapy is to help the person achieve, through a special relationship with a therapist, good communication within himself. Once this is achieved, he can communicate more freely and more effectively with others. We may say then that psychotherapy is good communication, within and between men. We may also turn that statement around and it will still be true. Good communication, free communication, within or between men, is always therapeutic.

It is, then, from a background of experience with communication in counseling and psychotherapy that I want to present two ideas: (1) I wish to state what I believe is one of the major factors in blocking or impeding communication, and then (2) I wish to present what in our experience has proved to be a very important way of improving or facilitating communication.

Barrier: the tendency to evaluate

I should like to propose, as a hypothesis for consideration, that the major barrier to mutual interpersonal communication is our very natural tendency to judge, to evaluate, to approve (or disapprove) the statement of the other person or the other group. Let me illustrate my meaning with some very simple examples. Suppose someone, commenting on the discussion, makes the statement, "I didn't like what that man said." What will you respond? Almost invariably your reply will be either approval or disapproval of the attitude expressed. Either you respond, "I didn't either; I thought it was terrible," or else you tend to reply, "Oh, I thought it was really good." In other words, your primary reaction is to evaluate it from *your* point of view, your own frame of reference.

Or take another example. Suppose I say with some feeling, "I think the Republicans are behaving in ways that show a lot of good sound sense these days." What is the response that arises in your mind? The overwhelming likelihood is that it will be evaluative. In other words, you will find yourself agreeing, or disagreeing, or making some judgment about me such as "He must be a conservative," or "He seems solid in his thinking." Or let us take an illustration from the international scene. Russia says vehemently, "The treaty with Japan is a war plot on the part of the United States." We rise as one person to say, "That's a lie!"

This last illustration brings in another element connected with my hypothesis. Althought the tendency to make evaluations is common in almost all interchange of language, it is very much heightened in those situations where feelings and emotions are deeply involved. So the stronger our feelings, the more likely it is that there will be no mutual element in the communication. There will be just two ideas, two feelings, two judgments, missing each other in psychological space.

I am sure you recognize this from your own experience. When you have not been emotionally involved yourself and have listened to a heated discussion, you often go away thinking, "Well, they actually weren't talking about the same thing." And they were not. Each was making a judgment, an evaluation, from his own frame of reference. There was really nothing which could be called communication in any genuine sense. This tendency to react to any emotionally meaningful statement by forming an evaluation of it from our own point of view is, I repeat, the major barrier to interpersonal communication.

Gateway: listening with understanding

Is there any way of solving this problem, of avoiding this barrier? I feel that we are making exciting progress toward this goal, and I should like to present it as simply as I can. Real communication occurs, and this evaluative tendency is avoided, when we listen with understanding. What does that mean? It means to see the expressed idea and attitude from the other person's point of view, to sense how it feels to him, to achieve his frame of reference in regard to the thing he is talking about.

Stated so briefly, this may sound absurdly simple, but it is not. It is an approach which we have found extremely potent in the field of psychotherapy. It is the most effective agent we know for altering the basic personality structure of an individual and for improving his relationships and his communications with others. If I can listen to what he can tell me, if I can understand how it seems to him, if I can see its personal meaning for him, if I can sense the emotional flavor which it has for him, then I will be releasing potent forces of change in him.

Again, if I can really understand how he hates his father, or hates the company, or hates Communists—if I can catch the flavor of his fear of insanity, or his fear of atom bombs, or of Russia—it will be of the greatest help to him in altering those hatreds and fears and in establishing realistic and harmonious relationships with the very people and situations toward which he has felt hatred and fear. We know from our research that such empathic understanding—understanding *with* a person, not *about* him—is such an effective approach that it can bring about major changes in personality.

Some of you may be feeling that you listen well to people and yet you have never seen such results. The chances are great indeed that your listening has not been of the type I have described. Fortunately, I can suggest a little laboratory experiment which you can try to test the quality of your understanding. The next time you get into an argument with your wife, or your friend, or with a small group of friends, just stop the discussion for a moment and, for an experiment, institute this rule: "Each person can speak up for himself only *after* he has first restated the ideas and feelings of the previous speaker accurately and to that speaker's satisfaction."

You see what this would mean. It would simply mean that before presenting your own point of view, it would be necessary for you to achieve the other speaker's frame of reference—to understand his thoughts and feelings so well that you could summarize them for him. Sounds simple, doesn't it? But if you try it, you will discover that it is one of the most difficult things you have ever tried to do. However, once you have been able to see the other's point of view, your own comments will have to be drastically revised. You will also find the emotion going out of the discussion, the differences being reduced, and those differences which remain being of a rational and understandable sort.

Can you imagine what this kind of an approach would mean if it were projected into larger areas? What would happen to a labor-management dispute if it were conducted in such a way that labor, without necessarily agreeing, could accurately state management's point of view in a way that management could accept; and management, without approving labor's stand, could state labor's case in a way that labor agreed was accurate? It would mean that real communication was established, and one could practically guarantee that some reasonable solution would be reached.

If, then, this way of approach is an effective avenue to good communication and good relationships, as I am quite sure you will agree if you try the experiment I have mentioned, why is it not more widely tried and used? I will try to list the difficulties which keep it from being utilized.

Need for Courage. In the first place it takes courage, a quality which is not too widespread. I am indebted to Dr. S. I. Hayakawa, the semanticist, for pointing out that to carry on psychotherapy in this fashion is to take a very real risk, and that courage is required. If you really understand another person in this way, if you are willing to enter his private world and see the way life appears to him, without any attempt to make evaluative judgments, you run the risk of being changed yourself. You might see it this way; you might find yourself influenced in your attitudes or your personality.

This risk of being changed is one of the most frightening prospects many of us can face. If I enter, as fully as I am able, into the private world of a neurotic or psychotic individual, isn't there a risk that I might become lost in that world? Most of us are afraid to take that risk. Or if we were listening to a Russian Communist, or Senator Joe McCarthy, how many of us would dare to try to see the world from each of their points of view? The great majority of us could not *listen;* we would find ourselves compelled to *evaluate,* because listening would seem too dangerous. So the first requirement is courage, and we do not always have it.

Heightened Emotions. But there is a second obstacle. It is just when emotions are strongest that it is most difficult to achieve the frame of reference of the other person or group. Yet it is then that the attitude is most needed if communication is to be established. We have not found this to be an insuperable obstacle in our experience in psychotherapy. A third party, who is able to lay aside his own feelings and evaluations, can assist greatly by listening with understanding to each person or group and clarifying the views and attitudes each holds.

We have found this effective in small groups in which contradictory or antagonistic attitudes exist. When the parties to a dispute realize that they are being understood, that someone sees how the situation seems to them, the statements grow less exaggerated and less defensive, and it is no longer necessary to maintain the attitude, "I am 100% right and you are 100% wrong." The influence of such an understanding catalyst in the group permits the members to come closer and closer to the objective truth involved in the relationship. In this way mutual communication is established, and some type of agreement becomes much more possible.

So we may say that though heightened emotions make it much more difficult to understand *with* an opponent, our experience makes it clear that a neutral, understanding, catalyst type of leader or therapist can overcome this obstacle in a small group.

Size of Group. That last phrase, however, suggests another obstacle to utilizing the approach I have described. Thus far all our experience has been with small face-to-face groups—groups exhibiting industrial tensions, religious tensions, racial tensions, and therapy groups in which many personal tensions are present. In these small groups our experience, confirmed by a limited amount of research, shows that this basic approach leads to improved communication, to greater acceptance of others and by others, and to attitudes which are more positive and more problem-solving in nature. There is a decrease in defensiveness, in exaggerated statements, in evaluative and critical behavior.

But these findings are from small groups. What about trying to achieve understanding between larger groups that are geographically remote, or between face-to-face groups that are not speaking for themselves but simply as representatives of others, like the delegates at Kaesong? Frankly we do not know the answers to these questions. I believe the situation might be put this way: As social scientists we have a tentative test-tube solution of the problem of breakdown in communication. But to confirm the validity of this test-tube solution and to adapt it to the enormous problems of communication breakdown between classes, groups, and nations would involve additional funds, much more research, and creative thinking of a high order.

Yet with our present limited knowledge we can see some steps which might be taken even in large groups to increase the amount of listening *with* and decrease the amount of evaluation *about*. To be imaginative for a moment, let us suppose that a therapeutically oriented international group went to the Russian leaders and said, "We want to achieve a genuine understanding of your views and, even more important, of your attitudes and feelings toward the United States. We will summarize and resummarize these views and feelings if necessary, until you agree that our description represents the situation as it seems to you."

Then suppose they did the same thing with the leaders in our own country. If they then gave the widest possible distribution to these two views, with the feelings clearly described but not expressed in name-calling, might not the effect be very great? It would not guarantee the type of understanding I have been describing, but it would make it much more possible. We can understand the feelings of a person who hates us much more readily when his attitudes are accurately described to us by a neutral third party than we can when he is shaking his fist at us.

Faith in Social Sciences. But even to describe such a first step is to suggest another obstacle to this approach of understanding. Our civilization does not yet have enough faith in the social sciences to utilize their findings. The opposite is true of the physical sciences. During the war when a test-tube solution was found to the problem of synthetic rubber, millions of dollars and an army of talent were turned loose on the problem of using that finding. If synthetic rubber could be made in milligrams, it could and would be made in the thousands of tons. And it was. But in the social science realm, if a way is found of facilitating communication and mutual understanding in small groups, there is no guarantee that the finding will be utilized. It may be a generation or more before the money and the brains will be turned loose to exploit that finding.

SUMMARY

In closing, I should like to summarize this small-scale solution to the problem of barriers in communication, and to point out certain of its characteristics.

I have said that our research and experience to date would make it appear that breakdowns in communication, and the evaluative tendency which is the major barrier to communication, can be avoided. The solution is provided by creating a situation in which each of the different parties comes to understand the other from the *other's* point of view. This has been achieved, in practice, even when feelings run high, by the influence of a person who is willing to understand each point of view empathically, and who thus acts as a catalyst to precipitate further understanding.

This procedure has important characteristics. It can be initiated by one party, without waiting for the other to be ready. It can even be initiated by a neutral third person, provided he can gain a minimum of cooperation from one of the parties.

This procedure can deal with the insincerities, the defensive exaggerations, the lies, the "false fronts" which characterize almost every failure in communication. These defensive distortions drop away with astonishing speed as people find that the only intent is to understand, not to judge.

This approach leads steadily and rapidly toward the discovery of the truth, toward a realistic appraisal of the objective barriers to communication. The dropping of some defensiveness by one party leads to further dropping of defensiveness by the other party, and truth is thus approached.

This procedure gradually achieves mutual communication. Mutual communication tends to be pointed toward solving a problem rather than toward attacking a person or group. It leads to a situation in which I see how the problem appears to you as well as to me, and you see how it appears to me as well as to you. Thus accurately and realistically defined, the problem is almost certain to yield to intelligent attack; or if it is in part insoluble, it will be comfortably accepted as such.

This then appears to be a test-tube solution to the breakdown of communication as it occurs in small groups. Can we take this small-scale answer, investigate it further, refine it, develop it, and apply it to the tragic and well-nigh fatal failures of communication which threaten the very existence of our modern world? It seems to me that this is a possibility and a challenge which we should explore.

Part II

In thinking about the many barriers to personal communication, particularly those that are due to differences of background, experience, and motivation, it seems to me extraordinary that any two persons can ever understand each other. Such reflections provoke the question of how communication is possible when people do not see and assume the same things and share the same values.

On this question there are two schools of thought. One school assumes that communication between A and B, for example, has failed when B does not accept what A has to say as being fact, true, or valid; and that the goal of communication is to get B to agree with A's opinions, ideas, facts, or information.

The position of the other school of thought is quite different. It assumes that communication has failed when B does not feel free to express his feelings to A because B fears they will not be accepted by A. Communication is facilitated when on the part of A or B or both there is a willingness to express and accept differences.

As these are quite divergent conceptions, let us explore them further with an example. Bill, an employee, is talking with his boss in the boss's office. The boss says, "I think, Bill, that this is the best way to do your job." Bill says, "Oh yeah!" According to the first school of thought, this reply would be a sign of poor communication. Bill does not understand the best way of doing his work. To improve communication, therefore, it is up to the boss to explain to Bill why his way is the best.

From the point of view of the second school of thought, Bill's reply is a sign neither of good nor of bad communication. Bill's response is indeterminate. But the boss has an opportunity to find out what Bill means if he so desires. Let us assume that this is what he chooses to do, i.e., find out what Bill means. So this boss tries to get Bill to talk more about his job while he (the boss) listens.

For purposes of simplification, I shall call the boss representing the first school of thought *"Smith"* and the boss representing the second school of thought *"Jones."* In the presence of the so-called same stimulus each behaves differently. Smith chooses to *explain;* Jones chooses to *listen.* In my experience Jones's response works better than Smith's. It works better because Jones is making a more proper evaluation of what is taking place between him and Bill than Smith is. Let us test this hypothesis by continuing with our example.

What Smith assumes, sees, and feels

Smith assumes that he understands what Bill means when Bill says "Oh yeah!" so there is no need to find out. Smith is sure that Bill does not understand why this is the best way to do his job, so Smith has to tell him. In this process let us assume Smith is logical, lucid, and clear. He presents his facts and evidence well. But, alas, Bill remains unconvinced. What does Smith do? Operating under the assumption that what is taking place between him and Bill is something essentially logical, Smith can draw only one of two conclusions: either (1) he has not been clear enough, or (2) Bill is too damned stupid to understand. So he either has to "spell out" his case in words of fewer and fewer syllables or give up. Smith is reluctant to do the latter, so he continues to explain. What happens?

If Bill still does not accept Smith's explanation of why this is the best way for him to do his job, a pattern of interacting feelings is produced of which Smith is often unaware. The more Smith cannot get Bill to understand him, the more frustrated Smith becomes and the more Bill becomes a threat to his logical capacity. Since Smith sees himself as a fairly reasonable and logical chap, this is a difficult feeling to accept. It is much easier for him to perceive Bill as uncooperative or stupid. This perception, however, will affect what Smith says and does. Under these pressures Bill comes to be evaluated more and more in terms of Smith's values. By this process Smith tends to treat Bill's values as unimportant. He tends to deny Bill's uniqueness and difference. He treats Bill as if he had little capacity for self-direction.

Let us be clear. Smith does not see that he is doing these things. When he is feverishly scratching hieroglyphics on the back of an envelope, trying to explain to Bill why this is the best way to do his job, Smith is trying to be helpful. He is a man of goodwill, and he wants to set Bill straight. This is the way Smith sees himself and his behavior. But it is for this very reason that Bill's "Oh yeah!" is getting under Smith's skin.

"How dumb can a guy be?" is Smith's attitude, and unfortunately Bill will hear that more than Smith's good intentions. Bill will feel misunderstood. He will not see Smith as a man of goodwill trying to be helpful. Rather he will perceive him as a threat to his self-esteem and personal integrity. Against this threat Bill will feel the need to defend himself at all cost. Not being so logically articulate as Smith, Bill expresses this need, again, by saying, "Oh yeah!"

What Jones assumes, sees, and feels

Let us leave this sad scene between Smith and Bill, which I fear is going to terminate by Bill's either leaving in a huff or being kicked out of Smith's office. Let us turn for a moment to Jones and see what he is assuming, seeing, hearing, feeling, doing, and saying when he interacts with Bill.

Jones, it will be remembered, does not assume that he knows what Bill means when he says, "Oh yeah!" so he has to find out. Moreover, he assumes that when Bill said this, he had not exhausted his vocabulary or his feelings. Bill may not necessarily mean one thing; he may mean several different things. So Jones decides to listen.

In this process Jones is not under any illusion that what will take place will be eventually logical. Rather he is assuming that what will take place will be primarily an interaction of feeings. Therefore, he cannot ignore the feelings of Bill, the effect of Bill's feelings on him, or the effect of his feelings on Bill. In other words, he cannot ignore his relationship to Bill; he cannot assume that it will make no difference to what Bill will hear or accept.

Therefore, Jones will be paying strict attention to all of the things Smith has ignored. He will be addressing himself to Bill's feelings, his own, and the interactions between them.

Jones will therefore realize that he has ruffled Bill's feelings with his comment, "I think, Bill, this is the best way to do your job." So instead of trying to get Bill to understand him, he decides to try to understand Bill. He does this by encouraging Bill to speak. Instead of telling Bill how he should feel or think, he asks Bill such questions as, "Is this what you feel?" "Is this what you see?" "Is this what you assume?" Instead of ignoring Bill's evaluations as irrelevant, not valid, inconsequential, or false, he tries to understand Bill's reality as he feels it, perceives it, and assumes it to be. As Bill begins to open up, Jones's curiosity is piqued by this process.

"Bill isn't so dumb; he's quite an interesting guy" becomes Jones's attitude. And that is what Bill hears. Therefore Bill feels understood and accepted as a person. He becomes less defensive. He is in a better frame of mind to explore and re-examine his own perceptions, feelings and assumptions. In this process he perceives Jones as a source of help, Bill feels free to express his differences. He feels that Jones has some respect for his capacity for self-direction. These positive feelings toward Jones make Bill more inclined to say, "Well, Jones, I don't quite agree with you that this is the best way to do my job, but I'll tell you what I'll do. I'll try to do it that way for a few days, and then I'll tell you what I think."

CONCLUSION

I grant that my two orientations do not work themselves out in practice in quite so simple or neat a fashion as I have been able to work them out on paper. There are many other ways in which Bill could have responded to Smith in the first place. He might even have said, "O.K., boss, I agree that your way of doing my job is better." But Smith still would not have known how Bill felt when he made this statement or whether Bill was actually going to do his job differently. Likewise, Bill could have responded to Jones in a way different from my example. In spite of Jones's attitude, Bill might still be reluctant to express himself freely to his boss.

The purpose of my examples has not been to demonstrate the right or wrong way of communicating. My purpose has been simply to provide something concrete to point to when I make the following generalizations:

(1) Smith represents to me a very common pattern of misunderstanding. The misunderstanding does not arise because Smith is not clear enough in expressing himself. It arises because of Smith's misevaluation of what is taking place when two people are talking together.

(2) Smith's misevaluation of the process of personal communication consists of certain very common assumptions, e.g. (a) that what is taking place is something essentially logical; (b) that words in themselves apart from the people involved mean something; and (c) that the purpose of the interaction is to get Bill to see things from Smith's point of view.

(3) Because of these assumptions, a chain reaction of perceptions and negative feelings is engendered which blocks communication. By ignoring Bill's feelings and by rationalizing his own, Smith ignores his relationship to Bill as one of the most important determinants of the communication. As a result, Bill hears Smith's attitude more clearly than the logical content of Smith's words. Bill feels that his individual uniqueness is being denied. His personal integrity being at stake, he becomes defensive and belligerent. As a result, Smith feels frustrated. He perceives Bill as stupid. So he says and does things which only provoke more defensiveness on the part of Bill.

(4) In the case of Jones, I have tried to show what might possibly happen if we made a different evaluation of what is taking place when two people are talking together. Jones makes a different set of assumptions. He assumes (a) that what is taking place between him and Bill is an interaction of sentiments; (b) that Bill—not his words in themselves—means something; (c) that the object of the interaction is to give Bill an opportunity to express freely his differences.

(5) Because of these assumptions, a psychological chain reaction of reinforcing feelings and perceptions is set up which facilitates communication between Bill and him. When Jones addresses himself to Bill's feelings and perceptions from Bill's point of view, Bill feels understood and accepted as a person; he feels free to express his differences. Bill sees Jones as a source of help; Jones sees Bill as an interesting person. Bill in turn becomes more cooperative.

(6) If I have identified correctly these very common patterns of personal communication, then some interesting hypotheses can be stated:

(a) Jones's method works better than Smith's, not because of any magic, but because Jones has a better map than Smith of the process of personal communication.

(b) The practice of Jones's method, however, is not merely an intellectual exercise. It depends on Jones's capacity and willingness to see and accept points of view different from his own, and to practice this orientation in a face-to-face relationship. This practice involves an emotional as well as an intellectual achievement. It depends in part on Jones's awareness of himself, in part on the practice of a skill.

(c) Although our colleges and universities try to get students to appreciate intellectually points of view different from their own, very little is done to help them to implement this general intellectual appreciation in a simple face-to-face relationship—at the level of a skill. Most educational institutions train their students to be logical, lucid, and clear. Very little is done to help them to listen more skillfully. As a result, our educated world contains too many Smiths and too few Joneses.

(d) The biggest block to personal communication is man's inability to listen intelligently, understandingly, and skillfully to another person. This deficiency in the modern world is widespread and appalling. In our universities as well as elsewhere, too little is being done about it.

(7) In conclusion, let me apologize for acting toward you the way Smith did. But who am I to violate a long-standing academic tradition!

QUESTIONS

1. What is the relationship of communication to psychotherapy?
2. What, according to Rogers, is the major barrier to communication? What does he recommend to avoid this barrier? What difficulties face his recommendation?
3. Why did the misunderstanding between Smith and Bill arise?
4. What does Roethlisberger recommend to facilitate communication?
5. Distinguish the approaches and the conclusions of Roethlisberger and Rogers.

AN EXPERIMENTAL APPROACH TO
ORGANIZATIONAL COMMUNICATION *

Alex Bavelas and Dermot Barrett

Communication as a critical aspect of organization has been attracting more and more attention. If one may judge from articles and speeches, much of the current thinking on communication centers around categories of problems which arise in day-to-day operations—"getting management's point of view to the workers," "stimulating communication up the line as well as down," "obtaining better communication with the union," "establishing more effective communication within management, and especially with the foremen." Knowing how such questions usually arise, it is not surprising that their discussion invariably resolves itself into considerations of *content* and *technique*: on the one hand, analyses of what management ought to be saying to the worker, the union, the foreman; on the other hand, descriptions of devices which can best say it—bulletin boards, letters, films, public address systems, meetings, etc. In its extreme form this approach becomes one of searching for a specific remedy for a specific ill. Helpful and practical as this may be, it is doubtful that such activity can lead to the discovery and understanding of the basic principles of effective organizational communication. Breakdowns and other difficulties at some point of a communication system are often only superficially related to the local conditions which appear to have produced them. They may, rather, be cumulative effects of properties of the entire communication system taken as a whole. But what are these properties, if, indeed, they exist?

Formal and informal systems

An organizational system of communication is usually created by the setting up of formal systems of responsibility and by explicit delegations of duties. These categories include statements, often implicitly, of the nature, content, and direction of the communication which is considered necessary for the performance of the group. Students of organization, however, have pointed out repeatedly that groups tend to depart from such formal statements and to create other channels of communication and dependence. In other words,

---

* From *Personnel*, Vol. 27, No. 5 (March, 1951), pp. 366-371. Copyright, 1951, by the American Management Association. Reprinted with permission of the American Management Association.

informal organizational systems emerge. One may take the view that these changes are adaptations by the individuals involved in the direction of easier and more effective ways of working, or, perhaps, not working. It is no secret that informal groups are not always viewed by managers as favorable to the goals of the larger body. Also, it is by no means obvious that those informal groupings which evolve out of social and personality factors are likely to be more efficient (with respect to organizational tasks) than those set up formally by the managers. Altogether, if one considers how intimate the relations are between communication channels and control, it is not surprising that the managers of organizations would prefer explicit and orderly communication lines.

Is there "one best way"?

Unfortunately, there seems to be no organized body of knowledge out of which one can derive, for a given organization, an optimal communication system. Administrative thinking on this point commonly rests upon the assumption that the optimum system *can* be derived from a statement of the task to be performed. It is not difficult to show, however, that from a given set of specifications one may derive not a single communication pattern but a whole set of them, all logically adequate for the successful performance of the task in question. Which pattern from this set should be chosen? The choice, in practice, is usually made either in terms of a group of assumptions (often quite untenable) about human nature, or in terms of a personal bias on the part of the chooser. The seriousness of this situation is illustrated by the following example.

Let us assume that we have a group of five individuals who, in order to solve a problem, must share as quickly as possible the information each person possesses. Let us also assume that there are reasons which prevent them from meeting around a table, and that they must share this information by writing notes. To avoid the confusion and waste of time of each person writing a message to each of the others, a supervisor decides to set up channels in which the notes must go. He strikes upon the pattern shown in Fig. 1.

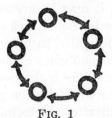

FIG. 1

In this arrangement each individual can send to and receive messages from two others, one on his "left" and one on his "right." Experiments actually performed with this kind of situation show that the number of mistakes made by individuals working in such a "circle" pattern can be reduced by fully 60 per cent by the simple measure of *removing one link,* thus making the pattern a "chain" as shown in Fig. 2. The relevance of such a result to organization communication is obvious, simple though the example is. The sad truth, however, is that this phenomenon is not clearly derivable either from traditional "individual psychology" or from commonly held theories of group communication.

F<small>IG</small>. 2

An integral process of organization

Perhaps some headway can be made by approaching the general problem from a somewhat different direction. In the affairs of organizations, as well as in the affairs of men, chance always plays a part. However good a plan may be, however carefully prepared its execution, there is a point beyond which the probability of its success cannot be increased. With the firmest of intentions, agreements and promises may be impossible to carry out because of unforeseen events. Nevertheless, an organization whose functioning is too often interrupted by unforeseen events is looked upon with suspicion. Bad luck is an unhappy plea, and it may well be that the "unlucky" organization is more to be avoided than the simply incompetent one. On the other hand, few things about an organization are more admired and respected than the ability to "deliver" despite widely varying conditions and in the face of unusual difficulties.

In a very broad sense, it may be argued that the principal effort of organizational activities is the making of favorable conditions for the achievement of certain goals. In other words, an effort is made to increase, as much as the economics of the situation will permit, the probabilities of succeeding. This is the essence of the manager's job. The development of training and selection programs, the improvement of methods and the specification of techniques, the organization of research and development activities, the designation of responsibility and the delegation of duties—all these processes have one organizationally legitimate purpose: to increase the chances of organizational success. Upon this point rest almost all of the notions by which we are accustomed to evaluate organizations—in part or as a whole.

An organization is, in short, a social invention—a kind of "machine" for increasing certain sets of probabilities. (Which sets of probabilities are given to it to increase, which it chooses, how freely and by what means will not be discussed here. These problems, although they lie well within the scope of this subject, are outside the range of this paper. We will confine ourselves to a consideration of the process by which an accepted set of probabilities is optimized.) Probabilities of success are increased, however, only by taking relevant and appropriate actions. For the manager, these actions reduce in most instances to the gathering and evaluating of information in the form of reports, schedules, estimates, etc. It is entirely possible to view an organization as an elaborate system for gathering, evaluating, recombining, and disseminating information. It is not surprising, in these terms, that the effectiveness of an organization with respect to the achievement of its goals should be so closely related to its effectiveness in handling information. In an enterprise whose success hinges upon the coordination of the efforts of all its members, the managers depend completely upon the quality, the amount, and the rate at which relevant information reaches them. The rest of the organization, in turn, depends upon the efficiency with which the managers can deal with this information and reach conclusions, decisions, etc. This line of reasoning leads us to the belief that communication is not a secondary or derived aspect of organization—a "helper" of the other and presumably more basic functions. Rather it is the essence of organized activity and is the basic process out of which all other functions derive. The goals an organization selects, the methods it applies, the effectiveness with which it improves its own procedures—all of these hinge upon the quality and availability of the information in the system.

Patterns of communication

About two years ago a series of studies was begun whose purpose was to isolate and study certain general properties of information handling systems. The first phase of this research program [1] is

---
[1] These studies are supported jointly by the Rand Corporation and the Research Laboratory of Electronics at M.I.T.

directed at a basic property of all communication systems, that of connection or "who can talk to whom."

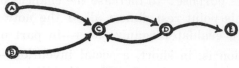

FIG. 3

This property of connection can be conveniently expressed by diagrams. The meaning of the picture in Fig. 3 is obvious. Individuals **A** and **B** can send messages to C but they can receive messages from no one; C and D can exchange messages; E can receive messages from D, but he can send messages to no one. The pattern shown in Fig. 3, however, is only one of the many that are possible. A group of others is shown in Fig. 4. An examination of these patterns will show that they fall into two classes, separated by a very important difference. Any pair of individuals in each of the patterns, d, e, and f can exchange messages either directly or indirectly over some route. No pair of individuals in each of the patterns a, b, and c can exchange messages. Patterns like a, b, and c obviously make any coordination of thought or action virtually impossible; we will be concerned from this point on only with patterns like d, e, and f.

Since the individuals in any connected pattern like d, e, and f can share ideas completely, should we expect that the effectiveness of individuals in performing group tasks or solving group problems would be the same in patterns d, e, and f except for differences in ability, knowledge, and personality? Should we expect differences in quality and speed of performance? Is it likely that the individuals

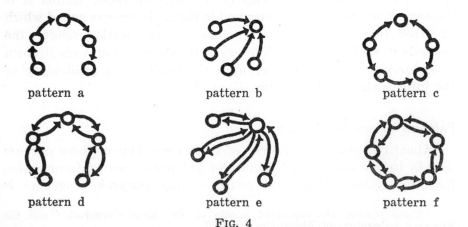

pattern a   pattern b   pattern c

pattern d   pattern e   pattern f

FIG. 4

working in one pattern would show significantly better morale than the individuals working in a different pattern? Sidney Smith and Harold J. Leavitt conducted a series of experiments [2] which yielded very definite answers to these questions. An experimental design was used which made it possible to equate the difficulty of the tasks which the groups performed, and which permitted the cancelling of individual differences by randomizing the assignment of subjects to patterns. Also, the experiment was repeated with different groups enough times to establish the consistency of the results. A brief summary of the findings is given in Fig. 5. The use of qualitative terms in Fig. 5 in place of the quantitative measurements which were actually made blurs the comparison somewhat, but it gives a fair picture of the way these patterns performed. Since the original experiments were done by Smith and Leavitt, this experiment has been repeated with no change in the findings.

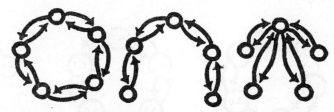

Speed	slow	fast	fast
Accuracy	poor	good	good
Organization	no stable form of organization	slowly emerging but stable organization	almost immediate and stable organization
Emergence of Leader	none	marked	very pronounced
Morale	very good	poor	very poor

FIG. 5

The question very properly arises here as to whether these findings can be "explained" in the sense of being related to the connection properties of the patterns themselves. The answer to this question is a qualified yes. Without developing the mathematical analysis, which can be found in Leavitt's paper, the following statements can be made:

For any connected pattern, an *index of dispersion* can be calculated. Relative to this index, there can be calculated *for each position in each pattern* an *index of centrality*, and an *index of peripher-*

[2] Harold J. Leavitt reports these experiments in detail in the January, 1951, issue of the *Journal of Abnormal and Social Psychology*.

ality. The data suggest strongly that the rapidity with which organization emerges and the stability it displays are related to the gradient of the indices of centrality in the pattern. In Fig. 6 these indices are given for each position. It should be added at this point that in the patterns in which leadership emerged, the leader was invariably that person who occupied the position of highest centrality.

The index of peripherality appears to be related strongly to morale. In Fig. 7 the indices of peripherality are given by position. Those individuals who occupied positions of low or zero peripherality showed in their actions as well as in self-ratings (made at the end of the experiments) that they were satisfied, in high spirits, and generally pleased with the work they had done. Those individuals who occupied positions of high peripherality invariably displayed either apathetic or destructive and uncooperative behavior during the group effort, and rated themselves as dissatisfied and critical of the group's operation.

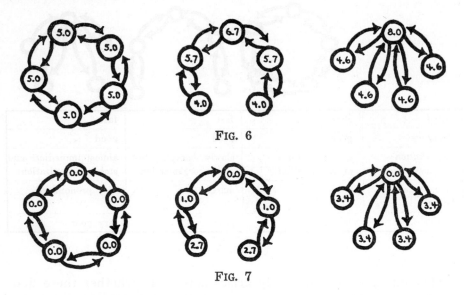

FIG. 6

FIG. 7

A word of caution should be given concerning the slow, inaccurate, but happy "circle" pattern. Subsequent experiments by Sidney Smith indicate that this pattern possesses unusual abilities for adaptation to sudden and confusing changes of task—a quality lacking in the other two patterns.

A promising field for research

Clearly, these experiments are only the beginning of a long story. The findings, although they promise much, settle nothing; but they do suggest that an experimental approach to certain aspects of organizational communication is possible and that, in all probability, it would be practically rewarding. As the characteristics of communication nets and their effects upon human performance *as they occur in the laboratory* become better understood, the need will grow for systematic studies of actual operating organizations. The job of mapping an existing net of communications even in a relatively small company is a complicated and difficult one, but it is not impossible. Some work is beginning on the development of field methods of observation. The importance of bridging the gap between the simple, directly controlled experiment and the very complex, indirectly controlled social situation cannot be overestimated.

QUESTIONS

1. What, apparently, does current thinking on communication center around? What are the limitations of this approach?
2. Describe the influence of informal systems on organizational communication.
3. Can an optimal communication system be derived for an organization? Why?
4. Explain what is meant by the statement "A basic property of all communication systems is that of connection."
5. Briefly outline the conclusions of this article.

STIMULATING UPWARD COMMUNICATION *

Earl G. Planty and William Machaver

Managers, by and large, have been relatively quick to perceive the problems of downward communication. The growth and complexity of modern industry have placed pressure upon management at all levels to develop effective means of transmitting to lower echelons information that is vital to the continuing, efficient operation of the business.

Executives and supervisors recognize, too, that misinformation and the resulting misunderstanding lessen working efficiency. Sharing information with subordinates at all levels of the organization tends to diminish the fears and suspicions that we all sometimes have in our work and toward our employer; it affords the security and feeling of belonging so necessary for efficiency and morale. In general, it may be said that *downward* communication is an integral part of the traditional industrial organization and is readily accepted and made use of—more or less effectively—by management.

The neglected other half

Unfortunately, however, some managers tend to consider communication a one-way street. They fail to see the values obtained from encouraging employees to discuss fully the policies and plans of the company. They do not provide a clear channel for funneling information, opinions, and attitudes up through the organization.

There are many values, however, that accrue to those managers who listen willingly, who urge their subordinates to talk freely and honestly. Upward communication reveals to them the degree to which ideas passed down are accepted. In addition, it stimulates employees to participate in the operation of their department or unit and, therefore, encourages them to defend the decisions and support the policies cooperatively developed with management. The opportunity for upward communication also encourages employees to contribute valuable ideas for improving departmental or company efficiency. Finally, it is through upward communication that executives and supervisors learn to avert the many explosive situations which arise daily in industry.

* From *Effective Communication on the Job*, ed. M. Joseph Dooher and Vivienne Marquis (New York: The American Management Association, 1956), pp. 141-157. Copyright, 1956, by the American Management Association. Reprinted by permission of the American Management Association.

If these advantages are to be achieved, we must realize that communication is dynamic. It must flow constantly up as well as down if it is to stimulate mutual understanding at all levels of the organization.

Faced as all industry is with the need for education in this complex and emotion-laden problem of upward communication, Johnson & Johnson and affiliated companies established a committee of operating executives to make a thorough investigation of the problems of upward communication. The personnel directors, a sales director, and two vice presidents in charge of manufacturing constituted the committee. They met, read, studied, interviewed specialists, argued the question among themselves, and then prepared the material which constitutes the body of the following report. Operating in panel style, they presented the report to the board of directors of the parent company, to the boards of affiliated companies, and to major operating executives, inviting their suggestions and criticisms.[1] Other committees similarly prepared themselves, presented reports, and invited discussions with middle and lower levels of management. Thus the report which follows represents practical recommendations dealing with the fundamentals and techniques of upward communication—a program developed by the joint effort of operating executives.

I. The Value of Effective Upward Communication [2]

A. Values to superiors

1. Many of management's best ideas are sown on cold and sour soil, not tilled and prepared in advance for the information. Where attitudes and feelings are transmitted freely upward, however, management is forewarned of possible failure and can better prepare the seed bed before its own ideas are broadcast. Upward communications tell us not only when our people are ready to hear our story, but also how well they accept our story when we do tell it. We have no better means than upward communication of knowing whether our downward communications have been believed.

---

[1] The writers wish to acknowledge the assistance of the following members of the committee who presented the report: E. A. Carlson, Controller at Johnson & Johnson; J. T. Freeston, Assistant Personnel Director at Johnson & Johnson; J. F. Kiley, Vice President, General Line Field Sales Force at Johnson & Johnson; W. S. McCord, Director of Industrial Relations at Personal Products; C. V. Swank, Vice President in Charge of Manufacturing at Johnson & Johnson; and H. A. Wallace, Vice President in Charge of Manufacturing at Ethicon Suture Laboratories, Inc.

[2] The points outlined in this section were developed by the panel in reply to the moderator's question, "What values may we expect in business and industry from improved upward communications?"

2. If we are to gain understanding and full acceptance of our decisions, subordinates must be given the opportunity to participate in their making or at least to discuss the merits and defects of proposed actions. Social scientists tell us that employee understanding and loyalty do not come solely from hearing facts, even true facts. Appreciation and loyalty result from self-expression in a situation in which the subordinate feels there is personal sympathy toward him and his views. Therefore the superior should encourage subordinates at any level to ask questions and contribute their own ideas. Above all, he should listen, sincerely and sympathetically, with intention to use workable ideas that are proposed.

3. From upward communication we discover whether subordinates get the meaning from downward communication that is intended by the superior. It is highly unlikely that a subordinate left completely to his own interpretation will understand a directive or an action just as the originator intended it. In the first place, management may phrase its messages vaguely or ambiguously. Second, recipients interpret even the clearest communication in the light of their own biases and experience. Even though it may seem to us most logical that they should draw only one conclusion, we can never be sure what subordinates think unless we get them to relay back to us their interpretations and reactions to what we do and say.

4. Finally, effective upward communication encourages subordinates to offer ideas of value to themselves and the business. The need here is to devise and use every form of upward communication that will draw these ideas from all who are qualified to make them.

B. Values to subordinates

1. Upward communication helps satisfy basic human needs. All subordinates look upon themselves as having inherent worth at least as great as the personal worth of their superiors. This is true even if they feel their own inferiority in managerial ability or in some other skill. They still think, just as you and I do, that because they are individual human beings they have certain values and rights. This sense of personal worth is always injured when people do not get a chance to express their ideas—when they are merely told, without opportunity to comment or reply. This principle applies even if the telling is very well done. We respect our employees' dignity only when we allow, or better still invite, them to express their reactions to what is told—preferably before action is taken.

2. Employees who are encouraged to talk directly and frankly with their superiors get a release of emotional tensions and pressures

which otherwise may find outlet in criticism to other members of the company and the community, or in loss of interest or efficiency. Some superiors feel that by listening to fanatics, crackpots, and neurotics they encourage their complaints. If complaints seem to arise from physical or mental ailments, treatment by a physician or psychiatrist may be necessary. But to the degree that the maladjustment lies in the man's work relations, listening to him may identify failures and sore spots in the organization that cause his problems. Moreover, it is well established that the right kind of listening enables many individuals to understand and solve their own problems. For the *normal* individuals in industry, it is likely that the more you listen willingly to what employees are inclined to tell you, the less time you will in the future be called upon to give.

3. Unlike the organizational structure of the church, the school, the local and even the national government, industry in its organization is essentially authoritarian. This makes it even more necessary in industry than in, say, education or government that every opportunity be given subordinates to express their views freely and to make their influence felt. Many think that business cannot continue to exist as we know it today unless more and more ways are found to bring the essentials of democracy into the workplace. Fortunately, the principles of democracy do not require that such business functions as financing, expansion or curtailment of production, and hiring be decided upon by vote of the majority. However, the fact that by nature we must be authoritarian in some matters makes it imperative that we be more democratic in those business matters where employee participation is appropriate. Nothing is more fundamental to democracy than upward communication in which the ideas of subordinates are given prompt and sympathetic hearing followed by such action as is desirable.

II. BARRIERS TO UPWARD COMMUNICATION

Even though management may appreciate the need for effective upward communication, it may not translate this need into action. It becomes apparent at once that to swim up the stream of communication is a much harder task than to float downstream. The currents of resistance, inherent in the temperament and habits of supervisors and employees and in the complexity and structure of modern industry, are persistent and strong. Let us examine some of these deterrents to upward communication.[3]

---

[3] Panel discussions with various groups revealed that until the obstacles to effective communications were clearly identified and accepted it was difficult to

A. Barriers involving business organization

1. The physical distance between superior and subordinate impedes upward communications in several ways. Communication becomes difficult and infrequent when superiors are isolated so as to be seldom seen or spoken to. In large organizations executives are located in headquarters or divisional centers, at points not easily reached by their subordinates. In smaller organizations their offices are sometimes remotely placed, or they hold themselves needlessly inaccessible.

2. Complexity also delays communication up. Suppose there is at the employee's level a significant problem that eventually must be settled at the top. The employee tells his supervisor. They talk it over and try to settle it. This takes a day or two. Then it goes to the department head. He requires some time to hear the case, thinks about it a day or two, and then tells the divisional manager, who holds the case a week while he investigates, unwilling to bother the vice president with it. Since there may appear to be an admission of failure in passing the problem up, each level of supervision is reluctant to do so, thus causing more delay. By the time the problem reaches the top echelon, months may have elapsed since it first arose.

3. Movement of information through many levels dilutes or distorts it. Since each supervisor consciously or unconsciously selects and edits the information he passes up, the more levels of supervision, or filter stations, it passes through before it reaches the top, the less accurate it becomes. Also, in a large company with a hierarchy of management, contacts become fewer and more hurried as one ascends in the organization. A group leader contacts his workers more often than a president contacts his vice presidents.

B. Barriers involving superiors

1. The superior's attitude and behavior in listening will play a vital role in either encouraging or discouraging communication up. If the boss seems anxious to get the interview over with or appears to be impatient with his subordinate, or annoyed or distressed by the subject being discussed, this attitude will place an insurmountable communications barrier between them in the future.

---

discuss techniques and methods profitably. A clear understanding of what impedes upward communications must precede removal of obstructions. In many cases an open channel is all we need for ideas and attitudes to flow upward. It was the thought of the syndicate that more could be gained by first emphasizing the removal of barriers than by first putting out enticements and formal devices for stimulating communication upward. Group meetings, written reports, and individual contacts become mere window dressing and will fail in their purpose if superiors have not first dispelled completely any feeling of disinterest or impatience with what their subordinates are telling them.

2. A boss may fall into the familiar error of thinking that "no news is good news," whereas lack of complaint or criticism is often a symptom that upward communication is working in very low gear; or he may assume, often wrongly, that he knows what subordinates think or feel; or he may have such an exaggerated sense of duty that he feels it disloyal to listen to complaints, especially if made intemperately. This attitude tends to discourage employees with justifiable complaints from approaching their superiors.

3. We all have a natural defensiveness about ourselves and our actions. As managers, we are prone to resent and resist communications which indicate that some of our actions have been less than perfect. Where this attitude is evident, loyal workers who could be most helpful to us sometimes withhold information. In such cases communicating is of necessity done by the less loyal workers and the maladjusted. In other words, unless we are willing to hear criticism freely, much we learn about our organization comes from those who are the least loyal to it.

4. Superiors often resist becoming involved with the personal problems of their subordinates. This resistance to listening may affect the subordinates' willingness to communicate up on other matters more directly related to the job. Moreover, job problems and personal problems are often closely linked, and it is difficult to discuss the one without the other.

5. One of the strongest deterrents to communication up is the failure of management to act on undesirable conditions previously brought to its attention. The result is that the workers lose faith both in the sincerity of management and in the value of communication.

6. Listening is time-consuming. Many executives feel that they are too involved with daily problems and responsibilities to provide adequate time for listening fully to their subordinates' ideas, reports, and criticisms. Nevertheless, many time-consuming problems could be minimized or eliminated if superiors were free to listen to their employees, for in listening they can discover solutions to present problems or anticipate causes for future ones. The subordinate who has free access to his boss can get the answers to many budding problems and thus eliminate heavier demands made when the problems have gotten complex, emotion-laden, and possibly out of control.

A man's philosophy of management determines the value he places upon communications and the time he gives to it. A manager who has freed himself of much of his routine responsibilities and is

engaged in building individual subordinates and developing teamwork in his group will rank communications high in priority and will
allow time for it, since it is the nerve center of such a leader's
management. In contrast, the boss who acts alone, solves most of his
department's problems himself, and lets the growth of subordinates
take its own course may well be too busy to communicate.

C. Barriers involving subordinates

1. Communication down may run more freely than communications up because the superior is free to call in the subordinate and
talk to him at will. The subordinate does not have the same freedom
to intrude upon the superior's time. A man is discouraged from
going freely over his boss's head or from asking appeal from his
decisions by the line of authority that prevails in industry.

2. Neither the facilities available nor the rewards offered to the
subordinate for upward communication equal those for messages
downward. Management can speed the flow of information down by
the use of company publications, in-plant broadcasts, meetings, bulletin boards, form letters, etc. By praise, promotions, and other signs
of recognition management can reward subordinates who act upon
communications down, as it can penalize those who fail to act. Few
such facilities or incentives for encouraging communications upward
are available to the employee.

3. Communications from subordinate to superior cannot be prepared with as much care as those that move down. A sales manager,
for example, may address a message to a dozen men—a message
resulting from the combined thinking of his staff, strengthened by
research, careful writing, editing, and visual aids. He and his staff
are free to give that message far more time and thought than a
salesman in the field can expend on a message back to the sales
manager.

4. Because tradition, authority, and prestige are behind communications down, they flow more easily in that direction than do
communications up. In communicating up, the subordinate must
explain himself and get acceptance from one who has greater status
and authority. The subordinate's difficulties are greater also because
he is likely to be less fluent and persuasive than the man who communicates down to him.

The semantics barrier is likewise greater for the subordinate.
His superior, probably having worked at one time on the subordinate's job, knows the attitudes, the language, and the problems of

that level. On the other hand, the man who is communicating up faces the difficulty of talking to a person with whose work and responsibilities he is not familiar.

5. Like all of us, employees are emotional and prejudiced. Their feelings mix freely with their facts, creating further barriers to objective upward communications. Their observations and reports to management are prejudiced by their own personal habits and sentiments. The establishment of rapport through judicious listening will help the superior to understand and interpret what employees are trying to tell him. The superior, of course, must recognize and minimize his own prejudices and idiosyncrasies before he can do this.

6. Unless superiors are particularly receptive, subordinates generally prefer to withhold or temper bad news, unfavorable opinions, and reports of mistakes or failures. Because some managers are defensive about listening to bad news, those who like and respect them withhold information or minimize omissions and errors out of friendly motives; others keep back information from fear, dislike, or indifference.

III. What Should Be Communicated Upward?

Many executives are satisfied if communications from below inform them about such matters as the following:

A. What subordinates are doing; highlights of their work, achievements, progress, and future job plans.
B. Outlines of unsolved work problems on which subordinates now need aid or may require help in the future.
C. Suggestions for improvements within the department or company.
D. How subordinates think and feel about their jobs, their associates, and their company.

The first three points deal with work-centered matters about which the alert executive normally tries to keep himself well informed. The fourth area—that of subordinates' personal feelings and attitudes—has not, however, received equal attention, though of equal or even greater importance. Consequently, it may be valuable to spell out in detail some of the things under "D" (above) which an executive should learn through upward communications.

1. Feelings about the job

a. Are people satisfied with their pay in relation to other jobs in the company, similar jobs in the industry or community? (How do you know? What have you done to find out?)

b. Are working hours and shift rotations felt to be reasonable? (From whom do you get your information?)

c. Do employees feel that the workload is fairly distributed? (What positive evidence have you of this?)

d. What do employees think about the quality and adequacy of tools, equipment, and office furniture? (Do they tell you this?)

e. Is there confusion between people in closely related jobs as to who is to do what? Is authority clearly stated and understood? (On what do you base your opinions? Is it more than wishful thinking?)

f. Are there formal standards for personal appearance? Are these well known and accepted? Do subordinates believe that "bosses" observe the rules and regulations that they expect subordinates to follow?

g. Do subordinates feel that all possible candidates for promotion from within are given full and honest consideration? (Have you asked them lately?)

h. Do employees think that people are laid off or discharged unreasonably? Is employment stable, or does the company hire and fire frequently? Do older employees feel secure in their jobs?

i. What do subordinates think of the willingness of the company to discuss policies, plans, and actions that affect their jobs?

j. Do subordinates feel that their superiors are interested in helping with personal or family problems that may influence attitudes at work? (How did you determine their feeling in this matter?)

2. Feelings about associates: superiors, subordinates, or equals

a. What do they think of the efficiency of the boss, the department, the company? (What plan do you have for discovering this?)

b. Do employees feel that the boss has favorites?

c. How adequately do the employees believe they are supervised? (Sales and merchandising have a variety of devices for determining customer satisfaction. What do you use with your subordinates to find out their opinions about your services to them?)

d. Do your subordinates feel they are being prepared to grow and advance? Do subordinates feel that they are pigeonholed? Are individuals counseled about their weaknesses and given the opportunity for personal growth and development?

e. Do subordinates feel that superiors resist new ideas of their subordinates without evaluating their worth? Are individuals afraid to present honest complaints to their bosses?

f. Are employees satisfied that grievances are handled promptly and fairly? That there are opportunities for transfer? Opportunities for a second chance for the person who gets into difficulties?

g. Do employees feel that you understand their needs and desires?

h. Do superiors know how subordinates get along with fellow employees?

3. Feelings about the company

a. What do subordinates think about the company's integrity and fairness as an employer—the degree to which company actions live up to promises and expressed policies?

b. What do employees think of the standing of the company—its financial strength and ability to maintain its competitive position?

c. What is the company's reputation in the community? (Who tells you this? How sure are you of the facts?)

d. What do employees' families and associates think of their jobs and of their opportunities with the company? (Have you ever reviewed how you determine this? Is it left to chance?)

e. Do people feel that they know far enough in advance about serious changes so that they can adjust to them?

f. Do employees feel that equal pay is given for equal work? How do they think the white-collar earnings compare with those of wage workers?

g. How often do people say: "The wage employees have got an increase—why can't I have one? The people out in the shop make more money than I do; yet you have to have a college degree to hold my job."

h. Do employees say: "Our products must be pretty good. They're the only ones you see in the stores." Or, "Why do our 'whatzits' cost so much? We make them by the million."

i. Do employees know and accept personnel practices regarding illness, leave of absence, vacation, military leave, etc.?

j. Do subordinates believe in the fairness and adequacy of health, insurance, and retirement programs? (If you are interested in what they think, you have no doubt established communication plans to find out.)

k. Do employees feel that adequate recreational and educational facilities are available? (Did you ever make a survey on this?)

l. Do your employees understand the annual report, or do they think it is written for accountants? Is the information presented in your company paper interesting to its readers?

m. Do employees consider cafeteria food prices fair and quality good?

IV. Principles for Communication Upward

A. Coverage must be systematic and balanced

1. Some managers feel that upward communication can be achieved by open-minded receptivity, without systematic planning. Spontaneous communication, however, may be neither balanced nor comprehensive. A few glaring weaknesses or successes may get all the attention. Voluble, aggressive spokesmen for some departments of the organization may claim frequent hearings, while others get none. The executive or supervisor who relies upon spontaneous communication alone receives neither a true picture of conditions nor the information he needs to forestall trouble and improve conditions. Free communications upward cannot be left to chance. Superiors must stimulate, encourage, and find ways to facilitate their movement.

2. A program for upward communication must provide for continuity. The flow of information upward cannot be turned on and off at the whim or to the advantage of either party if it is to be effective. The boss must try to listen on stormy days and with problems on his mind just as freely as he does when his world runs well. The subordinate, too, must communicate upward when the wheels run smoothly as well as when they squeak.

B. The flow of communications must be directed

1. Wherever possible, communications should move step by step upward through the organization. Ideally it should not be necessary for the bottom level of employees to communicate directly with those who are several levels higher in the organization. This is not to deny the opportunity for anyone at any level to be heard at any other level. Although such opportunity should exist, it will seldom be used where communications are strong at each level.

2. To be effective, communication must flow upward until it reaches that person who is responsible for, or who can take action upon, the conditions mentioned in the communication. If he can handle the problem effectively, there will be little need for detailed communication to go to a higher level.

C. Listening must be sensitive

1. It is a well-established principle of social science that people in different occupations and in different positions of responsibility within occupations have different outlooks on life. They see and interpret things through different-colored glasses and with different meanings and values. We cannot expect employees to look upon the

importance of efficiency, productivity, profit, and other such matters exactly as we do. They rarely will think exactly as we do, nor we as they do, although through education we can come somewhat closer. Therefore, listening to employees, trying sincerely to get their interpretations and ideas, and acting on the basis of what they think, not what we think, or what we wish they would think, are absolutely essential to realistic management. Serious mistakes are made when management assumes that a certain set of facts will or should lead to the same conclusion in the employee's mind as it does in the manager's mind.

2. Often in making complaints, the complainant is not aware of, or will not reveal, the true cause of his criticism or irritation. It is human nature to cover up the real cause of complaints and to attach an attitude of resistance to some wholly unrelated subject. The superior must strive to learn the real cause for brickbats and bouquets. Frequently it will be something very different from what the employee says or even thinks it is.

3. Experienced executives know that employees tell their boss what they think he wants to hear. They know that subordinates, even the most candid ones, sift out that which will hurt his feelings or reflect upon his ability. The superior must realize that anything he hears has passesd through a sieve designed to select that material which will gain the communicator's end, or win him as much approval as possible.

As we have seen, subordinates hesitate before they pass up unpleasant information. They ask themselves whether this information will annoy or offend their superior, whether they will be thought disloyal for listening to such criticism, or for passing it upward, whether their superior is secure enough himself to hear bad news. Since this is so, the wise manager may have to be constantly alert to, if not searching for, criticisms, complaints, and other evidences of dissatisfaction.

4. Subordinates are especially alert to all physical cues and non-verbal signals. A superior's actions, such as movements of the head and body, grimaces, silences, smiles, and scowls, are as important as words in encouraging or discouraging free reporting upward. A setting of the jaw, a reddening of the face, or a stiffening of the body are the subtle red lights in upward communication that say, without a word being spoken, "Stop, this is going too far!"

5. Upward communication is never highly effective if it appears to be "upward" communication. The concept of the dignity of man and the concept of the worth of employees as persons, having ideas

in many respects as valuable as their superior's, demand that we accept ideas from below without condescension. We should be as sensitive to them as we would be to the opinions of friends or associates.

6. There are occasions when we must be particularly sensitive to what is being communicated upward. In an atmosphere of frequent and unusual changes, it is especially important that all executives and supervisors work diligently to see that there are open and complete channels for upward communication. When a new plant is being opened, new systems installed, new production of sales problems, new policies established, economic retrenchment under way, then is the time to tune the communications receptors most delicately and listen in most often.

D. Listening must be objective

1. If upward communication is to be effective, the listener must show a constructive, receptive attitude toward direct or implied criticism of himself and his department, no matter how bad the news or how hostile the critic. A superior's willingness to listen is revealed by the amount of time he gives to hearing subordinates, his ability to put them at ease, and the absence of tension.

2. Sometimes we listen freely because it is to our advantage to find out employee sentiments and feelings. If communications up are to be successful, we must listen with equal interest when it is obvious that the advantage lies with the subordinate. Good upward communication includes those things subordinates want us to know for their benefit, as well as those things which we want to know for our own advantage.

3. We must guard against selecting only those communicators we want to hear from. Conscious or unconscious favoritism in choosing reporters whose ideas and opinions we hold in high regard gives us a distorted picture of conditions and may discourage other employees from correcting that picture. Line men must listen to staff assistants, top management to junior executives, union stewards to foremen, and vice versa, with the same interest that they would listen to their colleagues.

4. It is unwise for executives to state their positions or proposals first and then ask subordinates to suggest contrary or alternate points of view, or to comment upon their superior's opinions. Don't let your own position be known if you seek truly free opinions.

5. The person who listens to communications up with the certainty that he is right and the subordinate is wrong will accomplish little.

Unless the superior possesses and reveals an open mind and a willingness to change if shown to be wrong, he might as well not listen.

E. Listening implies action

1. A popular fallacy is that if we permit a man to blow off steam, the complaint will automatically be dissipated. Where adjustments in company policy or executive action are necessary, listening in the absence of any corrective action is not of much help. The superior who feels that he can listen long and willingly to justifiable complaints and reduce their disturbing effect within the complainant without taking action is fooling himself. Although listening and non-directive counseling may be valuable in helping subordinates to find and solve their own problems, they are not to be relied upon completely if the main cause of the trouble lies outside the individual.

2. When you are receiving communications up, be sure that you do not verbally agree or appear to the listener to do so if, at the same time, you do not intend to take corrective action. Your words or sympathetic listening may lead him to think that you plan to take an action which you do not contemplate. When your action does not follow, the subordinate is properly resentful. If a good idea cannot be put into effect at the time, or if a bad situation cannot then be improved, tell the individual and give him the reasons.

V. Media and Methods

By far the most effective method of tapping the ideas of subordinates is sympathetic listening in the many day-to-day, informal contacts within the department and outside the workplace. There are no full-blown systems that will do the job in any easier manner. No delegation of a manager's responsibility to know the thoughts and attitudes of his subordinates is possible. This is a job which must in the main be done individually, painstakingly, and with understanding and sympathy. It is not something to be accomplished by a high-pressure drive or through a mechanical system. Nothing can equal a manager's willingness to hear. Given this, however, some of the devices listed below have been found helpful in further encouraging free upward communication.

A. Various social gatherings of the employees through departmental parties, birthday parties, luncheons, outings, picnics, sports, and recreational events are fine opportunities for informal, casual communications. Unplanned, chance meetings taking place at the water fountain or beginning on the elevator or in the hallways may also provide opportunity for subordinates to be heard.

B. Staff personnel within the department have many opportunities to observe and talk with line employees. As a result, they sometimes can contribute to the supervisor's knowledge of what his subordinates think and feel. The alert manager is responsive to comment that such staff members may offer him about the operations and personnel of his department. Of course, he will not treat such communicants as informers; he will not expect them to reveal names or to violate confidences.

C. In any organization, there are some persons who, because of special insights and experiences, are particularly good at listening to and interpreting what employees say. Since some people can listen all day without really comprehending what they hear, it is important that we listen carefully to those who have some responsibility for morale and who possess peculiar skill in gaining insight into the real motives, feelings, and thoughts behind what people say.

D. In unionized companies, management can learn something about employee attitudes from union publications and union officials. If relations with the union are good, if union officials and shop leaders have been informed of what management wants, and if they have confidence in its motives, a study of union publications can be of great assistance in revealing what employees are thinking.

E. A checklist may also be helpful to supervisors who control a large number of subordinates. At the end of the day, on mimeographed lists of their employees, they can check off the men they have contacted. Mechanical as it seems, a quick review of the sheets covering a weekly or monthly period will show which employees have been neglected. Still other supervisors schedule their contacts. One division head in a production unit, for example, has a scheduled monthly visit with every employee in his department in addition to the informal contacts which grow out of the work situation.

F. In counseling after merit rating or evaluation of an employee, the superior who listens carefully and questions tactfully has many opportunities to discover what the subordinate thinks and feels about a wide range of subjects.

G. Grievance procedures are important means of getting ideas upward. However, we cannot expect them to do the major job; the main thing we want from upward communication is an awareness of the normal day-to-day ideas and attitudes of employees. A grievance may be considered an abnormal upward communication, the basis of which is misunderstanding. It is important, of course, to have a means of communicating serious misunderstandings upward for all levels of employees and supervisors. However, informal upward communication should be so good that this abnormal means of communication is rarely needed. To depend upon a grievance procedure as the main source for our knowledge of how employees feel limits us to knowing their thoughts only when they are negative, critical, or sharply different from our own.

Before any of the foregoing media and methods can be profitably exploited, however, management must be persuaded of the value of upward communication. It must also learn where, when, and how to listen and what to listen for.

VI. RESULTS OBTAINED FROM EFFECTIVE UPWARD COMMUNICATION

The general objectives achieved through strong upward communications are, as we have seen, the growth of democracy and leadership in the workplace, the development and strengthening of individuals through the satisfaction of the human need for self-expression and participation, and the promotion of loyalty and respect for the company. For those managers who encourage a free flow of upward communication there are, in addition, more immediate rewards:

The supervisor or executive gets an improved picture of the work, accomplishments, problems, plans, attitudes, and feelings of his subordinates.

Before becoming deeply involved, the manager can spot individuals, policies, actions, or assignments which are likely to cause trouble.

By welcoming upward communication, management strengthens the only device for tapping the ideas and help of its subordinates. This gives management a better answer to its problems and eases its own responsibility.

By opening the channels upward, management helps the easy flow and acceptance of communications down. *Good listening makes good listeners.*

QUESTIONS

1. Briefly outline the values of upward communication.
2. What are the deterrents to effective upward communication?
3. Discuss the basic principles for communicating upward.
4. How can effective upward communication be achieved? Which is the most effective method?
5. What basic part does management play in upward communication? Why?

MAKING CONSTRUCTIVE USE OF
THE OFFICE GRAPEVINE *

Keith Davis

The impression I have gained in discussing the office grapevine before different management groups is that most managers would rather avoid the subject entirely. They have, of course, their good reasons. The grapevine is intangible, and it is much easier to deal with tangible matters. Anyway, managers lack control of it. So why not ignore it altogether, and devote the time to matters which can be more directly controlled? Most managers are not even sure they have any responsibility concerning the grapevine in their department. Their job description does not say so; it is not shown on the organization chart; and *their* manager usually has not mentioned it (except, occasionally, to wish it were dead). Yes, indeed—managers have good reasons for ignoring the grapevine or pretending it is not there.

The situation is much like that in one of Aesop's fables. You will remember that a fox sought some grapes which grew so high on the vine that he could not reach them. At last, he decided: "Those grapes are sour and aren't worth having anyway." In the same manner, many an office manager has decided that there are only sour grapes to be found on the office grapevine. Here are some comments I have gathered from actual discussions with office managers:

> "The grapevine never gives us anything but trouble; so I stay away from it as much as I can."

> "Don't talk to me about communicating through the grapevine. I wouldn't trust it for any purpose."

> "If I could get rid of the grapevine in my office, my troubles would be over."

Admittedly, this last manager has a good idea. The grapevine is a thorn in the side of every office manager. It regularly offers resistance to his formal orders, or amends them, or creates rumor. It is, in the true sense, a *troublemaker*. How easy and convenient it would be if an office manager could simply abolish the grapevine! Perhaps he could place a notice on the bulletin board, saying: "Effective at 12:00 noon tomorrow, the grapevine in this office is abolished." But we are daydreaming. If there is one thing all of us have learned from our experience and research, it is that *homicide is not a solution to the grapevine.* It cannot be abolished, rubbed out, hidden under a basket, chopped down, tied up, murdered, or stopped. If we suppress it in one place, it pops up in another. If we cut off one of its sources, it merely moves to another—much the way we change from channel to channel on a television set. It is as hard to kill as the mythical glass snake which, when struck, breaks itself into fragments and grows an entire new body out of each piece. In a sense, the grapevine is man's birthright, because whenever men congregate in groups of two or more the grapevine is sure to develop. It may involve smoke signals, jungle tom-toms, taps on the prison wall, ordinary conversation, or some other method—but it will always be there.

What Is the grapevine?

The grapevine is the communication system of the *informal organization* in business. Typically, a business is divided into two great organizational systems—one formal and one informal. The *formal* organization is the one usually shown on organization charts, and it is built by means of a chain of command in which authority is delegated successively from one person to another. The maintenance of this chain of command requires an elaborate network of orders, instructions, and reports, which constitute the formal communication system of the business. The *informal* organization, on the other hand, arises from the social relationships of people. It is neither required nor controlled by management. To serve this informal organization, an informal communication system arises. It is variable, dynamic, and fickle, running back and forth across organizational lines and rapidly changing its course. Hence, the term *grapevine* arose to describe its meandering, hither and yon, back and forth, like its vegetable namesake.

In a recent issue of *The Indianapolis Star Magazine*, Joseph K. Shepard described the grapevine in somewhat poetic terms:

> With the rapidity of a burning powder train, information flows like magic out of the woodwork, past the water fountain, past the manager's door and the janitor's mop closet. As elusive as a summer zephyr, it filters through steel walls, bulkheads, or construction glass partitions, from the sub-basement to the rafters, from office boy to executive. . . . It carries good news and bad, fact as well as fancy, without discrimination. It cares nothing about reputation, nothing about civil rights; it has no respect for persons or for prerogatives of management; it will carve up and serve the big brass, the shop foreman, and the stenographer with fine impartiality.

The important point which we must recognize is that the grapevine is a *natural, normal activity*. It is an essential part of the total
human environment. There is nothing inherently evil about the
grapevine, just as there is nothing inherently evil about the weather.
To be sure, we gripe and groan about the weather, but we would all
perish without rain, sun, and the other ingredients which comprise it.
Some authorities have suggested that, in a similar manner, businesses
would perish if they did not have a grapevine to fill in the gaps
existing in the formal communication system. Consider, if you will,
your own business and how you would feel if you were absolutely
sure that the grapevine was "dead" in your company. You would
almost certainly be worried. Your ability to build teamwork, motivate
your people, and create identification with the company would be
severely restricted. Indeed, if employees are so uninterested in their
work that they do not engage in shop-talk about it, we usually consider them maladjusted. And if they are so disinterested in their
associates that they do not discuss who will get the next promotion and
why Martha was late to work, we often suspect they are abnormal.
The definite conclusion for the office manager, then, is: *Be glad you
have a grapevine*. You would have a "sick" office without it.

How does the grapevine operate?

Managers occasionally get the impression that the grapevine
operates like a long chain in which *A* tells *B,* who tells *C,* who in turn
tells *D,* and so on until, 20 persons later, *Y* gets the information—
very late and very incorrect. Sometimes the grapevine may operate
this way, but research shows that it generally follows a somewhat
different pattern. *A* tells three or four selected others (such as *B, R,*
and *F*). Only one or two of these receivers will then pass on the
information, and again they will usually tell more than one person.
Then, as the information becomes older and the number of those
knowing it grows larger, it gradually dies out because those who
receive it do not repeat it. In professional literature, I have called
this network a "cluster chain," because each link in the chain tends
to inform a cluster of other people instead of only one person.

If we accept the idea that this cluster chain is predominant, then
it is simply a matter of logic to conclude that only a few persons are
active communicators on the grapevine for any particular bit of
information. If, for example, 87 clerks in your office know that Mabel
got married secretly last Saturday, the word was probably spread
to these 87 by only 10 or 15 of your clerks. The remainder knew the
information, but did not spread it. These persons who keep the

grapevine active are called "liaison individuals" in the professional literature. For example, in one company which I studied, when a quality control problem occurred, 68 per cent of the executives knew about it, but only 20 per cent of them spread the information. In another case, when a manager planned to resign, 81 per cent of the executives knew about it, but only 11 per cent passed the news on to others.

Up to this point, my picture of the grapevine network is probably consistent with the common image. The typical reaction, at this point, is probably somewhat as follows: "Martha is one of those liaison individuals. If I could just hush her, maybe we could get some work done around here." I doubt, however, that the problem is that simple. If you "hush" Martha, someone else will probably take her place on the grapevine, because the grapevine is more a product of the *situation* than it is of the person. In my own research, I have uncovered no strong evidence that any one person or group consistently acts as liaison agent to the exclusion of all others. It is true that some of us are more active on the grapevine than our associates, but the evidence is clear that—*given the proper situation and motivation—any of us tend to become active on the grapevine.* In three successive surveys I made of one group of 60 executives, for example, the liaison agents were completely different in each instance.

Most people tend to be active on the grapevine when they have *cause* to be. This means that they are acting partly in a predictable way. This element of cause and predictability is important because it offers management a chance to influence the grapevine. What are some of these causes? For one thing, we know that any group tends to be most active on the grapevine during periods of excitement and insecurity—during, for example, a layoff or the introduction of automation into the office. At such times, the grapevine is a beehive of activity, which means that it must be watched with extra care and "fed" the right information to keep it from getting out of hand.

People also are active on the grapevine when their friends and work associates are involved. This means that if Mary is to be promoted or Beatrice is fired, the other employees should be told the full story as soon as possible. If they are *not* informed, they will fill in the gaps with their own conclusions—and there you have the start of another rumor. People also tend to be most active on the grapevine when they have news, as distinguished from stale information. Research shows that the greatest dispersion of information occurs immediately after it is made known; therefore, it is important to get out the right story in the beginning.

The grapevine exists largely through word of mouth and observation; hence, if you have procedures which regularly bring people in contact, you can expect these people to have an active grapevine. In one company, for example, the chief link between two officers was the manager's secretary, who stopped at the other office after lunch each day to pick up reports. In another case, the link was an accounting clerk who every morning telephoned 300 yards across the company property to get some cost data. In a similar manner, employees having adjacent desks are likely to be in closer communication than two employees in separate buildings. Thus, the office manager partly determines the nature of the grapevine by the office layouts and procedures which he establishes.

One grapevine characteristic with which we are all familiar is its function as a carrier of rumor, which is defined as *untrue* grapevine information. Some persons look upon the grapevine as nothing but a rumor-manufacturing machine. Research, however, suggests that we greatly overplay the rumor aspects of the grapevine. We are inclined to remember the few times it brings us rumors and to forget the many times it brings us facts—which leads us to the erroneous conclusion that the grapevine carries mostly rumors. Actually, the reverse is true. If we took a cross section of the grapevine, we would see that much more than half of its information is correct. Though I do not have enough cases to present statistically reliable figures, my research indicates that, in normal business situations, between 90 and 95 per cent of grapevine information is correct. Occasionally the grapevine has the correct information *even when the boss does not.* In one company, for example, an office supervisor learned by the grapevine that his job was to be abolished. He did not at first believe this, but later learned it was true. In another company, a field salesman learned of his transfer from a friend who was in the real estate business. The real estate man knew the information because the new salesman's wife had contacted him, seeking a new house in the community.

Another marked characteristic of the grapevine is the speed with which it functions. The cluster chain makes it easy for a few people to reach many others in a short time. Furthermore, through modern air travel and electronic communication, it is possible for the grapevine to leap hundreds of miles very quickly. To offer an example, a man we shall call Joe Smith, who worked for a manufacturing company, was on a year's leave of absence in Florida. One day, in the home office up North, a company official came into the president's office and said that he had heard that Joe was quitting to go with another company. "You must be wrong," said the president. "I talked to Joe, long distance, the day before yesterday, and he said he would be back on the first of the month." At that point, the president's secretary brought in the morning mail. Right on top was a special-delivery letter from Joe Smith submitting his resignation in order to take a job with a rival company. Investigation disclosed that Joe had happened to meet an out-of-town friend just after he made his sudden decision to resign. He told his friend, who in turn called home that evening and told his wife—and the grapevine was under way!

With regard to the above illustration, and other examples cited in this study, another characteristic of the grapevine is evident. For although many of my illustrations involve office girls and wives at home, the grapevine is not exclusively a function of women. Men are quite active on it also. It should be borne in mind that the grapevine is a coeducational institution.

Benefits of the grapevine

One fact which research has disclosed is that the grapevine provides a number of benefits and that many managers, either intuitively or consciously, already make use of these benefits. As mentioned earlier, the grapevine is a primary means for development of group identification and interest in work. It also helps the company complete its job of communication. Most employees probably get as much company information by way of the informal grapevine as through formal communication. In fact, it would be almost impossible for management to transmit formally all the variety of company information which is necessary to help employees feel a part of the company. They depend on the grapevine to help them understand their environment.

Some managers use the grapevine additionally as a tactical maneuver. This is a common device in collective bargaining. As an example, one company reached a stalemate with its union, and, in order to speed up negotiations, it had one of its representatives drop the rumor that the company's wage offer would be withdrawn at the end of the week if the union continued to ignore it. Needless to say, this word reached the union quickly, and the parties were back at the bargaining table the next day. (It should be observed that the union makes good use of this tactical device, too.)

The grapevine is also a primary source of upward communication, especially information about what people are doing and how they feel toward certain situations. The grapevine brings to a manager both facts and feelings, rumor and truth, and it is the manager's task to sort and interpret them. Another benefit of the grapevine is that it is probably the best emotional safety valve yet devised. When Mary gets irked at the office manager, she isn't likely to tell him— but she does need to tell *someone* in order to get the problem off her mind.

Situations such as these prove that the grapevine has many useful functions around the office. Given the proper environment, it can "earn its board and keep." Though it is a problem, it is not by any means *all bad*.

Using the grapevine constructively

At this point, we have recognized at least three major facts about the grapevine:

It is here to stay.
It is a normal part of our organization.
It offers certain benefits.

If we accept these ideas, then common sense dictates that *we should learn to live with the grapevine*. It can be especially helpful if we give it some guidance. That is a large order, but we know we must fulfill it because the grapevine is roughly half of our communication system. We can no more ignore it than we can ignore half of our markets or half of our company policies. Our first step in living with the grapevine, therefore, is to become aware of it. It is a part of our decision-making environment. We must regularly ask ourselves: How will this action affect the grapevine? What precautions do I need to take? Can the grapevine help implement this action?

Our next step is to learn something about the grapevine, so that we will know how to deal with it. If we are professional managers, we will try to prepare ourselves professionally. Most of all, each of us must study his own company, so that he can get some feel of the channels of communication and the role which the grapevine plays. If possible, it is desirable to support research on the subject or do it oneself, because there is not adequate coverage of this subject in the professional literature.

Third, we should tune in to the grapevine—listen and learn. Actually, there is not *one* grapevine, but *hundreds* passing back and forth around us every day. What are the management grapevines saying? The union grapevines? The employee grapevines? A word of caution, however, is in order here: It is necessary to sift and interpret what is heard on the grapevine. Management's task is to look for the *meaning,* not merely the words. To illustrate, a man we shall call Jones supervised nine claims adjusters in an insurance office. Jones tried to listen to the grapevine, and one of the messages that came through was: "Your men don't feel busy enough. They want more work to do." Jones knew that each man had an adequate workload, so he finally concluded that the grapevine had garbled the statement before it reached him. Investigation disclosed that Jones *heard* right but made a wrong interpretation. He took the words at face value instead of relating them to the people who stated them. These men felt that one or two of Jones' favorites were getting all the large claim adjustments, which carried more prestige. Therefore, his men really wanted *fairer* work assignments, but not *more* work. Then why didn't they say so? Evidence indicated that they did not dare to ask directly for fairer assignments, for three reasons: First, such action would be openly charging Jones with favoritism. Second, it would be openly taking prestige cases away from fellow workers, which might create internal conflict. And, finally, prestige was a measure of employee "feeling" about claims, and management gave no recognition to this aspect of claims. Having these good reasons, the men asked for more work, hoping that with the extra work they would get more prestige cases or that Jones would finally perceive what they wanted. The conclusion which we may draw from this example is that we should listen to the *meaning* which the grapevine conveys rather than to the *words* it uses.

A fourth step in living with the grapevine is to discover its leaders and work with them when the occasion demands. All of us take part in grapevines, but there are some "thought leaders" who generally mold the group's opinions. If, for example, some complicated organizational changes are being made and you know that your people do not understand them even after you have tried to explain them, perhaps you should solicit the support of one of your key men in the informal organization. He may be able to re-interpret your ideas through the grapevine in terms which make more sense to workers. Of course, you may not formally ask this man to help you, but you can make sure that he does understand the changes and feels free to convey them to others. This kind of approach works only if the thought leader has a favorable attitude toward the company; therefore, you should do all in your power to cultivate cooperative attitudes among the informal thought leaders of your office. It is useless to try to ignore these thought leaders, because to do so is simply to bury one's head in the sand like an ostrich. They *are* there, and they will influence people's reactions to what management does.

A fifth step in working with the grapevine is to feed it facts, so that it will have something useful to carry. The grapevine is as active and restless as waves on a seashore. Minute by minute, hour by hour, as people contact each other throughout your office, the grapevine is operating. Thus, there exists tremendous capacity for carrying information. Whether what is carried is useful or useless depends considerably on management. You can keep news bottled up in your executive ranks, in which case the grapevine carries much useless speculation about company activities *because employees do not know the real facts*. Or, you can take the better approach and communicate what the workers want and need to know about the company so that some grapevine energies can be devoted to carrying and interpreting these company facts. In other words: *Feed and water the grapevine.* Supply it with useful facts today so that you do not harvest sour grapes tomorrow. Help the grapevine to be usefully productive.

Dealing with rumor

Learning to live with the grapevine means that we must know how to deal with rumor. My opinion is that we should strike back at it firmly and consistently. But we should know *how* and *what* to strike. It is a serious mistake to strike at the grapevine as a whole merely because it happens to be the agent which carries rumor. That approach is somewhat the equivalent of doing away with people because they transmit disease to each other.

Rumor originates for a number of reasons. One cause is plain maliciousness, but it is probably not the most important. A more frequent cause is employee anxiety and insecurity. When people are poorly placed, emotionally maladjusted, or inadequately informed about their environment, they often react by circulating rumor. This is a normal human effort to make their situation more meaningful and secure. On other occasions, rumor serves as a means of wish fulfillment or applying pressure upon management. For example, Mary and Joan start a rumor that everyone in the office will get a $20 monthly raise. Saying this makes them feel better, and they hope that if it is said long enough and loud enough perhaps it will come to pass. Employees are wise, and they sometimes use rumor as a tactical maneuver. Given the proper situation of poor employee communication, they plant an undesirable rumor in order to "smoke out" the true facts from a reluctant management. In this case, management has mostly itself to blame, because it failed to provide the facts on time or to explain why it could not provide them.

If we are going to strike back at rumor, our best approach is *to get at its causes* rather than to attempt to kill it after it has already started. We should prove that we are professional managers by practicing *preventive medicine*. My opinion is that a well-managed office has very little rumor mongering, for the simple reason that people have little cause to start rumors. We have all seen offices and shops like this. When each worker feels reasonably secure, believes himself to be a part of the team, and understands the things that matter to him, there are few rumors.

But in spite of all you can do, rumors do start. Then what? In general, one should try to halt those rumors that are important enough to be of concern. They should be stopped as early as possible, because research shows that, once a rumor's general theme is known and accepted, employees distort future happenings to conform to the rumor. Thus, if employees accept the "scuttlebutt" that you are planning to move your offices to a new building, then every minor change thereafter will be interpreted as a confirmation of that rumor. If the rumor were dead, these same changes could be made without any employee upset at all.

It seems to me that a firm's communication policy should distinguish between two types of rumors. It is a waste of time to strike at all rumors, and to do so makes a mountain out of a molehill. Company policy *should* make it clear, however, that employees are not to spread so-called "subversive" rumors—those which tend seriously to reduce morale, destroy teamwork, decrease productivity, or maliciously attack a person's dignity and integrity. Employees who spread this type of rumor do just as much harm as if they threw sand into a gearbox, and, when they are rated or screened for promotion, their record on this matter must be considered.

Rumors are stopped by means of public-address system announcements, rumor columns in plant newspapers, bulletins, and similar devices. The most effective method, however, is face-to-face introduction to the facts by each manager. In this approach, it is wise to give the facts directly, without first mentioning the rumor, because research suggests that, when a rumor is repeated at this time, it is remembered just as well as the refutation.

Regardless of a rumor's importance, managers should listen to it carefully, because—even though untrue—it usually carries a message. Each manager should ask himself: Why did that rumor originate? What does it mean? In every case, there is some *cause* which the manager needs to understand. If, for example, the grapevine has it that the only meat available in the cafeteria all next week will be wieners, it may mean that too many wieners are being served, or that the cafeteria's wieners are wonderful, or that Friday fish day is not adequately respected, or something else—or nothing at all. The manager's job is to try to take meaning from the hodgepodge of rumors as they pass by. Perhaps this approach is unrealistic for some managers or for everyday usage, but occasionally managers with keen insight have made valuable interpretations from rumors on the grapevine. One such case was that of the labor relations director who, during a strike, listened carefully to what the workers said management was going to do. He knew these were rumors because management had not *decided* what to do, but he listened just the same, because these rumors gave him insight about worker attitudes toward management and about how far the workers would go.

Need for management training

I have been talking about how to live with the grapevine, and my final point is that it is necessary to train managers and supervisors in grapevine communication just as thoroughly as they are trained in formal communication. Most of the communication training programs I have seen in business give very little attention to informal communication. This is a serious oversight which requires correction. Apparently it is assumed that managers already know how to deal with the grapevine, and therefore should be trained chiefly in formal communication. I suspect, however, the reverse of this assumption is more accurate. At any rate, training about grapevine communication is badly needed. Improvement in employee communication is going to be slow until our managers learn more about how to make constructive use of the grapevine.

In summary, I have made four points which I urge every manager to consider carefully:

> The grapevine is here to stay.
> It is a normal group activity.
> We can make constructive use of it because it is not all bad.
> To make better use of it, we need to give our managers more training in informal communication.

QUESTIONS

1. Why do many managers dislike the grapevine?
2. What does the term "grapevine" mean?
3. What are the basic characteristics of the grapevine?
4. Discuss the advantages of the grapevine.
5. Explain how the grapevine can be used effectively.

General Questions on Part 5

1. Discuss the relationship of communication to leadership and human relations.
2. Explain what is meant by "two-way" communication.
3. What is the basic reason for communication?
4. What are the fundamental dimensions of communications? Which of these dimensions is most important to organizational efficiency? Why?
5. Why do misunderstandings arise between people?
6. Prepare a list of barriers to communication.
7. How important is listening to communication? Why?
8. What effect does rumor have on organizational efficiency? How can rumors best be handled?
9. Explain the basic process of communication.
10. Prepare a list of the communication media that can be used in a typical organization.

Bibliography for Part 5

Articles

BENEVENTO, P. "Administrative Communication and its Relationship to Leadership," *Journal of American Society of Training Directors,* Vol. 13, No. 5 (May, 1959), pp. 9-16.

BRETH, R. D. "Human Relations and Communications are Twins," *Personnel Journal,* December, 1952, p. 259.

CHASE, STUART. "Executive Communications: Breaking the Semantic Barrier," *Management Review,* Vol. 46, No. 4 (April, 1957), pp. 58-66.

DAVIS, KEITH. "Communication Within Management," *Personnel,* Vol. 31, No. 3 (November, 1954), pp. 212-217.

——————— "Management Communication and the Grapevine," *Harvard Business Review,* September-October, 1953, pp. 43-49.

DRUCKER, PETER. "Communications—What Are Employees Really Interested In?," *Advanced Management,* Vol. 16, No. 2 (February, 1951), pp. 7-9.

FISCHER, F. E. "A New Look at Management Communication," *Personnel,* May, 1955, pp. 487-495.

HOSLETT, SCHUYLER D. "Barriers to Communication," *Personnel,* Vol. 28, No. 2 (September, 1951), pp. 108-114.

HOUSTON, N. S. "Create a Proper Communication Atmosphere," *Office Executive,* Vol. 32, No. 2 (February, 1957), pp. 21-23.

MCMURRY, R. N. and RUTH G. SHAEFFER. "Foundations for Better Communications," *American Business,* Vol. 27, No. 7 (July, 1957), pp. 23, 40.

NICHOLS, R. G. "Listening Is A Ten-Point Skill," *Nation's Business,* Vol. 45, No. 7 (July, 1957), pp. 56-60.

PIGORS, PAUL. "Communication in Industry: A Cure or Conflict?," *Industrial and Labor Relations Review,* Vol. 6, No. 4 (July, 1953), pp. 497-509.

TARNOPOL, LESTER. "Attitudes Block Communications," *Personnel Journal,* Vol. 37, No. 9 (February, 1959), pp. 325-328.

WANCE, W. W. "Supervisors Must Know 'How to Listen,'" *Journal of American Society of Training Directors,* March-April, 1955, pp. 19-21, 54.

Books

Effective Communication On the Job. New York: American Management Association, 1956.

GARDNER, B. B. and D. G. MOORE. *Human Relations in Industry.* Homewood, Ill.: Richard D. Irwin, Inc., 1945.

HERON, A. R. *Sharing Information With Employees.* Stanford, California: Stanford University Press, 1942.

REDFIELD, C. E. *Communication In Management.* Chicago, Ill.: University of Chicago Press, 1953.

WHYTE, W. F. *Is Anybody Listening?* New York: Simon and Schuster, Inc., 1952.

PART 6. PARTICIPATION

Whatever his duties or responsibilities may be, the typical American workman of today is surrounded by a complex technological maze. This means he must reconcile systems and procedures, understand and execute company policies, delevop essential technical skills to perform his job properly, and so forth. Quite clearly he faces an extremely difficult task.

One factor that has contributed greatly to this complex task is the corporate form of organization. Layer upon layer of "managers" has been added to what was originally a simple business structure. Lines of communications have become complicated and easily snarled; confusion has arisen as to responsibility and authority; and, most important of all, the social and physical distances between managers and workers have become greater and greater.

The result of this has been that for some people a job is only a job—work that must be performed in order to earn a living. Resigning themselves to the complexity of the maze, workers lose interest, not only in their work, but in the company as well. Some become chronic "job shoppers," whereas others develop apathy towards their work and perform at a level that is just good enough to keep them employed. Still others become agitators, endeavoring to stir up malcontentment in their departments by constant complaining or by disseminating false information. Thus, the corporation and its evolving technology, although largely responsible for unprecedented prosperity, have also fostered much discontent and unrest.

Now we are not making the claim that this is generally true of all industry. Obviously it is not; certainly many of us are well satisfied with our jobs, do our best at them, and do not as a rule fall into the categories just described. So the question arises: "Why this difference between workers? Why are some of us inspired by our job and its responsibilities while others find themselves wallowing in the doldrums?"

Needless to say, a myriad of answers may be offered. Volume upon volume has been written along these lines, and a great portion of this book is devoted to just this subject. Our concern in this part, however, is with something so basic to any and all organizations that, indeed, it is possibly the most vital link between the worker, his job, and the company.

We are referring, of course, to *employee participation*—psychologically as well as physically—in the many phases of the management process. It has been shown in countless numbers of studies that participation on the part of employees exerts profound effects on quality of work, acceptance of changes, and on over-all morale. Furthermore, employees who are psychologically and mentally involved in their jobs display a much greater degree of identification with the company and its goals, thereby creating a climate conducive to individual growth and development. In turn, it is this very growth and development that so vitally affects the expanding company and the business economy as well.

A Theoretical Framework for Participation

One of the truly perplexing problems we face as we go through life is that we cannot always prove, with facts and figures, all of our opinions and ideas. Many things in life we have to accept at face value or on the basis of sheer faith alone. For example, what about the advantages to be derived from going to college? Can one actually prove conclusively that he will have a better life if he obtains an academic degree and becomes a lawyer, businessman, or politician? The answer is fairly simple—no, he cannot. But he can obviously *assume* that a college education will help him to achieve goals that will make him a more satisfied, happy person.

The same thing can be said of quite a few of the practices and procedures that one uses as a manager or executive in the business world. Everything cannot simply be measured in terms of dollars and cents, in inches and feet, or in terms of absolute cost. In short, the benefits to be derived from many practices and/or policies have to be assumed and taken for granted. Certain indirect measurements are frequently utilized, but exclusive reliance upon them is not feasible. Employee fringe benefits are a good example. Although management assumes that benefits contribute to productivity and morale, the extent of their contribution cannot be directly and exactly ascertained.

The theory behind securing employee participation in group endeavor is of the same nature. It remains an impossibility to measure or calculate exactly the benefits attained by running an organization on a participative-democratic basis rather than on a highly autocratic basis. Because the best measurement we have to date is accomplishment, it is along these lines that leading enterprises of today's economy, utilizing participative management, rank first and foremost in terms of profits, assets, research and development, and so on. As Gordon Allport points out in his article, these companies have devised ways and means for achieving ego-involvement on the part of workers within the organization. And it is upon this ego-involvement that the success of participative management depends, for people will only take an active interest in the forces that shape their industrial destinies if they are given free opportunity and encouragement to do so.

Industrial organizations, because of their form of organization, are highly autocratic. As was shown in Part 2, leaders or managers are appointed to their leadership positions and are vested with authority to compel obedience from their subordinates. Consequently, many employees have little or nothing to say about the whole procedure, except perhaps the freedom to quit their jobs, although circumstances usually preclude this. In other words, they have little choice but to accept their appointed "boss," even though the goals that each party seeks to attain are probably directly opposing. Because successful leadership is heavily contingent upon leaders and followers viewing each other as "mutual means" for achieving similar goals, a serious dichotomy arises.

Those of us fortunate enough to have been born and raised in the democratic atmosphere of the United States have gone through a long process of inculcation in democratic processes. Consequently, we expect to have something to say about actions and plans that affect our way of life in industry and society. If others attempt to deprive us of this right, we will do all in our power to do something about it.* The growth of unionism, for example, shows how this has affected industry.

We are not trying to say that the autocratic type of industrial organization is essentially bad or purposefully opposed to democracy. Obviously, certain authority relationships are necessary to provide direction and coordination in any organization. Our principal claim, however, is that by introducing and blending into this autocratic structure as many participative devices as are feasible, advantages will accrue that tend to minimize some of the effects of autocracy.

---

* The authors are fully aware of the limits of reality; certainly our democratic processes are imperfect and often leave much to be desired. Nevertheless, this does not disqualify the basic assumptions upon which such processes rest, nor does it imply that, because some imperfections exist, the entire system is imperfect.

Just how much participation is feasible will depend upon individual managements and their philosophies. Once again, Allport demonstrates that proper focus on participation enhances democratic action. The last twenty years have shown that industry is fully aware of these potentialities. The critical question now becomes one of how far management is willing to go with participative management.

Although our thoughts have so far been directed towards management's approach to participation, the individual employee deserves equal attention. Tannenbaum and Massarik's article states that "the subordinate must be capable of becoming psychologically involved in the participational activities." In other words, not only must he be conditioned to participating in decisions that affect him in his work, but he has to possess the necessary intelligence and desire to do so. Thus, several conditions have to be met by both the management and the worker before participative management can successfully be applied in any enterprise.

In summary, it is important to bear in mind the psychological basis upon which employee participation rests. The psychologist has proven most conclusively that people are more creative, exhibit greater degrees of initiative, and become more responsible when given the opportunity to express themselves and share in the decisions affecting them. Not only is this true of our democratic society as a whole, but of industry as well. Therefore, industry must provide means for allowing employees to participate actively—psychologically as well as physically—in their work. The problem of "how" is the subject of following sections.

PARTICIPATIVE LEADERSHIP

Part 2 has already sketched the different approaches one can take towards leadership. Admittedly, it is a vast and complex subject. If we were to query a random sample of successful executives about the worthwhileness of using the participative approach in directing the work of subordinates, unquestionably a variety of answers would be received. Depending upon their background and function, some would undoubtedly be highly in favor of such techniques, while others would be quite skeptical.

We can see also that managerial attitudes will differ for varying reasons. The old-line manager who insists he "came up the hard way" will consider participation as nonsense, insisting that workers are paid to do, not think. He gives the orders and makes the decisions. Or an executive's personality may be such that he cannot relinquish any of his authority. Furthermore, he may fear that increased participation will result in his authority being taken away from him or that it will give the union more and more power.

These and many other negative attitudes regarding participation still persist in the industrial scene. However, they are slowly but surely changing with the passage of time. As the old-timers begin to relinquish the reins to younger men, the latter tend to bring newer concepts of management into their jobs, among them being the idea of securing subordinate participation. Recognition is given to the fact that authority really flows from the bottom up and not exclusively from the top down. Today employees are better educated and therefore expect more from their boss and from the company as a whole. Jobs are not scarce, and man power is at a premium. All in all, people know more and want more. The democratic system has instilled in the majority of us the desire to get ahead and to improve our way of life. Once we have had the taste of opportunity, we are not likely to give it up.

So the modern executive has to admit to his own limitations. He cannot do all that has to be done by himself. He must, of necessity, depend upon others. No longer is he the indispensable man, what with the emergence of the management profession. This does not imply, however, that he can pass on his responsibilities to those below him. Indeed, participative management does not lighten the executive load, for he still must make final decisions and be accountable for performance and getting the work done. It simply means he must now be willing to share his authority and responsibility with his subordinates.

To practice participative leadership, the executive or supervisor has to admit that his people have talents and abilities other than what they can do with their hands. He must recognize that his subordinates have the ability to think, to come up with new ideas, and to initiate new procedures and ways of doing things. In fact, countless numbers of innovations have stemmed directly from employees on the assembly line. As more executives and their companies open their minds to this talent and allow it to express itself, productivity will increase in rapid strides.

But it must be emphasized that participation is not a one-way street. Participation requires joint response on the part of *both* superior and subordinate. Both have to share a zone of interest, recognizing that theirs is a joint endeavor. In today's technical world, the manager and the worker cannot walk separate paths. The success of one depends upon the success of the other. The assembly line, for example, cannot roll unless the salesman gets the order, the engineer designs the product, the supervisor lays out the needed processing, and the worker performs his diverse functions.

The modern executive job is thus increasingly becoming one of a participative nature. Executives and supervisors are today turning to their subordinates for more help in the decision-making process. How far to extend this participation throughout the organization now becomes a perplexing question. There is no simple solution here. It depends upon the individual situation and how ready the organization and its people are for participation. Certain limits have to be established, but the question of where and how to draw the line is a problem for top management to resolve.

TYPES OF PARTICIPATION

Multiple management

"Multiple management" is a term coined to describe a certain type of participation. It best describes how some companies establish permanent committees to assist and advise operating executives.

These companies, for example, establish committees at different levels made up of representatives from many different departments. Such committees exist to give advice to key executives in particular functions. Perhaps the vice-president in charge of sales will have a sales committee made up of people from personnel, finance, production, the legal department, and so on, which will meet at intervals to discuss with the vice-president various policies or actions that he has taken or possibly will take. Ordinarily these committees have no decision-making power. Instead, their job is to recommend, discuss, and review. One of their principal advantages is that they serve as a fine training technique for people in different functions. By participating in these committee meetings, people from different jobs learn more about the sales function, its responsibilities and problems.

Consultative management

The multiple management type of participation is found in a relatively few number of firms. Other companies, however, have found that committees do serve as an excellent device for obtaining participation, although these companies do not ordinarily set up such an elaborate system of committees as do firms utilizing the multiple management concept. Rather than set up formal, standing committees, their preference, especially at the middle and lower levels of the organization, seems to be for *ad hoc* committees. To distinguish between the two different approaches to using committees, we can label the latter approach "consultative management."

Regardless of what committee system is used, of fundamental importance is the fact that committees do serve as excellent providers for participative effort. Through them, people are asked to share in solving problems, to discuss and analyze various situations, and to add their ideas to the ideas of their peers and superiors. Along these same lines, many companies urge supervisors to hold periodic staff conferences and meetings for attaining the same results. Here people are informed of past and coming events that may affect them in their work. Again their comments and ideas are solicited and their opinions are asked for. This, too, is a part of consultative management.

Suggestion systems

Company-wide suggestion systems are another technique for obtaining participation, especially at the rank-and-file level. Some persons undoubtedly feel that suggestion systems are of little importance, and in some companies this might be entirely correct. The success of such systems depends heavily upon how well they are implemented and administered, and upon a firm belief by management in their importance. If management displays a sincere interest in the system, it can be a very effective participation device. If, however, it is installed just because it looks good to have one and because other companies have them, employees are quick to sense these attitudes, and the results will probably be solely on the negative side.

These are but a few techniques a business can use to encourage active participation on the part of all employees. Many other techniques, too numerous for special mention here, are also available to the progressive concern. Of the utmost importance, however, is not what specific techniques to use, because they will depend upon the situation, but rather that the manager-leader realize that the desire to participate is a basic drive in all employees, and thus certain conditions must prevail before this need can be accommodated. We shall now look at these in some detail.

ORGANIZATION STRUCTURE AND PARTICIPATION

Before any kind of participative leadership or consultative management can be applied in an organization, there must be a firmly rooted belief on the part of the executive class that participation by employees is not only desirable but essential as well. In turn, executive attitudes regarding participation will depend upon whether their company is highly centralized or whether it is decentralized in terms of authority.

The highly centralized company, of course, restricts managerial authority to the uppermost levels of management. All important decisions, and many unimportant ones as well, are reserved for top officials and are, for all practical purposes, divorced from the operating manager who should be making them. His job is to implement whatever the decisions might be. When this is the situation, how can operating managers be expected to invite participation on the part of their own subordinates when their own superiors do not offer them this opportunity? Indeed, active, ego-involved participation will be virtually nonexistent in this type of organization.

The decentralized structure presents a different picture, however. When managers are given full authority to make decisions commensurate with their responsibility, they are more likely to extend this policy to their subordinates and to invite active participation by subordinates to the mutual advantage of all. Decentralization of managerial authority is really one of the broadest phases of participation that any company can indulge in. It is an open challenge to managers to motive them to higher standards of performance, and it encourages them to extend the same principle to their subordinates.

The degree of participation in any company will thus hinge on top management's orientation towards the whole concept of authority. Participation tends to be higher and more active when the formal structure is decentralized, with the reverse being true when the structure is centralized. Chris Argyris has a penetrating analysis of this point in his article, and he makes some salient observations concerning the formal structure and the degree of participation.

PARTICIPATION AND UNIONISM

All of us are aware of the tremendous importance of labor unions in today's economy. There is no doubt that a large number of workers identify themselves principally with their union and not their company. Their major efforts are directed towards enhancing the status of their local and its membership, and towards increased participation in union affairs.

Progressive labor leadership during the past twenty-five years has fostered a growing amount of participation on the part of members. Workers are encouraged to hold office in the local and to participate in all types of union activities. Because the union provides many benefits for its members and does all in its power to protect their rights and welfare, workers soon begin to sense that they are a part of something, that through their union they are given more say-so over the factors influencing their behavior on the job. In short, through the outlet for participation that the union provides, some workers completely shift their allegiance from their company to their union.

Most modern-day unions realize that in the main their success depends upon the success of the companies they have organized. Therefore, they actively strive to participate more in certain managerial activities. Although the subject of union inroads into management prerogatives is always a hotly debated one and one with extensive ramifications, it nevertheless cannot be denied that in many firms unions now participate rather freely in such activities as time and motion study for determining job content and for setting production standards, job evaluation for determining wage rates, and the handling of grievances. In addition, they exert profound influences on personnel activities, such as hiring, layoffs, promotions, transfers, and so on. All of this is achieved by union policies aimed at increasing the amount of union participation in the affairs of the company.

Union leaders, however, frequently look with disfavor upon management's attempts to secure more worker participation. They fear that such attempts will shift worker loyalty from the union to the company. Hence, union leaders often oppose such efforts, claiming they are paternalistic or anti-union in nature. Management's job, therefore, frequently becomes one of convincing union officials that worker participation on behalf of the company will benefit the union as well as the organization. Clearly, mature attitudes are required on the part of both sides to implement successfully this kind of participation.

It is necessary to realize that unions, at least at the rank-and-file level, do sometimes complicate the problem of participation. On the one hand, they tend to offer an outlet for a person's basic need to participate, and in so doing they attract loyalty to the union rather than to the company. On the other hand, they may deliberately oppose management attempts to solicit more worker participation. In many instances, management invites such actions because of its own resistant attitude towards unionism, although this is slowly but surely becoming a thing of the past.

BENEFITS OF PARTICIPATION

The role of participation in American industry has become increasingly important over the past few decades. During this time period, the theory underlying participation and its many benefits has been transformed into actual practice, and it has been proven rather conclusively that participation will work and will result in advantages to both employers and employees.

One of the major results of participation is that it aids in making people more mature and responsible individuals, both on and off the job. By being allowed to express himself in his work, rather than being absorbed into a complex system of procedures and systems, the individual assumes a feeling of dignity and status. If he knows he can express his opinions and ideas, a personal sense of gratification and involvoment takoo plaoo within him and tonds to manifoet itsolf in his personality.

Participation also leads to increased understanding throughout the organization. People learn that others have problems besides themselves. If the workers are invited to share in these problems and to work towards common solutions, a greater degree of organizational balance occurs because of decreased misunderstanding and individual and group conflict. This also holds true when a union is involved. Mutual interest is brought to the forefront. The future holds great promise for peaceful and beneficial labor relations if both parties will lean towards increased participation.

Individual creativity and response to job challenges are also enhanced by participation. If given the opportunity to question and suggest instead of always having to follow a rigid set of instructions, an employee's natural ingenuity and ability are allowed expression. Hence, he is given the opportunity to grow and to develop himself. In discussing the advantages of participation and training in his article, Jennings shows that the two must go together to obtain the best results for purposes of development.

Studies further show participation to be a leading factor in getting people to accept changes. People who are consulted about changes, who are allowed to participate in decisions about the changes, are normally people who best adjust to such decisions. So it can be seen that participation along these lines greatly facilitates individual adjustment and satisfaction.

Although there are many other advantages to be realized from participation, they are far too numerous to be covered here. But it should be emphasized how tremendously important this subject is to today's managers. Many possibilities lie ahead for utilizing participation in management. It remains to be seen just how far companies are willing to go. Obviously there are limits here, but it is up to the individual concern to adapt to these.

THE PSYCHOLOGY OF PARTICIPATION *

Gordon W. Allport

John Dewey has shown that psychological theories are profoundly affected by the political and social climate prevailing in any given time and place. For example, an aristocracy produces no psychology of individual differences, for the individual is unimportant unless he happens to belong to the higher classes.[1] Dualistic psychology, he points out, flourishes best when one group holds a monopoly of social power and wishes to do the thinking and planning while others remain the docile, unthinking, instruments of execution.[2] And apologists for the status quo, he adds, are the ones who most readily declare human nature to be unalterable.

"The ultimate refuge of the stand-patter in every field, education, religion, politics, industrial and domestic life, has been the notion of an alleged fixed structure of mind."[3] It was no accident that psychological hedonism flourished as a justification for Nineteenth Century laissez-faire, or that reflexology blended with dialectical materialism dominated Russian psychology after 1917. All of us watched with dismay the abrupt perversion of German psychological science after 1933.[4] With such evidence before us can we doubt that American psychology too bears its own peculiar stamp of political and social dependency?

It is not my purpose to examine the thesis that social and economic determinism has been decisive in the history of psychology, nor the countercontention that the facts about human nature must be true regardless of any politico-ethical frame that we may hold. Dewey boldly declares democracy and sound psychology to be forever coextensive; it is impossible to have one without the other. He would frankly banish all psychological postulates that are not democratically oriented.[5]

---

* From *The Psychological Review*, Vol. 52, No. 3 (May, 1945), pp. 117-132. Reprinted with permission.

[1] J. Dewey, *Psychology as Philosophic Method* (Berkeley: University Press, 1899).

[2] J. Dewey, *Human Nature and Conduct* (New York: Holt & Co., 1922), p. 72.

[3] J. Dewey, "The Need for Social Psychology," *Psychological Review*, Vol. 24, 1917, p. 273.

[4] F. Wyatt and H. L. Teuber, "German Psychology Under the Nazi System—1933-1940." *Psychological Review*, Vol. 51, 1944. pp. 229-247.

[5] G. W. Allport, "Dewey's Individual and Social Psychology," Chapter 9 in *The Philosophy of John Dewey*, ed. by P. A. Schilpp (Evanston: Northwestern University Press, 1939), especially pp. 281, 283, 290.

Alluring as this whole problem is, let us limit our consideration to one distinctive, culturally-conditioned feature of American psychology.

I. American Psychology Predominantly a Motor Psychology

It will take but a moment's reflection for us to agree that the genius of American psychology lies in its stress upon action—or in slightly dated terminology, upon the motor phase of the reflex arc. Of all schools of psychological thought that we might name only behaviorism, in both its muscle-twitch and operational versions, is primarily American. Functionalism is American (rather than German or British) chiefly in its motor emphasis. Capacity psychology and mental testing in America deal primarily with accomplishment, activity, performance. The individual differences that are said to be a typical American interest have to do chiefly with measurable operations. We seldom record, for example, an individual's unique and subjective pattern of thought-life.

Of the many potential lines of development laid down in James's *Principles* over 50 years ago, the threads that were picked up were the radical motor elements, leading in the hands of Holt, Washburn, and Langfield to a *motor theory of consciousness;* in the hands of Dewey to a psychology of *conduct, adjustment,* and *habit.* James himself established *pragmatism,* a doctrine that invites attention almost exclusively to the motor consequences of mental life. When James waxed ethical, as he frequently did, his moral advice was generally, "If you really care about something, you should *do* something about it." Even Josiah Royce whose thought is often said to be the opposite of James's, agreed (like a good American) with his emphasis on *action.* Loyalty, said Royce, "is complete only in motor terms, never in merely sentimental terms. It is useless to call my feelings loyal unless my muscles somehow express this loyalty. . . . Nobody can be effectively loyal unless he is highly trained on the motor side." [6]

Returning on every ship from Europe (until ten years ago) were fresh young American *Doktoranden.* Their intellectual luggage was filled with European theories and concepts. But when unpacked at our motor-minded laboratories, these importations looked alien and were promptly subjected to a strenuous course in Americanization. *Feelings of innervation,* for example, were promptly dubbed outlandish. *Innervation* would do, but feelings were *de trop. Ideo-motor*

---

[6] J. Royce, *Race Questions, Provincialism, and Other American Problems* (New York: Macmillan Co., 1908), pp. 239, 241.

theory arrived, and though given a hospitable welcome by James, made little headway. *Ideas,* as the sovereign source of movement, smacked too much of the divine rights of Herbart. When ideas were offered to American psychologists, they commonly replied, "Keep them: stimulus and response will do quite nicely, thank you." *Empathy* arrived in a portmanteau packed in Munich. It was embedded in a whole self-psychology and in an epistemology of *Wissen von fremden Ichen.* Everything went into the ash can save only a greatly oversimplified version of what Lipps originally intended. *Motor mimicry* was all we wanted. What would we be doing with a "mental act that held a guarantee of the objectivity of our knowledge"?

Importations in the psychology of thought were so roughly handled that they scarcely survived at all. What was *unanschaulich* in Würzburg became *anschaulich* in Cornell. To think without images seemed mildly treasonable; but to think *with* them gradually became unpatriotic. Better to think with our larynx, hands and viscera, or better still in recent years with our action currents. To explain volition in Würzburg an impalpable decision factor, a *Bewusstheit,* was needed. But it all became so much simpler in Berkeley—a mere matter of rat-vibrissae quivering with VTE at a choice point in a maze.

Other transformations were equally drastic. Of the countless dimensions for the study of personality proposed by Stern, the IQ alone was picked up. Wertheimer died perplexed by the selective attention Americans were paying to the visible, tangible portions of his work.[7] The entire *Geisteswissenschaft* is known in this country chiefly through an absurd little pencil and paper test leading to the inevitable profile. Small wonder that Spranger explained, "Die grösste Gefahr Deutschland's ist die Amerikanizierung." [8]

One might think that phenomenology, since it derives from *Akt* psychology, might take hold in this country. But *mental* acts are not popular; it is *motor* acts that count. Or one might suppose Americans would take to Intentionality, a concept dealing with the orientation of the subject toward an object from which one might predict his future action. But such a concept is still too subjective. It is hard for us to even understand what it means. *Attitude* we will admit— it can be operationally defined—but intentionality is just too Central European.

---

[7] W. Kohler, "Max Wertheimer: 1880-1943," *Psychological Review,* Vol. 51, 1944, pp. 143-146.

[8] Cf. E. Spranger, *Kultur und Erziehung* (Leipzig: Quelle & Meyer, 1923), p. 199.

In short, we as Americans have motorized psychology. Our theories of human nature transform meditative functions into active functions. The process clearly reflects the demand of our culture that inner life issue quickly and visibly into tangible success: that closures be reached both overtly and swiftly.

Do I seem to deplore the one-sidedness of our approach? I do not mean to. Quite the contrary: it is our way of going at things. Our preference for action, for objectivity, has carried us to new levels of attainment, and will carry us still further. In the future European models will be followed even less than formerly. What we produce must be indigenous within our culture and must harmonize with our active orientation. It is especially true in social psychology, I think, that our derivations from Europe are virtually at an end. What may have been valid in Wundt, Durkheim, Le Bon, Tarde, Pareto, will in the postwar era find better expression in the fresher, behavioral approach of America. *It will do so, that is, if our psychology of social action expands to give fuller play to the activities of the total organism than has been customary in the past.* Even though subjective categories do not appeal, we need to find better ways of linking our psychology of action to the central regions of personality. Up to now little progress has been made in this direction.

II. Motor Activity and Higher Mental Processes

True, American psychologists have to their credit the discovery that motor activity plays a pivotal role in higher mental functions. Take as an example, *learning:* we have repeatedly insisted that learning is "not passive absorption but an active response!" In the classic experiment by Gates, learning scores jumped 100 per cent when four-fifths of the subject's time was devoted to recitation rather than to passive reading.[9] Haggard and Rose, recently reviewing many learning studies, including those that have to do with the simple conditioning of reflexes, report that in all cases learning seems to be facilitated if the subject himself overtly takes part, perhaps by turning the switch that rings the conditioning bell, or by drawing a line to accompany the apparent movement of the autokinetic phenomenon, or even by clenching the fist while memorizing nonsense syllables. These authors generalize these studies under a *Law of Active Participation*, ". . . when an individual assumes an active role in a learning situation (a) he tends to acquire the response-to-be-learned more

---

[9] A. I. Gates, "Recitation as a Factor in Memorizing," *Arch. of Psychology*, Vol. 6, No. 40, 1917.

rapidly, and (b) these response-patterns tend to be more stably formed, than when he remains passive." [10]

How to permit such helpful motor activity to go on in a classroom where 50 pupils are busy learning, is a large-sized pedagogical problem. "The chief source of the 'problem of discipline' in schools," says Dewey, "is that the teacher has often to spend a larger part of the time in suppressing the bodily activities" of the children.[11] The situation is wholly abnormal in that the teacher tries to divorce bodily activity from the perception of meaning; and yet perception of meaning is incomplete without full manipulation and adequate bodily movement.

Memory for material learned in school and college is notoriously poor, so poor that educators are forced to console themselves with the wistful adage which holds education to be "what you have left when you have forgotten all you learned in school." Perhaps a few studious attitudes, a few analytical habits are left; but should *content* disappear from the mind as rapidly as it does? We know that content acquired through personal manipulation does not seem to evaporate so rapidly.

I recently asked 250 college students to write down three vivid memories of their school work in the 8th grade. Afterward I had them indicate whether the memories involved their own active participation in the events recorded. Were they reciting, producing, talking, playing, arguing, or were they passively listening, watching, not overtly involved? Three-quarters of the memories were for situations in which the subject himself was actively participating, even though the percentage of time actually spent in participation in the average 8th grade room must be small.

We may mention also the problem of *voluntary control*. Although America has contributed little enough to the psychology of volition, what it has contributed is typical—namely the finding of Bair [12] and others, that a large amount of excessive, and apparently futile, motor involvement is necessary before one can gain control voluntarily over a limited muscular segment of the body. We know that a considerable overflow of effort is needed before fine skills can be differentiated, and before the individual can develop any satisfactory degree of self-determination.

---

[10] E. A. Haggard and R. J. Rose, "Some Effects of Mental Set and Active Participation in the Conditioning of the Autokinetic Phenomenon," *Journal of Experimental Psychology*, Vol. 34, 1944, p. 56.

[11] J. Dewey, *Democracy and Education* (New York: Macmillan, 1919), p. 165.

[12] J. H. Bair, "Development of Voluntary Control," *Psychological Review*, Vol. 8, 1901, pp. 474-510.

In the realm of modern *therapy* self-propelled activity plays an increasing part, as the "Rogers technique" becomes more and more widely applied.[13] Analogously, the Kenny treatment for infantile paralysis requires the patient to take more and more responsibility and to be more and more active, otherwise, it is discovered, the suggestions given by the therapeutist will not accomplish their purpose.[14] Angyal refers to the universal experience of psychiatrists that healthy ideas can be easily conveyed to the patient on the intellectual level without the slightest benefit accruing. The difficulty is to induce a state in which the idea "permeates the personality and influences the behavior."[15] In this war we have learned the importance of reconditioning at the front, that is, of allowing the patient himself quickly to work out his *own* relations with the terrifying environment that shocked him.

Facing the problem of *reëducation* in Germany, Lewin points to the impossibility of ideological conversion until requisite experience is available. "To understand what is being talked about," he says, "the individual has to have a basis in experience." No amount of verbal defining will convey the meaning of such concepts as "his Majesty's loyal opposition" or "fair play." To most Germans loyalty is identified with obedience; the only alternative to blind obedience is lawless individualism and laissez-faire.[16]

One of the chief problems confronting the AMG to-day is to keep the inhabitants of liberated countries active in shaping their own destiny.[17] Handouts beget apathy, and apathy prevents an interest in one's own future. How much better it was for Parisians to retake their own city than for the Allies to have done all the work, handing over the finished product. In his excellent new book *Mental Hygiene*, Klein expresses the point: "Without action there is no shift from the wish to the deed. There is motive, but no purpose. There is yearning without striving; hence the potential self-improvement dies stillborn."[18] To be sure, we must not over-simplify the problem of rescue and emergency relief for Europe's dazed and demoralized citizens.

---

[13] C. R. Rogers, *Counseling and Psychotherapy* (Boston: Houghton Mifflin, 1942).

[14] C. Bohnengel, "An Evaluation of Psychobiologic Factors in the Reeducation Phase of the Kenny Treatment for Infantile Paralysis," *Psychosomatic Medicine*, Vol. 6, 1944, pp. 82-87.

[15] A. Angyal, *Foundations for a Science of Personality* (New York: Commonwealth Fund, 1941), p. 326.

[16] K. Lewin, "The Special Case of Germany," *Public Opinion Quarterly*, Vol. 7, 1943, pp. 555-556.

[17] G. W. Allport, "Restoring Morale in Occupied Countries," *Public Opinion Quarterly*, Vol. 7, 1943, pp. 606-617.

[18] D. B. Klein, *Mental Hygiene* (New York: Henry Holt, 1944), p. 319.

Yet the only rule to follow, so far as it is at all practicable, is to allow them to participate fully in their own rescue and rehabilitation.

III. Activity Versus Participation

Facts of this sort prove to us that people have to be active in order to learn, in order to store up efficient memories, to build voluntary control, to be cured when they are ill, restored when they are faint.

But implied in much American work is the proposition that one activity is as good as any other activity. It is *random* movement, according to much of our learning theory, that brings the organism to an eventual solution. And according to one experimentalist, "If the body muscles are tense, the brain reacts much more quickly and intensely, if they are relaxed, it may react weakly or not at all." [19] The implication seems to be that tenseness of any kind makes for mental alertness. Activity as such is approved.

Random movement theories of learning, muscular tension theories of efficiency, speed theories of intelligence, and motor theories of consciousness do not make a distinction that seems to me vital, namely, the distinction between mere *activity* as such and true, personal *participation*.

Before we examine this distinction as it affects psychological theory and practice, I should like to point out that the self-same distinction occurs in the economic and social life of the common man.

Take, for example, Citizen Sam who moves and has his being in the great activity wheel of New York City. Let us say that he spends his hours of unconsciousness somewhere in the badlands of the Bronx. He wakens to grab the morning's milk left at the door by an agent of a vast Dairy and Distributing system whose corporate maneuvers, so vital to his health, never consciously concern him. After paying hasty respects to his landlady, he dashes into the transportation system whose mechanical and civic mysteries he does not comprehend. At the factory he becomes a cog for the day in a set of systems far beyond his ken. To him (as to everybody else) the company he works for is an abstraction; he plays an unwitting part in the "creation of surpluses" (whatever they are), and though he doesn't know it his furious activity at his machine is regulated by the "law of supply and demand," and by "the availability of raw materials" and by "prevailing interest rates." Unknown to himself he is headed next week for the "surplus labor market." A union official collects

---

[19] A. G. Bills, *The Psychology of Efficiency* (New York: Harper & Bros., 1943), p. 23.

his dues; just why he doesn't know. At noontime that corporate monstrosity, Horn and Hardart, swallows him up, much as he swallows one of its automatic pies. After more activity in the afternoon, he seeks out a standardized day-dream produced in Hollywood, to rest his tense, but *not* efficient mind. At the end of his day he sinks into a tavern, and unknowingly victimized by the advertising cycle, orders in rapid succession Four Roses, Three Feathers, Golden Wedding and Seagram's which "men who plan beyond tomorrow" like to drink.

Sam has been active all day, immensely active, playing a part in dozens of impersonal cycles of behavior. He has brushed scores of "corporate personalities," but has entered into intimate relations with no single human being. The people he has met are idler-gears like himself meshed into systems of transmission, far too distracted to examine any one of the cycles in which they are engaged. Throughout the day Sam is on the go, implicated in this task and that,—but does he, in a psychological sense, *participate* in what he is doing? Although constantly *task-involved,* is he ever really *ego-involved?*

Now this problem is familiar to all of us, and one of the most significant developments of the past decade is its entrance into both industrial and social psychology. The way the problem has been formulated by industrial psychologists is roughly this:

The individual's desire for personal status is apparently insatiable. Whether we say that he longs for *prestige,* for *self-respect, autonomy,* or *self-regard,* a dynamic factor of this order is apparently the strongest of his drives. Perhaps it is an elementary organismic principe as Angyal [20] and Goldstein [21] would have it; perhaps it is rather a distillation of more primitive biological drives with social competitiveness somehow added to the brew. For our purposes it does not matter.

What the industrial psychologist has discovered is that when the work-situation in which the individual finds himself realistically engages the status-seeking motive, when the individual is busily engaged in using his talents, understanding his work, and having pleasant social relations with foreman and fellow-worker, then he is, as the saying goes, "identified" with his job. He likes his work; he is absorbed in it; he is productive. In short, in McGregor's terms he is industrially *active;* that is to say, he is participant.[22]

---

[20] A. Angyal, *Foundations for a Science of Personality* (New York: Commonwealth Fund. 1941).

[21] K. Goldstein, *Human Nature in the Light of Psychopathology* (Cambridge: Harvard University Press, 1940).

[22] D. McGregor, "Conditions of Effective Leadership in the Industrial Organization," *Journal of Consulting Psychology,* Vol. 8, 1944, pp. 55-63.

When, on the other hand, the situation is such that the status-motive has no chance of gearing itself into the external cycles of events, when the individual goes through motions that he does not find meaningful, when he does not really participate, then come rebellion against authority, complaints, griping, gossip, rumor, scapegoating, disaffection of all sorts. The job-satisfaction is low. In McGregor's terms under such circumstances the individual is not active; he is industrially *reactive*.

In the armed forces, in federal employment, in school systems, the same principle holds. Ordinarily those at the top find that they have sufficient comprehension, sufficient responsibility, and sufficient personal status. *They* are not the ones who gripe and gossip. It is the lower-downs who indulge in tendency-wit against the brass hats, who complain, who go AWOL, become inert, or gang up against a scapegoat. When in actual combat, all the energies and training, all the personal responsibility of which a soldier is capable, are called upon, then egos are engaged for all they are worth. Men are active; they have no time to be reactive; nor have they reason to be.

Accepting this analysis as correct the problem before us is whether the immense amount of reactivity shown in business offices and factories, in federal bureaus, in schools, can be reduced, as it is when men at the front are using all their talents and are participating to the full in life-and-death combat.

We are learning some of the conditions in which reactivity does decline. Friendly, unaffected social relations are the most indispensable condition. Patronizing hand-outs and wage-incentive systems alone do not succeed. Opportunities for consultation on personal problems are, somewhat surprisingly, found to be important. And as members of this Society have shown, group decision, open discussion, and the retraining of leaders in accordance with democratic standards yield remarkable results. One of Lewin's discoveries in this connection is especially revealing. People who dislike a certain food are resistant to pressure put upon them in the form of persuasion and request; but when the individual himself as member of a group votes, after discussion, to alter his food-habits, his eagerness to reach this goal is independent of his personal like or dislike.[23] In other words, a person ceases to be reactive and contrary in respect to a desirable course of conduct only when he himself has had a hand in declaring that course of conduct to be desirable.

[23] K. Lewin, "The Dynamics of Group Action," *Educ. Leadership*, Vol. 1, 1944, pp. 195-200.

Such findings add up to the simple proposition that people must have a hand in saving themselves; they cannot and will not be saved from the outside.

In insisting that participation depends upon ego-involvement, it would be a mistake if we were to assume that we are dealing with a wholly self-centered and parasitic ego that demands unlimited status, and power for the individual himself.[24] Often, indeed, the ego is clamorous, jealous, possessive and cantankerous. But this is true chiefly when it is forced to be *reactive* against constant threats and deprivations. We all know of "power-people" who cannot, as we say, "submerge their egos." The trouble comes, I suspect, not because their egos are unsubmerged, but because they are still reactive toward some outer or inner features of the situation which are causing conflicts and insecurity. Reactive egos tend to perceive their neighbors and associates as threats rather than as collaborators.

But for the most part people who are participant in coöperative activity are just as much satisfied when a teammate solves a common problem as when they themselves solve it.[25] Your tensions can be relieved by my work, and my tensions by your work, provided we are co-participants. Whatever our egos were like originally, they are now for the most part socially regenerate. Selfish gratifications give way to coöperative satisfaction when the ego-boundaries are enlarged.

Nowadays we hear it said by our own colleagues that Americans will never participate in a postwar world union unless it is shown clearly to be to their self-interest to do so. Undoubtedly the statement is true, but self-interest is highly extensible. A revealing study by Lt. Leighton conducted at a Japanese relocation center makes this point clear.[26]

When the Japanese were asked to pick cotton in nearby ranches to help save the crop, very few responded. The reason was that they were expected to donate all wages above $16.00 a month to a community trust fund, to be used for the common good.

There was as yet insufficient community feeling; the over-all trust fund seemed too big, too distant, too uncertain. All that happened was endless argument for and against the trust fund, while the cotton stood in the fields.

---

[24] H. D. Spoerl, "Toward a Knowledge of the Soul," *The New Phil.*, Vol. 47, 1944, pp. 71-81.

[25] H. B. Lewis, "An Experimental Study of the Role of the Ego in Work. I. The Role of the Ego in Cooperative Work," *Journal of Experimental Psychology*, Vol. 34, 1944, pp. 113-126.

[26] A. H. Leighton *et al.*, "The Psychiatric Approach in Problems of Community Management," *American Journal of Psychiatry*, Vol. 100, 1943, pp. 328-333.

At this point the schools asked to be allowed to go picking and to use the money for school improvements. This request was granted, and soon church groups, recreational societies and other community units showed themselves eager to go on the same basis; and the project was a success.

What we learn from this study is that self-interest may not extend to include an object so remote and impersonal as a community trust fund, but may readily embrace school improvements, church and recreational centers. For most people there is plenty of ego-relevance to be found in teamwork provided the composition of the team and its identity of interest are clearly understood.

Americans will endorse international coöperation in the future (as they do at the present moment) provided they continue to see its relevance to their own extended egos, and provided they feel that in some way they themselves are participating in the decisions and activities entailed.

Nearly everyone will bear testimony to the superiority of satisfaction that comes from successful teamwork as contrasted to solitary achievement. Membership in a group that has successfully braved dangers and surmounted obstacles together is a membership that is ego-involved, and the egos in question are not parasitic but are socialized.

An important by-product of participation, as I am using the term, is the reduction of stereotypes. Sam's mind we can be sure was a clutter of false stereotypes concerning the Dairy company, the transportation system, the abstract corporation for which he works, concerning economic laws, federal regulation, to say nothing of the tabloid conceptions begotten in Hollywood and by advertisers. Had he really participated in his employment his notions of "the Company," of surpluses, of labor unions would have become realistic. In recent years for some of us a job in Washington has happily shattered our previous stereotypes concerning sovereignty, bureaucracy, and other alleged attributes of "the government." One of the favorable results of the war will be the fact that men who have shared a common destiny, participating together in bombing crews, in life-and-death assaults, will at last be freed from their tabloid assumptions regarding the nature of Jews, Negroes, Catholics, and other American minorities.

IV. PARTICIPANT DEMOCRACY

At the time of a presidential election we know that only about three in every five eligible voters go to the polls. At primary time the ratio is more likely to be one in every four. Yet voting is the irreducible minimum of participation in political democracy. People who do not vote at least once in four years are totally non-participant; those who vote only in a presidential election—these comprise at least a third of all voters—are scarcely better off. And if we wished to complicate matters we might ask whether those who go to the polls are really participating with the deeper layers of personality, or whether their voting is, so to speak, a peripheral activity instigated perhaps by fanfare or by local bosses. It would not be hard to prove that participation in political affairs, as well as in industrial, educational, and religious life, is rare. In this respect most people resemble Citizen Sam.

Two contemporary social psychologists have concerned themselves deeply with this problem. They see that increasingly since the days of the industrial revolution individuals have found themselves in the grip of immense forces whose workings they have no power of comprehending, much less influencing. One of the writers, John Dewey, states the problem in this way:

"The ramification of the issues before the public is so wide and intricate, the technical matters involved are so specialized, the details are so many and so shifting, that the public cannot for any length of time identify and hold itself. It is not that there is no public, no large body of persons having a common interest in the consequences of social transactions. There is too much public, a public too diffused and scattered and too intricate in composition." [27]

Dewey has spent many years seeking remedies for this situation. Chiefly he has laid emphasis upon the need for face-to-face association, for evolving democratic methods within school and neighborhood so that citizens may obtain in their nerves and muscles the basic experience of relating their activities in matters of common concern. Some political writers, e.g., Mary P. Follett,[28] have held that the solution lies in reconstituting political groups on a small enough scale so that each citizen may meet face-to-face with other members of a geographical or occupational group, electing representatives who will in turn deal face-to-face with other representatives. Though the town may no longer be the best unit for operation the spirit of the town-meeting is thus to a degree recaptured. "Democracy," says

---

[27] J. Dewey, *The Public and Its Problems* (New York: Holt & Co., 1927), p. 137.
[28] M. P. Follett, *Creative Experience* (New York: Longmans, Green & Co., 1924).

Dewey, "must begin at home and its home is the neighborly community." [29]

Central to Dewey's solution also is freedom of publicity. To obstruct or restrict publicity is to limit and distort public opinion. The control of broadcasting and of the press by big advertisers is an initial source of distortion. Other groups need freer ventilation for their views, in order to reduce rigidity, hostility, and reactivity.

The second social psychologist, F. H. Allport, states the problem rather differently. He asks how an individual enmeshed within innumerable cycles of activity all imposed upon him from without can retain his integrity as a person? Like Sam, he finds himself a cog in countless corporate machines. State, county, federal governmental systems affect him, as do economic cycles, the impersonal systems known as private enterprise, conscription in wartime, social security; so too city transportation, milk production and delivery, consumption, housing, banking. But he does not affect them. How can he? F. H. Allport points to an inherent contradiction that seems to lie in Dewey's position.[30] The latter hopes that the individual will participate in every public that his own interests create in common with others. That is to say, Sam should join with others who are affected by the same municipal, banking, transporting, feeding, housing cycles and work out common problems. But Sam would be a member of hundreds of segmental types of public. And in dashing from one "common interest" meeting to another, he would not find his interests as an individual truly fulfilled by being partially included in multiple groups. He would still be a puppet of many systems. As complexities increase under modern conditions, total inclusion of the personality in specialized publics becomes increasingly difficult to achieve.

Like Dewey, F. H. Allport has given various suggestions for the solution of the problem, but chiefly his emphasis has been upon the creation of a scientific spirit in the common man encouraging him to call into question the corporate fictions, the sanctity of the economic cycles, which, unthinkingly, he takes for granted. By questioning the transcendental reality commonly ascribed to nationhood, to "consumer competition," to institutional fictions, and by substituting direct experience with the materials affecting his life, the individual

[29] J. Dewey, *The Public and Its Problems* (New York: Macmillan, 1919), p. 213.
[30] F. H. Allport, *Institutional Behavior* (Chapel Hill: University Press, 1933), Ch. 5.

may himself eventually work out a measure of integrity and wholeness within himself.[31]

Both Dewey and F. H. Allport seem to agree that the only alternative to a keener analysis of the behavioral environment and more active participation in reshaping it, is to give way progressively to outer authority, to uniformity, to discipline, and dependence upon the leader. This battlefield exists here and now within each of us. The answer to growing complexity in the social sphere is renewed efforts at participation by each one of us, or else a progressive decline of inert and unquestioning masses, submitting to government by an èlite which will have little regard for the ultimate interest of the common man.

Now, drawing together the threads of this problem, we are confronted with the following facts:

1. Since the industrial revolution there has been increasing difficulty on the part of the ordinary citizen in comprehending and affecting the forces which control his destiny.

2. Potentially the individual is a member of many, many publics, defined as groups of people having a common interest, for example, as voters, motorists, veterans, employers, consumers, co-religionists.

3. No public includes all of an individual's interests.

To these facts we add our earlier conclusions, namely, that

4. Activity alone is not participation. Most of our fellow citizens spin as cogs in many systems without engaging their own egos even in those activities of most vital concern to them.

5. When the ego is not effectively engaged the individual becomes reactive. He lives a life of ugly protest, finding outlets in complaints, strikes, above all in scapegoating; in this condition he is ripe prey for a demagogue whose whole purpose is to focus and exploit the aggressive outbursts of non-participating egos.

V. Toward a Solution

It is risky indeed to suggest in a few words the solution of such an immense social problem. Certainly it will require the combined efforts of educators, statesmen, and scientists to rescue the common man from his predicament.

But from our preceding discussion one line of thought stands out as particularly helpful.

---

[31] F. H. Allport, "The Scientific Spirit and the Common Man," *Proceedings of the Conference on Scientific Spirit & Democratic Faith* (New York: 2 West 64th St., 1944).

Is it not true that all of us find coercive demands upon our motor systems imposed by the corporate cycles in which we move, generally *without* serious frustration resulting? Speaking for myself, only the outer layers of my personality are engaged in my capacity as automobile owner, insurance holder, Blue Cross member, consumer of clothing, patron of the IRT. Perhaps, you say, I should be more interested in these cycles, but I reply one must choose, and other things are more important to me. In this age of specialization all of us are willing to delegate expert functions to experts. We simply cannot be bothered about the innumerable technical aspects of living that are not our specialty. To be sure, in matters of broad political or ethical policy-making the story is different; we cannot so easily avoid responsibility. Political reforms making possible good schools, recreation, and health are presumably the concern of all people. National policy in securing a lasting peace is a matter of great moment for each one of us. But even among these broad social and political issues I find some that excite me more than others.

What I am saying is that I cannot share Dewey's dismay at our failure to create innumerable self-conscious publics wherever there are common interests. In the first place, these publics need operate only on the broadest policy-forming level; and, in the second place, a relatively *few* members of a group can often serve adequately as representatives of others who are likeminded. I do not mean that a few public spirited citizens should do all the work. There should be wider distribution of responsibility. But my point is that talents differ. *What warms one ego chills another.*

Now assuming that the major fields of activity open to all normal people are the economic, the educational, recreational, political, religious and domestic, we might assert that a healthy ego should find true participation in all of them. Or allowing one blind spot to the bachelor, to the constitutional hater of sports or of politics, to the agnostic, there is still need for a balanced diet of participation in, say, five fields.

Against some such norm we might test our present situation. Do we find Citizen Sam truly participating in some *one* political undertaking; in some *one* of his economic contacts (preferably, of course, in his job where he spends most of his time) ; is he really involved in *some* religious, educational, recreational pursuits, and in family affairs? If we find that he is not actively involved in all of these areas of participation, we may, as I say, grant him a blind spot or two. *But unless he is in some areas ego-engaged and participant his life is crippled and his existence a blemish on democracy.*

In brief, it is neither possible nor desirable that all of our activities and contacts in our complex social order should penetrate beneath the surface of our personalities. But unless we try deliberately and persistently to affect our destinies at certain points, especially where broad political policies are concerned, and in some of the other representative areas of our life, we are not democratic personalities, we have no balance or wholeness, and society undergoes proportionate stultification.

VI. New Directions for Social Psychology

Returning to our starting point, my contention is that the earlier emphasis of American psychology on motor activity as such is now changing into an emphasis upon ego-involved participation. As time goes on it will mark increasingly the essential differences that exist between movement initiated at the surface level and at the deeper levels of personality.[32] To do so will not be to abandon our dependence on the social climate in which we work. Quite the contrary: at last the genius of American psychology will be brought into line with the century of the common man.[33]

What concretely are the roles that psychologists will play in this process? At least half a dozen can already be fairly well defined:

1. To those who serve in some consulting or guidance capacity Citizen Sam will come as a client. He will have this symptom or that —perhaps resentment, depression, bewilderment, or apathy. Among college students, a certain unpublished study suggests that 20 per cent are apathetic, complaining that they have no values whatever to live by. It calls for great therapeutic skill to lead such clients to commit themselves unreservedly to something. I have suggested that a balanced personality needs deep-rooted participation in all or most of the six spheres of value: the political, economic, recreational, religious, cultural-scientific, and domestic. But commitments cannot be too comprehensive. It is not politics or economics as a whole that evokes participation, but merely some one limited and well-defined issue in the total sphere. The democratic personality needs to influence *some* but not all of the factors that influence him in representative fields of his activity.

2. The consultant may go one step further. Sam should feel not only that he is a citizen participating at crucial points in common

---

[32] G. W. Allport, "The Ego in Contemporary Psychology," *Psychological Review*, Vol. 50, 1943, pp. 451-478.
[33] C. J. Friedrich, "The Role and the Position of the Common Man," *American Journal of Sociology*, Vol. 69, 1944, pp. 421-429.

activities, but he should be oriented as well toward the inner crises that will occur, for example, in middle age when vitality recedes, when his furious activity can no longer be sustained, when he faces old age and death itself. Sam, if I may put it in this way, needs to find that metaphors and images are more important ultimately than motor gyrations. In other words, the consulting psychologist has responsibility for encouraging subjective richness in personality. For in the broader sense participation extends beyond the days when active citizenship is possible. The ego needs to be wholesomely attached to life even after efficiency of action declines.

3. Industrial psychologists and group workers have already found a rewarding line of work in educating management, foremen, and employees in respect to the conditions that increase efficiency through participation in the job. The same type of effort is also yielding returns in other directions—especially in recreational and educational enterprises.

4. I would call attention specifically to the forum movement in this country which is one of the symptoms of the common man's awakening. Problems of group discussion lie at the very core of social psychology, and we shall do well to seize the opportunity now offered for investigation and social action in this field. I suggest that public opinion polls be geared to these neighborhood discussion meetings. Opinion recorded cold on a front porch is likely to be different and less enlightened than that recorded after an hour's participation in a people's policy forum.

5. As teachers, both in college and in adult centers, we have a job to do in encouraging the participation of the public in the progress of science itself. The layman now finds it impossible to keep pace with science. Dazed by the benefits of radio, auto, airplane and vitamins, all of which regulate his life, he stands on the sidelines and cheers as the procession of science goes by. He has little real contact with the material from which his life is fashioned and little understanding. Exhibitions, demonstrations, and simplified experiments will help him understand.[34] But the layman needs even more; he needs to know how to control the applications of science. While bestowing upon him many blessings, science has also given its bounty to tyrants and to the self-appointed èlite, with the result of fabulous fortunes for the few, slums and squalor for the many, violent wars and suffering beyond endurance. The common man has not chosen

---

[34] F. H. Allport, *Institutional Behavior* (Chapel Hill: University Press, 1933).

these consequences. He was never consulted, was never participant in guiding the applications of science.

It would not be difficult to expand this list of services that psychology can provide in leading the common man into more effective participation during the democratic renaissance that lies ahead. The fact that so many of us have had active war experience guarantees that devices and techniques, as well as the requisite purpose, are available for this work.

Before listing my sixth and last suggestion, may I digress for a moment to call attention to the present training that psychologists are obtaining as participants?

VII. Psychologists as Participants

The Office of Psychological Personnel tells us that within the current year, approximately one-quarter of the 4500 psychologists listed are in the armed forces (64 per cent if we count only male psychologists between 18 and 38) ; another quarter works full or part time for the federal government or war agencies.[35] Impressive as these figures are they do not include many others who are closely linked to the common effort through unreported community work and personal sacrifice. On the other hand, to be sure, some nominally engaged in war work may be mere idler-gears accomplishing little. Though they spin in the total chain their egos are not engaged. For the most part, however, the involvement is authentic and the experience gratifying.

One wonders what the youthful portion of the profession will do with their training. Some have lost their taste for academic life and will remain in "practical" work. Among those who return to teach we can anticipate that the content and form of their instruction will be affected by their experiences. One of our ablest young social psychologists writes me that he intends, if it can be arranged, to teach six months in the year and spend the other six in an advertising business where social psychology is put into practice. In doing so he is not forsaking science; quite the contrary: he knows that only by observing the *installation* of psychological science can its facts be separated from its fantasies.

What the war has done for the majority of social psychologists is to provide them with a direction for future work, a direction that will not be lost in our generation. Committed to advancing democracy, we have found tools to work with, specialties that we

[35] D. G. Marquis, "The Mobilization of Psychologists for War Service," *Psychological Bulletin*, Vol. 41, 1944, pp. 469-473.

mean to continue to use. There are polling, content analysis, group decision, leadership training, devices for alleviating minority tensions, and many other useful techniques.

There are also negative lessons we have learned. One of these has impressed me constantly since the excited summer of 1940. I dare say we have all had the experience of seeing plans manufactured too rapidly. Most of the blue-prints we drew up have become waste paper. Quick and alert minds meet in a committee; good rapport is established; solutions are rapidly designed at the verbal level. They are plausible solutions, and often seem much better than the policies and practices that eventuate under the auspices of less expert groups. An example of what I mean is the 500 page blue-print prepared by the Committee for National Morale early in 1941 for a Federal Morale Service. It seemed like a more adequate plan than the stammering series of arrangements that followed, the OFF, COI, OSS, OWI. But obviously the blue-print was not geared to political realities. How many other plans fail because they are not suitable to the existing situation?

Granted that plans of men, like those of mice, "gang aft agley," should the plans of social scientists suffer as large a proportion of casualties as they do? There are plans for community work, plans for international coöperation, plans for reorganization of a faculty, for postwar rehabilitation, for this and for that. My impression is that the plans devised by social psychologists are unusually fluent, plausible, and reflect a high "verbal factor." But for the most part these good intentions fail in action. Our thoughts leap heavenward; our muscles remain below. Conceding that intellectual leaders should often point to goals above present probabilities of attainment, that they should be didactic, imaginative, still the mortality rate of their plans in these times of crisis is too high.

There are many occasions when an academic social psychologist evolves a bright idea, does the exploratory work, obtains rather convincing results on a limited scale, and then finds himself blocked in getting his ideas used. His participation is excellent up to a point, but it falls short of application—which means it falls very short indeed. The final chapter to the sad story is sometimes that his ego ceases to be active, and becomes reactive. He feels frustrated, becomes critical, bites at the brass hats, the Foundations, and lapses into apathy.

The roots of his difficulty are probably three in number. (1) Though he has sensed a need, no responsible organization has signified its intention to use his results. He has proceeded without adequate coöperation and guidance. (2) He has not learned to write simple, convincing, action-compelling reports of his research. (3) He is too much of a solipsist, unable to realize that because results are fascinating and significant to him, they will not appeal to men who make policies and initiate action unless these men too are worried about the problem in question, and unless the results reach them at the right *time* and in a clear *way*.

A social psychologist must not expect people to applaud his neat study because it is a neat study. Public policy will never mesh itself into the tempo of the laboratory or into the style of our technical journals. To be effective social psychology must go 100 per cent of the way in meeting the demands of policy-forming agencies in respect to the content, the style, and the timing of its work. It is sad to note that our profession, by and large, is not adept at the task of installation, whether in government bureaus, industry, or the community.

There are, of course, striking individual exceptions. In these fortunate cases the psychologist becomes effective because of his ability to combine in his own person the functions of both "fact finder" and "operator." [36, 37]

VIII. Conclusion

My final point is a plea that in future theoretical and systematic writing social psychologists give due consideration to the historical trend I have outlined. Reduced to the briefest possible statement it is this:

Half a century ago psychologists characteristically ascribed to the personality certain governing agencies: the will, the soul, the self, the moral sentiments, or some other ruling faculty. Subsequent emphasis upon the motor processes, especially in America, resulted in a kind of entropy for personality. Being deprived of its self-policing functions personality seemed to dissolve into endless cycles of motor activity controlled by stimulus or by habit. Like a taxicab its successive excursions had little relation to one another. Then gradually some principles of self-regulation returned to psychology, a bit timidly and not too clearly, under the guise of "integration," "vigilance," "homeostasis."

"Ego-functions" too were introduced to provide for a re-centering of personality with an increase in its stability. Ego-functions, as I

[36] G. W. Allport and H. R. Veltfort, "Social Psychology and the Civilian War Effort," SPSSI Bulletin, *Journal of Social Psychology*, Vol. 18, 1943, pp. 165-233.
[37] G. R. Schmeidler and G. W. Allport, "Social Psychology and the Civilian War Effort: May 1943-May 1944," SPSSI Bulletin, *Journal of Social Psychology*, Vol. 20, 1944, pp. 145-173.

have shown elsewhere, are of many kinds, and the ego is susceptible of many definitions.[38]

Perhaps the most important distinction concerns reactive ego-functions which are resistant, contrary, clamorous, as opposed to active ego-functions which find full expression in participant activity. When participating the individual discovers that his occupational manipulations grow meaningful; his community contacts are understood and appreciated. He becomes interested in shaping many of the events that control his life.

Participation, as opposed to peripheral motor activity, sinks a shaft into the inner-subjective regions of the personality. It taps central values. Thus in studying participation the psychologist has an approach to the complete person.

Random movement, derived from the sensori-motor layer of the personality, has too long been our paradigm for the behavior of man. It fails to draw the essential distinction between aimless activity and participation. The concept of random movement denies dignity to human nature; the concept of participation confers dignity. As American psychology increasingly studies the conditions of participation it will elevate its conception of human nature, an event, we can be sure, that will at last gratify the man in the street.

In focusing upon problems of participation social psychology will also be advancing democracy, for, as Dewey has shown, the task of obtaining from the common man participation in matters affecting his own destiny is the central problem of democracy.

Skills learned by at least half our profession during this war are well-designed to carry out this purpose. Psychologists can employ them in diverse ways as consultants, group workers, personnel executives, teachers, writers, and community leaders. And in following this road psychologists as individuals will find their own salvation, for—common men that they are—they will discover that they too are participating in the march of democracy.

[38] G. W. Allport, "The Ego in Contemporary Psychology," *Psychological Review*, Vol. 50, 1943, pp. 451-478.

QUESTIONS

1. Why do you thing that this somewhat theoretical article was included in this section?
2. What is the relationship between idustrial productivity and participation?
3. What does the term "ego-involvement" mean?
4. What are the advantages of securing employee participation?
5. Do you feel that the typical executive would agree with Allport's conclusions?

PARTICIPATION BY SUBORDINATES IN THE MANAGERIAL DECISION-MAKING PROCESS *

R. Tannenbaum and F. Massarik

I. INTRODUCTION

The role of "participation" by individuals or groups in American culture in general and in industrial organizations specifically has been treated by many writers. Its implications for political theory as well as for a theory of human relations in formal organizations are numerous. However, in spite of this academic and extra-academic interest, a clear-cut, operational definition of the concept, or a precise set of hypotheses regarding its dynamics, has not been developed. While to do so will be the object of this paper, the treatment will not be completely operational. The development of appropriate methods of measurement is conceived as a next step that should follow the preliminary one of conceptual clarification undertaken in this paper.

A review of the literature indicates that three major approaches have been taken in dealing with "participation":

(1) *The Experiential Approach.* This approach is exemplified by writers who in the course of their experience in enterprising work have obtained a "feel" for the role of participation in the decision-making process and have put down their experiences in article or book form.[1] Writings such as these provide a set of insights and hunches whose verification in any systematic fashion has not been attempted. The actual referants from which these formulations are derived often are single sets of observations in a single or in a few enterprises—observations generally made in an uncontrolled fashion.

The experiential approach, operating outside the bounds of scientific method, nonetheless adds to scientific knowledge indirectly by providing the raw material from which hypotheses may be moulded. The precise structure of these hypotheses is not stated neatly by the experiential writers, but rather remains to be formulated.

---

* From the *Canadian Journal of Economics and Political Science*, Vol. 16, No. 3 (August, 1950), pp. 408-418. Reprinted with permission.

[1] For example: H. H. Carey, "Consultative Supervision and Management" (*Personnel*, Mar., 1942); Alexander R. Heron, *Why Men Work* (Palo Alto, 1948); Eric A. Nicol, "Management through Consultative Supervision" (*Personnel Journal*, Nov. 1948); James C. Worthy, "Changing Concepts of the Personnel Function" (*Personnel*, Nov., 1948).

(2) *The Conceptual, Non-Experimental Approach.* This approach characterizes the writings of authors who are, essentially, academicians with strong theoretical backgrounds. It is typified by writings that deal with "conditions," "functions," and other abstractions, generally of a socio-psychological nature, that attempt to explain the dynamics of participation.[2] The conceptual, non-experimental approach at its best is the process of theory or hypothesis formulation. Ideally it lays the groundwork for actual testing and experimental work, but much of this type of technical literature so far published on participation lacks the clarity of conceptual definition necessary to make it useful as a basis for experimental work.

(3) *The Experimental Approach.* This approach is found in the writings of authors who have seen fit to apply experimental techniques either to especially constructed social situations involving participation, or else in natural settings in which participational activities prevail.[3] With adequate controls and with a meaningful theoretical structure within which individual findings may be placed, this approach is doubtless the most fruitful. Ideally it indicates what will happen under specified sets of conditions and with what degree of probability. Unfortunately, up to now experimental work on the dynamics of participation in the decision-making process has been sporadic.[4]

The present paper is of the conceptual, non-experimental type. Participation in the decision-making process is conceived here as an instrument that may be used by the formal leadership of an enterprise in the pursuit of its goals. No attempt will be made to examine it from an ethical standpoint or in terms of its consistency within the frame of a democratic society, although it is by no means assumed that such considerations are less important than the ones set forward here.

II. Definition of Participation

It is essential, in dealing with participation, to make clear the meaning which is to be attached to the concept. One must specify both who the participators are and in what they are participating.

---

[2] For example: Douglas McGregor, "Conditions for Effective Leadership in the Industrial Situation" (*Journal of Consulting Psychology*, vol. VIII, Mar.-Apr., 1944); Gordon W. Allport, "The Psychology of Participation" (*Psychological Review*, May, 1945).

[3] For the concept of the "natural experiment," see F. Stuart Chapin, *Experimental Designs in Sociological Research* (New York, 1947), and Ernest Greenwood, *Experimental Sociology* (New York, 1945).

[4] For a good summary of relevant experimental work, see Ronald Lippitt, "A Program of Experimentation on Group Functioning and Productivity" (in *Current Trends in Social Psychology*, Pittsburgh, 1948).

Too frequently in the available literature on the subject the reader must determine these matters for himself since no explicit statements bearing on them are made by the writers.

As already indicated, this paper is primarily concerned with participation as a managerial device. Attention is therefore focused on the subordinates of managers in enterprises as the participators. It is important to note that these subordinates may be either non-managers or managers.[5] If they are managers, they are subordinates of superior managers in the formal organization of the enterprise in addition to having subordinates who are responsible to them.

Because of space limitations, consideration of the participation of individuals as union members in specific activities of an enterprise is excluded from the scope of this paper. Suffice it to say here that in those cases where the participation of union members is direct and personal, the benefits to be derived by the enterprise are similar to those derived from participation within the superior-subordinate relationship. However, in those cases (which are the greatest in number) where the participation of the union member is indirect and impersonal, it is doubtful if such is the result. It is our conclusion that most of the statements which follow are relevant to the former cases.[6]

What then is the meaning of participation, and with what type of participation by subordinates are we here concerned? An individual participates in something when he takes a part or share in that thing. Since taking a part or sharing is always involved, participation takes place in a social context. Managerial subordinates in formal enterprises are responsible to their superiors for the performance of designated tasks. In such performance, they are participating in the production of the good or service of the enterprise. They also participate (share), through the receipt of wages or salaries, in the distribution of the total revenue received by the enterprise. These types of participation are common to all enterprises. But there is another type of participation which is much less frequently encountered, although its use as a managerial device has, of recent years, grown rapidly in importance. This type involves participation by subordinates with their superiors in the managerial decision-making process.

---

[5] For definitions of these terms as used here, see Robert Tannenbaum, "The Manager Concept: A Rational Synthesis" (*Journal of Business*, Oct., 1949).

[6] In connexion with this discussion, it should be noted that when participation takes place within the superior-subordinate relationship, managers have primary control over the nature of the activity; when it takes place as part of the manager-union relationship, they may or may not, depending upon the relative power of the two parties.

Decisions are made by managers in order to organize, direct, or control responsible subordinates to the end that all service contributions be co-ordinated in the attainment of an enterprise purpose.[7] Since managers are those who accomplish results through subordinates, the latter are always directly and intimately affected by managerial decisions and therefore may have a considerable interest in them. Because of this possible interest, subordinates may have a strong desire, particularly in a nation with deeply-ingrained democratic traditions, to participate in the determination of matters affecting them. It is of importance, therefore, to consider the form which such participation might assume.

Decision-making involves a conscious choice or selection of one behaviour alternative from among a group of two or more behaviour alternatives.[8] Three steps are involved in the decision-making process. First, an individual must become aware of as many as possible of those behaviour alternatives which are relevant to the decision to be made. Secondly, he must define each of these alternatives, a definition which involves a determination of as many as possible of the consequences related to each alternative under consideration. Thirdly, the individual must exercise a choice between the alternatives, that is, make a decision.

In enterprises, managerial subordinates, as subordinates, can participate in the first two steps of the managerial decision-making process. They cannot participate in the third step. The actual choice between relevant alternatives must be made or accepted by the manager who is responsible to his superior for the decision.[9] However, subordinates can provide and discuss with their manager information with respect both to relevant alternatives and to the consequences attendant upon specific alternatives. In so doing they are participating in the managerial decision-making process.[10]

---

[7] See Tannenbaum, "The Manager Concept: A Rational Synthesis."

[8] This discussion of the decision-making process is based upon Robert Tannenbaum, "Managerial Decision-Making" (*Journal of Business*, Jan., 1950).

[9] In a democratic group, the choice can be made through a vote participated in by the rank and file. But, in such a case, the leader is organizationally responsible to the rank and file, and the members of the rank and file are not properly, in so far as the decision is concerned, subordinates of the leader.

Members of a democratic group, making the final choice in matters directly affecting them, may be more highly motivated as a result thereof than managerial subordinates who are granted the right to participate only in the first two steps of the managerial decision-making process. For evidence of the motivational effects of group decision, see Kurt Lewin, "Group Decision and Social Change" (in T. M. Newcomb and E. L. Hartley (eds.), *Readings in Social Psychology*, New York, 1947).

[10] It is this type of participation that most writers, who deal with human relations in enterprises, have in mind when they use the concept. The following examples illustrate this contention: "One of the most important conditions of the

The participation with which we are here concerned may take place in two different ways. First, it may involve interaction solely between a subordinate and his manager.[11] This would be the case where a worker originates a suggestion which he transmits to his boss. Secondly, it may involve interaction between a group of subordinates and their manager. This would be the case where a manager calls his subordinates together to discuss a common problem or to formulate a recommendation.[12]

III. POSSIBLE ADVANTAGES OF PARTICIPATION AS A MANAGERIAL DEVICE

It becomes useful to inquire why managers might find it advantageous to use this device. In other words, what are the possible benefits which might accrue to an enterprise whose managers made it possible for subordinates to participate in the decision-making process? In providing an answer to this question, it is first necessary to indicate the criterion which would guide the managerial choice relating to the use of participation.

A manager of an enterprise (profit or nonprofit) who behaves rationally will attempt to make a selection from among alternatives related to any problem which will maximize results (the degree of attainment of a given end) at a given cost or which will attain given

---

subordinate's growth and development centers around his opportunities to express his ideas and to contribute his suggestions before his superiors take action on matters which involve him. Through participation of this kind he becomes more and more aware of his superiors' problems, and he obtains genuine satisfaction in knowing that his opinions and ideas are given consideration in the search for solutions" (D. McGregor, "Conditions for Effective Leadership in the Industrial Situation," p. 60); "I am not suggesting that we take over intact the apparatus of the democratic state. Business cannot be run by the ballot box. . . . We must develop other inventions, adapted to the special circumstances of business, which will give employees at all levels of our organizations a greater sense of personal participation and 'belonging'" (J. Worthy, "Changing Concepts of the Personnel Function," p. 175); "Action initiated by the responsible head to bring his subordinates into the picture on matters of mutual concern is not a sharing of prerogatives of authority. Rather, it is an extension of the opportunity of participation in the development of points of view and the assembly of facts upon which decisions are made" (H. Carey, "Consultative Supervision and Management," p. 288).

[11] The concept of interaction as used here is not restricted to direct person-to-person, two-way communication (as in the process of superior-subordinate discussion), but encompasses more indirect forms (such as, for example, written communication) as well.

[12] It may be observed that participation in the latter way, where there is communication between participators and where the act of participation is carried out through the medium of the group (as in cases of "group decision"), may often yield the more useful results. The level of derivable benefits may be higher than if participation had proceeded through channels in which there had been no inter-participator communication. Some factors important in this context are the following: (a) the feeling of "group belongingness" obtained by means of "action together" and (b) the role of norms, set as a result of group discussion, toward which behaviour will tend to gravitate.

results at the lowest cost.[13] This is the criterion of rationality. Guided by this criterion, rational managers will find it advantageous to use participation whenever such use will lead to increased results at a given cost or to the attainment of given results at a lower cost.

There are many advantages which *may* stem from the use of participation as a managerial device. The following are the principal ones:

(1) A higher rate of output and increased quality of products (including reduced spoilage and wastage) as a result of greater personal effort and attention on the part of subordinates.[14]

(2) A reduction in turnover, absenteeism, and tardiness.

(3) A reduction in the number of grievances and more peaceful manager-subordinate and manager-union relations.

(4) A greater readiness to accept change.[15] When changes are arbitrarily introduced from above without explanation, subordinates tend to feel insecure and to take countermeasures aimed at a sabotage of the innovations. But when they have participated in the process leading to the decision, they have had an opportunity to be heard. They know what to expect and why, and they may desire the change. Blind resistance tends to become intelligent adaptation as insecurity is replaced by security.

(5) Greater ease in the management of subordinates.[16] Fewer managers may be necessary, the need for close supervision may be reduced, and less disciplinary action may be called for. Subordinates who have participated in the process leading toward a determination of matters directly affecting them may have a greater sense of responsibility with respect to the performance of their assigned tasks and may be more willing to accept the authority of their superiors.

---

[13] The term *cost* is here used in its highly precise form to refer to whatever must be given or sacrificed to attain an end. See "Price," *Webster's Dictionary of Synonyms.* The term *end* is broadly conceived to embrace whatever factors (monetary or nonmonetary) the managers themselves define as the formal ends of the enterprise.

[14] For examples, see Lippitt, "A Program of Experimentation on Group Functioning and Productivity"; John R. P. French, Jr., Arthur Kornhauser, and Alfred Marrow, "Conflict and Cooperation in Industry" (*Journal of Social Issues,* Fed., 1946); *Productivity, Supervision and Morale* (Survey Research Center Study no. 6, Ann Arbor, 1948).

[15] See, for example, Alex Bavelas, "Some Problems of Organizational Change" (*Journal of Social Issues,* Summer, 1948); Elliott Jacques, "Interpretive Group Discussion as a Method of Facilitating Social Change" (*Human Relations,* Aug., 1948); Lewin, "Group Decision and Social Change."

[16] See, for example, L. P. Bradford and R. Lippitt, "Building a Democratic Work Group" (*Personnel,* Nov., 1945); O. H. Mowrer, "Authoritarianism vs. 'Self-Government' in the Management of Children's Aggressive (Anti-Social) Reactions as a Preparation for Citizenship in a Democracy" (*Journal of Social Psychology,* Feb., 1939, pp. 121-6).

All managers possess a given amount of formal authority delegated to them by their superiors. But formal authority is not necessarily the equivalent of effective authority. The real source of the authority possessed by an individual lies in the acceptance of its exercise by those who are subject to it. It is the subordinates of an individual who determine the authority which he may wield. Formal authority is, in effect, nominal authority. It becomes real only when it is accepted. Thus, to be effective, formal authority must coincide with authority determined by its acceptance. The latter defines the useful limits of the former.[17] The use of participation as a managerial device may result in a widening of these limits, reducing the amount of resistance to the exercise of formal authority and increasing the positive responses of subordinates to managerial directives.

(6) The improved quality of managerial decisions. It is seldom if ever possible for managers to have knowledge of *all* alternatives and *all* consequences related to the decisions which they must make. Because of the existence of barriers to the upward flow of information in most enterprises, much valuable information possessed by subordinates never reaches their managers. Participation tends to break down the barriers, making the information available to managers. To the extent that such information alters the decisions which managers make, the quality of their decisions may thereby be improved.

These, then, are the principal advantages which *may* stem from the use of participation as a managerial device.[18] The conditions under which it *will* accomplish them—under which participation will lead to motivation—is the concern of the section which follows.

IV. The Psychological Conditions of Effective Participation

All managers of an enterprise are faced with the problem of eliciting service contributions from their subordinates at a high level of quality and intensity. These service contributions are essential if the formal goals of the enterprise are to be attained. What induces subordinates to contribute their services? What motivates them?

A motivated individual is one who is striving to achieve a goal; his activity is goal-oriented.[19] But it should be stressed that motivation is only *potential* motion towards a goal. Whether or not the goal

---

[17] This concept of effective authority is expanded upon in Tannenbaum, "Managerial Decision-Making."

[18] These advantages will henceforth be referred to as enterprise advantages.

[19] A goal is defined as a result which, when achieved, has the power to reduce the tension of the organism that has caused the organism to seek it.

is reached depends not only upon the strength of the force in the direction of the goal, but also upon all other forces (both driving and restraining) in the given situation.[20] To illustrate, a person may be motivated to produce 200 units of an item per day, but the restraining force in the form of machine failure or a quarrel with the foreman may lead him to attain an output of only 150 units.

In enterprises, the goals towards which individuals strive may be of two kinds. They may be the formal goals of the enterprise, or they may be other goals which are complementary to the formal goals. The latter is the typical case. Individuals may strive for monetary reward, prestige, power, security, and the like; or they may strive for certain psychological gratifications through the very act of doing the job (that is, they work because they like their work). The primary reason why they contribute their services is to attain these latter goals. In attaining these desired goals, they make possible the attainment of the formal goals of the enterprise which to them are simply means to their own ends. In this sense, the desired goals and the formal goals are complementary.

In the former case, the goals desired by the individual and the formal goals are the same. The individual contributes his services primarily because such contribution makes possible the attainment of the formal goals of the enterprise which coincide with his own personal goals. To the extent that this coincidence of goals exists, the necessity for managers to provide complementary goals for subordinates is thereby lessened, and related costs are reduced. It is suggested that participation tends to bring about a coincidence of formal and personal goals.[21] It may be that through participation, the subordinate who formerly was moved to contribute his services only because he sought, for example, security and financial rewards, now comes to be moved additionally because he recognizes that the

---

[20] Thus, motion in the direction of goals may be achieved not only by adding forces in the goal-direction, but also by reducing forces impeding such motion. See K. Lewin, "Frontiers in Group Dynamics" (*Human Relations*, vol. I, no. 1, 1947, pp. 26-7).

[21] It must be noted that participation as used in this context is only one device which may lead to additional motivation by bringing about a coincidence of formal and personal goals. For example, some other devices that under certain conditions may result in motivational increases and their derivative benefits to the enterprise are permitting personal discretion to the person to be motivated and stimulation of a sense of pride of workmanship. In the former context, managers in all enterprises must always decide the amount of discretion to permit to subordinates. Many considerations naturally underlie this decision. For present purposes, it is important to emphasize that in many circumstances, the granting of considerable discretion may lead to substantial increases in motivation. Several devices may be used concurrently, and the dynamics of the devices themselves are interrelated. For example, use of discretion may bring about an enhanced pride-of-workmanship feeling.

success of the enterprise in turn will enhance his own ability to satisfy his needs.[22]

Whether one conceives of participation as involving separate subordinates with their superiors or subordinates-in-groups with their superiors, in the final analysis one must not lose sight of the fact that the subordinate is a unique human being with a given personality. This implies that whether or not participation will bring forth the restructuring of his goal pattern (incorporating the formal goals within the scope of the personal goals) will depend upon a set of dynamic psychological conditions, the primary ones of which are outlined below:

(1) The subordinate must be capable of becoming psychologically involved in the participational activities. He must be free from "blockages" which may prevent him from re-arranging his particular goal pattern in the light of new experience. He must possess some minimum amount of intelligence so that he may grasp the meaning and implications of the thing being considered. He must be in touch with reality. If he responds to a dream world, any "real" developments, such as opportunities to take part in certain decision-making processes, may not penetrate without gross distortion and as a result miss their point.

(2) The subordinate must favour participational activity. In other words, the person who believes that "the boss knows best" and that the decision-making process is none of his business is not likely to become strongly motivated if given an opportunity to participate. It is apparent that for personality types shaped intensely by an authoritarian system, opportunities for participation may be regarded as signs of weakness and leadership incompetence and on that basis may be rejected unequivocally.[23]

(3) The subordinate must see the relevance to his personal life pattern of the thing being considered. When he realizes that through participation he may affect the course of his future in such a fashion as to increase its positive goal elements and to diminish the negative ones, he will become motivated. For example, a person who can see the relationship between "putting his two bits" into a discussion of a new way of using a stitching machine and the fact that this may mean greater job security and increased pay for himself may be motivated.

---

[22] It must be recognized that typically goal configurations, rather than single goals, act as motivating agents.

[23] For example, see A. H. Maslow, "The Authoritarian Character Structure" (in P. L. Harriman (ed.), *Twentieth Century Psychology*, New York, 1946). For more detailed treatments see the major works of Erich Fromm and Abram Kardiner.

(4) The subordinate must be able to express himself to his own satisfaction with respect to the thing being considered. He must be psychologically able to communicate; and, further, he must feel that he is making some sort of contribution. Of course, if he cannot communicate (owing to mental blocks, fear of being conspicuous, etc.), by definition he is not participating. If he does not feel that he is contributing, he may, instead of becoming motivated, come to feel inadequate and frustrated. This presupposes that not only is he articulate, but that he has a certain fund of knowledge on which to draw. Participation may fail if it involves considering matters that are quite outside the scope of experience of the participators.

All of the above conditions must be satisfied to some minimum extent. Beyond this requirement, however, the conditions may be mutually compensating, and a relatively low degree of one (although necessarily above the minimum) may be offset somewhat by an extremely high degree of another. For example, if a subordinate is unusually anxious to take part in participational activity (perhaps for reasons of prestige desires), he may come to be quite involved in the process of restructuring his goal pattern so that it will include some of the formal goals, even though he is not always certain as to whether or not he is really contributing anything worthwhile. Further, the relationships specified by the conditions are essentially dynamic. Opportunities for participation, reluctantly used at first, ultimately may lead to a change of mind and to their enthusiastic acceptance.[24]

It is apparent that individual differences are highly important in considering the effectiveness of participation as a motivational device; however, the "amount of participation opportunities" made possible by the managers is also a variable quantity. Thus, it is necessary to enquire what the limits to opportunities to participate are in terms of maximum results.

Common sense experience indicates that when some subordinates are given too many opportunities for participation, or too much leeway in participating, they may tend to flounder; they may find themselves unable to assimilate effectively the range of "thinking

---

[24] It should be stressed that "life spaces" of individuals (that is, their conceptions of themselves in relation to the totality of a physical and psychological environment) and their readiness for action in the light of these conceptions are never static. Constant change and "restructuring" take place, making for an essentially dynamic patterning of behaviour. For alternative definitions of the concept "life space" see Robert W. Leeper, *Lewin's Topological and Vector Psychology* (Eugene, 1943), p. 210.

opportunities" with which they are faced.[25] On the other hand, if they are given little or no opportunity to take part in the decision-making process, by definition they will not come to be motivated by participational activity. For each individual, an amount of participation opportunities lying somewhere between these two extremes will result in a maximum amount of motivation. A hypothesis stemming from this formulation is that for effective operation of participation as a motivational device in a group situation, the members of the group must respond similarly to given amounts of participation, for wide divergences of response may bring forth social tensions and lack of team work within the group.

Of course, many factors act together to motivate an individual. Therefore, the usefulness of the conceptualization advanced depends upon the possibility of breaking down the total of motivational forces into those owing to participation and those owing to other factors. Experimental control methods, matching of cases, and similar devices may have to be utilized to make such an analysis possible. Whether or not the increment of motivation owing to participation is worthwhile depends to an important extent upon the level of intensity of motivation that prevailed previous to introduction of the device of participation. No doubt, there are upper limits to intensity of motivation, and, if motivation has been strong all along, the effect of participation may not be very great.

V. Extra-Participational Conditions for Effective Participation

Beyond the factors governing the relationship between participation and possible resultant motivation, certain conditions "outside" the individual must be considered by the managers in deciding whether or not this particular device is applicable.[26] It would be possible to distinguish a great number of such outside conditions that may determine whether or not the use of participation is feasible in a given situation. Those here indicated are suggestive rather than fully definitive. All are viewed with this question in mind: "Granting that participation may have certain beneficial effects, is it useful in a given instance if the ends of the enterprise are to be achieved?"

---

[25] For the belief that "thinking" as a solution for the industrial problem of motivation is usable more effectively on the supervisory level, but less applicable on the "lower levels" of the organizational hierarchy, see Willard Tomlison, "Review of A. R. Heron, *Why Men Work*" (*Personnel Journal*, July-Aug., 1948, p. 122).

[26] For analytical purposes, this article differentiates between conditions regarding the dynamics of participation as a psychological process and all conditions outside this psychological participation-to-motivation link. The latter category of conditions is treated under the present heading.

To answer this question affirmatively, the following conditions must be met:

(1) *Time Availability.* The final decision must not be of a too urgent nature.[27] If it is necessary to arrive at some sort of emergency decision rapidly, it is obvious that even though participation in the decision-making process may have a beneficial effect in some areas, slowness of decision may result in thwarting other goals of the enterprise or even may threaten the existence of the enterprise. Military decisions frequently are of this type.

(2) *Rational Economics.* The cost of participation in the decision-making process must not be so high that it will outweigh any positive values directly brought about by it. If it should require outlays which could be used more fruitfully in alternative activities (for example, buying more productive though expensive equipment), then investment in it would be ill-advised.

(3) *Intra-Plant Strategy.*

(a) *Subordinate Security.* Giving the subordinates an opportunity to participate in the decision-making process must not bring with it any awareness on their part of unavoidable catastrophic events. For example, a subordinate who is made aware in the participation process that he will lose his job *regardless* of any decisions towards which he might contribute may experience a drop in motivation. Furthermore, to make it possible for the subordinate to be willing to participate, he must be given the feeling that no matter what he says or thinks his status or role in the plant setting will not be affected adversely. This point has been made effectively in the available literature.[28]

(b) *Manager-Subordinate Stability.* Giving subordinates an opportunity to participate in the decision-making process must not threaten seriously to undermine the formal authority of the managers of the enterprise. For example, in some cases managers may have good reasons to assume that participation may lead non-managers to doubt the competence of the formal leadership, or that serious crises would result were it to develop that the subordinates were right while the final managerial decision turned out to be in disagreement with them and incorrect.

(4) *Inter-Plant Strategy.* Providing opportunities for participation must not open channels of communication to competing enter-

---

[27] See Chester I. Barnard, *Organization and Management* (Cambridge, 1948), p. 48.

[28] See McGregor, "Conditions for Effective Leadership in the Industrial Situation," *passim.*

prises. "Leaks" of information to a competitor from subordinates who have participated in a given decision-making process must be avoided if participation is to be applicable.

(5) *Provision for Communication Channels.* For participation to be effective, channels must be provided through which the employee may take part in the decision-making process. These channels must be available continuously and their use must be convenient and practicable.[29]

(6) *Education for Participation.* For participation to be effective, efforts must be made to educate subordinates regarding its function and purpose in the over-all functioning of the enterprise.[30]

It must be stressed that the conditions stipulated in this section are dynamic in their own right and may be affected by the very process of participation as well as by other factors.

VI. Effects of Participation as a Function of Time

An area of research that still remains relatively unexplored is that relating to the variation of the effects of participation with time. Some experimental studies have examined these effects in terms of increased productivity over a period of several weeks or months and found no appreciable reductions in productivity with time; while other evidence indicates that in some cases participation may have a sort of "shock" effect, leading to a surge of interest and increased motivation, with a subsequent decline.[31] Inadequate attention seems to have been given to this rather crucial question, and the present writers know of no studies that have traced the effects of participation (or other motivational devices) over periods as long as a year. However, on a priori grounds, and on the basis of experiential evidence, it would seem that, after an initial spurt, a plateau of beneficial effects will be attained, which finally will dissolve into a decline, unless additional managerial devices are skilfully employed.

---

[29] For a rigorous mathematical treatment of channels of communication within groups see Alex Bavelas, "A Mathematical Model for Group Structures" (*Applied Anthropology*, Summer, 1948, pp. 16 ff.).

[30] See French, Kornhauser, and Marrow, "Conflict and Co-operation in Industry," p. 30.

[31] For evidence of no decline in the motivational effect of certain participational procedures in an industrial re-training situation after a relatively brief time period subsequent to initiation of participation had elapsed, see. for example, L. Coch and J. R. P. French, "Overcoming Resistance to Change" (*Human Relations*. vol. I. no. 4, pp. 522-3). Also Lewin, "Group Decision and Social Change," pp. 338 and 343. For the hypothesis that under certain conditions decline may occur with time, see Heron, *Why Men Work*, p. 180.

QUESTIONS

1. Historically, what have been the three approaches for dealing with the problem of participation?
2. How do these authors define participation?
3. What advantages do they claim participation offers as a managerial device?
4. List and explain the psychological conditions that are needed to secure effective participation.
5. Does this article tend to agree or disagree with Allport's? In what ways?

ORGANIZATIONAL LEADERSHIP AND PARTICIPATIVE MANAGEMENT *

Chris Argyris

IMPORTANCE OF PARTICIPATION

"Participative management" and "democratic leadership" are phrases that are currently in the limelight in most management circles. These phrases are taken to mean that the subordinates should be given an opportunity to participate in the various decisions that are made in their organization which affect them directly or indirectly. Many executives, consultants, and research scientists, including the author,[1] have written and continue to write about the advantages of participative management. These people encourage supervisors and executives to increase the employees' participation in various organizational activities, especially in the decision-making process. They point out that, among other things, studies show that participative management tends to (1) increase the degree of "we" feeling or cohesiveness that participants have with their organization; (2) provide the participants with an over-all organizational point of view instead of the traditionally more narrow departmental point of view; (3) decrease the amount of conflict, hostility, and cutthroat competition among the participants; (4) increase the individuals' understanding of each other which leads to increased tolerance and patience toward others; (5) increase the individual's free expression of his personality, which results in an employee who sticks with the organization because he (i.e., his personality) needs the gratifying experiences he finds while working there; and (6) develop a "work climate," as a result of the other tendencies, in which the subordinates find opportunity to be more creative and to come up with ideas beneficial to the organization.

Although these trends are admittedly desirable, many supervisors and executives ask, "Exactly how far can this notion of participation and democracy be carried out?" Lately we have been asking ourselves the same question. Although we cannot answer it completely within the space of this paper, we would like to present for the reader's consideration some preliminary thoughts on the matter.

---

* From the *Journal of Business*, Vol. 28, No. 1 (January, 1955), pp. 1-7. Reprinted with permission.

[1] Argyris, "Techniques in Member Centered Training," *Personnel*, XXVIII, No. 3 (November, 1951), pp. 236-46.

Factors Influencing the Successful Introduction of Participative Management In An Organization

Much attention has been given and continues to be given to (1) the executives' feelings and attitudes about participative management; (2) the small informal groupings within the organization; and (3) the personnel policies of the organization. The assumption is that these are the three crucial factors in making participative management work.

We agree that these three factors are crucial, but we would like to add another. It seems to us that the kind of organizational structure within which these factors operate is also crucial. It is this factor that we propose to examine further.

How may we characterize the nature of most modern industrial and business organizations? One way to answer this question is to note the underlying rules or principles used by administrators to create and administer these organizations.

Simon defines some of the more common principles of administration upon which organizations are based as:

> 1. Administrative efficiency is increased by a specialization of the task among the group. [Specialization.]
> 2. Administrative efficiency is increased by arranging the members of the group in a determinate hierarchy of authority. [Unity of Command.]
> 3. Administrative efficiency is increased by limiting the span of control at any point in the hierarchy to a small number. [Span of Control.] [2]

These principles serve as the basis for the definition of organizational structure. They point out the kind of organization within which we usually try to introduce participative management programs. The question arises, "What problems can we predict will tend to arise when we try to introduce participative management to such an organization?"

In order to answer this question, we find it necessary first to re-examine and perhaps to redefine exactly what we mean by "organization."

A Concept of Organization

We may begin by defining an organization as an aggregate of parts (e.g., individuals, departments) integrated into an organized "whole." [3]

---

[2] Herbert A. Simon, *Administrative Behavior* (New York: Macmillan Co., 1947), pp. 20-21.

[3] More specifically, an organization may be defined as (1) any aggregate of parts (2) in a hierarchical order (3) co-existing (4) and interrelated in such a

How do these parts (e.g., individuals) become integrated into an organized whole? Research at the Yale Labor and Management Center indicates that the following *organizational processes* must be performed if an aggregate of individuals is to become an organization:

1. A *Work-flow Process* to define the behavior sequence that the parts of the organization must accomplish to achieve the objective (e.g., in a shoe factory a series of behavior sequences must be set up which people must perform in order to produce shoes)
2. A *Reward and Penalty Process* to induce people to do the work the organization assigns to them (in other words, the Reward and Penalty Process "taps" human motivation by rewarding or penalizing according to the acceptability of the actions performed)
3. An *Authority Process* to direct the employees in order that the organizational requirements be met
4. A *Perpetuation Process* to maintain and replenish the basic resources of organization (men, materials, and ideas)
5. An *Identification Process* to select and define clearly understood emotionally toned symbols, concepts, or other such aspects which will help individual employees identify with the organization as a whole, which in turn automatically helps to point out the uniqueness of the organization in the larger environment in which it is imbedded
6. A *Communication Process* to provide media and paths for communication

In other words, according to this scheme, we assume that an organization cannot exist unless someone performs at least these essential (but not sufficient) processes. We may now begin to understand how the principles of specialization and unity of command affect the possibilities of successfully initiating "participative management" in organizations.

Let us assume that we have a plant all set up to manufacture shoes. We have purchased the plant, the equipment, and the materials necessary to produce our product. We now need only "labor" to make the shoes. We hire these employees, and, if we administer our organization according to the modern management principle of task specialization, we will assign them to the specific task (or set of tasks) of making shoes. In terms of our outline this means that we assign them to tasks in the work-flow process.

But, according to our definition of organization above, these employees cannot be welded into an organization because they lack

---

unique manner (5) that the parts are able to maintain themselves only through this unique interrelatedness; (6) and simultaneously these parts work together in order to achieve the purpose which the organization is intended to achieve. (7) And to achieve Nos. 5 and 6 by adapting, within the limits, to any external influences, thereby (8) maintaining the characteristic interrelated state of these parts (i.e., maintaining organization).

the remainder of the organizational processes (e.g., authority, reward and penalty, etc.). In order to provide these processes and thus create an organization out of this aggregate of people, we create a new job containing the missing processes. We give the person who takes this job control over the authority, reward and penalty, perpetuation, and other processes. We call this person the "organizational leader." Now, the employees who are making the shoes can be welded into an organized unit. But, to do so, they must by definition become dependent upon the organizational leader for the missing processes of organization. They must turn to him for their authority, reward and penalties, perpetuation, etc. Thus the principle of unity of command is now "translated" into the principle that the subordinates are to report to one leader and are to be dependent upon him for certain crucial activities.

In other words, the scheme suggests that what is customarily called "the principle of unity of command" is actually the principle of inducing the subordinates to follow the leader by making them dependent upon him and by paying them to accept this dependence. There is, therefore, a "built-in" sense of dependency of the subordinates upon the organizational leader.[4] This dependency, we suggest, is inevitable if we follow the principles of task specialization and unity of command.

Do Dependence and Participation Go Together?

The question arises, "How truly participative (i.e., how spontaneous and free) can subordinates be if they are to be dependent upon their leader?" "How much democracy can we have if the power lies in the one who leads and not in the ones who are led?" Or, if we take the leader's point of view, "How democratic can he be if his job *is* to control the processes of organization?" Unfortunately, these and other similar questions are not answered by the many interesting and provocative studies in small-group dynamics from which so much of our information about the value of participation stems. The reason is that most of the research is based upon experimentally created or actual groups whose basic purpose is *not* to give any one leader a "life-or-death grip" (to quote an employee) on the other members of the group. Leadership in these groups seems to arise at any given time from the individual's ability to fulfil the needs of the other members of the group. It does not arise because of any predeter-

---

[4] The leader is dependent upon the subordinates in terms of the work flow; he depends upon them to produce.

mined power of any one member over the other members of the group.

Although we also do not have a clear-cut answer to the question of "How much participation is possible?" there are some implications in our analysis which might be useful in eventually helping us to arrive at an answer. We discuss some of these implications below.

A BASIC CONFLICT BETWEEN ORGANIZATION DEVELOPMENT AND PERSONALITY DEVELOPMENT

If the modern management principles (e.g., unity of command, task specialization, span of control, etc.) are to obtain *ideal* expression in an organization, the management would have to assign non-supervisory employees to a job which tends to (1) permit them little control over their work-a-day world; (2) place them in a situation where their passivity rather than initiative would frequently be expected; (3) lead them to occupy a subordinate position; (4) permit them a minimum degree of fluidity (variety) and emphasize the expression of one (or perhaps a few) of the agent's relatively minor abilities; and (5) make them feel dependent upon other agents (e.g., the boss).[5]

The problems that would tend to arise if we assign people to such jobs can be seen by asking the following questions, "What sorts of personality characteristics do people in our culture tend to exhibit?" Or, to put it another way, "What needs do relatively normal adults in our culture have?" "Would these needs be able to find some such expression in a job situation as the one we describe above?"

A somewhat detailed analysis of much of the material available on the development of the human personality suggests that people in our culture (1) tend to develop from receiving and incorporating aspects of culture as an infant to controlling, using, redefining, and helping others incorporate these aspects of culture as an adult; (2) develop from a state of being passive as an infant (i.e., having other people initiate action for them) to a state of being increasingly active as an adult (i.e., they initiate action as much or more than other people toward them); (3) develop from being capable of behaving only in a few ways and in a rigid manner as an infant to being capable of behaving in many different ways and behaving in a flexible manner as an adult; (4) develop from being in a subordinate position in the family and society as an infant, to occupying a more

---

[5] F. W. Taylor, *Scientific Management* (New York: Harper & Bros., 1947), and R. Urwick, *The Elements of Administration* (New York: Harper & Bros., 1944).

equal and/or superordinate position in the family and society as an adult; and (5) develop from a state of high dependence on others as an infant to a state of independence and finally to a state of inter-dependence in their society as an adult.[6]

If we assume, for a moment, that the people who come to work for us are relatively normal, then may we not conclude that these people will tend to desire to find work which will help them fulfil some combination of the above trends? (The exact combination naturally depends on the individual.) In order to accomplish this, an individual would require a job in which he can (1) define for himself a ratio of activity (initiation of action) to passivity where activity is greater than passivity (passivity defined as others initiating action for the individual); (2) define for himself a position equal and/or superordinate to the other people with whom he interacts; (3) define for himself tasks where he is able to provide expression for the many learned ways of behaving that are important to him (this includes the expression of important abilities, needs, sentiments, and personal goals); (4) define for himself a sense of fluidity and flexi-bility that is comparable to his personality fluidity and flexibility; (5) express feelings of independence and interdependence in rela-tion to the other people in the organization; (6) feel that he has the respect of other individuals who are important in his life; and (7) obtain from his job a degree of creature sufficiency he desires.[7]

Thus, relatively normal individuals are characterized as "having built into them (through the process of growing up) tendencies to

---

[6] Chris Argyris, *Personality Fundamentals for Administrators* (rev. ed.; New Haven: Yale Labor and Management Center, 1953).

[7] It seems necessary that we pause for a moment and make a few important comments concerning the listing just presented.

First, we want to emphasize that the exact combination of these requirements and the degree to which each one of them is to be fulfilled for any given indivi-dual can be ascertained only by analysis of that individual case. Thus, it is possible that Individual A, for example, requires primarily 1, 2, and 4, with an emphasis on 1. On the other hand, Individual B may require that all the above be fulfilled, with an emphasis on 5 and 6.

It is also conceivable that Individual C may desire 1 *not* to be active, *not* to have an equal or superordinate position; 2 *not* to desire to feel independent; 5, etc. According to our viewpoint, this adult would have to be classed as "not matured." He is still at a more childlike stage of development. Psychologists may call him "fixated" at an earlier stage of development. This individual would not require a function which permits him to accomplish the items suggested in 1-7.

The point we want to emphasize is that we are *not* eliminating individual differences, nor are we imposing our developmental scheme on everyone. This is not a "budding rosebud" theory. We are simply suggsting that a normal individual, living in and interacting with our culture, will tend to exhibit these developmental trends but in his own unique combination. If the individual does not depict any of these trends, then we would suggest that, broadly speaking, he is not mature and that he will tend to be in equilibrium in the kind of function in which a mature individual will not be in equilibrium.

be active, to be independent, to be flexible, and to express their many and varied abilities," etc. Job situations, on the other hand, are described as requiring an individual to be passive, to be dependent, and to express only one or two abilities.

The job requirements are clearly different from, and in some cases antagonistic to, the requirements of relatively normal individuals. However, they *are* substantially similar to the requirements of an infant in our culture.

Thus, we are led to conclude that it would be difficult for the organization to place relatively normal adult individuals in "ideal" job (i.o., from the organization's point of view) situations without creating difficulties. Similarly, it would be difficult for the individual to obtain ideal personality expression without blocking the efficient expression of the organizational principles.

There are a number of ways out of such a dilemma for both the employees and the management. For example, some recent research at the Yale Management and Labor Center indicates that employees may adapt to their working situation in various ways. Individuals may (1) leave the organization; (2) accept the frustration on the assumption that if they work hard they will eventually be raised to a leadership position; (3) become apathetic and not "give a damn" about their work; (4) create informal activities and informal groups to help them adapt (if the groups are found to be effective, the individuals may desire to stabilize them and make certain that these groups will always exist; this might be accomplished by the individuals bringing to bear upon the work situation power which is inherently theirs, i.e., that which comes from the political, social, and economic privileges given to all people in this country; thus, the groups may be stabilized in the form of trade-unions); and (5) come into the organization prepared (through culture training) to expect no high degree of personality expression; this expectation tends to act to reduce the negative effects of the actual lack of personality expression obtained on the job.

Management, on the other hand, may act to minimize the difficulties by decreasing the employees' dependence upon the organization leader.[8] This is one of the main objectives of increased employee participation in decision-making. The point we would make is simply

---

[8] Management may also decrease the negative effects of specialization through "job enlargement." In terms of our framework, this means giving employees more work-flow tasks. Our research suggests that an increase in work-flow tasks does not necessarily lead to better-adapted individuals. It is the inclusion of authority, reward and penalty, and perpetuation tasks that really counts.

that, if we are to use participation to decrease dependency, then we may also have to change the nature of our organization. Our organization is no longer being administered by the principles described above. In short, participative management implies a different set of organization principles.

If what we have said to date makes sense, then clearly there are some interesting implications for executive training. First, is there not a need for a reexamination of the basic structure of organization as defined by traditional administrative principles? Perhaps a different type of organization structure is necessary if "participative management" is really to work. Until such basic changes are made, might it not be more realistic to teach participative management principles to executives *after* they have been helped to understand the effects that this basic dependency relationship has upon the employees? We could teach them to understand the nature of a dependency relationship and point out how it conflicts with normal personality needs.[9] This would help the supervisors gain more insight into the "why" of the often-observed apathetic, disinterested behavior on the part of employees. It would help the supervisor to understand the *adaptive value* of the many informal activities that employees create but which management may dislike. For example, what would happen if the supervisor is helped to realize that apathy may be a healthy way to adapt to the type of work situation in which a person is usually placed? Would it not lead the supervisor to ask himself, "How can I minimize this dependency relationship and reduce the number of personality-blocking aspects of the organization without detracting from the efficient management of the organization?" He would do this *before* he spent hours making "morale" speeches about "everybody getting on the team."

Moreover, would not this knowledge help us to learn to set realistic limits to participative management, thereby making the supervisors more secure in its use? It seems to us that one reason many supervisors resist participative management is that they feel that there are no limits to its use. Also, would it not help to alleviate, or at lease to decrease, the often-produced feelings of inadequacy and perhaps guilt that supervisors have after listening to how democratic they ought to be?

---

9 For further discussion of these points see the author's "Executive Leadership: Developing It in Yourself and in Others," speech before the Harvard Business School Club of New York, February, 1954 (to be published as a chapter of a monograph by the McKinsey Foundation for Management Research, Inc.).

We close with this point. Let nothing in this paper be construed to mean that we are implying that modern management principles are "bad" or that apathy and indifference on the part of members of organizations are "good." We are simply trying to spell out what *is*. It seems to us, if we all (employees and executives) understand the basic difficulties inherent in organization, there should result a greater tolerance for and patience and understanding of the organization's problems, our own problems, and the problems of others.

QUESTIONS

1. Why does Argyris feel that participative management is so important?
2. What is the relationship between dependence and participation according to this article?
3. What is the conflict between organization development and personality development?
4. What remedies does Argyris suggest for the conflict between organization development and personality development?
5. Do you agree or disagree with Argyris' criticisms of management principles?

MANAGEMENT BY PARTICIPATION *

Keith Davis

Participation is an overworked word in the business environment, but it is a much underworked activity. The idea sounds good to most businessmen, but they are frequently unsure what to do with it. Some grossly misinterpret what it is, and others are not sure when to apply it or how far to go with it. One reason for all this confusion is that managers have not had much experience with the modern style of participation. As they practice it, they usually develop confidence in its benefits and attain the skill that customarily comes with experience. Another reason for confusion is that there are many new ideas about participation. Only recently have social scientists and managers begun to devote substantial professional attention to its use in business. Participation, though ancient in the history of mankind, is comparatively new in the modern business culture.

THE NATURE OF PARTICIPATION

Participation is defined as mental and emotional involvement of a person in a group situation which encourages him to contribute to group goals and share responsibility in them. There are three ideas in this definition which are important to businessmen who will practice the art of participation.

First, and probably foremost, participation means mental and emotional involvement, rather than mere muscular activity. Some managers go through the motions of participation, but nothing more. They hold meetings, ask opinions, and so on, but all the time it is perfectly clear to employees that their manager is an autocratic boss who wants no ideas. This is busy work, not participation.

A second important idea in participation is that it motivates persons to contribute to the situation. They are given an opportunity to release their own resources of initiative and creativeness toward the objectives of the organization. In this way, participation differs from "consent," which uses only the creativeness and ideas of the manager who brings his ideas to the group for consent. The consenters do not contribute; they merely approve. The practice of "consent" allows some degree of useful communication (mostly one-

* From the *Management Review*, Vol. 46, No. 2 (February, 1957), pp. 69-79. Copyright, 1957, by the American Management Association. Reprinted by permission of the American Management Association.

way), but it does not provide participation in which all members of the group can contribute their ideas.

A third idea in participation is that it encourages people to share responsibility in an activity. Because they are self-involved in an organization, they want to see it work successfully. Participation helps them become responsible industrial citizens, rather than non-responsible, automatons.

Managers often ask, "If by means of participation I share authority and responsibility with my personnel, don't I lose some of my own authority? I can't afford to lose authority because I am responsible, and if I am responsible, I must have the authority." This is a perfectly normal worry, but it is hardly justifiable, because the participative manager still retains his authority to decide. He shares his problem with the group by means of a process which may be called social delegation. Social delegation in the human relations domain is comparable to formal delegation in the organization domain. Formal delegation does not weaken a manager's organizational authority; neither does social delegation weaken his authority. No modern manager objects to formal delegation. In fact, it is his stock-in-trade; it is the act which makes him a manager. No manager of the future, say 20 years hence, will under normal conditions object to social delegation through participation. It, too, will be his stock-in-trade—that which makes him a participative manager.

BENEFITS OF PARTICIPATION

Participation is not just a theory derived by someone looking for a new idea in human relations. There is ample evidence that it works in practice. The great danger with participation, as with scientific management, is that its practitioners will get lost in the procedures of participation while overlooking its philosophy.

Procedures do not make participation; rather, when they are used in the right time and circumstance, they make it possible for participation to develop in the minds of employees. The substance of participation is a set of attitudes among employees which encourages teamwork and satisfies their need for human dignity as respected, contributing members of their organization.

Participation offers many advantages. It is valuable in many areas other than job performance, such as working conditions, community relations, and employee benefits; consequently, its use may produce widespread benefits to a company as a whole. The principal advantages of participation may be summarized briefly as follows:

1. It encourages better decisions.
2. It uses the creativity of all employees.
3. It restores a measure of human dignity, motivation, and mutual interest.
4. It encourages people to accept responsibility.
5. It improves morale and teamwork.
6. It encourages acceptance of change.

As a consequence of these general benefits, certain more specific production and economic benefits tend to occur. Note that they are a result of the general benefits and do not occur independently, which means that participation works indirectly through the minds and emotions of men to bring its benefits to the production floor.

Among the specific benefits are: (1) higher rate of output; (2) improved quality of product; (3) fewer grievances and conflicts; (4) reduced turnover, absenteeism, and tardiness; (5) increased income for distribution to those who are involved in the enterprise.

In the words of William Seward, who studied participative practices in industry, "The experience of those concerns who have made participation a tenet of policy shows that, when all employees are treated as participants in the business, that business can provide greater rewards."

Prerequisites of Effective Participation

Participation's success is directly related to how well certain prerequisite conditions are met. Some of these conditions occur in the participants; some exist in their environment. Taken together, these conditions mean that participation works better in some situations than others—and in certain situations it does not work at all. These conditions are:

1. There must be time to participate before action is required. Participation is hardly appropriate in emergency situations.

2. The financial cost of participation should not exceed the values, economic and otherwise, that come from it. Employees cannot spend their full workday participating, to the exclusion of all other work! To take another example, if participation causes disastrous competitive leaks of information, the cost may be too high.

3. The subject of participation must be relevant to the participant's organization or something in which he is interested, else he will look upon it merely as busy work.

4. The participant should have the ability, such as intelligence and knowledge, to participate. It is hardly advisable, for example,

to ask the janitor in a pharmaceutical laboratory to participate in deciding which of five chemical formulas deserve research priority; but he might participate in other problems related to his work.

5. The participants must be able mutually to communicate—to talk each other's language—in order to be able to exchange ideas.

6. Neither party should feel that his position is threatened by participation. If a worker thinks his status will be adversely affected, he will not participate. If a manager feels that his authority is threatened, he will refuse participation or be defensive. Participation, therefore, thrives best in a company culture which truly accepts it all the way from the top down.

7. Participation for deciding a course of action in an organization can take place only within the group's area of job freedom. Some degree of restriction on sub-units is necessary in any organization in order to maintain internal stability. Each separate sub-unit cannot make decisions which violate company policy, collective bargaining agreements, legal requirements, and similar restrictions. The area of job freedom for any manager is his area of free decision remaining after all outside compulsory restrictions have been applied. With regard to the restricted area, he and his men may participate in deciding that a change should be made, but they alone cannot make the change.

DEGREES OF PARTICIPATION

Any manager who tries to set up participation in his company will recognize that there are degrees of participation ranging from zero to infinity, and that the lesser degrees are easier to reach. Considerable skill is needed to attain advanced degrees of participation, but there are always places to begin. There are three important degrees of participation. The first is the *mutual-understanding degree,* and its purpose is to help all members understand each other's functions and attitudes so that they will develop better teamwork. They become more self-involved, more creative, and more responsible members. The *advisory degree* is built upon the mutual-understanding degree, because members are hardly ready to give sound advice until they understand the situation. In advisory participation an individual can help make decisions and offer creative suggestions, but he lacks authority to apply his ideas. The leader finally decides the course of action after giving suitable weight to ideas of participants. The *authoritative degree* of participation actually gives the group a degree of power to effect its decision. This power may be formal, as when a manager delegates decision-making authority on a safety matter to his group, or informal, as when the group makes decisions subject to the manager's right to veto, but his veto is hardly ever invoked. An example of the latter is multiple management, which will be discussed later.

THE UNION'S ROLE

A labor union often has definite policies regarding what areas and degrees of participation it thinks are desirable. Even if the union institution has no explicit policies, its leaders usually have definite viewpoints toward participation. Some unions, for example, favor joint participation in job evaluation; others do not.

Many union leaders feel that if they participate in helping management decide courses of action, the union's ability to challenge these actions is thereby weakened. These union leaders would prefer to remain aloof, having complete freedom to express disagreement with management and challenge it at any time. The opposite point of view, held by some leaders, is that participation gives them an opportunity to get on the inside and to express their viewpoint before action is taken, which is superior to disagreement and protest after a decision is made. In actual practice, most union viewpoints are somewhere between these two extremes; some types of participation are acceptable, but others are not. Much depends on the existing state of company-union relations, the degree of participation proposed, the stability of the union, and similar influences. Good faith on the part of both parties is essential.

An important distinction to unions is the difference between (1) employee participation in the role of union representative, such as having a union representative on the job-evaluation committee, and (2) participation by an individual employee, such as in a shop safety committee. Unions are much more hesitant about the former, because they are officially involved. They look more favorably upon the latter practice, as long as matters covered in the collective-bargaining contract are excluded, and usually they will not formally object if management wishes to establish practices of this type.

TECHNIQUES OF ENCOURAGING PARTICIPATION

The participative methods discussed below represent new developments and examples of the wide applicability of participation. Some methods, for example, work best with managers; other plans apply to employees. Some use formal committees; others work informally.

The plans are consultive supervision, democratic supervision, production committees, suggestion programs, and multiple management.

CONSULTIVE PARTICIPATION

Consultive supervision, also called consultive management, is the term which best describes a manager's general efforts to develop informal participation, with minor emphasis on formal committees and procedures. It is the kind of participation which a manager can apply even though his boss does not apply it. No new company policies are required, and the existing authority-responsibility relationships in his firm are not affected. Consultive supervision, as the name implies, means that the manager consults with his employees on key problems which affect them, in order to get them to think about the problems and contribute their own ideas before he makes decisions. This approach requires that a manager be genuinely receptive to ideas of his men so that they can perceive that their ideas are useful. A manager applying consultive supervision must have the humility to admit that he does not know more than all his men together and that his ideas are not always best. His attitude is the important factor, rather than the procedure itself, because his men will quickly perceive the superficiality of any procedure which is not underwritten by a genuine desire for employee ideas.

Consultive supervision does not weaken a manager's formal authority, because he still retains the right to decide. It normally should strengthen his informal authority, because his consultation with employees and response to their ideas help to make him their representative as well as the company's. A number of important by-products, such as better communication and grievance settlement, come from consultive supervision, because both parties better understand each other's problems.

DEMOCRATIC SUPERVISION

Democratic supervision, also known as democratic leadership, is often used as a synonym for consultive supervision, but, in a narrower sense, democratic supervision is something different. It makes a greater shift of decision-making responsibility to the group. In some instances, the supervisor "delegates" decision-making authority to his group to the extent that he does not proceed until group decision is reached on matters referred to it. If the group does not decide, this is the supervisor's cue that no action should be taken. Although he theoretically retains ultimate authority, in practice he shares it with his group.

The democratic supervisor obviously does not let his group make all decisions affecting it. In the first place, decisions can occur only within the area of job freedom, as described earlier. Each group in a coordinated production unit, for example, cannot determine its own days and hours of work. In the second place, only a few of the total number of decisions are brought to the group; otherwise, it would spend its whole day deciding. What is meant is that the democratic supervisor brings to his group a sufficient number of problems to cause them to feel that their creativity is being used and that they are adequately involved in determining the affairs which affect their work. The feeling or climate of participation is the important factor, not the number of decisions.

PRODUCTION COMMITTEES

Production committees are groups formally organized to consider work problems and composed jointly of worker and management representatives. They have been used for decades, especially in railroading and clothing manufacturing; and on occasion they have produced excellent results. But production committees have had a checkered record of success. In some industries they have been successful, but not in others. Some companies have used them for a while, then dropped them.

One reason for the poor performance record of production committees is that management and labor have lacked the human relations skill to ulitize them. This impediment will be removed in time, but other impediments are not so easily pushed aside. Some union leaders feel that production committees are a surreptitious device for a speed-up. Others believe that unions should not become involved in "management work" related to production, because it will weaken the union's role. A number of employers object to "letting the union (or workers) manage the plant." As a further deterrent, there is the ever-present possibility that the committees will become bogged in red tape, lose continuity because of infrequent meetings, or otherwise become impotent. Because of these problems, production committees may continue to play a minor participative role in business under normal conditions. Other practices, such as informal consultive supervision, tend to be more widely applicable.

SUGGESTION PROGRAMS

Though suggestion programs have been more successful than production committees, they need careful "feeding and watering" in order to flourish. One human relations weakness is that they exist primarily by written communication; hence the motivation that comes from face-to-face interaction is lacking. The employee seldom participates in the consideration of his ideas; other persons do that for him.

A second suggestion-program weakness is the tendency of the average foreman to resent employee suggestions, because he looks upon them as criticism of his ability and efficiency.

One answer to this problem is the kind of higher-management support which gives a foreman credit for a high suggestion rate in his department and which sells him on the philosophy that all employees can have good ideas. Another answer is to give the foreman some financial return for suggestions accepted in his department, such as 10 per cent of total payments to his men.

Just as foremen resent suggestions, specialized staff personnel may resent them even more when the suggestions apply to their specialty. Experience has shown that industrial engineers especially tend to object to suggestions affecting processes for which they are responsible. Many a good idea has died, not because someone failed to suggest it, but because some specialist rejected it partly for emotional reasons.

An even more difficult problem with suggestion programs is the employee's reluctance to suggest any improvement which will make production more efficient and thus deprive fellow workers of employment. He also hesitates to make any proposals which cause other employees to have to produce more (even though the work is made easier) because he knows they may retaliate by rejecting him socially or using other pressures. The result in many instances is that employees do not dare to make production suggestions. Instead, they emphasize personal needs, such as better locker space.

Suggestion programs are workable and have a place in participative management; however, their role is limited because of their narrow scope (i.e., only suggestions) and their emphasis on the written word. Face-to-face practices have broader usefulness in participative management.

MULTIPLE MANAGEMENT

Multiple management is a participative practice started in 1932 at McCormick & Co., Inc., primarily for junior executives. It has been used successfully around the world in hundreds of companies, both unionized and nonunionized. Its central core is a junior board of directors which is given the opportunity to study any company problem and to recommend courses of action. Company information is made freely available to them, and their meetings are unrestrained by the presence of any senior executives. Members set their own by-laws and rotate their membership. Only two "brakes" are put upon the board. First, all recommendations must be unanimous, which encourages the board to recommend only the better ideas on which all can agree, and which places responsibility for the recommendation on each member. Second, no recommendation becomes effective until the president or senior board approves it, which is a means of retaining ultimate top-management control. In practice, this second "brake" is seldom needed when the plan is working well. At McCormick & Co., to cite one example, only six out of 2,109 recommendations were rejected in the first five years of multiple management.

As the practice eventually developed at McCormick & Co., multiple management also used specialized junior boards, such as a factory board, sales board, and institutional sales board. The use of these specialized boards depends somewhat on the size of a firm and its own particular problems. Obviously, a small company of only 300 persons would have no need for the additional specialized boards.

Multiple management has proved itself as a participative practice for management, especially for the sometimes-overlooked middle managers. It is an excellent way to bring new blood into the top-management structure and to train men as they move up. It taps the reserve of creativity which middle managers seldom get to use, and it encourages them to take on responsibilities as rapidly as they are able. The result is a plan which helps meet their age-old desire to participate, and does so in a way that benefits managers, workers, stockholders, and customers alike. As with any plan, there have been occasional failures. Two prime reasons are lack of genuine support by top management and suppression of free committee discussion because senior executives attend meetings.

DEVELOPING EFFECTIVE PARTICIPATION

The five participative plans discussed—consultive supervision, democratic supervision, production committees, suggestion programs, and multiple management—are examples of the many ways in which management can develop participation among its employees. There is now considerable evidence that participation can increase productivity and morale, along with other beneficial side effects. It offers an unlimited potential for improvement in business, but this potential is tempered by the fact that it cannot be suddenly (and rashly) "installed." As part of the culture of the plant, it is a change which must come about slowly; and since it is a human relations change, great skill is needed to apply it. Management should therefore proceed with caution, building each improvement upon a past success—but by all means, management should proceed!

QUESTIONS

1. How does Davis define participation? What are some of the implications of this definition?
2. Why does participation work better in some situations than in others?
3. What is the difference between democratic supervision and consultative supervision?
4. Do you think that participation weakens a manager's authority?
5. Why does the application of participative techniques require a great deal of skill?

DEVELOPING PARTICIPATION:
SOME FUNDAMENTAL FORCES *

Eugene Emerson Jennings

Human relations training in business and industry is becoming increasingly popular and necessary. It is usually offered in a group situation, and ever since Lewin reported the superiority of the discussion method in contrast to the lecture method, great emphasis has been given to trainee participation.

In Lewin's study the objective was to change housewives' entrenched food habits. In some groups the nutritionists used the lecture method and gave an informative account of the possibilities and the ways of preparing the recommended food. In other groups the nutritionists allowed discussion among the housewives while the same information was presented. A follow-up showed that only three per cent of the housewives in the lecture groups served one of the recommended foods in contrast to 32 per cent in the discussion groups. Greater involvement was the deciding factor.

Lewin's studies were conducted during the last war and since then training programs have made participation as important as content. The training director knows the value of the interplay of thoughts and words of the trainees on learning and behavior change as they discuss a provocative problem and decide upon a solution. Involvement through participation helps to overcome many obstacles that otherwise might preclude training. A group of trainees have been known to agree upon a course of action in spite of the fact that their backgrounds, predispositions, and attitudes would normally prevent agreement. Why and how does consensus of opinion occur among a group of trainees who are uniquely different from each other?

Judging by the emphasis many training directors place upon participation, one would think that that is the sole answer. However, there are different kinds and amounts of participation. The unbridled kind is probably less effective than organized and guided participation. The self-oriented kind probably is less satisfying than the problem-oriented. Furthermore, there is no guarantee that participation will stimulate learning.

* From the *Personnel Journal*, Vol. 35, No. 5 (October, 1956), pp. 166-170. Reprinted with permission.

AMIABILITY NOT ENOUGH

Because of these questions, the current tendency is to go deeper than mere participation and create a climate or atmosphere which leads the trainees to desire to participate. Stress is placed upon a climate wherein personal relationships are pleasant, the air is permeated with tolerance, effort and achievement are recognized, and there is the greatest freedom of expression.

However, these elements, although worthy, are not in themselves basic to a participant-group climate. Creating the right climate calls for a great deal more than good intentions and a general amiability among the trainees. Whenever a group comes together to work on a common undertaking, powerful tendencies, which I shall call theories, are brought into operation and play a decisive role in determining the value of the participation. These "theories" vary in complexity from the simple observation that group behavior and isolated behavior are substantially different, to the profound observation that a psychological unity exists among trainees in perception of and responses to various subject matter.

Creating a climate conductive to participation requires recognizing and organizing the basic tendencies that arise in a group and which, when repressed or allowed unorganized expression, serve to limit both participation and learning. Theories regarding some principles relative to the degree of participation are discussed in this article of the series and will be followed in the next by a discussion of the principles relative to direction of participation.

RELEVANCY OF THE PROBLEM

To begin with, the most elementary theory relates to the relevancy of the training problem. If the human relations problem bears upon the trainees' dominant needs and goals, participation is likely to be greater than if less relevant needs and goals are involved.

This theory is supported by Schacter, who introduced a problem which was relevant to some groups and largely irrelevant to other groups. The differences in participation between the two sets of groups were very striking. In the groups discussing a relevant problem the trainees made larger individual contributions to the discussion and there were fewer prolonged pauses in the discussion. The conclusion was apparent that when the problem touched upon the needs and goals of the group the tendency to participate was stronger.

TRAINEES SHOULD FEEL NEED

Studies also suggest that unless the trainees have a felt need for training they will not be sensitive to a climate conducive to participation. In my opinion, this theory is commonly disregarded. Many training programs are conducted as if the supervisor, foreman, or other trainee has an aroused need for human relations training when he takes a seat in the training room. This is not true. Some time should be devoted to showing the trainees the importance of the subject. At present this is usually done for introduction purposes and is not sufficient to motivate.

Furthermore, it is not uncommon for training programs to be conducted as if the trainees were predisposed to drawing a relationship between the training material and their problems on the job. Bridging this gap is very important in creating relevancy and should be done by the trainees while in the training program. Only a brief association with supervisors and foremen would reveal that many are not sensitive to a need for human relations training. When put through a human relations program they may make a distinction between what is said in the training room and what is practical in the job situation. Many supervisors never see a relationship between the two, or see value in discussing situations with each other.

Another factor that prevents showing the relevancy of the problem is that the trainees are often reluctant to state their needs and fears and anxieties, especially those that have an intimate bearing upon the problem. Unless they can bring themselves to state these relationships, the chances are that they will not be made nor understood. Participation will be limited to the degree that the trainees perceive the relevancy of the problem.

DIFFERENCES OF OPINION

Participation is likely to increase as differences of opinion are perceived to exist among the trainees. Note what happens when a wedge is driven into a group of people, dividing them into two sides where complete agreement existed before. Participation is not only bound to be more intense but also of a different type. It will be more persuasive than informative, more directed than unled.

In several of my classes I found that participation increased in proportion to the number of conflicting opinions. When only two people were perceived as antagonists, participation was considerably less than when I was able to get another student to interject a different viewpoint. Not only did more students participate who before did not express their views, but the two students who were the original antagonists became more aggressive and emphatic. Instead of the students perceiving only two possible viewpoints they went away thinking about several sides of the question. The participation was not only greater but more broadening.

COHESIVENESS ENCOURAGES PARTICIPATION

Participation is likely to increase as cohesiveness of the group increases. By "cohesiveness" I mean the attraction that the training group offers the individual trainee. Such things as friendship, status, and recognition are elements offering attraction. Thus, a cohesive group is one in which these elements are commonly felt by the trainees.

This aspect was studied by arranging subjects so that there were several highly cohesive groups and several low-cohesive groups. During the discussion the groups with high cohesiveness proceeded at a more intense rate and attempted to influence each other more. In addition, the group members made a greater effort to participate somehow.

Another study suggests that as members place an increasing value on participation, their satisfaction in participation increases. Thebaut, studying under-privileged groups, revealed that people with low status and recognition were prone to disassociate with the group when difficulties were encountered.

In a training situation the low-status members are the first to withdraw from participation when a block is encountered. This is usually true excepting for the individual who, because of low status, attempts to create the block by a form of participation. In any event it seems that, by increasing the attractiveness of membership in the group to each member, one can increase participation.

WHEN TRAINEES GROUPED THEMSELVES

I studied this possibility with a group of trainees who were allowed to move from group to group as they desired. The study revealed that communication increased as the group members became more friendly. Most of the trainees seemed to get more satisfaction from interacting with others whom they liked. It was easier to participate and this participation was greater than when the trainees were randomly grouped without regard to their likes and dislikes of each other. The tendency of friendship to increase ease of participation is supported by Festinger, Cartwright, and others, who found that where friendship did not exist participation was restrained.

These data suggest that one way to acquire greater participation is to allow the trainees to group themselves as much as possible. So many programs arrange the trainees into groups and then do not allow them opportunity to go to another group. As will be shown later, training groups are usually too large and should be divided into smaller groups. This subdividing not only facilitates discussion, but also encourages moving about by providing more groups from which to choose associates.

ENTHUSIASM BREEDS ENTHUSIASM

In passing, it might be mentioned that the more eager some of the trainees are to participate, the greater will be the group's participation. This principle merely means that a group that has enthusiasm and interest attracts other people who, without knowing the nature of the activity, nevertheless want to be a part of it. The more interest and enthusiasm is shown by some trainees, the more others, who might normally be disinterested, become interested. The relevancy of the problem is often brought out and emphasized because some group members have interest and enthusiasm.

Insofar as the problem actually has relevancy, interest and enthusiasm will compound on such relevancy. I cannot point to direct evidence of this tendency. However, in the Lewin studies previously mentioned, one reason why group participation was more successful than the lecture method was that the desire to participate—in any kind of group and about any kind of subject—was satisfied. This was not the case in the lecture groups. Discussion of the problem by some created interest in others, whose interest in turn stimulated discussion. It is a sort of chain reaction.

Certainly if the training director were to rely solely upon the interest and enthusiasm generated only by the nature of the problem, at times he would find little participation. The ability to capitalize on the interest shown by a few of the trainees at the outset, and to use this interest as a lever for building interest in others, is an effective way of spreading the urge to participate.

Another theory that has wide application to training is related to the size of training groups. Participation will tend to be greater and more uniformly distributed in small groups than in large groups. Simmel in a study of small groups recognized the importance that size has in stimulating participation.

SIZE OF GROUP AFFECTS PARTICIPATION

In study groups of Boy Scouts, Hare concluded that too little chance to participate not only reduces participation substantially but that members in groups of twelve also feel more rushed than members in groups of five. Leaders in small groups reported too much time in some cases, while leaders in large groups reported too little time. There were more chances to speak in the small groups than in the large. Hare suggests that the reason members in large groups tend to participate less is that, where there are many more members, their opinions count less; in small groups individual opinions count more.

Bales indicates that groups of four or five tend to have a more even distribution of participation between members, while in larger groups participation is more apt to be confined to a few. He suggests that the best size group for participation is probably five. When the group is larger than seven, the trainees with low participation tend to either stop talking or they center their remarks on a few. In the smaller group each member tends to say at least something to each other member.

My research with both small groups, the size of three and five, and large groups, as many as twelve and twenty, indicates that the same number of outstanding participators will be found in both large and small groups. That is, in a group of twelve usually three or four will evolve as the outstanding participants, whereas in a group of six or seven the same number will stand out. This, of course, varies considerably with the group and subject material. In small groups the tendency to focus on a few is just as great as in the large groups. But of course the percentage of participants is greater in small groups.

These studies have tremendous application to human relations training. The *poorest way* to motivate the low participators, and the *best way* to give the more vocal trainees influence, is to put them in a large group. Many training groups number around fifteen to twenty people and this seems much too large if the aim is to elicit participation as an aid to learning. Care should be taken to provide equal opportunity to participate if the success of the training program depends on the trainees' participation.

DISSATISFACTION RELATED TO PARTICIPATION

The lack of sufficient opportunity to participate will result in dissatisfaction with the training. Preston and Heintz found that, where both leaders and non-leaders participated more nearly equally, the members reported the discussion to be more interesting and satisfying. Where the leaders merely presented the problem and withdrew from active participation, the leaders and non-leaders were less satisfied with the results. Hare found that after group discussion the trainees who were the most dissatisfied were those who felt little opportunity to speak. He also found that, because less opportunity exists in large groups of about twelve or more, more dissatisfied members will exist in them than in small groups of five or seven.

This theory does not suggest that the objective of the training director should be to obtain equal participation from the trainees. On this subject Bales states that participation does not necessarily mean that the trainees should talk an equal amount. "As a matter of fact," he says, "even approximate equality of actual talking time among members is very rare; and when it does appear, it is usually associated with a free-for-all conflict." Shaw studies the question of whether groups could obtain a larger proportion of correct solutions to certain problems than individuals could. She concluded that groups could; and also noted that members in groups with both correct and incorrect solutions did not participate equally.

Participation Need Not Be Equal

The important factor to note concerning group training is this: that, more important than whether or not one has equal participation, is whether or not every member feels equal opportunity to participate. Participation is necessary before many members will affirm the group's solution; it is necessary because it makes them feel that the group's decision is their own, and their participation is satisfying. For some members there is no substitute for some actual verbal participation, no matter how slight.

Whereas too little participation results in too few ideas and suggestions, too much participation creates a feeling of competition. Deutsch studies the effects of a competitive versus a cooperative climate on group productivity. His results show that generally when competition is present among members of a group, whether because of participation or the presence of mutually exclusive goals, greater personal insecurity and expectation of hostility from others is present. That is, competition resulting from too much participation will tend to make more members feel tense and insecure. Furthermore, competitive participation often marks self-centered activity rather than group-centered activity. As mentioned previously, self-centered behavior is usually less satisfying and should be avoided as much as possible. These possibilities should be borne in mind by the training director, since training can be affected by too much participation as well as too little.

QUESTIONS

1. What is the relationship between participation and training activities?
2. Based upon your own experience, do you think that learning is enhanced by participation? In what ways?
3. When is participation likely to be greater in the training situation?
4. How does group size affect participation?
5. When participation is thwarted, what are the usual results?

GENERAL QUESTIONS ON PART 6

1. After reading the preceding articles, summarize and digest what you think the chief benefits of participative management to be.
2. What is the union's role when it comes to employee participation?
3. In what ways does organizational authority enter into the problem of participation?
4. What are the principal factors that complicate the development of participative management?
5. Compare Argyris' article with Tannenbaum and Massarik's. In what ways do they differ?
6. How do executive attitudes influence the degree of participation?
7. What type of organizational structure is most conducive to effective participation?
8. Do you think informal groups affect participation in any way? How?
9. Are there any limits to the degree of participation practiced in a firm? If so, what are they?
10. How does participation enter into the over-all area of human relations?

BIBLIOGRAPHY FOR PART 6

Articles

JENNINGS, E. E. "Forces That Lead to Group Agreement and Decision," *Personnel Journal*, Vol. 35, No. 7 (December, 1956), pp. 250-253.

KAHN, R. L., and A. S. TANNENBAUM. "Union Leadership and Member Participation," *Personnel Psychology*, Vol. 10, No. 3 (Autumn, 1957), pp. 277-292.

LAWRENCE, L. C., and P. C. SMITH. "Group Decision and Employee Participation," *Journal of Applied Psychology*, October, 1955, pp. 334-337.

PRESTON, M. G., and R. K. HEINTZ. "Effects of Participatory vs. Supervisory Leadership on Group Judgment," *Journal of Abnormal and Social Psychology*, Vol. 44, 1949, pp. 345-355.

PURCELL, T. V. "Dual Allegiance to Company and Union," *Personnel Psychology*, Spring, 1954, pp. 48-58.

ROFF, H. E. "Subvision: The Art of Managing From Below," *The Management Review*, Vol. 45, No. 6, pp. 435-437.

STAFF. "Group Decision-Making: Pro and Con," *Dun's Review and Modern Industry*, Vol. 73, No. 5 (May, 1959), pp. 96-98.

STAFF. "Better Operating Results from Participative Management," *Management Methods*, October, 1955, p. 66 ff.

Books

DAVIS, K. *Human Relations in Business.* New York: McGraw-Hill Book Company, Inc., 1957.

METCALF, H. C. and L. URWICK. *Dynamic Administration.* New York: Harper and Brothers, Publishers, 1940.

PLANTY, E. G. and T. FREESTON. *Developing Management Ability.* New York: Ronald Press Company, 1954.

HAIRE, M. *Psychology In Management.* New York: McGraw-Hill Book Company, Inc., 1956.

PFIFFNER, J. M. *The Supervision of Personnel.* Englewood Cliffs, N. J.: Prentice-Hall, Inc., 1951.

PART 7. RESISTANCE TO CHANGE

In order to remain stable and flexible and to insure long-run success, most organizations must operate within a dynamic environment. This means, in essence, that management must be alert to, must plan for, and must adapt itself, the company, and employees to myriad changes that are necessary for the efficient operation of a business enterprise. If this is not done—that is, if dynamism, flexibility, and adaptability do not exist—then there is great danger that complacency and stagnation will set in. The result, particularly in highly competitive industries, could well be serious damage to or even death of the organization concerned.

Why People Resist Change

Because change of every conceivable type and form is highly important to the success of an organization, it is unfortunate that many people have the tendency overtly or covertly to resist it, frequently to the extent of seriously impeding or completely thwarting its effectuation. Perhaps a basic reason why this resistance occurs, whether it is manifested in the form of apathy and indifference or in the form of opposition and rebellion, is because most changes disturb the equilibrium of the situation and environment in which individuals and groups exist. To overcome this disequilibrium and to return to a state of balance requires people to go through a period of adaptation and adjustment to the change. If this inevitable process of adjustment is facilitated, especially prior to initiation of the change, so that a new state of equilibrium can be quickly achieved, then little or no resistance usually results. On the other hand, if management ignores this fundamental facet of human behavior and does nothing to help people adjust, then resistance will occur and a state of disequilibrium will continue to exist. How serious this situation will be is, of course, impossible to say, because it will depend upon the nature of the people and the change concerned.

Although disequilibrium is the result of change and the cause of resistance, it is important to recognize that the state of disequilibrium which exists is actually an imbalance in need satisfaction. The assumption here is that prior to a change the individual exists within an environment in which the satisfaction of his needs has reached a high degree of stability. When a change occurs, particularly in the absence of adjustment facilitation, there is immediately manifested a threat to motive satisfaction. In other words, there now occurs the possibility that the change may prevent or decrease need satisfaction. Whether or not the change actually has this result makes no difference at this stage. The important point is that, until proven otherwise, the person believes or assumes that this threat will materialize. As a consequence, he feels his needs are no longer satisfied to the degree that they were satisfied and a state of imbalance exists. Only when he recognizes that the change will not affect his need satisfaction, or when he adapts himself to a change that in fact does decrease or prevent the satisfaction of a need, will equilibrium return and resistance disappear. In either case, however, some degree of adjustment must occur.

Types of Changes That Create Disequilibrium

The types and kinds of changes that cause disequilibrium and resistance are legion in number. They range in nature from attitudinal changes, such as a supervisor changing a positive attitude toward a subordinate into a negative attitude, to fantastic technological advancements, such as a new machine that will displace twenty old machines. Because it would be impossible to consider here every conceivable form of change, we shall devote our attention only to those types of changes that are likely to occur in most organizations. No attempt will be made to rank them in order of importance, because changes affect people in different ways; consequently, a change that causes great resistance in one person may create little or no disequilibrium for another individual.

Changes in tools, machines, and equipment

Almost every organization has experienced difficulty with employees who resist the installation of new tools, machines, and equipment. Whether such changes are the result of technological advancement or managerial efficiency makes little difference—a threat to security, status, and other basic needs has occurred. Consequently, even if the change is potentially beneficial to the employee, resistance usually results.

Like all changes, those concerning the mechanisms and devices with which people work establish an element of the unknown. In the case of a new machine, for example, especially one that has the potential to displace workers, people resist its introduction because they do not know how it will affect them. Accordingly, they begin to wonder about things such as whether or not the machine will displace them, if they will have the skill required to operate it, and so on. Until these unknowns are resolved, people will assume without realizing it that their fears and suspicious will be confirmed. This is particularly true of any change in machines that actually poses a threat to job security. In fact, it could be said that resistance to automation is one of the chief areas of resistance that management is faced with today, primarily because the results of technological advancement have actually resulted in the displacement of people and the loss of jobs.

Changes in methods and procedures

It is frequently said that we are creatures of habit. Although this statement connotes a detrimental characteristic of man, it should be recognized that habit, especially in the context of a business organization, does possess several distinct advantages. Perhaps one of the most important of these concerns the fact that the way we habitually do things, assuming that these habits are correct and efficient, can lead to the development of greater proficiency in doing work. In other words, by doing the same thing over and over, we can acquire a high degree of skill in performing various aspects of our jobs.

When a change occurs in a method or a procedure that we have been habitually accustomed to using, we have the tendency to resist it because it may decrease our proficiency and hence the pride we take in our work. In addition, we sometimes feel that the change was directed at us, that is, that we were not performing the job correctly and that we have lost face because we did not perceive and effectuate the change in the first place. Although such reactions sometimes border the ridiculous, they are nevertheless very real to those who experience them and hence are powerful motivators of behavior. How many times, for example, have we heard someone say "it won't work" when we know very well that the individual concerned definitely does know it will work? Changes in methods and procedures, therefore, like all other changes, establish many unknowns that must be clarified if adjustment is to take place.

Changes in personnel

A change that frequently results in a great deal of covert resistance in many organizations occurs when a subordinate is placed under the supervision of a new superior. Usually the degree of resistance developed in such a situation is correlated with the length and the satisfaction of the previous superior-subordinate relationship. In other words, the longer and more satisfied we were with our "old boss," the more we visualize and fear the unknowns created by the appearance of a new boss, especially if he is a total stranger. Until proven otherwise, we suspect and fear the worst about his ability to perform his job and to perceive our proficiency. Most important of all, we wonder what sweeping changes he will make (as many new bosses do) and what effect they will have on us. Without being able to express what has happened to us, we have lost in one moment much of the feeling of stability we had in need satisfaction. Until we bring back into balance our desire for belonging, recognition, status, and other motivating forces, we shall continue to view the new man with suspicion. Unfortunately, the attitudes that result from these fears become the very barriers that hinder the new superior in proving his worth to his employees and in providing the means or opportunity to satiate their basic needs.

Changes in formal organization structure

The creation of a formal structure, as the section on organization pointed out, establishes lines of authority and responsibility in an organization. Along with these lines there are also created channels of communication and interpersonal relationships. When changes in this formal structure occur, unknowns about future lines and relationships develop. We wonder, for example, who will be responsible for what and why, who our new boss will be, what opportunities it will take away from us or create for us, and so on. The result of these worries is that we no longer maintain equilibrium in our need satisfaction. Consequently, faced with the possibility of loss of status, prestige, belonging, recognition, and so forth, we become involved in a state of imbalance and resist the change.

Another aspect of formal structure concerns the question of who has the authority to make a change. Quite frequently employees resist changes, not because of the change *per se*, but because of the person who initiated or requested it. An example of this would be the foreman of Department B telling a worker in Department C to use a new procedure in the performance of his work. Although the new procedure may be very efficient and acceptable to the employee, he resists it because the foreman has no authority over him. The same type of reaction also occurs when changes are made by people who have the authority to make changes but whose authority is not known or accepted by the worker. This frequently happens when staff people have been delegated the authority to initiate changes. An illustration would be the industrial engineer who has been given the task of developing and installing better job methods. Because the employee tends to view his own boss as the only person who has a right to tell him what to do, he also tends to resist and reject any change proposed by the engineer.

Changes in informal organization

The informal relationships established between people in an organization become a very important part of our existence, basically because many of our primary motivational forces find their satisfaction in these relationships. Our urge to belong, for example, finds satisfaction in the many informal groups and cliques with which we associate. Our desire for recognition is satisfied by the accord given to our skills, talent, and abilities by various friends and acquaintances in the organization. Likewise, our needs for prestige, status, achievement, and many other basic sociological and psychological motives depend to a great degree on various aspects of informal organization for their satisfaction. Consequently, when management makes any change that disturbs the informal relationships established between people, there is bound to be created a state of imbalance and, hence, resistance to the change.

Of all the classes of changes that can disturb informal relationships, perhaps one of the most important for management to recognize and understand is that type of change which results in the separation of groups and individuals. Whenever people find it difficult or impossible to continue or maintain informal relationships, they find it equally difficult or impossible to maintain stability in need satisfaction. The reason for this, of course, is because the means to need satisfaction, namely, the people with whom we associate informally, no longer is present or easily accessible after the change. The result is that stability in motive satisfaction disappears and resistance sets in. It is no wonder, therefore, that people resist changes such as transferring an employee from one department to another or the simple moving of a clerk from one end of an office to the other end.

How People Resist Change

Resistance to change can take many forms. At one extreme, people suffer a temporary disequilibrium in need satisfaction, ask a few questions about the change, quickly adjust to it, and resume their previous behavior. At the other extreme, reaction can take the form of open opposition, rebellion, and even destruction. In between these extremes lie many other forms of behavior, such as apathy, indifference, and antagonism. What type of reaction occurs in a particular situation is a function of the nature of the change and the people concerned. It is especially a function of how well adjustment to the change was facilitated.

Whatever general form resistance to change may take, it is important for managers to recognize that human behavior will always be influenced by it. This means that immediately or ultimately the change will exert an impact on employee performance. Depending upon the nature of the resistance, therefore, behavior can be reflected in such things as quantity and quality of production, absenteeism, tardiness, turnover, grievances, accidents, strikes, and so on. Unfortunately, many of these concrete results of resistance are very difficult to relate to the change that caused them, not only because of physical and organizational elements, but also because they are frequently so subtly manifested by employees that it is difficult to observe and measure them in the first place. This is just another reason why management must make every effort possible to effectuate the change properly and to facilitate adjustment to it.

Facilitating Adjustment to Change

Although the following articles consider in detail methods of overcoming resistance to change, several important points deserve mention here. One of the most important of these concerns the fact that preventing and overcoming resistance demands that managers respect and understand employee reaction to change. Altogether too frequently, people in leadership positions assume that, because a change will definitely be beneficial to people, it will be acceptable to them. Actually, nothing could be farther from the truth. Consequently, whether threats to need satisfaction are real or imagined, they must always be recognized as powerful motivators of behavior. As such, some manner or form of adjustment facilitation must take place.

Another important point for managers to understand is that there is no one simple panacea for preventing or overcoming resistance to change. Although it may be possible in one situation to rely exclusively on one particular method, such as participation, for example, it is most unlikely that such a technique will be universally and solely applicable in all resistance problems. What is more likely is that the manager (the leader) must utilize many different methods, techniques, and procedures to prevent and to remedy resistance to change situations. This means that, in addition to participation, he may certainly have to counsel and train employees, particularly if a change actually results in the prevention or decrease of need satisfaction. It may also mean that if the situation warrants it, he will have to dispense with the change or completely adjust his thinking about it. Most fundamentally of all, however, it means that he must determine and communicate to his employees the things they consciously and subconsciously want and need to know to resolve the unknowns that pose the real or imagined threat to the satisfaction of their motivating forces. In other words, preventing and remedying resistance to change demands efficient leadership and the practice of human relations.

Although the literature on resistance to change is not as complete as one would like it to be, there are, nevertheless, several outstanding articles on this subject. McMurry's article, for example, contains a useful appraisal of resistance to change as a handicap to industrial progress. Zander, in his article, discusses the nature of resistance, the conditions that are associated with its development, and ways of preventing or decreasing it. Lawrence's article contains an interesting analysis of resistance from a social viewpoint and a critique of participation as a solution to it. Dorwin Cartwright offers an excellent statement of some principles of achieving change in people. J. M. Juran discusses experiences that indicate that cultural patterns are a vital factor in resistance to technical change, and he shows how these experiences have direct application to problems of change involving line and staff relationships. Floyd C. Mann analyzes some of the problems of conducting research on change and shows how we can create and study it.

THE PROBLEM OF RESISTANCE TO CHANGE IN INDUSTRY *

Robert N. McMurry

A medium-sized Middle Western manufacturing company recently installed a new and greatly improved wage incentive plan at a cost in excess of $20,000. The work was done entirely by outside engineers. These engineers did an excellent job technically and management was satisfied; the only difficulty was that three weeks later the new plan had been completely abandoned and the investment of $20,000 had been totally lost. Why was this?

Industrial progress finds one of its greatest handicaps in the frequent resistance of both management and workers to change of any sort. This is especially marked if the change is introduced without proper advance notice and explanation to those whom it will affect. Even innovations which are obviously advantageous are often objects of attack. Where the changes threaten either the status or job security of either workers or management, their reaction is certain to be quick and violently negative. In those organizations where employee and supervisory insecurity is present, even minor revisions of policies or procedures may evoke profoundly disturbing reactions among individuals and groups. An effort is made at once either to block the introduction of the new methods or to discredit them after their installation and force their removal.

Even ordinarily honest and loyal workers and executives will sometimes lie, misrepresent, and engage in outright sabotage of the new procedures, so bitter are the antagonisms aroused. Nor are these manifestations limited to individuals. Large groups of employees may react with equal violence when their security or status is at stake. An example of this is the frequent reaction of white employees to the introduction of Negroes into the work force. The latter are a threat both to their security (the Negroes are considered as competitors in the labor market) and to their status (the whites resent being grouped with the Negroes whom they regard as of lower status). Actually the Negroes may be highly desirable as employees and may contribute to the welfare of the organization as a whole. Nevertheless, their introduction is violently resisted. While it is customary to attribute these resistances to the reluctance of

* From the *Journal of Applied Psychology*, Vol. 31, No. 6 (December, 1947), pp. 589-593. Reprinted with permission.

people to change well-established habits, it is probable that the chief causes lie far deeper.

The principal root of this hostility to anything which threatens security or status is *fear* (frequently reinforced and rationalized by accumulated resentments and rivalries). The hostility which this fear generates, in turn, leads to attacks upon the sources of the anxiety. The amazing feature of these attacks is that many of them come from employees who, because of their rank or long service, have no real ground to fear for either their status or security. Nevertheless, quite without adequate justification, many feel extremely insecure. This is because deep-seated fears exist within the individual himself. Everyone knows fear. Even the infant is prey to this emotion because it is innate, inborn. Furthermore, everyone is constantly faced by very real and tangible grounds for anxiety and insecurity. Nature is cruel. The law of the fang prevails to a greater extent than many recognize. The world at large is no place for the weakling. Even business is highly competitive. Rivalries and conflicts exist within nearly every business. Realistically regarded, life is far from a bed of roses for most people.

Hence, the real and justifiable fears which beset the average person are legion. There is always somewhere in the future the danger of economic disaster, of another depression with its threat to savings, to the home, to security. Everyone is faced with the problem of old age and its attendant likelihood of illness, suffering, and dependence. Even in youth and the prime of life, there is always the immediate possibility of illness, of accidents, and the inevitability of death. Nor are these real grounds for fear confined to the individual himself. There is also the fear of misfortune to loved ones; a fear, again, which the war years have greatly stimulated. Finally, there is almost always the more or less immediate danger to everyone of loss of his job or of being displaced or demoted, with its attendant loss of prestige, "status," and earnings.

It must be kept in mind that the average rank-and-file employee in industry today, unlike his counterpart of fifty years ago, does not even own his own tools. The only commodity he has to sell is his labor or some readily replaceable skill. He is, therefore, much more dependent economically upon his job tenure than was the case with the man who could, if necessary, set up in business for himself. In addition, the longer he has remained with a particular company, often the greater his difficulty in getting work elsewhere. This is because the bulk of the routine jobs in industry today do not require great skill; certainly not in the sense of the old-time master craftsman. Consequently, the employee who has spent ten to twenty-five years in a particular line of work has gained little that is saleable, but has lost his youth, his vigor, and his adaptability to new lines of endeavor. He has given the best years of his life and often has little of vocational value to show for it.

It is because of this that there is such a feeling of need for some sort of job security among most working people (whether it be seniority or some other form of property rights in the job). For the same reason, anything which threatens job security or hard-won status, such as it is, is desperately feared and resented.

Unfortunately, these real and understandable grounds for fear are not the only ones which contribute to employee insecurity. Nearly all persons also suffer to a greater or less degree from neurotic anxieties and fears which have no basis in reality whatever. Among these latter are the insecurities which grow out of the passive dependent tendencies of the emotionally immature. Others grow out of the repeated rejections to which the individual may have been subjected during childhood or youth. Still others have their origin in an over-strict conscience, resulting from too rigorous an upbringing. (Nearly everything such persons do makes them feel guilty.) Likewise, many neurotic anxieties have their basis in buried but powerful hostilities toward loved ones and others which produce a free-floating sense of guilt and anxiety and lead to constant worrying.

Many of these fears, regardless of their nature, are too painful to be faced; they cannot be lived with. Hence, they have been thrust out of the center of the individual's consciousness; they are vaguely present on the periphery. They are not entirely repressed; merely out of sharp focus. Nevertheless, they continue to exist in a latent state, their power to disturb quite undiminished. Their presence constantly disturbs the individual's emotional equilibrium and makes its balance a precarious one. When any new challenge to his status or security occurs, it accentuates his existing anxieties and feelings of insecurity. These added fears almost inevitably upset his emotional balance. His latent fears, having been reinforced, once more threaten to become painfully conscious. This must be avoided at any cost. Hence, he has powerful incentive to rid himself of the source of danger to his status and security.

Fears which even trivial changes arouse are often so powerful that they are overwhelming. The fear thus induced is so real and poignant that it may even induce a state of actual panic. At this point, the victim ceases to be entirely rational, in spite of the fact that he may appear outwardly calm and possessed. If it appears politically expedient, he may even indicate a high degree of favor for the very changes which have excited his anxiety. Nevertheless, he will stop at nothing to save himself. (This attitude of superficial acceptance of an innovation is sometimes barefaced hypocrisy; more often the individual's fears are so acute that he cannot take an open stand against anything.)

Because of the highly emotional character of these resistances to change, a direct, logical presentation of the merits of the change is often futile. The more they are discussed, the more violent the anxieties they are likely to arouse and the greater the individual's need to discredit and eliminate them. Even worse, however, is to attempt to explain to him the *sources in himself* of his antagonisms to the projected change. This only makes him react more violently because it mobilizes fresh anxieties within him and breaks down his defenses against them. It not only forces him to face his naked fears himself, but makes him aware that others know his weaknesses. This adds to his anxieties—and to his aggressiveness.

In view of the foregoing circumstances, great caution must be exercised in making any changes in organization or methods, even those which are obviously and badly needed. It will never be possible wholly to eliminate anxieties in workers and supervisors with consequent resistances to change for its own sake and as a threat to their status or security. Hence, it is essential that any modification of product, procedures, organization, or policies which may affect status or may be interpreted as an implied threat to job security should be considered carefully before it is made. It is particularly important that its implications be considered from the standpoint of the insecurities and possible anxieties of the employees affected. It must always be kept in mind that, regardless of the facts, those who will be affected may interpret it somehow as a threat to them and respond accordingly.

Sometimes it is better, in the long run, not to make moderately needed changes because the disturbance they will occasion may be more costly in the end than will a continuance of the *status quo*. In those cases, where there is some real threat to an employee's status and security in the change, it will prove wiser and cheaper to "kick him upstairs" to some "advisory" job (thus retaining his status and job security), rather than risk the organization-wide disturbance of morale which his demotion or other "face" destroying course of action might bring with it. It is entirely possible for *one* individual, if sufficiently aroused, to disrupt the morale and smooth functioning of an entire segment of a business by pointing out that what has happened to him *could* happen to many others.

If it is finally decided that a change must be made, it is wise to move very slowly. Only one innovation should be introduced at a time; ample warning must precede it, and a full statement must be given of the reasons for it and the benefits which are expected to result from it. If this is done, there is less likelihood that the emotional equilibrium of the individual or group will be upset. Informing the employee in advance will do much to allay the fears that a sudden change might otherwise arouse. There will always be some anxiety, but this will help to minimize it.

Further to allay the fears of those affected, they should be given maximum opportunity to participate in the discussion and planning of proposed changes in advance of their introduction. They should also have some voice in deciding how and when they will be made effective. This gives them a feeling of having had at least some part in the determination of their own destinies. This tends to minimize their feelings of helplessness and consequent anxiety in the face of the changes. At the same time, it will give them a better insight into, and understanding of, the conditions calling for the innovations and the way in which they will be of personal benefit to those affected. This, in turn, will allay their anxieties and discourage the development of resistances and hostilities.

Finally, if a program calling for other than minor changes is to gain acceptance and use, it is imperative that ready outlets be provided for the expression and relief of the hostilities which will almost inevitably arise. Under the best of conditions, some of those affected will be disturbed and unhappy. Therefore, it will be necessary to provide these employees with easily accessible facilities to "talk out" their anxieties and resentments from time to time. They will not be aware that it is largely *fear* which stimulates their aggressions and needs for reassurance; all they will know is that having talked about them, they will feel better. Periodic, informal meetings between small groups of the affected employees and a representative of top management are to be recommended for this purpose. He must be patient and sympathetic and give the employees' complaints about the changes, no matter how absurd or unreasonable, a fair hearing. This thus provides a release for their accumulated tensions. Such meetings, by bringing resistances out into the open, have the advantages both of relieving the rancor of the disgruntled worker or supervisor before he has had a chance seriously to disrupt departmental morale, and of reviewing the worthwhileness of the new procedures and methods. Sometimes it will be indicated that even further changes are necessary.

The resistance of workers, supervisors, and executives to change is irritating and often frustrating. This is especially true when the improvements are designed specifically to help them and the company as a whole. However, if it is recognized that it is their basic anxieties and insecurities which underlie and stimulate their lack of cooperation, not sheer stubbornness, selfishness, and stupidity, a more understanding and sympathetic view can be taken of the problem. These resistances will probably never be totally overcome, but through the awareness of the basic fears and the application of the principles outlined above, an informed and constructive course of action can be undertaken to insure the acceptance and continued use of the new procedures and policies, even though they may incorporate a number of radical innovations.

QUESTIONS

1. Explain why people resist change.
2. Why is it difficult to overcome resistance to change?
3. What cautions must be exercised in making changes?
4. Why is it sometimes better not to make a change? Do you agree?
5. What does McMurry recommend to make changes effectively?

RESISTANCE TO CHANGE— ITS ANALYSIS AND PREVENTION *

Alvin Zander

In order to derive the benefit from research in industrial relations, someone must plan a program of action to apply them. When one begins implementing, he must change the social system in some way. The creation of this change can cause the development of resistance in those influenced by the change.

First, we shall look at what resistance is; second, the conditions that appear to be associated with its development; and third, some means whereby resistance may be prevented or decreased.

Nature of resistance

Let us look at some examples of resistance growing out of administrative changes.

A large number of foremen in a company were given training in how to treat their men like human beings. They liked the course and were eager to apply their learnings on the job. The company found, however, that relatively few of the foremen are really behaving any different on the job. They know their stuff but do not use it.

In one of the paper-shuffling government agencies a new data form was developed which all admitted was briefer, more logical, and easier to use. Yet, this department found that the employees often omitted much of the data needed on this form, their speed of work decreased, and they objected to it on many insignificant grounds.

Our favorite example of resistance was furnished by a farmer in the TVA area. He assured us that he knew all about contour plowing, the rotation of crops, and the use of what he called "phosaphate" for improving the soil. He allowed as how these were good ideas, "But," he said, "I don't do it that way."

These examples have one common denominator which might serve here as a definition of resistance. They describe behavior which is intended to protect an individual from the effects of real or imagined change. This reaction might be to either real or imagined change since the resister might be reacting to things that were really not changed but he thinks were, or fears that they might be. If a person

* From *Advanced Management*, Vol. 15, No. 1 (January, 1950), pp. 9-11. Reprinted with permission.

believes a change has been made, or fears potential change, it makes no difference whether or not it is true in fact. He will act as though there has been a change.

How can one recognize when resistance is working? Unfortunately, there is no list of typical behavior which can be described as the symptoms of resistance, which, if present, indicate that one is dealing with this phenomenon. It is the protective function which the behavior is providing which determines whether or not a person is resisting, rather than the kind of thing he does. By the same token, all behavior which opposes change is not necessarily resistance. Some opposition to change may be perfectly logical and grounded on well-supported reasons. The behavior must be attempting to protect the person against the consequences of the change in order for it to be resistance. This may be clearer if we look at the origin of the concept.

The hostility pattern

The term and the concept we are using here has been borrowed from psychotherapy. When a therapist is attempting to change the behavior of the patient, he expects resistance from him. The therapist takes the position that the pattern of behavior used by the patient (which makes him a "sick" person) is a means to some satisfaction for him even though it also may make him ineffective or unhappy. Resistance occurs in the patient when the process of change (therapy here) comes close to being successful. When faced with the unpleasant necessity of giving up the behavior he does not like, but somehow needs, he begins to balk. He becomes silent, blushes, changes the subject, tells fibs, comes late to appointments, becomes angry with the therapist, or any of a number of similar things. The therapist watches for the context in which these signs of resistance occur since these indicate the crucial problems in the way the patient sees and deals with his world.

For the administrator, resistance may occur under fairly similar conditions. When he attempts to create a change the administrator may develop, unintentionally, many threats to the person or groups with whom he works. The behavior used by the resister may take many forms.

It may take the form of hostility either openly expressed or obliquely implied. The aggression may be directed against the change itself or against the administrator. What is done depends on how the person can safely resist without further endangering himself in that situation. Other symptoms of resistance may be sloppy effort after the change has been made, or fawning submissiveness which is a hybrid of applepolishing and apathy. It can occur by lowering the level of aspiration to an inefficient degree, discouragement, or the development of unhappy cliques and outspoken factions. It is important, however, to remind ourselves, that it is the function which such actions are performing for the person that makes them resistance rather than what they look like.

Where resistance starts

It will be helpful if we look at a few conditions conducive to resistance.

1. Resistance can be expected if the nature of the change is not made clear to the people who are going to be influenced by the change. In one of the largest government agencies, a change required one department which originally had the responsibility of processing papers involved in contacts with certain industries to share this task with another office. Announcement of the change was issued in a brief statement. The immediate reaction was violent objection, even though some of the workers privately admitted that it was a wise and necessary move. They were reacting to incomplete information. Many people fear incomplete information about changes which influence them. It is more comfortable to know exactly where one stands.

There is some evidence to support the hypothesis that those persons who dislike their jobs, will most dislike ambiguity in a proposed change. They want to know exactly what they must do in order to be sure to avoid the unpleasant aspects of their jobs. Some administrators may attach too much importance to the value of information itself. Apparently they reason that people "ought not" to resist the way they do because the administrator has told them everything he thinks is important for them to know about the impending change.

2. Different people will see different meanings in the proposed change. Some of the resistant reaction described above came about because some workers saw the change as an indication that they had been doing a poor job, others assumed it meant their office would soon be abolished, still others were troubled since they were losing some of the power they had formerly controlled. We tend to see in our world the things that we expect to see. Complete information can just as readily be distorted as incomplete information, especially so if the workers have found discomfort and threats in their past work situation.

3. Resistance can be expected when those influenced are caught in a jam between strong forces pushing them to make the change and strong forces deterring them against making the change.

4. Resistance may be expected to the degree that the persons influenced by the change have pressure put upon them to make it, and will be decreased to the degree that these same persons are able to have some "say" in the nature or direction of the change. In a garment factory a change was required. The switch meant that workers would be asked to change their jobs and, in many cases, to develop working relationships with new people. An experiment was made in which three different styles of introducing this change were tried out. One group of workers were simply informed about the change and were allowed to ask questions. They developed the most resistance as measured by turnover, absenteeism, and slowness in learning the job. Resistance was *less* in those groups who sent representatives to a meeting in which the nature of the change was discussed and all persons present made plans to carry out the change.

Resistance was *least* in the groups in which those to be affected discussed the nature of the change, laid plans for making it, and as a total group made decisions which were satisfactory to the entire group. In this latter group everyone participated. They had an opportunity to develop their own motivation instead of making the change only on the basis of orders from the boss. The fact that they were able to develop their own understanding of the need for the change and their own decisions about how to do it, reduced resistance most effectively.

5. Resistance may be expected if the change is made on personal grounds rather than impersonal requirements or sanctions. A supervisor posted the following notice:

> I have always felt that promptness is an important indicator of an employee's interest in his job. I will feel much better if you are at your desk at the proper time.

Employees responded to this notice by appointing a committee to get information which would justify their late arrival at the office. Many administrators can expect trouble in establishing a change if it is requested in terms of what "I think is necessary"; rather than making the request in the light of "our objectives," the rules, the present state of affairs, or some other impersonal requirement.

6. Resistance may be expected if the change ignores the already established institutions in the group. Every work situation develops certain customs in doing the work or in the relations among the

workers. The administrator who ignores institutionalized patterns of work and abruptly attempts to create a new state of affairs which demands that these customs be abolished without further consideration will surely run into resistance.

These are a few of the conditions in which resistance might be expected to occur. There probably are many others.

Decreasing resistance

Some procedures on the part of the administrator might be useful in preventing or decreasing the resistance which arises in a changed situation. Let us look at a major principle in preventing resistance and some of its basic implications:

Resistance will be prevented to the degree that the changer helps the changees to develop their own understanding of the need for the change, and an explicit awareness of how they feel about it, and what can be done about those feelings.

This principle implies that the administrator can use resistance as an important symptom. Specifically, he can use the nature of the resistance as an indicator of the cause of resistance. It will be most helpful to him as a symptom, if he diagnoses the causes for it when it occurs rather than inhibiting it at once. The same resistant behavior, for example, may indicate that one person feels that he has lost prestige by the change, to another it may mean that he has lost power over an area of influence which he formerly controlled, and to still another it may mean that he fears that his friends will think less well of him. An administrator must know what the resistance means in order that he may effectively lessen it by working on the causes instead of the symptom.

There has been a good deal of experience in recent years in staff meetings and in work conferences like the National Training Laboratory for Group Development with the use of a group observer. This observer gives to the group, and the leaders, information about the group and the nature of any resistance. In these cases, the data about itself is made common group property for all members to discuss and to use in planning better work relations.

This communication must go in both directions. If two-way communication is not maintained, negative attitudes created during resistance will tend to persist.

Restoring understanding

In a utility company a new office was formed with a new set of supervisors. The entire staff of supervisors called the workers together and scolded them for shortcomings in their performance. The tone used by the supervisors was so aggressive that the employees found it difficult thereafter to discuss anything with them except those topics directly related to the effectiveness of production. The workers kept themselves at a distance from the supervisors and the supervisors made no move to close the gap. The result was that distance between these two groups made it impossible for them to come to any new understanding of each other. This mounting hostility was lessened only when the personnel department advised a number of "gripe-sessions" with small groups of workers in which the two levels developed a new understanding of each other.

Another implication in the above principle is that there is value in blowing off steam. The psychologists call this a "catharsis." There is good evidence that new attitudes can be accepted by a person only if he has a chance to thoroughly air his original attitude. Resistance to accepting the rigid, and often apparently meaningless, rules of military life, showed itself in flagrant violation of the rules, often in a most aggressive manner. Punishment only increased the resistance. Relief was provided by group sessions in which men were able to thoroughly gripe. After this relief of tension, they were able to turn to a reasonable discussion about what they could do to learn to live in terms of these requirements. It is as though new air can be put in the tire only after the old air is released.

A third implication of the earlier expressed principle is that resistance may be less likely to occur if the group participates in making the decisions about how the change should be implemented, what the change should be like, how people might perform in the changed situation, or any other problems that are within their area of freedom to decide. The experiment in which three ways of introducing a change were tried out showed that the workers, who had a chance to make a group decision about the ways in which the change should be made, developed much less resistance than did those who were simply called together to be told about the change and have all of their questions answered. What is important here is that the workers feel that they have a chance to discuss the major factors involved in the change, a chance to understand the nature of the fears they have in facing this change, and a chance to plan what they will do to calm their fears.

Self-diagnosis gets action

Still another implication is that resistance will be less likely to develop if facts which point to the need for change are gathered by the persons who must make the change. A number of high level supervisors in a utility industry came to feel that the workers had many negative attitudes about their jobs which were due to poor supervisory practices. Each supervisor, quite naturally, felt that other supervisors were at fault. Top management set up a number of study groups in which the supervisors first learned how they could diagnose the causes of these negative attitudes. Each supervisor then returned to his own work place and gathered facts that would be necessary for him to analyse the causes of negative attitudes he could spot among his workers. Later the supervisors came together to report their findings. At this meeting their enthusiasm for change in their own practices was high because they had participated in gathering the facts which best described their problems. People will be more likely to act in terms of information they gather themselves than in terms of information gathered by others and delivered to them. If it is clear that a change is indicated in a given state of affairs, but the people who must abide by the change are resisting the shift, they can come to see it themselves by obtaining the facts which properly "case" the situation.

To summarize, we have said that resistance is a problem which any person who is responsible for social change must face. Even though it is strange and unexpected behavior, there are causes for the development of this phenomenon. These causes may be understood, and resistance may be prevented, if the administrator will help the changees develop their own understanding of the need for change and explicit awareness of how they feel about it, and what can be done about those feelings.

QUESTIONS

1. Describe resistance to change in terms of human behavior.
2. How can one recognize when resistance to change is working?
3. What conditions are conducive to resistance to change?
4. Discuss the ways resistance to change can be prevented or decreased.
5. What part does communication play in resistance to change?

HOW TO DEAL WITH
RESISTANCE TO CHANGE *

Paul R. Lawrence

One of the most baffling and recalcitrant of the problems which business executives face is employee resistance to change. Such resistance may take a number of forms—persistent reduction in output, increase in the number of "quits" and requests for transfer, chronic quarrels, sullen hostility, wildcat or slowdown strikes, and, of course, the expression of a lot of pseudo-logical reasons why the change will not work. Even the more petty forms of this resistance can be troublesome.

All too often when executives encounter resistance to change, they "explain" it by quoting the cliché that "people resist change" and never look further. Yet changes must continually occur in industry. This applies with particular force to the all-important "little" changes that constantly take place—changes in work methods, in routine office procedures, in the location of a machine or a desk, in personnel assignments and job titles. No one of these changes makes the headlines, but in total they account for much of our increase in productivity. They are not the spectacular once-in-a-lifetime technological revolutions that involve mass layoffs or the obsolescence of traditional skills, but they are vital to business progress.

Does it follow, therefore, that business management is forever saddled with the onerous job of "forcing" change down the throats of resistant people? My answer is *no*. It is the thesis of this article that people do *not* resist technical change as such and that most of the resistance which does occur is unnecessary. I shall discuss these points, among others:

> (1) A solution which has become increasingly popular for dealing with resistance to change is to get the people involved to "participate" in making the change. But as a practical matter "participation" as a device is not a good way for management to think about the problem. In fact, it may lead to trouble.
> (2) The key to the problem is to understand the true nature of resistance. Actually, what employees resist is usually not technical change but social change—the change in their human relationships that generally accompanies technical change.

* From the *Harvard Business Review*, Vol. 32, No. 3 (May-June, 1954), pp. 49-57. Reprinted with permission.

(3) Resistance is usually created because of certain blind spots and attitudes which staff specialists have as a result of their preoccupation with the technical aspects of new ideas.

(4) Management can take concrete steps to deal constructively with these staff attitudes. The steps include emphasizing new standards of performance for staff specialists and encouraging them to think in different ways, as well as making use of the fact that signs of resistance can serve as a practical warning signal in directing and timing technological changes.

(5) Top executives can also make their own efforts more effective at meetings of staff and operating groups where change is being discussed. They can do this by shifting their attention from the facts and so forth, to what the discussion of these items indicates about developing resistances and receptiveness to change.

Let us begin by taking a look at some recent research into the nature of resistance to change. There are two studies in particular that I should like to discuss. They highlight contrasting ways of interpreting resistance to change and of coping with it in day-to-day administration.

Is Participation Enough?

The first study was conducted by Lester Coch and John R. P. French, Jr., in a clothing factory.[1] It deserves special comment because, it seems to me, it is the most systematic study of the phenomenon of resistance to change that has been made in a factory setting. To describe it briefly:

The two researchers worked with four different groups of factory operators who were being paid on a modified piece-rate basis. For each of these four groups a minor change in the work procedure was installed by a different method, and the results were carefully recorded to see what, if any, problems of resistance occurred. The four experimental groups were roughly matched with respect to efficiency ratings and degree of cohesiveness; in each group the proposed change modified the established work procedure about the same degree.

The work change was introduced to the first group by what the researchers called a "no-participation" method. This small group of operators was called into a room where some staff people told the members that there was a need for a minor methods change in their work procedures. The staff people then explained the change to the operators in detail, and gave them the reasons for the change. The operators were then sent back to the job with instructions to work in accordance with the new method.

The second group of operators was introduced to the work change by a "participation-through-representation" method—a variation of the approach used with the third and fourth groups, which turned out to be of little significance.

[1] See Lester Coch and John R. P. French, Jr., "Overcoming Resistance to Change," *Human Relations*, Vol. I, No. 4 (1948), p. 512.

The third and fourth groups of operators were both introduced to the work change on a "total-participation" basis. All the operators in these groups met with the staff men concerned. The staff men dramatically demonstrated the need for cost reduction. A general agreement was reached that some savings could be effected. The groups then discussed how existing work methods could be improved and unnecessary operations eliminated. When the new work methods were agreed on, all the operators were trained in the new methods, and all were observed by the time-study men for purposes of establishing a new piece rate on the job.

Research findings

The researchers reported a marked contrast between the results achieved by the different methods of introducing this change.

No-Participation Group. The most striking difference was between Group #1, the no-participation group, and Groups #3 and #4, the total-participation groups. The output of Group #1 dropped immediately to about two-thirds of its previous output rate. The output rate stayed at about this level throughout the period of 30 days after the change was introduced. The researchers further reported:

> "Resistance developed almost immediately after the change occurred. Marked expressions of aggression against management occurred, such as conflicts with the methods engineer. . . . hostility toward the supervisor, deliberate restriction of production, and lack of cooperation with the supervisor. There were 17% quits in the first 40 days. Grievances were filed about piece rates; but when the rate was checked, it was found to be a little 'loose'."

Total-Participation Groups. In contrast with this record, Groups #3 and #4 showed a smaller initial drop in output and a very rapid recovery not only to the previous production rate but to a rate that exceeded the previous rate. In these groups there were no signs of hostility toward the staff people or toward the supervisors, and there were no quits during the experimental period.

Appraisal of results

Without going into all the researchers' decisions based on these experiments, it can be fairly stated that they concluded that resistance to methods changes could be overcome by *getting the people involved in the change to participate in making it.*

This was a very useful study, but the results are likely to leave the manager of a factory still bothered by the question, "Where do we go from here?" The trouble centers around that word "participation." It is not a new word. It is seen often in management journals, heard often in management discussions. In fact, the idea that it is a good thing to get employee participation in making changes has become almost axiomatic in management circles.

But participation is not something that can be conjured up or created artificially. You obviously cannot buy it as you would buy a typewriter. You cannot hire industrial engineers and accountants and other staff people who have the ability "to get participation" built into them. It is doubtful how helpful it would be to call in a group of supervisors and staff men and exhort them, "Get in there and start participation."

Participation is a feeling on the part of people, not just the mechanical act of being called in to take part in discussions. Common sense would suggest that people are more likely to respond to the way they are customarily treated—say, as people whose opinions are respected because they themselves are respected for their own worth—rather than by the stratagem of being called to a meeting or asked some carefully calculated questions. In fact, many supervisors and staff men have had some unhappy experiences with executives who have read about participation and have picked it up as a new psychological gimmick for getting other people to think they "want" to do as they are told—as a sure way to put the sugar coating on a bitter pill.

So there is still the problem of how to get this thing called participation. And, as a matter of fact, the question remains whether participation was the determining factor in the Coch and French experiment or whether there was something of deeper significance underlying it.

RESISTANCE TO WHAT?

Now let us take a look at a second series of research findings about resistance to change. Recently, while making some research observations in a factory manufacturing electronic products, a colleague and I had an opportunity to observe a number of incidents that for us threw new light on this matter of resistance to change.[2] One incident was particularly illuminating:

> We were observing the work of one of the industrial engineers and a production operator who had been assigned to work with the engineer on assembling and testing an experimental product that the engineer was developing. The engineer and the operator were in almost constant daily contact in their work. It was a common occurrence for the engineer

---

[2] For a complete report of the study, see Harriet O. Ronken and Paul R. Lawrence, *Administering Changes: A Case Study of Human Relations in a Factory* (Boston, Division of Research, Harvard Business School, 1952).

to suggest an idea for some modification in a part of the new product; he would then discuss his idea with the operator and ask her to try out the change to see how it worked. It was also a common occurrence for the operator to get an idea as she assembled parts and to pass this idea on to the engineer, who would then consider it and, on occasion, ask the operator to try out the idea and see if it proved useful.

A typical exchange between these two people might run somewhat as follows:

Engineer: "I got to thinking last night about that difficulty we've been having on assembling the x part in the last few days. It occurred to me that we might get around the trouble if we washed the part in a cleaning solution just prior to assembling it."

Operator: "Well, that sounds to me like it's worth trying."

Engineer: "I'll get you some of the right kind of cleaning solution, and why don't you try doing that with about 50 parts and keep track of what happens."

Operator: "Sure, I''ll keep track of it and let you know how it works."

With this episode in mind, let us take a look at a second episode involving the same production operator. One day we noticed another engineer approaching the production manager. We knew that this particular engineer had had no previous contact with the production operator. He had been asked to take a look at one specific problem on the new product because of his special technical qualifications. He had decided to make a change in one of the parts of the product to eliminate the problem, and he had prepared some of these parts using his new method. Here is what happened:

He walked up to the production operator with the new parts in his hand and indicated to her by a gesture that he wanted her to try assembling some units using his new part. The operator picked up one of the parts and proceeded to assemble it. We noticed that she did not handle the part with her usual care. After she had assembled the product, she tested it and it failed to pass inspection. She turned to the new engineer and, with a triumphant air, said, "It doesn't work."

The new engineer indicated that she should try another part. She did so, and again it did not work. She then proceeded to assemble units using all of the new parts that were available. She handled each of them in an unusually rough manner. None of them worked. Again she turned to the engineer and said that the new parts did not work.

The engineer left, and later the operator, with evident satisfaction, commented to the original industrial engineer that the new engineer's idea was just no good.

Social change

What can we learn from these episodes? To begin, it will be useful for our purposes to think of change as having both a technical and a social aspect. The *technical* aspect of the change is the making of a measurable modification in the physical routines of the job. The *social* aspect of the change refers to the way those affected by it think it will alter their established relationships in the organization.

We can clarify this distinction by referring to the two foregoing episodes. In both of them, the technical aspects of the changes introduced were virtually identical: the operator was asked to use a slightly changed part in assembling the finished product. By contrast, the social aspects of the changes were quite different.

In the first episode, the interaction between the industrial engineer and the operator tended to sustain the give-and-take kind of relationship that these two people were accustomed to. The operator was used to being treated as a person with some valuable skills and knowledge and some sense of responsibility about her work; when the engineer approached her with his idea, she felt she was being dealt with in the usual way. But, in the second episode, the new engineer was introducing not only a technical change but also a change in the operator's customary way of relating herself to others in the organization. By his brusque manner and by his lack of any explanation, he led the operator to fear that her usual work relationships were being changed. And she just did not like the new way she was being treated.

The results of these two episodes were quite different also. In the first episode there were no symptoms of resistance to change, a very good chance that the experimental change would determine fairly whether a cleaning solution would improve product quality, and a willingness on the part of the operator to accept future changes

EXHIBIT 1. TWO CONTRASTING PATTERNS OF HUMAN BEHAVIOR

	Change		
	Technical aspect	*Social aspect*	*Results*
Episode 1	Threatening the customary work relationship of operator	Sustaining the customary work relationship of operator	1. No resistance 2. Useful technical result 3. Readiness for more change
Episode 2	Clean part prior to assembly	Use new part in assembly	1. Signs of resistance 2. No useful technical result 3. Lack of readiness for more change

when the industrial engineer suggested them. In the second episode, however, there were signs of resistance to change (the operator's careless handling of parts and her satisfaction in their failure to work), failure to prove whether the modified part was an improvement or not, and indications that the operator would resist any further changes by the engineer. We might summarize the two contrasting patterns of human behavior in the two episodes in graphic form; see EXHIBIT 1.

It is apparent from these two patterns that the variable that determines the result is the *social* aspect of the change. In other words, the operator did not resist the technical change as such but rather the accompanying change in her human relationships.

Confirmation

This conclusion is based on more than one case. Many other cases in our research project substantiate it. Furthermore, we can find confirmation in the research experience of Coch and French, even though they came out with a different interpretation.

Coch and French tell us in their report that the procedure used with Group #1, the no-participation group, was the usual one in the factory for introducing work changes. And yet they also tell us something about the customary treatment of the operators in their work life. For example, the company's labor relations policies are progressive, the company and the supervisors place a high value on fair and open dealings with the employees, and the employees are encouraged to take up their problems and grievances with management. Also, the operators are accustomed to measuring the success and failure of themselves as operators against the company's standard output figures.

Now compare these *customary* work relationships with the way the Group #1 operators were treated when they were introduced to this particular work change. There is quite a difference. When the management called them into the room for indoctrination, they were treated as if they had no useful knowledge of their own jobs. In effect, they were told that they were not the skilled and efficient operators they had thought they were, that they were doing the job inefficiently, and that some "outsider" (the staff expert) would now tell them how to do it right. How could they construe this experience *except* as a threatening change in their usual working relationship? It is the story of the second episode in our research case all over again. The results were also the same, with signs of resistance, persistently low output, and so on.

Now consider experimental Groups #3 and #4, the total-participation groups. Coch and French referred to management's approach in their case as a "new" method of introducing change, but from the point of view of the *operators* it must not have seemed new at all. It was simply a continuation of the way they were ordinarily dealt with in the course of their regular work. And what happened? The results—reception to change, technical improvement, better performance—were much like those reported in the first episode between the operator and the industrial engineer.

So the research data of Coch and French tend to confirm the conclusion that the nature and size of the technical aspect of the change does not determine the presence or absence of resistance nearly so much as does the social aspect of the change.

ROOTS OF TROUBLE

The significance of these research findings, from management's point of view, is that executives and staff experts need, not expertness in using the devices of participation, but a real understanding, in depth and detail, of the specific social arrangements that will be sustained or threatened by the change or by the way in which it is introduced.

These observations check with everyday management experience in industry. When we stop to think about it, we know that many changes occur in our factories without a bit of resistance. We know that people who are working closely with one another continually swap ideas about short cuts and minor changes in procedure that are adopted so easily and naturally that we seldom notice them or even think of them as change. The point is that because these people work so closely with one another, they intuitively understand and take account of the existing social arrangements for work and so feel no threat to themselves in such everyday changes.

By contrast, management actions leading to what we commonly label "change" are usually initiated outside the small work group by staff people. These are the changes that we notice and the ones that most frequently bring on symptoms of resistance. By the very nature of their work, most of our staff specialists in industry do not have the intimate contact with operating groups that allows them to acquire an intuitive understanding of the complex social arrangements which their ideas may affect. Neither do our staff specialists always have the day-to-day dealings with operating people that lead them to develop a natural respect for the knowledge and skill of these people. As a result, all too often the staff men behave in a way that threatens and disrupts the established social relationships. And the tragedy is that so many of these upsets are inadvertent and unnecessary.

Yet industry must have its specialists—not only many kinds of engineering specialists (product, process, maintenance, quality, and safety engineers) but also cost accountants, production schedulers, purchasing agents, and personnel men. Must top management therefore reconcile itself to continual resistance to change, or can it take constructive action to meet the problem?

I believe that our research in various factory situations indicates why resistance to change occurs and what management can do about it. Let us take the "why" factors first.

Self-preoccupation

All too frequently we see staff specialists who bring to their work certain blind spots that get them into trouble when they initiate change with operating people. One such blind spot is "self-preoccupation." The staff man gets so engrossed in the technology of the change he is interested in promoting that he becomes wholly oblivious to different kinds of things that may be bothering people. Here are two examples:

> In one situation the staff people introduced, with the best of intentions, a technological change which inadvertently deprived a number of skilled operators of much of the satisfaction that they were finding in their work. Among other things, the change meant that, whereas formerly the output of each operator had been placed beside his work position where it could be viewed and appreciated by him and by others, it was now being carried away immediately from the work position. The workmen did not like this.
>
> The sad part of it was that there was no compelling cost or technical reason why the output could not be placed beside the work position as it had been formerly. But the staff people who had introduced the change were so literal-minded about their ideas that when they heard complaints on the changes from the operators, they could not comprehend what the trouble was. Instead, they began repeating all the logical arguments why the change made sense from a cost standpoint. The final result here was a chronic restriction of output and persistent hostility on the part of the operators.
>
> An industrial engineer undertook to introduce some methods changes in one department with the notion firmly in mind that this assignment presented him with an opportunity to "prove" to higher management the value of his function. He became so preoccupied with his personal desire to make a name for his particular techniques that he failed to pay any attention to some fairly obvious and practical considerations which the operating people were calling to his attention but which did

not show up in his time-study techniques. As could be expected, resistance quickly developed to all his ideas, and the only "name" that he finally won for his techniques was a black one.

Obviously, in both of these situations the staff specialists involved did not take into account the social aspects of the change they were introducing. For different reasons they got so preoccupied with the technical aspects of the change that they literally could not see or understand what all the fuss was about.

We may sometimes wish that the validity of the technical aspect of the change were the sole determinant of its acceptability. But the fact remains that the social aspect is what determines the presence or absence of resistance. Just as ignoring this fact is the sure way to trouble, so taking advantage of it can lead to positive results. We must not forget that these same social arrangements that at times seem so bothersome are essential for the performance of work. Without a network of established social relationships a factory would be populated with a collection of people who had no idea of how to work with one another in an organized fashion. By working *with* this network instead of *against* it, management's staff representatives can give new technological ideas a better chance of acceptance.

Operators' know-how overlooked

Another blind spot of many staff specialists is to the strengths as well as to the weaknesses of firsthand production experience. They do not recognize that the production foreman and the production operator are in their own way specialists themselves—specialists in actual experience with production problems. This point should be obvious, but it is amazing how many staff specialists fail to appreciate the fact that even though they themselves may have a superior knowledge of the technology of the production process involved, the foreman or the operators may have a more practical understanding of how to get daily production out of a group of men and machines.

The experience of the operating people frequently equips them to be of real help to staff specialists on at least two counts: (1) The operating people are often able to spot practical production difficulties in the ideas of the specialists—and iron out those difficulties before it is too late. (2) The operating people are often able to take advantage of their intimate acquaintance with the existing social arrangements for getting work done. If given a chance, they can use this kind of knowledge to help detect those parts of the change that will have undesirable social consequences. The staff experts can then go to work on ways to avoid the trouble area without materially affecting the technical worth of the change.

Further, some staff specialists have yet to learn the truth that, even after the plans for a change have been carefully made, it takes *time* to put the change successfully into production use. Time is necessary even though there may be no resistance to the change itself. The operators must develop the skill needed to use new methods and new equipment efficiently; there are always bugs to be taken out of a new method or piece of equipment even with the best of engineering. When a staff man begins to lose his patience with the amount of time that these steps take, the people he is working with will begin to feel that he is pushing them; *this* amounts to a change in their customary work relationships, and resistance will start building up where there was none before.

The situation is aggravated if the staff man mistakenly accuses the operators of resisting the idea of the change, for there are few things that irritate people more than to be blamed for resisting change when actually they are doing their best to learn a difficult new procedure.

MANAGEMENT ACTION

Many of the problems of resistance to change arise around certain kinds of *attitudes* that staff men are liable to develop about their jobs and their own ideas for introducing change. Fortunately, management can influence these attitudes and thus deal with the problems at their source.

Broadening staff interests

It is fairly common for a staff man to work so hard on one of his ideas for change that he comes to identify himself with it. This is fine for the organization when he is working on the idea by himself or with his immediate colleagues; the idea becomes "his baby," and the company benefits from his complete devotion to his work.

But when he goes to some group of operating people to introduce a change, his very identification with his ideas tends to make him unreceptive to any suggestions for modification. He just does not feel like letting anyone else tamper with his pet ideas. It is easy to see, of course, how this attitude is interpreted by the operating people as a lack of respect for their suggestions.

This problem of the staff man's extreme identification with his work is one which, to some extent, can only be cured by time. But here are four suggestions for speeding up the process:

(1) The manager can often, with wise timing, encourage the staff man's interest in a different project that is just starting.

(2) The manager can also, by his "coaching" as well as by example, prod the staff man to develop a healthier respect for the contributions he can receive from operating people; success in this area would, of course, virtually solve the problem.

(3) It also helps if the staff man can be guided to recognize that the satisfaction he derives from being productive and creative is the same satisfaction he denies the operating people by his behavior toward them. Experience shows that staff people can sometimes be stimulated by the thought of finding satisfaction in sharing with others in the organization the pleasures of being creative.

(4) Sometimes, too, the staff man can be led to see that winning acceptance of his ideas through better understanding and handling of human beings is just as challenging and rewarding as giving birth to an idea.

Using understandable terms

One of the problems that must be overcome arises from the fact that the typical staff man is likely to have the attitude that the reasons why he is recommending any given change may be so complicated and specialized that it is impossible to explain them to operating people. It may be true that the operating people would find it next to impossible to understand some of the staff man's analytical techniques, but this does not keep them from coming to the conclusion that the staff specialist is trying to razzle-dazzle them with tricky figures and formulas—insulting their intelligence—if he does not strive to his utmost to translate his ideas into terms understandable to them. The following case illustrates the importance of this point:

> A staff specialist was temporarily successful in "selling" a change based on a complicated mathematical formula to a foreman who really did not understand it. The whole thing backfired, however, when the foreman tried to sell it to his operating people. They asked him a couple of sharp questions that he could not answer. His embarrassment about this led him to resent and resist the change so much that eventually the whole proposition fell through. This was unfortunate in terms not only of human relations but also of technological progress in the plant.

There are some very good reasons, both technical and social, why the staff man should be interested in working with the operating people until his recommendations make "sense." (This does not mean that the operating people need to understand the recommendations in quite the same way or in the same detail that the staff man does, but that they should be able to visualize the recommendations in terms of their job experiences.) Failure of the staff man to provide an adequate explanation is likely to mean that a job the operators had formerly performed with understanding and satisfaction will now be performed without understanding and with less satisfaction.

This loss of satisfaction not only concerns the individual involved but also is significant from the standpoint of the company which is trying to get maximum productivity from the operating people. A person who does not have a feeling of comprehension of what he is doing is denied the opportunity to exercise that uniquely human ability—the ability to use informed and intelligent judgment on what he does. If the staff man leaves the operating people with a sense of confusion, they will also be left unhappy and less productive.

Top line and staff executives responsible for the operation should make it a point, therefore, to know how the staff man goes about installing a change. They can do this by asking discerning questions when he reports to them, listening closely to reports of employee reaction, and, if they have the opportunity, actually watching the staff man at work. At times they may have to take such drastic action as insisting that the time of installation of a proposed change be postponed until the operators are ready for it. But, for the most part, straightforward discussions with the staff man in terms of what they think of his approach should help him, over a period of time, to learn what is expected of him in his relationships with operating personnel.

New look at resistance

Another attitude that gets staff men into trouble is the *expectation* that all the people involved will resist the change. It is curious but true that the staff man who goes into his job with the conviction that people are going to resist any idea he presents with blind stubbornness is likely to find them responding just the way he thinks they will. The process is clear: whenever he treats the people who are supposed to buy his ideas as if they were bullheaded, he changes the way they are used to being treated; and they *will* be bullheaded in resisting *that* change!

I think that the staff man—and management in general—will do better to look at it this way: When resistance *does* appear, it should not be thought of as something to be *overcome*. Instead, it can best be thought of as a useful red flag—a signal that something is going wrong. To use a rough analogy, signs of resistance in a social organization are useful in the same way that pain is useful to the body as a signal that some bodily functions are getting out of adjustment.

The resistance, like the pain, does not tell what is wrong but only that something *is* wrong. And it makes no more sense to try to overcome such resistance than it does to take a pain killer without diagnosing the bodily ailment. Therefore, when resistance appears, it is time to listen carefully to find out what the trouble is. What is needed is not a long harangue on the logics of the new recommendations but a careful exploration of the difficulty.

It may happen that the problem is some technical imperfection in the change that can be readily corrected. More than likely, it will turn out that the change is threatening and upsetting some of the established social arrangements for doing work. Whether the trouble is easy or difficult to correct, management will at least know what it is dealing with.

New job definition

Finally, some staff specialists get themselves in trouble because they assume they have the answer in the thought that people will accept a change when they have participated in making it. For example:

> In one plant we visited, an engineer confided to us (obviously because we, as researchers on human relations, were interested in psychological gimmicks!) that he was going to put across a proposed production layout change of his by inserting in it a rather obvious error, which others could then suggest should be corrected. We attended the meeting where this stunt was performed, and superficially it worked. Somebody caught the error, proposed that it be corrected, and our engineer immediately "bought" the suggestion as a very worthwhile one and made the change. The group then seemed to "buy" his entire layout proposal.
>
> It looked like an effective technique—oh, so easy—until later, when we became better acquainted with the people in the plant. Then we found out that many of the engineer's colleagues considered him a phony and did not trust him. The resistance they put up to his ideas was very subtle, yet even more real and difficult for management to deal with.

Participation will never work so long as it is treated as a device to get somebody else to do what you want him to. Real participation is based on respect. And respect is not acquired by just trying; it is acquired when the staff man faces the reality that he needs the contributions of the operating people.

If the staff man defines his job as not just generating ideas but also getting those ideas into practical operation, he will recognize his real dependence on the contributions of the operating people. He will ask them for ideas and suggestions, not in a backhanded way to get compliance, but in a straightforward way to get some good ideas and avoid some unnecessary mistakes. By this process he will be treating the operating people in such a way that his own behavior will not be perceived as a threat to their customary work relationships. It will be possible to discuss, and accept or reject, the ideas on their own merit.

The staff specialist who looks at the process of introducing change and at resistance to change in the manner outlined in the preceding pages may not be hailed as a genius, but he can be counted on in installing a steady flow of technical changes that will cut costs and improve quality without upsetting the organization.

Role of the Administrator

Now what about the way the top executive goes about his *own* job as it involves the introduction of change and problems of resistance?

One of the most important things he can do, of course, is to deal with staff people in much the same way that he wants them to deal with operators. He must realize that staff people resist social change, too. (This means, among other things, that he should not prescribe particular rules to them on the basis of this article!)

But most important, I think, is the way the administrator conceives of his job in coordinating the work of the different staff and line groups involved in a change. Does he think of his duties *primarily* as checking up, delegating and following through, applying pressure when performance fails to measure up? Or does he think of them *primarily* as facilitating communication and understanding between people with different points of view—for example, between a staff engineering group and a production group who do not see eye to eye on a change they are both involved in? An analysis of management's actual experience—or, at least, that part of it which has been covered by our research—points to the latter as the more effective concept of administration.

I do not mean that the executive should spend his time with the different people concerned discussing the human problems of change as such. He *should* discuss schedules, technical details, work assignments, and so forth. But he should also be watching closely for the messages that are passing back and forth as people discuss these topics. He will find that people—himself as well as others—are always implicitly asking and making answers to questions like: "How will he accept criticism?" "How much can I afford to tell him?" "Does he really get my point?" "Is he playing games?" The answers to such questions determine the degree of candor and the amount of understanding between the people involved.

When the administrator concerns himself with these problems and acts to facilitate understanding, there will be less logrolling and more sense of common purpose, fewer words and better understanding, less anxiety and more acceptance of criticism, less griping and more attention to specific problems—in short, better performance in putting new ideas for technological change into effect.

Questions

1. What is the basic thesis of Lawrence's article?
2. What does Lawrence think of participation as a solution to resistance to change? Why does he think this way? Do you agree?
3. What are the basic aspects of change? Which of these aspects, according to Lawrence, actually causes resistance to change? Why?
4. Discuss what executives and staff experts "need" to facilitate change.
5. What steps can management take to deal effectively with resistance to change?

ACHIEVING CHANGE IN PEOPLE: SOME APPLICATIONS OF GROUP DYNAMICS THEORY *

Dorwin Cartwright

I

We hear all around us today the assertion that the problems of the twentieth century are problems of human relations. The survival of civilization, it is said, will depend upon man's ability to create social inventions capable of harnessing, for society's constructive use, the vast physical energies now at man's disposal. Or, to put the matter more simply, we must learn how to change the way in which people behave toward one another. In broad outline, the specifications for a good society are clear, but a serious technical problem remains: How can we change people so that they neither restrict the freedom nor limit the potentialities for growth of others; so that they accept and respect people of different religion, nationality, color, or political opinion; so that nations can exist in a world without war, and so that the fruits of our technological advances can bring economic well-being and freedom from disease to all the people of the world? Although few people would disagree with these objectives when stated abstractly, when we become more specific, differences of opinion quickly arise. How is change to be produced? Who is to do it? Who is to be changed? These questions permit no ready answers.

Before we consider in detail these questions of social technology, let us clear away some semantic obstacles. The word "change" produces emotional reactions. It is not a neutral word. To many people it is threatening. It conjures up visions of a revolutionary, a dissatisfied idealist, a trouble-maker, a malcontent. Nicer words referring to the process of changing people are education, training, orientation, guidance, indoctrination, therapy. We are more ready to have others "educate" us than to have them "change" us. We, ourselves, feel less guilty in "training" others than in "changing" them. Why this emotional response? What makes the two kinds of words have such different meanings? I believe that a large part of the difference lies in the fact that the safer words (like education

* From *Human Relations*, Vol. 4, No. 4 (1951), pp. 381-392. Reprinted with permission.

or therapy) carry the implicit assurance that the only changes produced will be good ones, acceptable within a currently held value system. The cold, unmodified word "change," on the contrary, promises no respect for values; it might even tamper with values themselves. Perhaps for this very reason it will foster straight thinking if we use the word "change" and thus force ourselves to struggle directly and self-consciously with the problems of value that are involved. Words like education, training, or therapy, by the very fact that they are so disturbing, may close our eyes to the fact that they too inevitably involve values.

Another advantage of using the word "change" rather than other related words is that it does not restrict our thinking to a limited set of aspects of people that are legitimate targets of change. Anyone familiar with the history of education knows that there has been endless controversy over what it is about people that "education" properly attempts to modify. Some educators have viewed education simply as imparting knowledge, others mainly as providing skills for doing things, still others as producing healthy "attitudes," and some have aspired to instil a way of life. Or if we choose to use a word like "therapy," we can hardly claim that we refer to a more clearly defined realm of change. Furthermore, one can become inextricably entangled in distinctions and vested interests by attempting to distinguish sharply between, let us say, the domain of education and that of therapy. If we are to try to take a broader view and to develop some basic principles that promise to apply to all types of modifications in people, we had better use a word like "change" to keep our thinking general enough.

The proposal that social technology may be employed to solve the problems of society suggests that social science may be applied in ways not different from those used in the physical sciences. Does social science, in fact, have any practically useful knowledge which may be brought to bear significantly on society's most urgent problems? What scientifically based principles are there for guiding programs of social change: In this paper we shall restrict our considerations to certain parts of a relatively new branch of social science known as "group dynamics." We shall examine some of the implications for social action which stem from research in this field of scientific investigation.

What is "group dynamics"? Perhaps it will be most useful to start by looking at the derivation of the word "dynamics." It comes from a Greek word meaning force. In careful usage of the phrase, "group dynamics" refers to the forces operating in groups. The investigation of group dynamics, then, consists of a study of these forces: what gives rise to them, what conditions modify them, what consequences they have, etc. The practical application of group dynamics (or the technology of group dynamics) consists of the utilization of knowledge about these forces for the achievement of some purpose. In keeping with this definition, then, it is clear that group dynamics, as a realm of investigation, is not particularly novel, nor is it the exclusive property of any person or institution. It goes back at least to the outstanding work of men like Simmel, Freud, and Cooley.

Although interest in groups has a long and respectable history, the past fifteen years have witnessed a new flowering of activity in this field. Today, research centers in several countries are carrying out substantial programs of research designed to reveal the nature of groups and of their functioning. The phrase "group dynamics" has come into common usage during this time and intense efforts have been devoted to the development of the field, both as a branch of social science and as a form of social technology.

In this development the name of Kurt Lewin has been outstanding. As a consequence of his work in the field of individual psychology and from his analysis of the nature of the pressing problems of the contemporary world, Lewin became convinced of society's urgent need for a *scientific approach* to the understanding of the dynamics of groups. In 1945 he established the Research Center for Group Dynamics to meet this need. Since that date the Center has been devoting its efforts to improving our scientific understanding of groups through laboratory experimentation, field studies, and the use of techniques of action research. It has also attempted in various ways to help get the findings of social science more widely used by social management. Much of what I have to say in this paper is drawn from the experiences of this Center in its brief existence of a little more than five years.[1]

II

For various reasons we have found that much of our work has been devoted to an attempt to gain a better understanding of the ways in which people change their behavior or resist efforts by others to have them do so. Whether we set for ourselves the prac-

---

[1] D. Cartwright, *The Research Center for Group Dynamics: A Report of Five Years' Activities and a View of Future Needs* (Ann Arbor: Institute for Social Research, 1950).

tical goal of improving behavior or whether we take on the intellectual task of understanding why people do what they do, we have to investigate processes of communication, influence, social pressure—in short, problems of change.

In this work we have encountered great frustration. The problems have been most difficult to solve. Looking back over our experience, I have become convinced that no small part of the trouble has resulted from an irresistible tendency to conceive of our problems in terms of the individual. We live in an individualistic culture. We value the individual highly, and rightly so. But I am inclined to believe that our political and social concern for the individual has narrowed our thinking as social scientists so much that we have not been able to state our research problems properly. Perhaps we have taken the individual as the unit of observation and study when some larger unit would have been more appropriate. Let us look at a few examples.

Consider first some matters having to do with the mental health of an individual. We can all agree, I believe, that an important mark of a healthy personality is that the individual's self-esteem has not been undermined. But on what does self-esteem depend? From research on this problem we have discovered that, among other things, repeated experiences of failure or traumatic failures on matters of central importance serve to undermine one's self-esteem. We also know that whether a person experiences success or failure as a result of some undertaking depends upon the level of aspiration which he has set for himself. Now, if we try to discover how the level of aspiration gets set, we are immediately involved in the person's relationships to groups. The groups to which he belongs set standards for his behavior which he must accept if he is to remain in the group. If his capacities do not allow him to reach these standards, he experiences failure, he withdraws or is rejected by the group and his self-esteem suffers a shock.

Suppose, then, that we accept a task of therapy, of rebuilding his self-esteem. It would appear plausible from our analysis of the problem that we should attempt to work with variables of the same sort that produced the difficulty, that is to work with him either in the groups to which he now belongs or to introduce him into new groups which are selected for the purpose and to work upon his relationships to groups as such. From the point of view of preventive mental health, we might even attempt to train the groups in our communities—classes in schools, work groups in business, families, unions, religious and cultural groups—to make use of practices better designed to protect the self-esteem of their members.

Consider a second example. A teacher finds that in her class she has a number of trouble-makers, full of aggression. She wants to know why these children are so aggressive and what can be done about it. A foreman in a factory has the same kind of problem with some of his workers. He wants the same kind of help. The solution most tempting to both the teacher and the foreman often is to transfer the worst trouble-makers to someone else, or if facilities are available, to refer them for counselling. But is the problem really of such a nature that it can be solved by removing the trouble-maker from the situation or by working on his individual motivations and emotional life? What leads does research give us? The evidence indicates, of course, that there are many causes of aggressiveness in people, but one aspect of the problem has become increasingly clear in recent years. If we observe carefully the amount of aggressive behavior and the number of trouble-makers to be found in a large collection of groups, we find that these characteristics can vary tremendously from group to group even when the different groups are composed essentially of the same kinds of people. In the now classic experiments of Lewin, Lippitt, and White [2] on the effects of different styles of leadership, it was found that the same group of children displayed markedly different levels of aggressive behavior when under different styles of leadership. Moreover, when individual children were transferred from one group to another, their levels of aggressiveness shifted to conform to the atmosphere of the new group. Efforts to account for one child's aggressiveness under one style of leadership merely in terms of his personality traits could hardly succeed under these conditions. This is not to say that a person's behavior is entirely to be accounted for by the atmosphere and structure of the immediate group, but it is remarkable to what an extent a strong, cohesive group can control aspects of a member's behavior traditionally thought to be expressive of enduring personality trains. Recognition of this fact rephrases the problem of how to change such behavior. It directs us to a study of the sources of the influence of the group on its members.

Let us take an example from a different field. What can we learn from efforts to change people by mass media and mass persuasion?

[2] K. Lewin, R. Lippitt, and R. K. White, "Patterns of Aggressive Behavior in Experimentally Created 'Social Climates'," *Journal of Social Psychology*, Vol. 10 (1939), pp. 271-299.

In those rare instances when educators, propagandists, advertisers, and others who want to influence large numbers of people, have bothered to make an objective evaluation of the enduring changes produced by their efforts, they have been able to demonstrate only the most negligible effects.[3] The inefficiency of attempts to influence the public by mass media would be scandalous if there were agreement that it was important or even desirable to have such influences strongly exerted. In fact, it is no exaggeration to say that all of the research and experience of generations has not improved the efficiency of lectures or other means of mass influence to any noticeable degree. Something must be wrong with our theories of learning, motivation, and social psychology.

Within very recent years some research data have been accumulating which may give us a clue to the solution of our problem. In one series of experiments directed by Lewin, it was found that a method of group decision, in which the group as a whole made a decision to have its members change their behavior, was from two to ten times as effective in producing actual change as was a lecture presenting exhortation to change.[4] We have yet to learn precisely what produces these differences of effectiveness, but it is clear that by introducing group forces into the situation a whole new level of influence has been achieved.

The experience has been essentially the same when people have attempted to increase the productivity of individuals in work settings. Traditional conceptions of how to increase the output of workers have stressed the individual: select the right man for the job; simplify the job for him; train him in the skills required; motivate him by economic incentives; make it clear to whom he reports; keep the lines of authority and responsibility simple and straight. But even when all these conditions are fully met we are finding that productivity is far below full potential. There is even good reason to conclude that this individualistic conception of the determinants of productivity actually fosters negative consequences. The individual, now isolated and subjected to the demands of the organization through the commands of his boss, finds that he must create with his fellow employees informal groups, not shown on any table of organization, in order to protect himself from arbitrary

---

[3] D. Cartwright, "Some Principles of Mass Persuasion: Selected Findings of Research on the Sale of United States War Bonds," *Human Relations*, Vol. 2, No. 3 (1949), pp. 253-267.

[4] K. Lewin, *Field Theory in Social Science* (New York: Harper and Brothers, 1951), pp. 229-236.

control of his life, from the boredom produced by the endless repetition of mechanically sanitary and routine operations, and from the impoverishment of his emotional and social life brought about by the frustration of his basic needs for social interaction, participation, and acceptance in a stable group. Recent experiments have demonstrated clearly that the productivity of work groups can be greatly increased by methods of work organization and supervision which give more responsibility to work groups, which allow for fuller participation in important decisions, and which make stable groups the firm basis for support of the individual's social needs.[5] I am convinced that future research will also demonstrate that people working under such conditions become more mature and creative individuals in their homes, in community life, and as citizens.

As a final example, let us examine the experience of efforts to train people in workshops, institutes, and special training courses. Such efforts are common in various areas of social welfare, intergroup relations, political affairs, industry, and adult education generally. It is an unfortunate fact that objective evaluation of the effects of such training efforts has only rarely been undertaken, but there is evidence for those who will look that the actual change in behavior produced is most disappointing. A workshop not infrequently develops keen interest among the participants, high morale and enthusiasm, and a firm resolve on the part of many to apply all the wonderful insights back home. But what happens back home? The trainee discovers that his colleagues don't share his enthusiasm. He learns that the task of changing others' expectations and ways of doing things is discouragingly difficult. He senses, perhaps not very clearly, that it would make all the difference in the world if only there were a few other people sharing his enthusiasm and insights with whom he could plan activities, evaluate consequences of efforts, and from whom he could gain emotional and motivational support. The approach to training which conceives of its task as being merely that of changing the individual probably produces frustration, demoralization, and disillusionment in as large a measure as it accomplishes more positive results.

A few years ago the Research Center for Group Dynamics undertook to shed light on this problem by investigating the operation of a workshop for training leaders in intercultural relations.[6] In

[5] L. Coch and J. R. P. French, Jr., "Overcoming Resistance to Change," *Human Relations*, Vol. 1, No. 4 (1948), pp. 512-532.
[6] R. Lippitt, *Training in Community Relations* (New York: Harper and Brothers, 1949).

a project, directed by Lippitt, we set out to compare systematically the different effects of the workshop upon trainees who came as isolated individuals in contrast to those who came as teams. Since one of the problems in the field of intercultural relations is that of getting people of good will to be more active in community efforts to improve intergroup relations, one goal of the training workshop was to increase the activity of the trainees in such community affairs. We found that before the workshop there was no difference in the activity level of the people who were to be trained as isolates and of those who were to be trained as teams. Six months after the workshop, however, those who had been trained as isolates were only slightly more active than before the workshop whereas those who had been members of strong training teams were now much more active. We do not have clear evidence on the point, but we would be quite certain that the maintenance of heightened activity over a long period of time would also be much better for members of teams. For the isolates the effect of the workshop had the charactertic of a "shot in the arm" while for the team member it produced a more enduring change because the team provided continuous support and reinforcement for its members.

III

What conclusions may we draw from these examples? What principles of achieving change in people can we see emerging? To begin with the most general proposition, we may state that the behavior, attitudes, beliefs, and values of the individual are all firmly grounded in the groups to which he belongs. How aggressive or cooperative a person is, how much self-respect and self-confidence he has, how energetic and productive his work is, what he aspires to, what he believes to be true and good, whom he loves or hates, and what beliefs and prejudices he holds—all these characteristics are highly determined by the individual's group memberships. In a real sense, they are properties of groups and of the relationships between people. Whether they change or resist change will, therefore, be greatly influenced by the nature of these groups. Attempts to change them must be concerned with the dynamics of groups.

In examining more specifically how groups enter into the process of change, we find it useful to view groups in at least three different ways. In the first view, the group is seen as a source of influence over its members. Efforts to change behavior can be supported or blocked by pressures on members stemming from the group. To make constructive use of these pressures the group must be used *as a medium of change*. In the second view, the group itself becomes the *target of change*. To change the behavior of individuals it may be necessary to change the standards of the group, its style of leadership, its emotional atmosphere, or its stratification into cliques and hierarchies. Even though the goal may be to change the behavior of *individuals*, the target of change becomes the group. In the third view, it is recognized that many changes of behavior can be brought about only by the organized efforts of groups *as agents of change*. A committee to combat intolerance, a labor union, an employers association, a citizens group to increase the pay of teachers—any action group will be more or less effective depending upon the way it is organized, the satisfactions it provides to its members, the degree to which its goals are clear, and a host of other properties of the group.

An adequate social technology of change, then, requires at the very least a scientific understanding of groups viewed in each of these ways. We shall consider here only the first two aspects of the problem: the group as a medium of change and as a target of change.

The group as a medium of change

Principle No. 1. If the group is to be used effectively as a medium of change, those people who are to be changed and those who are to exert influence for change must have a strong sense of belonging to the same group.

Kurt Lewin described this principle well: "The normal gap between teacher and student, doctor and patient, social worker and public, can . . . be a real obstacle to acceptance of the advocated conduct." In other words, in spite of whatever status differences there might be between them, the teacher and the student have to feel as members of one group in matters involving their sense of values. The chances for re-education seem to be increased whenever a strong we-feeling is created.[7] Recent experiments by Preston and Heintz have demonstrated greater changes of opinions among members of discussion groups operating with participatory leadership than among those with supervisory leadership.[8] The implications

---

[7] K. Lewin, *Resolving Social Conflicts* (New York: Harper and Brothers, 1948), p. 67.

[8] M. G. Preston and R. K. Heintz, "Effects of Participatory vs. Supervisory Leadership on Group Judgment," *Journal of Abnormal and Social Psychology*, Vol. 44 (1949), pp. 345-355.

of this principle for classroom teaching are far-reaching. The same may be said of supervision in the factory, army, or hospital.

Principle No. 2. The more attractive the group is to its members the greater is the influence that the group can exert on its members.

This principle has been extensively documented by Festinger and his co-workers.[9] They have been able to show in a variety of settings that in more cohesive groups there is a greater readiness of members to attempt to influence others, a greater readiness to be influenced by others, and stronger pressures toward conformity when conformity is a relevant matter for the group. Important for the practitioner wanting to make use of this principle is, of course, the question of how to increase the attractiveness of groups. This is a question with many answers. Suffice it to say that a group is more attractive the more it satisfies the needs of its members. We have been able to demonstrate experimentally an increase in group cohesiveness by increasing the liking of members for each other as persons, by increasing the perceived importance of the group goal, and by increasing the prestige of the group among other groups. Experienced group workers could add many other ways to this list.

Principle No. 3. In attempts to change attitudes, values, or behavior the more relevant they are to the basis of attraction to the group, the greater will be the influence that the group can exert upon them.

I believe this principle gives a clue to some otherwise puzzling phenomena. How does it happen that a group, like a labor union, seems to be able to exert such strong discipline over its members in some matters (let us say in dealings with management), while it seems unable to exert nearly the same influence in other matters (let us say in political action)? If we examine why it is that members are attracted to the group, I believe we will find that a particular reason for belonging seems more related to some of the group's activities than to others. If a man joins a union mainly to keep his job and to improve his working conditions, he may be largely uninfluenced by the union's attempt to modify his attitudes toward national and international affairs. Groups differ tremendously in the range of matters that are relevant to them and hence over which they have influence. Much of the inefficiency of adult education could be reduced if more attention were paid to the need that influence attempts be appropriate to the groups in which they are made.

[9] L. Festinger *et al.*, *Theory and Experiment in Social Communication: Collected papers* (Ann Arbor: Institute for Social Research, 1950).

Principle No. 4. The greater the prestige of a group member in the eyes of the other members, the greater the influence he can exert.

Polansky, Lippitt, and Redl [10] have demonstrated this principle with great care and methodological ingenuity in a series of studies in children's summer camps. From a practical point of view it must be emphasized that the things giving prestige to a member may not be those characteristics most prized by the official management of the group. The most prestige-carrying member of a Sunday School class may not possess the characteristics most similar to the minister of the church. The teacher's pet may be a poor source of influence within a class. This principle is the basis for the common observation that the official leader and the actual leader of a group are often not the same individual.

Principle No. 5. Efforts to change individuals or subparts of a group which, if successful, would have the result of making them deviate from the norms of the group will encounter strong resistance.

During the past few years a great deal of evidence has been accumulated showing the tremendous pressures which groups can exert upon members to conform to the group's norms. The price of deviation in most groups is rejection or even expulsion. If the member really wants to belong and be accepted, he cannot withstand this type of pressure. It is for this reason that efforts to change people by taking them from the group and giving them special training so often have disappointing results. This principle also accounts for the finding that people thus trained sometimes display increased tension, aggressiveness toward the group, or a tendency to form cults or cliques with others who have shared their training.

These five principles concerning the group as a medium of change would appear to have readiest application to groups created for the purpose of producing changes in people. They provide certain specifications for building effective training or therapy groups. They also point, however, to a difficulty in producing change in people in that they show how resistant an individual is to changing in any way contrary to group pressures and expectations. In order to achieve many kinds of changes in people, therefore, it is necessary to deal with the group as a target of change.

[10] N. Polansky, R. Lippitt, and F. Redl, "An Investigation of Behavioral Contagion in Groups," *Human Relations*, Vol. 3, No. 4 (1950), pp. 319-348.

The group as a target of change

Principle No. 6. Strong pressure for changes in the group can be established by creating a shared perception by members of the need for change, thus making the source of pressure for change lie within the group.

Marrow and French [11] report a dramatic case-study which illustrates this principle quite well. A manufacturing concern had a policy against hiring women over thirty because it was believed that they were slower, more difficult to train, and more likely to be absent. The staff psychologist was able to present to management evidence that this belief was clearly unwarranted at least within their own company. The psychologist's facts, however, were rejected and ignored as a basis for action because they violated accepted beliefs. It was claimed that they went against the direct experience of the foremen. Then the psychologist hit upon a plan for achieving change which differed drastically from the usual one of argument, persuasion, and pressure. He proposed that management conduct its own analysis of the situation. With his help management collected all the facts which they believed were relevant to the problem. When the results were in they were now their own facts rather than those of some "outside" expert. Policy was immediately changed without further resistance. The important point here is that facts are not enough. The facts must be the accepted property of the group if they are to become an effective basis for change. There seems to be all the difference in the world in changes actually carried out between those cases in which a consulting firm is hired to do a study and present a report and those in which technical experts are asked to collaborate with the group in doing its own study.

Principle No. 7. Information relating to the need for change, plans for change, and consequences of change must be shared by all relevant people in the group.

Another way of stating this principle is to say that change of a group ordinarily requires the opening of communication channels. Newcomb [12] has shown how one of the first consequences of mistrust and hostility is the avoidance of communicating openly and freely about the things producing the tension. If you look closely at a pathological group (that is, one that has trouble making deci-

---

[11] A. J. Marrow and J. R. P. French, Jr., "Changing a Stereotype in Industry," *Journal of Social Issues*, Vol. 1, No. 3 (1945), pp. 33-37.

[12] T. M. Newcomb, "Autistic Hostility and Social Reality," *Human Relations*, Vol. 1, No. 1 (1947), pp. 69-86.

sions or effecting coordinated efforts of its members), you will certainly find strong restraints in that group against communicating vital information among its members. Until these restraints are removed there can be little hope for any real and lasting changes in the group's functioning. In passing it should be pointed out that the removal of barriers to communication will ordinarily be accompanied by a sudden increase in the communication of hostility. The group may appear to be falling apart, and it will certainly be a painful experience to many of the members. This pain and the fear that things are getting out of hand often stop the process of change once begun.

Principle No. 8. Changes in one part of a group produce strain in other related parts which can be reduced only by eliminating the change or by bringing about readjustments in the related parts.

It is a common practice to undertake improvements in group functioning by providing training programs for certain classes of people in the organization. A training program for foremen, for nurses, for teachers, or for group workers is established. If the content of the training is relevant for organizational change, it must of necessity deal with the relationships these people have with other subgroups. If nurses in a hospital change their behavior significantly, it will affect their relations both with the patients and with the doctors. It is unrealistic to assume that both these groups will remain indifferent to any significant changes in this respect. In hierarchical structures this process is most clear. Lippitt has proposed on the basis of research and experience that in such organizations attempts at change should always involve three levels, one being the major target of change and the other two being the one above and the one below.

IV

These eight principles represent a few of the basic propositions emerging from research in group dynamics. Since research is constantly going on and since it is the very nature of research to revise and reformulate our conceptions, we may be sure that these principles will have to be modified and improved as time goes by. In the meantime they may serve as guides in our endeavors to develop a scientifically based technology of social management.

In social technology, just as in physical technology, invention plays a crucial role. In both fields progress consists of the creation of new mechanisms for the accomplishment of certain goals. In both fields inventions arise in response to practical needs and are to be evaluated by how effectively they satisfy these needs. The relation of invention to scientific development is indirect but important. Inventions cannot proceed too far ahead of basic scientific development, nor should they be allowed to fall too far behind. They will be more effective the more they make good use of known principles of science, and they often make new developments in science possible. On the other hand, they are in no sense logical derivations from scientific principles.

I have taken this brief excursion into the theory of invention in order to make a final point. To many people "group dynamics" is known only for the social inventions which have developed in recent years in work with groups. Group dynamics is often thought of as certain techniques to be used with groups. Role playing, buzz groups, process observers, post-meeting reaction sheets, and feedback of group observations are devices popularly associated with the phrase "group dynamics." I trust that I have been able to show that group dynamics is more than a collection of gadgets. It certainly aspires to be a science as well as a technology.

This is not to underplay the importance of these inventions nor of the function of inventing. As inventions they are all mechanisms designed to help accomplish important goals. How effective they are will depend upon how skilfully they are used and how appropriate they are to the purposes to which they are put. Careful evaluative research must be the ultimate judge of their usefulness in comparison with alternative inventions. I believe that the principles enumerated in this paper indicate some of the specifications that social inventions in this field must meet.

QUESTIONS

1. What is "group dynamics"?
2. What, according to Cartwright, is a basic reason why we have encountered trouble in explaining resistance to change?
3. What principles of achieving change in people are emerging from the application of the group dynamics theory?
4. What influence does the group exert on the individual?
5. Are the principles of achieving change in people flexible? Why?

IMPROVING THE RELATIONSHIP
BETWEEN STAFF AND LINE *
An Assist from the Anthropologists   J. M. Juran

Industrial effectiveness has been greatly aided by the use of the "staff" concept, under which "staff" personnel, making use of time, perspective, objectivity, and special skills seldom available to line supervision, have carried out a host of vital tasks. Staff *advisors* have given legal, financial, economic, and other forms of counsel. Staff *coordinators* have prepared sales plans and production schedules. Staff *control* men have inspected the product and audited the books. Staff *utility service* men have conducted process research, run the employment department, written insurance, and maintained the physical plant.[1]

The price that is commonly paid for this improved effectiveness is often a strained relationship between line and staff personnel. There are multiple causes of this strain in the organization—honest differences on jurisdictional boundaries, empire-building tendencies, confusion as to extent of "authority," and so on. But implicit in all of them, and running through all the forms of staff work, is the fact that the line supervisor is called upon to *adapt himself to changes proposed by the staff specialist.*

This is a difficult situation. The staff specialist exhibits a fierce loyalty to his brain child. The line supervisor is no less loyal to the habits and traditions he knows and understands. Small wonder that the resulting differences sometimes erupt into charges about impractical theorists, or backward old-timers.

Now, from an unexpected quarter, comes a flash of illumination.

For some years, numerous technical experts employed by the United Nations Educational, Scientific and Cultural Organization (UNESCO) have been introducing technical changes into industrially "backward" countries. These technical changes have involved agriculture, transportation, power development, public finance, public health, etc. The problems faced by these experts in the "purposive

---

* From *Personnel*, Vol. 32, No. 6 (May, 1956), pp. 515-524. Copyright, 1956, by the American Management Association. Reprinted by permission of the American Management Association.

[1] For a penetrating discussion of what is "staff," see *Papers of the 9th International Management Congress, Brussels, 1951*, Section 1, "The Structure of Large Enterprises," pp. 5, 6.

introduction of technical change" are brilliantly analyzed in a new book,[2] *Cultural Patterns and Technical Change,* edited by the eminent anthropologist, Margaret Mead.

This venture into anthropology has much to do with the staff and line relationship in industry. The common problem is the impact of new technical ideas on members of established societies ("cultures"). But the UNESCO analysis is more comprehensive, more incisive, and more practical in its exposition of principles than any related study in industrial literature. This same set of principles, translated into industrial dialect, might well constitute a code of practice for industry's staff specialists. So far as the writer is aware, nothing in industrial literature so admirably covers the needs.

The concept of culture

The starting point of the UNESCO book is the concept of a "culture." "Culture" is a "body of learned behavior," a collection of beliefs, habits, practices, and traditions, shared by a group of people (a society) and successively learned by new members who enter the society. A "culture," as thus defined, can be found in a factory, an office, a mine, a warehouse, a company. The older the institution, the more certain it is to have developed such a "body of learned behavior."

Culture is not a kettle full of loose, disconnected pieces. Rather, it is a unified whole, no element of which can be disturbed without repercussions on a wide scale. As the book points out:

> . . . Once an agricultural specialist has included in his expectations the possibility that in his attempt to get land organized in fields sufficiently large for the use of agricultural machinery, he may have to take account of graves and ghosts, sacred trees, oracles, shrines, dowries, sex habits and unborn children, as well as inheritance, property laws, rights of way, and "ancient lights," he will then be more ready to follow out the implications of any particular resistance which he meets in the foreign country where he goes as a specialist.[3]

The existence of this unified culture requires that before change is made, the whole culture must be taken into account. Failing this, there is a risk that the members of the culture will be forced to make the unhappy choice of either accepting the destruction of traditions that are important to them or sabotaging the program of change.

---

[2] Margaret Mead, Ed., *Cultural Patterns and Technical Change,* United Nations Educational, Scientific and Cultural Organization (Paris, 1953). Reprinted as a "Mentor Book" by the New American Library, 1955.

[3] *Op. cit.,* p. 21.

The technical expert convinced of the logic of his proposed changes (from *his* point of view) and oblivious of the unity of the culture he is disrupting is inevitably headed for trouble.

The UNESCO book describes several whole cultures. These descriptions are of value not merely because they reveal the broad spectrum of human behavior; they are valuable also because many seemingly strange human practices have startling counterparts in modern industry.

Among the Tiv of Nigeria, for example, health is not a separate concept or body of know-how. Disease, accident, death are all regarded as part of the mystic potency (*tsav*) of individuals. The man with plenty of *tsav* can conquer disease; lacking *tsav*, he goes under. Likewise, today, in one company after another, we find the comment "Show me a good operation and I'll show you a good branch manager (or foreman)." As with the Tiv, management success is attributed to the "savvy" of the individual, rather than to skill in the use of a body of management know-how.

The Burmese have had difficulty in accepting government by precedent. Likewise, many companies today have had difficulty in adopting "standard practice."

To the Greek peasant, self-esteem is paramount. To suggest that he is backward and needs the help of an expert violates this self-esteem. So it is with many of today's shop supervisors.

The Palau island elite have some interesting trappings of authority such as the right to five entrances to their houses and a special type of hair comb, right of way on the village paths, and so on. Of the same order are the symbols of status of the modern industrial elite: the office carpet, the stall in the company garage, and the key to the executive washroom.

Equally recognizable is the defense of the Palauan when accused of violating regulations. "Fabrication of the facts was and still is a well-developed art. A more common procedure is to acquiesce overtly to any orders given but actually to evade their execution while verbally simulating compliance. The order might even be enthusiastically applauded and then either 'misunderstood' or worked at without ever being quite accomplished." [4] Similarly, the "yes" of the Spanish-American workman often means "You are the boss, so I agree." In the same way, modern industry harbors yes-men who "go doggo," "act dumb," or "drag their feet."

---

[4] *Op. cit.*, p. 137.

Psychological principles influencing acceptance of change

From this series of studies in the introduction of technical change into established cultures, the UNESCO book develops the *psychological principles* to be observed by staff experts. Expressed in industrial language, and exemplified, these principles are as follows:

1. *The staff specialists who propose change must understand that the premises on which they base their proposals are merely products of the culture in which the expert happened to be reared. They are not necessarily universal truths.*

A foreman retires and there is need to appoint a new foreman. The superintendent offers the job to a qualified workman and is shocked when the promotion is declined. In the same way, a scientist may prefer the laboratory to the directorship; a professor may prefer the classroom to the deanship. It is stupid to accuse such men of "no ambition" because they elect to follow a way of life which is preferable to them.

2. *The culture of the line supervisor serves him well by providing him with precedent, practices, and explanations. These things, however unenlightened, have the advantage of predictability and thus assure, to some degree, peace of mind. The more the staff specialist recognizes the real values this culture has for the line supervisor (instead of disparaging it as "ignorance," "stubbornness," "too-old-to-learn," etc.) the better will he be able to prepare his case.*

An accountant worked up a financial report to improve control of the inventory of copper rod. The rolling mill superintendent never read the report. Instead, he continued to rely on two stripes painted on the wall of the storage shed. Years ago he had given the foreman orders to keep the pile of stored rod high enough to cover the lower stripe, but not so high as to cover the upper one. By this method, he was able to review the inventory situation at a glance on his daily trip through the shop. The system had never failed, and the varying price of copper had never bothered him. Had the accountant translated his report into suggested changes in the height of the paint stripes, he might have gotten somewhere.

3. *The staff specialist should examine his proposals from the viewpoint of the line supervisor, since that is what the latter is bound to do anyhow.*

A manufacturing engineer, under pressure to reduce manufacturing costs, concluded, after studying competitors' products, that his own company's specifications were needlessly tight and thus not competitive. He then proposed to the manufacturing vice president that a joint study be undertaken by the manufacturing, sales, and engineering departments to confirm or deny this conclusion. Despite the engineer's evidence, the manufacturing vice president rejected the idea because manufacturing performance was currently under fire from the president. The manufacturing vice president felt that before he could make such a proposal (which could be construed as muddying the water) he would first have to solve some of the more purely manufacturing troubles.

4. *The staff specialist must avoid the temptation to deal with a localized problem through a sweeping master plan which goes far beyond immediate needs. If he urges the sweeping plan, he risks rejection of the entire proposal, including the solution to the localized problem as well.*

A procedures analyst was assigned the job of working up a plan for delegating approval of purchase orders. The company was ready for such a plan, and the analyst put together a good one. However, he succumbed to the temptation of extending it to cover the delegation of authority for approval of capital expenditure projects also. The climate was not right for securing action on the latter. As a result, his plan for purchase orders lost out too.

5. *Unless the line supervisor is genuinely convinced that the change should be made, he is likely to return to his old ways rather than endure the tensions of frustrations brought about by the change.*

A staff quality-control engineer succeeded in convening a meeting of company executives to hear him out. He put on an entertaining, convincing display, using pin-ball machinery, dice games, charts, etc., and aroused a highly favorable reaction among the executives. The plant superintendent honestly didn't understand what the engineer was driving at. However, he was unwilling to get in the way of anything which had so favorably impressed top management. The engineer went to work but, swept away by his own enthusiasm, he spent his energies devising numerous charts which had little relation to the actual problems faced by the shop. The shop faced many real quality troubles which required diagnosis and solution through a variety of remedies. The engineer had only one remedy and was trying to apply it to all the company's troubles. Within two years, the charts had fallen into disuse and the whole program was discredited. All that was left was widespread confusion and irritation in the shop.

The tensions and frustrations brought about by change may lead to a variety of unwelcome consequences:

    (a) Return to former practices, less satisfactory though they are.
    (b) Immature, even childish, behavior.
    (c) General belligerence, verbal attacks, anger.
    (d) Substitute outlets for energies—alcohol, gambling.
    (e) Flight from reality in the form of blaming others, chronic bad health, etc.

A change may make old, valued habits obsolete, may deny what a man has been saying for years. It is not difficult to understand why the UNESCO report approaches frustration as a mental health problem.

What acceptance of change involves

How, then, can technical changes be made acceptable? Logical explanation alone is not the answer, since this is no substitute for the emotional satisfactions of the present order. Criticism of the existing order is even worse. It is an attack on long-standing beliefs and thus an attack on the believer. A staff specialist giving vent to such criticism makes himself disliked and renders himself ineffective no matter how meritorious his proposals may be technically.

Acccepting technical change involves two activities for the learners:

    (a) *Unlearning* old habits, attitudes, beliefs.
    (b) *Learning* the new.

Unlearning the old, a painful process at best, is made easier by clothing the new learning in familiar dress, so that there is no chasm to cross—only small fissures.

For example, a company sold its goods in a market which gave price diffcrentials in favor of "wholesalers" over "retailers." However, the wholesalers' original functions (buying in quantity, and breaking bulk) were no longer being performed. Yet the price differential was being maintained after the reason for it had disappeared. Direct learning of this fact of life was difficult. The company's sales executives found it hard to accept this new situation in actuality, even though they had no answer to the logic. It was necessary to teach them indirectly, by computing their costs of selling to the two kinds of customers. In the same way, the military in World War II had great difficulty in dealing with civilian consultants until the device of "simulated rank" was adopted. In a culture as rank-conscious as the army, this simplified contacts greatly.

Learning the new is encouraged by "consistent, prompt attachment of some form of satisfaction." The forms of satisfaction are familiar enough—praise, approval, increased status, sense of participation, material reward.[5]

Stress is laid on the satisfaction of learning a new skill, of belonging to a particular social group. Moreover, the learning must be by actual doing, by experiencing, by "living through a long series of situations in which the new behavior is made highly satisfying— without exception if possible—and the old not satisfying."

Analyzing the pattern of behavior

"One of the necessary tools of the expert . . . is some way of analyzing the traditional behavior, so as to be able to estimate just where the changes are going to fall, which habits are going to change, which beliefs are going to be threatened, which attitudes will have to be altered." [6]

The analysis of traditional behavior requires a study and an understanding of the customary pattern of life. This study should be long enough in time to include weekends as well as work days. It should be wide enough in scope to embrace activities off the job as well as those on the job. It should disclose not only the activities of individuals when alone, but also the activities of the group.

As this pattern of behavior becomes known, each change under consideration can then be examined as to its likely effect on the pattern.

A company needs to expand the chemical laboratory, and puts up a new building on part of the parking lot. The displaced cars must find parking space on the overcrowded public streets. Men have to leave home earlier to find a place to park. Their wives and children have to adapt themselves to this new routine. New car pools are formed, creating some fresh social groupings, tearing others apart. Wide waves of disturbance begin to spread from so innocent a beginning as the need to relieve the congestion in the chemical laboratory.

Another example can be drawn from a common problem in human relations. A plant industrial engineering staff works up a plan for putting the production workers on piecework. Painstakingly, they debate numerous questions of methods, standards, pay scales. But as

---

[5] Those who place stress on a high material standard of living are due for a shock here. The anthropologists point to many peoples who work only to meet immediate needs, and to many cultures in which the habit of "working," as Western society defines it, is not considered a virtue.

[6] *Op. cit.*, p. 280.

the date for introducing the change approaches, there is a protest from the maintenance trades, who are not even involved. They point out that there has always been a difference in pay between production and maintenance workers; the proposed change will close the traditional gap, and something will have to be done for the maintenance people to retain the old relationship.

Recommendations

Some of the recommendations of the UNESCO report are thoroughly familiar to industry. Others are only occasionally followed, while some are virtually unknown.

1. *Secure the active participation of those who will be affected, both in the planning and in the execution of a change.*

The current wave of interest in industrial "communication" includes this principle.

2. *The planning should include participation not only by the advocates and by those who will be affected; the planning should also include third parties who can supply balance and objectivity.*

As yet, industry has made little use of this idea.

3. *Strip off all technical cultural baggage not strictly needed for introducing the change.*

There have been numerous violations of this principle in industry. An accountant assigned to work up a company training course in cost control may want to "lay a foundation" of general and cost accounting. Personnel people have urged courses in psychology as essential supervisory training background for a company venture into employee testing. The recent insistence of many quality-control specialists on supervisory training courses in statistics, and the current emphasis by operations research specialists on mathematical tools are of the same order. The situation was well summed up by one harassed supervisor: "If education is that painful, I prefer to remain ignorant."

4. *When the long-standing habits of the line are used as a vehicle for introducing change, such use should be planned and applied by a member of the line who is sold on the change.*

This is another way of saying that only the line people know the habits of the line. But involved here is also a useful hint on where the staff leaves off and the line takes up.

5. *Reduce the impact of changes by weaving them into an existing broader pattern of behavior, or by letting them ride in on the back of some acceptable change.*

A company was in customer trouble because of broken delivery promises. When the staff people recommended a more centralized production control function, the departmental production control men argued against the change. Seeing trouble ahead, the staff people made it their business to include in their plan remedies for some long-standing needs of the production control department, such as increased clerical assistance, improved paperwork, and mechanical aids. That did it.

6. *Put yourself in the other fellow's place.*

Any individual derives his attitude toward change from *his own* point of view, not from the view of the proponent of change.

An American visiting in England proposed to a British firm of silversmiths that they explore getting around the American import duty on finished silverware by bringing American-owned silver into England, performing their operations, and shipping the finished goods back duty-free. The immediate reaction of the British firm was to reject the idea. The rejection had nothing to do with import technicalities; it was based on the fact that in England a silversmith company that works on silver it does not own occupies a much lower social status than a company that owns the silver it fabricates. (A similar caste distinction prevails in American industry generally, as between prime contractor and subcontractor, or between manufacturing companies and manufacturing service companies.)

It is when the proponent of change runs into seeming blind opposition (you gotta have north light; the blue grinding wheels cut better; we tried plastic handles years ago and they didn't work, etc.) that he must move most cautiously. "Blind opposition" is how it looks to the staff man. It may only mean that the staff man has failed to grasp the situation as viewed by the line.

7. *Make use of the wide variety of methods available for dealing with resistance to change.*

There are many ways of overcoming resistance to change. You may:

(a) Try persuasion to secure change. Much depends here on the extent of prior participation and on the extent to which the individual is *treated with dignity.*

In one company, an important executive was in the habit of using new ideas, especially those suggested by employees, as a basis for taunting supervisors with the question. "How is it that you didn't think of this during all these years?" The result was a "freeze" by supervisors to all proposals for change, employee suggestions or otherwise.

Then someone went to work on the important executive and convinced him that he was doing a lot of damage. He revised his policy and began to "accentuate the positive," holding up as good examples those supervisors who showed improvements through change. Within a year, the supervisory freeze had fully thawed out.

(b) Change the environment in a way which makes it easy for the individual to change his point of view.

Company X contemplated putting up a new hosiery mill in a Southern community. Conditions were generally favorable. However, the past record of industrial companies in the community had been unenlightened. In consequence, factory work was low in the social scale, and candidates for factory work contained a high percentage of undesirables.

The company not only put up a modern air-conditioned factory building; they provided a handsome recreation room and permitted employees to use it out of hours for social events. Because this recreation room was the best facility of its kind in the area, it became an important social center in the community. The employees of Company X, far from being under the social stigma of factory workers, were looked up to because of the high standing which the company had earned in the community. As a result, Company X enjoyed a wide choice of candidates for employment.

(c) Remedy the causes of the line man's resistance.

In the early days of the study of industrial accidents, injuries caused by dropping something on the foot stood high on the list. The safety shoe was developed as a protective device. Safety directors had ample data and logic on their side to demonstrate the value of the shoes. Yet workmen turned them down, primarily because of their strange appearance. When the safety shoe was redesigned so that it looked much like a dress shoe, worker acceptance increased markedly.

(d) Create a social climate which favors the new habits.

A familiar example is the stimulation of patriotic feeling during a war. In industry, it may be observed when group incentives replace individual incentives. The machinist no longer stands by waiting for the craneman to finish; he is now willing to help the craneman who, for his part, is now less likely to enforce jurisdictional boundaries. A similar situation develops between functional divisions when a company decentralizes into product divisions. A new spirit of collaboration arises because the social climate demands it.

This social climate includes specific recognition, e.g., service pins, which bestow dignity and status on career employees. The awards for safety, housekeeping, etc., fall into the same category.

(e) Provide sufficient *time* for mental changes to take place.

This vital rule is often violated and needlessly. There are numerous ways of applying it. For example, in suggesting changes, propose distant effective dates to allow time for all to become familiar with the idea before being subject to the change itself. If a proposed change is rejected, let some time pass before bringing the subject up again.

The importance of *time as an ingredient of change* is well known to the chemist, the politician, and many others. The industrial staff man needs to grasp this principle firmly.

(f) Start small and keep it fluid.

To protect both the staff and line man, the unexpected should be provided for. Change should be introduced slowly and gradually, so that, if necessary, the original plan may be modified as experience dictates.

Industry uses this principle extensively. The pilot plant, the test town, the trial period are all means of trying out on a small scale, and of learning at little risk, before taking the big plunge.

8. *No surprises.*

One of the main reasons why a culture develops is that it makes life predictable. It is true that even an established culture includes patterns of change, e.g., progression from apprentice to journeyman, the annual model, periodic collective bargaining. But the type and pace of these changes are also predictable in the established culture.

It is the unexpected change—the one that defies explanation— which breeds chaos, and drives the individual to find a way to relieve his tension.

This rule of no surprise is closely related to the rule of providing enough time for mental changes to take place.

9. *Provide a measure of effectiveness.*

The success with which a change has been introduced is measured by the extent to which it is accepted as part of the way of life of the people who are affected by it. To measure the extent of acceptance, and to reduce the risk of relapsing into the old ways, standards should be set up. These can be a goal to the line, and enable it to judge progress.

While industry often provides for the measurement of results (cost, quality, service) it does little to provide for measuring the rate at which changes are accepted, and the permanence of this acceptance.

10. *Treat people with dignity.*

Technical change may appear to be concerned solely with things. However, technical change has much impact on people, whose dignity as persons must be respected.

The classic example in industrial history is the Hawthorne experiments. A test room was created to study the effect of illumination on factory work. The assemblers in the test room considerably outperformed the assemblers in the regular department. However, no reason for this could be found in the variation in illumination. The superior performance of the handful of test-room operators was found to stem from the new sense of importance they felt.

Conclusion

The UNESCO experiences make it clear that cultural patterns are a vital factor in resistance to technical change, and that there are established ways for the technical expert to deal successfully with these cultural patterns.

These same experiences and solutions have direct application to the industrial problems of the staff and line relationship. In fact, the universal nature of the principles involved suggests their adoption as training material for business schools, executive training programs, and company training programs generally.

Questions

1. Concerning the concept of change, what, according to Juran, is the relationship between line and staff people?
2. What part do cultural patterns play in resistance to change?
3. What principles should staff specialists observe when introducing change?
4. What does acceptance of technical change involve?
5. State and discuss the recommendations of the UNESCO report. Do you agree with these recommendations?

STUDYING AND CREATING CHANGE:
A MEANS TO UNDERSTANDING
SOCIAL ORGANIZATION *

Floyd C. Mann [1]

Social organizations are functioning entities with interdependent structures and processes. They are not fixed, static structures, but rather continuously moving patterns of relationships in a much larger field of social activity. To understand what their essential elements and dimensions are, what it is that gives an organization its unity, it is necessary to study and create social change within organizational settings.

Relatively little is known about organizational change. Social scientists stress the study of the dynamic in social systems, but few [2] accept the risks involved to gain the knowledge and skills needed to create and measure changes in functioning organizations. This is not surprising, for research within large-scale organizations is at such an early stage that the social scientist knows little about how (1) to gain access to these research sites, (2) to initiate and sustain organizational change, and (3) to measure such changes. We have only begun the systematic codification of the working knowledge and skills necessary for the researcher to get into, and maintain himself within, the social science laboratories of functioning organizations. [3] Systematic, quantitative measurement of change processes in complex organizational settings is in its infancy. Longitudinal studies are rare—social scientists seldom attempt to obtain more than a single "before" and "after" measurement and are often content to try and decipher findings from *ex post facto* study designs. The actual steps and skills necessary to initiate and sustain changes within an organization are not only relatively unknown, but there is even some suspicion that knowledge of social action and an ability to engineer change are not appropriate for the social scientist.

* From *Research in Industrial Human Relations*, ed. Arensberg *et al.* (New York: Harper & Brothers, 1957), Chapter X, pp. 146-167. Reprinted with permission.

[1] Drs. Rensis Likert, Daniel Katz, Robert Kahn, and Norman R. F. Maier have made especially helpful suggestions concerning the organization and presentation of this material. They can, of course, in no way be held responsible for the shortcomings which remain.

[2] For an account of a conspicuous exception to this, see N. C. Mare and E. Reimer, "The Experimental Manipulation of a Major Organizational Variable," in *Journal of Abnormal and Social Psychology* (1956).

[3] F. Mann and R. Lippitt, eds., "Social Relations Skills in Field Research," *Journal of Social Issues*, Vol. 8, No. 3, 1952.

While social scientists are not spending any sizable proportion of their time in learning how to change interpersonal and intergroup relations in functioning organizations, a wide variety of practitioners are. These include at the one extreme the consultants or the "operators" who take over organizations which are failing and rebuild them, and at the other extreme, the "human relations" trainers. Most of these men know very little theoretically about processes of organizational, attitudinal, and behavioral change, but they do know a great deal intuitively about the problems of changing people in an organization. This is especially true of the training men.

This suggests that there should and can be a closer working relationship between those concerned with actually *changing* organizational structure and processes and those researchers concerned with *understanding* organizational change. Social scientists have not begun to take advantage of their opportunities for learning about organizations from those in the "practicing professions"—those who are *doing*.[4] Observations and systematic measurements around the practitioner's efforts to alter systems of relationships in organizations can provide the researcher with valuable insights into the dynamics of organization. Gaps in knowledge become excruciatingly apparent; new sources of data and problems for research emerge. In turn, social scientists can contribute to practitioners by helping them assess what effect their actions as change agents have. Most practitioners—and especially those trainers who are concerned with changing the human relations skills of supervisors—have very little systematic, and no quantitative, evidence on the success of their efforts to create changes in individuals or organizations. It seems clear that there is a broad basis for cooperation here. Systematic studies of the work of those attempting to change the way things are done in an organization may contribute to our understanding of social organizations. And developments in measurement and the procedures used by researchers to understand organizations better may contribute to the working knowledge of trainers and others in the "practicing professions."

In this chapter we will focus on the description and evaluation of several different types of procedures designed to change interpersonal and intergroup relations in complex organizations. We will first look at two human relations training programs whose effects have been systematically and quantitatively studied. Then we will

---

[4] Donald Young, "Sociology and the Practicing Professions," *American Sociological Review*, Vol. 20 (December, 1955), pp. 641-648.

describe briefly the development and evaluation of a change procedure with which we are experimenting to increase the understanding,
acceptance, and utilization of survey research findings. At the close
of the chapter these two specific types of procedures for creating
change in organizational settings are contrasted as a first step in
identifying facets of change processes which merit greater experimentation and in providing insights into the structure and functioning of organizations.

CHANGING INTERPERSONAL RELATIONS THROUGH TRAINING SUPERVISORS

Recurrent opportunities for social scientists to study a change
process within an organizational setting are provided by human
relations training programs for supervisors. As change procedures,
these programs are formal, rational, purposeful efforts to alter institutional behavior. In contrast to the day-to-day attempts of management to bring about change, they are bounded in time and
organizational space, and are thus easily studied intensively.

Because of the several historical developments described in
Chapters I, II, and XIII, management by the late forties began to
be convinced that training might be useful for their supervisors, and
there has since been a wholesale adoption of human relations training programs. While there was and still is a remarkable range in
the content, methods, and settings of these programs, nearly all of
them have centered around improving supervisory skills in dealing
with people—either as individuals or in face-to-face groups. They
are frequently directed at teaching the supervisor how to work with
an employee as an individual, occasionally at working with employees as members of a small group, but only rarely at understanding
and working within the complex social system of the large corporation or factory. Another way of saying this is that the courses
have drawn heavily from psychology, to a lesser extent from social
psychology, and usually not at all from sociology.

There are no commonly agreed-upon ways by which these programs can be described. The following headings are, however, useful: objectives, content, methods, setting, training leader, and
training unit. For example, the objectives of these programs are
usually very general and quite ambitious: "to assist supervisors in
developing the skills, knowledge, and attitudes needed to carry out
their supervisory responsibilities," or "to improve morale, increase
production, and reduce turnover." Their contents usually include
human nature, personality, motivation, attitudes, and leadership, and

other information about relevant psychological principles and research findings may also be included. More often than not the methods of training are some variant of the "lecture-discussion method." The settings are frequently in a classroom away from the job. The trainers are generally staff men whom the trainee did not know before the training; the trainees, first-line supervisors or foremen meeting with other supervisors from other parts of the organization.

Few systematic, quantitative studies have been made to investigate the effectiveness of these programs.[5] This is not to say that there has been no interest in evaluation. Any review of the literature will indicate many such attempts and many testimonials about the relative advantages of different procedures of training. Mahler and Monroe [6] reported a number of "evaluative studies" after reviewing the literature and conducting a survey of 150 companies known to have training programs. While these studies almost without fail acclaim the many benefits of such training, few of them meet more than a fraction of the requirements necessary for a rigorous test of the basic underlying assumptions.

What are these assumptions? In general, they are that training supervisors in human relations will result in changes in the supervisors' attitudes and philosophy, that these changes will be reflected in their behavior toward employees on the job, that this changed behavior will be seen by the employees, and that they will in turn become more satisfied with their work situation, then more highly motivated, and, ultimately, more productive workers.

While there is a good deal of evidence that human relations training programs do meet part of these assumptions—e.g., they do appear to change the verbal veneer of supervisors—there are few scientifically rigorous, quantitative studies which have demonstrated that these changes in what supervisors *know* affect their attitudes and behavior as seen or experienced by their subordinates. Few studies show that human relations training of supervisors is related to changes in the attitudes or productivity of employees under those supervisors.

---

[5] A nonquantitative, but extraordinarily thorough and insightful study of foreman training was made by A. Zalenznik, *Foreman Training in a Growing Enterprise* (Boston: Graduate School of Business Administration, Harvard University, 1951).

[6] W. R. Mahler and W. H. Monroe, *How Industry Determines the Need for and Effectiveness of Training*, Personnel Research Section Report 929 (Washington: Department of the Army, 1952).

It is not possible to make a complete review of these studies here.
A review of the findings from several recent, major evaluative studies
will, however, provide a good deal of evidence concerning the effectiveness of certain types of training programs. The findings will certainly emphasize the need for more systematic, quantitative research
to assess the most effective combinations of content, methods, settings, training units, and trainers.

The Canter-Tyler studies

In 1949, Canter [7] developed a human relations training course for
first-line supervisors in the home offices of a large insurance company. The three objectives of the course were "(1) to establish facts
and principles concerning psychological aspects of behavior and
group functioning to enable supervisors to become more competent
in their knowledge and understanding of human behavior; (2) to
increase supervisors' capacities for observing human behavior; and
(3) to present personality adjustment concepts to aid in integration
of achievements made in the first two objectives." This training was
designed to provide a foundation of information on which to build
later through additional practice and "technique" training. Specific
content was primarily psychological: human nature, personality,
motivation, attitudes, leadership, and group structure. Method was
lecture-discussion. The training occurred in the conference rooms
of the company; Canter himself was the trainer. The trainees were
eighteen supervisors whose superiors had participated in a preliminary run for executives. The course was presented in ten two-hour
weekly sessions.

To determine the influence of this training, Canter employed a
battery of paper-and-pencil questionnaires and tests which were
given before and after training to two groups of supervisors: an
experimental group of eighteen from one department who received
the training, and a control group of eighteen from two other departments who did not receive training. The two groups were similar in
type of work performed, age (about thirty), education (thirteen
years), and proportion of men and women. While the control group
had more years of service with the company (7.5 and 4.6, respec-
tively) and higher mean scores on a mental alertness test, the statistical technique used in the final analysis did not require prematched
individuals or groups.

---

[7] R. R. Canter, "A Human Relations Training Program," *Journal of Applied
Psychology*, Vol. 35 (February, 1951), pp. 38-45.

Six tests, yielding a total of twelve separate scores, were used. (1) General Psychological Facts and Principles; (2) "How Supervise"; (3) General Logical Reasoning; (4) Social Judgment Test; (5) Supervisory Questionnaire; and (6) Test for Ability to Estimate Group Opinion. The major findings were that the trained supervisors obtained mean scores on all tests better than would have been predicted on the basis of the performance of the untrained group alone. For five out of the twelve measures, the differences were statistically significant at the 5 per cent level; for two other measures, differences were significant at the 10 per cent level. Other important conclusions were that trained supervisors became more similar in abilities measured by the tests and more accurate in estimating the opinions of employees in their departments, but not their sections. It was also found that those holding highest scores initially gained the most on all measures except the Test of Ability to Estimate Group Opinion, where the opposite result was obtained.

While Canter assumed in his design that cognitive training—i.e., an ability to understand human relations concepts and principles— would have to precede any behavioral training in supervisory skills, practices, and attitudes, Tyler [8] designed a companion study to measure any changes in employee morale which might be attributed to this training. Her morale surveys indicated improvement in employee morale scores for *both* the experimental and control departments. Morale improved by an average of 11 points per section (range 2-25 points) in five of seven sections in the experimental group, and decreased slightly in two others. "In the control groups, morale increased in eight of the nine sections by an average of 14 points (range 5-32 points). The decrease in the other section was seven points. The only category which showed a somewhat consistent change among sections was 'supervision' on which scores for over half of the sections decreased." After warning the reader of the possible effect of the before-test experience, she notes: "Undoubtedly, the difference in change in morale between the control and the experimental groups is not large enough to be significant" (page 47). Canter, however, points out that in Tyler's study "morale was quite high initially, which might account for the lack of any improvement in the experimental department over the control."

The strength of the Canter-Tyler studies is that they used both *before* and *after* measures for experimental and control groups.

[8] B. B. Tyler, "A Study of Factors Contributing to Employee Morale" (Master's thesis, Ohio State University, 1949).

Canter's use of multiple criteria against which to evaluate the various sub-goals of the training program is also noteworthy. The use of Tyler's perceptual and employee morale measures in conjunction with Canter's attitudinal and cognitive measures permits an evaluation of the course's effectiveness at two levels: the supervisor's intent, and his on-the-job performance. The findings from this combination of studies make it obvious that classroom learning does not guarantee the translation of such learning into job performance. It should be remembered, however, that Canter did not set out to change supervisors' skills and practices, but only their understanding of human relations concepts and ideas.

Fleishman-Harris studies

Working with the education and training staff of a large company manufacturing trucks and farm machinery, Fleishman [9] developed a study design and a battery of research instruments for measuring the continuing effectiveness of leadership training. The general objectives of this training [10] were to change understanding, attitudes, habits, and skills of foremen by giving them solid foundation in four basic areas of industrial knowledge. These areas were personal development, human relations, economics, and company operations. The method was primarily lecture-discussion. The training staff included full-time instructors, former supervisors, and part-time university faculty. The training was given to foremen who were taken from a wide variety of operations and plants and sent to a central school in Chicago for two weeks of eight-hours-a-day intensive development.

To determine the effects of this course on foremen from one motor-truck plant who had taken this training, Fleishman employed an *ex post facto* design with four groups of about thirty each. One group had not received the training; the other three had, 2-10 11-19, and 20-29 months earlier. The groups were alike on a number of background characteristics: age (early forties), education (eleven years), length of service (sixteen years), supervisory experience (seven years), size of work group (about twenty-eight), and supervisory experience with present work group (six years). Seven paper-and-pencil questionnaires were used to obtain opinion, expectation, and perceptual data about leadership practices from the trainees,

---

[9] Edwin A. Fleishman, "Leadership Climate, Human Relations Training, and Supervisory Behavior," *Personnel Psychology*, Vol. 6 (Summer, 1953), pp. 205-222.

[10] Charles L. Walker, Jr., "Education and Training at International Harvester," *Havard Business Review*, Vol. 27 (September, 1949), pp. 542-558.

their superiors, and their subordinates. This battery gave Fleishman an opportunity to investigate the differences between supervisory beliefs as reported by the foreman himself and supervisory practices as reported by his employees, and to explore the interaction of training effects with the supervisor's "leadership climate." Each questionnaire contained two independent leadership dimensions which had been identified by factor analysis: "consideration"—the extent to which the supervisor was considerate of the feelings of employees; and "initiating structure"—the extent to which the supervisor defined or facilitated group interactions toward goal attainment.

The results obtained by giving attitude questionnaires to foremen on the first and last days of their training in Chicago provide evidence of how the topics stressed in this leadership training affected these two dimensions. The results obtained from these before and after measures showed a significant increase in "consideration" (.05 level) and an even more marked decrease in "initiating structure" (.01 level). The on-the-job effects of the training, however, appeared to be "minimal." "The training did not produce any kind of permanent change in either the attitudes or behavior of the trained foremen." The employees under the most recently trained foremen actually saw them as *less* considerate than the employees under the untrained foremen saw their superiors. This statistically significant finding was supported by other trends toward more structuring and less consideration by those foremen who had the training. Thus, while the human relations approach was stressed in the course and understood at least well enough to be registered as an opinion change on a paper-and-pencil questionnaire, it was not evident in what trained foremen said they did, or what their employees saw them doing in the actual work situation.

The most important variable found to affect leadership was the climate within which the foreman worked. In fact, the kind of superior under whom the foreman operated seemed "more related to the attitudes and behavior of the foremen in the plant than did the fact that they had or had not received the leadership training."

These results, showing that the training was not meeting its objective of making foremen more human-relations oriented in the plant, left two alternatives open: redesign the course, or initiate an intensive criterion study relating supervisory behavior to group effectiveness. The latter alternative was chosen, and Harris [11] de-

---

[11] E. F. Harris, "Measuring Industrial Leadership and Its Implications for Training Supervisors" (Doctoral thesis, Ohio State University, 1952).

signed a study in the same plant to investigate (1) the relationship between these two dimensions of leadership behavior and various measures of work efficiency, and (2) the effects of a training course planned as a brief refresher for the central school training in Chicago. It is the findings from this second objective in which we are primarily interested here.

The course, lasting one week, was given at a small nearby college. The effects were evaluated by field experimental design with before and after measures for experimental and control groups. Two groups of thirty-one foremen were established through matching on a number of variables, including length of time since attending the central school (almost three years), scores on before measures (including leadership climate), and other personal factors. One group was given the training. Questionnaires, similar to Fleishman's, were used to obtain information from employees and foremen about the foremen's attitudes and behavior.

Harris used several different methods of analyzing his findings. His most rigorous method indicated there were no statistically significant differences in the foremen's own leadership attitudes or the workers' descriptions of their foremen's behavior—before and after this additional refresher course. The only significant difference he found was a decrease in the degree to which the foremen in the *control* group showed structuring in their leadership behavior as described by their employees. Building on Fleishman's gradual decreases in structuring and increases in consideration the longer the foreman is back on the job, Harris suggests this finding might be interpreted to mean that the refresher course may have "tended to retard a general decrease in structuring."

Harris and Fleishman [12] in analyzing the data from both of their studies in the same plant have uncovered one finding which tends to qualify the general, completely negative conclusion of their findings regarding the effectiveness of this training. This finding concerns the stability of leadership patterns of individual foremen who did not have the training in contrast to those foremen who had the training. They find there is *less* stability in the pre-post measures for the foremen who had the training than for those foremen who did not have training. This suggests that the courses had markedly different effects on different foremen, and that "large individual

---

[12] E. F. Harris and E. A. Fleishman, "Human Relations Training and the Stability of Leadership Patterns," *Journal of Applied Psychology*, Vol. 39 (February, 1955), pp. 20-25.

shifts in scores occur in both directions." They conclude that their research findings show no significant changes in *group* means among trained foremen and that future research should be directed toward investigating personal and situational variables which interact with the effects of training.

At best, these two studies suggest that this type of training has little or no general effect on the behavior of foremen in the plant. At worst, they suggest that the unanticipated consequences of separating foremen from their work groups and making them keenly aware of their role in management more than offset the anticipated consequences of making the foremen more considerate of employees as human beings. Fleishman's finding that *leadership climate* appeared to be a better predictor than *training* of foremen's plant attitudes and behavior underscores the importance of considering the constellation of expectation patterns in which the trainee is embedded. Training which does not take the trainee's regular social environment into account will probably have little chance of modifying behavior. It may very well be that human relations training—as a procedure for initiating social change—is most successful when it is designed to *remold the whole system of role relationships of the supervisor.*[13]

The findings from these four studies suggest that trainers, researchers, and others interested in social change need to rethink what forces are necessary to create and sustain changes in the orientation and behaviors of people in complex systems of relationships. There is a good deal of evidence that management and trainees are enthusiastic about these training courses in general. Management's enthusiasm may be an index of whether the training will continue, but it does not indicate whether training is achieving changes in behavior. And while trainee satisfaction and acceptance may be important as an antecedent to learning, these factors do not indicate whether the training will produce attitudinal and, more significantly, on-the-job behavioral changes.

It should be stressed that the criterion which has been used here for measuring the effects of human relations training is not easily met. There is ample quantitative evidence in the preceding studies that supervisors' information about, and verbal understanding of, human relations principles can be increased. There is much less evi-

---

[13] For a full account of these two studies combined, see E. A Fleishman, E. F. Harris, and H. E. Buntt, *Leadership and Supervision in Industry* (Columbus: Personnel Research Board, Ohio State University, 1955).

dence that these courses have an effect on the trainee's on-the-job behavior as seen by those working under him. And the hard fact remains that there are no quantitative studies which indicate that these courses in leadership affect workers' job satisfactions or motivations.

FEEDBACK: CHANGING PATTERNS OF RELATIONSHIPS BETWEEN SUPERIORS AND SUBORDINATES BY USING SURVEY FINDINGS

Long-range interest in the actual varying of significant variables in organizations has necessitated that members of the Human Relations Program of the Institute for Social Research, University of Michigan, not only study existing programs for training and changing people in organizations, but that we *develop* new techniques for changing relationships, and that we learn how to *measure* the effects of such changes within organizations. As a result, we have invested a good deal of professional effort in exploring the effectiveness of different procedures for changing attitudes, perceptions, and relationships among individuals in complex hierarchies without changing the personnel of the units. The latter is an important qualification, for we have found that the changes in subordinates' perceptions and attitudes which follow a change in supervisory personnel are frequently of a much larger order than those generated by training or other procedures for changing the attitudes or behavior of incumbents.

Exploratory and developmental phase

One procedure which we developed and subsequently found to be effective in changing perceptions and relationships within organizations has been called "feedback." This change process evolved over a period of years as we [14] tried to learn how to report findings from human relations research into organizations so that they would be understood and used in day-to-day operations. Work began on this process in 1948 following a company-wide study of employee and management attitudes and opinions. Over a period of two years, three different sets of data were fed back: (1) information on the attitudes and perceptions of 8,000 nonsupervisory employees toward their work, promotion opportunities, supervision, fellow employees,

---

[14] A number of people contributed to the design of this feedback process during its developmental phase. They included Sylvester Leahy, Blair Swartz, Robert Schwab, and John Sparling from the Detroit Edison Company, and Rensis Likert, Daniel Katz, Everett Riemer, Frances Fielder, and Theodore Hariton from the Survey Research Center.

etc.; (2) first- and second-line supervisor's feelings about the various aspects of their jobs and supervisory beliefs; and (3) information from intermediate and top levels of management about their supervisory philosophies, roles in policy formation, problems of organizational integration, etc. We had several aims in this exploratory phase: (1) to develop through first-hand experience an understanding of the problems of producing change; (2) to improve relationships; (3) to identify factors which affected the extent of the change; and (4) to develop working hypotheses for later, more directed research.

The process which finally appeared to maximize the acceptance and utilization of survey and research findings can be described structurally as an interlocking chain of conferences. It began with a report of the major findings of the survey to the president and his senior officers, and then progressed slowly down through the hierarchical levels along functional lines to where supervisors and their employees were discussing the data. These meetings were structured in terms of organizational "families" [15] or units—each superior and his immediate subordinates considering the survey data together. The data presented to each group were those pertaining to their own group or for those subunits for which members of the organizational unit were responsible.

Members of each group were asked to help interpret the data and then decide what further analyses of the data should be made to aid them in formulating plans for constructive administrative actions. They also planned the introduction of the findings to the next level. The meetings were typically led by the line officer responsible for the coordination of the subunits at a particular level. Usually, a member of the Survey Research Center and the company's personnel staff assisted the line officer in preparing for these meetings, but attended the meetings only as resource people who could be called upon for information about the feasibility of additional analyses.

These meetings took place in the office of the line supervisor whose organizational unit was meeting, or in the department's own small conference room. All of the survey findings relative to each group were given to the leader and the members of his organizational unit; they decided what to consider first, how fast to work through each topic, and when they had gone as far as they could and needed to involve the next echelon in the process.

---

[15] F. Mann and J. Dent, "The Supervisor: Member of Two Organizational Families," *Harvard Business Review*, Vol. 32 (November-December, 1954), pp. 103-112.

This feedback change procedure was developed in an organization where a great amount of effort had already been invested in the training of management and supervisors. During the war the company had participated in the various J-programs sponsored by the War Manpower Commission, and more important, during the several years we were experimentally developing the feedback process, Dr. Norman R. F. Maier was working with all levels of management to improve their understanding of human relations and supervision.[16] The supervisors with whom we were working to increase their understanding of their own organizational units therefore had a great deal of training in the application of psychological principles to management.

Our observations of the feedback procedure as it developed suggested that it was a powerful process for creating and supporting changes within an organization.[17] However, there was no quantitative proof of this, for our work up to this point had been exploratory and developmental.

A field experiment in accounting departments

In 1950, when eight accounting departments in this same company asked for a second attitude and opinion survey of their seventy-eight supervisors and eight hundred employees, we [18] had an opportunity to initiate the steps necessary to measure the effects of this organizational change process. The questionnaires used in this resurvey were similar to those used in 1948 and provided the basis for a new cycle of feedback conferences. The general plan for the handling of these new resurvey data was to let everyone in the departments—employees and department heads—see the over-all findings for eight accounting departments combined as soon as they were available, and then to work intensively on their use in *some* departments, but not in others until there had been a third survey.

While our objective was to test the effectiveness of the basic pattern of feedback developed during the preceding two years, we encouraged department heads and their supervisors to develop their own variations for reporting data to their units and maximizing their use in the solution of problems. After the all-department meetings

---

[16] For a thorough description of this training, see N. R. F. Maier, *Principles of Human Relations* (New York: Wiley, 1952).

[17] F. Mann and R. Likert, "The Need for Research on Communicating Research Results," *Human Organization*, Vol. 11 (Winter, 1952), pp. 15-19.

[18] F. Mann and H. Baumgartel, *Survey Feedback Experiment: An Evaluation of a Program for the Utilization of Survey Findings*, monograph in preparation, Survey Research Center, University of Michigan.

had been concluded, the chief executive of the accounting departments held a meeting with each department head in the experimental
group. At this meeting, the findings for the department head's unit
were thoroughly reviewed. The findings included comparisons of
(1) changes in employee attitudes from 1948 to 1950, (2) attitudes
in that department with those in all other departments combined,
and (3) employees' perceptions of supervisory behavior with supervisory statements about their behavior. Department heads were
encouraged to go ahead with feedback meetings as soon as they felt
ready, tentative next steps were discussed, and assistance from the
researchers and the company personnel staffs was assured. Four
departments launched feedback activities which were similar to each
other in purpose but somewhat different in method. The programs
varied in duration (13-33 weeks), in intensity (9-65 meetings), and
in the extent to which nonsupervisory employees were involved in
the process. During the eighteen months that these differences were
unfolding, nothing was done in two of the remaining four departments after the first all-departments meetings. This was done so
they might be available as "controls." Changes in key personnel
eliminated the remaining two departments from any experimental
design.

A third survey of attitudes was conducted in these departments
in 1952 after the natural variations in the feedback programs had
run their courses. In 1950 and 1952 surveys were then used as
"before" and "after" measurements, the four departmental programs
as "experimental variations," with the two inactive departments as
"controls."

Our findings indicate that more significant positive changes occurred in employee attitudes and perceptions in the four experimental departments than in the two control departments. This was
based on two measures of change: (1) a comparison of answers
to sixty-one identical questions which were asked in 1950 and 1952,
and (2) of a comparison of answers to seventeen "perceived change"
questions in which employees had an opportunity to indicate what
types of changes had occurred since the 1950 survey. In the experimental group, a fourth of the sixty-one items showed relative mean
positive changes, significant at the .05 level or better; the change for
another 57 per cent of the items was also positive in direction, but
not statistically significant. Major positive changes occurred in the
experimental groups in how employees felt about (1) the kind of
work they do (job interest, importance, and level of responsibility);
(2) their supervisor (his ability to handle people, give recognition,

direct their work, and represent them in handling complaints) ; (3) their progress in the company; and (4) their group's ability to get the job done. The seventeen perceived-change items were designed specifically to measure changes in the areas where we expected the greatest shift in perceptions. Fifteen of these showed that a significantly higher proportion of employees in the experimental than in the control departments felt that change had occurred. More employees in the experimental departments saw changes in (1) how well the supervisors in their department got along together; (2) how often their supervisors held meetings; (3) how effective these meetings were; (4) how much their supervisor understood the way employees looked at and felt about things, etc. These indicate the extent to which the feedback's effectiveness lay in increasing understanding and communication as well as changing supervisory behavior.

Comparisons of the changes among the four experimental departments showed that the three departments which had the two feedback sessions with their employees all showed positive change relative to the control departments. The change which occurred in the fourth was directionally positive, but it was not significantly different from the control departments. In general, the greatest change occurred where the survey results were discussed in both the departmental organizational units *and* the first-line organizational units. The greater the involvement of all members of the organization through their organizational families—the department heads, the first-line supervisors, *and* the employees—the greater the change.

Implications of these findings

The basic elements of this feedback process described above are not new. They involve (1) the orderly collection of information about the functioning of a system, and (2) the reporting of this information into the system for (3) its use in making further adjustments.

Work by Hall [19] and others who have had considerable practical experience with the use of information about a system for creating change show a similarity in both action steps and basic approach. This suggests there are certain psychological and sociological facts which must be taken into consideration in attempting to change

[19] Milton Hall, "Supervising People—Closing the Gap Between What We Think and What We Do," *Advanced Management*, Vol. 12 (September, 1947), pp. 129-135.

the attitudes and behavior of an *individual* or a *group of individuals* in an *organizational setting.*

1. Attitudes and behavior of an individual are functions of both basic personality and social role. *Change processes need to be concerned with altering both the forces within* an individual and the forces in the *organizational situation* surrounding the individual.

2. Organizations, as systems of hierarchically ordered, interlocking roles with rights and privileges, reciprocal expectations, and shared frames of reference, contain tremendous forces for stability or change in the behavior of individuals or subgroups. Change processes need to be designed to harness these forces for creating and supporting change. *As forces already in existence, they must first be made pliable, then altered or shifted, and finally made stable again to support the change.*

3. Essentially, unilateral power and authority structures underlie the hierarchical ordering of organizational roles. *Expectations of the superior are therefore more important forces for creating change in an individual than the expectations of his subordinates.* Also, those with a direct authority relationship—line superiors—have more influence than those without direct authority—staff trainers.

4. The attitudes, beliefs, and values of an individual are more firmly grounded in the groups which have continuing psychological meaning to him than in those where he has only temporary membership. The supervisor's role of interlocking the activities of two organizational units requires that he have continuing membership in two groups: (a) the organizational unit directed by his superior in which he is a subordinate along with his immediate peers; and (b) the organizational unit for which he is responsible. *Change processes designed to work with individual supervisors off the job in temporarily created training groups contain less force for initiating and reinforcing change than those which work with an individual in situ.*

5. Information about the functioning of a system may introduce a need for change. This is especially true when the new data are seen as objective and at variance with common perceptions and expectations. Change processes organized around objective, new social facts about one's own organizational situation have more force for change than those organized around general principles about human behavior. *The more meaningful and relevant the material, the greater the likelihood of change.*

6. Involvement and participation in the planning, collection, analysis, and interpretation of information initiate powerful forces for change. Own facts are better understood, more emotionally acceptable, and more likely to be utilized than those of some "outside expert." *Participation in analysis and interpretation helps by-pass those resistances which arise from proceeding too rapidly or too slowly.*

7. Objective information on direction and magnitude of change—knowledge of results—facilitates further improvement. *Change processes which furnish adequate knowledge on progress and specify criteria against which to measure improvement are apt to be more successful in creating and maintaining change than those which do not.*

Comparison of "Classroom" Human Relations Training and Organizational Feedback

This is only a partial listing of the points with which a scientifically based technology of social change in organizational settings will have to be concerned. Our conceptualization and the identification of the relevant individual and organizational variables and their interrelationship is at a primitive stage. The systematic quantitative investigation of the effectiveness of different change procedures has scarcely begun. Even at this early date, however, a comparison between the structure and process of feedback and "classroom" human relations training as two different types of change procedures may be a useful exercise. It may help identify variables or facets of change processes which merit greater experimentation and investigation both by the practitioners and by those researchers interested in organizational change. By a "classroom" human relations program we mean a training which would consist of a series of classroom-like meetings in which supervisors from many different points of the organization meet to listen to a presentation of psychological principles which a trainer from the personnel department thinks they ought to know about and be ready to use on the job after a brief discussion following the training. This kind of training experience differs from the feedback process in a number of respects. These differences are stated to keep the comparisons reasonably brief and to sharpen the contrasts.

1. What are the objectives?

"Classroom" Training—Improve supervisor-subordinate relations through changing the supervisors' understanding of human behavior, attitudes, and skills.

Organizational Feedback—Improve organizational functioning through changing understanding, attitudes, and behavior among all members of the organization.

2. What is the setting in which change is being attempted?

"Classroom" Training—Trainees are taken off the job and out of the network of interpersonal relationships in which they normally function for training in an "encapsulated" [20] classroom-like situation.

Organizational Feedback—Change is attempted as a regular part of the day's work in established organizational relationships.

3. What is the informational content?

"Classroom" Training—General psychological principles of human behavior, case materials, or data from outside the training group and

---

[20] M. Haire, "Some Problems of Industrial Training," *Journal of Social Issues*, Vol. 4, No. 3 (1948), pp. 41-47.

often the organization, only occasionally using problems from the group's own experience.

Organizational Feedback—Objective quantitative information about attitudes, beliefs, and expectations of the trainees themselves, or the subordinates in their own organization.

4. What is the method?

"Classroom" Training—Lectures, presentations, films, skits, and occasionally role-playing followed by discussion on how to apply what has been learned back on the job.

Organizational Feedback—The progressive introduction of new information about the problems within the groups for which the trainees are responsible. Group discussions of the meaning and action implications of the findings, followed by group decisions on next steps for changing or handling the situation.

5. Who are the trainees?

"Classroom" Training—First-line supervisors and foremen whose superiors may have, but more often have not, had the course.

Organizational Feedback—Everyone in the organization from the top down [21]—the president, top management, intermediate and first-line supervision, *and* employees.

6. What is the training unit?

"Classroom" Training An aggregate or collection of individual supervisors from different departments throughout the organization. A functional conglomerate without continuing psychological meaning for the individuals. Frequently seen as a "group" simply because the individuals are in close spatial proximity to one another.

Organizational Feedback—An organizational unit whose members have an organizational function to perform and whose members (a superior and his immediate subordinates) have continuing psychological meaning perceptually and behaviorally to one another as a team or family.

7. Who is the change agent?

"Classroom" Training—An outsider—an expert, a staff man—who has no direct, continuing authority or power over the trainee and few recurrent opportunities to reinforce the training.

Organizational Feedback—The organizational unit's line supervisor, who is given some help through pre- and post-meeting coaching by the expert outsider.

8. How is the pace or rate of change set?

"Classroom" Training—The trainer sets the pace, attempting to gear the training to average trainee's ability to comprehend and assimilate the material.

Organizational Feedback—The members of the group move from one topic to another as they are ready for the next step.

---

[21] N. R. F. Maier, "A Human Relations Program for Supervision," *Industrial and Labor Relations Review*, I (April, 1948), pp. 443-464.

9. How long does the change process continue?

"Classroom" Training—A fixed number of days or weeks, seldom less than 16 or more than 80 hours.

Organizational Feedback—No fixed length of time, the change procedure usually continues over a period of months—6 to 24 months.

10. How much tension is there?

"Classroom" Training—Usually relatively little, most trainees feel they already know a good deal about human behavior and how others feel.

Organizational Feedback—Frequently considerable, as objective information and particularly the differences between supervisory beliefs and practices come into a focus so sharp that complacency is shattered and the security about what is social reality is shaken.

11. What assumptions are made about attitudes and how they are changed? [22]

"Classroom" Training—The primary assumption is that the trainee does not know certain facts, that his previous organization of relevant information will be altered when he understands the new facts. Attitudes are seen as a function of the range of information available to the trainee; they are changed by altering cognitive structure.

Organizational Feedback—Here the assumptions are that the trainee already has satisfying ways of seeing things and relating to others, that attitudes and behavior can be changed only by altering their motivational bases. Norms of psychologically relevant groups are seen as more important determinants of attitudes than cognitive processes.

12. How is effectiveness of the change measured?

"Classroom" Training—Usually by informal comments of trainees, occasionally by interviews or questionnaires with the trainees after the training.

Organizational Feedback—By changes in employees' perception of their supervisor's behavior.

The differences drawn between these two types of procedures for creating change in an organizational setting may not be as marked as presented here. Human relations training programs do vary tremendously from company to company and from time to time. There is no single pattern. Since we know little about the frequency of different species of human relations training programs, the specific mix of content, method, setting, etc., which we used as the basis of our contrast may no longer be found in organizations. Our comparison aimed to emphasize the extent to which various characteristics of change processes vary on the basic dimension of *motivation for change*.

---

[22] I. Sarnoff and D. Katz, "The Motivational Bases of Attitude Change," *Journal of Abnormal and Social Psychology*, XLIX (January, 1954), pp. 115-124.

Different contents, different methods, different settings, different training units, and different change agents contain different motivational impacts for change. What constitutes the most effective combination for changing behavior in organizations is not known. Few practitioners have really done any bold experimenting; almost none have combined measurement and experimenting to search for the most significant dimensions and variables in change processes. This is an area in which there is a great need for social experimentation and social invention.

In the social sciences, as in the physical sciences, invention plays a crucial role. Inventions in social technology—skills and processes for creating change—and innovations in measurement both contribute speedily to progress in understanding social phenomena. The responsibility of experimenting with different methods of measuring change and with new procedures for investigating the interrelationship of functioning organizational processes rests heavily with the students of social organization. The rate at which knowledge about organization is developed will probably be closely correlated to the rate at which we try new approaches to the study of problems in this area.

QUESTIONS

1. What part are social scientists playing in the process of change? What can social scientists contribute to practitioners in this area?
2. How can change be created and studied? Cite an example.
3. Explain what is meant by "feedback"? Is it a useful process for creating and supporting change? Why?
4. What psychological and sociological facts must be taken into consideration in attempting to change attitudes and behavior?
5. How does the "classroom approach" differ from organizational feedback? Which is best for creating change in an organization?

GENERAL QUESTIONS ON PART 7

1. What effect does change have on people? Why?
2. Why is resistance to change a problem in industry?
3. Explain the difference between social and technical change. Which has the greatest influence on the human being? Why?
4. How does resistance to change differ from reaction to frustration?
5. Prepare a list of specific changes that affect people.
6. What approach would you follow when a necessary change actually results in disequilibrium in need satisfaction of employees?
7. Discuss the ways in which people resist change. Illustrate with examples from your own experience.

8. Explain how resistance to change is related to leadership and human relations.
9. How would you initiate a change? Show where your approach agrees or differs with the approaches indicated in the articles in this part.
10. Can resistance to change be prevented? Why?

BIBLIOGRAPHY FOR PART 7

Articles

COCH, LESTER and J. R. P. FRENCH. "Overcoming Resistance to Change," *Human Relations*, Vol. 1, No. 4 (August, 1948), pp. 512-532.

MOORE, LEO B. "Too Much Management—Too Little Change," *Harvard Business Review* (January-February, 1956), pp. 41-48.

STALEY, JOHN D. "There'll Be Some Changes Made," *Supervisory Management*, Vol. 3, No. 2 (February, 1958), pp. 9-14.

TANNENBAUM, ROBERT. "When It's Time for a Change," *Supervisory Management* (July, 1956), pp. 51-56.

Books

RONKIN, H. R. and P. H. LAWRENCE. *Administering Changes*. Cambridge, Mass.: Harvard University Press, 1952.

SELEKMAN, B. M. *Labor Relations and Human Relations*. New York: McGraw-Hill Book Company, Inc., 1947.

DAVIS, K. *Human Relations in Business*. New York: McGraw-Hill Book Company, Inc., 1957.

CARTWRIGHT, D. and A. ZANDER. *Group Dynamics*. Evanston, Ill.: Roe, Peterson and Company, 1956.

HOSLETT, S. D. *Human Factors in Management*. New York: Harper and Brothers, Publishers, 1946.

PART 8. COUNSELING

One of the more significant conclusions of the now-famous Hawthorne Study pointed to the need for procedures whereby employees could be aided and assisted in adjusting to their over-all social environment. It was shown that employees were, after all, human beings—that they have feelings, emotions, and attitudes that directly influence the quality and caliber of their work.

The student should recall that the Hawthorne Study was conducted at the Western Electric Company in Chicago and endeavored to ascertain the major factors influencing the productivity of employees. This was a lengthy study in terms of time, and the significant conclusions concerning productivity, to the amazement of most people, centered around the work-place and its social nature rather than around the physical factors influencing worker output.

To a large degree, the research indicated that mental attitudes are shaped by the immediate work situation. However, it also strongly emphasized that the individual worker brings with him to his job certain patterns of behavior, hopes, fears, and emotions, all of which exert tremendous influences on his work performance. In short, our "mental setting," which really controls the quality of our work and our industrial behavior, is influenced by a multiplicity of emotional factors both directly and indirectly related to our job. To these emotional factors we, as workers, must adjust.

To aid individuals in this emotional adjustment to their jobs, the Western Electric Company originated an extensive personnel counseling program, which evoked a great deal of interest at that time. Other companies inaugurated similar programs, and extensive work and research on the part of many people—notably Carl Rogers and associates—greatly helped in developing counseling techniques that were soon incorporated into the industrial sphere.

The current status of counseling as a managerial tool, at least as far as industry is concerned, is somewhat hazy. Among supervisors and managers, the concensus would probably be that in theory it is fine but in reality it is not very practical. They would likely respond that they do not have the time or the skill to act as counselors and that it should be the job of some college-trained specialist.

Harold Mayfield, in the first article of this section, illustrates a philosophy and approach towards counseling that one company has taken in dealing with employees and their problems. He presents counseling as a vital solution for aiding supervisors in establishing harmonious relationships with their subordinates. It is his contention that, through the nondirective method of counseling, managers are encouraged to listen to people and to talk out their problems with them, thus encouraging a greater degree of understanding as well as serving as a technique for preventing future problems.

The manager must be aware of the fact that wherever a superior-subordinate relationship exists, counseling situations will inevitably arise. The more complex and demanding these relationships become, the higher up in the organization they occur, and the more skilled and independent the personnel who are involved, so also will the difficulty of the counseling situation become. Over the years since the Hawthorne Study, different techniques and approaches to this problem have been developed. We shall now examine these in some detail.

COUNSELING TECHNIQUES

The old-time foreman of twenty-five or thirty years ago would have thought it ridiculous to talk over emotional problems, or for that matter any problems, with his subordinates. Fortunately, we have over the years developed new theories of human behavior that have greatly enhanced our understanding of why people act the way they do. We recognize now that behavior is caused, and therefore counseling can frequently help not only supervisors but workers as well in understanding individual behavior and its many manifestations.

Many different techniques have been and still are utilized to counsel workers. For the sake of simplicity, we can break these down into two major categories:

(1) Directive (structured) methods
(2) Nondirective method

Directive methods

These are the "old-style" approaches to a counseling situation. They usually appear to the neophyte supervisor to be the easiest course of action in bothersome situations. They are quick and require little skill; hence, undue reliance is usually placed on them. They can be classified as follows:

(1) *Advice*. This is probably the most commonly used approach in a counseling situation. It is relatively easy for any of us to give advice to a counselee—assuming, of course, that we know what advice to give. But always remember that in a counseling situation you are dealing with a person's emotions; indeed, you are trying to get a person to see his emotions and to understand his own behavior. The giving of advice assumes that the counselor understands exactly what the counselee's problem is, what has caused it, and the best solution to the problem. Yet this is seldom the case, for we are not always able to understand someone else's problems or to suggest solutions to them. Hence, the giving of advice tends to breed dependency, does not free emotions, and really does not enable the counselee to see and understand his own problems. Consequently, it hinders the development of necessary insight and self-understanding.

This does not mean that the counselor should avoid providing direct answers for certain types of questions. Obviously, factual answers should be given when required. It is only when emotional problems are present that we should avoid direct advice and instead place principal reliance on skillful discussions and questions to direct the counselee towards a greater awareness of himself and his own solution to his problem.

(2) *Forbidding*. Many supervisors, when faced with a counseling situation, resort to the easiest possible method—that of forbidding or admonishing. How many times do we hear the phrase: "I warned him what would happen. . . ." Unfortunately, this type of counseling rarely, if ever, achieves a permanent change in behavior. Perhaps it accomplishes a temporary change; but as soon as the feeling of fear wears off, old behavior patterns begin reoccurring. Forbidding or threatening only effects short-lived changes, breeds resentment and animosity, frequently requires reinforcement by actual punishment, and does not usually succeed in changing terminal attitudes. Why, then, keep individuals living and working in constant fear; why keep fostering attitudes of resentment when other means—positively oriented—exist that accomplish more permanent results with a greater degree of mutual satisfaction?

(3) *Exhortation*. Another familiar approach is the pep-talk, which we call exhortation. Often this works wonderfully well in the locker room between halves of the football game. However, few teams go through a complete season with an undefeated record. So even here it takes more than the coach's exhortations to accomplish this goal. Billy Sunday used to be a great exhorter, especially on

week ends. He succeeded in building up a head of steam in people, albeit a short-lived one. And this is the principal difficulty with the exhortation approach, namely, that it has only a short-lived effect and therefore seldom accomplishes permanent behavioral changes. It does not clarify emotional problems nor does it encourage us to take a closer look at ourselves, at our attitudes, and at our actions. It only makes weak people weaker and disturbed people more disturbed if used too often.

(4) *Explanation.* Still another easy approach for the boss is to explain the employee's problem to him. The boss assumes a patriarchal position, listens to the employee talk for a few minutes, and then launches into a lengthy dissertation on the problem in a completely different light from that in which the employee sees it—if he can perceive it at all. To explain something to someone else necessitates complete knowledge of facts, which, in most instances, the counselor does not have. Likewise, it assumes that the counselee will accept the facts as given, including the counselor's proposed solution. However, people, especially emotionally disturbed people, will not always accept facts and solutions. Motivation is essential here, and the best motivation is to clear away the emotions and feelings that are blocking self-perception. Explaining things will not usually accomplish this.

(5) *Reassurance.* The last directive method that we shall note is the pat-on-the-back or reassurance approach. Now there is nothing wrong with reassuring people at times. We all need periodic reassurance; certainly it is a necessary aspect of the recognition for which we all strive. But the same objections are raised against reassurance as a counseling technique as were raised against previous approaches, namely, that overdependence on it does not enhance the counselor's objective of achieving permanent effects in a person's behavior and that it does not provide for needed "psychological drainage" to remove pent-up frustrations and emotions.

Reassurance and encouragement tend to build up our egos. We like to hear that we are doing better or that things will improve in the future. But as Carl Rogers, one of our foremost experts in this field, points out, reassurance is essentially repressive. In short, it really denies that the counselee has a problem, and by creating a rosy hue the counselor may prevent the real problem from being brought out into the open. If this is the case, then what improvement results? In simple terms—nothing.

These five methods, therefore, comprise what are called the directed methods. We can also label them the "old-style" methods of counseling. Their shortcomings rest on the following highly questionable assumptions: (a) that the counselor quickly understands the employee's problem, (b) that he knows all the facts and issues involved, (c) that he knows the best solution, and (d) that he can get the counselee to perceive his own situation and accept the counselor's proposed solution. Obviously there are many pitfalls here; consequently, the value derived from the directed methods is severely limited.

Nondirective counseling

This is the newer approach to counseling. It is not necessarily new in terms of the historical time element, but only in the sense of actually being used in industry.

To remedy the shortcomings of the directive methods, more and more people are turning to this nondirective type of counseling. Although it is explained very well in a subsequent article by Leonard Himler, it should be noted that the nondirective interview places heavy emphasis on "psychological drainage" or "catharsis" as its foundation. It focuses principally on the emotions that surround and usually prevent an individual from seeing and understanding his problems in their true perspective. It is predicated on the assumption that if by skillful interviewing a counselor can succeed in getting the counselee to "purge" or release his emotions—hence the term catharsis—then the counselee will be able to recognize his own problems and the appropriate solution to solve them with a minimum of direction and advice from the counselor.

This method stresses the importance of understanding-listening on the part of the counselor. It becomes the counselor's task to encourage the counselee to talk, thus forcing the counselee's pent-up emotions to be released. Before any attempt is made to clarify and define the problems involved, these emotions must be recognized by the counselee. So the principal focus is on the counselee, on how he perceives his problem and how he thinks it should be handled. The interviewer remains neutral, not arguing or forcing his own opinions. The counselor attempts to establish what professional counselors term a "permissive relationship," encouraging the employee to talk freely and, through skillful listening, helping the counselee to detect and clarify his negative and positive feelings. The ultimate goal of nondirective counseling is to stimulate the subordinate to self-recognition and self-acceptance of the need for change, and from that point to lead him to work out his own program for self-improvement. To achieve this goal, certain attitudes are essential:

(1) A belief that the individual is responsible for himself and is mature enough to keep that responsibility.

(2) A belief that a person is capable of solving his own problems once he recognizes them.

(3) A belief that people want to be understood, not judged. True feelings can only be expressed by developing a permissive attitude.

(4) A belief that the individual is important to you, hence the creation of a feeling of acceptance.

(5) A deep-seated respect for the feelings of the subordinate. Disagreement and argument will not enhance this respect. Only by trying to understand the man's feelings can a mutual respect be created.

CONDUCTING THE NONDIRECTIVE INTERVIEW

There are several major steps to be observed in conducting a nondirective interview, among them being the following:

(1) *Be prepared.* If you, either as a professional counselor or as a supervisor of some type, are aware that a particular individual is coming in later in the day to discuss a problem, it is always wise to know as much about the man as possible. In most companies, handy reference can be made to a person's personnel folder. If the man appears unannounced and no advance preparation is possible, it is always best to be prepared for such happenings by a periodic review of your subordinates. In this way some knowledge of your people is always with you.

(2) *Put the man at ease.* There are many ways for achieving this. Hold the interview in comfortable surroundings where you can both sit and relax, perhaps smoking or enjoying a cup of coffee. People are always willing to talk more fully in surroundings conducive to personal comfort.

(3) *Establish rapport.* This refers to establishing a friendly, rather intimate relationship between yourself and the counselee. Let the man know that you want to listen to him, that what he says will be held in the strictest confidence. In Himler's words, there must be "a mutual feeling of friendliness and sympathetic unity." You must convey to the individual that you want to share his problem with him and aid him in deciding on a definite course of action.

(4) *Don't argue or admonish.* If you start either one of these, immediately the man will assume a defensive position. If he senses that he is in any way wrong, he will become even more emotional than he was at the start of the interview. This only defeats the purpose of the interview. If he becomes defensive in attitude, issues become hazy and more involved.

(5) *Don't display authority.* Avoid exerting any authority before this man, not only organizational authority but intellectual authority as well. People resent social subordination, so do not command or confuse. Talk with the man, not to him. Seek to understand and be understood.

(6) *Listen carefully.* This is essential to nondirective interviewing. Listen critically for negative and positive feelings. Don't interrupt. Encourage the man to speak fully and openly without fear. *Echo his statements back to him* by careful questioning, by facial expressions, and by body movements. And remember to listen with eyes as well as ears. Seek to understand through good listening.

(7) *Don't advise.* Try to avoid giving the man advice even though he may emotionally ask: "But what should I do?" Keep encouraging him to speak; in this way emotions are cleared away. Sooner or later he will offer his own advice. Seize upon this and encourage more probing. You can answer some questions about company policies and procedures, perhaps, but offer as little as possible direct advice for solving his problem. Keep him talking so self-awareness and insight can begin occurring.

(8) *Help clarify positive courses of action.* When the man does start making positive suggestions, encourage him to continue to go further and to recognize the consequences of his behavior. An occasional suggestion might help when he reaches this stage. Let him know that you agree when he gets on the right track; help him, again by questioning, to see various alternatives for solving his problem, but let him make his own choice.

These are but a few simple, elementary steps in the nondirective procedure. However, they are fundamental to counseling. Because most of us are not clinical psychologists or therapists and for the most part do not run into serious mental cases in the industrial situation, we do not have to concern ourselves here with involved techniques. Successful application of the eight points will yield amazing results in most cases.

INSIGHT WILL DEVELOP

Carl Rogers, one of the original pioneers of nondirective counseling, asserts that if the counselor recognizes negative and positive expressions and then echoes them back to the counselee during the interview, the latter then begins to develop insight or awareness into his own behavior and problems. He will see relationships and facts that had previously been clouded by his emotions. Until this happens, that is, until insight starts to develop, the man will think and talk defensively and negatively. But when insight does occur, he will view his behavior in a new perspective and positive action can ensue. In the summary to his article, Rogers presents the following conclusions to support his contention:

(1) In nondirective counseling, new perceptions and self-understanding will occur in a somewhat spontaneous fashion.

(2) These insights will vary in type, some simple and some complex, but will enhance the understanding of behavior.

(3) Insights develop gradually but will culminate in a peak towards the end of the interview. They will be followed by positive plans and decisions.

(4) Insights are not likely to occur if the counselor attempts to direct the interview to any great extent, thus creating a defensive attitude on the part of the counselee.

The Supervisor as a Counselor

We stated earlier that many supervisors shun any type of counseling if they possibly can. However, the number of companies that employ full-time, professional counselors is relatively small, meaning that more and more responsibility for this duty is falling on the shoulders of the supervisor or the manager. After all, it seems reasonable to assume that he knows his people better than anyone else and is in more frequent contact with them; hence counseling should be primarily his responsibility.

As to why supervisors may shy away from this duty, several reasons exist. In the first place, they frequently lack training in the non-directive technique and this, coupled with a lack of top-management support, or interest, tends to retard or dull supervisory interest. Secondly, supervisors and managers are usually first and foremost job-oriented; hence indifference to employee problems develops. Third, discussing personal problems with individuals is not a very pleasant task, especially if supervisors have had no training along these lines; so the obvious alternative is to ignore such problems completely or to refer them to someone else, typically the personnel department. Lastly, counseling takes time, and time being a very precious thing to most supervisors, harassed as they are by production demands, counseling becomes one of the less important details.

Often one will encounter in a company a situation where a great deal of employee counseling is carried on by the personnel department. Supervisors encourage this as it appears to relieve them of the responsibility. However, current emphasis continues to place principal responsibility for this duty squarely on the line organization rather than "passing the buck" to the personnel department. It is the latter's job to train line personnel in counseling techniques and to sell them on the importance of carrying this duty out to the best of their ability. Often representatives of the personnel department may sit in on some types of counseling interviews, such as performance reviews, exit interviews, and so on, to help and assist the line supervisor. Nevertheless, this does not relieve the latter of his basic responsibility.

COUNSELING SITUATIONS

So far we have been concentrating our discussion on the more general aspects involved in counseling with employees. Perhaps it now would be best to identify some of the specific situations that arise which typically require some type of counseling.

No doubt there will be many times that different employees will want to talk to their boss about some aspect of their jobs that is disturbing them. Personality clashes will occur between employees, necessitating a conference with the supervisor. Complaints may center around working conditions or some other specific job duties. In short, myriad situations relating to a man's job can occur that require some counseling.

On the other hand, some individuals may want to talk to their immediate superior about personal problems not directly related to their jobs. Problems in a man's home life may be seriously disturbing his work. Because people will hesitate to come directly to their boss with these problems, supervisors need to be on the watch for people whose work might not be up to par and, if necessary, to approach them and encourage them to talk. Quite often, these deep-seated emotional problems are hidden causes of serious job complaints or disorders. Supervisors have to be constantly on the alert for this type of thing.

If personal problems appear to be extremely serious, supervisors should refer these people to others more professionally qualified to assist them. If legal or medical advice is needed or if the man appears to have a somewhat serious mental disorder, the supervisor should direct him to appropriate help. It is not the supervisor's job to interfere in cases like this except to refer the man to other people.

A combination of directed and nondirective counseling is required in discussing performance reviews with subordinates. Earl Planty and Carlos Efferson, in a very stimulating article at the end of this part, discuss briefly some of the fundamental assumptions underlying this type of counseling. They list some very practical guides for aiding supervisors and managers in conducting an evaluation interview. Although it is not our purpose to discuss here merit rating or performance reviews, we do recognize that these procedures are indispensable for enhancing and improving worker performance. And the success and effectiveness of performance rating is heavily contingent upon how well a supervisor communicates his ratings to individual employees. Here is where skill in counseling assumes a dramatic role. If he can convincingly communicate rating results to employees and show them in a positive way where improvement is needed, changes in attitudes and behavior can and most likely will occur.

Other instances where counseling procedures may be employed are as follows:

(1) Exit interviews
(2) Employment interviews
(3) Job evaluation interviews
(4) Disciplinary cases
(5) Studies of work methods
(6) Morale surveys

Benefits Realized from Counseling

There are many advantages to using counseling procedures in dealing with employees. First, proper counseling on the part of managers and supervisors can go a long way towards developing a deeper understanding of and respect for their subordinates. Too frequently we forget that those working for a company sail in the same boat. It is truly amazing how far a willingness to listen to one's subordinates can go in influencing positive attitudes on the part of these same people. The social distance between boss and worker can be markedly reduced, not only by advocating the open-door policy, but by really taking the time to talk with and listen to workers. Unless a superior can establish this needed support, his own job success will be severely handicapped.

Secondly, good counseling is an indispensable aspect of "preventive management." By sincerely talking with people, many problems that might occur in the future can be found out and prevented. Unfortunately, this is a point too often overlooked, with the result that supervisors spend a great deal of time as "fire fighters." Many problems could be prevented if we would only take the time to listen properly.

Third, as was mentioned earlier, good listening makes good listeners. If employees know that their supervisor sincerely does his best to listen to and talk over problems with them, they are likely to be more receptive to his communications. His orders and requests will be received by attentive ears, not rejecting ones. Cooperation, not conflict, will result.

And last, good counseling aids in developing more mature, independent workers. When employees are able to get their complaints and problems out into the open, they become less dependent on their supervisor and are normally willing to assume more responsibility. They adjust themselves to their fellow workers and to their jobs, showing more initiative and self-reliance.

THE COUNSELING FUNCTION
IN MANAGEMENT *

Harold Mayfield

A company is an organization consisting of people, not of buildings and machines. If the leaders of a company are to be successful, they must deal with their people successfully. One of the first requirements of human relations is a reasonable degree of skill in talking with people. This skill and a willingness to deal with people on a human plane are needed in American industry today.

To illustrate that need, we can look at the history of industry. A few years ago, Elton Mayo of Harvard, the leading spirit behind the famous Hawthorne study of people at work, said, "While material efficiency has been increasing for 200 years, the human capacity for working together has in the same period continually diminished."

This is an alarming statement. Although you may not be acquainted with the long historical trend, I think your own experience will confirm that the human stresses and strains in business are increasing day by day.

Now, what I am suggesting is not merely that technology has advanced at a faster rate than our skills in human relations, rather that technology in some respects has advanced at the expense of human relations. I am suggesting that some of the advances in efficiency tend to thwart human inclinations. Consider some of the side effects of the devices by which we have advanced in efficiency. Some of these devices are mechanical; the assembly line is perhaps the most conspicuous example. Some of these devices are human; some you will recognize by the names "work simplification" and "specialization." Peter Drucker has pointed out that these devices, at worst, treat the human being as a machine and a rather inferior machine at that. Even at best, many of these devices bring a reduction in human satisfactions at work.

It is my view and the view of most modern psychologists that the normal human being is on the whole a friendly and communicative person—when free of fear and compulsion. He is this kind of person not just in his hours of relaxation, but every minute of the day—if he is allowed to be so. Yet, if you will reflect, you will see many

* From *The Personnel Administrator*, Vol. 3, No. 1 (February, 1958), pp. 23-25. Reprinted with permission.

influences in business which make it difficult for the individual to express these inclinations at work.

Production pressure, manifest in a thousand ways and possibly reaching its maximum in machine pacing, makes it difficult or impossible for a person to keep up with his job and at the same time respond humanly to the people around him. We have many methods and devices in industry to increase individual concentration on the task and at the same time make it less interesting. Many of our arrangements have the effect of isolating people from one another—and this, too, goes against the grain of human nature. We isolate people by distance, by partitions, by mechanical noise.

Modern efficiency even tends to separate the foreman from his people; it often makes the foreman so busy that he can not pause to communicate and, in some very progressive businesses, the foreman may even be provided with a motor scooter which threatens to make his inaccessibility complete.

Please understand, I am here looking at the seamy side of progress. I am not denying that many things we value highly in our lives have been placed within our reach by efficient business methods. I am not proposing we step backward in time. Increased efficiency has brought us human gains as well as material reduction in backbreaking toil.

But it is a sobering thought that most of the benefits of industrial progress have improved our situations while off the job, not on the job itself. Therefore, we are challenged to look at the workplace and see if we can build into the job more of the human satisfactions that people crave.

Consider for a moment how the attitude of the factory worker differs from that of the farmer. True, the farmer works long hours and there are many frustrating things about his job, especially the weather. But the farmer enjoys great freedom in his work. If he wishes to whistle while he works, he does so. If a neighbor passes, he is likely to stop and chat a moment. If he wants to hear the ball score or the grain quotations, he goes into the house and turns on the radio.

A somewhat similar attitude toward work prevailed in the craft shops, which were the forerunners of industry at an earlier period in history. There the atmosphere of the workplace was almost recreational. The shoemaker made the complete shoe. Usually he was proud of his skill. He worked at his own speed. He gave individual touches to his work. The workplace was a kind of living room. Usually he had a helper or two, as much for companionship as for economic gain. Dogs ran through the workroom. Children played in it. If there was a noise outside in the street, everyone dropped their work to see what was happening.

That is the way people work if left to their own devices. That attitude toward work on the part of primitive people is the despair of American contractors building military installations in far parts of the world. That, indeed, is an attitude far removed from the modern factory. Perhaps we have gone too far in some respects.

My object here is to offer a few ideas about humanizing the workplace—that is, a few suggestions that I believe will help us work with human nature and not against it.

Sometimes I think we are annoyed by the fact that human problems on the job are inevitable.

The whole man comes to work, not just the part of him you want. From home he brings his worries, attitudes he developed before you knew him, poor health, fatigue, and an endless list of other conditions that you may wish he had left at home.

At work, too, he picks up attitudes that are beyond your control. He develops emotions, draws conclusions, and picks up alleged facts from the grapevine that you probably deplore. But the fact remains that you have to deal with this man as he is—with the whole man.

We might prefer not to deal with certain awkward problems. Unfortunately we do not have that choice. Directly or indirectly, we must deal with people's problems when we deal with people. Even in ignoring the problems, we are actually dealing with them in a certain way. The only real choice before us is to select one of several possible methods.

It is my firm belief that we are wise to deal helpfully, rather than by ignoring them or repulsing them. Yet I do not advocate this course purely out of altruism. I suggest that it is good business. I propose a down-to-earth, practical goal; namely, to get the individual back to work in a frame of mind to do a good job.

I am willing to concede that there are more ways than one of dealing with human problems and that no two of us would handle the same problem in exactly the same way. In a given situation, there may be several approaches that yield reasonably good results, and yet none of them that completely satisfy us.

However, I believe there is one kind of approach that holds more promise than others. It is the method that has been most clearly identified and described by the school of nondirective counseling.

At this point I feel the need of a word of caution and explanation. I am talking about a general approach to human problems on the job—problems I consider inevitable. I do not mean to imply at any time that those of us in managerial jobs should become counselors in the professional sense. In fact, I believe we should avoid becoming counseling therapists. I am proposing merely that we can learn from the professionals an approach to human problems that may be more effective than the methods most of us use when we do what comes naturally.

I see two important merits in the nondirective (or active listening) approach to human problems.

First, it has long-range benefits. Although it may seem time-consuming today, it holds promise of saving a great deal more time tomorrow. It aims at giving the individual increased resources within himself to meet future problems when they arise. In contrast, if we attempt to provide solutions to other people's problems, we invite the danger that they will become dependent upon us. Although a quick word of advice may relieve the pressure of the moment, it may result in an endless succession of repetitions.

A second great virtue of active listening is that you can do little harm with it. This may seem faint praise but, in view of the modest counseling skills that we can expect to have in positions of management, it is important. Our potentialities for harm are considerable if we use unsound methods.

In giving this endorsement to counseling methods, I do not want to imply that the majority of contacts with your people are to be handled nondirectively. Most of your contacts should be handled in direct and factual ways. The need for the active listening role is signalled when there is strong emotion present.

For example, if a man says to you, "Mr. Supervisor, where shall I take this load of stock?", tell him, "Take it down to the basement." If a man asks, "What time is it?", tell him, "It is ten minutes after five."

On the other hand, if the man says to you, "Mr. Supervisor, why don't you get off my back?," any attempt to handle this question directly or by factual information obviously misses the point. The reality with which the supervisor has to deal is not contained in the words used. The real problem is emotion—in this case, anger or irritation.

From the man's opening sentence in this instance, you have no way of knowing what lies behind his outburst. If you wish to deal with the problem constructively, you must get more information. This you will not get by a sharp retort, by a lecture from you, nor by any response that silences him. Unless you can get him to open up further, you have little hope of making progress with him.

The special power of the nondirective approach lies in the fact that people talk and think more clearly when they have a good listener. They can grapple more successfully with their own problems in the presence of an understanding person. Probably we have all had experience that illustrates this principle. Certainly we have all felt the need of achieving understanding with our people.

In our own company we have recognized that the counseling approach is plainly needed in performing two duties that are a part of every supervisor's job. As I have implied previously, every supervisor is confronted from time to time with an emotional person— an angry man or a tearful woman. In addition, he may invite a situation with overtones of emotion in a program of routine interviews. In this instance, the supervisor takes the initiative and schedules a private conversation with each of his people, asking them for their comments about their job and their future hopes in it.

Members of a personnel department probably encounter more occasions when they need skills in listening than most other staff people. In our company for years we have urged that one of the most important functions of the personnel department is that of the "listening ear." By this we mean that the personnel department must stand ready to give highest priority to individual problems over the clerical routine of the department.

In our plants, the personnel director is fairly accessible, and many people think of him as their first recourse when they do not get satisfaction from their own boss. The employment manager, the first person many people meet on the job, is a source of counsel, particularly by new people. The nurse is brought into personal problems as a result of her health and first-aid work.

In addition to these jobs which might be considered normal in business, our company has another position that is even more clearly recognized for its counseling function. In departments employing a large number of girls, say 200 or more, we have a woman assigned to each shift. She is called a counselor, but might more descriptively be called "house mother." She is located in the women's lounge, where the girls are provided with comfortable chairs, radios, magazines, and other comforts. Here the girls spend their spare time before and after work, during rest periods, and perhaps at lunch.

Although these women may perform minor clerical jobs and assist in the plant recreation program, their main function is to be friendly and helpful to the girls when unforeseen problems arise. Although we call them counselors, I am reluctant to use that term outside the company because we do not pretend that they are counselors in the professional sense.

They have had a little training, but we would not want them to attempt to handle the kinds of cases that would be routine in a counseling center. They are mature women usually selected from among the working group, and picked for their judgment and ability to be good listeners. Normally, they report to the Women's Director in the plant (the woman who assists the Personnel Director on women's problems). She handles their training, mostly through regular meetings.

Although we have recognized the counseling need of our supervisors for many years, we have not yet uncovered any miraculous devices to help them acquire this skill. The subject has been given attention in supervisory meetings at various times, but we have never developed a course on counseling. Fortunately, we think many supervisors have considerable latent skill in this respect and respond well to encouragement.

In our search for a training device, we brought a number of our plant personnel to a meeting at the University of Chicago Counseling Center two years ago. In a three-day meeting, we attempted to give twenty of our people (we limited attendance to one person from each unit represented) an over-view of nondirective methods, in the hope they they could translate this knowledge into an educational program for supervisors and others in the plant.

In summary, I am convinced of our need for humanizing our relations with people in industry. I believe this task falls principally upon the supervisors, but is shared also by staff people in management, particularly those in the personnel department. An essential part of this process is the improvement of our skills in talking with people in situations charged with emotions.

Human problems of this kind are inevitable in business. They are a consequence of the elementary fact that the whole man comes to work, and we have to deal with all of him if he is to become an effective member of the organization.

The variety of personnel problems confronting us in business is endless. No two of us will meet the same problem in exactly the same way. At first glance, this may make the counseling approach seem impossibly difficult. But, fortunately, there are a few simple principles whose importance transcends technique. The essence of the counseling approach to human problems is contained in these three words: friendly—understanding—listening. If any of the three is missing, the process will fail. People tend to unfold in a friendly atmosphere. But it is not enough simply to be friendly, as most of us are surrounded by friendly people. It is a rare experience for most people to feel that they are understood; but in the presence of understanding, most people see their own problems with increased clarity. And, finally, we need constantly to remind ourselves that the prerequisite of understanding is listening, not talking.

In this approach to human problems, we have some degree of assurance that we are working with human nature rather than against it.

QUESTIONS

1. Why is counseling so important to the typical business firm?
2. How has modern technology complicated the relationship between the worker and his job?
3. What is the special attraction of nondirective counseling as set forth by Mayfield?
4. In what area of the business are counseling skills most apt to be needed?
5. Evaluate this article in light of your own work experience. Do you agree or disagree with the author's major conclusions?

THE DEVELOPMENT OF INSIGHT IN A COUNSELING RELATIONSHIP *

Carl R. Rogers

In dealing with adolescent and adult clients, one question which faces the worker—whether psychologist, case worker, psychiatrist, or educational counselor—is, "How may this individual come to an effective understanding of himself?" It is recognized that once the individual genuinely understands his behavior, and accepts that understanding, he is able to adopt a more realistic and satisfactory control of his actions, is less likely to hurt others to gain satisfactions, and in general can become more mature. But how to reach this goal?

This understanding of self we customarily call insight. We find rather general agreement that the achievement of insight is the keystone of the process of therapy. Whether we are dealing with a student who is maladjusted, or a marriage which is skidding toward failure, or a war neurosis, the essentials of a therapeutic experience seem to be the same. First comes the experience of release—the pouring out of feelings, the loosening of repressions, the unburdening of guilt, the lessening of tension. There follows, if progress is to be made, the understanding of self, the acceptance of one's impulses, the perception of relationships. which we classify under the term insight. Then, out of this more accurate view of the inner life, out of this new understanding of the web of personal adjustments, come new plans, new choices, new and more satisfying ways of meeting the realities with which the individual is faced. While each of these three steps is essential, and no one can take place without the other, the middle step, the achievement of insight, is a crucial one and deserves much more attention than it has had in the past.

In the counseling and the research on counseling which is being carried forward at Ohio State, we are gradually accumulating more information about this important aspect of psychotherapy. We are finding that in counseling relationships governed by a non-directive viewpoint, highly significant insights develop with a spontaneity and vigor which is astonishing.[1] We are also becoming more and more convinced, though as yet research evidence is meagre, that such spon-

---

* From the *Journal of Consulting Psychology*, Vol. 8, No. 6 (November-December, 1944), pp. 331-341. Reprinted with permission.
[1] Carl R. Rogers, *Counseling and Psychotherapy* (Boston: Houghton Mifflin, 1942).

taneous insight is not characteristic of other counseling approaches. We find that the directive procedures which are characteristic of so much educational guidance do not produce insight of this sort. Our evidence would also point to the conclusion that spontaneous insight is a rare occurrence in the more interpretative approaches such as psychoanalysis. Consequently, it appears to be worth while to present both examples and research evidence regarding the achievement of self-understanding as we are seeing it.

Insight, as it is coming to be defined through our practical experience and research findings, involves such elements as (1) an acceptance of one's impulses and attitudes, good or bad, including attitudes previously repressed; (2) an understanding of the patterning of one's behavior, the perception of new relationships; (3) a fresh perception of reality made possible by this acceptance and understanding of the self; (4) the planning of new and more satisfying ways in which the self can adjust to reality. Since this definition grows out of examination of the data, not from armchair speculation, an attempt will be made to let the data speak for themselves.

Where problems are not too deep-seated, simple and partial insights may come very quickly. A father, concerned about his ten-year-old daughter, is encouraged to talk out his attitudes, and arrives at these insightful reactions in a single interview.[2]

> Father. She's awful pokey—awful pokey. You just can't get her going. Of course, maybe it's been our fault. It's been easier to do things for her than to teach her to do them. She hasn't enough to do. She ought to have more responsibility.
> Counselor. That's a splendid idea . . . You feel you haven't given her a chance to learn?
> Father: Yes. She gets an allowance, but the trouble is she spends it. And then it comes time to go to the show and she hasn't any. And I haven't the heart—I give it to her. (Pause) Of course when I was a boy I didn't have any money at all—I had to earn everything.
> Counselor. You think it would have been better if someone had given it to you?
> Father. Well, it wouldn't have hurt. My parents could have . . . (Pause) I know I give in to her and she knows it, see?

This may seem like a minimum degree of insight. It could be briefly stated in these terms "She should have more responsibility, but I don't give it to her because I feel sorry for myself as a boy." It is a simple insight, yet it is effective. Before the father leaves he says, in a hesitating manner, "I kinda think tomorrow morning when

[2] Helen Sargent, "Non-directive Counseling Applied to a Single Interview," *Journal of Consulting Psychology*, Vol. 7, 1943, p. 186.

she wakes up she's going to find she has some things to do!" One
year later the school principal, talking to the psychologist about this
child, knowing nothing of the above, says, "Well, she seems better.
. . . And the attitude of the parent seems different. They seem to be
giving her more responsibility in various ways." This illustrates one
of the points which I would like to make—that partial insights, spontaneously arrived at, are surprisingly effective in bringing about
alteration of behavior.

Another illustration of such simple and partial insight might be
given. A young bride has been troubled by guilt feelings about an
experience previous to her marriage in which she had been intensely
in love with a young man who regarded her as "just a passing fancy."
She is troubled about keeping this experience from her husband. She
talks out her attitudes in one contact, getting considerable release.
In a second brief contact she shows how much insight she has
gained.

> I guess I needed to talk to someone about it. I think I can see where
> I stand now. If I were to tell Nick it would merely mean that I was
> selfish. I would be telling him to help myself, not because of anything I
> feel I owe to him. It would be "passing the buck" to him. I see now
> that it was merely an experience that hurt me—hurt my ego. It's only
> natural that I should feel queer about it. But that feeling queer is
> my own burden. Certainly it's unfair to pass it on to Nick. It would
> certainly be foolish of me to endanger our relationship, too. Time will
> cure my "conditioning" to this very small unpleasant segment of my life
> —and my marital happiness will hasten this time. I already feel my
> perspective changing—the present looms larger and larger and the rest
> dwindles.

Here we find that the insight achieved involves a better acceptance of attitudes previously denied—the hurt to her ego—a clearer
perception of the patterning and significance of her own desire to
tell her husband, and finally a choice of a new method of handling
the problem.

As might be expected, a working insight is not always so easily
achieved. Much depends on the complexity of the problem, and the
extent to which attitudes are repressed. In the case of an aviation
cadet who was failing in his solo flights, counseling brought to light
an intense and hitherto denied hatred for his unreasonably strict
father. The gradual perception of a relationship between his attitude
toward his father and his reactions during his flights covers several
interviews. Brief excerpts from the fifth, sixth, and tenth interviews
will illustrate the development of this insight.

From fifth interview:

S. You know after the last interview I wondered what made me tell you the things that I did. Could it be possible that the instructor is a symbol of my father? Is that hatred coming back to blot my memory? Could that possibly be significant?

C. You wonder if perhaps the instructor might be a symbol of your father.

S. Yes, he was telling me what to do just like Dad always did. I fully intended to carry out the instructor's directions; I couldn't *not* want to do them. Maybe I forgot because I thought of Dad and wanted to forget.

From the sixth interview:

S. On the basis of what we've done thus far the instructor may have been considered in the role of my father and as he was telling me what to do I probably didn't want to because I thought of him as my father—but I don't know—I'm not sure.

C. You're not absolutely sure that that's the answer to your problem.

S. I'm not positive but that's what it seems to be at the present time. If *you* said it was I would know it. Then recognizing that fact, I wouldn't be bothered in the plane any more.

C. If I should say that was the solution to your problem and you didn't thoroughly believe it yourself, that wouldn't do much good, would it? Or if I told you that wasn't the solution to your problem, and you thought that perhaps it was, then my telling you wouldn't do a bit of good either.

S. (Smiling) I see your point. I guess you're right.

From the tenth interview:

The cadet tells of a recent failure to do well. The counselor recognizes his feeling.

C. You didn't follow his instructions up in the air even when he was telling you.

S. It seems that way. If you could apply that to other maneuvers it might be. I really want to fly though. Maybe that's why I haven't done so well—a dislike to follow directions. Gee, that's pretty well tangled up. Let me try and draw a parallel there. My instructor is to my father as my instructor's directions are to my father's directions. Even though I thought I wanted to, I really didn't want to.

C. You feel there's a parallel to your father's and instructor's directions.

S. I wanted to fly badly. That may be the block. That's probably the answer to the question. I guess I didn't have it formulated before I came here today, but I sure do now.

C. You feel that may be at the center of your problem.

S. That's right. Flying is grand. By George, why did I have to get an instructor that reminded me of father? If I got an easy instructor all the way through would it have been easier? There's a good possibility I would have been the best in the group.

In this material the insight which is gained is primarily a new perception of relationships between past repressed attitudes and present experiences. It should be pointed out that neither in this case, nor in any of the cases cited in this paper, has the counselor ever suggested these insights in any way. The counseling has been non-directive, with the counselor reflecting, in an understanding fashion, the attitudes and feelings expressed. The understanding of self springs from the client, not from the counselor.

In other instances the insight consists largely of an acceptance of the denied portions of the self. Illustrations of this type of insight may be taken from the case of Mrs. S., a young, highly educated mother, who comes for assistance because she is having trouble with her child and is losing the affection of her husband. Some of the points at which she comes face to face with her own feelings may be given. First she faces her basic rejection of her child.

> Mrs. S. I'm afraid I'd have to say this of myself, I really didn't want Buddy. We were married two years, and I had a job. My husband didn't want me to work. We thought children would be the best solution. We felt social pressure too. With the birth rate up in the lower groups, college graduates should have children. In a limited way we were emotionally interested in him, but not deeply. And I've never adjusted to having him! It's terrible to say this!

Later she sees the relationship of this rejection, and of her difficulty with her husband, to Buddy's behavior.

> Mrs. S. He senses the tension in us, lacks security. That probably explains it all. I used to put myself into working for social causes. Now I've given myself all to my husband, none to Buddy. I pat him and tell him I love him, but I wonder if he doesn't know.
> C. You feel perhaps he realizes you don't love him much.
> Mrs. S. Say not 'til now. But with the situation as it is—how will it come?
> C. You want to love him.
> Mrs. S. Yes, very much. I'm not just coldblooded.

At another point she begins to accept the role of being a women, rather than merely an intellectual. Talking about her husband, she says:

> Mrs. S. I spend my time worrying about him, discussing with him his feeelings and emotions. Instead I should take an interest in myself, my clothes, my hair. I've never been that sort of person—I hate to fuss with my hair. I shouldn't say that—after I'm through, and look in the mirror, I like myself better. That's the first time I've thought of it that way.
> C. Instead of being tense about him, you feel you should take an interest in yourself, and you find that doing that, like fussing with your hair, is not as foreign to your nature as you thought.
> Mrs. S. Yes. I have more hope now than I have felt to this moment.

In regard to her relationship to her husband, this woman also gains much insight in which she sees the problem in a new frame of reference, and also decides what she can do about it.

Mrs. S. I'm more firmly convinced than ever that what I have to look at is myself, rather than Bill, do something about my own faults and shortcomings. I thought a lot about it last night; I realized a person can only be responsible for oneself, not for the other person's feelings and emotions. I wasn't treating him as an individual—my emotional involvement makes that hard. I tried to think and feel for him, take over his problem and work it through for him.

C. Now you feel you can be responsible for yourself, and can let him be responsible for himself.

Mrs. S. Yes. Things may break down, but we can build them up again.

C. While things may not go smoothly, you feel more basic security.

Mrs. S. Yes. I've got to look at myself, to see how I'm dressing and behaving with him.

C. You feel those are your responsibility.

Mrs. S. Yes. And the children—I'm not excusing myself about them. I thought it was impossible for anyone to take care of a house, and herself, and find time to play with the children, but I think now I can. I'd assumed some things were impossible, but they were not.

In these excerpts, being able to accept as a part of herself her rejecting attitudes, and her desire to be a woman, enables her to achieve a more detached and realistic attitude toward the reality of her husband and his behavior. It also frees her to choose new patterns of reaction.

In the instances which have been given the insights which were achieved were relatively simple, though definitely significant. In some cases insights are much more involved, and the achievement of them is a more gradual process. A series of excerpts from the case of Alfred will indicate something of the richness which this insight process may have. Alfred was a very withdrawn student, the seclusive sort who was living largely in fantasy when he first came in. The possibility of a schizophrenic break seemed very real. There were twenty interviews, and during that period he altered in a most striking fashion in his behavior and attitudes. He became independent and socially adjusted, indeed something of a social leader. His adjustment has been further tested by two years in the army, to which he has reacted very well. There are in his case many threads of insight which would be intriguing to follow. One which has been selected is his gradual achievement of understanding of his daydreaming. His gropings toward this insight are a fascinating process to watch. It is unfortunate that only brief excerpts can be given from the phonographic recordings of the contacts.

In the seventh interview Alfred first shows a real understanding of the fact that his daydreaming was compensatory.

Alfred. I always had the idea that I would make up for a lot of the things I didn't do—like being an Edison or a Lincoln some day. Yet I never did enjoy the real happiness that kids were having at the present time. I always kidded myself along by thinking that "I'm going to be a great man some day." And when you get to college, and really find out how many brilliant people there are you realize you've been kidding yourself. You certainly never could become important if you were to go on in the past, instead of concentrating and studying and everything. I think maybe if I could be as happy as this I could amount to something—probably not an Edison or Lincoln, but I could hold a position. It would certainly be through an entirely different set of plans than I planned on the other way of doing it.

In the tenth interview he brings out more forcibly how much the fantasy meant to him, and how difficult has been the process of bringing it into the full light of consciousness.

Alfred. So anyway I do believe coming over here is helping me, because these things don't bother me as much as they used to. And I used to carry them around with me. For instance, that daydreaming. Boy, it just about killed me the first time I tried to tell that to anybody, but I suppose that if I tell it about twenty-five times I'll really begin to laugh at it.

In the eleventh interview he expands the insight gained. He is able to face the fact that the satisfactions of fantasy existed not only in the past, but even during the initial stages of counseling. He also faces frankly the fact that his fantasy goals are impossible.

Alfred. I just used to comfort myself at school by telling myself that I would be a very famous person some day, and I didn't just say that as a sort of compromise, I actually believed that that was right, and even when I was coming here I still did think that. I remember one time I said to myself, "If I were happy I would be another Abe Lincoln," but if your mind is really normal and out in the world, you realize how really big the world is and you realize that . . . maybe you aren't going to accomplish as much as you want.

In the fourteenth interview Alfred makes the final link in this chain of insight when he becomes genuinely willing to face and accept the prospect of being only an average person in the real world, rather than a great person in a fantasy world of his own making.

Alfred. I might desire to be an awfully great person, but really just to be average and to be normal is something to be very appreciative of, because I was thinking it could very easily be that I could grow up to be a *bum*. I was watching some of the newsies, men about 35 or 40, selling their papers, and I thought, "Gee, just to be average really isn't such a little thing." For a man to have a respected position, he really doesn't need to be known even in his own community as a great figure, but to be average is really a very high position compared with how low a person could fall in the opposite direction where he would be a bum.

In these excerpts we see Alfred openly accepting his fantasies, and able to bring them fully into consciousness, recognizing that they are compensatory, recognizing that he has used them as a means of satisfaction right up to the present, perceiving the difference between fantasy satisfactions and the less glamorous but more substantial satisfactions of real goals, and finally accepting a realistic goal as his own. This is a rich, deep, and thoroughly effective instance of spontaneous insight.

In this same case there is still another thread of insight which is worthy of our attention. He was, as his been mentioned, a very withdrawn young man, with no satisfying contacts of a social nature, standing on the brink of creating his own private world in the form of a psychosis. A few of his statements, as he comes to see himself more clearly in this respect, will both illustrate the achievement of insight, and reveal the way the world looks to a highly seclusive individual. During the seventh interview he indicates something of his isolation, and the dawning realization that he might be able to deal with it.

> Alfred. It's like a curtain in a theatre, something that shuts me off from the players in the rest of the play. Just completely isolates me. Until I pull that curtain away and look at myself as being one of the players the same as anyone else, I won't be able to get very far. At times when I really get to looking at these things the way I should, I wonder why I don't jump in and get in the stream of life.

In the eleventh interview he begins to see this isolation as being partially in the past, giving a vivid picture of the way he felt. He also recognizes that he is changing, living more in a world of social reality.

> Alfred. I just withdrew a little more each year until things had gotten to a point that around Christmas time I started to wonder for fear I was the only person that was alive. I must have gotten away from the present world that much, that everything just kind of disappeared, kinda, and I felt as if I were standing on a hill all alone or something, and everything was gone, and here I was all alone. But the more I start going back in the group, why—I know the other day I was thinking about something, I don't know, I had my mind on something else, and I suddenly got the idea, "Well, how in the world could I have gotten the idea that I was the only person existing. Here this person is every bit the same as I am."

As might be supposed, it is not an easy matter to face all these deep problems within the self, and reorient to new goals, yet growth was steadily made during the interviews. In the sixteenth interview Alfred gives a picture of the two opposing forces within himself, the desire for growth and the desire to withdraw from life. His descrip-

tion of the constructive turmoil into which his life has been thrown
has the genuine literary quality which only accompanies a struggle
to say deeply significant things.

> Alfred. I certainly think in a way the problem is a lot clearer
> than a while ago, yet—maybe - - It's like the ice breaking up on a
> pond in the spring, it's—while things are a lot nearer to—While the
> pond is a lot nearer to being nothing but clear water, yet things are
> much more unstable now, possibly, than when the pond was covered
> with ice. What I'm trying to bring out is that I seem to be so much in
> a terrible fog all of the time lately, but I do feel a lot better off than
> I was before, because then I didn't even realize what was the matter.
> But maybe all this fog and so-called trouble is due to the fact of two
> opposing forces in me now. You know it's not really a case of just
> letting one be superior, but it's kinda breaking up and reorganizing
> that's going on now that makes things seem so doubly bad. So maybe
> I'm better off than I think.

The person who is skilled in therapy will realize that this is a
deep and genuine insight, and will not be surprised that in the next
interview Alfred made a definite decision to obtain a job as junior
counselor in a summer camp, a step he had contemplated before, but
about which he had been unable to come to a clear decision.

In this second train of insightful thinking, which could be illustrated with many other examples from the recordings, Alfred sees
clearly his icebound, frozen, isolated personality, and comes to see
also the attractiveness of life in a social, real, world. Though he also
perceives the pain and difficulty of such a radical reorganization of
life, he is able to face this and to take steps in the direction of social
life and social responsibility.

As may have been noted, these spontaneous insights, wrought out
of the individual's struggle to see himself more clearly, have a depth
and a sincerity and an individual quality which are quite lacking in
attempts on the part of the counselor to "give" the client insight.
This is the person seen from within, rather than without, and the
difference is very striking. As an illustration of the attempt to give
insight, a portion may be taken from an electrically recorded psychoanalysis, conducted by a reputable psychoanalyst. This example could
be duplicated hundreds of times in the course of the 424 interviews
of the analysis.

The patient, a schizophrenic young man, has been telling, in the
fourth interview, about vaguely guilty feelings which he had while
in the cafeteria, and the thought that if he did not eat much for
lunch, he could later go to the candy counter, but then remarks that
these ideas are foolish. The interview continues:

Analyst.   What does eating candy make you think of?

Patient.   Home, right away now. That's what it means.

Analyst.   And what does home make you think of?

Patient.   My mother.

Analyst.   And what does your mother make you think of?

Patient.   Oh, children, babies. Those ideas are put in my head. I don't know. I've got those thoughts again in my head.

Analyst.   Yes. And as you think of babies, what comes into your mind?

Patient.   Girls, I guess. Barbara Royce.

Analyst.   Barbara Royce?

Patient.   Yes. (very long pause).

Analyst.   You see, you have a guilt about Barbara Royce. You undoubtedly have sex feelings about her and something within yourself has been trying to convince you that this is wrong. That same part of your personality is making you feel guilty about eating, about going down to the cafeteria, about asking for a second course, about eating candy. You see, it connects right up with the thoughts that come, that somehow you—one part of you is trying to make you believe that all of that is wrong. Well, we know it isn't. (Pause) Why shouldn't you feel that way toward girls?

Patient.   Well, I don't see any reason why I shouldn't. That's just a - - Well, it's all right. (Long pause.) [3]

Here it seems all too clear that any seeing of relationships, any perception of pattern, is in the mind of the analyst, not in the mind of the patient. The nearest he comes to accepting his own feelings is a passive acceptance of the analyst's attitude, by saying, "Well, it's all right." This is pale indeed alongside of the spontaneous insights which we have been examining. It lacks any of the internal conviction which they carry. It shows how weak are attempts to *give* insight, when compared with the client's *achievement* of insight.

Our knowledge regarding insight comes not only from such examples as have been given, but from research studies which have been made. Three of these investigations have findings pertinent to the topic of insight. Snyder [4] has made an objective study of the characteristics of non-directive counseling in six complete counseling cases. He devised an objective list of 38 carefully defined categories and classified each of the nearly 10,000 client and counsel responses into one of these categories, thus making possible a statistical study of the counseling process. Raimy [5] has studied the changing concepts

---

[3] From an analysis recorded under the auspices of the Yale Institute for Human Relations.

[4] Wm. U. Snyder, "An Investigation of the Nature of Non-Directive Psychotherapy," unpublished Ph.D. thesis, The Ohio State University, Columbus, Ohio, 1943. A condensation of this thesis is shortly to be published in the *Journal of General Psychology.*

[5] Victor C. Raimy, "The Self-Concept as a Factor in Counseling and Personality Organization," unpublished Ph.D. thesis, The Ohio State University, Columbus, Ohio, 1943.

of the self which the individual exhibits in counseling. His study is
based on 14 recorded cases. Curran [6] has made an exhaustive analysis
of the case of Alfred, with particular reference to the problem of
insight. From these three studies certain findings in regard to self-
understanding in non-directive counseling may be briefly stated, with
the source in parenthesis.

1. Insight primarily follows outpourings of material with a negative emotional content, colored by such attitudes as hostility, self-
criticism, and hopelessness. (Curran)

2. Insightful responses are most likely to follow immediately upon
counselor responses of simple acceptance. They tend *not* to follow
interpretation, persuasion, or other directive counselor responses.
(Snyder)

3. An important aspect of insight is the seeing of relationships
between issues heretofore regarded as unrelated. (Curran)

4. Another important aspect of insight is the alteration of concepts of the self. Individuals who come for counseling tend to see
themselves in a strongly negative light as worthless, bad, inferior,
etc. As insight is gained and the self is accepted, the self-concept
is reorganized and a strong positive valuation is placed on it. The
individual sees himself in much more positive terms. (Raimy)

5. As insight is gained into given problems or issues, those problems tend to drop out of the client's conservation. (Curran)

6. Insight and the making of independent plans and decisions
both constitute a very small fraction of the client's conversation at
the outset of counseling, but rise to become a significant part of the
concluding interviews. These two categories taken together constitute 12.5 per cent of the client responses in initial interviews, 30.5
per cent of the middle interviews, and 42.5 per cent of the final counseling interviews. (Snyder)

With the evidence thus far given, indicating that spontaneous
insights do occur in non-directive counseling, that they exhibit themselves in a variety of ways, and that they are significant in altering
the client's concept of himself and his way of behaving, it becomes
important to ask ourselves, Under what conditions is this spontaneous insight most likely to be achieved?

A careful examination of a growing body of data brings one to
the conclusion that there is one primary principle operative. When
the client is freed from all need of being in any way defensive, spon-

6 Charles A. Curran, "An Analysis of a Process of Therapy Through Counseling and Its Implications for a Philosophy of Personality," unpublished Ph.D.
thesis, The Ohio State University, Columbus, Ohio, 1944.

taneous insight comes bubbling through into consciousness. When the client is talking through his problems in an atmosphere in which all his attitudes are genuinely understood and accepted, and in which there is nothing to arouse his desire to protect himself, insight develops.

Some workers will feel disappointed in the simplicity of this conclusion. They will feel that they have always dealt with clients in an accepting fashion. The fact is however that most of the procedures actually used in counseling contacts are such as to make clients defensive. This is clearly shown by our study of recorded interviews. It is not enough for the worker to have an accepting attitude, though this is important. The techniques used must also be such that defensiveness will not be aroused. Let us look at some of the methods actually employed by most workers.

Questions, for example, constitute one of the methods most frequently used in counseling. They may be simple questions such as, "When was that?" "Did he like it?" Or they may constitute an attempt to get deeper into attitudes expressed by asking, "Why did you feel that way about it?" "Why did you think that was bad?" "Why do you think these things happen?" Or questions may be of a highly probing nature, "What did you think about your mother?" "Will you behave next time the way you did this time?" In varying degrees all these questions arouse the psychological defenses of the client. There is always the fear that the questions may go too far, may uncover the attitudes which the client is afraid to reveal even to himself. Snyder's study showed that counselor questions tend to be followed frequently by rejection of the question by the client.

Evaluation responses are another familiar aspect of counseling. We have learned long ago that negative evaluations—comments which imply criticism, which question motives, which pass judgment on the client—tend to freeze the situation, and to make spontaneous expression difficult. We have not sufficiently learned that reassurance, agreement, and commendation have the same effect to a lesser degree. "I agree with you," "You're certainly right," "You've done very well," "You don't need to feel guilty about that," are the sort of well-intentioned comments which actually make it more difficult for the client to bring contradictory attitudes into the relationship. They show that the counselor is passing judgment on the client. These particular attitudes are judged favorably, but the client fears that there may be attitudes which will be judged unfavorably, and hence is unable to bring his thinking fully into the interview.

Advice and suggestions are, we know, freely given even by those who protest strongly that they do not wish to guide the client's life. "Of course you will want to make your own decision, but I think you might try . . . " is one of the many subtle ways by which we introduce our own solutions to the client's problems. Such procedures cut off free expression. In two ways they make the client defensive. If he brings out deeper attitudes it would seem to imply that the counselor had *not* solved the problem. It would also bring the possibility that the counselor would try to solve these deeper problems in ways which the client did not want.

Interpretation of the client to himself is a technique used somewhat by psychologists and social workers, and very heavily by psychiatrists and analysts. The more shrewd the interpretation, the more it hits the mark, the greater the defensiveness it arouses, unless the client has already reached that point of insight himself. Snyder found that interpretation, even when made by skilled counselors, is most likely to be followed by client responses which deny the interpretation. The client is thrown on the defensive.

To sum it up, most of the procedures which we customarily use in counseling tend to put the client subtly on his guard. As we analyze our psychotherapeutic contacts there are only two techniques which are actually in accord with the accepting viewpoint which most workers profess. These are simple acceptance—"Yes," "M-hm," "I understand"—and recognition and clarification of feeling. The first needs no explanation, but there is no doubt that it serves an important part in developing a permissive atmosphere where the client can discover insight.

The procedure of recognizing and clarifying attitudes is one which also has a deceptive simplicity. It consists in mirroring, reflecting for the client the feelings he has been expressing, often more clearly than he has been able to do for himself. Two examples might be given. The first one is a very simple reflection of a straightforward attitude, taken from the case of the aviation cadet mentioned earlier.

> Cadet. I should have soloed long ago. And here is something. Before I joined the Navy I was an overhead electrical crane operator, and that takes depth perception, coordination, and alertness; and I'm positive that I can apply that to my flying.
> Counselor. You feel that your training as a crane operator should help you in your flying.
> Cadet. That's right. And here's something else. . . .

This simple recognition of feeling serves the purpose of making expression of attitude easy, and of interposing nothing which will make the client in any way defensive. It makes him feel that he is understood, and enables him to go on to another area of emotionalized attitude, until gradually he has worked into the deeper and really significant realms.

Responses which might be termed clarification serve a further purpose of assisting the client to understand himself, but without any trace of an approach which would arouse defensiveness. A brief example from a case in which the man was disturbed over his tendency to gamble excessively will illustrate this point.

> Mr. R.   One thing I have thought of vaguely, that might be the cause of everything; I have had the props knocked out from under me so many times since I went into business. After I got out of the University I went into business in L - -, and had a good practice there, but my family didn't want me to stay there. They kept after me until I gave it up and came home. I worked for my father then, and had just gotten up to a decent job when I was let out for no particular reason. Next time I set up a lease that was profitable, and just at the time when I was about ready to profit from it, they cancelled the lease.
> Counselor.   You feel that the breaks have been against you.

Here the counselor's response puts briefly, and in clearer form, the underlying attitude which the client has been expressing. It is as such recognition and clarification of feeling frees the client from all need for defense, since it never in any way attacks the ego, that expression becomes freer, deeper attitudes are brought forth, and insights are developed. The justification for the development of these non-directive attitudes, and the skills which implement them, lie in the results which they bring.

This material has certain clear implications for the worker who deals with maladjusted clients in need of help. If deeper degrees of insight are deemed desirable, if it is important that the client reorganize his concept of himself, if he needs to find fresh and more satisfying ways of dealing with his problem, then the worker will increase the likelihood of this by adopting certain viewpoints and procedures. The worker will need to cultivate a tolerant, accepting attitude which quite genuinely accepts the individual as he is. Furthermore the worker will need to utilize in the counseling situation only those techniques, which prevent defensiveness from arising. Aside from simple acceptance, the major technique is that of mirroring for the client the emotionalized attitude which he is expressing. Snyder found that these two types of responses constituted nearly 75 per cent of the counselor's statements in non-directive counseling. Their use and the counselor's accepting attitude are undoubtedly the primary reason for the development of the spontaneous insights which have been discussed, insights which deeply alter the client's way of living.

SUMMARY

1. It has been found that in counseling situations of a non-directive character, new perceptions and understandings of self develop in spontaneous fashion.

2. These insights are of various types, some relatively simple, some highly complex and going to the root of the behavior patterns of the individual.

3. Research shows that these insights develop gradually in a non-directive counseling situation and mount to a peak toward the conclusion of the counseling experience. They follow free expression of negative emotion. They are closely connected with a positive change in the self concept. They are accompanied or followed by plans and decisions which involve the alteration of behavior.

4. Insights are not likely to follow counselor procedures which evaluate, question, probe, advise, or interpret. They are likely to develop if the counselor uses responses which are accepting and clarifying. Procedures which make defensiveness on the part of the client completely unnecessary, but which make the client feel that he is deeply understood, are most successful.

QUESTIONS

1. To what does the term "insight" refer in the context that Rogers explains it?
2. What are some of the better techniques for the counselor to employ that tend to eliminate the creation of a defensive attitude on the part of the counselee?
3. List and explain the major conclusions of this article.
4. Of what value is the development of self-understanding in the counseling situation?
5. What is the fundamental basis for recognizing and clarifying attitudes in a counseling situation?

THE COUNSELING INTERVIEW *

Leonard E. Himler

One of the things that we are learning more and more in this industrial age is that we cannot separate the human being on the job from the human being at home. Try as he will, the individual himself cannot prevent his relationships on the job from influencing his home life, or vice versa. It would be most helpful if every employee could check his personal problems in the cloakroom and then devote himself fully to his job during the remainder of the day. We know that doesn't happen; if it did, we could probably dispense with many of our managers. In reality, whether they realize it or not, much of the time of managers is spent in getting people to work together efficiently in spite of the personal problems, attitudes, and motives which they bring with them.

It has been estimated that in the aggregate around 60 or 70 per cent of the time of a business executive is spent in direct consultation with other people. Many of these contacts are private and of the type that we call interviews. This word "interview" is in some ways inadequate for our discussion, since it is somewhat cold and doesn't hint at all of the rich meaning that I should like to give this subject. The term "inter-personal contact" sounds more technical but I think expresses more fully what we are trying to discuss. The word interview has been used so much in connection with employment techniques that many take it for granted that we are concerned almost entirely with such procedures. But it should be emphasized that there are many other types besides employment interviews. There are counseling interviews, interviews concerning salary increase, warning interviews, interviews in regard to referring an employee to another place or person, discharge interviews, job evaluation interviews, exit interviews, and so on. As a matter of fact new uses for interviews in industry are constantly being developed. Employee opinion interviews can be mentioned as an example. Questionnaires without the aid of interviews always fall short of revealing the true picture in getting employee opinions. It is true, of course, that in the hands of some individuals interviews also fail in some respects to get at the most significant factors. But until something

* From *Addresses on Industrial Relations*, Bulletin No. 16, 1945, pp. 63-74, Bureau of Industrial Relations, University of Michigan. Reprinted with permission.

better comes along, interviews remain the best instrument for getting close to a human being to find out what he thinks and what he wishes, how he feels and what motivates him, and how you can influence him constructively for your benefit as well as for his own.

Another new use for the interview technique is in connection with employee appraisal studies. The older term "merit rating" is being discarded, since it has come to be associated with the unpleasant thought of passing sentences on employees. But, in the interest of productivity, we need to make periodic appraisals of employees. We can get rid of the idea of passing judgment on someone with the possibility that he might be treated unfairly, if we think of the appraisal interview as an instrument that attempts to evaluate his services and then helps him to help himself. In effect this is the goal of all counseling interviews. The appraisal interview offers a most effective channel through which an employee can be taught and motivated to so organize himself in relation to his job that everyone, including himself, will profit.

In order to do a proper "man analysis" of this sort it is of course necessary to have specific interviewing techniques which make it possible to get into effective personal contact with the man. The psychiatrist's approach is also based on a private face-to-face conversation, and in his analysis the evolution of a person's emotional life constitutes the core of the discussion. In business and industrial relationships when employer and employee try to solve their problems by similar personal contacts, the goal is to improve job efficiency, but emotional factors inevitably crop up and they must also be handled. Obviously the outcome of all inter-personal contacts, whether on the skilled professional level or whether on the business supervisory level, will depend on the interplay of many complex factors. Most important are the knowledge of people and the philosophy of human nature which the interviewer possesses, and secondly, the skill and effectiveness with which he puts into practice certain specific techniques used to study, appraise, influence, and motivate his fellow human beings.

Considering not only skill but also time limitations, there is always some question as to just how accurately the true facts of a given situation can be determined in the ordinary interview. Obviously when an inexperienced interviewer abruptly demands of an employee, "Now what's on your mind?" there is not much likelihood of uncovering more than surface resentments. Even with experienced interviewers the possibility always exists of getting only symptoms and interesting sidelights on a problem rather than its basic underlying factors and causes. The challenging question before us is, how can we best employ the interview as an instrument to give us all that we're after, provided of course, that we recognize the heart of a problem when it is disclosed. By and large, in the average interview, one can expect to get more in the nature of symptoms and complaints than causes. The skillful interviewer has learned how to distinguish smoke from fire, and above all, how to avoid being lost in the smoke screen which often conceals the true facts.

Five main steps in interviewing

There are at least five main steps to be kept in mind in conducting interviews. First, of course—and I don't want to dwell on this because you all understand that there are many ways of doing it—it is important to put the person at ease. That in itself should certainly not be difficult. It is often said that one of the quickest ways to put a person at ease is to ask him to sit down. No one is comfortable for long while standing up, and anger and irritation are more quickly aroused in that position. You may have noticed that when anyone bristles with anger at a conference he rises from his chair almost automatically. When a person gets angry the nervous system mobilizes energy to support him in a fighting position. And of course, under such conditions he is in anything but the best position for constructive motivation by some other human being. Hence the necessity of putting the individual at ease, even if the subject is highly controversial.

The next step is to instill confidence in the person being interviewed, and for this psychiatrists and psychologists are accustomed to use the word "rapport," which refers to a mutual feeling of friendliness and sympathetic unity. That is, the aim is to have the interviewer and interviewee share a feeling that they are working together on a common problem involving both of them, even if some points are in definite disagreement at the outset. It is possible for a psychiatrist, for instance, to get "rapport" even with a wildly disturbed, insane person. Even under such extreme conditions he can still make that person feel that he has come to help, regardless of the patient's insistence that there is nothing wrong and that he is being detained against his will. It is often amazing how one who is experienced can establish rapport even with a person who is practically out of touch with reality, who is emotionally uncontrolled, or is hearing voices. If this is true of mental patients, it is certainly more true of the contact between two normal human beings if the significance of it is but recognized.

Thirdly, in order to get information, it may be necessary also to give some information, but it should never be forgotten that effective interviews are mostly designed to draw out information and permit the other fellow to do the talking. How to minimize irrelevant conversation and how to get the basic and significant information is, of course, the great challenge, and doing this effectively requires knowledge of the various interviewing techniques.

Another step, stressed more in psychiatric work than in industry and business, has to do with giving insight, that is, making the person understand the problem a little differently and from other angles than he did before. This involves much more than just giving advice. It is more then just telling him what you think or what you would do if you were in his place. Giving insight means using the interview technique to stimulate him to see his problem a little differently, and as a result he comes to a new conclusion about the thing that's bothering him. That may be a request for promotion, transfer, increase in salary, or any of the multitude of daily problems which if not properly handled accumulate and undermine efficiency and cooperation.

The fifth step which is closely tied up with giving understanding or insight, involves motivating the individual to carry out a different or at least improved type of action than that which he might have originally performed. For instance, let us say that he asks for an increase in wages, and that under existing conditions the request cannot be granted. The interviewer's responsibility certainly should go beyond merely giving a curt refusal, since the object is to keep up the employee's interest and cooperation even if he does not get the increase. This cannot be achieved by merely "stalling," although there are still some men in business who think that interviewing under such circumstances is just a matter of putting the other fellow off with a wordy sermon or with vague and empty promises. On the contrary, if the interview is properly conducted, the individual goes away richer from the experience, and sometimes even more effectively motivated than if he is simply given the increase in a perfunctory way. Merely bestowing a raise or a promotion does not in itself assure a better performance.

As an instrument for human motivation, the interview has power that goes above monetary gain. Cash, to be sure, is a tangible measure of a man's value, but there is much more in the final satisfaction which he gets from his work than his pay check. It should be apparent that the interview relationship can create as well as destroy common bonds of loyalty and inspiration. Much more is involved in interviewing than merely giving in to pressure on the one hand or showing the other fellow that you not afraid of him (when you really are) on the other. The interview can establish influences and emotional bonds which are powerful factors in an industrial enterprise. Money alone cannot match that.

The Hawthorne technique

Everyone in business should be familiar with the experiments carried out at the Hawthorne plant of the Western Electric Company, and with the book, "Management and the Worker," by F. J. Roethlisberger and W. J. Dickson, which describes the technique developed as a result of this work. It might be helpful at this point to review briefly some of the main points of the so-called Hawthorne technique of interviewing.

In that approach the interview is regarded as a social experience in itself, in the sense that has been mentioned above. It is an experience involving two people which has effects beyond just getting the immediate job done. It should have a quality all of its own, and the ability to give it this quality can be studied and learned. Some people, apparently without any special effort, seem to have a natural ability to make their contacts with others meaningful and effective. But on the basis of my own experience and of observations of students in training, I believe that anyone who has a genuine interest can, in the process of time, steadily improve in practicing this art. It is important not merely to copy the techniques of those who are successful in interviewing, as that would be stilted and artificial, but it is valuable to study both the spirit and the methods used, then put your own coloring on the process. There is of course no substitute for personal experience, and in interviewing one must also learn sometimes by one's mistakes. On the other hand if you are not conscious of the need constantly to improve, you will miss many opportunities to learn new techniques from others.

The chief responsibility of every executive is to influence more people to a greater extent than is possible if interviewing techniques are disregarded. Many men in business and industry are elevated to jobs involving administrative duties over other people, but often not because or account of possessing that ability. Men who are worthy of promotion because of skill and technical knowledge have not always picked up all the devices which would make them more effective in handling people. That technique is something that is not taught in school, and it must be acquired and absorbed as one goes along. It is distressing to see executives who have tremendous power over others administering it as they would the laws of physics instead of the laws of human nature. It is understandable, but it is not so readily overlooked or forgiven that some of these men have been too busy with their engineering problems to bother about human psychology. But it should not be forgotten that an executive must be an engineer of human beings, and this requires some skill, at least some thought, which the text books on engineering simply don't give. Nor will job analysis, as such, give you all this. The science of man analysis should be increasingly helpful.

To go on with the Hawthorne technique: First, it is fundamentally a listening technique. You take a friendly, patient, receptive attitude toward another human being. You are not biased in any way. You're neutral, and yet you're more than neutral because you are friendly at the same time. You are intelligently critical, as it has been well expressed. That means you are objective. You have a scientifically detached, and yet at the same time a warm human attitude. That, in brief, is the listening method. It's not as easy as it sounds. The mere word listening does not encompass all of the technique. There is more to it than merely bending a sympathetic ear to all that is said. Interviewing involves also selection of what to pay attention to, discovering information which needs to be emphasized and amplified, and quite often redirecting the stream of conversation into significant channels. You have to select those topics which it is important to bring into the open, and you must be able to sidestep features that are not pertinent, but which, of course, may come along with the story as it unfolds under your sympathetic guidance. The art consists in doing that with an economy of time, and still not getting too far away from what you wish to accomplish in the end.

Along with this you must always be aware of a number of "don'ts." I should like to mention at least five of them, all involving the letter "a," which makes it easier to remember them. Don't argue; don't admonish; don't advise; don't display authority; and don't let the other person's feelings affect yours. You must remain calm, yet not so calm that you are sublimely unaffected or untouched by his feelings. You must be in communication with him, but without being infected with his anger, fear, or defensiveness. You must be careful not to get yourself maneuvered into a position where you're defending yourself. That is arguing, not interviewing. If an individual can't attack the capitalistic system which he vaguely feels is responsible for his frustration singlehanded, he may feel justified in attacking the personal representative of the system, which in this case may be yourself, his employer. You for the moment are a much more tangible target for resentment and abuse. Now in such an event do you rise up in righteous indignation, justifying yourself with the thought, "He can't talk to me that way; who does he think he is; I'll put him in his place," etc. If you do, that is the end of the Hawthorne technique right there for you, because you have slipped into the natural instinctive response of raising your fists in response to his. You see that this is not the interviewing approach we are trying to describe here. Situations of this type serve to illustrate again that this non-directed technique which stresses listening as its main ingredient is not so easy as it sounds, and it often calls for reserve powers of control and good judgment.

Then besides listening, you have to talk at least to some extent. But you almost have to ration what you say. You ought to talk just as I'm talking into this microphone, aware that any slip will be on record for all time, and this realization naturally exerts a little restraint on anything I say. That is the way you should go into the interview, yet you must not freeze up with the disease known as "interview fright," which corresponds in some ways to "mike fright." The rule to remember is that you should talk in a well-conducted interview only to help the other fellow talk. That is the whole goal of your conversation—to help him talk about things that you want him to talk about or that he wants to say but may not be able to say unless you help. There are many problems that a person can't discuss unless he is in an atmosphere that encourages it.

Here is a simple example. A short time ago I had an opportunity to interview a young girl who had been happily married only a year when her husband was sent to the South Pacific, where he was killed in battle. The girl was an average, normal, healthy young adult, not in any sense a psychiatric case. She was working at her old job in an office when the sudden bad news came. She took it bravely and, after a few weeks absence, returned to her work. Months went by, during which all she received to remind her of her broken dreams were her own letters returned one by one. Her friends respected her as the wife of a man who died in fulfilling his duty, but the loneliness of life without a strong emotional tie was beginning to weigh heavily upon her. Then one day, just after she had been sent the purple heart, she suddenly broke down at work, stated she was unhappy in her job, and without any other plan, insisted that she had better quit.

What should the employer do in such an instance? Take the distraught girl's word for it and release her? Offer her an opportunity to transfer to another department as a willingness to help? Refer her to a psychiatrist? Obviously none of these possibilities will entirely take care of the immediate situation that has flared up in an acute emotional episode. There is need for a genuine counseling contact here. The counselor must help this girl get rid of some of her excessive tension and help her to face her problem with more hope. Right here is where some men make an error in their technique. When a woman is sobbing, many men think, "I must do everything possible to stop those tears." So these men attempt to handle the problem by saying, "Don't cry. Buck up. Everything will turn out all right," or words to that effect, which of course aim merely at getting rid of the problem, not solving it. For this girl everything obviously isn't turning out right, and such misdirected reassurance only adds to her sense of desolution and discouragement.

. . . Rather than offer stereotyped reassurances, the technique of using a respectful period of silence—what I like to call an "expectant pause"—is often much more effective. When you sit by quietly and do little or no talking you have prepared the way for a talk in which the girl unburdens herself, at least of the most immediate worries. In this instance the girl responded by talking about her inner sense of loneliness, how she missed the love and attention which her husband had given her, and how she despaired of ever again being happy. She didn't want to be disloyal to the memory of her husband, but she is still quite young and her needs are for more than just grief over what is gone and past. As she talked it became more and more clear that she was not crying so much out of grief as she was because normal love and affection had been denied her.

You may say at this point that it certainly isn't the girl's employer's place to supply the missing emotional needs. That is of course true. But if he has merely listened to her this far, he has already helped her. By providing a sympathetic atmosphere in which she can say some of these things, matters that at first sound a little like disloyalty and selfishness, you have really done an expert bit of counseling. Your respect for her right to try to express what is troubling her removes the first obstacle in her path, a path which will eventually lead her to a reconstructed social and emotional life.

She's entitled to that; no one would argue this, her dead husband least of all. By helping her to see all this you have given her an experience from which she can raise her head again and go on clear-eyed. The tears recede without any entreaty to stop them by effort of will. It is very satisfying a few weeks later to find such a case happily back on the job, grateful for your human interest, and hopeful again that somehow life can go on. The counselor helped to make that possible, even though he had no ready-made answers as to just how she must manage the rest of her life. It's good for her that he doesn't.

Men too can be troubled by worries and insecurities which do not cause an outburst of tears, but result in a show of anger and irritability over little trifles. A man, may, for example, have a veritable tantrum over a small bookkeeping error, but the real cause of all the emotion is not the mistake in the office, but the problems he brought with him from home. This sort of difficulty is not at all rare. When the counselor has the proper point of view toward personality flareups of this kind, his mind is open to indications which lead to the real trouble, and it is surprising how soon this comes out if he will but use the listening technique. But if you try to stop the tears or fight back before you hear the story out, you are violating the principle of the Hawthorne method.

And you don't have to give advice or lectures on the advantages of controlling one's temper. You just have to give the person concerned the right to say privately what's bothering him. Speech is used only to smooth the ground for inter-communication and occasionally to point out good points in the situation. It is not wise to dish out praise too freely or to praise the individual for every statement he makes, but it is helpful to praise accurate observations or statements that are undoubtedly true and valid. Praise often opens the way for further confidence, just as suspiciousness closes it. The counselor almost needs to bite his tongue to stop any tendency to lecture or moralize at length, for that is simply interrupting and interfering with the effective use of the listening technique.

The interviewer should always be prepared to listen first to what is uppermost in the individual's mind. It is seldom possible to make good progress unless this "head of steam" is permitted to escape at the beginning of the interview. The interviewee may in the process tend to wander off and talk about subjects that, as far as you can see at the moment, have no relationship to the important problem of being efficient on the job. On such occasions it is sometimes necessary to guide the conversation back into the main channel. On the other hand, every once in a while a little exploring of the by-ways is richly rewarded by revelations which come quite unexpectedly. It takes alert attention, skill, and judgment to keep open the channels of communication when the information seems to be dammed up. There are a number of people like the girl mentioned, who simply cannot talk at once about the things that are bothering them, but who respond quite readily after a little encouragement. Like getting a small splinter out from under the skin, emotional troubles at first resist being explored, and it may even hurt a little when this has finally been accomplished. Then healing can take place from the bottom up, which is the kind of healing a physician always strives to bring about.

Some emotional experiences, such as those which soldiers have to go through, become more deeply buried, and this is why it is hard for some of these men to even talk about them. It is obvious that deep-seated, repressed experiences can become quite disturbing, and the treatment of such problems may require the skill of a psychiatrist. The listening technique, rather than too much curiosity or too many questions, is to be preferred in dealing with returning veterans. It is natural to be curious about some of his war experiences, but the technique of being attentive to what he says and being willing to listen before becoming inquisitive or prying is always the best approach.

This then is the method which has been called the Hawthorne technique. It involves listening, it involves some don'ts and it involves a little, sometimes very little talking. One could give a number of scientific names for each of these steps, but in essence that's all there's to it. In practice, however, it's not so easy as it sounds.

Emotional transference in interviewing

One point worthy of special mention concerns the interviewer's own emotions. He should not be overly disturbed if he sometimes feels neutral or even a little reluctant to begin an interview. It is perfectly natural to feel some resistance to beginning interviews which have every indication of being difficult or even downright unpleasant, at least in part. We all have this kind of reluctance for instance when we are forced to take an arrogant employee to task. She has to be talked to about her manners, her telephone voice, her errors, her absences, or whatever it may be, and this is not an enviable assignment. Or suppose this same girl keeps coming in every two weeks with a request for an increase in salary. Since you do not enjoy the experience, you might be tempted to assume a brusque, dictatorial manner in the hope of getting rid of the problem by intimidation.

Inexperienced interviewers are sometimes distressed by the initial reluctance they feel in dealing with difficult personalities, and it is good to know that they need not feel ashamed or inferior because of this unpleasant reaction. It must be accepted as part of the experience. Often the more reluctance one feels at the beginning of an interview, the more of the opposite emotion there is potentially in the situation, after the process has been carried past that first hurdle. Shared emotional experiences go through many shifting changes of intensity, even to the point of reversing the original attitudes. This does not mean that the two people have to wind up falling in love with each other in order for the interview to be successful. We must not jump to that erroneous conclusion, as some do who have read a smattering of Freudian psychology. The word for this shared emotional experience is "transference." Whether it is fully understood or not, there is a transfer of emotions during the interview, and the important point is that both parties feel it.

This matter of mutual feeling during the interview is a delicate subject, and just to what degree you must feel certain emotions is difficult to describe, and certainly impossible to express in any mathematical terms. But sometimes I've felt that the amount of feeling you get out of it is in reverse proportion to the reluctance you have to start with. At any rate this should give encouragement to those who dread the first few minutes of an interview.

A well-conducted interview is an emotional experience and that means that it is work. After a day of it you can be as tired as if you had dug a six-foot ditch, half a block long. In some ways it is even harder. This is true especially if you are dealing with persons who are hostile, irritable, annoyed, critical, or ready to bite your head off if you make a false move. It is understandable why some executives and supervisors tend to avoid such interviews, or try to carry them on in an entirely aloof, mechanical way, refusing to become enmeshed in any emotional entanglements, and remaining securely within their own shell. This may be self-protection, but it's not interviewing. Before you finish a good interview you have felt something, and the other fellow also undergoes a similar experience. This is a feature of interviewing which surpasses in importance the mechanical steps which were outlined in the previous section.

Psychological blind spots

One simply cannot talk about interviewing, whether it is for employment, for an appraisal, or for a salary increase, without mentioning certain limitations, certain obstacles that constantly present themselves. It is worthwhile to think of these in advance. In psychology some of these limitations to effective interviewing are called blind spots. You all know that the human eye is a well-nigh perfect instrument, but there is one small spot, just to the outer side of the direct line of vision where it is blind. This spot is so small that for all practical purposes it is negligible, but psychological blind spots— those things in life which you don't see or understand—can be much bigger. Some people have such strong opinions and prejudices that they never even see the person opposite them for what he is. They are blinded by their own preconceived notions about that person.

So often a supervisor has such a deep-seated conviction against an employee that even if the employee miraculously lost all his faults it would not even register with his supervisor. Too often we think our set opinions about people are unchangeable. This attitude becomes a great handicap in interviewing and counseling. People who try to simplify their relationships with others by such preconceived fixed notions almost defy you to find any other interpretation of the other fellow's behavior. They never give another human being any credit for change, and, it follows of course, they often change very little themselves. They want to go through life without modifying any of their ideas. People with blind spots of that kind are the world's worst counselors.

All of us have some pet theories or ideas which in certain situations may amount to blind spots. A counselor should always try to understand his own and then try not to let them interfere with his efforts to help the other fellow. Take for instance your own ideas about drinking. Depending on your habits and your attitude toward alcohol, you are quite apt to immediately form an opinion or pass judgment on another if his practices differ from yours. Even though a man's drinking habits may need correction, that in itself is not a sound basis for judging his ability on a job. You must be careful not to carry over conclusions from one area into another whether they pertain to drinking or creed or race or some other matter. Those can become tremendous blind spots. Even one's opinion concerning another's political beliefs can become an influence which goes way beyond its actual importance.

Other psychological mechanisms which influence interviews

In the field of applied psychology the term "mechanism" refers to more or less standardized or systematized units of behavior which a person uses to attain his ends. In business and industry the one mechanism which influences the behavior of many ambitious young men is "identification." If you grew up under an employer whom you respected, who had an efficient way of doing business, you naturally admired him and tended also to be like him and use his methods, even to the point of being unimpressed or impatient with any other ways of conducting business affairs and contacts.

Let us suppose however that you grew up under an industrialist who used the iron fist ruthlessly in his climb to the top and that you served this man twenty or thirty years ago. In those times human beings could be bought cheaply, there was always a big bullpen full of them asking for work, and none of them were veterans with employment rights. It wasn't necessary to have any special technique for dealing with employees—power and authority and money, combined with engineering skill were all more important than interviewing skills. If you identified yourself with an executive of that era you might find it hard to accept any other formula for dealing with people. The techniques we have been discussing would seem "soft" and ineffectual. Even though the times have changed, you might find yourself clinging to the outworn techniques with which you identified yourself. Your identifications then have become blind spots for you, and they are now handicaps in your interrelationships with people. This example may seem overdrawn, but it serves to illustrate how all of us have had experiences in our past life which continue to influence our present contacts and which are shaping our techniques, sometimes in a very subtle way.

If you regard an interview as a truly dynamic, new experience, you must be prepared to feel yourself changing in your attitude and opinions about a person. You must be prepared to modify, even reverse your first impressions, all of which are based on past experiences, but in the present situation they may be entirely misleading and erroneous. Far from going through the interview merely to prove that your preconceived notions are right, you should welcome a change in feeling regarding the other person when you have had an opportunity to hear what he says and judge him for what he really is. That is what I meant awhile back when I said you too are undergoing emotional experiences at the same time the person who is talking to you is releasing his.

Another important limitation in interviewing is of course its cost in time. Interviewing is a time consuming procedure, but if insufficient time is allowed for doing it right, the individual will come back with more problems later, and in the end the time loss may even be greater. Suppose that an office manager never really took the time to counsel a "problem-employee," and yet every day that employee's inefficiency cost him fifteen or twenty minutes, not only of her time, but probably also of that of others around her. Emotional difficulties cannot be sidestepped by saying there isn't time to work them through, since they only grow rather than disappear if they are not faced frankly and treated correctly.

One little disagreeable after-effect of interviewing is the possibility of being misquoted or misrepresented to someone else by the individual who was interviewed. I could give you some very rich examples from my own experience of the unconventional if not actually illegal advice I'm supposed to have given in interviews. The human tendency to misquote at the other fellow's expense will crop up in this work every now and then. You have to run that risk. It doesn't mean that counseling only makes a bad matter worse. It's natural and perhaps in some cases forgiveable for human beings to turn things about and discredit the counselor a bit in order to save face. In psychology, this is the mechanism of projection.

Another limitation in interviewing is the temptation we all have to tell our own experiences. There are so many kind and well-meaning executives whose conceptions of a counseling interview consists of giving out a long story of their own rise to fame, then adding, sometimes even audibly, "Take a look at me. See what I've done. Now you go out and do the same thing." And they really believe that is counseling and that an employee gets inspiration by listening to them. It helps, but not in the way such a person thinks, because he's the one who has enjoyed the emotion of seeing his own reflection as he talks, after which he very probably has softened up to any proposal which the employee may have up his sleeve. The therapy here was for the person who did the interviewing rather than for the person who listened. Once in awhile an employee gets a little out of those long-winded stories, but it is only fair to warn you that this is a very weak way to counsel. It's almost as bad as giving too much advice.

Another pitfall in interviewing is to be maneuvered into a position where you make a promise you can't keep. Take the example of the foreman who steps into a beer garden and gets a little too friendly with people under him. In such a situation he could easily be maneuvered into a discussion in which statements are made that might weaken his relationships on the job. Obviously situations of this kind can more easily be prevented than corrected.

A professional psychiatrist can very comfortably establish a zone of neutrality in his office in which his patient can feel free to complain against anybody or anything—the more the merrier. In the employer's office this same individual cannot feel free. He cannot forget that you are his employer and that you have the hiring and firing authority over him. In other words, your authority stands in the way of his freedom to tell you fully what he thinks and how he feels. The Hawthorne technique is helpful, but it does not fully eliminate this obstacle. It was developed in a neutral atmosphere divorced from the Personnel Department, and the counselors using this technique stand aside pretty much like a physician who takes a kindly interest and respects your confidence without pretense of any authority over you.

But most employers, and especially those in a small organization, must do some counseling notwithstanding the fact that they have authority. They can't step out of their role as employer while trying to help individuals who come to them or are referred to them for interviews. Fortunately this dilemma is not always as disturbing as it sounds, but it does serve to point out the need for full awareness of authority as a limitation in interviewing and counseling.

An employer who freely displays his authority or uses it as a club would scarcely rate higher than thirty per cent so far as the effectiveness of his interviews are concerned. Such a man never realizes how poor he is. If he could hear himself described by those he thought he was helping, he might be made uncomfortably aware of his inadequacy. Some of these men have no security unless they are expressing authority, and you can feel it the minute you enter their offices. Underneath, such men are really afraid. The more they wield the policeman's club the more they reveal it. It is sometimes helpful to keep this in mind when dealing with such men.

Another limitation in counseling has to do with the age factor. You will notice that good counseling techniques are usually illustrated with case histories of young people. It is true that it is easier to modify the attitudes of people before they have reached the age of thirty or thirty-five. People of forty, forty-five or fifty are less amenable to great change even with the best techniques. After a man has passed fifty he is pretty well hardened into a pattern which cannot be greatly modified. Counseling is a less effective agent with older persons.

The salary interview

Now let us take for an example a salary interview. This type of interview comes up again and again, and I believe provisions should be made to meet it before waiting for the inevitable recurrence of the request for a raise. My own feeling is that an employer ought to talk salary to every important employee at least once every six months.

One of the ways to discourage an employee, of course, is never to discuss salary. He either gets discouraged and quits, or keeps bringing the subject up, getting more frustrated and inefficient each time. Obviously not everyone can have a raise every time he asks for it. And the people who are most persistent in asking are often not the ones who ought to get the increases. It is unfortunate but true that many salary increases are given to those who raise a hue and cry; the increases are given to get relief from the clamor. Those persistent demands should be stopped by a good interview technique.

There are endless methods of getting rid of the person who asks for an increase when it cannot be granted. One is the "stalling technique" of at first acting receptive, then seizing the first opportunity to divert him from the subject, until pretty soon he finds himself out in the hall, but without what he wanted. You may say, "Well, I got rid of that one easily." But did you? The man was not even given the courtesy of a direct answer, and he is bound to resent being put off, no matter how adroitly it was managed. Remember too that this man has to face his wife and she is not going to appreciate the sleight-of-hand he was given. All this means that he will probably be discontented on the job, that he will do no more than is expected, and will in effect be on a sort of sit-down strike for a time until he cools off, gets another job, or can pull a "squeeze-play" to match your technique in getting what he wants. If his work falls off and he is reprimanded for that, he becomes all the more convinced that he'll never get the rate, and so the downhill spiral goes on. This sort of thing happens to people who are potentially valuable employees. It isn't only the unworthy ones that get the treatment.

The most effective way to meet a salary request, whether it is granted or not, is to conduct a proper interview. The goal should be to send the individual out of your office, realistically facing his situation, satisfied that he has had a square deal, that his problem has been given fair consideration, and that there is something in the future to look forward to. This can be done even if he is not granted the increase.

In contrast to this is the method of getting rid of a wage demand by saying that due to war conditions the employee's wages are frozen, and so your hands are tied, etc. This stirs up as much resentment as the sarcastic remark, "Don't you know there's a war on?" It attempts to get rid of responsibility by taking refuge in authoritative rulings, and even if the answer is true, it must be covered with an interview technique which does justice to the employee's individuality.

In a properly conducted salary interview you should find out why the employee wants the raise, why he feels entitled to it, what problems he has that a raise, in his mind, will solve, and so on. As he does the talking, he will develop other aspects of his plans in your organization, his future, his home, and his activities outside the business. In the course of the conversation you lead him to weigh the alternatives of an immediate raise against the possibilities of promotion in the long run. The degree of long-range planning that an employee does is an excellent gauge of his value, and a good salary interview will bring this out.

My argument is that whether a person deserves a raise or doesn't deserve it, whether he gets it or doesn't get it, he should walk away from the salary interview satisfied that he has had a hearing, that his complaints have been listened to, that the reasons he thought were adequate for the raise were carefully considered, even if they were not strong enough to be convincing. Instead of regarding such interviews as a necessary evil, the employer should approach them with an element of expectation. He might ask himself, "How well can I handle this difficult situation in which I'm going to frustrate this individual? He isn't going to get what he wants. Yet I'm going to make him walk away with a substitute that is equivalent or even better than just giving him a little raise. Perhaps I need to show him that he ought to prepare himself for life more realistically, more in terms of his own eventual good and that of the organization with with he is identified."

To be sure, the war has interfered with the real meaning of this argument to the effect that the best things in life come in the long pull and not in a sudden gift without merit. This of course makes the interview today just that much harder—the fact that an employee can go somewhere else and get more wages because of the manpower shortage. But you've got to sell him on long-range values even in the face of a short gain that he can get without effort.

It should not be forgotten that even if they cannot phrase it in other ways, most people are working for something more than mere money. If you think that dollars and cents are all that your interview must be concerned with, you are missing much in your understanding of what motivates people. You do not come to grips with the real issues if you just talk money. What the employee is searching for is what he feels money can do for him, the love he can get with it, and the respect and prestige it will bring. The more basic needs of security, opportunity, and long-range gains can be woven into an interview without giving the employee a long lecture on how long it took you to get where you are, that he shouldn't live beyond his means, etc.

The returning veteran is interesting in this respect. With his recent experiences still fresh and his knowledge that life can be lost in a few seconds, he may be a little impatient with people who talk about long-range values, and may be more intensely interested in the immediate rewards and opportunities which in some respects are due him. With him, even to a greater extent than with other employees, we should avoid stalling techniques or other evasive methods. The need is for interviews which give definite, concrete answers and which motivate men the way military life did in building up a team spirit.

"R. S. V. P." in counseling

In summing up, we might express the four chief aims of an effective interview in the letters R. S. V. P., which stand for Reassurance, Suggestion, Ventilation, and Participation. These procedures are especially useful in dealing with individuals who have a need for counseling, who are nervous and high-strung, and who are not adjusting themselves satisfactorily.

In giving Reassurance, the counselor tries to give a person a feeling of security, even though the person is emotionally upset and feeling quite insecure. This is often achieved by the process of being allowed to speak about the problem and everything that is disturbing the individual. The physician can use reassurance on the basis of his examination and knowledge that there is no organic disease. Employees who are afraid that they will be fired, who don't know where they stand, who are fearful of making mistakes, and all those who are excessively insecure on the job, need and profit most from reassurance, even if this can only be given provisionally.

Another approach is through the use of Suggestion. As was implied in the discussion of salary interviews, suggestion is used when ideas are mentioned that focus the individual's attention on other points besides those he considers of first importance. The employee may come into your office with just one thought: "I want that $5.00 raise." And what do you do? You throw out other possibilities: other aspects which he is not thinking of at the moment or may not even have thought of at all; questions relative to his future with the company; other ways of giving service which he has neglected; and other satisfactions which he is getting from his job besides his wages. Office work for instance is getting many little satisfactions which are not present in factory work, and even though the pay is less, the long-range security is better. Attention is drawn to these features with the implication that there are other advantages to the present work besides the salary.

You should be prepared to use suggestion just as the physician does in dealing with a nervous patient who is overconcerned about his heart palpitation. Energy which is being directed toward the function of one organ needs to be dispersed, and this is the way tension is alleviated, whether the organ in question is really diseased or not. By reminding a person of other features of his life which also are worthy of attention, we relieve him of worry over only one disturbance, and he is then free to get relief which comes through balanced activity. That in brief is the art of suggestion. The goal is to throw the attention away from things that bother a person excessively even if these things have a certain amount of basis in reality. Suggestion then is controlled attention, by means of which thought and energy is redirected into another more constructive channel.

This technique is useful every once in awhile when you must deal with an unhappy employee. Some individuals get disturbed over one aspect of their job and they may accumulate so much tension over it that their entire efficiency is undermined. As in renaming a "draft" a "circulation of air," you can bring attention to other aspects of the identical situation which is causing the trouble and change a person's attitude toward it. This is a useful technique, provided the original situation is an average one and the individual does not have too many other problems.

The "V" of these four initials refers to Ventilation. This is sometimes spoken of as "psychological drainage." It refers again to permitting the person to talk out his problem. If it happens to be worry over a draft, for instance, as he talks he may very likely develop the idea that drafts cause various diseases, and he may reveal that this fear of diseases was suggested to him by someone who was merely repeating hearsay. The interview permits him to work out the conclusion that in a state of anxiety or apprehension he was too quick to seize upon a complaint which is only incidental to his working conditions, and not a cause of his trouble at all.

And finally, the most important thing to be accomplished in the interview is to enlist the individual's Participation in the solution to his problem. You do not order or command him to solve his own problem, but you indicate and suggest in various ways that he can and should take an active part himself in bringing about a better end-result. This should be a part of every interview, and can best be emphasized toward the concluding part, as the interview progresses and the employee is first shown that the end he desires involves a number of other aspects. He is then asked to focus on one particular aspect which seems most likely to be helpful in arriving at the desired end. For instance, an employee who needs to improve his skills before he is qualified for the pay increase he desires could improve himself by attending night school. One cannot order people to improve themselves in this way, but the suggestion can be made and then, when there is opportunity for another interview, it will be evident whether or not the employee was interested in helping himself by making special effort.

The person who participates in constructive suggestions of this type is usually the more valuable employee, and he should be rewarded accordingly. The diagnosis of the person who demands something that he makes no effort to earn soon becomes apparent if regular follow-up interviews are made available, whether these are concerned specifically with salary or any other topic. From then on it's much easier to handle the requests for salary increase. Persons who do not accept suggestions and opportunities for cooperative participation can be shown why their requests must be denied.

No interview is complete unless some effort is made in the direction of a follow-up, even if it involves only showing interest in subsequent outcomes or developments. Even if you cannot begin to solve every employee's problems through interviews, you should always strive to convey to them your continuing interest in their efforts to help themselves and in your willingness to assist them.

SUPPLEMENT

PRACTICAL STEPS IN CONDUCTING COUNSELING INTERVIEWS

The general aim of the counseling interview is to establish a "zone of neutrality" in which the employee can talk out rather than act out his troublesome impulses. An essential requirement in counseling is skill in the art of listening. This is much more difficult to put into practice than it may seem, since it involves not only breaking habits required in ordinary conversation, but also recognizing what to listen to. The interview must be skillfully but unobtrusively guided along channels which will touch on basic factors, not merely superficial aspects of the problem which may at the moment seem to be causes for complaint and emotional disturbances.

The object is to guide the employee into thinking through, planning and talking out steps which he himself can put into effect, so that in this way he participates actively in the solution of his own problem. The properly conducted interview frees him from the painful and bewildering aspects of his situation so he can again tackle it more effectively in his own way. Counseling thus offers no ready-made solutions, but motivates individuals to self-guidance and healthy self-directed action. In short, it helps them to help themselves.

An interview has aptly been defined as "a conversation with a purpose." In counseling interviews it is especially important to keep both the general and the specific purpose clearly in mind. This is the first step in the recommended advance preparations for this type of interview. The second step requires the interviewer to refresh his mind concerning all that is known about the personality, previous experience, and work record of the individual to be interviewed.

The interview itself

There are a number of other steps in conducting interviews which should constantly be kept in mind and practiced until they become second nature. It is especially important that these measures be utilized in conducting the initial interview with an employee. Obviously the process can be simplified and will be less time consuming in follow-up interviews. As far as it is practicable, the following general procedures should govern the interview, no matter whether the counselor or the employee initiated it:

1. First, see that the employee is physically comfortable and at ease. Recognize the importance of privacy. Nobody likes to talk confidentially in an atmosphere which does not permit him to feel at home.

2. There is no place for excessive dignity or ceremony in the counseling interview. The best rule is to be natural and informal. Above all, the interviewer must have a genuine, not a merely casual or forced interest in the employee and the problem he brings.

3. It is good policy to begin the interview with some comment of a more or less favorable nature which makes the employee feel he is noticed and appreciated for himself. This rather naturally opens the way to a talk about things affecting his job in which he is interested.

4. Make a point of using a quiet tone, slow speech, plain language, and a courteous manner. Make the employee feel clearly that even if he is at a disadvantage your object is not to "put him on the spot" or "pin something on him." On the contrary, show him that your object is to share with him your thinking about problems in which you have a mutual interest.

5. At about this point the conversation can be guided into channels which will enlist his thoughts concerning other aspects of the situation than those he is complaining about or habitually uses as the single explanation of his difficulties. But always remember that you are counseling, not prosecuting.

6. In the course of listening to the employee's story, the counselor often gains confidences and confessions of a personal nature. This may be helpful but it is not necessarily the only goal of the interview. The factors must be singled out which have direct or indirect influence on job efficiency, the criterion by which the success of the interview will be measured.

7. The interviewer must constantly seek to get the employee to define in his own words, the aspects of the problem he has avoided or overlooked. The following are examples of the "who-what-when-where-how" questioning which emphasizes the part the employee himself must play in remedying the situation:

> What are your ideas concering the causes of the difficulty?
> What have you done in an effort to improve the situation?
> What changes in personnel might improve the situation?
> If you were in charge of the department, what would you do?
> What steps would increase the efficiency of your department?
> How can your own efficiency be improved?
> What stands in the way of doing a better job yourself?
> Do you have someone to whom you can take your problems?
> Do you know what your supervisor thinks of your work?
> How are the human relations in your department?
> What do you see ahead for yourself in your present job?
> In what way do you think the interviewer could be of help?

8. Animate your talk with expressions of interest in new ideas, with expectant pauses, requests for specific examples, brief summarizations of what the employee has said, and written notes outlining the main points. Switch to neutral topics if the employee gets excessively emotional or "closes up" on any one subject. When the tension has subsided, gingerly return the conversation to that topic, either in the same or a subsequent interview.

9. Avoid interrupting or giving long-winded advice before the employee has had an opportunity to fully explain his side of the story. Resist the temptation to lecture or moralize.

10. Invite the employee to frankly discuss his feelings, even if some of them are definitely negative. Attempt to divert excessive emotion into a feeling of team-sense and loyalty to the organization and to yourself personally.

11. Never commit yourself to promises which you may not be able to keep. But you can promise to investigate further any problem which the employee feels is an obstacle to his full cooperation.

12. The point to which you must constantly return toward the end of the interview is that there surely must be some way in which the two of you working together can improve the situation. Even if all elements of the disagreement cannot be cleared away, the opportunity to come to grips with the issues has already advanced the employee one step further to the solution.

13. Be fully acquainted with the referral system in your organization. Avoid any implication that you attempt to solve employee problems single-handed. Whenever the possibility for securing outside help comes up, emphasize the part which other counselors, supervisors, physicians, or members of the family may play in bringing about a solution. Offer to consult with the individual to whom the employee is referred, but indicate that this will be done only with his consent and permission.

Follow-up interviews

Not all counseling problems require follow-up interviews, but it is usually a good plan for the interviewer to express his willingness to continue the discussion at a later time. It is often effective to "hit the iron again while it is hot" and seek the employee out in order to inquire briefly as to progress, after an interval of a few days. Counselor-initiated contacts of this kind carry a distinct advantage over the other method of waiting until the employee returns with another problem. Follow-up interviews in general are seldom as time-consuming as the initial interview, and the results of the little added effort which is required in following through is more than rewarded by the response it elicits.

Interview records

Notes taken during interviews should be in plain view of the employee. They should be limited to listing dates, figures, or facts, or illustrating graphically some aspect of the situation, such as the organizational framework within which the employee works. As soon as convenient after the interview is over, it is desirable to make a condensed summary of the problems presented, issues faced, issues unsettled, positive steps initiated, and referrals made. This report should include mention of contacts made with others concerning the employee. Notes of this type help to refresh the memory preparatory to subsequent follow-ups. It is obviously helpful to include those aspects of the problem which give the most effective entry in succeeding contacts.

QUESTIONS

1. List some of the more important uses of the "interview" as Himler uses the term.
2. Summarize the five major steps that Himler presents for conducting the counseling interview.
3. What does the term "emotional transference" mean?
4. What does R. S. V. P. in counseling mean? Explain.
5. Contrast Himler's article with that of Rogers. What significant differences do you note?

COUNSELING EMPLOYEES AFTER
MERIT RATING OR EVALUATION *

Earl G. Planty and Carlos E. Efferson

For various reasons, supervisors and executives are often reluctant to sit down and talk frankly with their subordinates about their job performance and to analyze their strengths and weaknesses. One reason may be that they don't quite know how to begin what appears to be a complex, difficult job—a job which, because of its psychological implications for the ratee and its demands upon the rater, they may feel ill-equipped to undertake. Understandably enough, therefore, they tend to avoid a planned approach to counseling on performance and development and, instead, let chance take its course.

There are, however, certain principles and techniques of counseling for improvement which *can* be put to practical use by executives and supervisors. Most of this chapter describes simple techniques which can be applied in an orderly, deliberate, and scientific manner to such counseling.

Before examining the techniques, we might outline four assumptions or principles upon which the success of such counseling depends.

FUNDAMENTAL ASSUMPTIONS

One of the principles that must guide us is the old truism that we do not see ourselves as others do. In counseling after evaluations, we must proceed as though it is very unlikely that a subordinate will evaluate himself and all parts of his work as his superior does. We must accept it as completely natural that a man who appears to us to be good in personal relations may think himself a miserable failure in this function. We should also expect that the reverse may be true, and, in either case, we should not label the man "maladjusted" or "weak" but, rather, "human." We should expect to find people who, *in our eyes*, are not contributing enough, but who *themselves* think they are contributing more than their share. We must not be at all surprised to find men with insatiable ambition for advancement whom we look upon as mediocre. We must not be surprised if we find here and there a man who expects a promotion when we thought he knew he was not even doing his present job satisfactorily.

* From *Effective Communication On the Job*, ed. M. Joseph Dooher and Vivienne Marquis (New York: The American Management Association, 1956), pp. 173-190. Copyright, 1956, by the American Management Association. Reprinted by permission of the American Management Association.

Because these things are so, we must counsel regularly with our people, for it is most unlikely that *our* evaluation of their work matches *theirs*. Now, as simple as this principle seems and as long as it has been recognized in our literature and in our own personal relationships, most of us in business do not use it in our day-to-day operations. Instead, most of us let our subordinates roll along more or less unaware of their failures or their successes, of their mediocrity or their outstanding characteristics. Thus we miss the greatest possible opportunity for strengthening the weak and making stronger those who are already successful. Some of us rationalize that if our subordinates are "good" men they will make an objective judgment of their own progress and personality. Others believe that "no news is good news" and think that their subordinates will also accept this negative sort of approval.

There are other important principles underlying counseling which find their roots in the blindness of man to himself. One of them is that we must counsel slowly and carefully, using the "feel" approach, recognizing that insight into one's own behavior comes slowly, sometimes not at all, and hardly ever completely. We must recognize that we ourselves may have as many false definitions as does the man with whom we are talking, and that it is impossible to recognize and allow for our own biases completely. Even when we are certain of the direction in which we want to lead the subordinate, we must remember that it may take him many interviews to see in himself what we see in him; we must lead the man into only as much self-criticism and suggestion at one time as his personality can absorb without disintegrating effects.

We must ever remember that the purpose of counseling is more one of development than of discipline. The approach must be positive, and our outlook on this score will go far to determine our success or failure. When the subordinate sees that the purpose of counseling is his own good, one of the major obstacles to mutual understanding is overcome. He will see that our purpose is to help him if we keep in mind that people need to hear about their good points as well as the weak points, and if we make clear our intention to use his strengths and reward him for them while we simultaneously help him discover and overcome his weaknesses.

Of course, one of the most fundamental assumptions upon which we must proceed is the belief that most people can, if properly assisted, change their attitudes and behavior for the good. Contrary to the belief of many, success or failure is not born in a man, but comes in part as a result of the use to which he puts his talents and the way he is helped to develop them, however limited or liberally endowed he may be. Performance counseling, in addition to letting the subordinate know where he stands, helps by providing encouragement and assistance while improvement is taking place. The foregoing has attempted to explain a few assumptions regarding counseling for improvement. The remainder of this chapter will deal with specific counseling suggestions and guides that have been worked out and applied with good results in Johnson & Johnson.

PRACTICAL GUIDES FOR COUNSELING

I. Definition

We are referring to the interview and counseling which follow evaluation. In some cases, this counseling will be clear and direct; in other cases, it may be subtle and non-directive. In some cases a meeting will be called specifically for counseling. In other cases a less formal, more casual approach will be made.

II. Purposes of counseling following evaluation

A. *Getting the subordinate to do a better job* through making clear your standards of performance. Remember that you too have peculiar traits and expectancies. Here is a chance for the subordinate to learn your preferences in quality, quantity, and methods of work and to understand your reasons for these standards.

B. *Giving the employee a clear picture of how he is doing* with emphasis upon strengths as well as weaknesses. Showing how well he meets your standards. Much trouble results in business and industry from subordinates whose self-rating is sharply at variance with their superior's evaluation.

C. *Discussing together plans for improvement* and projects for better utilization of the subordinate's strengths.

D. *Building strong, personal relationships* between superior and subordinate in which both are willing to talk frankly about the job, how it is being done, what improvement is possible, and how it can be obtained. Improving human-to-human understanding so that closer, stronger relationships exist.

E. *Eliminating or reducing anxiety*, tension, and uncertainty which may exist where individuals do not have the advantages of planned counsel.

III. Preparing for the interview

    A. Assuming that the rating has been done and that some brief time has passed between the evaluation and the interview, it is well to do a little reviewing before meeting with the subordinate.

        1. Restudy the job of the man to be counseled and what it takes to do it.

        2. Think about the man, his personality, record, experience, and training. Have his personnel file available.

        3. Also review in your mind how you rated him in the light of his job requirements.

            a. Review and weigh the factors which entered into your evaluation.

            b. Review *why* you rated him as you did.

            c. Bring to mind specific facts or illustrations from his job performance to substantiate your opinions.

    B. Determine what you want to accomplish in the interview and prepare a plan of discussion for doing so. You might wish to accomplish some of the following:

        1. Leave the man with more *will to work* than he previously had.

        2. Send him away with as much knowledge of his *specific strengths* and *weaknesses* as his personality can take.

        3. Leave him with a specific or general *statement of his overall effectiveness.* Example: "Adding it all up, John, we feel that you are an asset (or a distinct asset) to the company, and we hope you stay on with us for years," or, "John, I think your work compares so favorably with other similar work in the company that we should soon begin to look for new opportunities for you," or, "Your performance is not adequately meeting the needs of the position and suggested improvement is expected."

        4. Work out with the subordinate a few specific steps that both of you are to undertake for his betterment. This might include your giving him a special assignment in a field where he thinks he is weak, assigning him to a committee or to a training program, etc.

    C. After the first meeting has been held and cooperative relations established, some managers like to inform the subordinate of the time and subject of the next meeting so that he can anticipate the discussion and consequently be better prepared psychologically for it.

D. Plan to meet in private, and without interruption.

E. If this is the first interview, anticipate some curiosity, tension, or anxiety in the individual. Prepare to reduce it.

F. Decide in advance how to use whatever rating form, narrative description, or questionnaire you have recorded your data upon. In some instances the rating form itself is used as a guide in the interview. The supervisor may, in such a case, show the employee his rating sheet and discuss it with him. However, there are certain disadvantages in this approach:

1. The form may come to be the principal issue of the interview. Discussion may center on the language of the rating form, or such technicalities as the weighting of factors or the definition of degrees.

2. The older employee may be so resistant to a written record that he also resists any corrective efforts. He may feel that he is condemned unalterably because of the written record.

3. The employee may be so concerned with the end rating, the alphabetical or numerical score, that he never hears the constructive suggestions of the interview. (Some feel, in the light of the above, that the form should never be shown. Whether or not he sees the form, the subordinate should eventually know how he has been evaluated.)

G. Visualize how you might lead into your points, indirectly at first.

IV. Manner for the interview

A. Acceptance depends heavily upon the interviewer's manner. Create the impression that you have time for the interview and that you consider it highly important.

B. Throughout the interview, place primary interest upon development and growth for the individual. The executive must see that the individual feels that the activity is a constructive, cooperative one. Minimize evaluation, rating, recording of evidence. Avoid implications that the meeting is or could be used for disciplinary purposes.

C. Create the impression that your evaluation or opinion is not unalterable and permanent. Let it be known that you realize men are dynamic and ever changing, and that your opinions, too, are open to change.

D. Be open-minded to the opinions and facts presented by the one being counseled—be prepared to change your estimation in the light of additional or new evidence. Be willing to learn about him.

E. Don't dominate or cross-examine. Avoid argument. Listen. Listen attentively as well as politely. Listen to sift the important points from the detail, to separate facts from opinions, to identify information and know when it is presented as such and when it is used to persuade and influence toward the teller's own objectives.

F. Remember that the subordinate must do almost all the talking at some points in the interview: in bringing his opinions and feelings to the surface and to your attention; in getting a better understanding of himself; and in making plans for self-improvement.

V. The interview

A. Setting the stage for and beginning the interview.

1. Pick the right time, day, and place. Counsel should not occur shortly after a disciplinary action or an argument. Pick a time when the relationship is strongest, when you are in a good mood, and have reason to believe the subordinate feels likewise.

2. At the outset relieve tension to make the man feel at ease and receptive.

a. Get the man to talking.

b. Then explain the objectives of evaluation; point out that everybody is involved; invite the man to raise questions and introduce his own problems; give him a feeling of security. Say that your interest is in helping him with his job or his future.

B. Techniques.

1. Talk about some of the good things first. Show appreciation of past successes.

2. Talk generally about the man's status at the outset.

3. Some executives ask the man to evaluate himself as a starter.

4. Get away from past failures as quickly as you can. Get the discussion into prevention of future failures, into plans for success. Build upon strengths.

5. In almost every instance allow for "face saving." If you are dealing with a "first offense" or a very good man, you may even share some of the blame. With repeated failures, however, you will need to be sterner.

6. You, however, should guide the interview. Invite the subordinate back from detours, escapes, fruitless conversation.

7. *Just how directly the subordinate should be told or led to see (a) his strengths and weaknesses and (b) the over-all quality of his performance depends upon the levels in the organization which are being worked with, personal traits of the individuals involved, the subordinate's degree of success or failure on his job, the counselor's objective, etc. How directly must be determined in each individual case. Remember, however, that improvement is most rapid where an employee learns from counseling to understand himself, and where he himself makes judgments about his abilities. The skillful executive leads the employee to better evaluations of himself. He does not make them up for him. It is what the subordinate sees for himself and accepts that he does something about.*

8. Some specific suggestions for handling various reactions to the counseling are given below. It is true that typing like this is not completely realistic since some reactions will fall in more than one category. Allowing for this, however, good results have followed from use of these suggestions.

a. *The man accepts your evaluation and indicates a willingness to improve:*

(1) With the average competent employee the reaction described above will be the ordinary one, occurring more often than all the other reactions mentioned hereinafter.

(2) The subordinate may express genuine surprise at some parts of your evaluation of him and his work, but his response will be positive and friendly rather than defensive or antagonistic, for most subordinates admire their superiors, respect their opinions, and want to please them.

(3) When the subordinate is told that his work is satisfactory, and when plans for self-improvement and growth are invited or suggested, the response is usually highly enthusiastic. There is no greater motivating force for an employee than for his superior to lay plans with him for improvement and security in his present position or for eventual advancement in the organization.

(4) The average person when being counseled about his work is likely to ask for elaboration of any constructive criticisms. This gives the counselor a chance to talk over the full story, though it appears to the counseled that the information is in response to his own request.

(5) We can look for most people to try to improve immediately after counseling, and we can expect them to come back with evidence of their improvement, asking for further suggestions and help.

(6) The normal subordinate can be expected to accept his full share of responsibility for failure in departmental operations. In fact, people tend to feel more responsibility for operations than their functions prescribe, and they are usually quite ready to work on cooperative plans for improvement.

(7) We can expect frank and honest counseling to gain for the superior a reputation among his subordinates for being a "square-shooter." This can be of great help in efficient and cooperative performance of normal day-to-day operations.

(8) The subordinate is very likely to feel that an evaluation of his performance comes to him somewhat as a personal favor from his superior. All kinds of relations are likely to be closer and smoother where the superior has shown a genuine interest in letting a subordinate know his strengths and weaknesses and has helped him with the latter. An alert supervisor does not shut off other close personal relations which a subordinate is likely to invite following a good evaluation.

(9) Even successful people need frequent reassurance that their work is satisfactory. Some of your best

men may appear somewhat over-eager for this re-assurance.

b. *The man can't agree with your evaluation or the con-structive criticisms; has evidence to show your evaluation in some respects is not accurate; disagrees constructively and unemotionally:*

(1) Don't try too hard to get agreement the first time, or even the first few times counseling is undertaken. Let your first job be to state your position; getting acceptance of your point of view may take more time.

(2) His disagreement with you may come from his own personal make-up, his experience on the job, and other factors which are entirely within him and which it will be difficult for you to understand at the outset.

(3) Be prepared to expect some disagreement based upon the difference in your personality and role within the company and his. Such disagreement should not handicap regular communications between you. No one of us completely agrees with any of the persons with whom we cooperate daily. *Full* agreement is impossible and unnecessary. It is impossible to ex-pect people to have the identical motivation, values, definitions, outlooks, and so forth.

(4) Listen carefully to find out why the man does not agree. Check the reliability of your own facts and of his criticisms. Prepare yourself for future dis-cussions with additional evidence about the man's performance.

(5) Say that you will look into this matter and give him every benefit of the facts. At the same time raise any questions which you have about the reliability of his own information. Send him away to think over his own position while you do the same with yours.

(6) Realize that experienced men who have done a great deal of evaluation and counseling agree that they frequently learn from those they are evaluating. Many experienced men know that they have some time or other been given false steers and colored

information, and they are happy to receive any additional facts which may improve their judgments.

(7) Be willing to change your evaluations in the light of more evidence. Evaluations are not static things. Just as men change constantly, so should opinions about them.

c. *The man agrees completely and almost too easily. You suspect he does not understand or is reserving his objections:*

(1) Get him to state the condition as you stated it to him; get him to sum up what you've discussed.

(2) In this case be sure that his agreement is fundamental, that it is not a device for complimenting the counselor, and thereby avoiding emphasis upon his need to improve. Some people use a device of easy agreement when criticized. In accepting easily like this, they seem to think there will be less stern insistence upon their taking some direct and immediate steps for improvement.

(3) Emphasize what is to be done about change, improvement, or development. Get the man who appears to have accepted your evaluation to commit himself strongly about doing something regarding it. Outline how you plan to follow up on his plans for improvement. This check-up may be the very help he needs.

d. *The man is too eager for promotion or financial reward:*

(1) If the subordinate uses your favorable evaluation of him to insist upon immediate financial reward, you may remind him that a man has to perform in a highly successful fashion for some period of time on any job before thinking of advancement.

(2) Outline the promotional route which he may expect to follow. Discuss in general or specific terms when you think he may be ready for advancement, and following readiness how long it has taken men in similar positions to find an opportunity.

(3) His insistence on promotion or salary increase in return for a good rating may reveal his desire to see some tangible evidence of the success which you

have told him he enjoys. Be sure that you have made full use of intangible rewards—assignment to committees working on difficult problems on higher levels; release from routine operations to attend conferences, training schools, etc.; minor improvements in office facilities, secretarial services, and personal attention in a variety of ways.

(4) If too many of your men insist upon overly rapid rewards, perhaps you are stressing opportunity, promotion, and advancement too much. We should evaluate people *first* to improve their performance on their present job and only secondarily to prepare for promotion. Present success in the full meaning of the word must precede promotion. Put your emphasis upon it. People can, and should, be motivated to superior performance on their own job before there is promise of advancement.

(5) Review your salary schedules and rate of promotion to assure yourself that the man has been treated fairly.

(6) The man may not deserve advancement. It is the purpose of your counseling to get him to see this. Do not be surprised if you do not accomplish it at the first meeting.

(7) Wives are sometimes responsible for husbands' impatience. Your counseling may have to include her, too.

(8) If your salary schedules are adequate, over-frequent requests for pay increases may indicate that you are not providing enough intangible rewards. The subordinate may be compensating for their lack in demanding excessive financial returns in their place.

e. *The man avoids blame, which is manifestly his, shifts the criticism to others—possibly to other people he works with, to you, or to company policy.*

(1) At the outset, listen to him rather than halt his recital. To do the latter might merely send him somewhere else with his complaints.

(2) Speak and act so as to create the impression that you are impartial and fair-minded and want him to take

only that responsibility which is his. Above all, guard that his irrational conduct does not upset and annoy you; at any rate, do not let your words or actions convey your distress if you feel it.

(3) Try to find why he blames others. What inadequacy does he have that makes it impossible for him to accept justifiable blame?

(4) Then ask yourself how you can help him to feel more successful so that he will not need to use such an escape or excuse to provide for his requirements. Find out what taste of success you will have to help him achieve so that he will not find it necessary to deny *all* blame.

(5) Directly or indirectly compliment him for his willingness to assume responsibility where you find any evidence that he has done so. Let him realize that acceptance of blame, when accompanied with determination to improve, will not be a disadvantage to him.

(6) Watch carefully from meeting to meeting with him to see whether he grows in willingness to assume responsibility for his failures.

(7) Following a few sessions handled in this way, determine whether his blame-avoidance is basic in his personality and requires psychological counsel, or whether it is based on factors in his environment which you can help him to recognize and improve upon.

(8) Sometimes it helps to put the man in closer contact with the individuals or groups he is criticizing. Give him special projects, find other ways to throw him into closer association with capable people whose abilities he underestimates.

f. *The man wants to quit. He is a good man, and you would like to keep him:*

(1) Find out why he wishes to leave. He may not be too clear on this himself. Perhaps the emotional release he gets in reviewing his reasons will satisfy him. If his reason for leaving is based on some failure which you recognize within the organization, take some

prompt action to correct it. If this comes as a surprise, it may mean that you have failed to keep close enough touch with your subordinate.

(2) Do not be afraid to assure him of your respect for his ability. Some men talk of leaving only because they are not sure they are wanted in their present jobs. Remember, too, that success is not enough in itself to reassure a man. He must hear from *you* that you consider him successful. Too many executives feel that "He should know he's doing all right unless I tell him different."

(3) If the man is accepting temporary advancement with some other company in place of an ultimately better future with you, outline the growth possibilities in his present position. Make sure he sees all the inducements you have to offer.

(4) If he has a better offer elsewhere and you truly wish to retain him, look carefully at your own rewards, tangible and intangible. Can they be increased, now or in the future?

(5) Steer the conversation so that the man does not commit himself definitely to leaving and so that he does not make statements so harsh that he will feel that all confidence in him has been lost by his management.

g. *The man loses his temper. Becomes emotional, angry, or abusive:*

(1) Listen.

(2) Don't argue. Don't show disapproval.

(3) Be sure to let the man know that his loss of temper or emotional behavior is not a permanent black mark against him. It is very important that you let him leave realizing that you still have a friendly feeling toward him. Next time you meet him be especially cordial.

(4) Call him back a few days later. If he is still in the same mood, listen, don't argue. Call him back once more.

(5) If there is no improvement, you must soon state your case.

h. *The man seems determined to argue. Denies most of your facts, evidence, and opinions:*

(1) Let him talk freely. While he is talking, try to find out what it is basically that is bothering him. Since all behavior has some reason for being, listen carefully. Try to find the cause of his resistance.

(2) Thank him for calling his point of view to your attention. Say that you will look into it and talk with him later.

(3) Avoid being drawn into an argument which may arouse emotions that might block or seriously delay an understanding.

(4) But don't retreat. Be sure he understands your point of view and your insistence upon it. Do this tactfully, moderately, without arguing.

(5) Close the interview tactfully. Try it again when he may be in a better mood, or when you have taken whatever constructive action is possible about the fundamental cause of his resistance. He may be completely cooperative and understanding in the next interview.

i. *The man is surly, not cooperative, resentful, or he is just passive and unresponsive:*

(1) Try to figure out why he acts this way. Is it normal for him? Is he giving careful attention to what you say? Is it self-protection? Does he fear to reveal his own attitude, or something in his job?

(2) Don't be afraid of a certain amount of silence. Give him ample time to think and respond.

(3) Watch carefully for any spark of interest in what you are saying. Try to get him to talk about anything you have said that seems to strike even a small response. Ask his opinions about things important to him: "What do you think about so and so?" or "What would you do in this case . . . ?"

(4) Reassure him early in the interview. Talk about as many of the complimentary things as you can at the outset.

(5) He may think that you think he is worse than he really is.

(6) Don't push or try to persuade too much at one sitting. He may change his attitude by the next sitting, or you may learn more about why he is as he is.

(7) He may resist the whole idea of evaluations and counseling following them. Go over your reasons again. Show how he can profit from knowing where he stands and from laying plans for improvement. Long-service men sometimes see no merit in evaluations. Anticipate some of this and explain the reasons for the scientific evaluations. Ask the man's objections.

(8) He may feel that you are trying to change habits within him which exist of his own personal choice. He may resist your discussing what he thinks are personal matters and none of your affair. He may not realize that certain habits (courteousness, personal appearance, punctuality, modesty, for example) relate closely to success on the job. Show him how this is so.

j. *The man is obviously nervous and sensitive:*

(1) Apparently you have not put him at ease. Both before and during the interview, talk about the things he knows best and feels most free about—the new home he is furnishing, a good idea he recently submitted, his service in a local fund-raising drive, etc.

(2) If he is not participating, try to get him to do so; make it a two-way communication.

(3) Explain the purpose and constructive values that may come from evaluations and counseling.

(4) Don't talk about him—instead, talk about his work or his job. Begin by referring to actual work situations in which he has done well—a new system he helped to install, a quality improvement he suggested, a report he prepared.

k. *You have nearly given up the idea of improvement of the man. This may be the last or the next to last interview before he leaves. You are now thinking more of separating him pleasantly with good public relations and with constructive help for him in his future employment than you are of improving him so that he may stay on:*

(1) Talk frankly and directly about his leaving. It will be some shock to him at first, but getting him to face the facts realistically will make his remaining days much easier and will minimize his future employment troubles.

(2) If there is evidence that he is not perfectly clear about his failures, review them. Ask him to recall your previous conversations, your recommendations for improvement and what he thinks he has done about it. If possible, get him to state what he has been told previously about past failures.

(3) Review assets in the man which may make him valuable in some other company. Talk about these places and how he can get contacts with them.

(4) Tell him just what kind of work you will recommend him for. Give him the proper names in the organization to use as references.

(5) Refer the man to the proper sources in the organization which will help him prepare résumés, register with agencies, or otherwise look for employment.

(6) Some like to review "the second chance." Discuss what he has learned from the failures, what he intends to do differently.

(7) Leave your mind open as to the possibility that the man may still change for the good.

C. Closing the interview.

1. Review the points made in the interview and encourage the subordinate to summarize them or put them in his own words.

2. Always reassure the man as to your interest in his progress and indicate willingness to take up the discussion again at any time.

3. You should close when you have made clear whatever points you intended to cover, when the younger or junior executive has had ample time to review his problems and release any emotional tensions that exist, when plans of action have been cooperatively developed, and when you and the subordinate are at a natural stopping point. It is particularly good to close when both of you have a feeling of satisfaction about the results obtained.

VI. Evaluation and follow-up

A. Following the interview you may wish to make a few notes before the facts brought out and the plans developed are forgotten.

B. Some managers follow up the interview by a visit—stopping by the man's workplace or calling him into their office on some detail or other—wherein the subordinate has opportunity to get any additional help he may require.

C. In the interim between interviews, keep careful, but unobtrusive, watch over the man's progress or lack of it. Early in the next interview review what the subordinate has done toward the recommended self-understanding or improvement and how effective his efforts have been.

Conclusion

The scientific, objective approach to improving executive performance is simple and practical, including only three steps:

I. Setting performance standards.

II. Rating, measuring, judging—as objectively as possible—how close a particular executive comes to the standards. Learning where the man exceeds requirements, where he meets them, and where he misses them.

III. Counseling with the subordinate regarding the findings of step two above.

There is no magic or mystery to these steps. They are simple, straightforward, practical. In a great many cases the first two steps are undertaken and completed more or less objectively and fully. But how rarely is the third step undertaken—with what timidity, anxiety, and reluctance is it approached. The list of excuses for procrastination in counseling is long:

> The man being counseled will react badly—he may argue; he may be upset and made insecure; or he may get a conceited notion of his own importance.
> The man will reveal the content of his counseling, particularly that part which is complimentary, and thus provoke jealousy in the group.
> Busy managers don't have time for counseling. The men really know where they stand from hints and suggestions given them.
> Lower-level executives and supervisors are not skillful enough to counsel with their subordinates.

Rarely, if ever, has the truest objection to counseling come out: Managers, as we emphasized earlier, do not know how to begin what appears to be a complex, difficult job and possibly an unnecessary one for them. Yet counseling with subordinates about performance *is* necessary, and a man's own superior is the logical person to do it. For how can a man develop on the job unless he and his superior recognize specifically his strengths and his weaknesses *and cooperatively lays plans for growth and improvement?*

QUESTIONS

1. State the fundamental assumptions that underlie evaluation interviews.
2. What are the best ways to prepare for an interviewing situation?
3. What are some of the typical results of a well-conducted evaluation interview?
4. How do you handle the type of man who is dissatisfied with his job and wants to quit?
5. Do you feel it is necessary to counsel with employees after they have been evaluated? Why or why not?

GENERAL QUESTIONS ON PART 8

1. What are the two major approaches to counseling? Explain.
2. Explain why nondirective counseling is becoming increasingly important in industry.
3. List some of the more essential steps to be followed when conducting a nondirective interview.
4. What attitudes should a good counselor bring to his job?
5. What are the principal values to be realized from effective counseling procedures?
6. How does a counselor go about attempting to develop insight on the part of a counselee?
7. How does Planty and Efferson's article differ from the other articles in this section of the book?
8. What situations are most likely to occur in a firm that makes counseling procedures mandatory?
9. What is your opinion of counseling as a managerial tool?
10. What attitudes should management adopt toward employee counseling?

BIBLIOGRAPHY FOR PART 8

Articles

EILBIRT, HENRY. "A Study of Current Counseling Practices in Industry," *Journal of Business*, Vol. 31, No. 1 (January, 1958), pp. 28-37.

KOSIAK, PAUL. "Commonsense Counseling," *Personnel Journal* (April, 1947), pp. 343-352.

MOYER, N. A. "Using the Non-Directive Interview," *Supervisory Management*, Vol. 2, No. 7 (June, 1957), pp. 28-39.

SPEROFF, B. J. "There's Danger in Trying to Make Every Supervisor a Counselor," *Personnel Journal* (March, 1955), pp. 376-377.

ZANDER, ALVIN, and JOHN GYR. "Changing Attitudes Toward a Merit Rating System," *Personnel Psychology* (Winter, 1955), pp. 429-448.

Books

GARDNER, B. B., and D. G. MOORE. *Human Relations in Industry.* Homewood, Ill.: Richard D. Irwin, Inc., 1945.

ROGERS, C. *Counseling and Psychotherapy.* Boston: Houghton Mifflin Company, 1942.

ROBINSON, G. P. *Principles and Procedures in Student Counseling.* New York: Harper and Brothers, Publishers, 1950.

BALINSKY, B., and R. BURGER. *The Executive Interview.* New York: Harper and Brothers, Publishers, 1959.

PART 9. PRACTICING HUMAN RELATIONS

Throughout this book little attention was given to the art of practicing human relations. Instead, every effort was made to provide for the reader an opportunity to study the fundamental aspects of human relations, such as leadership, motivation, communication, and so on, which are foundational to its practice. The reason for doing this is, of course, obvious: the skill with which any function of the manager's job is practiced is directly correlated with the practitioner's knowledge and understanding of that function.

FUNDAMENTAL ASPECTS OF PRACTICING HUMAN RELATIONS

Although the major purpose of this section is to discuss some of the more concrete aspects of practicing human relations, it is necessary first to give brief consideration to several basic points that have not been discussed in previous sections but that are equally fundamental to the practice of human relations. Perhaps the most important of these points concerns the fact that the successful practice of human relations requires the manager to know and understand the basic needs of people and to do everything in his power to arrange and construct the work environment so that employees can find the means and the opportunity to satisfy their physiological, sociological, and psychological motives. This does not imply, incidentally, that the practice of human relations is solely dependent upon motivation *per se*. On the contrary, it merely indicates that motivation is the core of influencing employee behavior. Practicing human relations successfully still requires the manager to know and understand the impact of organization and change upon people; the importance and influence of communication, counseling, and participation; and the integrating and coordinating nature of leadership. Most important of all, it requires the manager to use his knowledge of these areas to design and modify a work environment that is conducive to need satisfaction.

Another important point upon which rests the successful practice of human relations is that of empathy. Although Robert N. McMurry discusses this subject in detail in a following article, it should be mentioned here that one of the chief reasons why we fail to practice human relations successfully is because we are too easily inclined to assume we know how people think and feel about things. Studies by the score have indicated that what we think about the attitudes and needs of people is altogether too frequently in direct contrast with what people themselves actually say their thoughts and needs are. This is particularly true of the superior-subordinate relationship. Consequently, to think you know what people want or need at any point in time is indeed a dangerous assumption. The only way to practice human relations effectively, therefore, is to know what the attitudes and motives of your employees are. This means you must empathize, that is, put yourself in the shoes of your employees. From a more practical viewpoint, it means you must find out directly from your subordinates what they think and feel about the many facets of their jobs and work environment and then act accordingly.

A third basic point upon which the practice of human relations rests concerns the fact that managers, in addition to knowing and understanding the motives of their subordinates, must be definitively acquainted with their own wants and needs. As Robert Tannenbaum points out in his article, our behavior, and hence the way we practice human relations, is greatly influenced by our own needs. This means, in essence, that what we do to satisfy our own motive forces may be the type of behavior that thwarts the satisfaction of the needs of our subordinates. When this situation arises, the manager, if he wishes to motivate his people effectively, must obviously adjust his actions accordingly. Whether or not he is willing to do this depends, of course, on his ability both to restructure his needs and, when necessary, to subordinate them to the needs of his employees.

A fourth and final fundamental aspect of practicing human relations is concerned with the hierarchical nature of human needs. As the section on motivation pointed out, motivating forces are structured according to their importance to the human being. Obviously, therefore, physiological needs take precedence over all other motives. When these needs are satisfied, other forces, namely, sociological and psychological needs, take precedence. Unless the manager recognizes this, he is apt to commit the common error of assuming that employees are more interested in wages and fringe benefits than they are interested in the more subtle aspects of their working environments. Practicing human relations on this assumption means, of course, that little attention would be paid to such important forces as belonging, acceptance, and so forth, and that consequently employees would not be properly motivated.

Constructing a Proper Work Environment

It is self-evident that if employees are to behave and produce effectively, they must find while working in the organization the means to satisfy their basic needs. This means that the practice of human relations must be directed toward the construction and maintenance of a work environment that is conducive to need satisfaction. Furthermore, it means that managers are responsible for arranging and combining the factors that make up and influence the environment in which an employee works because they, more so than any other people, have control over most of these factors.

Unfortunately, the factors that make up and influence the work environment are legion in number. They range in nature from personal contact with human beings to inanimate and inarticulate things such as policies, procedures, equipment, and the basic duties and responsibilities inherent in jobs. Even the color of paint and the level of illumination have been proven to exert an effect on human behavior. Because it would be impossible to discuss in this text all the known factors that influence and are a part of the working environment, attention shall be given only to those factors over which managers have the most control and which are most directly related to need satisfaction.

Policy

Undoubtedly the basic starting point in the actual practice of human relations is to formulate, determine, and communicate to all personnel explicit and concise statements of human relations policy. As every student of management knows, policy is a statement of intention, a guide to action that gives course and direction to the carrying out of any function. Because the importance of human relations as a managerial function is neither greater nor less than the importance of other functions in an organization, it should also be based on a strong foundation of policy. If this is not done, the actual practice of human relations, particularly with respect to the design of procedures and other factors that influence human behavior, will be left to the whims and fancies of the managers involved. Quite frequently the result of this is complete inattention to the impact of procedures, techniques, and so forth on the human being. It should be stressed, therefore, that human relations will be practiced uniformly and successfully only when it is the avowed intention of the organization to do so. In other words, the practice of human relations is correlated with—in fact, dependent upon—the strength and the effectiveness of policy statements concerning this basic function.

Recruitment

Seldom recognized by many people is the fact that the practice of human relations commences when a prospective employee comes in contact with the organization for the first time. This indicates that recruitment, which is the function of finding candidates for employment, plays an important role in employee motivation. The nature of the advertisement that is first used to contact him, the treatment he is accorded when he applies for a job at the employment office, the physical condition of the organization—these and many other aspects of this function exert a tremendous impact on behavior. If any of these facets creates doubt about opportunity for need satisfaction, there is a good chance, especially during periods of full employment, that candidates will seek jobs elsewhere. This is why, for example, so many of the recruitment advertisements we see today stress points such as "good supervision," "nice people to work with," "opportunity for advancement," and so on, in addition to "good wages" and "benefits."

One of the basic reasons why effective recruitment is so important in human relations is because at this point in time the prospective employee knows little if anything about the organization; consequently, a great many unknowns about need satisfaction exist in his mind. What he "sees" in the advertisement, therefore, is basically what he "sees" in the organization. This is particularly true of the treatment he receives at the employment office. If the receptionist he meets is dour and impolite, he will frequently tend to assume that this person is representative of all the employees in the organization and that, consequently, the people he may work with will be equally discourteous. Illogical as this may be, it is a well-known aspect of human behavior.

Selection

Selection is the function of screening candidates for employment and hiring those who are best suited for the jobs to be filled. This function is an important part of the work environment, and hence of human relations, for two reasons. First of all, like recruitment, the treatment the candidate receives while being screened by interviews, tests, and physical examinations exerts a tremendous influence on his behavior. If he is treated curtly or bombarded with examinations that confuse and frighten him, there will arise within him doubt concerning many of his basic needs.

A second fundamental reason why the selection function is important to the practice of human relations is because it is the point in time when an employee is matched to a job. If care is not given to equate a person's knowledge, skill, and ability with those demanded by the job, there is danger that many motivating forces will go unsatisfied. For example, if an individual is placed on a job for which he is neither presently nor potentially qualified, he is likely to become frustrated when his behavior fails to achieve a level of performance that is necessary for pay raises, promotions, and so on. On the other hand, an individual who is placed on a job for which he is over-qualified frequently fails to achieve a sense of accomplishment and, as a consequence, finds many of his basic needs, especially psychological motives, going unsatisfied. The only solution to this important problem is to screen definitively all candidates for employment and to hire only those whose talents meet the requirements of the job. This means, of course, that managers must in the first place know what the various jobs demand of people. In other words, it means that all jobs must be analyzed and that accurate and complete job descriptions and job specifications must be written and used.

Induction

The moment an individual becomes an employee of an organization, he faces a process of adjustment that is extremely critical to his behavior on the job. He must, for example, adjust himself to the people with whom he will work and adapt himself to myriad policies and rules. If this period of adjustment is facilitated so that he successfully conditions himself to his new work environment, there is every reason to expect that he will become a properly motivated employee. If, however, managers pay little attention to this critical aspect of employment, there is every reason to expect that the new employee will encounter many situations that are not conducive to need satisfaction.

Induction, the process of facilitating adjustment to a new work environment, therefore becomes an extremely important function of management. New employees must be properly introduced to their jobs and their fellow employees. They must be acquainted with policies and procedures that affect the work they do and the level of performance expected of them. They must be shown where their job fits into the whole and what is expected of them in terms of quantity and quality of production. They must, in effect, be given all the information they need to know and want to know to perform their jobs effectively. Unless these things are done, they will not feel that they are members of the organization and, consequently, will experience dissatisfaction in needs like acceptance and belonging. Furthermore, lacking the information they need for successful performance, they will soon discover that it is extremely difficult, if not impossible, to behave on the job in the manner necessary for need satisfaction.

Training

There are at least two reasons why there is no such thing as an employee, whether he be the chief executive or the janitor, who needs no training or development. In the first place, learning is a continuous process. Because training is the direction of learning, it must also be continuous, especially if we want people to learn things properly and efficiently. In the second place, within every organization there are constantly occurring situations that demand training of some type or kind. New employees must be acquainted with duties, responsibilities, and job methods. Present employees must be introduced to new techniques, processes, and equipment. Junior executives must be groomed for higher-level responsibilities. And so on.

Although training is obviously necessary for organizational efficiency, it is also equally necessary for successful human relations. There are several reasons why this is true. First of all, proper training, in conjunction with good recruitment and selection, should result in employees who are better able to perform their duties and responsibilities. This means, in essence, that people will have the ability to perform at a level necessary to obtain recognition, acceptance, achievement, status, and so forth. Secondly, proper training can facilitate goal achievement on the part of employees. Many people, for example, have the potential to work at higher levels in an organization. This potential usually results in a desire to attain these higher levels for various reasons. To achieve these responsibilities, however, requires that potential be developed by proper training and experience. In other words, potential must be converted into capability. If this is done successfully, then there is reason to expect that people will be better equipped to achieve their higher goals. If it is not done, that is, if training is not keyed to the development of potential, then employees will find it impossible to achieve the objectives they have set for themselves. The result, of course, as Part 3 pointed out, will be frustration.

Employee rating

Most employees prefer to know where they "stand" in an organization. They want to know, for example, if they are performing at a level necessary for wage increases and promotions. They want to know their strengths and weaknesses, particularly the latter, so that they can direct their energies toward improving themselves. Most important of all, they want to know that their superiors are aware of their capabilities, potential, and performance, and that they are being measured by a consistent, uniform, and fair set of standards.

Organizations that have not established a formal employee rating system cannot guarantee these things to their employees. They cannot, for example, base promotions on a foundation of ability. They cannot consistently grant wage increases on a basis of merit. They cannot, in any way possible, guarantee that superiors will be aware of the true worth of their subordinates. Most important of all, they cannot practice human relations successfully. Only when managers are definitively and accurately aware of employee performance can they possibly influence the behavior of their employees in an effective manner. Until an efficient rating system is established, therefore, it can be expected that people will not be able to achieve the degree of satisfaction they desire for needs such as recognition, achievement, security, fairness, and so on.

Promotions

Although the subject of promotions has been alluded to several times in this section, it should be pointed out again that most employees have as basic needs the opportunity for advancement and achievement for physiological, sociological, or psychological reasons. Because of this, a great deal of their behavior will be directed toward getting "ahead" in the organization. Although it has been stated that behavior of this type can be induced and facilitated by effective rating systems and training, it must be recognized that an equally important requirement is a sound systematic promotion program.

Systematic promotion refers to the fact that lines of relationship have been established between jobs. Based on accurate job descriptions and job specifications, these lines indicate which jobs lead to other responsibilities and what skills and knowledges are needed to be promoted. They in no way, it should be noted, guarantee that employees will automatically be moved in accordance with their direction. But they do point out with emphasis that management has established a promotion system based on need and ability, rather than on whim and bias. When joined with proper training and employee rating, such a system has obvious human relations implications.

Employee compensation

It was pointed out earlier in this section that too many managers give too much thought and attention to the monetary aspects of the work environment. Basically, the major reason for this is failure to recognize the hierarchical nature of human needs. As a consequence, these people overemphasize the quantitative aspects of employee compensation.

Unfortunately, the number of dollars *per se* an employee receives for his services is not the only facet of compensation that is important to him. What is frequently more important is the relationship of his wage to the wage another individual receives for the same or a different job. If, for example, another employee is receiving more for the same work, and factors such as experience, length of service, and merit do not account for this difference, then imbalance in need satisfaction occurs. This same result occurs when a person on a less difficult job is paid more than an individual who is working on a more difficult job.

Another aspect of compensation that is extremely and fundamentally important to the individual concerns the relationship of his pay to his contribution on the job. If he feels, rightly or wrongly, that he is underpaid for his services, a decrease in satisfaction of needs will obviously result. The effect of this is frequently a reduction in performance.

The solution to human relations problems that stem from employee compensation is, of course, a sound wage and salary administration program. In other words, among other things, job analysis and job evaluation must be used so that the pay of jobs is based in part on the relative worth of jobs. And employee rating must be used so that pay and raises can be based on performance and merit. Only when proper management techniques such as these are used will it be possible to build an effective compensation program.

Supervision

Although the subject of supervision was discussed in the section on leadership, because every supervisor is a leader, it must be noted here that managers are responsible for the selection of supervisory personnel. Because we know today that the major responsibility of a supervisor is to lead people, that is, to get work done through subordinates, every effort must be made to employ leaders who are skilled in motivation and other basic aspects of human relations. This means, consequently, that the age of promoting the best worker, technician, or specialist to a supervisory position has long since disappeared. The effective motivation of employee behavior requires leadership ability, not technical skill. Although technical ability may be an important requirement of some supervisory jobs, it is certainly in no way correlated with leadership skill. The selection of supervisors, that is, the hiring of people who must successfully practice human relations, must therefore be based on a sound recruitment and screening program. It must also to a great extent be based on proper training and development.

Jobs

It would be impossible to discuss here the nature of the various duties and responsibilities that people have in business and industry. Yet it is extremely important for managers to recognize that the work people do greatly affects and influences employee behavior. At one extreme, for example, people can obtain a great deal of satisfaction, such as status, prestige, achievement, and so forth, in the work they do. At the other extreme, jobs can make people become bored, listless, apathetic, and indifferent. This latter point is particularly true of the thousands of routine, menial, tedious tasks that exist in many organizations today.

Although it is undoubtedly impossible to design jobs that are challenging and interesting to all employees who must perform the tasks involved, there are several things managers can do to make the work more satisfying. In the first place, greater attention can be given to the selection of individuals who must work on these so-called nonchallenging jobs. This means that, in addition to considering the knowledge and skill needed for the job in question, attention must also be given to the level of mental ability and the type of personality that the job requires. By doing this, a much better matching of job and employee will occur.

Among other things managers can do to make jobs more interesting and challenging to people is to offer them opportunity for a change in their routine. For example, instead of having them do the same thing over and over, their duties and responsibilities can be rotated periodically so that, for a time at least, boredom and monotony can be alleviated. This technique is, in fact, almost a necessity for motivating junior managers who are destined for future high-level responsibilities. It is extremely difficult to keep motivated, indeed at times to keep employed, future executives who for the time being must be kept employed at tasks that do not challenge their abilities.

FUNDAMENTALS OF MANAGEMENT

In the section on leadership it was pointed out that the manager has many responsibilities in addition to motivating his subordinates. He must, for example, plan, organize, coordinate, and control the work to be done. Only when he does all these things, and does them well, will his organization be operated successfully.

Because it was impossible to consider in this book all the important factors that make up and influence the work environment, it should be stressed at this point that the successful practice of human relations demands that the manager give explicit attention to the human element when he designs the work to be done and the procedures, techniques, equipment, and so on that will be used to implement it. In other words, when he plans, organizes, coordinates, and controls work, he must, in addition to consideration of the technical and mechanical factors involved, give full attention to the impact of these things on the human being. Most important of all, he must fully recognize and understand that, in the final analysis, only people get work done. Only when the manager does this and gives weight to it in the design of the organization and work environment can he hope to practice human relations successfully.

The articles that follow were picked to provide a foundation for the practice of human relations. McMurry's and Tannenbaum's articles were chosen because they point out the necessity for empathy and understanding of our own basic needs. Schwab's article was included because it gives some practical examples of putting human relations research results to work. The article by McGregor was selected because it clearly analyzes the staff role in the practice of human relations. Lastly, the article by Elizabeth and Francis Jennings was included because it is an excellent treatise on the understanding necessary to guide the practice of human relations.

EMPATHY: MANAGEMENT'S
GREATEST NEED *

Robert N. McMurry

From time to time George French has wondered why he is so manifestly and inescapably unpopular. He cannot understand it. He has always tried to do the right thing. In fact, he has often gone out of his way to be helpful.

As a department head with the Booth Manufacturing Company, he has regarded it as his duty to help his subordinates to improve themselves in every way. As a result he has always made it his practice periodically to counsel with them and point out their shortcomings to them. That they have not always been wholly receptive to his constructive criticisms is one of the crosses he has had to reconcile himself to bear. Nevertheless, in spite of this, he still feels it is his duty to help them in this way.

His father, whom he has always greatly admired and tried to emulate, had always told him that one of his greatest obligations in life was to help his fellow man. In consequence, he has persevered, even though his subordinates have not only frequently failed to follow his advice, but some have gone so far as to nickname him the "Broadaxe of Dept. 126."

All his life he has dedicated himself to doing his duty, however painful though it might be. Early in his life his father gave him a set of maxims which he has tried to follow faithfully, regardless of how strongly he might be tempted to swerve from the path of duty. These maxims are:

1. Always respect your superiors (they have had more experience and know their jobs or they would not be in them).

2. Always follow instructions as given (there is a good reason for every rule).

3. Always be honest and forthright in your dealings with others (while some may not like it, they will respect you for it).

4. Always put the interests of your employer before your own (this is one of the best ways to make progress on your job).

5. Always try to help others, even though they may not be appreciative of it.

* From *Advanced Management*, Vol. 18, No. 7 (July, 1953), pp. 6-11, 34. Reprinted with permission.

It has not always been easy for George to follow his father's admonitions. Some of his decisions have been hard for him to make. There was, for example, the case of old Pete Rogers. Pete had been with the company for 35 years. When it came time for him to retire, a review of his personnel file revealed that, due to a clerical error, he had never been officially listed as an employee with the insurance company which administered the retirement trust.

In consequence, technically Pete was not eligible for a pension. George had tried to explain to Pete that while it *was* unfortunate, mishaps of this character did occur and that there was nothing that he could do to help him. When Pete protested, he had even shown him the contract with the insurance company which stated explicitly the conditions under which employees were eligible for a pension, and had explained why he was ineligible. He hadn't liked to deal with such situations, but a rule is a rule.

Then there was the case of Molly Stevenson. Molly was a clerk in his department handling the first step in processing orders received from customers. With the help of the company's methods expert, he had worked out performance standards for each clerk's activities. In this way he knew exactly what each girl should be expected to produce.

Molly had originally been one of his best and most faithful performers. Her work was accurate, and she spent little time in the washroom or in idle talk with the other girls. But over a period of time, her work had begun to deteriorate both in quantity and quality. He had spoken to her about it on several occasions. Each time she had promised to improve and for a short time she had. Later, she had slipped back, each time a little further.

In the meantime, he had heard that Molly's widowed mother, of whom she was the sole support, was suffering from cancer and that Molly was attempting to care for her at night to save the cost of a nurse. He suspected that this might be the reason her work was suffering. Hence, when he next talked to Molly he had told her that she would have to find someone to care for her mother at night because it was affecting her work.

Molly burst into tears and said she would try but she didn't know whether she could because doctor bills were already taking everything she earned. He had said that he understood, but that she must remember that her work must come first if she expected to stay in his department. She promised that she would try and for a while did show some improvement.

Ultimately, however, her performance had shown a further retrogression and it had been necessary for him to call her in and release her. He had explained and she agreed that he had given her fair and ample warning. He had hated to do this, but his conscience was clear. She had been unable to meet the department's production standard; she had been warned; she had to be replaced.

Persons like George are not intentionally cruel. They are not overt sadists; they derive no immediate personal satisfaction from making others unhappy. They are, of course, pleased with the *power* they have over others. If the exercise of this power results in suffering, they may even feel a momentary pang of regret that it is they who have been chosen as the instruments through whom circumstances or a higher authority have chosen to act. Such experiences are unpleasant, they admit, but they are all part of the day's task. They constitute one of the less pleasant aspects of the supervisor's work.

In short, such persons are neither vicious nor vindictive; they are simply incapable of *empathy*, of emotional resonance, of the capacity to put themselves in the place of another and respond as he does. In simple terms, *they are completely and totally insensible to the needs or feelings of others.* They have no insight into or real interest in people.

They regard people in the same casual, detached impersonal manner that they think of inanimate objects or animals. If a pair of shoes wears out, they are discarded; if a pet develops distemper, he is destroyed; if an employee ceases to be productive, he is taken off the payroll. It is this quality of complete conscienceless unconcern for others which reaches its apex, its finest flowering, in the ruthless dictator, e.g., Stalin; in the "torpedo" (the professional killer); or in the master of a mass extermination establishment such as Buchenwald.

Most individuals who lack empathy are not inhuman in a calculated manner; they are simply persons who find it difficult or impossible to form attachments to people. They cannot make even minimal emotional investments in others. Their capacity for affection, even interest in anyone outside of themselves, is usually quite limited.

What little warmth and love they have is jealously hoarded within their own egos and is lavished almost exclusively on themselves. Such persons are frequently not unfriendly; they may even be quite affable, especially with superiors and associates. Often they are very public-spirited and generous, but always in a rather impersonal manner.

Hereditary or environmental?

No one knows precisely why some individuals have a marked capacity for empathy, some less, and some practically none at all. It is probable that constitutional (inherited) factors may have a part to play. It is more likely, however, that early environmental factors have a vital influence in determining the degree of empathy of which a person may be capable.

Where the child has been reared in a cold, loveless, rigid, and overdemanding environment or one in which he has known little emotional security (his parents may have given him material benefits but little or uncertain affection), he may have feared to invest love or even interest in others for fear that it would not be reciprocated. Living always under the threat of emotional rejection by those from whom he seeks support and love, he dares not risk permitting himself to become too closely attached to others. They might (and perhaps have done so) reject his timid advances. In such instances, it is safer to hoard one's love within oneself.

People vs. things

Under such circumstances, it is natural for an individual to turn his field of interest from people to *things*. Things are not expected to be a source of love; therefore, they cannot reject and hurt. *They are emotionally safe.* In addition, in a scientific age such as the present, things can be both fascinating and challenging. In consequence, they have tremendous appeal to many, particularly those who are especially sensitive to rejection.

Also in the American society of today, a preoccupation with *things* is highly acceptable socially. This is the "scientific age," and science, until very recently, has concentrated its activities almost exclusively on *things* rather than on people. It is not surprising, therefore, that business and industry with their emphasis on production, research, accounting, engineering, and finance have had unusual appeal to "thing-minded" persons.

Even sales work, which presumes to deal with people, has been largely mechanized through the introduction of research designed to determine the best means of exploiting the public wants and needs through advertising and other standardized marketing techniques.

In consequence, business and industry probably have a higher concentration of predominantly thing-minded persons than do many of the professions, e.g., medicine, the church, and the arts. And from a purely materialistic point of view this is probably advantageous.

A single-minded concentration on *things* by management with less regard for humanitarian considerations has probably contributed largely to the industrial development of this country. It has doubtless resulted in a vast contribution to the national product and the tremendous improvement in the American standard of living which has accompanied it. Whether this growth and increase in efficiency has also sometimes been at the cost of human well-being is a debatable question.

Certainly many of the frictions and conflicts which now plague business and industry may be attributed to the extent to which business management today is permeated with George Frenches—dynamic, efficient, loyal, and creative administrators who are also largely or totally insensitive to the needs, problems, and anxieties of the people with whom they work and whom they supervise.

The union as defender

Probably the best evidence of the acuteness of this problem is to be seen in the rapidity of the growth of the labor movement, once the social and legal shackles were removed from it. There are many conditions which influence workers' decisions to join unions. But one of the chief of these is the feeling on their part that management's points of view and attitudes lack an understanding for and appreciation of employee needs and problems. This, they recognize, is due in part to failures of intra-company communication—management is literally ignorant of much that affects its people. But even when improved communication techniques have been introduced so that management is adequately informed, it is still often reluctant to take what the employees regard as needed action. Hence, many feel that they need a union as a defense against management's ignorance, indifference, or intransigence.

It is not that most workers distrust management's basic motives: The old stereotype of the capitalist as a hard-eyed, blood-sucking leech, mercilessly exploiting the helpless proletariat, has been relegated chiefly to Communist propaganda circles. Most employees are sufficiently sophisticated to know that top and middle management is composed of hired hands whose positions are fundamentally no different from theirs, except that the pressures are greater.

What they resent is management's blithe assumption that it already knows, on an *a priori* basis, what its subordinates need and how their problems should be handled. Too many management policies reflect either a complete ignorance of what is actually transpiring at the worker level or a total disregard for employee sensibilities and needs.

Typical of this latter type of thinking was that shown by the manager of an eighty-year-old plant which was being closed because it was no longer competitive. He told his employees, many of whom had over 30 years' service, that he would give separation allowances *only to those who were too old and feeble to obtain employment elsewhere.*

This manager was not deliberately and willfully attempting to be cruel. He was simply shortsighted. By excluding all but those who were manifestly incapable of other employment, he (by profession an engineer) estimated that he could save his employers approximately $30,000.

It never occurred to him to consider what $200 or $300 would mean to an aging employee who had given the best years of his life to the company. This was because *he was completely without empathy.* He lacked entirely the capacity to put himself in his people's shoes. He was a rational automaton to whom people are merely ciphers and are to be treated as such.

It is largely because industry has more than its quota of such executives that the unions have had such a rapid growth and continue to have the support of their members. The union, after all, constitutes their sole defense against such management.

The schism in attitudes

More immediately, however, this lack of empathy by supervisors and executives at every level is productive of many misunderstandings and conflicts in the course of day-to-day operations. These arise out of what may be termed "conflicts of attitudes."

An example may be seen in the difference between management and union attitudes toward incentive compensation based upon time studies. Management considers such incentives to be quite legitimate, even somewhat generous, since they enable the employee to share in the rewards of any additional effort which he expends. The unions, on the other hand, as well as many employees, regard them as instruments for the "speed-up," the conscienceless exploitation of the worker through appeals to his avarice.

Here may be seen the same technique of management as looked at from two violently opposed points of view: Those of management and labor. The attitudes of management are enthusiastic; that of labor is bitterly in opposition. Furthermore, neither has either sympathy or understanding for the other's point of view. Nor is either desirous of learning to understand the bases for the other's attitudes. Each group is monolithic in its opposition to the viewpoint of the other.

Furthermore, this conflict is based on no coldly rational difference of interpretation of the evidence; it is highly toned emotionally. Feelings run riot on both sides. Arguments pro and con are vigorously impassioned; factual evidence gives way to elaborate rationalizations; the level of discourse ascends higher and higher on the ladder of abstraction.

As the contestants become farther and farther removed from reality in their discussions, the higher and shriller becomes the emotional tone of their arguments. Ultimately, an impasse is reached. The parties to the conflict are so far apart that there is no hope for its resolution. The outcome is an uneasy state of armed truce. The net result is that time study rates become in themselves a symbol of management-labor conflict. Obviously, this does not enhance their effectiveness as incentives. (On the average, 70% of union grievances center on time study rates.)

This illustrates the fact that a lack of sympathy for others' points of view is not confined to supervisors and company executives. It is equally common among rank-and-file workers and their union representatives. Neither they nor members of management are able successfully to place themselves in the positions of those with whom they are in disagreement or are even desirous of attempting to do so.

In short, the cause of much industrial strife is to be found less in the specific practices and policies at issue and more in the *attitudes* of their protagonists and opponents toward them. It is not *the thing in itself* which is significant but the *feelings* which are associated with it. It is they which cause and perpetuate the difficulty. Therefore, if the conflict is to be resolved, the first step is to change the parties' attitudes toward the matter at issue.

Changing antagonistic attitudes

Superficially, this appears to be easy. It would seem to be only a matter of the clarification of misunderstandings. Given all of the facts it should not appear to be difficult for both parties to see the logic of the situation and reach an agreement. This would be true if both could observe the identical facts from the same perspective, i.e., objectively and without bias. This, unfortunately, is where the difficulty arises.

No one can ever be entirely objective about anything: He is always to some degree the prisoner of his preconceptions. In short, he has an *attitude* toward every issue with which he comes into contact. Further, each attitude has some (usually considerable) emotional toning or coloring. In other words, everyone is likely to feel at least reasonably strongly on nearly every issue toward which he has a well-established attitude.

If these feelings were strictly rational, they might be amenable to influence by logic. Unfortunately, they are not. Two factors influence them. The first of these is the *displacement of affect*. By this is meant the extent to which attitudes which are generated by one set of circumstances and which may well have been appropriate and justified are shifted or "displaced" on to other quite foreign and often inappropriate objects.

A common example is the young man who (entirely unconsciously) displaces his hostilities toward his father onto his foreman. The father may have been an unconscionable autocrat, the foreman a mild, ineffective, and well-intentioned nonentity, but both are "authority figures." The young man's resentments toward authority, as embodied in his father, can easily, and frequently do, displace onto the foreman. This is not because the foreman is arbitrary or demanding. It is simply because he, like the father, symbolizes authority. (This, incidentally, explains why so many young people are drawn to Communism which purports to be dedicated to the destruction of intrenched authority.)

The second factor influencing feelings is the extent to which these attitudes are the products of deep-seated needs (many of which are not socially acceptable), hostilities, and anxieties. The high emotional toning which many of them carry likewise gives them a somewhat irrational quality. This is because their roots extend far back into the individual's infancy, and they have retained many of the prelogical characteristics of the child's thinking. They have been formed and colored by early environmental and subsequent cultural influences.

Among these influences are such factors as the individual's cultural heritage, economic level, occupational status, education, character of associates, political beliefs, and specific experiences on the job (relations with supervision, the union, etc.). Of particular significance also are the characteristics of the persons with whom he has identified himself in the course of his development. (If the ideal he strove to emulate was John D. Rockefeller, he would have radically different attitudes toward management than would be the case had John L. Lewis been his hero.)

The menace of inflexibility

Because the roots of most of everyone's attitudes are deeply buried in his past, their sources, even their very existence, are almost entirely unknown to him. Furthermore, because of their long standing they are also practically immutable. They have become firmly embedded in his personality. The holder will, in consequence, defend them literally to the death. He does not know he acquired them; he is not even too greatly concerned about their consistency or logic. He is convinced of one thing only: *What he believes is right.* Such mental sets as these are encountered frequently in the field of politics, e.g., the unreconstructed Democrat who still votes as his pappy did and whose motto is: "Right or wrong, I'll always be a Democrat." Unfortunately, such firmly held attitudes are not confined to politics; they are equally common in the field of labor-management relations.

As a result, neither workers nor their union representatives nor members of management can approach most of the issues on which conflict exists objectively and with an open mind. Each has his own particular constellation of attitudes on every topic. Furthermore, each is not only convinced that his attitudes are the only right ones, but that any opinions which differ from his are *irrevocably and indisputably wrong.* This makes agreement almost completely impossible.

Since neither party to the dispute actually has much solid, factual ground for his opinions (he is probably discussing the "interpretation" of the facts at issue), he is more likely chiefly to be expressing his *attitudes.* Hence, it is obvious that any meeting of the minds will be difficult to bring about. Not only will each party to the dispute find it difficult to place himself in the position of the other, but assuming that one or the other tries, he will still have difficulty in accepting the viewpoint of his opponent.

Thus, the major problem facing industry, if it is to enjoy labor peace and benefits of good employee morale, is a twofold one: First, it must stimulate a higher degree of empathy in its supervisors and executives to improve their immediate handling of their interpersonal relationships. Secondly, it must arouse management to a clearer awareness of the part that *its own* attitudes play in clouding and biasing its analysis of the labor relations problems with which it is faced.

Management initiative

Most important, it must recognize that *the initiative for improvement in this area must come principally from management itself,* first, because emphathy is one of the prime requisites for success as a supervisor or executive and secondly, because neither the mass of the workers nor their union representatives, generally, have any reason to be aware that there may be an element of illogic in their attitudes and beliefs.

The unions, being part of a "movement," rarely question the essential rightness of their goals and the means employed to gain them. The majority of the workers and their representatives are still comfortably but implacably convinced that *their* viewpoints are invariably the only correct ones. Hence, they cannot be expected to see any need to question the soundness of their beliefs, much less take the initiative to change them in any way or to recognize that the employer's position may have any merit whatever.

Even within a presumably enlightened management group, the difficulties of stimulating a greater degree of empathy will be great. To begin with, if a supervisor's or executive's insensitivity to the feelings and needs of others is actually symptomatic of a deep-lying personality deformation, of a basic incapacity to invest affection in others, no amount of training or admonition will be of much help. Such persons must be recognized as inherently incapable of empathy. Situations such as this must be faced realistically. A George French can never be given much empathic insight.

On the other hand, if supervisors such as he are recognized as empathic cripples, their capacity for harm can be minimized. As far as possible, they can be taken out of line, administrative positions and given staff responsibilities. There they will have little contact with people, but can concentrate all of their efforts on *things* (production, engineering, accounting, etc.). If it is impossible to relieve them of administrative responsibilities, their personnel activities can be audited periodically by contacts with their subordinates (using exit interviews, follow-up interviews, counseling sessions, and periodic opinion polls) to discover, correct, and forestall their more egregious blunders in the field of human relations.

Where there *is* demonstrated capacity for empathy among them, much can be accomplished to make middle and top management aware of its nature, the need for it, and what it can accomplish in bettering human relationships. At the same time, it is essential that a recognition be given top and middle management of the magnitude of the differences which may exist between their beliefs and attitudes on various aspects of company operations and those of lower level supervision and the rank-and-file employees.

Since the nature and range of these differences are frequently unknown to both parties, it is desirable to bring them to management's attention. This will often eliminate sources of misunderstanding and friction and at the same time illustrate, often dramatically, the variety and character of existing differences in attitudes between groups.

Both of these objectives can be attained by conducting a study designed to measure objectively and quantitatively the nature and extent of empathic differences at varying levels in a business organization. Either as a part of an employee opinion poll or independent of it, a series of identical attitude questions are asked of members of top and middle management and of hourly rated employees.

Typical of such questions is the following: "Do you believe that the Taft-Hartley Law is a 'slave labor act'?" Each respondent is asked to give a categorical "yes" or "no" answer to indicate his personal opinion relative to the issue. Following this, he is asked to indicate what answer ("yes" or "no") a majority of his associates and peers will give to the same question. Next (if he is a member of top management) he is asked to state how a majority of the members of his middle management (supervisory) and hourly-rated employees will respond. Members of middle management are asked to indicate how they believe top management and the rank-and-file employees will answer, as well as to state their own opinions. The hourly-rated group is asked to report similarly on middle and top management as well as on themselves.

Assessing the differences

When these responses are tallied it becomes possible to measure the extent to which:

1. Absolute differences in attitude toward each issue exist among the three groups.

2. Members of each group understand (are empathic to) the attitudes of:

a. Their own (their peer) group.

b. Groups ranking above and below them in the organization.[1]

---

[1] For a discussion of the problem and the potentialities of this technique, see H. A. Rammers, "A Quantitative Index of Social-Psychological Empathy," *American Journal of Orthopsychiatry*, 520, 1950, pp. 161-5, and A. M. Anikeeff, "Reciprocal Empathy: Mutual Understanding Among Conflict Groups," *Purdue University Studies of Higher Education*, 77, 1951, pp. 1-48.

It is often a shock to members of the various groups, particularly those in top management, to discover the magnitude of existing differences in attitudes at the various levels. They are frequently even more seriously disturbed to learn the degree of their own errors in estimating the attitudes of the members of other groups. Findings of this character, as indicated, present graphically and dramatically the range of the differences in opinion existing among employees of different levels in the enterprise and the frequent lack of insight into the attitudes of others by various management and worker groups. These findings can then serve as a basis both for training top and middle management in the nature and importance of empathy and for highlighting significant differences in attitudes among employee groups. Once these distinctions have been established, management can take constructive steps to discover the reasons for them and to minimize their effects.

Empathy is a critical factor in a wide variety of activities. The physician with a fine "beside manner" is merely an individual with a strong inherent "feel" for his patients' needs, problems, and anxieties. He senses them largely by intuition, but, as a result, is able to respond to them with keener insight and hence greater effectiveness than does his colleague to whom his patients' complaints represent merely a formal catalogue of symptoms.

Most truly successful salesmen are empathic to a high degree. While they are rarely aware of the part empathy plays in their effectiveness, its contribution is a major one. It enables them intuitively to sense the prospects' true (as distinct from *stated*) needs. They then direct their sales presentations to showing how their products satisfy these more basic needs. In short, they have a resonance, a sensitivity, to the prospects' emotional as well as rational needs and respond predominantly to the former.

They then use logical appeals only to *rationalize* (justify on logical grounds) the use of their products to gratify needs which are never even made articulate but which the salesman can sense empathically. Such persons are invariably more successful than those who, being incapable of empathy, must rely wholly on purely logical appeals directed at obvious needs.

Element of leadership

All really successful leaders, including every dictator, have great empathic sensitivity. The essence of leadership of the masses is the development of an intuitive awareness of what they need and want.

As most groups of this type are notoriously inarticulate, the leader must sense their needs instinctively, i.e., by empathy. He does this by placing himself in their positions and thinking what he himself would want under those conditions.

Knowing their needs, he can then chart a course designed to give them what they want and also justify his program. He may claim authorship for his plan himself, but the true roots of the appeal of his program are to be found in his *empathic awareness of what the group wants.* He insures that his followers will respond to his commands because in so doing, *they are actually only doing what he has sensed they have wanted to do anyway.*

This was the secret of Hitler's power over the German masses: Being of lower middle class background himself, he knew what they needed and wanted. He simply promised that if they followed him they would have what they wanted. The secret of his success lay in the fact that he was *emotionally in tune* with his followers. In consequence, whatever he demanded of them was what they desired to do anyway, regardless of its illogic, its nature, or its consequences.

Because of the tremendous power of this intuitive type of leadership and the great, albeit ordinarily unrecognized, cost of the failure of management and supervision to see others' problems from their points of view, the need for empathy must be of constant concern to management at all levels. Top management must look at itself objectively and appraise its own capacity for empathy.

In evaluating the competence of members of middle management, the ability to understand and respond to the needs and problems of others must be given a weight equal to that given to technical skills and productivity. Great reluctance must be shown to promote anyone to an administrative or supervisory position who has demonstrated an appreciable incapacity for empathy. Regardless of his other qualifications, if he is an empathic cripple, he will experience difficulty in handling people. He can never be truly effective as a leader without some ability to sense his subordinates' needs and problems. He can function only as a dictator in a completely regimented, authoritarian autocracy.

But as all totalitarian regimes have discovered to their sorrow, slave labor is rarely efficient and productive. *Participation* by subordinates is vital if their creativity and effort is to be maximized. But participation is impossible in an autocracy, particularly where the supervisor is incapable of empathy. If participation is to be encouraged, the leader must be capable of establishing and maintaining rapport with his subordinates. This he cannot do if he has no capacity for empathy. Therefore, empathic sensitivity is vital to effective leadership at all levels. Without it, no supervisor or executive can get the most from his people.

Even more vital is the role of empathy in resolving the conflicts which arise from differences in *attitudes* toward specific issues or company practices. If management representatives are incapable of empathy, it will be natural for them to assume that there is no question concerning the essential rightness of *their* positions on every issue. In short, they will be completely intolerant of the opinions and positions of their subordinates and the latters' union representatives.

Because a lack of empathy for management's viewpoint is also to be expected on the part of these employee and union groups, the result can rarely be other than a continuing and bitter deadlock. Often the consequences of such conflicts are both costly and distressing, taking as they do the form of slowdowns, work stoppages, limitations of output, theft, insubordination, abuse of equipment, and generally substandard morale.

A reasonable approach

Granting that management personnel has at least some empathic sensitivity, its reaction to a conflict situation will be to attempt to be reasonable. When confronted with a conflict of attitudes as in the case of time studied incentive rates or promotions on merit rather than on seniority, it will not immediately adopt a two-valued orientation, i.e., assume that everything is absolutely right or absolutely wrong and that it has a monopoly on being in the right. It will grant that not everything is completely black or white; there may be some grays. It will further admit that it may be at least partly in the wrong. Most important, it will seek to ascertain not only what the employees and their union representatives believe and want, *but why they have these particular opinions and make these demands.*

Furthermore, its approach to such conflicts will not be doctrinaire. It will honestly seek the truth; it will not be looking solely for substantiation of its firmly held convictions. Such management really wants to learn the facts, even though they may perhaps be personally embarrassing and may pose difficult problems. In short, this type of top management may discover that its people actually have compelling and valid reasons for their beliefs and for making their demands. It can also discover that many of its own cherished opinions are not only incorrect, but are positively harmful.

It's up to management

The key to the resolution of these attitudinal conflicts lies, there-fore, in the ability and willingness of those who determine company policy to try objectively and without passion to see both sides of the problems which face them. And, as already indicated, the *initiative must come from management*. Only management is in a position to correct many of the conditions which create or exacerbate employee ill-will and feed the fires of their hostility toward itself and what it stands for.

This, in turn, presupposes that relatively clear channels of com-munication exist between top company executives and the workers. The most empathic executive in the world is not going to be able to put himself in his subordinates' places if he is unable adequately to communicate with them. While it is customary to think of the chain of command, the hierarchy of supervision, extending from president to laborer, as offering a clear channel of communication, a little reflection will indicate that this is rarely the case.

There are too many barriers to communication and sources of distortion in such a hierarchy. (The chief of these is the desire of each of those in each echelon to impress *his* superiors with the super-lative quality of *his* performance. Hence, nothing is permitted to come to his superior's attention which might raise embarrassing questions about *his* competence.) Therefore, the line organization must be supplemented as a dependable channel of communication.

Likewise, for a number of reasons, the union hierarchy rarely provides a clear channel of management-employee communication. To begin with, the union is rarely an impartial, disinterested agency. Many of the issues in a conflict situation are ones toward which it is vehemently partisan. Furthermore, many unions themselves are rife with factionalism and internecine strife. Precisely what will be com-municated will depend greatly upon which faction is in power. These internal difficulties, therefore, seriously affect a union's value as a dependable medium of management-worker communication.

"Talking it out"

If management is to obtain a comprehensive and valid picture of its employees' opinions and attitudes and their sources, it must pro-vide facilities for them to talk them out freely, at length, and without reservation. This generally excludes counseling conferences with supervision (relatively few foremen, department heads, and even executives have the skill, time, patience, and empathic sensitivity to make such contacts successfully).

Only persons who have demonstrated a high degree of empathy and who have been trained in the use of the unstructured, open end or nondirective interview can be used. Interviews of this type should be conducted with all employees (including supervisors) at regular intervals. All new employees should be interviewed a few weeks after starting on the job; older employees should have a counseling interview at least once each year, and all employees on leaving should be given an exit interview.

Ideally, an opinion poll should be conducted biennially to provide a static cross-section of employee and supervisory attitudes as a control on the findings of the less formalized procedures. From these several sources, data can be assembled and collated which will provide management with a detailed, explicit, and fluid picture of precisely what each employee wants and believes, and why he wants and believes what he does.

"Do unto others . . ."

If, on the basis of the information obtained in this manner, management will then take the initiative in trying to see its people's problems *from their perspective*, it may discover that there is merit in many of their beliefs and demands. It may likewise learn that many of their complaints are justified.

Of the greatest significance, however, it will find it easier to resolve many management-worker conflicts of interest and attitude, some of which at first seem quite irreconcilable. It will not always be easy for management to accept others' (particularly the unions') points of view; and efforts in this direction may well be looked upon with suspicion by many in business—if for no other reason than that an approach of this nature is a distinct novelty in most companies.

It will be charged that this is a "soft," "appeasing," way to handle these problems. (It is *not*, because seeing the other person's side does not necessarily imply weakness—it does not preclude disciplining.) Most significant, where an open-minded, albeit firm, atittude toward employee problems has been tried, the results have almost invariably been good. In nearly every instance where an enterprise has been consistently free from labor trouble, it has had top management which has applied this philosophy.

And why should the results not be good? The principle on which this method is based is at least 2,000 years old. It is simply the application in modern industry of the Golden Rule, "Do unto others as ye would have others do unto you."

QUESTIONS

1. Explain what is meant by empathy.
2. What misunderstandings and conflicts arise because of lack of empathy?
3. Why must the initiative for improvement in labor-management relations come principally from management itself? Do you agree?
4. How is empathy related to leadership and communication?
5. What must management do to obtain a valid picture of employee opinions and attitudes?

DEALING WITH OURSELVES BEFORE
DEALING WITH OTHERS *

Robert Tannenbaum, Ph.D.

Frequently when we talk to executives about the problems they face in dealing with other people, these leaders will point the finger at some one else. A usual comment after a session such as this is: "You know, this is most helpful but my boss should have been here." Frequently, too, executives will ask how to deal with a particular person whom they describe, but rarely do they talk about themselves. Nevertheless, the place to begin human relations is at home—that is, with ourselves.

Analogy from the craftsman

In the area of interpersonal relations, an analogy can be drawn from the craftsman on the job. When the craftsman works at his machine, he has to ask himself three questions: What do I use this instrument for? How do I use this instrument? What is the result of using this instrument? In interpersonal relations, the instrument is ourselves, and we have to ask the same questions.

As for the first question, some executives might say: "Well, I am responsible for attaining certain organizational objectives. Therefore I use myself for whatever influence potential I have for bringing about organizational goals." Other executives might say: "We have so many *wiggits* to turn out per hour. I use myself in relation to my subordinates or in relation to the line in order to get this organizational goal accomplished."

Still others might give this answer. "I use myself to help other people realize their own potential as fully as possible." And some individuals who particularly like to work in a group participatory way might say they use themselves to facilitate the attainment of the group goal.

But let's not be too hasty here. As we watch many executives at work, we find in reality they often consciously think they are using themselves to attain the kind of objectives mentioned but in fact are trying to attain unconscious personal goals. Here are a few instances.

Often we, as executives, get up to a certain point in the organization. We attain a certain title, and this title becomes a source of

* From *Office Executive*, Vol. 32, No. 8 (August, 1957), pp. 29-30, 35. Reprinted with permission.

security that helps us to block off many threats or potential threats that might come our way in our relations with subordinates. We use our status to block communications upward, for often our subordinates, particularly those who are on the make, have ideas that may be better than ours.

If a subordinate passes an idea up the line, he may in a sense show us up in a bad light. He makes us feel uncomfortable. We feel his hot breath on our neck. We are afraid he will take our job over. Therefore we try to make it difficult for him to really communicate his ideas upward. Or, we use our status to put him in his place.

For example, suppose a subordinate offers a criticism about something we have just done. We turn to him, using our status, and say: "Look, Joe, I have been through the ropes. I know this work a lot better than you do. It seems to me I should be calling the shots here."

Probably, consciously, we would justify talking to him this way because, after all, our time is important. Of course, we know the real answer for our response, but we do use rationalization of this kind. The reality may well be that we use our status to put Joe in his place or to frighten him.

Dependency relationship

Consider another instance. We managers give a great deal of lip service daily to the importance of developing our subordinates—really helping them to grow. Yet, most of us tend to keep people in the dependency relationship with respect to us. We are careful about giving individuals wide latitude and freedom in which they will have the opportunity to grow and develop. We are even cautious about giving them an opportunity to make mistakes as a basis for learning.

Having people look up to us satisfies our ego. We prefer individuals who turn to us for the answers, individuals who can't make a move until we call the shots for them. To play the role of the puppet-man, keeping the employee at the end of the dangling strings so that he moves only when we make the appropriate gesture, gives our egos satisfaction.

Our rationalization here is that we have to direct the fellow closely because he just does not know how to work. Or, he has not had sufficient experience. Or, "I know more than he does about what he is doing. And because I know more, I am watching him closely, directing him rather sharply to further organizational objectives." Often we are afraid to look at our own real motivations.

Typically when we behave in this way we are meeting primarily our own needs—needs for security; needs for status; needs for comfort in the work situation. Such behavior on our part represents our own immaturity, our own inability to be actually big in a psychological sense in relation to those with whom we deal.

Hence, when we ask how we use ourselves as an instrument, we have to look behind or deeply beneath the usual rationalization we come up with. We have to ask ourselves: "Am I really meeting my own needs when I behave the way I do?"

A great temptation

Consider the second question—How do I use this instrument that is myself? A great temptation here is to ask for a few do's and don't's to use as the *open sesame* in interpersonal relations. But the reality of success in interpersonal relations is by no means this simple. Dealing effectively with other people depends upon not only what we are but also upon the nature of the people with whom we are dealing and the situation. Different kinds of behavior are called for in different situations.

Effectiveness in interpersonal relations depends on two essential qualities—*social sensitivity* and *behavioral flexibility*. *Social sensitivity* means the ability to accurately understand another individual. People differ from each other rather markedly in this ability. Some persons are much more accurate in their perception of other people. Most of us have real blind spots when we look at other individuals. We tend to see only what we want to see or have to see in order to feel comfortable in our relations with another person.

Frequently, for example, time and method study men, accountants, production managers and marketing specialists see individuals through a lens or filter that distorts the reality that is there. They see only what they want to see or have to see to feel comfortable.

Behavioral flexibility means the ability to behave appropriately in the light of the understanding of the other person. While some individuals are socially sensitive, they have little behavioral flexibility, and the reverse is true.

What differentiates people who are low in behavioral flexibility and social sensitivity from those who are high in these qualities? The person who is relatively mature emotionally, the person who has worked through many personality problems, is the individual who tends to be high in both traits. On the other hand, the person who is relatively immature emotionally is the individual who is lacking in high performance in these two traits. Persons wishing to develop greater social sensitivity must become aware of the need they are serving when they distort the mechanism they set up; otherwise they will continue to see things inaccurately.

For instance, in a recent executive training period one of the participants gave a lengthy discussion on the "listening technique." He suggested to the group that a good idea would be for the members to each listen to one of their employees for one week and then report on the experience at the next meeting. The idea was accepted, and the man who made the recommendation was the first to give a report.

"You know," he said, "I learned a lot about myself when I tried this experiment with the employee. I found as I tried to listen that I was extremely uncomfortable. As I look back at this discomfort, I realize that when I gave the other person an opportunity to do the talking, I was no longer in the position of control. The other person was determining what was being said. I discovered when I hit these periods of silence that I couldn't wait them out. I couldn't stand it. I had to start talking."

Unconstructive situation

This executive hit on two areas that got in his way from the standpoint of behaving in a new manner. First was his need to control people; second, which he did not understand at the time, was his discomfort in what might be called an unconstructive situation. The situation was not carefully defined. Nothing is as unconstructive as a period of silence.

We find in training sessions, for instance, that if we do not follow an agenda, if we as trainers don't tell our trainees what to do, a certain number of us feel uncomfortable because the meeting lacks structure. In other words, the executive who finds silence uncomfortable has unresolved personality problems within himself. These problems get in the way of his being more effective when he tries to listen. Hence, for such an executive to behave more effectively and flexibly, he would have to take care of the unresolved problems.

Consider next the third question. What is the result of the use of this instrument, ourselves? Few individuals really know what their impact is on other individuals—how other people see them, respond to them or feel about them.

One time, for example, in a training activity with eight top men, I interviewed each one individually. At the end of each interview I asked this question: "How do you think the other seven fellows in this group see you?" If you were in this particular spot in your own organization and knew that I would be talking with the other seven men about how they really saw you, what would your answer be? If your answer is a question mark, as in the case with many persons, the situation is serious.

For years as office managers, you have been talking about the importance of all types of managerial controls as far as office procedures are concerned. You have argued that statistical and accounting controls are essential if you are to run a business effectively. You set your goals or standards, and you need a quick report on the accounting, statistical and other operating data so that you can quickly check performance against goals.

People who work with guided missiles know these missiles have to have a control device or feed-back that will detect deviation of the missile from the target. Yet, in our interpersonal relations, we rarely, if ever, have any control mechanism or feed-back. A feed-back mechanism could let us know how other people see us. It could be a means of telling us whether we are on the target or not.

Why don't we find out exactly how other people feel about us? Perhaps finding out would make us too uncomfortable. Maybe intellectually we would like to know but emotionally we don't want to. The idea makes us shudder.

We go around like ostriches

Hence we go around like ostriches, believing what we really want to believe of ourselves rather than believing what reality would tell us. Our inability to get feed-back on our impact on other people stems from our own inability to permit other people to call the shots as they see them.

How, then, can we improve this instrument, ourselves? More and more training classes are being designed to help executives gain the kind of increased insights into themselves to help them become more effective along the lines previously mentioned. The American Management Association, for instance, has set up special training programs for executives. In addition, the National Training Laboratory is available at Bethel, Maine, and many other training laboratories in group development have been set up. The University of California at Los Angeles has a special program called "Sensitivity Training for Management."

However, special programs are not the only types of activity that can be used as a means for improving oneself in greater emotional maturity. The listening skill referred to is a key in self-development. This skill has many other beneficial outcomes. We can't really understand ourselves better unless we get the feed-back that we need from other people—the people with whom we interact. If we never give these individuals an opportunity to tell us what they think, we deny ourselves much useful information needed in our own personal growth and development.

The direction each of us needs to grow is in the direction of real listening skill—the ability to develop an atmosphere around ourselves, an atmosphere of security, lack of threat, of acceptance and warmth that makes it possible for other people to feel comfortable and free of negative reaction.

Listening isn't easy. It can not be accomplished by turning the right knob. The ability to listen takes time to acquire but pays off when developed.

QUESTIONS

1. What are the essential qualities for effectiveness in interpersonal relations?
2. Why do people who have social sensitivity lack behavioral flexibility?
3. Why do many executives keep employees in a dependency relationship?
4. What part does emotion play in social sensitivity and behavioral flexibility?
5. What does Tannenbaum recommend we do to improve our social sensitivity and behavioral flexibility?

MOTIVATION AND HUMAN RELATIONS PRINCIPLES *

Robert E. Schwab

My role in this discussion is to give some practical examples of putting human relations research results to work. During the past five years the Detroit Edison Company has been closely associated with the Institute for Social Research in its human relations program. We have participated in research projects and naturally have had an active interest in the findings. However, we have been more concerned with how to apply what we learn through research to the solution of human relations problems and the building of an effective organization.

The problem which faces all of us in industry is how to create the kind of conditions under which our employees will direct their best efforts toward the objectives of the enterprise. Widespread concern over a fair day's work is just one indication that active cooperation and enthusiasm for industry's objectives doesn't just come naturally.

The role of research

That's where people like our friends at the Institute for Social Research and others doing research in human relations come into the picture. Not that they have any secret formulas for winning friends and influencing people. The interesting thing about research in human relations is that the researchers are simply telling us what, of the things we now do, gets the kind of results we want and why. That's a very important thing for us to understand, because our human relations are going to improve only when we start doing more of the things that result in desirable attitudes and actions on the part of others and avoiding the things that result in undesirable attitudes and actions. That puts the problem right where it should be, in the hands of every man in industry who is responsible for getting things done through other people, including the president and every level of supervision between him and the fellow who runs the machine or drives the truck or pulls the switches or gives the service.

Another interesting thing about human relations research is that it can tell us what we do that builds good team spirit, high morale,

* From *Personnel Series No. 155*, The American Management Association, 1953, pp. 30-39. Copyright, 1953, by the American Management Association. Reprinted by permission of the American Management Association.

and high productivity in our workforce, but it hasn't told us much yet about how to get more of our supervisors at all levels to accept and use good human relations principles. Unfortunately, human relations principles don't solve human relations problems without a lot of help from each of us. When we make a new discovery in engineering or technology, we can usually put it right to work to solve problems or improve methods. But, when we learn more about how to motivate others, it usually calls for some change in us. Since it is human nature to resist change, we too often give little more than lip service to those things which require changes in our own traditional ways of thinking or acting. We in industry have been much too inclined to look for plans, programs, gadgets, and gimmicks, which, when applied to the other fellow, result in his seeing things our way and putting as much enthusiasm into doing what we want done as we ourselves would do.

Putting research results to work

Dr. Likert, Dr. Zander and Dr. Kahn have been telling us about some of the things we do in industry that result in high morale and high productivity in work groups. One of the things they tell us about ourselves is that the kind of leadership we provide in our companies has a very important influence on the attitudes and actions of our employees. Now, this isn't a particularly new thought. We've always known that some supervisors got better results with their people than others. When we begin to look objectively at the supervisor who is building highly motivated work groups—or a division—or a department, we find he is likely to be the sort of fellow who

- Goes to bat for his employees;
- Shows an interest in how they get along;
- Lets his employees know what he thinks of their work; and
- Gets his employees' ideas and does something about them.

These are only typical of the personal characteristics of the supervisor who gets best results with his work group. The significant finding is that sincere concern for the employee as an individual and consideration for his point of view are essential elements in motivation. We can hardly expect the other fellow to be concerned with our point of view unless we show a little interest in his.

In examining further the human relations principles which are present in the high-morale, high-productivity situations, we find one kind of activity that is almost always present. There is a good deal of sharing of problems and plans with those who will be most affected by decisions. This is a practice which most top managements recognize as valuable for building a strong top-management team, but we have not been fully aware of its importance for high motivation at every level in the organization. Granted, the kinds of problems shared at each level may differ, but the important thing seems to be that the principle of participation is employed all the way down. Jimmy Durante is always saying that "Everyone wants to get into the act," and Jimmy, being a pretty good judge of human nature, has apparently put his finger on an important principle of motivation. Our problem is to find effective ways to let supervisors and employees "get into the act."

Evidence of the importance of the principle of participation led us to consider further how it might be applied in our company. It was recognized that many supervisors had always talked work problems over with their groups. There were also top management groups and committees who discussed and recommended action before final decisions were made on matters of engineering, policy, etc. This degree of participation was well accepted. Our problem was gradually to extend problem-sharing to more subjects and to include more people. This could be done only as acceptance and understanding of the principle, and skill in its use, could be developed. And at each step of the way it had to meet the practical test that it worked—that it got better results. Human relations research said it was so, but few of us change our traditional ways of operating unless we find from personal experience that some other way gets better results for us.

Belief in the principles of good human relations and awareness of the special significance of participation has led us during the past five years to extend our understanding and activity in these four ways:

1. The training of all supervisors, from top management down, in human relations in supervision. The purpose of the training was to develop understanding of and skill in sharing certain job problems with employees.

2. The involvement of all supervisors and, on occasion, employees in the development of a number of company personnel policies and benefit plans.

3. The feedback of results of a company-wide attitude survey to supervisors and employees for consideration, comments, and recommendations.

4. Continuing investigation of the relationship between participation and desirable attitudes or action on the part of supervisors and employees.

Human relations training

I believe it will help us to understand how human relations principles can be extended in any organization if I discuss each of these briefly. First, as to the training of supervisors. Starting with top management and going down through successive levels, all supervisors were given intensive human relations training. The principles of good supervision, based on results of research, were presented for their consideration. In small groups and with their own line superior they discussed the application of the principles to the solution of their own day-to-day problems.

Evidence was presented to show that groups sharing decisions showed reasonable and even high production standards. They set high quality goals, and their decisions were characterized by accurate judgments. They sometimes introduced facts which supervisors might have overlooked. They normally gave management problems sound consideration, and their decisions were effectively carried out in practice. Several factors directly related to motivation were found to be present where work groups shared in the decisions that were to be made.

1. There is increased satisfaction. The groups derive satisfaction in solving problems.
2. The attitudes and objections can be voiced and receive recognition.
3. Cooperation results in constructive use of social pressure within the group.
4. Each individual in the group feels responsible for the success of the decisions.
5. The individuals do not feel ordered about. They do unpleasant tasks more willingly.
6. In participating, each individual feels he is part of the company.
7. Goals are specified by the group, and progress toward those goals is experienced by each member.

Once the effectiveness of participation was demonstrated, ways of sharing problems with the group were discussed, and supervisors were encouraged to try the method on their own problems. A great many examples of the successful application of participation to the solution of problems in work groups resulted. As supervisors experienced success in using this method, they began using it more in their relations with their subordinates. Some problems successfully solved in this way included:

1. Distribution of disagreeable jobs.
2. Selection of vacation periods.
3. Office arrangement.
4. Reduction of paperwork.

5. Lunch schedules.
6. Equal distribution of work.
7. Care of equipment.
8. Correction of errors on bills of material.
9. Responsibility for company-owned tools.
10. Wash-up time.
11. Selection of men to be transferred.

Three examples will illustrate the effect of sharing job problems on the accomplishment of a fair day's work.

1. A traditional problem in our type of business is that of working outside in unfavorable weather. In some instances "inclement weather," as it is called, makes such jobs as work on overhead lines more hazardous. The question of when weather is inclement is a matter of judgment and frequently subject to difference of opinion between the supervisor and the union steward. Following the principle of sharing such problems with the group, a foreman and union steward agreed to submit the question to the crew on each occasion of questionable weather conditions. Following this agreement, discussions between the foreman and his men resulted in an increase in the number of times the crews worked during border-line weather conditions.

2. In the face of a potential shortage of coal, it was felt necessary to stock an extra supply. This would require increased daily quotas from the group of 37 men who were doing the coal stocking. The supervisor called his men together and told them the facts. The need for additional coal was explored and the problem of stocking an additional amount discussed. Among the other things, it developed that it would be desirable that vacations be postponed for a three-month period, during which time the additional coal was to be stocked. The supervisor agreed to make whatever concession seemed desirable for vacations at a later date. The group finally decided that they could stock 60 cars in each shift. This was even more than had been expected. The figure of 55 cars had been thought likely by the supervisor. During the three-month period involved, the men worked seven days a week plus overtime and maintained or exceeded the figure they had set for themselves. In addition, the supervisor reported a notable improvement in team spirit in the group. Other problems were put to them for group decisions with good results.

3. In one large accounting department, the department head has been increasing the efficiency of his operations through what he calls "job enlargement." By combining routine and highly specialized jobs, he is able to build back into them more variety and responsibility.

Employee interest and motivation are thereby increased, and higher morale and production result. The workforce is more flexible, also, and can be shifted to meet peaks. The department head attributes his success in making these changes to the fact that employees concerned have been consulted in the changes and help plan the revised jobs. In one case, a supervisor planned to replace an employee who was leaving. She was encouraged to talk it over with the group, and they suggested a rearrangement of the machines and work which made the replacement unnecessary. This could happen only where mutual respect and cooperation had been developed through application of good human relations principles.

These examples are typical of day-to-day administration which, when multiplied many times through many supervisors, result in increasingly effective operation. I wouldn't want to leave the impression that all problems are easily resolved in this way or that all supervisors are equally proficient in their use of participation. There are naturally differences in the degree to which supervisors are willing to share decisions with their group. Some have not developed the necesary skill of working with a group in this way. Others feel they share problems but, in the eyes of employees, actually do not.

Other problems arise out of the fact that, once employees have the satisfaction of being "in" on things, they tend to resent it when, for some reason, they are not consulted. These limitations have not offset the advantages that have been gained and are perhaps the result more of limited understanding and skill on our part than of any basic fault in the principle itself.

We are continuing to train new supervisors in the principles of participative leadership, and others are encouraged to extend its use in their day-to-day work-group problems.

Participation in the development of personnel policies

To be really effective, participation must be experienced at every level of the organization, including middle and lower supervisory levels. Understanding and agreement with company objectives and a feeling of personal responsibility for company success among all members of management are essential prerequisites to developing a sense of responsibility and motivation among employees. Positive steps to extend participation in the management group must be part of any plan to increase organizational effectiveness.

For several years now, some of our major personnel policies have been developed with the participation of all supervisors and, in a few

instances, employees. This procedure has resulted in a better understanding of the problems involved, better acceptance, and, we think,
better administration of the policy once installed. Policies which have
been developed in this way include a disciplinary procedure and a
complaint procedure for all employees except those represented by a
union; a company safety policy; a hospitalization plan; a transfer
and promotion policy; assignment of parking space, and a major
revision to the company's retirement plan. In each case, detailed discussions were carried on with supervisors and their ideas and opinions reflected in the final policy.

In the case of both the company hospitalization plan and its pension plan, an attitude survey had revealed that employees were not
well satisfied with the benefits provided, even though the plans were
superior to many in industry. The sessions with supervisors and
employees about their attitude toward the plans and the possibilities
for revision resulted in improvements, being made in both instances,
with considerable betterment in the attitude of employees toward
those two important benefits. Meetings with supervisors on the need
to improve promotional opportunities throughout the company led to
the adoption of a job-posting plan for all employees except those in
top-level staff and administrative positions.

Recently, a series of meetings have been completed with all supervisors in small groups to solicit their reactions to the status of
employee relations in the company, and to discuss with them changes
in policy and practice which they felt would improve the opportunity
for building an effective organization. They were asked to comment
frankly on problems which they felt limited their effectiveness as
supervisors. In addition to their own top line superiors, other representatives of top management were present in the meetings. Groups
of 25 to 50 supervisors were broken into small "buzz" groups for
deciding on questions and comments. Discussions were frank, sometimes critical of top management. In several meetings the president
of the company was present to discuss problems which involved major
company policies and organization. Questions that could not be
answered in the meetings were referred for study and subsequent
reporting. As a result of these meetings, several changes in policy
have been made and others are being studied. Management's willingness to consider supervisors' attitudes and take action on their suggestions has resulted in favorable comment and improved attitudes in
some instances where misunderstanding existed.

Two areas of concern revealed in these meetings with supervisors
have been followed up by additional meetings on these specific sub-

jects. One is a discussion of the company's absence policy and its administration, and the other a discussion of the company's financial position and the need for effective and economical operation in the face of rising costs of doing busines. Although these discussions have only recently been completed, there is already evidence that increased understand will lead to fuller cooperation and more effective administration.

In some instances, discussions with supervisors and employees have been accompanied by similar discussions with committees representing the unions. These were not the regular negotiating committees, and discussions were held outside negotiating periods. Changes in the hospitalization plan and the retirement plan, for example, have been negotiated with the unions following such discussions with their representatives. Talking over such matters with union representatives away from the bargaining table has proved worth while in gaining mutual understanding and cooperation and in facilitating negotiations later.

Another current activity which provides opportunity for employees and supervisors to work together to improve the effectiveness of company operations is work simplification. Many of us are familiar with the basic principles involved in this approach to methods improvement. Supervisors and employees are trained in methods of analyzing their own work, in contrast to bringing in methods experts, as is commonly done in traditional methods programs.

The satisfaction and recognition which supervisors and employees get from improving their own jobs greatly increases their willingness to accept new methods and their desire to make the better way work. Frequently the motivation resulting from this approach is as important as the actual improvement in the technique itself.

Feedback of attitude survey results

Early in our association with the Institute for Social Research, its Survey Research Center made an intensive survey of the attitudes of our employees and supervisors. Written questionnaires were administered to all non-supervisory employees, and all supervisors and members of management were interviewed concerning their work attitudes. In addition, 10 per cent of the non-supervisory employees from groups identified through the questionnaire as having high or low morale were given personal interviews. The resulting information about attitudes of employees toward their jobs, their supervisors, company benefits, pay, their chances for promotion, and various other factors in the work situation was sent back down the line for discussion. Comparisons between departments and work groups were made available, and both supervisors and employees were asked to interpret the results and make recommendations for the solution of problems which were present. Here again many changes were made which resulted in better understanding and improved working effectiveness.

In one department, a controlled experiment was set up in which supervisors of certain work groups held a series of discussions with employees about their own group attitudes as revealed by a survey. In other work groups the results were reported back to employees but without the opportunity for group discussions led by the supervisor. In those groups where discussions were held over a period of several months, there was a measurable improvement in the attitude of the employees toward their jobs, their supervision, their opportunities in the company, and various other factors in the work situation. In those groups in which discussion was not held, relatively little change in attitude took place.

This experiment would seem to indicate that sharing of a group's own problems with them and freedom to discuss such problems with the supervisor result in more favorable attitudes in the work group. Another very interesting fact was that greater change in employees' attitudes occurred in this situation than in other departments where employees' attitudes were studied after their supervisors were given training in human relations.

Training men should see in this the need to carry their training in human relations well beyond instruction in principles and supervisory techniques.

Further investigation of relationships

Any sound approach to developing good human relations requires continuing review of the effectiveness of the methods being used. A series of studies made for us by the Institute for Social Research gave us the following information about participation in our company:

1. In work groups where morale was highest, a high percentage of employees felt that the company took considerable interest in their ideas and suggestions. Very few in low-morale groups felt this way.
2. In high-morale groups, most employees felt that group discussions with their supervisors were worth while. Not so in low-morale groups.
3. Both supervisors and employees felt that group meetings resulted in increased job interest and the group's working together more as a team.

4. Supervisors who held meetings with employees which employees felt were worth while in general looked on their supervisor as being good at handling people. If the supervisors held meetings, but employees didn't think them worth while, they generally felt their supervisor wasn't good at handling people.

5. In work groups having low absence rates, employees felt relatively free to discuss job and personal problems with their supervisor. In low-absence groups, meetings were held more frequently than in high-absence groups, and employees thought their work group had high group pride and good team spirit.

6. Supervisors who are given quite a good deal of "say" in spending money budgeted to them are more cost-conscious than those who don't have much "say."

7. Supervisors who were appraised by their superiors as doing a good job, and who were considered best qualified for promotion, met frequently with their employees and, in turn, participated frequently in decisions with their superiors.

These and other findings throw additional light on the nature and value of participation. Reports on some of our studies, such as those on absence, costs, and supervisor appraisals, have been prepared to help supervisors understand the importance of the way they work with their people in developing good teamwork.

Summary and conclusions

Research in human relations can help us understand and develop motivation in an organization. One significant finding is that the kind of leadership we provide is one of the major factors in high-morale, high-productivity work groups.

Effective leadership is characterized by sincere concern for the employee as an individual and acceptance of him as a full member of the team. There are many ways in which this attitude reflects itself in day-to-day relations between superior and subordinates. One important element is the extent to which problems are shared with those who will be affected by decisions.

The practice of participation exists to some extent in every organization. The principle can be extended consciously in many ways. Full understanding and acceptance of the values of participation must be accompanied by increased skill in using it in day-to-day relations between all levels of supervision and between supervisors and employees.

There are no perfect solutions to human relations problems. Some difficulties and failures must be expected in moving toward this type of leadership. However, objective measurement of results should show benefits in terms of higher morale and higher productivity.

This treatment of motivation as being related to leadership may not be satisfying for those who are looking for quick, easy ways of speeding up a production line or to those who view labor as a commodity for which a price should bring value received. Nor will it be very impressive to those who are looking for a new program which they can delegate to their personnel department to install and administer.

This is a concept for executives who recognize the importance of their personal leadership in building a strong industrial team. It is for those who really believe that industry must meet the needs of all employees for a sense of personal worth in their work. Such executives know that only through development of a feeling of personal responsibility on the part of all employees can their business really be successful. In some types of business this common aim and cooperative spirit are the only factors which cannot be fully duplicated by competitors and, therefore, survival may depend on them.

Those who would succeed in building good working relationships in this way must be sincere, for any who look on this approach as just another technique for getting people to work harder will find the essential element for motivating others to be absent. The average person gets his personal satisfactions and a sense of worth out of doing a good job and contributing his best efforts to worth-while activities. If conditions have developed in our companies which result in many employees not "doing what comes naturally," we need to examine closely what we as leaders of industry and work groups do or fail to do which results in restriction of output and resistance to our company objectives.

The employee's satisfaction with his part in industry not only is important to the effectiveness of his company but perhaps, in a larger sense, is necessary to his continued support of free enterprise itself. A system which does not furnish basic work satisfaction to its members cannot expect to continue for long. This is especially so in a democracy where widespread individual dissatisfaction can quickly be registered at the voting place. Now, particularly, when we are seeking to establish the values of individual freedom in the world, must American industry clearly stand for those values which workers everywhere can subscribe to.

The principle of participation in industry is especially significant because of its presence as an important element in all other phases of our living in a democracy. In fact, democracy in industry is perceived by some to be determined by the extent to which the employee shares in decisions on matters which affect him. If, indeed, there is some similarity and if democracy is to survive, it must be increasingly used by more and more people in more phases of our day-to-day living. The democratic principle must be extended, and it has to meet the common everyday practical test that it works, that it gets better results for all concerned. The need that we have today is not so much for a reaffirmation of our faith in democracy as for the actual application of its principles and methods in our day-to-day human relationships with other people.

The application is difficult, especially in problems involving very large groups; but, on the other hand, it is a very challenging problem, and if it is skillfully and capably handled it can be very rewarding and productive. Through research in human relations we have learned some of the principles of developing good teamwork and motivation, but we need to know much more. We need to invent new ways to apply these principles. The good executive will accept greater responsibility for improved human relations not only through a sincere belief in democratic principles but in learning, inventing, and applying specific human relations methods and skills in his personal relationships and in seeing that they are used throughout his organization.

The trustees of the Ford Foundation recently put it this way:

> The democratic course is the choice of the people in free countries of the world, and perhaps the hopes of tens of millions who are now citizens of totalitarian states. But the making of the choice is not a single, simple act of selection; it is a way of total living, and to choose it means to choose it again and again, today and tomorrow, and continuously to reaffirm it in every act of life.

That choice is for us and the leaders of industry whom we represent.

Questions

1. What is the major thesis of Schwab's article?
2. What part does training play in applying human relations principles?
3. Discuss the advantages of having supervisors participate in the development of personnel policies.
4. Explain what is meant by an atttiude survey and discuss the advantages of revealing to supervisors the results of such a survey.
5. Why is a continuing review of human relations methods and practices necessary?

THE STAFF FUNCTION IN
HUMAN RELATIONS *

Douglas McGregor

It is common practice today for organizational management to use the services of staff experts in dealing with problems of human relations. Departments of personnel administration are created, or outside consultants are hired, not only by industrial and business concerns, but by governmental agencies, philanthropic and educational institutions, and even to a limited extent by religious organizations and community groups. Many managements have not been entirely successful, however, in attempting to make effective use of these services. In some instances the staff expert has created more problems for the organization than he has solved. Relatively few managements have clearly determined what function they want the staff man to perform. Haphazard trial and error has frequently directed developments. The results have not always been happy.

There are as yet no final answers to the questions thus raised. Nevertheless, we are beginning to acquire some understanding of the nature of the effective staff role. It is my objective in this discussion to present, in a tentative fashion, certain conclusions reached by a group of staff men [1] who have worked in a variety of situations and observed many others, and who have been discussing critically among themselves and with other people over a period of several years the significance of their experiences. The emphasis in this discussion will be on the staff role in industrial organizations because that is where our experience has been widest. We believe, however, that our conclusions have implications for other kinds of human organizations.

Textbook discussions of the staff role are today usually expressed in about these terms: Line management has the full and final responsibility for directing the activities of the people who comprise the organization because line management is directly responsible to the founders or owners for achieving results through those people. Con-

---

* From the *Journal of Social Issues*, Vol. 4, No. 3 (Summer, 1948), pp. 6-23. Reprinted with permission.

[1] The members of the Industrial Relations Section at M.I.T., especially my colleagues Irving Knickerbocker, Alex Bavelas, Mason Haire, Charles Myers, Paul Pigors and Douglass Brown. Some of these problems have also been discussed at length with a group of experienced industrial personnel administrators and educators who are fellow members of the American Management Association.

sequently, line management must retain the full authority to carry out the function for which it is held responsible. This authority cannot be successfully delegated except within the line management organization. The staff role, on the other hand, is one of counsel, service and advice. The staff expert should have no authority over any part of the line organization, nor should he take any action which will interfere with line management's performances of its role.[2]

These conceptions are accepted as sound theory by a fair proportion of managements, but practice and theory do not always coincide. The head of the engineering department in one company—a man who had under him not only engineering and drafting, but large construction and maintenance units—recently expressed considerable dissatisfaction with the department of personnel administration in his company. He stated his position somewhat as follows:

> "I wish we could hire someone to take these personnel problems off my hands and solve them. I know that good human relations are important. However, my subordinates and I have so much to do that we can't afford the time we are spending on grievances, personnel policies, negotiations, promotions, and individual wage adjustments. What's more, I'm sick of those interminable management meetings where we discuss petty questions like wash-up time, holiday shut-downs, disciplinary warnings and so on. Why don't we get a competent man, give him freedom to hire whatever staff he needs, and then let him handle all these matters? An expert could do a far better job than we are doing, and leave us free to get on with our work."

The point of view expressed by this man is widely held, even by members of line management who would subscribe to the textbook statement above. They tend to separate the management function into two distinct categories. On the one hand are the planning, the making of decisions, the giving of orders, the assigning of responsibilities and the supervision necessary to get the job done. Oddly, they do not seem to regard these matters involving human relations. They are "management"; they are "getting out the production." In the other category are the problems that arise (such as complaints and grievances, worker objections to supervisors' actions, the negotiation of labor agreements) and the work necessary to prevent such problems from arising (such as planning and formulating policies, training supervisors, establishing shop rules, promoting employee cooperation). These things to them are human relations, and not management. They would gladly delegate the responsibility for the

---

[2] See Pigors and Myers, *Personnel Administration* (New York: McGraw-Hill, 1947), especially Ch. 2, for a clear statement of this distinction between line and staff. See also "Function and Scope of Personnel Administration," *Personnel*, July, 1947.

second category to "experts" who presumably have the skill and knowledge to handle them.

This functional division is psychologically absurd and in practice unworkable. An industrial organization is an efficient way of producing goods because it takes advantage of the possibilities of specialization of mechanical and human effort. However, as soon as specialization occurs there arises the necessity for integrating and directing the activities of people toward the ultimate objective of the whole organization; namely, the production and sale of goods at a profit. That integration and direction of specialized human activities is the function of line management.

It is in practice impossible to separate the function of assigning work to people from the function of settling the problems which arise in getting them to perform that work. If a worker objects to his work assignment, or to the working conditions or the shop rules, shall we ask a personnel "expert" to hear and settle the grievance? If we do, we are giving authority to someone who is not the worker's boss to tell him what he may or may not do. How long will the foreman retain control of his men if this authority is given to someone else? The foreman is responsible for the performance of his workers; the personnel man is not. (Obviously, the difficulties which will arise if we attempt this splitting of unitary functions will ultimately destroy the very integration of activities which it is line management's job to maintain.)

The whole idea is about as sensible as if a symphony orchestra conductor placed two podiums on the platform, hired a second conductor, and said: "You conduct the men in the orchestra who don't like my interpretation of the music; I'll conduct the others."

Line managers have a tendency to become unduly frustrated by the fact that human beings are somewhat less docile than materials and machines. The plea of the engineering department head which was outlined above is an unrealistic attempt to escape that frustration. It is, nevertheless, the expression of an attitude which is widespread among line managers. Moreover, many companies attempt to operate along lines similar to those proposed by that engineer. The results are seldom happy.

Frequently this idea is expressed more subtly. The manager, for example, may try to get the personnel man to make a decision for which the manager himself should take the responsibility. Perhaps he will consult the staff man on a disciplinary matter, or a new shop rule, and then ask the staff man to take the action decided upon—to impose the penalty on the erring worker, or to sign and post the rule.

The staff expert who expresses unwillingness to accept such responsibilities may find himself charged with failure to fulfill the requirements of his job. The logic of textbook statements is of little help at times like this. It serves merely to arouse resistance and antagonism from the line manager. On the other hand, the staff expert who accepts such line responsibilities is likely soon to find himself in an impossible position.

There are, of course, certain things which a competent staff department can and should do for line management. These "services," however, are distinctly limited to ones which do not infringe on line authority. They must be carefully scrutinized to make sure they are not in one way or another usurping responsibilities which can only be successfully assumed by line management.

For example, staff departments may successfully handle the preliminary screening of applicants for employment who meet qualifications determined by line management; they cannot successfully assume responsibility for hiring. Staff departments may successfully help line managers to plan training programs and teach them how to teach; however, except in a very limited sense the staff departments cannot successfully undertake to train line people in the performance of their jobs. The staff man can gather facts for and interpret policy to the line managers who hear and settle grievances; he cannot "handle" grievances without undermining line management. Staff men can aid in developing methods and procedures for wage and salary determination which will be administered by line management; they cannot successfully administer wages and salaries themselves.

A second conflict between practice and theory stems from the attitudes of staff men themselves. Some personnel administrators have (and insist that they must have) authority over the line organization. Subject to the approval of the president, or of an operating vice-president, they make decisions on grievances that have been heard by lower levels of management, negotiate labor agreements, formulate, install, and police the administration of personnel policies and practices, retain final approval of wage and salary increases, promotions, transfers, disciplinary penalties, discharges and layoffs. The degree of authority exercised by such staff men runs a wide gamut. It may often be camouflaged. For example, it is relatively common practice to give line management final authority in adopting or rejecting policies formulated by the staff, but in the same breath to give the staff responsibility for obtaining line conformity with those policies, once adopted. The term usually employed is "to co-ordinate" the administration of policies. "Co-ordination" very often in practice becomes "policing."

Even in organizations where the staff role is explicitly stated to be purely advisory, the staff man sometimes exercises considerable authority over the line organization in round-about ways. For example, it is generally accepted that the personnel administrator can be little more than a clerk unless he is given the prestige of a position in top management. Accordingly, he may report directly to the president or to an executive vice-president. From this "staff" position it is possible for him to exercise indirectly a remarkable degree of authority over the line. Suppose he is unsuccessful in getting members of middle or lower management to follow his advice. If he discusses his difficulty with the line officer to whom he reports, the result may be an order from the line officer to his subordinates which accomplishes the purpose desired by the staff man. Personnel administrators presumably possessing no authority have often been directly responsible for the demotion or even removal of intractible members of line management, or for the adoption of policies or procedures which they have previously been unsuccessful in "selling" to lower levels of management. Under such conditions it is not unusual for the staff department to be regarded by lower and middle line management as a powerful Gestapo.

There are large differences in this respect from organization to organization. Almost regardless of position in the organization, or of defined responsibilities, some staff men exercise authority over the line organization. When this happens the net effect, from the line manager's point of view, is like that of the worker whose foreman said to him: "I want your whole-hearted co-operation; you co-operate with me, or else. . . ." The line manager feels as though the staff man had said: "I am here solely to advise and counsel with you; you take my advice, or else. . . ." From the line manager's point of view the staff man is exercising authority whether he admits it or not.

On the other hand—again almost regardles of position or defined responsibilities—some staff men are genuinely believed by line management to exercise no authority over them whatever. They are regarded as advisors, and the line manager expects to be able to take the advice or reject it without pressure from his own line superiors.

The objective which management has in mind in establishing a personnel department or hiring a personnel consultant is in general much more clearly understood than are the methods by which to achieve it. The objective is to create and maintain healthy human relations in the organization. In the light of the discussion above, it is apparent that the achievement of this objective requires more than the establishment of a personnel department.

Fundamentally, the creation and maintenance of healthy human relations require certain kinds of behavior on the part of line management. The philosophy, attitudes and skills of all members of line management, as these are reflected in their every-day behavior, are the ultimate determinants of the quality of the human relations in the organization. Stated in the terms used above, the quality of the human relations will be directly determined by the way in which line management goes about integrating and directing the behavior of the people who comprise the organization.

The function of the staff expert in human relations is necessarily indirect. Nevertheless, if the staff expert's aid is to be effective, it must in many cases result in changes in line management's behavior. The common "tools" of the staff expert—the techniques of personnel administration such as systems for wage and salary administration, employee benefit programs, suggestion plans, employee publications and the like—are only for the purpose of implementing a sound line management philosophy and a high order of line management skill in directing the activities of people. These techniques cannot create or maintain that philosophy or those attitudes and skills. They cannot in themselves create healthy human relations.

The staff man, then, faces a dilemma. His task is to get line management to adopt the philosophy, develop the attitudes and acquire the skills which will create and maintain healthy human relations. However, in doing so he must not seek or accept authority over line managers, nor in any way relieve them of their primary responsibility for directing the behavior of the people comprising the organization.

In the light of these considerations, just what is the staff role? How can "advice and counsel" bring about the necessary changes in the behavior of line management? How can the staff man stay out of the trap of accepting responsibility for line functions without being justly accused of shirking his own responsibilities to the organization? How can he accomplish what he is supposed to accomplish without exercising authority over line management in some fashion?

These are difficult questions. There are no simple rule-of-thumb answers. Perhaps we can obtain a somewhat better understanding of the nature of the effective staff role by turning our attention for

a moment to a few basic conceptions about human behavior which
have direct relevance to the problem.

------

1. All human behavior is directed toward the satisfaction of
needs.[3] From birth to death the individual is engaged in a constant
attempt to satisfy his varied, complex, and sometimes conflicting
needs. Any given behavior is a resolution of forces arising in part
within him and in part in the environmental situation.

2. It follows from the first assumption that the individual will
change his established ways of behaving for one of two reasons: to
gain increased need satisfaction or to avoid decreased need satisfaction. Changes in his behavior for either of these reasons are inevitably a consequence of the way he perceives the situation. The
expected increase or decrease in need satisfaction may be illusory
(from the observer's point of view). The individual may rationalize,
delude himself, ignore or misinterpret facts. Nevertheless, he
behaves always in accordance with his perception of his own needs
and of the possibilities for satisfying them in the environmental
situation.

3. Therefore, if an individual, A, wishes to bring about a change
in the behavior of another individual (or group), B, he can do so by
effecting an "augmentation" in the possibilities of need satisfaction
as B sees them, or alternatively by effecting a "reduction" in the
possibilities of need satisfaction as B sees them.[4] The many variants
of method for inducing a behavior change—suggestion, threat,
promise, physical force, reward, punishment, propaganda, education,
etc.—resolve themselves ultimately into these two.

4. A can utilize augmentation or reduction to induce a behavior
change only if from B's point of view he possesses or controls means
which B can use for his own need satisfaction. There are many such
means, of course. Among the more common ones are money and

------

[3] We believe the assumptions stated in this and the following paragraphs are
virtually self-evident. They are stated somewhat dogmatically in order to avoid
too much verbiage. Moreover, certain qualifications of the statements are ignored
in the interests of brevity and simplicity. These qualifications are not important
for our present purposes.

The point of view expressed here stems from current "dynamic" psychology,
from modern psychoanalytic theory, and from our own efforts to develop a workable, integrated theory of human behavior in organizations. We have been materially influenced by such people as Kurt Lewin, H. A. Murray, Thomas French,
Franz Alexander (and their many associates and students), Margaret Mead,
Gardner Murphy, Edward Bibring, Walter Langer, John Dollard, Carl Rogers.

[4] This symbolic notation is adopted to prevent later confusion. A always
refers to the individual (or group) who is attempting to induce a behavior
change, and B always refers to the individual (or group) whose behavior is
affected.

other material possessions, knowledge, skill or specialized abilities, prestige, approval, love. A pay check, a promotion, a threat of disciplinary action, praise, criticism, an order, a request—all such things are possible ways of influencing *B's* behavior provided *A*, who uses them, controls means which *B* regards as important for satisfying his own needs. The pay check (or money) is a direct means for *B's* need satisfaction. *A* can provide or withhold it. The threat of disciplinary action depends for its effectiveness upon *A's* control of other means which *B* desires—for example, the job and its attendant rewards.

b. In every-day usage "authority" is equated with the reductive control of means. Thus to exercise authority is to attempt to induce a behavior change by the threat (implied or stated) to withhold, or by the actual withholding of means for *B's* need satisfaction. Whether it is the policeman, the priest, the boss or the parent who exercises authority, he does so by reduction, insofar as our common-sense notions of authority are concerned. The inference which *B* draws is that he must obey, or else suffer a reduction in need satisfaction.

It makes little difference how we define authority so long as we understand our use of the term. I shall use the phrase "reductive authority," first to remind the reader of the common usage, and second to distinguish this method of influencing behavior from methods involving augmentation. In most situations, *A* can utilize his control of means either augmentively or reductively. Actually he usually does both, but the emphasis is such that *B* perceives the one and ignores the other.

6. One final point requires elaboration before we return to our examination of the staff role. There is plenty of evidence (both experimental and common-sense) that emphasis upon reduction frequently does not induce the behavior desired by *A*. If one is riding a horse, it is wise to use the whip only if one holds the reins. Otherwise the horse may run, but not necessarily in the desired direction. When *A* utilizes reduction, he must remember that all behavior is directed toward need satisfaction. Unless *A* controls every alternative form of behavior available to *B*, the resulting behavior may satisfy *B* but not *A*! A threat often serves to eliminate a particular kind of undesirable behavior, but another equally undesirable behavior (from *A's* point of view) may be substituted for it. Moreover, reduction tends to be frustrating, and frustration typically creates aggression. *B* gets angry at *A*, which does not help the relationship, or increase *B's* docility.

Many industrial managements have emphasized reductive methods, deliberately or unwittingly, in attempting to modify workers' behavior, only to discover (1) that the desired behavior does not occur but undesired alternative behaviors do, and (2) that unexpected aggressive reactions occur. A good example is the emphasis on a purely reductive approach to discipline, or to the problem of obtaining conformity to standards of performance. Many so-called "protective clauses" in labor agreements are illustrative of the consequences.

There is today a growing recognition that success in inducing behavior change requires marked emphasis on augmentation. This is particularly true if A wants to continue the relationship with B. While it is impossible to eliminate the potentiality of reduction from any relationship in which B is at all dependent, it is almost always possible to throw the emphasis upon augmentation.

Reduction is an easy and natural method which is particularly likely to be overemphasized when A possesses much power in the relationship (i.e., when A controls important means which B requires for need satisfaction. The boss, for example, usually can replace a given worker with less reduction in his own need satisfaction than the worker will suffer if he "replaces" his boss). Excessive reliance upon reduction, however, is likely to be disappointing to A. The desired behavior too often does not occur, or the consequences in terms of aggression are unfortunate, and A discovers he has defeated his own purposes.

On the other hand, it must be admitted that the successful use of augmentation is neither simple nor easy. It requires considerable ingenuity. For example, the direct provision of means for B (high wages and other material benefits) such as is typical of paternalistic managements, is far less effective than the provision of opportunities by means of which B can *through his own efforts* achieve greater need satisfaction.

We may return now to our original problem.

The objective of the staff expert is to help line management to create and maintain healthy human relations in the organization. He seeks to increase his own need satisfaction by achieving this objective. In order to achieve it, he usually faces the problem of getting line managers at various levels of the organization to change their behavior. For our purposes, this "behavior" includes such things as the following: their philosophy, atittudes, decisions, methods of analyzing problems, use or acceptance of personnel techniques, ways of dealing with superiors, associates or subordinates.

It is now perhaps clear that the use of authority in the usual, reductive sense by the staff expert is an ineffective way of inducing behavior changes directed toward healthier human relations. This is perhaps the major reason for denying the staff expert "authority" over the line organization. He must limit himself to the use of augmentation just as completely as possible because only thus can he hope to achieve the objective for which he is hired. Any staff man who has used reductive methods has had the experience of watching the line manager comply with the letter of the law while violating its spirit. The line administration of personnel policies is a complex task in which the "how" is far more important than the "what." The correct "how," depending as it does upon a sound philosophy and upon the attitudes-behind-the-act, is rarely if ever induced by threats or punishment.

The use of augmentation by the staff expert is difficult in the extreme. The attitudes and habits of line management are the complex result of long experience with and adjustment to people. They are deep-rooted, heavily charged with emotion, frequently influenced by unconscious factors of considerable significance. If, under such circumstances, they must be changed, a high degree of professional skill is required of the staff man.

To begin with, B must have or acquire sufficient motivation to want to change his behavior.[5] Fortunately for A, line managers almost invariably are faced with problems in human relations which they have not solved to their own complete satisfaction. This gives A his opening. If he can get B to perceive him as a possible source of help in finding more effective solutions for B's human relations problems, A will be in a position to use augmentation to modify B's behavior.

Obviously the staff man who has demanded or accepted reductive authority over the line organization will not be perceived as a potential source of help. Quite the contrary! Nor will A be perceived as a source of help if he approaches B in terms of what he thinks B should be worrying about. He must be prepared to help B solve B's problems as B perceives them.

This is a particularly difficult point to get across to the personnel man who is excited over the potential value to the organization of his

---

[5] It will be helpful to utilize our symbolic device in the discussion which follows. A refers always to the staff man who is attempting to induce certain desired behavior (attitudes, skills, etc.) on the part of B, the line individual or group.

own pet project—say a training program, a suggestion plan, or a job evaluation program. That this important and valuable tool which he is prepared to offer to management, and which management obviously needs, should be put aside while he helps a superintendent or a vice-president with some trivial problem, arouses in him only impatience. If his manner reflects his impatience, he will very probably forfeit a real opportunity to begin to build an effective staff relation with the manager in question.

In the second place, *A* can rarely provide help to *B* simply by analyzing the problem for *B* and offering a solution. Sometimes, of course, this is desirable. However, if the problem really involves human relations, it is more than likely that *B's* perception of it reflects his own life-long history of dealing with people. His culturally determined political and economic attitudes, his emotional convictions and prejudices, his fundamental habits of adjustment in his line role (many of which have been unconsciously acquired) will all affect his perception of the problem. In fact, they may be the very factors which have until now prevented a successful solution of his problem.

Under such circumstances, an analysis and solution offered by *A*, however correct it may be objectively, may meet with immediate resistance. *B* feels he is being asked to abandon the only approach which in his eyes can yield need satisfaction: *i.e.* the one resulting from his perception of the situation. From *B's* point of view *A's* analysis will threaten reduction, not offer augmentation of need satisfaction.

Objective facts and logical conclusions drawn from them are important tools of the staff man *in their proper place*. The determining facts in most human relations problems, however, are the subjective facts of *B's* perceptual field and of *B's* needs as they relate to the problem. *A's* objective facts, introduced improperly or at the wrong time, will have a reductive rather than an augmentive impact on *B*. Knowledge and skill in analysis are important means controlled by *A*. He must be exceedingly careful how he uses them.

The personnel department in a large manufacturing company developed an on-the-job training course for workers which appeared to be highly efficient. A pilot experiment with the method was conducted. It yielded facts which showed quite conclusively that savings of $20,000 per year could be effected by adopting this training program for all new workers in certain departments. The facts were presented to management along with a recommendation that the program be adopted. It was turned down with some rather lame excuses, and the training department, for no apparent reason, found itself "in management's doghouse." The staff group did not discover why their facts had proved to be reductive to management. They lost an opportunity to provide real staff aid by failing to explore *B's* perceptual field before introducing their own factual analysis.

Experiences like this are more common than might be supposed. Usually the staff department's factual analysis is less "convincing" than in the case just mentioned, and therefore line management is in a position to rationalize a negative answer with little difficulty. Sometimes the staff expert, particularly if he is an outside consultant, never knows why his recommendations were not accepted. From his point of view they were obviously worth while. He is likely to rationalize his failure by concluding that management was just stupid.

Fundamentally the staff man—if he is to use augmentive methods to influence line management behavior—must create a situation in which members of management can learn rather than one in which they are taught. *B* must acquire his own insights, discover for himself (with *A's* sympathetic aid) why his behavior has been inadequate to the problem at hand, discover his own best answer, and ultimately accept full responsibility himself for making his solution work.

In this connection, *A* faces yet another trap. Awareness of the problem of *B's* perceptual field has led some staff experts to resort to a method of dubious value: If *A* has his own solution for a problem faced by *B*, he attempts to lead *B* to "discover" that solution as *B's* own. To be sure, masterminding of this kind works in many instances. However, it is potentially a dangerous boomerang. If *B* ever discovers or even suspects what is going on, the relationship may be seriously impaired. When *B* perceives *A's* actions as masterminding, *A* is promptly seen as a source of potential reduction. Protective behavior ("keep your neck in") and aggression will surely follow. Moreover, *A* is no longer trusted. *B* feels he has been tricked by dishonest tactics.

All in all, if the staff man is in a position where it is necessary that his solution be adopted by *B*, it is far safer to present his analysis openly, and face *B's* resistance, than to attempt the technique of masterminding. Unless the staff man has allowed himself to be put in an untenable role by the way his responsibilities have been defined, he will rarely find himself in a situation where *B* must be forced to accept his (*A's*) solution.

In certain respects the methods of the staff expert resemble those of the psychological therapist.[6] This is not surprising since the objectives of both are similar. The therapist attempts to aid individuals or groups to achieve healthy personal relations, and the staff expert attempts to aid individuals or groups to achieve healthy intra-organizational relations. Both are concerned not with imposing particular attitudes or particular kinds of behavior upon B, but with helping B to eliminate difficulties so that he can achieve health through his own efforts and in his own way.

In spite of these similarities in objectives, the role of the staff expert in an organizational setting should not be identified too closely with the role of the psychotherapist. The former confines his efforts to a very limited area—human relations within the organization—and even within that area he is primarily concerned with the problems involved in integrating and directing the activities of people. His emphasis is upon the more superficial aspects of human relations and not upon the deeper aspects of personal adjustment.

Sometimes, of course, deep-seated problems of personal adjustment may prevent B from coping successfully with his problems of organizational relations. This may present critical difficulties if B happens to be in a key position in management. In such cases, the staff expert is wise to limit himself to the task of getting B to seek competent psychiatric help outside the organization. Even if the staff man is himself a skilled clinical psychologist or psychiatrist, the situation is best handled in the way in which industrial medical departments handle cases requiring extended treatment: by reference to outside experts or agencies.

By and large, our experience indicates that the staff role in human relations is more happily identified with that of the educator than with that of the therapist. A's objective is to utilize his skill to create a situation in which B can learn, and to make his knowledge available so that B may utilize it to augment his own need satisfaction in ways consistent with the achievement of organizational objectives.

A way of thinking about the staff role, as conceived here, which some of us have found helpful is in terms of a succession of goals toward which the staff man works in any relationship with line management. These goals may be thought of narrowly, in terms of a specific problem of a single line manager, or broadly, in terms of a long-range program involving a whole management organization.

[6] Carl R. Rogers, "Significant Aspects of Client Centered Therapy," *American Psychologist*, Vol. 1, No. 10, 1946, 415-422. Franz Alexander, Thomas French, et al., *Psychoanalytic Therapy* (New York: Ronald Press, 1946).

They are stated as goals rather than "principles," first because the methods of reaching them will necessarily vary with the circumstances, and second because, although they may be approached, they are seldom reached in practice. It is one thing to state these complex and difficult objectives; it is another thing—at least as far as our experience goes—to possess the skill to achieve them in practice.

1. The staff expert, A, will seek first to establish with line management, B, individually and collectively, a relationship in which he is perceived as a source of possible help in solving probems of human relations. Whether he can establish such a relationship will depend partly upon his actions, partly upon the way he is fitted into the organizational structure, and finally upon the way in which his responsibilities are defined. Any hint of reductive authority attributed to him will make the achievement of this goal infinitely more difficult.

In establishing this relationship, A will be prepared to help B solve whatever problems B is concerned about. A's own notions of what B *should* be concerned about will be kept strictly in the background, at least until the relationship has progressed to the point where A can bring them up without becoming a potential threat to B. Outside consultants sometimes make a mistake in this respect when they utilize the device of the "survey" as a way of initiating the staff relationship.

2. When B desires his help, A will attempt to explore thoroughly with B the latter's "perceptual field." What is the problem *as B sees it*? What needs of B are involved? What does B see to be the difficulties, the obstacles, the possibilities in the situation? What are B's fears, hopes, uncertainties with respect to a solution?

At the same time, A will attempt to make clear to B his own perceptual field. What are A's objectives in his staff job? In what ways does A propose to be of help to B? What are A's relevant needs?

A will avoid making his own analysis of the problem, and developing his own solution. He will not attempt to "mastermind" B, but, genuinely to offer his knowledge and skill to B in a mutual exploration of the problem. Even if A thinks he knows an answer, he will reserve judgment because of a sincere belief that B's own intimate knowledge of the situation is the most likely basis on which the best answer can be developed. Genuine humility in the face of the inevitable complexity of problems of human relations is one of A's most valuable attributes. Too few staff experts recognize this important fact.

3. Together A and B will examine possible alternative approaches to the solution of the problem, seeking that solution which provides

the best *common* means for *mutual* need satisfaction. (*i.e.*, that action by *B* which simultaneously offers the greatest potential need satisfaction for *B* and best achieves *A's* objective of creating and maintaining healthy human relations).

During this process *A* may be able to introduce his own ideas, gather needed factual data, provide useful "tools" (e.g., relevant personnel techniques). He must be careful, however, to do so in a manner which *B* will perceive as augmentive. Any attempt on *A's* part to impose his ideas as the necessary answer, or to force *B* to accept his facts as correct, will certainly defeat *A's* purpose.

Compromises with theoretical perfection are inevitable in approaching this goal. A solution which is objectively best may in fact be poor if in *B's* eyes it offers too little need satisfaction. Industrial engineers, for example, often defeat their own purposes by insisting on the most "efficient" solution regardless of *B's* motivation.[7]

As a matter of fact, our experience has taught us that *B* will surprisingly often develop a better solution than *A* could have produced. *A's* most valuable function is to create a "permissive atmosphere" in which *B* can explore freely all possible alternatives and exercise his own ingenuity without fear of exposing his weakness. *A* seeks to help *B* to think out loud, guiding him where necessary with his own knowledge of the field.

In group situations especially, we have found that role playing can be a powerful diagnostic tool at this stage.[8] With it, *B* is able to see far more clearly than otherwise the advantages and disadvantages of alternative approaches to a solution, *including his own previous ones.*

4. Having explored together the alternative approaches to a solution and settled upon the "best" one, *A* will strive to give *B* whatever support he needs while *B* determines for himself in practice whether the agreed-upon solution is adequate. Often the solution calls for a pattern of behavior different from *B's* accustomed ones. In such cases *B may have some anxiety.* He may lack self-confidence, fear the possibility of loss of face. He may not possess the necessary degree of some essential skill. *A* can aid him in planning his actions by coaching him, evaluating the results of his efforts, and otherwise providing support before, during, and after the action.

---

[7] Peter F. Drucker, "The Way to Industrial Peace," *Harper's Magazine*, November and December, 1946, January, 1947.

[8] Alex Bavelas, "Role Playing and Management Training," *Sociatry*, Vol. 2, 1947, 183-191, and Leland Bradford and Ronald Lippitt, "Role Playing in Supervisory Training," *Personnel*, Vol. 22, No. 6, 1946, 3-14.

At this stage also, role playing may be an effective tool, but in a different way.[9] It affords the opportunity for pre-testing a proposed solution in a safe situation, "before the chips are down." It is a means by which B can acquire some degree of skill without exposing himself unduly. It may help B to acquire the necessary self-confidence to enable him to do something which he would otherwise be unwilling to attempt.

5. Finally, A will seek to help B gradually to assume full responsibility himself for the success of the agreed-upon plan. A's goal at this stage is B's independence, B's confident skill in handling this and other related problems himself.

It is dangerous for A, in providing help, to foster B's dependence. To the extent that B becomes or remains unduly dependent on A, A's power in the relationship is increased disproportionately. B soon arrives at a point where he makes quite unrealistic demands upon A for help. Then, no matter how unreasonable B's demands, any failure by A to provide the expected help will be seen by B as reduction.

Dependence, in some degree, of B upon A is inevitable if A's attempts to help are at all successful. The problem is to prevent that dependence from becoming too great or from lasting too long. A's goal is not to make himself indispensable, but to improve B's managerial competence toward the end of healthier human relationships in the organization.

In the light of the above it is perhaps clear that the staff expert's own emotional adjustment will be a critical factor in the successful performance of his role. If his own need for power is too strong, he will not be able to create or maintain an effective relationship with B. If he is over-anxious for recognition, he is likely to prevent B from achieving independence, or to destroy the results of his work with B by seeking credit for B's accomplishments. The sentimental "do-gooder" who is a familiar applicant for personnel jobs, is obviously miscast for the role outlined here. So is the "expert" who is over-confident of his own knowledge and skill.

_____

The fundamental purpose underlying all these sub-goals is to create, by the method of augmentation, opportunities for B to change his behavior (his attitudes, his philosophy, his skills) in a direction consistent with the creation and maintenance of healthy human relations throughout the whole organization. Unless A himself has some ideas about what _are_ healthy human relations, what philosophy of

_____

[9] Bavelas, _op. cit._

line management is essential to their development, what attitudes are desirable, what skills are necessary—he can hardly hope to accomplish this objective. Effective performance in the staff role requires some systematic theory of human relations in organizations. Without it, *A's* guidance of *B* will be blind indeed.

At the same time, *A* cannot impose his theories on *B*. If *A's* ideas are sound, *B* will adopt them because experience demonstrates that they provide better means for his own need satisfaction. If they are incorrect, or incomplete (as they must be at this stage of the development of the field of human relations), *B* can improve on them, and *A* can utilize his own experiences in the staff role as a basis for learning. This is perhaps the greatest challenge in the methods outlined above: they offer to *A* and *B* alike a valuable opportunity to learn.

When the answers are known, when human relations has become a science rather than an art, methods such as those here suggested will perhaps no longer be necessary or desirable. Today, however, the staff expert may forfeit his own opportunities to acquire greater competence if he assumes that only *B* can learn from the relationship.

In summary, the objective of the staff expert is healthy human relations in the organization. The staff man cannot achieve this objective himself; it can only be achieved by line management, whose function it is to integrate and direct the activities of all the people comprising the organization. The quality of human relations is directly determined by the way in which line management performs its function—by the philosophy and attitudes of line management, and the reflection of that philosophy and those attitudes in policies, procedures and above all in line managers' day-to-day behavior. Every phase of line management's job is accomplished through people; consequently, every act of management influences the quality of human relations in the organization.

Effective performance of the staff role involves getting line management to adopt a philosophy, attitudes and ways of behaving which will create and maintain healthy human relations. For reasons we have discussed, the staff expert must, if he is to be successful, confine himself to the method of augmentation and avoid reductive authority entirely. He possesses means (skills and knowledge) which the members of line management may use for the greater satisfaction of their needs and the simultaneous improvement of human relations. In order to make it possible for line managers individually or collectively to use these means augmentively, the staff expert strives in succession:

(1) To be perceived as a source of help.
(2) To work within the frame of reference of the line manager's perceptual field.
(3) To make it possible for the line manager to select, after joint exploration of alternatives, that course of action which offers him the greatest need satisfaction consistent with the objective of healthy human relations.
(4) To provide support in necessary ways while the line manager tests the selected method and acquires the necessary skill and confidence to use it.
(5) To guide the line manager toward the point where, having acquired competence and self-confidence, he will assume voluntarily the full responsibility himself for performing his line function in a way which will maintain healthy human relations.

The implication of these considerations for other relationships—for example, that of the line manager to his own subordinates, or that of the teacher to the student—are of more than minor significance. They cannot, however, be explored in the present context without taking us too far afield. A brief comment on one point, however, is perhaps pertinent.

If the fundamental assumptions outlined earlier in this discussion are sound, it can be argued with some force that effective line management requires the utilization of methods very similar to those which have been suggested as necessary for the effective performance of the staff role. Both the staff man and the line man are attempting to influence human behavior and human attitudes. The line manager, be he foreman or president, who carries the implications inherent in these conceptions of the nature of authority over to his own job, may gain new insight into his problems of integrating and directing the activities of people.[10]

The idea that successful performance of the line function requires heavy emphasis on reductive authority while successful performance of the staff function precludes it, demands careful and critical analysis. On the basis of our explorations of this problem we suggest that the only significant distinction between effective performance of the two functions is in terms of the means which *A* controls and which *B* desires for satisfying his needs, and not in terms of the way in which *A* exercises control.

The competent staff man controls knowledge and skills; the competent line man also controls knowledge and skills, and in addition material means (wages and other "benefits," opportunities for pro-

---

[10] The beginnings of such a trend in management philosophy are today apparent among the more progressive companies. Cf., for example, the "coordination committee" of the Standard Oil Company of New Jersey, and the practice of "consultative supervision" emphasized by General Foods Corporation.

motion, etc.). The successful performance of either the line or the staff function appears to require the creation of a relationship within which B can simultaneously increase his own need satisfaction and contribute more effectively to the achievement of organizational objectives. Emphasis upon augmentation rather than reduction is one important condition for the establishment of such a relationship. The genuine motivation of subordinates to cooperate with their superiors toward the achievement of organizational objectives will not occur so long as the line function is tacitly assumed to rest solely upon the line manager's exercise of reductive authority.

Thus the staff expert is challenged not merely to acquire skill himself in the performance of the staff role, but to use his skill in such a manner that line managers will seek voluntarily to adapt his methods to their own line function.

Questions

1. Distinguish between "line" and "staff."
2. What is the major thesis of McGregor's article? Do you agree?
3. What is the human relations objective of the staff expert? Can the staff man achieve this objective himself? Why?
4. Explain what effective performance of the staff role in human relations involves and requires.
5. Define "reductive authority" and show how it is related to the line-staff concept.

MAKING HUMAN RELATIONS WORK *

Elizabeth and Francis Jennings

The Robert Wood Johnson report, "Human Relations in Modern Business," published in the *Harvard Business Review* of September 1949, can be called a Magna Carta for management and the worker. As a set of guiding principles and ethical values collaborated upon by distinguished industrial, religious, and educational leaders, it is a significant accomplishment. It has long-range objectives which should become the keystone of full human productivity in commercial and industrial life.

The report necessarily deals with ideas and abstractions. It presents an ideal background for the social relationships in business which result in cooperative and integrated activity. But ideas in themselves do not live until they are incorporated in the daily life of people; they are not useful until they are put to test. Because the science of human relations is in its infancy, its language, drawn as it is from the psychosocial area, is obscure; the mind of management is therefore not prepared to use the generalities set forth in the report in concrete situations. Personnel representatives to whom management should look for such preparation have not yet, unfortunately, found a way to bridge the gulf between themselves and management which this psychosocial language has created.

The purpose of this article, based as it is on actual case experience, is to help bridge that gulf, so that management and workers may lay a foundation for the common understanding requisite to the establishment of human relations principles as a philosophy which will guide action.

Significance of Human Personality

The ultimate success or failure of any attempt to lay the foundation for common understanding depends on how people are valued. Progress has already been made in the establishment of procedures based on the evaluation of people. Progress has been made, but the concept behind this progress still is largely from the point of view that workers must be what management wants them to be. Manage-

* From the *Harvard Business Review*, Vol. 29, No. 1 (January-February, 1951), pp. 29-55. Reprinted with permission.

ment has considered what it can do to or for or with workers in order to achieve its purpose. (And management's attitudes toward people have been kindly, indulgent, protective, harsh, or arbitrary according to its feeling toward the individual worker.)

The trouble is that this point of view represents an authoritarian business structure in which the management has power to demand and the workers are under obligation to comply. In such a structure the management sets up policies and procedures for organized relationships which, no matter how sincerely cooperation is desired, exclude the possibilities of voluntary cooperation because they are, in essence, dictatorial; they fail to take the needs of the human personality into account.

Here is where the Johnson report makes such an important contribution: it is focused on the human personality. In the section which is a statement of principles, there is a warning that a society which fails to meet man's basic needs will perish. Policies and procedures, then, must take man's personality into account if the society represented by the business or industrial corporation is to be happy and productive.

Thus, the vital question for management to answer is: Are we fulfilling man's basic needs? And if not—as the following discussion should serve to demonstrate—what alterations in our management structure of operation are necessary in order to do so?

Basic human needs

Just what are the needs of the human personality? One section of the Johnson report, speaking of man's basic rights and needs, mentions his sense of dignity, the noble aims of his nature, the over-all purpose of his life, and his destiny in God's plan for the universe. Indeed, the section in question is entitled "The Dignity of Man."

Would it not be consistent with this idea of dignity, in fact a translation of it into terms of action, to say that life's over-all purpose is productivity—productivity in the sense of making the highest contribution of ourselves to society through the fullest utilization of our resources and powers—and that the aggregation of basic needs is toward this productivity?

The key word to man's productivity in this sense is environment; interactions between himself and his environment are the determining factor in its degree of fulfillment. Environment is not just the physical plant and surroundings; it is also the mental and emotional atmosphere inside the plant. It is the sum total of the contributions of experience made by every individual in the plant from the doorman to the president. It is the total of all the invisible contributions of voice, clothing, gesture, word, report, and report of report which every morning are behind every bench and desk, every ledger and typewriter, every wheel and tool in the organization. And every individual reacts according to the way his experience in his environment makes him feel. If he feels comfortable, mentally and physically, he will react favorably; if he is uncomfortable, his reaction will be unfavorable.

It is reasonable to conclude that the reactions which are conducive to growth and development are the reactions which are conducive to this productivity of the human personality; it is also reasonable to conclude that any environment which is most conducive to such productivity is the one which offers the worker the greatest number of opportunities to use his powers and resources to solve his own problems and make the majority of his decisions.

In today's business and industrial environment, the interacting pattern of contributions is not conducive to this kind of growth and development. On the contrary, it levels workers at the point which tends toward deterioration rather than progress because it does not offer opportunities for the utilization of their resources.

In order to grow and develop, we must have plans for fulfillment of goals; we must have a set of operating principles and disciplines on which to base decisions; we must seize upon all possible elements of progress. We must utilize our minds as well as our hands.

Today's business environment utilizes the worker's hands, but it does not utilize his mind, at least to anywhere near the same degree. Management and worker attitudes toward each other are partially responsible for this situation; mass production and mass living have made their significant contribution; but the great burden of responsibility rests largely upon those same institutions which collaborated on the Johnson report—business, church, and school—as *social institutions*.

Inadequacy of social institutions

These institutions have failed to help the worker develop a set of operating principles and disciplines on which to base his decisions and his personal conduct in work-a-day life. They have failed to show him how to make the best use of his mind, because as a result of their own conflicting values and standards of conduct they have left his mind in conflict.

Each of these institutions in its time has influenced the worker's personality, presenting to him its own set of values, but none of these values is consistent with the development of a basic philosophy which the worker can use on the job.

Sometimes the standards which he has learned are in total contradiction to those approved by the groups to which the worker belongs; sometimes they are the standards which appear to have the sanction of his group, but they are not the standards used by the successful worker.

The church, for example, lauds humility, self-effacement, self-sacrifice as personal virtues for man's personal use. Any worker who is self-sacrificing or self-effacing on the job is used by the group as a member who makes no demands for himself. The worker who wants to develop and progress dare not be self-effacing; he must be conspicuous, or he will be lost in the mass grouping of job activity. And yet, as we shall see, the worker who dares to be conspicuous in order to develop risks the disapproval of the group, for whom homogeneity is its most precious asset.

Confronted with such conflicting standards and values, it is extremely difficult for the worker to know which elements in his situation contribute to progress; it is difficult for him to make intelligent decisions. One worker stated this conflict clearly when she said, "I don't know what to do. You see, I was always taught to be polite and considerate of others, to think of myself last. But I am beginning to see that if I want to get anywhere on this job, I have to think of me first. The only reason I haven't started is that I would feel so guilty."

Problems of Conflicting Values

To understand the import of these conflicting values as they affect the human individual we must think in terms of actual work-a-day experience.

Multiple loyalties

The value of loyalty as an allegiance to a set of principles and disciplines evolved from concepts of right and wrong is perniciously construed on the job as loyalty to persons because they represent power and authority. The church and school teach workers to be loyal to something within themselves called conscience. The job teaches workers to be loyal to their boss regardless of his principles, character, or performance, regardless of the consequences of such loyalty to the workers themselves.

The Johnson report states in the section headed "Unions" that "life is full of multiple loyalty demands which can be adjusted by common sense." But the experience of anyone living realistically in his job environment is that these multiple loyalty demands result in tensions which frequently become unbearable. Consider the case of a young man, working in a delivery department, who had been called before the management for an inquiry into the delivery of a refrigerator which had crashed to the street from a fifth floor window:

> "I told Jack it wasn't safe," he said, "and he would not listen; he was in a hurry to get to the fights."
> We learned that Jack was the senior worker on the job. But where had the supervisor been?
> The worker asked that the information be kept confidential, then admitted that the supervisor had gone around the corner for a beer.
> The man was troubled about the black mark against his record; but he was also troubled because he had lied to the management, because he did not defend himself, and because his wife failed to understand his loyalty involvements.
> When asked why he did not tell the management the truth, he said uneasily: "Well, you see, Jack and I are brother union members. I can't bring Jack into it. And we have agreed we won't tell on Bill. Bill has to save his own skin. We told him we wouldn't tell."
> "But you have lied about the whole affair."
> "A man has got to be loyal to his boss," said the worker doggedly.
> "Has it ever occurred to you that in lying for the boss you are not protecting him? You are only hurting him. Suppose the next time a refrigerator crashes some one is injured or killed?"
> "You can't tell on a boss," he repeated, "I'm no squealer."

Where do the worker's loyalties lie in such an instance? What is common sense? Is it to protect and defend his own interests or silently accept rebuke and a reputation for carelessness? Shall he be loyal to unofficial demands inherent in union membership at the risk of his job future? Shall he comply with the demands of membership in his group despite the fact that they are in conflict with the implicit agreements made between himself and the management when his services were hired, or shall he ignore the group code of behavior, risk the isolation which would inevitably result, and tell management the true facts?

Perhaps the authors of the Johnson report by the use of the term "common sense" imply an adjustment which is best suited to purpose. It is certainly true that unless this worker clears himself of blame, he is not acting in his own interests, he cannot fulfill his own purpose which is to grow and develop in his job. He would need courage—more than he can summon, perhaps—to tell his friend and his boss that he proposes to defend himself before the management.

A discussion group to which this problem was submitted proposed two solutions for the worker. He could tell the management that he did his part, that the facts about the crash of the refrigerator can best be procured from the senior worker and the boss. "He will still have to take the black mark for carelessness," said one member, "but at least his conscience is clear." Another member suggested that the worker warn his friend and his boss "that he won't take the rap again."

One astute participant said that the individuals who represented the management during the inquiry had not been skilled in asking questions. "A skilled interrogator," he said, "would have got the truth out of the guy and protected him." "But he still has to live with his buddy and his boss," was a rejoinder.

An inevitable conclusion here is that there *was* more skill needed on the part of the interrogators, but there is a further serious implication. The worker did not feel that the union would support him. The management of unions is confronted with precisely the same problem that confronts the management of businesses. No responsible union management would want to see any worker accept unfair blame. If the union management has anticipated any of these conflicts in behavior standards, however, the worker has as yet not been helped toward a solution.

A union representative to whom this problem was submitted said that the management should have called in the union. Would the union, then, assume the responsibility of dictating to the worker what he must do?

Inconsistent honesty

The conflicts which arise as a result of inconsistent honesty values are perhaps the most serious of all these loyalty clashes. The maxim that honesty is the best policy is considered by the average employee to be an echo from his past, a phrase of exhortation delivered by clergymen and teachers who have never had to put the idea to work. But even in absentia, the maxim pricks his conscience; it gnaws his mind because he remembers that dishonesty practices are alleged to have dire results, yet his daily experience on the job is that dishonesty is a matter of course.

Some workers who have the privilege of sick leave still argue with their consciences about the misuse of sick leave, and their consciences win; other workers see to it that they use up every hour of sick leave by the end of the year. Some employees say they are too ill to come to work; they even succeed in producing a physician's statement that they are not well enough to work. It may be that their state of health demands a day's fishing, or hunting, or ocean breezes. But other employees state frankly that they want to take a day off to go fishing. The employee who lies is paid; the one who tells the truth is not. If the second employee, like the first, thinks only of immediate gains, he is likely to procure a physician's certificate next time he wants to go fishing.

But these are comparatively minor honesty conflicts when one considers the case of a young woman who stated that her boss was cleverly stealing from the management and that she must resign in order to report him:

> She revealed that she herself felt dishonest because she was aware of the dishonest practices of her boss. Asked why she must resign in order to report him, she replied: "I can't do anything else. If I report him while I am on the payroll, they will say I am disloyal."
> "You have not thought of talking this over with the boss himself?"
> "I don't understand."
> "Don't you have a responsibility to tell your boss what you have discovered?"
> "But I couldn't do that."
> "Why not?"
> "I just couldn't, that's all; it would be like I thought I was the boss."
> "But isn't it just as disloyal to talk about him among your friends as it would be to report him to the management, leaving him completely uninformed?"
> "He is a very important man; he would be angry. Besides, I'm not going to rat."
> "But you say you can prove he is stealing."
> "I can. I knew it more than a year ago. The man who told me told me not to tell. But I wasn't his assistant then."
> "And you feel that in order to bring this matter to the attention of the management you must resign?"
> "Yes. I don't want to be a squealer." (This is precisely what she does want to be. Anyone else in this situation would want the management to know that she is an honest employee while the trusted boss commanding a higher salary is dishonest. As long as she is under group controls, however, she feels that she cannot break the code. Resignation would remove her from the compulsion to obey the unofficial laws.)
> One week later, the employee stated that she had decided to stay on the job and keep quiet, hoping that the management would find out.

A group of workers to which this problem was presented was divided in a discussion of whether or not the employee was concerned about a matter which was none of her business. One section held that the employee should resign and write a letter; the other, that she should stay on the job, keep quiet, and hope that the management would discover the boss's dishonesty. "She has a moral responsibility to tell but not a job responsibility," was one curious remark. "But if you are going to be concerned with morals where you work, you would be better off scrubbing floors," rejoined a young man, who said he had worked during summers since he was fifteen.

The representatives of other kinds of institutional life to whom the situation was presented have said at once that the employee should discuss the situation with the boss, but not one member of the worker group made that suggestion. No one seemed to be concerned that she had discussed the matter with everyone but the man who was primarily involved. Apparently it was not considered disloyal to talk behind the boss's back, but only when he happened to be within hearing distance. Here are further comments in sequence:

A: "If she just wants to expose the guy, then she has no right to tell on him. If she is really concerned about loyalty to the management, although I doubt it—nobody can be really loyal to something so distant from personal experience—then let her go ahead. But it is not in her employment agreement that she go around reporting people."

B: "Where will she draw the line at stealing? We all know people who chisel about something—sick leave, expense accounts, stationery from the offices, loafing on the job, sick grandmother stuff. Where are you going to begin and end?"

C: "I have a similar problem, only my boss is just juggling figures, but I'm interested in my own welfare. I feel that it is not honest—what he is doing—but I don't dare butt in; I'm worried because my name countersigns the report, that's all."

D: "You should worry!" (This was a rejoinder to C's remark.) "Everybody juggles figures; management knows it; management has to be hypocritical about some things. You have to subordinate your feelings to the business."

C (protesting in turn): "But it's still dishonest."

D: "Then half the joint is dishonest." (With this bland observation, D shows for the second time that he is a person who has made an adjustment to his job environment. He is in no conflict about values; he feels no guilt. Only the institutions can decide whether society wants to educate for this kind of adjustment.)

C (still worrying, after the discussion was over): "I cannot understand why my generation is educated in a code of ethics which no one outside the cloistered walls believes in."

E: "The educators can hardly say that some kinds of dishonesty are condoned while others are not, can they?"

C: "Yes, they can, if that is the way they want it. There is not a day goes by that I am not mixed up on some ethical matter or other. I would hate to say this so vehemently to my father, but there is no doubt that the sacrifices he made for my education were in vain. I have had to throw overboard everything I learned at college."

RESULTING FEARS

The tensions which arise as a result of these value conflicts may take many forms—any one of which tends to limit the productivity of the worker as a human personality, and more often than not his actual output of work as well. Principally they show up as fear emotions.

Fear of authority

In the assistant's case just cited, for instance, we see the worker's fear of the individual who symbolizes authority. Management members are usually incredulous when it is suggested to them that the workers are afraid to express themselves, to speak the truth, to present a board of inquiry with the facts. One general manager said, "There is no logical reason for their fear." And he was right. But, like others in management positions, the manager is looking for logic in every situation. He forgets that in the past there has been logic in the workers' fear of the boss and that the past has continuing dominion over the present.

It is not the general manager as such that the employee fears, but what he represents. He is the symbol of authority. Authority has power to give and power to withhold. The worker is therefore determined to please the individual in authority so that he will give whatever it is that may happen to be wanted—the promotion, the new desk, the space by the window, the invitation to accompany him to the Atlantic City convention.

The desire to please, as we know, is learned by millions of little boys and girls before they become employees. In childhood the deprivations which authority can impose are not in terms of promotion and favors but in terms of candy, the movies, or rides on the pony at the seashore. The child soon learns that authority can deprive as well as give, and that authority gives only when it is soothed and propitiated. Then comes the realization that he must please authority to get what he wants. Eventually this idea is a fixed and integral element in his character structure and is carried over into his adult life.

It was early morning at the seashore when a youthful mother who wanted to read a mystery novel assured her small son, dressed in full Hopalong Cassidy regalia, that if he remained a good boy all day long, he would have another ride on the ponies tomorrow. No one would dare predict exactly what kind of employee little Hopalong will turn into without more details of his life with mamma, but one sure prediction is that he is not going to mature if mamma is consistent. And if he is subjected in his advancing years to the "get along with everybody" gospel, which is saturating our eyes and ears, his future is not bright.

In order to get along with everybody, the worker has to split himself into several selves—one for the job, one for the home and family, one for the church, one for the club, one for civic and state duty. The sociologist Pitirim Sorokin likens the individual who must identify himself with various groups, each with its own set of law norms, to a ball pushed in several directions by various forces.

This "get along with everybody" psychology is obviously a desire to avoid trouble. Mr. Keith Powlison, in the March 1950 issue of the *Harvard Business Review*, speaking of the losses which occur as a result of the avoidance of trouble, says that the attitude of the workers in this respect is caused by certain management attitudes. Management attitudes are clearly responsible in part, but the deeper causes are in our culture. These causes lie in the acute need for approval which is experienced by all of us at various stages of our personality development and for some of us throughout our entire lives.

Little Hopalong, for example, understands that if he interrupts mamma's novel too frequently, he will first bear the discomfort of her shrieking voice, then the wrath of her powerful hand. He recognizes mamma as the supreme authority. He will eventually transfer that identification of mamma's authority into any situation in which he feels the weight of authority—teacher, policeman, clergyman, the supervisor on the job, or any significant person in his experiences.

Fear of being one's self

When the worker's fear of authority and his resultant determination to please the boss are viewed in their wider aspects, they are perceived as the worker's fear of expressing and being himself. Instead of expressing his personal feelings and beliefs in the job situation, the worker says what he believes the management and his boss want him to say. Not only do the majority of workers rationalize their failure to progress on the basis that they dare not say what they really think and feel, but they believe that they will lose their jobs if they do so.

During the question period that followed a talk before personnel and management representatives, a member of the audience asked: "What can a man do when he feels he just cannot take any more from his boss?" It was suggested that the man must first try to examine his own attitude to discover how much he contributes to the unpleasant relationship, then must seek an opportunity to talk frankly with the boss around the fact that an unhappy worker is not fully productive. At that point one of the personnel men said, "That's fine in theory; but if we did that, where would all of us get new jobs?"

Whenever an employee expresses this kind of fear, and he is asked whether he can name anyone who lost his job because he told his boss or the management what he really believes to be the truth, the invariable answer is: "Oh, I can't prove it, but nobody dares to buck that guy. He wants a yes man."

It is undeniable that some of the destructive techniques of many members in high places have supported the concept that a worker has to be a "yes man." Even bosses who stoutly affirm that they want no yes man around will pound the desk, will shout interruptions, con tradictions, and denials before a subordinate is halfway through what he has to say. Yet, though there are supposed to be many instances in which a courageous subordinate was discharged because he spoke what he believed to be the truth, the allegation can rarely be proved.

What actually happens in most cases is that the alleged victim who is so sure the boss is "out to get me," "knife me in the back," "sell me down the river," himself creates the circumstances which result in his discharge or in his failure to progress. And of course an employee who has absorbed and believes these rationalizations of failure strongly resists the suggestion that no one can "sell him down the river" but himself.

Consider the case of an assistant (with a master's degree in sociology, incidentally) who had been instructed by the division head to prepare a report and to delete from it certain pertinent facts:

> The assistant feels that to do so would be not only against his ethical principles but against his professional principles as well. He has not been able to sleep. He has discussed the matter with officials in other divisions, one of whom told him, "It's not your funeral"; while another said, "Don't stick your neck out."
>
> "But it *is* my funeral, you see," he stated. "If anyone who really knows the field found out I prepared that report, he would think I didn't know my job."
>
> "These facts to be deleted are so important?"
>
> "They certainly are."
>
> "Then why do you not discuss the matter with your chief?"
>
> "One just does not imply that the boss doesn't know his job. The boss knows all the answers; and if I were to make an issue of it, he would think I wanted his job."
>
> "But couldn't you show him that it is in his own best interests to include these facts?"
>
> "Yes, but that would reveal that we have made some errors in judgment. And we have. I cannot put myself into the position of telling off the boss."

This young man is confronted with many problems as the result of his chief's orders. At home, he is trying to help his parents understand that his principles are involved, that he does not want to be dishonest, but neither does he want to be disloyal, nor be regarded as an assistant who does not know his job. His father warns that jobs are hard to get, that every worker's responsibility is to obey his chief. His mother says that if he loses his job, he will be a disgrace to the family, the first man in three generations to be discharged.

"They put me over the ropes last night; Dad thinks I'm crazy. He says there is no room for foolish ideals in business today, and of course mother wept; she isn't thinking about anything but the disgrace."

"Can't you convince her that there is no question of your losing your job because you are honest?"

He remained quiet for a moment, then replied, "I don't know about that. I'm not so sure."

"What do you mean?"

"I tell you my boss thinks he knows all the answers."

"But he would not consider discharging an employee with a record like yours."

"I'm not so sure."

"On such a petty pretext?"

"Well, one doesn't buck this guy."

"How do you know?"

"I have heard of a man who did and lost his job."

"You know that to be a fact?"

"Oh, yes. Everybody seems to accept that it happened that way. You're right—of course, I don't *know* it, but I do know my boss. He is inflexible. He is always right. Nobody can tell him anything. Arrogant is his middle name. And if he did not actually discharge me, he could make it hot for me."

(Here is a curious article in the industrial code of behavior. It is not a disgrace to resign because one is unable to accept the responsibilities of employment, because one has not become mature. It is unrealistic or stupid to resign because of involvement with ethical principles. But it is a disgrace to be discharged for any reason.)

A realistic adjustment for this problem situation would have been for the assistant to talk frankly with his chief. But instead he resigned, saying that his favorite philosopher, John Dewey, had helped him solve his problem: "Dewey says there is this distinction between a bad man and a good one—the bad man is the man who begins to deteriorate no matter how good he has been; the good man is the one who moves to become better."

It is not known whether the young man had ever studied John Dewey's philosophy with the aid of an instructor. Certainly, Dewey himself never expected to provide such comfortable self-deception. But the industrial soil is rich for this kind of failure to accept the challenge of being honest with oneself. The young man believes that he resigned rather than betray his principles; but he really resigned because he could not reconcile his loyalties, because he was afraid to be himself.

Fear of being different

This fear of being one's self is carried into every job situation in which the worker is involved. It becomes a fear of making mistakes, a fear of admitting ignorance, a fear of conflict. But the insurmountable fear it engenders is the fear of being different and therefore conspicuous. The employee who emerges from the group as successful is conspicuous. The success of any one member too frequently incurs hostilities on the part of unsuccessful employees. Many workers would rather remain secure in their group association than put to test the personal discomforts, the ridicule, the isolation which attend development.

There are as many negatives as positives in human possibilities; it is eternally true that the basic urge of the individual is to grow, to make something of himself, but he can unconsciously seize upon as many elements for failure as for success. If it is extremely uncomfortable to succeed, or to be conspicuous in development, he will be unable to comfort himself with the thought of eventual gains; he will choose the security of group approval. Consider the case of the women in a naval shipyard during the Second World War:

> Invariably these women rationalized their failure to achieve promotions, salary increases, and favorite assignments on the ground that only a girl who used her sex unscrupulously could get ahead.
> During a group conference designed to alter this attitude, there were pointed remarks directed toward one of the few women who had achieved the enviable distinction of welder first-class rating. (It was known that in retaliation the girls had put roaches in her lunch box, fouled up her lines, upset ink on her clothing, and sent her on fake errands. They had even planned to tell her that her husband had been killed overseas, but fortunately the supervisor heard of the plan and prevented its consummation.)
> The woman in question held her peace during the discussion. And when the conference was over, she said to the leader: "Don't let them think that you believe I got this first-class welder's rate honorably. They make it hard enough for me as it is. I prefer them to believe that I date all the supervisors; my husband would know it isn't true. I can take care of myself. I feel sorry for some of the women who really want to do a good job and do not dare."

Another quite similar case concerns a junior executive:

> During a class discussion among junior executives references were made to the humiliating methods of an unnamed senior executive. One member of the group, who had not risen to the defense of the senior executive during the class session, a few days later said: "You know, if those guys would just do what the big boy wants, there would be nothing to gripe about. All he expects is production. I admit he should use different methods, but I think sometimes he is so provoked he loses his head."

"It would have been helpful for you to make that comment in class."

"And have every man jack of them down on me for life? Why, if I got a promotion, they would accuse me of the old apple trick. I have to keep their goodwill."

The kind of maturity revealed by the woman welder and the junior executive is rare. There is no magic formula for it. It is there or it is not; and if it is not, management must help the worker try to develop it.

The very young worker is particularly inept in coping with group pressures, as demonstrated by the case of George who was just out of high school:

> When his employer announced a training program to develop a resource of junior executives, George told his co-workers that he intended to apply; his co-workers jeered at him, called him a softy, suggested he "get wise."
>
> "They said it was only a scheme to get more work out of us, and that only a guy who stood in with top bosses would get promoted anyhow."
>
> After three months had passed, the young man was unhappy because of the changed attitude of his friends on the job. When it was suggested that perhaps his own attitude had changed as a result of his new experience, he shook his head.
>
> "No, it's them. We used to go out Friday nights; they let me know they don't want me; they stop talking when I come around."
>
> "Are you sure this is not your imagination?"
>
> "Well, if it is, I didn't imagine my telephone call from my girl friend. She left a message for me, and the fellow I considered my best friend didn't give it to me. Fellows don't usually forget date messages, unless on purpose. You know, I wish I had never taken the course; I wish I could resign. If I don't get promoted, I'll never get back into the gang again."

Some management members find it hard to believe that workers can be cruel to each other. It is true that deliberate cruelty is uncommon, but unconscious feelings of envy, covetousness, or jealousy often gain expression in a disguised or covert manner. The person being cruel may not know it, but he feels inferior and threatened by his co-worker's success (the other worker's better appearance, material gains, intimacy with the boss, and so on), and he takes every opportunity to reduce the person to what he feels is his own level of accomplishment. With gossip, insinuation, or seemingly playful pranks he endeavors to place the co-worker in an unfavorable or ridiculous position. If his victim retaliates in a like manner, then a circle of strife is created in which the antagonists may recruit their friends, and eventually this conflict may be felt as a disruptive influence on the functioning of an entire department.

Fear of responsibility

The supervisor who is promoted from a work-group of which he has been a member to a position of authority in this group is particularly fearful of incurring the hostility of his former associates. He desires to maintain his former comfortable relationships with everyone; his fear, however, is colored by his recollection of how he felt toward bosses.

A supervisor who had just been promoted from within said to his assembled workers, "I'll never let you fellows down." He told a friend later, "I've never had any enemies and I'm not going to start making any now." This supervisor brought with him a determination to avoid trouble with his former fellow-workers; now, with the assumption of responsibility for their operations, he is unconsciously expressing a further dilemma with which he is confronted: How am I going to maintain the approval of my workers and the approval of my own bosses at one and the same time?

Most of us fear the responsibility of having authority over people, whether we arrive at that position from promotion or appointment. We meet the responsibility with whatever techniques have worked for us in the past when we were afraid of people. We have no known basis for these techniques; they are not of intellectual origin; we are seldom able to verbalize them; but they seem to work for us, to help us feel secure. Eventually these techniques become habitual methods which appear to be constructive because they produce immediately desired results.

Yet the end result is often proof that such methods are really destructive, as is shown in the following case of an industrial organization that was at a loss to explain the collapse of a division of 200 workers when the chief was transferred to another division:

> The president said: "John did not have an enemy in this place; he has been pre-eminently successful in establishing cooperative relationships. He started here when he was fourteen years old as a messenger. Everybody loves him. But suddenly, now that he has gone, we are having quarrels in the division, a great deal of absenteeism, errors, costly errors, tardiness. We cannot understand it."
>
> The president's words were the first clue to John's techniques. If John had actually given the management a sound technical performance, he would have made some enemies; it would have been impossible not to offend, impossible to mend all his personal-relationship breaks.
>
> Interviewing revealed that John had personally bought the cooperation of his people. He had developed a loyalty to himself, not to the organization, through the technique of intense activity in the personal lives of his employees. He never missed a graduation, a christening, a wedding, a funeral, or a birthday, with appropriate offerings to boot;

he knew every sorrow, every joy, every disappointment in the lives of his people; he patched up marriage troubles; he paid for divorces; he arranged wedding ceremonies under pressing circumstances; nobody had ever called him mister.

"John was a regular guy," said one of John's fortunates sadly. "He was always the same when you needed help, whether you lost your pay check or your aunt had to have her tonsils out."

John was actually a nonproductive supervisor. The productive supervisor develops his peoples' loyalty and responsibility to the company—not to himself. The productive supervisor can say "no" when it is necessary to do so. John could not say "no" lest he lose the approval of someone toward himself. He loved to say "yes" because so much less was required of him than if he were to say "no." John had no trouble with his people, but he sacrificed their personal resources to his own acute need for being approved and loved, just as the president said he was, by everybody.

In any of these case situations, the individual's behavior is based on what he believes the others want him to be, or what he feels he must be in order to assure approval toward himself. That he himself is a person with individuality to contribute to his environment˙does not occur to him; he absorbs the pernicious value system based on fear which subordinates the needs of the human personality to the rules of the game. As we shall see later, some of these rules are essential for efficient group functioning, but any rule or norm which makes man dependent upon forces entirely outside his own resources cannot be a contributing factor to progress.

When such fear emotions constitute the primary outside influence upon a man's behavior, then the sense of dignity that the Johnson report stresses so strongly is destroyed.

MANAGEMENT ATTITUDES

Although these fears have their roots largely in our culture conflicts, there are certain management attitudes which support and maintain them.

Destructive blame

It is here that the management attitude pointed out by Mr. Powlison plays its destructive role. When trouble occurs, management feels that someone must be blamed.

This attitude deprives management of the facts of experience which are essential to the solution of problems and to full productivity. A responsible attitude toward work calls for an awareness of experience, for the analysis of methods, testing of results, compilation of facts. Anyone who is afraid of being blamed if he presents the facts cannot develop this awareness and hence cannot develop a responsible attitude; he is too busy protecting himself from the possibility of blame and preparing his defenses in the event of blame. Avoiding experience in order to keep out of trouble, he is unable to accept experience and welcome it as a key to the solution of his problems and his own development.

The supervisor realizes that the mass-production principle has exposed him to the possibilities of unwarranted criticism. Since management must depend on reports of observations rather than on observation itself, and since the reports must proceed vertically through various interpreters, the supervisor is genuinely concerned lest the report present him in an unfavorable light and he be unable to defend himself. Protecting the vulnerability of his position, since he rarely finds that judgment has been withheld until all the facts are in, he classifies his employees as those whom he can trust and those whom he cannot, or as those who are likely to support his viewpoint in the event of trouble and those who may betray him. He verbalizes this attitude with the classifying of workers as loyal or disloyal. He holds his own supervisor in precisely the same category—as a man who will let him down or a man who will fight for him in the presence of top management.

During a question period which followed a talk before supervisors, someone asked, "Why is it that every level of supervisors considers the next level above a bunch of s.o.b.'s?" There was a quick retort from the audience, "Because they are." The reasons lie part in tradition, part in fact, a large part in the comfortable fiction with which workers rationalize their own failure, and a large part in suspicion that the supervisor will protect himself from management's wrath no matter who else is hurt.

It would be satsifying to be able to say that a good supervisor will not acquire the title of s.o.b., but we know that this is not true. The supervisor plays upon an unwilling instrument at the outset; the average worker, including each one of us, is glad when the working day is over. Consider for a moment what the supervisor must work with: the stubborn, the resentful, the sullen, the vindictive, the careless, the lazy, the indifferent, the moody, and the stupid. That is just an ordinary day's run of business. Rarely are more than a third of his subordinates responsible, alert, and interested. There is no more difficult task in the industrial world today than the task of promoting the interest, maintaining the enthusiasm, and developing the potentialities of the worker.

But the supervisor is handicapped in more ways. He is expected to be a leader of people who are unable to accept him in that capacity. A leader is, along with everything else that he may be, a person who readily assumes power and control when they are needed by the group and as readily relinquishes the power after the special need or crisis has passed. He is a resource.

The supervisor in the majority of industrial situations is not considered a resource by his workers. He is usually the last person on the job to hear of or to be consulted about a problem situation. The reasons for this lie partly in the worker's fear of admitting that he has misunderstood instructions, that he does not know a "how-to-do," that he is suspect of wanting someone's job if he asks questions, that he has not been trained to regard his supervisor as a resource; but there is another important reason—the supervisor will pass on the blame which has been communicated to him by management. It is a rare skill on the part of an executive to attack a problem situation with the atittude of, "What happened?" instead of, "What did you, the supervisor, do, or fail to do which resulted in this present troublesome situation?"

This compilation of fear emotions thus deprives management, the supervisor, and the worker of the analysis of experience which can prevent further occurrences of an undesirable stiuation. Instead of working together to use experience as a tool of control, the supervisor and the worker avoid each other in order to maintain what they erroneously regard as peace and harmony.

Presumably management's excessive use of blame is a kind of "keep him on his toes; if you praise him, he will relax his efforts" idea. As already indicated, this results in a laissez-faire operation which eventually nullifies itself. A laissez-fair method has its value, provided it is planned and coordinated with an intelligent use of pressure. But it is one thing to refrain from interference with a worker in order to develop the worker's own resources and skills in making decisions, yet being at hand when things go wrong; it is quite another to refrain from interference in order to avoid trouble. In the latter case, the supervisor attempts a sporadic solution to his problems; in the former, he uses problems as a continuing tool in supervision.

Hollow praise

At the same time praise can be just as destructive as blame. For often it means that the person who gives praise is presuming to pass judgment rather than to analyze. Consider the case of the branch manager of a sales corporation who was showing alarming signs of hostility toward the individuals in the home office:

Interviewing revealed that the manager's hostility had communicated itself to his people, but it was a cashier who had been many years with the firm who furnished the significant clue: "Fred's attitude changed after they had a dinner for the ten-year employees at the home office."

This was the manager's story: "If my wife wasn't so tied up here in church and social activity, I would have resigned. But she doesn't want to leave her friends. The home office never did have any faith in me.

"I found it out when I went to a banquet for the ten-year managers. You know what those things are. A lot of soft soap, more liquor, some good jokes, some bad, everybody shaking hands with the big boys. Well, I got into the spirit of it and found myself finally shaking the hands of the top man. He slapped my back, pumped both my hands, puffed his cigar, and let me have it, and anybody in the room could have heard it. 'You know, Fred,' he said, 'you're doing fine. And we all thought you couldn't make the grade.'

"All those years! They let me sweat blood to make this office a success, but not one of them ever believed I could do it. That boy will never know how near he came to a punch in the jaw. Maybe I am all wrong, but by golly, if I didn't have any faith in a man, I would get rid of him."

Undoubtedly, the "top man" in this case meant well, but his implied blame was more than the manager could accept. It came ten years too late in the form of a judgment instead of an analysis of potentialities at the beginning.

The blame-praise combination is often used as a method of control by executives who have become intellectually aware that they blame too often, so they try graciously to throw in a little praise. The result is graphically illustrated by a conversation overheard between two men during a lunch hour on a busy street: "Then he called us in and did one of those 'you're wonderful boys, but' jobs on us," said one of the men. The other replied, "I think he takes us for a bunch of school kids who want to feel that teacher loves them."

An executive with a habit of "wiping up the floor" with his people, as he himself phrased it (an expression of self-inadequacy of which he is unaware), said, "But I always pick them up and pat them on the back afterwards." This executive has no intellectual understanding that the pat on the back is symbolic of a superiority-inferiority acknowledgment; there is scarcely any kind of communication less dignified than this traditional gesture.

At the best, most of us feel slightly uncomfortable when we are praised, unless our need for approval is acute. And as for the obviously superior-inferior kind of praise, if we are not immediately concerned with the implied blame (from what blame did the praise arise?), we are likely to wonder what there was in our attitudes which indicated a need for praise.

Contrast with personality development

The blame-praise combination has a particularly serious effect upon control measures when it intensifies the worker's need for praise and makes him inordinately dependent upon approval in the form of praise, as in actual practice it so often does.

Unless we feel within ourselves that we are (or are not) doing a satisfactory job, we can become so dependent upon praise from the person in authority that we have to have it in order to sustain performance. Furthermore, if praise from the boss is the stimulus we need, then disapproval from him is likely to send us into a period of despair throughout which we are not productive; our self-approval feelings cannot be restored until the boss comes along and smiles upon us once more.

To understand the significant difference when the focus is on personality development, consider the case of a management which, planning to promote an executive to a top position, requested an investigation of his relationships with people:

> With the executive's permission, all the people who had worked with him closely were interviewed.
> Preliminary analysis of the statements made by the majority of interviewees indicated that the executive's relationships were destructive. He was alleged to carry whitewash in one hand, soap bars in the other; to be a thoroughgoing bastard," the type of man who would "cut his grandmother's throat without an apology to serve his own selfish ends."
> It was necessary to probe through the surface animosity toward this executive in order to arrive at the facts. Interviewing revealed that his alleged selfish ends were to make money.
> "He uses people to make money for himself."
> "In what way?"
> "He keeps you at it all day long."
> Another interviewee said: "Well, I tell you, he is strictly business. The other bosses do you favors, send gifts on holidays, buy tickets— that is, some of them do—but this guy gives you none of the trimmings. I think in some ways it's okay. Keeps you on your toes."
> One of the department's assistant managers said: "I think people miss being praised. For myself, I don't care. I'm not a child. I can measure my own success on a job. I want an over-all evaluation once a year, of course; but an evaluation is not necessarily praise; it is a critical analysis. In the long run the company is better off with a supervisor like ours, who expects the best a man has to give, than with one who will take as little as a man can give. He uses all our resources. But it's not enough for the average worker just to have his performance

evaluated—he wants to hear himself praised. I'm quite certain he does not give enough praise to satisfy most of his people."

(This speaker expresses precisely what is wrong with praise. Linked with the approval need of which we have already spoken, the need for praise is just another form of dependency on some agency outside ourselves. We all want to know how the management evaluates our performance, but this is not a need for praise; it is rather a need for appreciation and recognition. We *should* want this evaluation *in order to measure our own progress*, not in order to assure that we are pleasing the boss.)

Further interviewing revealed that although the executive rarely gave praise, neither did he humiliate his workers; nor did he call group meetings as a *disciplinary* crutch hoping that the individual who was his target would take the hint; nor did he fail to give constructive help when it was needed.

The interviewee who claimed that the boss would cut his grandmother's throat said during a second interview: "There is one thing, though; he does make you think out your own problems. He will let you make a mistake, and he won't bawl you out for it unless you make it twice. He is just hard to get used to."

(This worker was uttering a statement of major significance. Such an executive is hard to get used to because he treats his workers as though they are adults. He focuses attention upon the function of performance rather than upon himself. Because he is secure within himself, he builds loyalty to the organization rather than to himself. This executive frees the worker from fear of authority; he uses fear productively so that the worker has a fear of failing to do an adequate job rather than of failing to please the boss.)

This kind of supervision is fundamentally healthy. Not that it could not have been done better, or without quite so much apparent antagonism. But the point is that it is in ironic contrast to the kind of supervision described earlier in the case of the supervisor John or the kind of supervision of which many a top-management member boasts (with nothing more to back it up)—flowers at Easter, large sums of money at Christmas, birthday gifts and Thanksgiving offerings—the kind of supervision, with all its aura of apparent goodwill, where if the man is successful, his success is due to the workers' dreadful sense of obligation to him personally rather than any sense of obligation to the company as a whole.

It is in this area of supervision that the techniques which evolve from psychosocial principles are difficult to translate to groups of supervisors. The principle that a supervisor who is personally interested in his people is more likely to be successful in production than one who is not has had unlimited prescription as an antidote to the distress caused by non-human motives. It usually is learned and practiced, however, as a subjective method based on superiority-inferiority relationship rather than a principle based on a philosophy of personality development for those being supervised.

When the training is on an individual basis (the supervisor developing insight into his own behavior and thus into the behavior of his people, through the aid of a counselor), philosophical considerations can readily be used as a basis for the training. But where training is on a group basis, each supervisor tends to tie what he is learning to his own particular set of biases and prejudices, his own unconscious desires and dislikes, and reacts to the training according to his feelings of guilt if any remarks of the teacher appear to be addressed directly to him. (The most successful form of supervisory training is, of course, the discussion form where informal conversation with a skilled leader and with members of the group establishes a medium for self-expression.)

Until workers are released from the fears and inhibitions which limit their communication with supervisors and management, distortions of training principles will come to light only by accident, as in the case of a company which, on the point of rehiring a former woman supervisor, learned that she had been disliked by her workers:

> Inquiry revealed that the woman, Miss A, was disliked because of an alleged disinterest in the people with whom she worked. But analysis of these feelings led to the discovery that Miss B, the supervisor whom Miss A was now about to succeed, had on every Monday morning summoned each girl to her office with the query: "Have you any personal problems?"
>
> The workers' dislike of Miss A then took on a different coloring. And it was finally discovered that their real antipathy toward her stemmed from the fact that, in contrast to Miss B, she discouraged the use of business time for the discussion of inconsequential personal matters.

Undoubtedly these distortions will occur unless the supervisor has a conscious knowledge of himself as a person and begins to evolve a philosophy for living which will help him see that power and security techniques between himself and his workers are defeating his purpose.

AUTHORITY AS POWER

It is probable that the blame-praise technique, and all that goes with it, stems from certain management attitudes toward authority and responsibility. One of these attitudes is that authority evolves from positions on an organization chart. But real authority evolves from competence; and competence, in turn, from tested experience.

In the industrial period which preceded mass production, the supervisor, who through continuing experience with a total operation inevitably knew every detail of that operation instead of one unit of it, was perforce an authority. Actually, today, the supervisor is not an authority unless he proves his competence.

Yet management always introduces the worker to his supervisor instead of to his work—to the man to whom he is responsible rather than to the work for which he is responsible—and thus fixes the mind of the worker on an authority figure.

The difficulty here is that the word "authority" has in industrial usage connoted power. The mind of the worker is fixed on the supervisor as a power, on the next highest supervisor as a higher power, and so on up to the president as the highest power. We have already seen what the worker's attitude toward a power or authority figure does to his initiative and productivity.

Unfortunately, management has this same attitude toward authority, fixing upon itself the power to demand or to praise and blame, to indulge, protect, deprive, or discipline the worker, just as the father indulges or protects or disciplines the child according to his own judgment of what the child should be, rather than trying to find out what kind of person the child really is and developing his potentialities.

Protection of nonproductive employee

The attitude of holding the power or of being the father is clearly revealed in management's techniques with the nonproductive employee. If such an employee has influence, he is removed from the scene of actual production, given a title and salary commensurate with the quality of the influence; or he is left on the scene and given a strong assistant to carry out his own responsibilities. If he does not have influence, he is labeled a nuisance, a dummy, a troublemaker, or a problem employee; is left to his own resources until, from sheer frustration, he does make trouble; and then is transferred along with his label to another department, where he is again left to his own devices by an alerted supervisor who is already skilled in the art of avoiding trouble.

Some companies take pride in the 30-, 60-, 90-day follow-up program for new employees. Unfortunately, "follow-up" is usually all that it is. It is not a scientific analysis of the potentialities of the investment which the company and the worker are making in each other. It is not a study to determine whether there is a compatibility between what the worker can offer the company and what the company can offer him. It is not an inquiry into the adjustment of the worker to his job environment.

It is possible that management has a guilt conscience about the nonproductive employee, since the worker, if he is considered eligible for hire, can hardly have brought with him all the elements incidental to his failure to develop. As a matter of fact, experiments indicate that many workers considered hopelessly nonproductive by one supervisor have been fully developed by another.

The need, here, is for management's recognition that it is unfair to any individual to maintain him on a payroll unless he makes a contribution commensurate with his level of development. The only fair and protective policy is one which gives the nonproductive worker an opportunity to work elsewhere, in a different environment. Once it is determined that he has been given all the assistance the company can give him, it is better to discharge him than to submit and expose him to the indignities of nonrecognition and nonappreciation. That the discharge should take place before the worker has established his union membership is obvious; it is equally obvious that the worker should fully understand that he is not a failure.

This protection of nonproductivity can apply to employees in the executive ranks as well as to those at the bench or behind the counter. Consider the case of an executive, with his company for 17 years, who had a health problem:

> His physician had warned him that he must cut down his working hours or be prepared for a long illness. But he said that he could not cut his hours because he was doing his own work as an assistant plus the work of his division head, who had influence with the board of directors.
>
> "Have you talked with the division head about this situation?"
> "Well, no. Joe is a friend of mine. I don't want to hurt him."
> "But you are hurting yourself."
> "Yes, and I am also hurting my family, but—well, everybody knows about Joe. It won't do any good to discuss it with him. But the management is going to suffer eventually because I cannot keep this up."
> "Then you had better talk this over with Joe, in view of the fact that Joe knows you are doing his work, telling him that you cannot keep it up any longer."
> "I don't want to get anybody into trouble." (It is clear that the assistant wants his problem solved but does not want to solve it himself lest he himself get into trouble.)
> After a further long discussion, revealing that the assistant resents his good friend Joe whose influence with the board of directors is such that he need not make a contribution commensurate with his position: "Joe never did a stroke of real work in this place in his life."
> "You have some resentment against that, don't you?"
> "You bet I do. It isn't fair. My wife says I'm hard to live with; I'm grouchy; I'm so tired I am not a companion to her. We never go out any more. It's got me nearly crazy." (We begin to perceive that the worker's real problem is not the warning of the physician but the unpleasant relationships at home, and that his visit to the interviewer

was the result of an unconscious desire to express his hostility toward the division head rather than to discuss his long hours.)

Finally, at the end of the interview, "Well, I feel a little better about the whole thing; I'll try it a while longer."

Talking about the situation merely relieved the assistant's tensions. He remains a victim of management's policy toward the nonproductive worker and of his own fears.

But think, too, of what the employment record of Joe, the division head, might have been had the management had the courage to face the influential member on the board of directors with the facts, and had it separated Joe so that he could produce elsewhere instead of retaining him as a protected and patronized employee.

All the human rights are violated in Joe's case. He is permitted to receive a salary which he does not earn; he is referred to as "poor old Joe," "everybody knows about Joe"; he lives a parasitic life. He fulfills no purposes; he is the object of pity or contempt or resentment according to his co-workers' personal experiences with him. Even if Joe wanted to escape, he would not know how to do so, for his personal resources have atrophied from disuse. The management has solved all of Joe's problems except the most important problem of his existence—how to fulfill the purpose for which he was given life.

Managements which protect the nonproductive employee frequently use the union as a scapegoat for this failure to feet the situation. But good union leaders are the first to ask that management meet its obligation to utilize workers. The files of shop stewards are full of problem situations which come to their attention too late, solely because the management through its supervision has failed to meet the issues created in the situation. The procedure of discharge is an early obligation of management—not a late solution to a problem situation.

It is not going to be easy to convince workers, let alone executives, that in their own and the management's interests the management expects the fullest possible productivity. The workers are not yet aware of life's over-all purpose. They are aware of frustrations, tensions, vague and indefinable aches and pains, desires to escape, and invention of excuses for absenteeism and tardiness; but that any of these symptoms has its cause in their fear of self-expression and their need for self-realization is as yet beyond their full understanding. Furthermore, they have only their past experience with which to regard a new situation; they have seen nonproductive workers rise to high places; they believe that influence results in attainment, and they believe that the influence comes from "on high."

Consider the case of 110 workers who in an interviewing session made repeated references to a man who was bitterly resented by his co-workers:

In view of the fact that the interviewing was nondirective and that employees are always wary of naming names, the identity of this person did not appear for some time. Finally, the individual was named by an employee, who said: "Corney threw a book at me today."

A list of Corney's derelictions then emerged, including having beer with his lunches and returning to the office intoxicated, throwing anything at hand, sassing customers, refusing to answer the telephone, and calling people names. The only sin he had not committed was the sin of having favorites.

Yet Corney himself was a favorite, it appeared. Corney had influence. Some said the influence was Corney's uncle, but the identity of the influence remained a mystery.

"If it was any of the rest of us," said one individual angrily, "we would lose our jobs like this," snapping his fingers.

At the end of the interviewing program it was evident that the hostility toward Corney seriously interfered with production. Corney's immediate supervisor admitted that Corney was a problem, and he occasionally had too many beers. "But he is never really intoxicated; he is only slightly under the weather." The supervisor talked warily about Corney. He too was afraid of Corney's influence.

Corney's supervisor's supervisor said he knew all about Corney. "It's disgraceful, but nobody can do anything about it. He has been reported to the personnel department, but nothing happens."

The personnel department stated that Corney had been with the company for 22 years, that he had always been fond of beer with his lunches, had thrown books, bottles, anything at hand, and that he browbeat the girls. But before lunch and after the beer wore off, Corney was fine. The personnel department had a feeling that the division head did not want to come to grips with the problem of Corney.

The woman who was the division head said: "I could cheerfully wring his neck. He has a great deal of ability, but he does as he pleases because Mr. X is his uncle by marriage." She felt sure that Mr. X, who was vice president of the organization, would understand the situation. She said she would not mind at all if the matter were discussed with Mr. X.

Mr. X listened. "This is not a gag?" he asked. Assured it was a very serious interference with production, he promised to investigate the matter.

Investigation revealed that Corney's wife knew the uncle of Mr. X, and Corney had cannily let that be known. Finding that he was accorded new respect, Corney moved his story up a notch. His wife was the niece of Mr. X by marriage. Eventually, Corney himself became the nephew of Mr. X; Mr. X became Corney's lawful protector; and Corney became cock of the walk for 15 years.

When Corney was asked whether he knew Mr. X, he said solemnly, "Never spoke two words to him in my life." He knew that his long holiday was over. He substituted soft drinks for beer and upon return from lunch behaved with commendable decorum. The young lady who was tired of being Corney's target visited the interviewing office to say,

"Considering the way he was before, he is an angel now. It's like a miracle."

Indeed, it *was* a miracle—that an entire group of workers and supervisors could harbor resentment for 15 years which had never reached the ears of management because the workers were accustomed to seeing nonproductive members protected.

Fixing responsibility

A concomitant to management's attitude that authority evolves from persons because of their position on an organization chart is the attitude that responsibility for a total operation can be fixed at a certain level. The desirability of fixing responsibility as such is not disputed here. On the contrary, there are situations where specific responsibility can—and if it can, should be—pinned down to specific individuals. But there are also plenty of situations which, more than is often realized, pose the problem of collective responsibility. It is not practical to fix responsibility for a total operation at any level on an organization chart because no single official can obtain all the facts pertinent to all the details of his operation at any one time, nor can he function at all the levels of experience for which he holds responsibility.

It is at this point that it becomes vitally important to think in terms of functions rather than positions. The function of a merchandise manager in a department store, for example, is to manage a division; he holds the buyer responsible for assuring that the right merchandise is made available at the right price and at the right time in his division. But the buyer cannot be held responsible if the merchandise is not checked in and marked in time to go on sale. That is the function of the supervisor in charge of the receiving room. Neither can the buyer be held wholly responsible if the merchandise does not sell. The salesperson may not believe in the commodity value of the item and may not try to sell it; the salesperson may be unskilled in selling techniques. Training the salesperson is the function of the training department. We may say, then, that while responsibility for a function may be fixed at a certain level, responsibility for the operation is a collective matter.

It is obvious that since the individual supervisor fears the implications of responsibility because of the management's attitude toward trouble, it will be difficult to develop the attitudes which are requisite for a recognition of joint or collective responsibility. This is an attainable goal, however, provided management is willing to alter its attitude toward problem and conflict.

Constructive Integration

Just as management sees authority and responsibility in individual persons, management also sees trouble and conflict as the failure of an individual person rather than as the evolution of a situation. Conflict should provide stimulation for thought and a solid foundation for the solution of new problems; it usually provides uncomfortable relationships for everyone involved. Conflict should be the basis of integration; it is usually the source of disintegration.

Getting all the facts

Mary Parker Follett, whose lectures on business administration were as significant in the early part of the century as is the Johnson report at this time, said that there are three ways to treat conflict. The first is to dominate it; the second, to arrive at compromise; and the third, to integrate all the facts in order to discover the law of the situation. In her own words she used these "progressive differings" as a measure of success. But she emphasized that it is not possible to integrate conflict unless all the facts are brought out into the open.

Management's attitude toward trouble and conflict, then, must be altered from a praise-blame concept of control to a situational concept. Management must convince the workers that it welcomes a free exchange of ideas and experience. Actually, management must convince the workers that it desires free criticism whether or not management members are involved in this exchange of ideas. This is the first essential alteration in the worker's environment. He must believe that there will be no reprisals if he says what he really thinks and feels about a situation in which he is a participant. He must believe that management welcomes his experience as a contribution to administrative solutions.

The skills needed for integration of conflict evolve from concepts which psychologists call the doctrine of the wholes. Dr. Harold Lasswell, in his book, *Power and Personality*,[1] uses the phrase "contextual principle" for this concept—the principle that the detail has meaning only in relation to the whole of which it is a part.

The integrating process is to see all the points of view of the situation, to make available all the facts, to take time for all the ideas instead of only the ideas of the dominating personality, and to see the long-term needs of the organization as well as the immediate desires of the participating members. The skill, in short, is to refrain from

[1] London, Chapman & Hall, 1949.

taking sides until all the cards are on the table, and the total situation is recognized.

The vice president of an organization who summoned a meeting of his management associates for a discussion on changing the name of the company, and then sent word he was called out of town but was against the idea, is not "integration conscious."

While the ability to compromise should be part of our learning, since our daily lives are constantly demanding some compromise of us, to compromise when there are several points of view means that one or two sides give in and feel cheated because they have relinquished dearly held views. Furthermore, when there is a compromise, the solution rarely endures; whenever a similar situation arises, the same points of view are broached and fought for all over again.

However, even compromise is not possible if each side is determined to dominate the situation, without tolerance of what might be gained by integrating ideas. If groups are summoned for a discussion of mutual purpose, and one group arrives at the meeting with a determination to hold to the point of view that there can be no mutual purpose because management works for profits and workers for wages, and not to listen to any other viewpoint, there is no way to integrate the conflict; the discussion is a waste of time; the solution will be arrived at through domination on the part of the most powerful group.

Free expression

When, however, all members of the group have real freedom of expression (which includes honest listening to what others may express), viewpoints invariably alter in the light of the total experience presented, and the conflict can be integrated. What appear at first to be either-or situations, or all-or-nothing viewpoints, emerge as viewpoints which were colored by ignorance or misinterpretation of facts. Sometimes, of course, it is not possible to convince the participants that the decision is not already weighted by power. One member of top management who sincerely tried to introduce the integration process found that in his presence certain members would not express their views. It was not until he used a few choice words which are unacceptable in polite society to convince the members that he would not stand for their "pussyfooting" that the members really believed their president wanted their ideas whether or not they coincided with his own.

There is always a degree of emotional involvement in any conflict, but the tensions which involvement creates are considerably relieved once the viewpoints of everyone have been freely stated. Consider the case of what happened as the result of a 60-day leave of absence of a division head in a sales corporation:

> The company appointed a young man, new to the division, as a temporary head during the regular executive's absence. Only two weeks had passed before it was evident that the young man had unusual skills in developing cooperative relationships. The comptroller, who was responsible for the operation of the division, found that there was none of the usual loitering of young women and men in the hallways, none of the usual chatter among the women at their desks. Certain details of the operation which were usually behind schedule were now on time.
>
> The absent executive had considerable prestige with the company because of his relationship to one of the company's largest stockholders. The comptroller was aware of this when, sometime before the 60 days were over, he visited the manager to suggest that the temporary head be left in the position. The general manager said he appreciated the situation, "but there would be too much to explain and too many people to explain it to."
>
> The situation continued to improve, until by the time the absentee was due to return the comptroller was determined that he could not be so unfair to the workers and the company as to permit a return to the old laissez-faire routine. Several days after the absentee returned, the comptroller asked him if he had noted any change. The executive said that he had not. Then the comptroller told him frankly what had happened, hoping that the response of the executive to his own sincerity would be equally sincere.
>
> The result of this conflict was that at the executive's suggestion a meeting of the three division supervisors, himself, and the comptroller was held, with the executive opening the discussion: "There have been some changes during my absence which I think are good. I want to know how they came about and how we can continue this kind of progress."
>
> One of the supervisors said that there was a change in order-checking procedure: "It came about when we explained our method to the man who took over in your absence."
>
> The executive wanted to know if that was the only change.
>
> "You might as well know, since you asked," responded a woman supervisor, "that Mr. Y upheld us when we attempted to keep the women at their desks. Whenever we correct them, they run to you for sympathy, and frankly they usually get it. I know that you do not realize it makes our job that much harder. If you feel that we discipline the women too strictly, then you should tell us, not let them feel that you sympathize with them against us."

This is integration of an unusual order. As Miss Follett has stated, its success depends on getting all the facts into the open.

Use of conferences

Once working groups are convinced that management believes in the integration process as a tool of development, there are unlimited uses to which it can be put. The conference of an integrating nature is particularly useful in the settlement of personal disputes between supervisors and workers or between groups of workers. Consider the case of the supervisor of a selling department who discovered that the sales record for a period of 30 days for the entire department had fallen seriously below standard:

> On investigation he learned that a quarrel between two of the saleswomen was the cause of his difficulty. The 12 women in the department had taken sides, and having done so were instigating little quarrels of their own which became so intense that on one occasion the opinion of a customer was solicited by a young woman trying to prove her point.

> The supervisor had never held conferences of an integration nature, but he felt that nothing he could do could make the situation any worse than it already was. He arranged a dinner meeting in a private dining room. Observing that throughout the meal the affability was entirely too contrived, he waited calmly until the cigarettes were lighted after dessert before he broached the subject of the original quarrel.

> "At the end of two hours," as he described it, "I was exhausted, but they were going strong. Everything that was antagonistic had been aired; they seemed to forget that I was there although I assure you I was. I merely injected a word or two when the conversation got a little too rough. Finally, one of the girls said, 'What on earth started the whole thing?' They all began to laugh, and the meeting broke up with the former antagonists deciding to go elsewhere and have a drink to cement their renewed friendship. The girls thanked me for 'everything,' as one of them put it. But they have no idea what I owe them. I discovered that before the meeting began, I had unconsciously taken sides myself. As I listened, I knew that it was impossible to fix the blame on any of them. I will never take sides in my own mind again."

It is a little difficult to expect anyone not to take sides; we all unconsciously do so. Only the person who has no convictions at all refrains from doing so. The skill is to withhold judgment until all the facts are presented—and then, if necessary, to use intelligent pressure. As a matter of fact, *intelligent* pressure can be applied only when the situation or the supervision process is integrated. This is obviously the opposite of the negative solution of the supervisor about whom a worker said, when asked the reason for his ecstatic love of his boss, "He leaves me alone."

Once the organization is integration conscious, management will regard complaints in the spirit of, "What happened?" and "How can we prevent its happening again?" instead of, "Who is to blame?" Supervisors will consider, "What errors in judgment did I make?" and "What can I learn from this situation?" instead of, "How can I protect myself from blame?"

MANAGEMENT SELF-ANALYSIS

Management's success in convincing workers of its sincere intent to promote the free exchange of ideas and criticisms is dependent largely upon the degree to which management members will be willing to analyze and alter their own attitudes and behavior.

It is difficult for a top-management man to realize that the interacting pattern of influences in his company's environment begins with his own attitudes and relationships. He has forgotten the mental discomforts he experienced as a worker—what it feels like to be on the other side of the desk, to be publicly reprimanded, or to be humiliated. He has forgotten how many times he closed his lips over the words which crowded to be uttered, how many ideas he never spoke because of fear that the boss might think he wanted his job, how often he wished for an uninterrupted session with the boss during which he could say everything that was on his mind. He has forgotten that his own job performance was usually a reflection of the boss's attitude and behavior toward himself, that he was sensitive to every gesture, every tone of voice, every facial expression, and every word the boss uttered.

Part of the management member's lack of awareness of himself in relation to others is explained by the fact that he is seldom if ever confronted with himself, so successful is the conspiracy to keep him uninformed about the way his workers feel toward him. Unless he is habitually self-critical and analytical, he is likely to believe, when his relationships are unsatisfactory, that the other fellow was the one who would not cooperate.

Face-to-face relationships

One of the writers of this article talked before a group of personnel and management representatives, at the 1949 convention of the National Retail Dry Goods Association, on the need for self-expression in business and industry. In the context were seven reasons why workers do not talk frankly with their supervisors. It is significant that the seven reasons, sometimes with the total context, continue to be widely quoted in business and industrial magazines, and the speaker continues to receive letters requesting more information on the "telling the boss" speech.

One explanation of this response may be that all of us have a stereotyped idea of the supervisor-worker relationship, but a more likely explanation is that the seven reasons (and probably others like them) represent an experience to which every worker and supervisor can relate himself:

1. The supervisor does not have time to listen.
2. The boss who takes time to listen frequently does not really listen.
3. The boss often assumes that he knows all the answers because he knows what the answers ought to be.
4. The boss does not know how to encourage free exchange of ideas.
5. The face-to-face relationships which were a major success factor in business 50 years ago are not now adequately provided by the supervisor.
6. Many people who sit behind desks have not learned the facts are hard to get.
7. The employee who tells the boss feels that he is "ratting."

It is also significant that the third and fifth reasons in particular have occasioned comment. The third statement is expanded in the context to the point that management members especially are so remote from the concrete situation that they are unable to perceive the value of concrete experience. "Sometimes the higher level boss is so attached to the book answers that he will not relinquish them," the context proceeds; "this is the common complaint against the college-trained man who has enjoyed the luxury of expounding ideas and theories without ever being forced to make those ideas apply specifically."

For example, the management of a distributing company engaged the services of a warehousing expert at a very high figure, but it was soon experiencing losses much higher than his salary because of resentment against his attitude that he was never wrong. Absenteeism, accidents, careless handling, and illness resulted from his edict that everything in the warehouse was to be palletized despite the workers' protests that it was not practical from a time and space standpoint to palletize certain fast-moving items.

The resentment of the worker toward a supervisor who has had a formal education represents a very real problem in business and industry. Part of the resentment is in the worker's own feeling of inferiority and inadequacy. But a larger part is in the worker's recognition that the supervisor is unwilling to believe that some of his favorite theories do not apply in specific instances.

As for the fifth reason—that the face-to-face relationships which were a major success factor in business 50 years ago are not now adequately provided by the supervisor—judging by the flood of comments from individuals who wrote or spoke of their experiences with executives, here is a problem very "close to home" for many executives. Consider the following selected comments:

A: "He tells me to come into his office, then keeps me standing there for 10 or 20 minutes while he reads the papers on his desk. As if my time were less valuable than his!"

B: "My boss is always taking telephone calls when I am with him to try to get approval for an idea or a change. When I come out of his office, my insides are upside down with nervous tension."

C: "My boss is a nationally famous figure who makes speeches on employee-employer relations, but he doesn't seem to understand that the relations begin with himself. If I had a dollar for every time he uses the first person singular in his office, I would be a millionaire."

D: "A favorite technique of our boss is to call a group meeting, then bawl out those of us who have not pleased him. It is the old dunce cap trick with a new twist."

E: "The man who is my superior is continuously proving to himself that he has the right to hold the power of supervision. Whenever he has to criticize anyone, he waits until he has an audience, then he starts screaming. He is technically an able man, personally a sadist who takes out on all of us his hatred of himself. But he is not aware of any of it."

The woman who made this last comment has an unusual insight into the behavior of her supervisor. She is saying in effect that a man who hates himself hates others. She is also saying that this executive is afraid of himself in relation to individuals. He feels secure only when he has an audience, at which time he begins showing off—just as he showed off before his mother's guests when he was four years old.

Of course there are many executives whose face-to-face relationships with their people call forth responses of appreciation, cooperation, renewed effort, and loyalty to the company. But the nature of the response to the talk before the NRDGA has confirmed our judgment that they are outnumbered by less fortunate executives.

If it is true that the majority of executives, particularly those in top management, do not know how to promote satisfactory face-to-face relationships, what is the reason?

The reasons can be stated in various ways. It may be that the executive does not understand his function; it may be that he fears the responsibilities he has assumed, that he does not value people and so misuses them, that he is afraid he will lose his power, that he needs training—but any of these statements is reducible to this: that he is unaware of himself. If the executive were aware of himself in relation to others, he would make an attempt to alter his behavior.

Altering own behavior

We may ask whether it is possible for a man to become so aware of himself that he will attempt to alter his behavior. It *is* possible, but the success of his efforts is dependent upon the degree to which he is willing and able to look at himself. For even a man who is consciously self-critical is reluctant to give up his cherished ideals about himself.

Furthermore, few of us will attempt to alter our habits unless we are threatened with the possibility of failure or with failure itself. A top-management man who was convinced that he had not succeeded in arousing the interest of his subordinates, facing that kind of failure, set about altering his attitudes. Some executives are not alert to the lack of responsiveness on the part of their subordinates, and even those who are tend to think the lack of interest is hopeless. But this executive underwent the painful necessity of admitting failure, then the tedious and difficult ordeal of analyzing his own deficiencies, and, finally, the education of himself in a language which was new to him. It was on the day he summoned his people to a conference and opened it with the statement, "I have discovered that my methods have been wrong, and I intend to change them," that this man made it known he understood himself and his relationship to his employees.

There are many rating and training programs now offered to management for the development of executives and top men, but it is doubtful if any of these programs can be as effective as the executive's recognition of his own deficiencies and his sincere desire to know and understand himself.

The self-rating procedure which some organizations have installed is seldom effective because of a tendency to rate ourselves as we like to think we are, or as we would really like to be. For example, one management member rated himself and came to the conclusion he was a fine fellow. He is, when everything goes his way, when nobody contradicts him, when nobody talks except himself. He must have the center of the stage. If his associates and subordinates fail to give him the stage, everyone within the radius of his power feels the rage of his frustration. This man rated himself as he would like to be. No one has dared to tell him the kind of man he really is.

Other organizations have adopted preventive programs by way of selection techniques which are designed to screen the emotionally immature personality. But rarely are top executives selected through this procedure. Perhaps it is assumed that when a man gets to the top, his behavior is beyond reproach; perhaps that he will be insulted if his emotional maturity is questioned. A president who hired a top man on the basis of glowing references and then discovered the man had antagonized everyone with whom he came in contact, said, "I just did not have the nerve to send him to our psychologist. I was afraid he would be offended."

Later, in this same situation, the president said he could not understand why the man's references and reputation were of such high caliber. The answer is quite simple: none of this man's associates knew how his people felt toward him. Some executives have fine relationships with subordinates and are antagonistic toward their associates; others have fine relationships with associates and are antagonistic toward subordinates.

Incidentally (yet significantly), the executive who uses destructive methods unconsciously furnishes the organization with a scapegoat. The people who work with him and have had unpleasant experience in the association can always rationalize their failure to be fully productive on the basis of an attitude of, "You can't get anywhere with this guy, so what's the use?" Consider the case of the manager of a small plant who prided himself on his fine relationships:

> This manager was shocked one day to overhear a conversation in which he was described as a "so-and-so." When he told his wife about the incident, he was shocked again. Her response was, "Well you are, sometimes, particularly when people fail to meet your expectations."
> In view of the fact that the manager had always considered himself tolerant, he was unable to accept his wife's confirmation of the worker's statement. Seeking the aid of a counselor, he gradually began to understand the reasons for his intolerance and to change his methods.
> Some months later, feeling he could talk frankly with the worker whose comment he had overheard, he called the man to his office and related the story of his attempts to alter his attitude.
> "Well you see, sir," said the worker, "we have kind of noticed it, but we just don't believe it. We're waiting for you to change back. Somehow, we were more comfortable the other way."
> "You mean it was easier to hate me as a so-and-so than to like me as a good boss?" asked the manager.
> "Well, we could blame an awful lot on you," replied the worker.

Not all workers will respond productively to constructive techniques. Some workers are so emotionally immature that their responses are always negative. Fortunately, in the case just cited, the workers, who had become accustomed to blaming the manager for all their troubles and who therefore had to be educated to the acceptance of his new attitudes and methods, did respond to the change.

Concept of service

We have been using the word "leader" to designate the function of a supervisor or executive in order to nullify the boss-authority-power concept, but even this word "leader" is not adequate for activating the principles in the Johnson report. It cannot be overstated that these principles focus on man's basic needs. These needs are not to follow but *to be*—to be, first, an individual who lives in order to fulfill a purpose and, secondly, a member of a group which works for a common cause.

The Johnson report furnishes a key to a different concept about the executive function when it speaks of a mutual trusteeship between management and labor. The executive who accepts this concept will think of his function as a service to the organization and of his contribution to this service in terms of human relationships as well as technical skills and ability.

CREATING THE ENVIRONMENT

The problem, as posed at the beginning, is how to create an environment that is suited to man's basic needs. The Johnson report lists these needs as: self-esteem, recognition and appreciation, the respect of others, a chance to live, a social life, and assurance of economic security. It further states that concentration on any one of these needs leads to unhappiness and frustration. In the light of the preceding discussion, now, what can we do?

Inadequacy of techniques

In general, employment policies were not built around man's psychological needs until after the First World War, when the French word "personnel" had become part of the industrial vocabulary. The word was introduced to business and industry to cover the field of activities relating to the human personality, and a language was built around the word. Personnel representatives have too often concentrated on the techniques or on the language, without insight, without sufficient research into meanings, without sufficient endeavor to develop for themselves and for the management a philosophy based on the value of people.

From time to time special techniques have been acclaimed as *the* answer and have been absorbed (to an extent depending upon management's attitude about cost), to become fleshless and bloodless functions substituted for real human relations. Some of these techniques are turned into little tricks to keep people happy and productive, or to keep them at a status which management considers desirable.

One personnel director bases his success on the way he manipulates people in what he calls a "we-us" attitude. He says, "Let's all do this together"; even takes off his coat to make the idea realistic; but he has no intention of helping to do the job. Another director says, "I listen to everything they say and let them think I believe it." This attitude is commendable if he means he has no right to judge the truth or falsity or sincerity of statements without proof of intent to deceive, but his next remark indicates that his devices with people are designed to protect himself: "That way, I know everything that goes on, so when the big boy sends for me, I have all the answers ready."

Concentration on the language in the personnel field has led sometimes to such devotion to the abstractions that the practitioner in a company organization puts himself in the position of fighting for a personal cause, and indeed of directing his fight against management instead of working with the daily limitations which hinder the total application of the principles he holds so inviolate. This attitude, which is characteristic of too many persons with training in social sciences who work in the industrial and business fields, has led to such overemphasis on psychological needs that top management has really bought the idea, as one member put it, that "there are many things more important to workers than money."

Often, the now well-known Hawthorne experiment [2] is used to prove the value of these psychological needs. But actually it did not prove that money is not important. Nor did it prove that the needs of the individual are the paramount consideration for study, but rather that the relationship of people to each other is the field of inquiry to which the study of the human personality should be directed—not just the outward forms of behavior, but the relation of needs to behavior; not just the needs and drives, but the effects of these needs and drives upon cooperative relationships; not just the parts, but the whole. It would be difficult to analyze the relative importance of any of these human needs to each other or to the job, for they are interdependent just as the physical and biological properties of the human body are interdependent.

One of the reasons why personnel representatives have concentrated on techniques is that the management has been interested in the techniques rather than in a social philosophy or the relation of man's needs to the work environment. The personnel director has felt that he must be what management wants him to be. And yet some management members complain that their attitude of sufferance toward personnel directors is because they "go along, instead of giving guidance."

---

[2] Fritz J. Roethlisberger and W. J. Dickson, *Management and the Worker* (Cambridge: Harvard University Press, 1939).

One member of management said, "If I had my way, we would pay clerks to do the work our personnel director does; a high salaried personnel man or woman is just so much money down the drain." When asked for an explanation, he said, "Well the head of our outfit is a regular so-and-so who has no ideas about people except that they are to do his will; he belongs back in the dark ages. Do you think our personnel director will support us when we try to fight for some enlightenment in our policies and methods? No, he sits back and agrees with the big man. He is a perfect yes-no man."

The person who made this complaint is describing a director who has the same fears that inhibit the worker's courage and self-expression. If he has convictions, he is afraid to utter them lest he suffer disapproval; perhaps he is afraid of losing his job. It is possible, however, that he does not have basic convictions about people and life, and that, realizing the vulnerability of his position, he is afraid to seek outside help and guidance.

Psychosocial viewpoint

The Johnson report approaches human relations from a psychosocial viewpoint—the viewpoint that impulses, tendencies, and wants of biological origin are forces in the life of the individual which are continuously modified and reshaped by experience in interpersonal relationships—and the premise that a philosophy based on the dignity of the human personality is an imperative need if our democratic society is to endure. Within such an approach, personnel administration is inevitably related not only to the social structure in the organization but to the structure of society as a whole. Personnel administration, then, must begin to collaborate with our institutions for a uniform value system on what is socially desirable or undesirable.

It is not possible to utilize the Johnson report unless top management sees the need for such collaboration, for the philosophy based on the value of people must emanate from the top. No matter where a man stands in the hierarchy of the work world, he is first of all a person, then a man with special skills and knowledge. As a person, he has the same conflicts in values and standards which have been described in connection with the worker. And these conflicts manifest themselves in varying attitudes about people.

One management member may believe that people are sheep and parrots who want only to follow and to imitate; another, that people are little boys and girls who would rather not grow up; another, that people want to develop but because of circumstances entirely beyond their control are unable to do so; another, that people want to grow toward emotional maturity and will if given help. If all these members work out their own personality needs through these various concepts about people, the organization is already in a state of emotional chaos. Yet there are many businesses and industries trying to achieve the full productivity of employees by operating within such chaotic circumstances.

The real activation of the Johnson report will occur in the daily contacts between individual supervisors and individual workers. But this does not alter the fact that the personnel administration as such will necessarily have to strike a balance between the pragmatism which meets daily needs and the idealism which struggles against the recognition of practical necessity.

It is not proposed that management can create an environment which satisfies all the human needs, all at one time, for it is this which our contemporary society has been unable to do. To satisfy man's need to be recognized for his individual contribution, and at the same time satisfy his deep need to belong to groups, presents a seeming contradiction. There is a drive to be dominant in all of us, but there is also a need for protection and security which compels submission to authority and the curbing of self-expression; there is a drive to be intensely individualistic and to win as much for onself as possible, but there is also an urge for the recognition and approval of one's groups. The psychosocial scientists will say that man becomes a real person only as he begins to perceive his own self, and that perception of self emerges through the interpersonal relationships which comprise group association, but this is a language not readily translated into the layman's terms.

The problem of creating an environment which will suit these basic needs becomes one of how to develop individual personalities so that the organization will yield its own supervisors and executives and, concomitantly, of how to achieve the cooperative relationships which are essential for the accomplishment of interdependent function. Moreover, these goals must be met at the same time that it is desirable to maintain an equitable operating cost.

As we have already seen, the worker's problem is identical to management's. How does he maintain his individuality as a person, his basic rights and dignities, yet at the same time retain his group status? Confronted with the fact that he was never so variously dependent upon group association as he is today, man nevertheless continues the conscious or unconscious struggle to be independent.

Encouraging development

A further problem of management is that there are forces at work which influence the individual toward dependency and toward regarding those who speak of self-reliance with suspicion. And yet, if we look realistically at the industrial scene, we perceive that management can contribute only so much to the worker's development; the worker must be taught to contribute the remainder. Management can provide an environment which promotes growth and development, but only the worker can utilize that environment. Management can provide the opportunity for experience, but the worker must use the experience for his own progress.

For example, of two clerk typists who entered a hospital laboratory, one remained a clerk typist and the other became secretary to the chief technician. The former girl did no more work than was expected of her. The latter not only performed her work, but she volunteered her services to group conferences; she listened to professional conversations between doctors and nurses; she borrowed a medical dictionary. In short, not only did she contribute her individuality to the group performance, but she utilized her experience for development.

It can be said that the latter worker was more ambitious, more skilled in utilizing resources—this is undoubtedly the case—but the point here is that the laboratory management did provide the experience. As the girl herself says, "They have been wonderful to me; nobody ever got cross or impatient when I asked questions, and, believe me, I was really a nuisance. Everybody seemed eager to help me."

It can also be said that the latter worker had a stronger drive toward independence than the former, but, again, the point is that her job environment stimulated rather than stultified her initiative and energy.

Management has attempted to combat the influences toward dependency with communication and education programs designed to convince the worker, in essence, that the principles of individuation on which the capitalistic system is based are those which best suit his needs. Good enough, but such programs must guard against ignoring the psychological principle of stimulus and response. It is dangerous to undertake education and communication programs to sell capitalism unless the worker sees the facts which are communicated to him demonstrated in his own job experience. The worker will not absorb and believe just facts. He responds to those facts with his experience.

And he responds to the current educational programs with more distrust and suspicion than is already part of his attitude unless capitalism is made realistic to him and his family.

The real danger here is that management may, without realizing it, attempt to treat the symptoms without diagnosing the disease. In that event, the technique becomes one of administering sugar pills and pain killer in the hope that the operation need not be performed. If the program is handled carefully, on the other hand, the worker can be helped to see that the capitalistic system means something he can understand and experience; and as soon as that happens, he will accept it as the system in which he is most secure.

And it will mean something to him when he perceives that the only valid fear is the fear of not utilizing and developing his resources; when he is unafraid to express his opinions and to tell the truth when asked for facts; when he feels free to apply for a position in another department knowing that his supervisor not only welcomes his developmental activity but welcomes the opportunity to give new people training; when he sees cooperation as it is—a form of mutual aid.

The program for education which should be undertaken is one which helps the worker understand himself in relation to others, helps him recognize that he is happier and more productive when he is free to test and to find his own solutions. This kind of program conditions him for living effectively as a person not only on his job but in all of his activity.

Group participation

In order that group status may be assured, management must give the worker maximum opportunity through officially recognized group participation to express his personality. Cooperation in the sense of working toward a mutual goal, for self-advancement, for protection, is an active social process which is not yet a force in industrial life. Workers form groups, but these groups become exclusive and antagonistic; because of their homogeneity they exclude rather than aid the expression of individual opinion. Moreover, such groups become overorganized and thus nullify cooperation, as when there are too many committees, or when workers lunch together so frequently that they become bored with each other and can think of nothing to discuss except their problems.

The goal here is to develop group cooperation through which workers may pool their knowledge, develop strength as they hear their opinions voiced and begin to express themselves, give each other courage, satisfy their need for the esteem of others, promote enthusiasm and sound morale—and eventually group efficiency.

As the worker begins to participate in group activity, he realizes that management must set up an authority structure for conformity to certain standards without which the group cannot function satisfactorily, just as he has learned to accept standards without which civic groups cannot survive—standards of attendance, punctuality, safety regulations, responsibility for function, codes of conduct toward co-workers. In order to conform for the protection of the group, he must yield certain of his individual preferences, but he retains the right to self-expression, to live without fear of displeasing the boss, to ask questions, to challenge opinion. The experience of belonging to his group widens his horizons and alters his viewpoint. This is shown by the case of a young woman who had been six months on her first position as a supervisor:

> Because her family, educational, and religious life had developed within her a deep sense of values, she became seriously disturbed when she realized that she was absorbing certain ideas which her associates expressed in daily communication.
>
> At a division meeting, when asked by the head whether she had read certain source material, she replied that she had not had time to do so.
>
> At the close of the meeting, one of the supervisors said: "Don't ever tell him you have not read the material; it's one of his pet projects; he wasted a lot of money on that stuff, so we all let him think we read it. That is just good politics."
>
> The idea bothered her. "It isn't fair to lie to that old man," she said later, "and if I have to play politics in order to hold my job, I had better get out of here. It's vile. I hate liars."
>
> (Something unusual is happening to this young woman. No one has ever challenged her standards before, and she is reacting bitterly to people who do not believe and act as she thinks they should believe and act. Yet without this group experience, she would never have known the need to understand her rigid determination to mold individuals to her own liking and to judge their behavior.)
>
> She was asked to try an experiment. The next time she met the group, she was to express her opinions about their behavior toward the division head, without anger or judgment. As was to be expected, she found that others agreed with her but lacked the courage to say so individually.

Managements look with skepticism on group methods which integrate conflict and utilize maximum participation because they are a departure from custom. The president of an organization said, "Do you mean to tell me a stock boy can help me manage my business?" It is certainly not impossible that the stock boy could give the president some ideas, but the president is thinking of the stock boy sitting on the board of directors. This is not intended, and anyway the stock boy would be extremely uncomfortable. But a visit with the stock boy and some of his fellow workers for an exchange of opinions and experience would give the president some idea of how to manage the stock boys.

A simple application of group procedures in operating policy was used by an executive who had received frequent complaints about voluntary collection taking within departments:

> Collections were taken for engagement parties, wedding gifts, new babies, birthdays, anniversaries, families in financial distress, funerals, Christmas gifts to janitors and maids, bosses and co-workers, departure gifts, even something for individuals who had lost their pay envelopes. (One worker, when asked why she liked her job so much, replied, "Every time I lose my pocketbook, they take up a collection.")
>
> Not only were the collections unorganized and unsupervised, but anybody who desired to initiate a collection taking could do so. It took a courageous soul to ignore the collection basket—the ingenious collector saying casually, "We'll take anything you care to give," but carefully displaying a dollar bill on top of the pile—and there were quite a few who, lacking the courage to refuse but wanting to, went to the management for aid.
>
> The management resented this drain on employee income as much as the workers did. Instead of issuing an arbitrary policy, a top executive summoned a group of worker representatives for discussion, explaining that the management wanted to work out a policy which integrated everyone's viewpoint.
>
> The workers were at first reluctant to voice their opinions, but the chairman said, "We know that a discussion of this question is embarrassing because there is always a fear of being thought to be stingy, but we also know that it is a very real problem with many of you who have large families or only yourselves to depend upon. Large families require a lot of money these days."
>
> "That is just it," said one worker impulsively, and with her words the tension was broken. When the discussion was concluded, the members had decided to limit the occasions for which collections could be taken and to limit the amount which could be collected from one person at any one time. The workers retained the privilege of giving individual Christmas gifts and the management the privilege of discouraging gifts to bosses.
>
> The announced policy contained a paragraph that it had been written by workers' representatives in collaboration with the management. Had an arbitrary policy been issued, all that would have been needed to set hostile reactions in motion would be for one disappointed collector to say, "Who do they think they are, telling us what to do with our money?"

Here, in this case, is the essential difference between a dictatorial method of control and a participating method which utilizes the worker's individuality through the group's collective responsibility.

PRACTICAL IDEALISM

It may seem that the goals set here are impractical, that we seek through the realization of eternal virtues to establish a morality which has been struggling for acceptance and utilization in daily living for thousands of years, and that this same idea of morality is incompatible with the materialistic concepts in our civilization.

This may be felt especially by the management member whose thinking is largely influenced by the figures which represent cost and profit. But these same members are vaguely aware that something is wrong and that the tangible solutions have failed. Their difficulty is not that they are cost conscious—that is their responsibility—but rather that they are not sufficiently loss conscious. The losses in failure to develop the personal resources in industry and business are not inscribed on the ledger; they are in a large shadowy area which must be penetrated by creative thought.

The capacity for thinking creatively and for articulating creative thought is perhaps the ultimate development of man. We do not think creatively except in special spheres, when there is a special problem demanding immediate solution, and then the thinking is often in the form of the least resistance to new thought. Progress will be in the freeing of man's mind so that he will actually utilize known thought for thought about the unknown.

There is no real incompatibility between the *idea of making profits* and the *ideal* of the Johnson report. The report can and should be used within the framework of the profit motive, for the mutual purpose of management and labor is to establish organized relationships based on the democratic principle of faith in a man's personal worth, dignity, and potentialities. Only those who base their calculations *solely* on profit making, and their number is few rather than many, or those whose personal frustrations are such that they feel they must stem the tide of progress will be antagonistic to such mutual purpose.

Understanding between these two groups will be defined when the freeing of man's mind and personality for daily living and fulfillment is an accomplished fact rather than an unaccomplished abstraction. The continuance of our present form of government may depend upon the solidarities which can grow out of the working together for mutual purpose, for this is not only the purpose of labor and management—to make democracy a concrete reality—but it is also the purpose of the community, the state, and the nation.

Contemplation of the ground to be covered to achieve understanding is discouraging only when we are unable to keep our minds on the ultimate goal. There are ideas and ideals in profusion to be put to work, but we cannot expect that these ideas and ideals will function wholly; we must be patient as they function gradually, and thankful that they function partially toward accomplishment of mutual purpose.

There is much to be learned, much that is unknown, but there is also much that is known which can be applied within the daily limitations of the industrial scene. Skeptical as some managements may be of the contribution of social sciences to business and industry, we can no longer deny our need for their help. But that does not mean that we must turn the organization upside down to begin utilizing the whole man, or to find a sympathy between what the man is fit for and what the job can offer him, or to regard the whole field of behavior in the light of conscious and unconscious processes affecting relationships all at once. We would be unwise to make any but a simple beginning.

We can re-evaluate our supervision concept as having to do with job performance instead of having authority over people by beginning with one supervisor and his group. We can translate the desire to please the boss into a desire for the pleasure of fulfillment and of conforming to group regulations for our own and the group's benefit; we can begin with one group. We will find it necessary to reorganize the allocation of time, but we can begin with one integration procedure. We must set influences at work which convince workers that management is sincere; one top management member can start by welcoming and participating in free exchange of viewpoints.

What are our basic needs? Primarily to be ourselves, to think for ourselves, to ask questions if we do not understand, to alter our viewpoint in the light of total experience so that we may seize upon all the elements for growth and development, to desire nothing so much as fulfillment, and to dissolve all fears but the fear of unfulfillment, to be loyal to whatever it is within ourseves which makes us keep our agreement with God.

Perhaps the capacity to love, which our industrial selves have forgotten, is what we need and want more than anything else. When we recognize that need, the capacity to love will take on its real meaning. It will be a capacity to have knowledge of, to have understanding of, and to have respect for ourselves and each other.

QUESTIONS

1. Why does the ultimate success of human relations depend on how people are valued?
2. Why are there conflicts in our values of people? What problems and fears arise because of these conflicts? Why?
3. What part do management attitudes play in the tensions that arise as a result of value conflicts?
4. What do the authors mean by "constructive integration"?
5. How can an environment be created that is suited to man's basic needs?

GENERAL QUESTIONS ON PART 9

1. Who is responsible for practicing human relations? Why?
2. What does the successful practice of human relations require of the leader?
3. What part does research play in the practice of human relations?
4. Explain the importance of policy to human relations.
5. List the major factors that make up and influence the work environment.
6. Explain how organization and communication affect the practice of human relations.
7. Discuss how procedures and techniques influence the behavior of people.
8. Cite several examples of poor human relations. What would you do to improve these situations?
9. Can all managers practice human relations successfully?
10. Explain how planning, organizing, coordinating, and controlling are related to the practice of human relations.

BIBLIOGRAPHY FOR PART 9

Articles

CLEETON, G. U. "The New Approach to Employee Discipline," *Personnel*, Vol. 16, No. 4 (May, 1940), pp. 197-206.

FISCHER, F. F., and L. STRONG. "Building an Atmosphere of Acceptance," *Supervisory Management* (February, 1956), pp. 47-50.

HALL, MILTON. "Supervising People—Closing the Gap Between What We Think and What We Do," *Advanced Management*, Vol. 12 (September, 1947), pp. 129-135.

JARRAD, L. E. "Empathy: The Concept and Industrial Applications," *Personnel Psychology* (Summer, 1956), pp. 157-167.

JOINER, FRED H. "Making Employees' Work More Interesting," *Supervisory Management*, Vol. 2, No. 5 (April, 1957), pp. 17-21.

KATZ, ROBERT L. "Human Relations Skills Can Be Sharpened," *Harvard Business Review* (July-August, 1956), pp. 61-72.

NEWMAN, LOUIS E. "Some Philosophies of Management," *Advanced Management*, Vol. 24, No. 2 (February, 1959), pp. 6-8.

ROBIE, E. A. "Are Your Workers Bored with Oversimplified Jobs?," *Management Methods* (August, 1956), pp. 47-50.

SCHMIDT, FRED G. "Induction: Making Those 'First Impressions' Count," *Supervisory Management*, Vol. 2, No. 5 (April, 1957), pp. 29-32.

SMALL, S. M. "How to Motivate Good Work Attendance," *Manage* (August, 1955), pp. 5-11.

TRICKETT, J. M. "Fulfilling Individual Needs in Management Development," *Personnel*, Vol. 33, No. 6 (May, 1957), pp. 520-526.

WASHBURNE, N. F. "Good Leaders Do These Things," *Nation's Business*, Vol. 47, No. 3 (March, 1959), pp. 88-90.

WOLFF, JACK. "How to Use 5 Powerful Motivators That Cost You Nothing," *Management Methods*, Vol. 15, No. 4 (January, 1959), pp. 30-32.

WHYTE, W. H. "Social Science and Industrial Relations: How Management Can Use the Human Relations Specialist," *Personnel* (January, 1951), pp. 258-266.

Books

DAVIS, K. *Human Relations in Business.* New York: McGraw-Hill Book Company, Inc., 1957.

GRECO, M. C. *Group Life.* New York: Philosophical Library, Inc., 1950.

DRUCKER, P. *The Practice of Management.* New York: Harper and Brothers, 1954.

APPLEY, L. A. *Management in Action.* New York: American Management Association, 1956.

WHYTE, W. H. *The Organization Man.* New York: Simon and Schuster, Inc., 1957.

SAMPSON, R. C. *The Staff Role in Management.* New York: Harper and Brothers, 1955.

PART 10. HUMAN RELATIONS IN PERSPECTIVE

Today, the dynamics of American industrial progress are unchallenged throughout the world. Since the Civil War, the tremendous versatility of both men and production processes in adapting to technological changes ceases to be nothing short of unquestioned brilliance. These changing years have also brought forth successive generations of businessmen with differing philosophies of management and human relations.

As one looks back over the years, several distinguishable phases of the human relations movement in industry stand out. The first decade of the twentieth century, for example, showed management in somewhat of a pioneering stage, primarily concerned with developing systems and procedures for improving over-all corporate efficiency and with little attention paid to the human relations aspects of running a business. Principal concentration here focused on matters of finance and investment, and paternalism and "welfare management" were the approaches to personnel problems.

Next, industry entered into what can be termed the "engineering stage." Specialization became the vogue, and small distinction was made between men and machines. Technical innovations were rampant between World Wars I and II. Management concerned itself with costs, with production processes, and with product development. Once again, it was the human side of the enterprise that suffered. However, some progressive companies were beginning to establish personnel departments for dealing with certain aspects of employee relations. Research efforts also were directed along these lines.

But it really was not until the middle 1940's that the human relations movement blossomed out into full force. Paced by the emergence of the personnel function as a major aspect of company organization, this human relations movement has been gaining impetus for the past fifteen to twenty years. We are now beginning to recognize the vital importance of the behavioral sciences and their relation to the business environment. Study after study has delved into worker motivation, human behavior, group dynamics, and so on. Furthermore, increasing numbers of managements have expressed confidence in this human relations movement and the many benefits it has to offer.

THE EMERGING DISCIPLINE

Part 1 made explicit the point that we are using the term "human relations" as a focal point for explaining and discussing a new discipline that is slowly but surely beginning to take form. It is not our contention that such a discipline exists today in the sense that recognition is given to social sciences like economics, psychology, sociology, and so on. However, we do wish to emphasize that the application of these behavioral sciences to the business world has resulted in an increasing amount of both theory and empirical evidence regarding the behavior of industrial man.

As these social and behavioral sciences have developed, their sphere of interest has been greatly broadened. As a result, their penetration into corporations, small and large companies, governmental agencies and bureaus, service organizations, labor unions, and other organizations where human beings interact and whose efforts are directed and controlled by others is being crystallized into definite principles and concepts having a wide range of applicability. Experiments under controlled conditions with real-life working groups are conducted continuously to test the workability and the pragmatic aspects of principles and theories concerning human behavior. The march towards accumulating knowledge about man and his work moves relentlessly forward, never ceasing to uncover new information vital to industrial progress and productivity.

Part 1 also dealt in some detail with the interdisciplinary nature of management. It was explained there that the subject of human motivation is indeed a highly complex one. Furthermore, it was emphasized that a proper understanding of human motivation necessitates a drawing together of all the behavioral sciences. We labeled this as the interdisciplinary approach to the process of management. It is paramount that the student now recognize that a successful understanding and practice of human relations in the workplace is dependent upon the degree to which managers and leaders are able to draw together and apply the principles of these distinct, yet related, behavioral sciences.

It is now the goal of many researchers and academicians to help the manager in his task of better understanding of human behavior with all of its ramifications. Countless members of research efforts are continuously being directed along these lines. Many of our universities and foundations are sponsoring research within the industrial environment, constantly trying to test the hypotheses and the principles of the recognized behavioral sciences. Clearly, this is no simple task; numerous problems confront such efforts. For example, it is not always easy to convince business firms of the worthwhileness and values to be derived from participating in studies of this kind. They are expensive and time consuming, and in all truthfulness their results do not always pay off in monetary terms. Then too, when dealing with the human variable, it is not always possible to prove conclusively our assumptions concerning behavior. Frequently, we must generalize and recognize that prediction—as far as human behavior is involved—is not completely reliable.

But in the final analysis, while this emerging discipline of human relations can offer great aid to the businessman, it cannot replace the human judgment that each and every manager must bring to his job. By combining this judgment, however, with the valuable knowledge that is offered by the behavioral sciences, vast gains are to be reaped by both the manager and the worker. The latter will attain greater job satisfaction and a more complete integration with his work, while the former will find his own effectiveness in his work enhanced appreciably.

The authors also recognize, and fully admit, that as of this writing many challenges remain for developing awareness and appreciation on the part of the many for this new, formalized field of human relations. But the rapid strides made along these lines since the conclusion of World War II, and the ever-growing complexities and problems that continue to arise, make it mandatory that businessmen and leaders of business accord human relations the proper emphasis it deserves. Industrial progress of the future will ultimately depend upon how far industry is willing to go in establishing a community of mutual responsibility between the highest paid executive and the lowest paid production worker. One of the principal objectives of this human relations movement must be this needed integration.

THE CONTROVERSY OVER HUMAN RELATIONS IN INDUSTRY

In Malcolm McNair's article, which follows, the student will obtain a viewpoint strongly oriented towards a negative approach to the human relations function. And McNair does not stand alone here. Other prominent writers and scholars have, of late, been rather critically attacking many human relations teachings and principles.

Their criticisms are very diverse and range from one extreme to the other. McNair, for example, makes the claim that there is today a great overemphasis on the human relations aspects of work. The overtone of his article seems to be that industry has been invaded by the "happiness boys," bringing with them a bag of Freudian tools for achieving their ends. In his own words:

> Undue preoccupation with human relations saps individual responsibility, leads us not to think about the job anymore and about getting it done but only about people and their relations. I contend that discipline has its uses in any organization for accomplishing tasks. And this is especially true of self-discipline. Will power, self-control, and personal responsibility are more than ever important in a world that is in danger of wallowing in self-pity and infantilism.

McNair further claims that current emphasis on human relations training, especially at the college level, is virtually a waste of time; that only mature, seasoned executives can benefit by formal training as such. In retrospect, McNair presents many salient and provocative points, orienting his arguments against group dependency and manipulation, meanwhile stressing the need for strengthening and encouraging individual development and self-reliance.

Other critics have also questioned human relations principles along somewhat similar lines. Some contend that overdependency on human relations techniques breeds mass conformity within an organization, thereby stifling the initiative of creative individuals. They also state that most human relations practices are basically "manipulative" in nature, apparently assuming that people respond to this manipulation without realizing that they are responding to it. Others hold that the majority of human relations principles are not, and never will be, exact in nature; therefore, they feel that we should not rely on them to any great extent.

We could write extensively on these many criticisms of the human relations movement, but time limits us along these lines. Perhaps it is wisest to end this section by stating that anyone in any way connected with the teaching or the application of human relations principles fully admits the many shortcomings and inconsistencies along these lines. But this does not decry or in any way inhibit the tremendous advances that have been made in this area. Certainly a great deal of effort has yet to come forth. Some of our ideas do rest on shaky underpinnings; perhaps in some organizations human relations techniques are utilized to produce mass conformity. But in the final analysis, these are all questions that must be decided and that involve judgments that must be made by individuals directly concerned. It is easy to sit back and criticize, but still another thing to stand up and try to improve. This is the task now facing us—to strive constantly to improve our human weaknesses concerning human understanding.

THE CONTRIBUTIONS OF THE HUMAN RELATIONS MOVEMENT

In the succeeding articles of this part, the student will find excellent summaries of the advances made by human relations research. Donald Schoen, for example, sets forth many tangible benefits that can be realized by business executives with a proper orientation towards human relations. William Foote Whyte, long a recognized pioneer and expert in this area, presents what he terms a progress report on human relations theory and also indicates some of the still unsolved problems to be met. William Knowles, in a detailed and comprehensive article, draws together several of the more basic concepts in this field, including their limitations as well as their practical usefulness, and indicates just how far progress has been made in terms of their worthwhileness and applicability. And lastly, William Machaver illustrates how a successful businessman views the importance of the human relations function.

Underlying all of these articles are some critically important assumptions. One must recognize (1) that a business enterprise is primarily an organization of people; (2) that these people must be *motivated* to perform at peak efficiency; (3) that the objectives of workers and the objectives of the enterprise are not always the same and, indeed, are sometimes directly opposing; and (4) that business policies and procedures designed for achieving objectives have certain effects on people, and that these effects are not always those desired by the policymakers.

Human relations theory and principles, therefore, have developed in part to aid the integration of people with organizations. This body of knowledge attempts to understand human behavior in the workplace and to channel such behavior towards desirable ends, desirable in the sense that both the managed and the manager can realize goal and need satisfaction.

Furthermore, properly understood principles of human behavior can greatly enhance managerial effectiveness. The professional manager of today must assemble vast amounts of knowledge about people, why they are what they are, why they react like they do, to what environment forces they best respond, and so forth. This is no simple task. It demands a tremendous amount of time and effort. And even more basic, it demands a complete and unrelenting appreciation on the part of the manager for his fellow man and for the fact that theirs is a mutual endeavor. Consequently, the application of tested and proven human relations principles can and will bring about greater human understanding, provided that the above conditions are present. People can be motivated to higher and higher performance, human understanding can be broadened, and basic needs can be fulfilled if only both parties—the manager and the worker—will assume more responsibility in their roles as industrial citizens. Much yet remains to be accomplished. However, the road has been smoothed out by the accumulation of a large body of knowledge devoted to man and his work. A great deal of this knowledge has been assembled in the pages of this book for the interested student to read, ponder, and disseminate. And further progress in the management of men will depend heavily on the inquiring mind, on those who are willing to question and to change. Herein lies the great challenge to our industrial future—to find new and better ways to effect a common ground where men at all levels can understand and be understood.

THINKING AHEAD: WHAT PRICE HUMAN RELATIONS? *

Malcolm P. McNair

In 1956 the Inland Steel Company appointed a vice president of human relations. The Inland Steel Company, of course, is big business; but little business is not being neglected, for I note that the McGraw-Hill Book Company, Inc., is publishing a book on *Human Relations in Small Industry*. The Harvard Business School has had a chair of Human Relations since 1950; by now the number of courses in Human Relations in schools and colleges throughout the country has multiplied substantially. Even more marked is the rapid growth of executive development programs, some in schools, some in industry, but almost all of them placing emphasis on human relations.

Doctoral theses increasingly carry such titles as "A Case Study of the Human Aspects of Introducing a New Product into Production," "An Intensive Study of Supervisory Training in Human Relations and Foreman Behavior at Work," "A Case Study of the Administration of Change in the Large Modern Office," and "Emergence of Leadership in Manufacturing Work Groups." And recently the *Harvard Business Review* has reprinted a dozen articles on human relations, under the title "How Successful Executives Handle People, 12 Studies on Communications and Management Skills," which include such intriguing subjects as "Making Human Relations Work," "Barriers and Gateways to Communication," and "The Fateful Process of Mr. A. Talking to Mr. B."

It is obvious that human relations is very much the fashion in business thinking today. And fashions in business thinking are not a novelty; there have been many others. I can well recall that when I first joined the Harvard Business School faculty, the reigning vogue in business thinking was scientific management. Only a few years later, however, the grandiose claims of scientific management were sharply debunked. What was of solid worth remained—but a considerable amount of froth had been blown off the top.

Must we go through the same process—with all its waste and possible damage along the way—to get to what is worthwhile in human relations?

------

* From the *Harvard Business Review*, Vol. 35, No. 2 (March-April, 1957), pp. 15-39. Reprinted with permission.

My quarrel is not with the solid substance of much that is comprehended by the phrase "human relations," but rather with the "cult" or "fad" aspects of human relations, which are assuming so much prominence.

There can be no doubt that people are of absorbing interest to other people. To verify this fact you have only to look at what makes headlines in the newspapers. There is a fascination for most of us in speculating about people and their behavior. So it is not surprising that human relations has assumed so much prominence as a fashionable mode of thinking. But, as with any kind of fashion, it can be carried to the point where people accept it without questioning—and certainly this can be dangerous when we are dealing with such an important segment of man's activity.

Therefore, just because the tide has gone so far, I must make my points in the most emphatic manner possible. Though I feel I have not distorted the picture, I do not care whether businessmen accept my interpretation in full, or even in large part, *so long as they get stirred up to do some critical thinking of their own.*

Before going any further let me try to indicate the things in this area of human relations which are really basic and with which there is no conceivable quarrel. In the first place, there can be no dispute with research in the social sciences, including the behavioral sciences. Obviously such research is highly important to business management and to business education. Business management and education must seek to understand the behavior of people as workers, the behavior of people as members of organizations, and, of course, the behavior of people as consumers. In all these areas we need more and better understanding of human behavior.

Neither is there any dispute in regard to the things that are important for a man's conduct in relation to his fellow men. The foundation is good Christian ethics, respect for the dignity of the individual human being, and integrity of character. On these we should stand fast. Personally I have always liked this paraphrase of what Theodore Roosevelt once said in a commencement address: "On the Ten Commandments and the Sermon on the Mount, uncompromising rigidity; on all else, the widest tolerance." [1] But between acceptance of high moral principles and the exigencies of day-to-day conduct of affairs there can be, with the best intentions, a very wide gap.

---

[1] From the Introduction to *Theodore Roosevelt's America*, edited by Farida Wiley (New York: Devin-Adair Company, 1955), p. xxi.

This is the gap which by better understanding of human motivation we should try to fill.

Also there can be little dispute about the observations on the behavior of people at work which Professor Fritz J. Roethlisberger, the leader of the human relations group at Harvard, summed up half a dozen years ago:

> People at work are not so different from people in other aspects of life. They are not entirely creatures of logic. They have feelings. They like to feel important and to have their work recognized as important. Although they are interested in the size of their pay envelopes, this is not a matter of their first concern. Sometimes they are more interested in having their pay reflect accurately the relatively social importance to them of the different jobs they do. Sometimes even still more important to them than maintenance of socially accepted wage differentials is the way their superiors treat them.
>
> They like to work in an atmosphere of approval. They like to be praised rather than blamed. They do not like to have to admit their mistakes—at least, not publicly. They like to know what is expected of them and where they stand in relation to their boss's expectations. They like to have some warning of the changes that may affect them.
>
> They like to feel independent in their relations to their supervisors. They like to be able to express their feelings to them without being misunderstood. They like to be listened to and have their feelings and points of view taken into account. They like to be consulted about and participate in the actions that will personally affect them. In short, employees, like most people, want to be treated as belonging to and being an integral part of some group.[2]

In other words, "People behave like people." They have feelings. They don't always behave logically. The concept of the economic man can be a dangerous abstraction. Every individual wants to feel important, to have self-esteem, to have "face." Everybody likes to feel that he is "wanted." He likes to have a "sense of belonging." Group influences and group loyalties are important. The desire for psychological "security" is strong. People don't always reveal their feelings in words.

That all these human attitudes have important consequences for management is likewise not open to dispute. It is well accepted in management thinking today that leadership has to be earned, it cannot be conferred; that authority comes from below, not from above; that in any business unit there will be "social" groups which will cut across organization lines; that good communication involves both the willingness to listen and the ability to "get through" but not by shouting.

---

[2] From a speech entitled "The Human Equation in Employee Productivity" before the Personnel Group of the National Retail Dry Goods Association, 1950.

Dean Stanley F. Teele of the Harvard Business School recently made the statement, "As we have learned more and more about a business organization as a social unit, we have become increasingly certain that the executive's skill with people—or the lack of it—is the determining element in his long-range success or failure." [3] Here we are down to the nub of the matter. What is this skill? Can it be taught? Are there dangers in the teaching of it? Is skill an appropriate concept?

Perhaps I can give a clue to the line of thought which I am developing when I say that I am essentially disturbed at the combination of *skill* with *human relations*. For me, "human relations skill" has a cold-blooded connotation of proficiency, technical expertness, calculated effect.

There is no gainsaying the fact that a need long existed in many businesses for a much greater awareness of human relations and that, in some, perhaps in a considerable number, the need still exists. The very avidity with which people prone to fashionable thinking in business have seized on the fad of human relations itself suggests the presence of a considerable guilt complex in the minds of businessmen in regard to their dealings with people. So it is not my intent to argue that there is no need for spreading greater awareness of the human relations point of view among many businessmen. Nevertheless it is my opinion that some very real dangers threaten.

The world's work has to be done, and people have to take responsibility for their own work and their own lives. Too much emphasis on human relations encourages people to feel sorry for themselves, makes it easier for them to slough off responsibility, to find excuses for failure, to act like children. When somebody falls down on a job, or does not behave in accordance with accepted codes, we look into his psychological background for factors that may be used as excuses. In these respects the cult of human relations is but part and parcel of the sloppy sentimentalism characterizing the world today.

Undue preoccupation with human relations saps individual responsibility, leads us not to think about the job any more and about getting it done but only about people and their relations. I contend that discipline has its uses in any organization for accomplishing tasks. And this is especially true of self-discipline. Will power, self-

---

[3] From a speech entitled "The Harvard Business School and the Search for Ultimate Values" at the presentation to the *Harvard Business Review* of a citation from The Laymen's Movement for a Christian World, New York, October 25, 1955.

control, and personal responsibility are more than ever important in a world that is in danger of wallowing in self-pity and infantilism.

Most great advances are made by individuals. Devoting too much effort in business to trying to keep everybody happy results in conformity, in failure to build individuals. It has become the fashion to decry friction, but friction has its uses; without friction there are no sparks, without friction it is possible to go too far in the direction of sweetness and light, harmony, and the avoidance of all irritation. The present-day emphasis on "bringing everybody along" can easily lead to a deadly level of mediocrity.

We can accept the first part of a statement by Peter Drucker: "The success and ultimately the survival of every business, large or small, depends in the last analysis on its ability to develop people. . . . This ability . . . is not measured by any of our conventional yardsticks of economic success; yet it is the final measurement." Drucker, however, goes on to add a further thought, which opens more opportunity for debate. He says, "Increasingly from here on this ability to develop people will have to be systematized by management as a major conscious activity and responsibility." In this concept there is the familiar danger of turning over to a program or a course or an educational director a responsibility that is a peculiarly personal one.

The responsibility for developing people belongs to every executive as an individual. No man is a good executive who is not a good teacher; and if Drucker's recommendation that executive development be "systematized by management as a major conscious activity" is interpreted as meaning that someone trained in the new mode of thinking should be appointed as director of executive development, then the probable outcome will be simply another company program in human relations. While this may be good for some of the executives, no long-run contribution to the development of good people will be made unless the good individuals personally take the responsibility for developing other individuals.

Please do not misunderstand me. I am not talking about old-fashioned rugged individualism or the law of the jungle, and I am not holding up as ideals the robber barons of the nineteenth century, or even some of the vigorous industrialists of the early twentieth century. But I ask you to consider whether some of today's business leaders, well known to all of us—Clarence Randall, Gardiner Symonds, Neil McElroy, Tex Colbert, Earl Puckett, Fred Lazarus, and so on—are not primarily products of a school of friction and competitive striving. We need more men like them, not fewer. It may be appropriate here to cite the recent observations of Dean Teele on "inner serenity" and "divine discontent":

> Any realistic approach to the nature of top business management, and therefore to the problems of selection and development for top business management, makes abundantly clear that the balance between these two [attributes] is perhaps the most important determinant of success in top business management. Let me elaborate.
>
> Psychiatrists, psychologists, and religious advisers join with ordinary lay observers in noting how often human efficiency is greatly reduced by sharp inner conflicts—conflicts which usually center around value judgments. That is to say, conflicts as to basic personal purposes and objectives, as to the values to be sought in life, are far more often the barriers to effective performance than intellectual incapacity or lack of necessary knowledge. The goal then from this point of view is the development of that inner serenity which comes from having struggled with and then resolved the basic questions of purpose and values.
>
> On the other hand, in business as in the world generally, discontent is an element of the greatest importance. Dissatisfaction with onself, with one's performance, is an essential for improvement. So important to the progress of the world is discontent on the part of the relatively few who feel it, that we have come to characterize it as divine discontent. Here . . . the need is for both inner serenity and divine discontent—a need for both in a balance between the two appropriate for the particular individuals.[4]

To keep that important balance of inner serenity and divine discontent in our future business leaders, we need to focus educational and training programs more sharply on the development of individuals than is the fashion today. What is important for the development of the individual? Obviously, many things; but one prime essential is the ability to think, and the nurturing of this ability must be a principal objective of all our educational effort.

In the field of business education this ability to think, to deal with situations, to go to the heart of things, to formulate problems and issues, is not an innate quality. It has to be cultivated, and it requires long and rigorous and often tedious practice in digging out significant facts, in weighing evidence, foreseeing contingencies, developing alternatives, finding the right questions to ask. In all business education, whether at the college or graduate level or at the stage of so-called executive development, we must not omit the insistence on close analysis, on careful reasoning and deduction, on cultivation of the power to differentiate and discriminate.

There is a very real danger that undue preoccupation with human relations can easily give a wrong slant to the whole process of educa-

---

[4] "The Fourth Dimension in Management," an address to the American Management Association, New York, May 25, 1956.

tion for business leadership. For one thing, it tends to give a false concept of the executive job. Dealing with people is eminently important in the day's work of the business executive, but so are the processes of analysis, judgment, and decision making. It takes skill and persistence to dig out facts; it takes judgment and understanding to get at the real issues; it takes perspective and imagination to see the feasible alternatives; it takes logic and intuition to arrive at conclusions; it takes the habit of decision and a sense of timing to develop a plan of action.

On the letterhead of the general policy letters that are sent periodically to the managing directors of all 80-odd stores in the Allied Stores Corporation there is this slogan:

> To LOOK is one thing.
> To SEE what you look at is another.
> To UNDERSTAND what you see is a third.
> To LEARN from what you understand is still something else.
> But to ACT on what you learn is all that really matters, isn't it?

An executive's ability to see, to understand, to learn, and to act comprises much more than skill in human relations.

Awareness of human relations as one aspect of the executive's job is of course essential. But, in my view, *awareness of human relations* and the *conscious effort to practice human relations on other people* are two different things, and I think this is crucial.

As soon as a man consciously undertakes to practice human relations, one of several bad consequences is almost inevitable. Consciously trying to practice human relations is like consciously trying to be a gentleman. If you have to think about it, insincerity creeps in and personal integrity moves out. With some this leads by a short step to the somewhat cynical point of view which students in Administrative Practices courses have described by coining the verb "ad prac," meaning "to manipulate people for one's own ends."

A less deliberate but perhaps even more dangerous consequence may be the development of a yen for managing other people's lives, always, of course, with the most excellent intentions. In the same direction the conscious practice of human relations leads to amateur psychiatry and to the unwarranted invasions of the privacy of individuals.

Hence I am disturbed about the consequences to business management of human relations blown up into pseudoscience—with a special vocabulary and with special practitioners and experts. In fact, to my mind there is something almost sinister about the very term "human relations practitioner," though I am sure that all sincere devotees of human relations would vigorously disclaim any such imputation.

———

For me much of the freshness and the insight which character-ized a great deal of the earlier work in this field—exemplified by the quotation from Professor Roethlisberger which I cited in my intro-ductory statement—has been lost as the effort has progressed to blow human relations up into a science—something to be explored and practiced for its own sake.

I realize that many people in the human relations field—Professor Roethlisberger in particular—are also disturbed about this trend, and about its unintended repercussions. But it was almost inevitable that other people would run away with such a fruitful concept, and set it up as an idol with appropriate rituals of worship (usually called "techniques"). Once you throw yourself into trying to "listen," to "gain intuitive familiarity," to "think in terms of mutually independ-ent relationship," and so on, you can easily forget that there is more to business—and life—than running around plying human relations "skill" to plumb the hidden thoughts of everybody with whom you come in contact, including yourself.

This is the same mistake that some consumer motivation researchers make, as Alfred Politz has pointed out—trying to find out the attitudes, opinions, and preferences in the consumer's mind with-out regard to whether these factors are what determine how he will act in a given buying situation.[5] In his words, the "truth" that such researchers seek—and he always puts the word in quotes—is not only of a lower order than the scientifically established facts of how con-sumers react in real life, but it is also of less use to managers in making marketing decisions.

The whole thing gets a little ridiculous when, as pointed out in another article in this issue, foremen are assumed to have progressed when they have gained in "consideration" at the expense of some-thing called "initiating structure"—yet such was the apparent objec-tive of one company's training program.[6]

———

[5] Science and Truth in Marketing Research," *Harvard Business Review* (January-February, 1957), p. 117.

[6] Kenneth R. Andrews, "Is Management Training Effective? II. Measure-ment, Objectives, and Policy," *Harvard Business Review* (March-April, 1957), p. 63.

From the standpoint of developing really good human relations in a business context, to say nothing of the job of getting the world's work done, the kind of training just described seems to me in grave danger of bogging down in semantics and trivialities and dubious introspection. I am totally unable to associate the *conscious practice of human relations skill* (in the sense of making people happy in spite of themselves or getting them to do something they don't think they want to do) with the *dignity of an individual person created in God's image.*

Apparently this "skill" of the "human relations practitioner" consists to a considerable degree of what is called "listening." The basic importance of the ability to listen is not to be gainsaid; neither is it to be denied that people do not always reveal their inward feelings in words. But in the effort to blow human relations up into a science and develop a technique of communication, some of the enthusiasts have worked up such standard conversational gambits as "This is what I think I hear you saying," or "As I listen, this is what I think you mean."

No doubt there are times when a silent reaction of this kind is appropriate, but if the human relations practitioner makes such phrases part of his conversational repertoire, there are times when these cute remarks may gain him a punch in the nose. Sometimes people damn well mean what they are saying and will rightly regard anything less than a man-to-man recognition of that fact as derogatory to their dignity.

That a group of foremen who were given a course emphasizing human relations and thereafter turned out to be distinctly poorer practitioners than they had been before taking the course, as in the above case, would not, to my mind, be simply an accident. I think it a result that might well be expected nine times out of ten. In other words, the overemphasis on human relations, with all its apparatus of courses, special vocabulary, and so on, tends to create the very problems that human relations deals with. It is a vicious circle. You encourage people to pick at the scabs of their psychic wounds.

In evaluating the place of human relations in business, a recent incident is in point:

> At a luncheon gathering Miss Else Herzberg, the highly successful educational director of a large chain of stores in Great Britain, Marks and Spencer, Ltd., described at some length the personnel management policies of that concern and the high state of employee morale that existed. Throughout her description I was listening for some reference to human relations. I did not hear it, and when she had finished I said, "But, Miss Herzberg, you haven't said anything about human relations."

Immediately she flashed back, "We live it; we don't have to talk about it."

In point also is a recent remark of Earl Puckett, chairman of the board of Allied Stores Corporation, when in discussing a particular management problem he said, "Of course you treat people like people."

And so, although I concede that there is still too little awareness of human relations problems in many business organizations, I think that the present vogue for human relations and for executive development programs which strongly emphasize human relations holds some real dangers because it weakens the sense of responsibility, because it promotes conformity, because it too greatly subordinates the development of individuals, and because it conveys a one-sided concept of the executive job.

I turn now more specifically to the dangers to business education at the college level which seem to me inherent in the present overemphasis upon human relations. Business executives should have as much concern with this part of the subject as teachers—perhaps more, because they must use the young men we turn out; furthermore, they represent the demand of the market and so can have a real influence on what the educators do.

The dangers to the education of young men, in my opinion, are even more serious than the dangers to business executive development programs for mature men. After all, we are well aware that businessmen follow fads, and so fairly soon the human relations cult in business will begin to wane and operations research or something else will become the fashion. Also, as remarked earlier, there is still a substantial need in business for greater awareness of human relations, and more businessmen are sufficiently adult to separate the wheat from the chaff. Thus in advanced management training programs for experienced executives there is no doubt greater justification for courses in Human Relations than there is in collegiate and immediate graduate programs.

From the general educational standpoint perhaps the first question is whether human relations can be taught at all. I do not deny that something can be learned about human relations, but I do maintain that direct emphasis on human relations as subject matter defeats the purpose. When things must come from the heart, the Emily Post approach won't do; and if behavior does not come from the heart, it is phony. Clarence Budington Kelland, that popular writer of light fiction, in a recent *Saturday Evening Post* serial entitled "Counterfeit Cavalier," makes one of his characters say:

A very nice person has to start by being nice inside and have an aptitude for it. . . . They don't have to learn. It comes natural. No trimmings, but spontaneous. . . . If you have to think about it, it is no good.[7]

Good human relations do not lend themselves to anatomical dissection with a scalpel. How do people normally acquire good human relations? Some of course never do. In the case of those who do enjoy success in human relations and at the same time retain their sincerity, the result, I am convinced, is a composite product of breeding, home, church, education, and experience generally, not of formal Human Relations courses.

Hence in my view it is a mistake in formal education to seek to do more than develop an awareness of human relations, preferably as an integral part of other problems. This does not mean, of course, that the results of research in human behavior should not be utilized in the teaching of business administration. Certainly such results should be utilized (with due circumspection to avoid going overboard on theories that are still mostly in the realm of speculation). To take account of human relations in marketing problems and in personnel management problems and in labor relations problems and industrial management problems, and so on, of course makes sense. What I am decrying is the effort to teach human relations as such. Thus, I applaud the training of personnel managers, but I am exceedingly skeptical of training human relations practitioners.

I should like also to venture the personal opinion that human relations in its fairly heavy dependence on Freudian psychology is headed the wrong way. In the long history of mankind, the few centuries, dating perhaps from the Sumerian civilization, during which we have sought to apply an intellectual and moral veneer to man the animal are a very short period indeed as compared with the time that has elapsed since our ancestors first began to walk erect; and it seems to me that a large part of the job of education still must be to toughen and thicken this veneer, not to encourage people to crack it and peel it off, as seems to have been the fashion for much of the last half century. I suspect that modern psychiatry is in a vicious circle, that some of the principal causes of increased mental disease lie in morbid introspection, lack of strong moral convictions, and leisure that we have not yet learned how to use.

I believe that one of these days a newer school of thought in these matters will re-emphasize the importance of will power, self-control,

---

[7] May 26, 1956, p. 24.

and personal responsibility. I can well recall hearing Charles William Eliot, on the occasion of his ninetieth birthday, repeat his famous prescription for a happy life: "Look up, and not down, look forward and not backward, look out and not in."

Our present preoccupation with the emotional and nonlogical aspects of life seems to me in many ways responsible for the prevalent wishful thinking of the American people. As a higher and higher proportion of American youth goes to college, it might be supposed that intelligently realistic ways of looking at things would be on the increase, but the contrary seems to be true. As people we are more prone than ever to let our desires color our thinking. More and more the few people who have the courage to present realistic viewpoints on national and world affairs find that the public will not listen to what it does not wish to hear. Why isn't education bringing us a more intelligent outlook on life?

Can it be that one of the reasons is that education itself has surrendered so far to the ideas that are concerned primarily with the current fashionable interest in the emotional and nonlogical aspects of living? In reviewing Joan Dunn's book, *Why Teachers Can't Teach—A Case History*, E. Victor Milione remarks, "Our educational system has substituted training in life adjustment for education." [8] Obviously there are many analogies between the doctrines of the progressives in education and the overemphasis on human relations. Personally I prefer a more rigorous educational philosophy. I can well recall a remark of A. Lawrence Lowell that "the business of education is making people uncomfortable."

In any event, I think it is the job of education to push for more and not less emphasis on logics and morals in dealing with social problems. The following quotation from C. C. Furnas, chancellor of the University of Buffalo, makes much sense to me:

> We must recognize, of course, that it takes much more than pure intellect to answer social questions. Great problems involving many people are usually handled in an atmosphere of high emotion and the participants often show but little evidence of being rational human beings. But, even though it acts slowly, it is certainly true that intelligence can and does have some influence in shaping mass emotions. It is in this slow modification of mass emotional patterns that the average intelligent person can and should play a continuing role within his own sphere of influence. [9]

How can we do this if we encourage immature minds to regard the nonlogical aspects as the most important? Not that teachers

---

[8] *The Freeman* (March, 1956), p. 59.
[9] Ibid., p. 24.

necessarily intend it this way—though I am sure some have been carried so far—but simply that putting so much explicit emphasis on the emotional and irrational makes the student feel it is all-important. No protestation to the contrary can undo that impression—that perhaps *nonlogical* impression—which is exactly what an understanding of human behavior ought to lead us to expect in the first place.

But perhaps my principal quarrel with the teaching of human relations has to do with timing. Discussion of such problems as what men should learn, and how they should learn it, is probably as old as education itself, but much less attention has been given to the question, "When should men learn?"

The whole modern development of adult education has brought into disrepute the old adage that you can't teach an old dog new tricks. In fact, in the area of business administration it is quite plausible that teaching of certain managerial skills is best accomplished in later years, after men have gained considerable experience in business activities. William H. Whyte, Jr., the author of *Is Anybody Listening?* and *The Organization Man*, in discussing the Alfred P. Sloan Fellowship Program at the Massachusetts Institute of Technology, has this to say:

> But on one point there is considerable agreement: to be valuable, such a course should be taken only when a man has had at least five years' business experience. The broad view can be a very illusory thing. Until a man has known the necessity—the zest—of mastering a specific skill, he may fall prey to the idea that the manager is a sort of neutralist expediter who concerns himself only with abstractions such as human relations and motivation. Those who study these subjects after ten years or so of job experience have already learned the basic importance of doing a piece of work; in the undergraduate business schools, however, the abstractions are instilled in impressionable minds before they are ready to read between the lines and to spot the vast amount of hot air and wishful thinking that is contained in the average business curriculum.[10]

Among those managerial skills the specific teaching of which had better be left to later years is the handling of human relations. Thus I should not only rewrite the old adage in the form, "There are some tricks you can teach only to an old dog," but I should go on to the important corollary, "There are some tricks that you had better not try to teach to young dogs." The dangers in trying to teach human relations as such at the collegiate or immediate graduate level are

---

[10] *Fortune* (June, 1956), p. 248.

substantial. Indeed, by developing courses in human relations for college graduates in their early twenties without previous business experience we are essentially opening Pandora's box.

Such courses lead to a false concept of the executive's job. There is a de-emphasis of analysis, judgment, and decision making. Someone has said that the job of the modern executive is to be intelligently superficial. This statement is true in the sense that when a man reaches an important executive post, he does not have time to go to the bottom of every problem that is presented to him, and he certainly should not undertake himself to do the work of his subordinates. If he does these things, he is a poor executive. But if an executive has not learned at some stage to go to the bottom of problems in one or more particular areas, he will not in the long run be a successful manager.

Human relations expertise is not a substitute for administrative leadership, and there is danger in getting young men to think that business administration consists primarily of a battery of experts in operations research, mathematics, theory of games, and so on, equipped with a Univac and presided over by a smart human relations man. Undoubtedly many of the new techniques are substantial aids to *judgment*, but they do not fully replace that vital quality. One of the great dangers in teaching human relations as such at the collegiate or immediate graduate level is that the student is led to think that he can short-cut the process of becoming an executive.

The study of human relations as such also opens up a wonderful "escape" for the student in many of his other courses. Let's admit it: none of us is too much enamored of hard thinking, and when a student in class is asked to present an analysis of some such problem as buying a piece of equipment, or making a needed part instead of buying it, he frequently is prone to dodge hard thinking about facts in favor of speculation on the probable attitudes of workers toward the introduction of a new machine or new process.

For some students, as for some businessmen, the discussion of human relations aspects of business management problems can even lead to the development of the cynical "ad prac" point of view, which assumes that the chief end of studying human relations is to develop skill in manipulating people; this perhaps is the present-day version of high-pressure selling.

A different but equally dangerous result occurs in the case of the student who becomes so much interested in human relations that he turns himself into an amateur psychiatrist, appraises every problem he encounters in terms of human relations, and either reaches an unhealthy state of introspection or else develops a zeal for making converts to human relations and winds up with a passion for running over people's lives.

The sum of the matter is this. It is not that the human relations concept is wrong; it is simply that we have blown it up too big and have placed too much emphasis on teaching human relations as such at the collegiate and early graduate level. A sound program in business education, in my opinion, will of course envisage research in human behavior; it may, with some possible good results, venture on offering specific courses in Human Relations for mature executives; but for students in their twenties who have not yet become seasoned in practical business activities we should keep away from specific courses in Administrative Practices and Human Relations, while at the same time inculcating an awareness of human relations problems wherever they appropriately appear in other management courses. In other words, let us look closely enough at what we are doing so we can be sure that the gains we make in this area turn out to be *net* gains.

Finally, to express a personal conviction on a somewhat deeper note, I should like to refer again to Dean Teele's comments, cited earlier, on "inner serenity." The attainment of that all-important goal, in my opinion, is not to be sought through the present vogue of interest in human relations. Inner serenity is an individual matter, not a group product. As Cameron Hawley puts it, "A man finds happiness only by walking his own path across the earth." [11]

Let's treat people like people, but let's not make a big production of it.

---

[11] "Walk Your Own Path!" *This Week Magazine* (December 11, 1955).

Questions

1. List and explain McNair's criticisms of human relations teachings and principles.
2. Do you agree with his points of view? Why or why not?
3. What does McNair feel the essential skills of an executive to be?
4. In part McNair defends the human relations movement and in part he severely criticizes it. Explain.
5. Do you think that the point of view prevailing in this article is the one most commonly found in industry? Why or why not?

HUMAN RELATIONS:
BOON OR BOGLE? *

Have business and business education gone overboard in their current interest in "human relations"? Is an interest in human relations to be equated with tender-mindedness, sentimentality, and an unrealistic desire to make everyone happy? Does the concept of "human relations skill" imply cynical manipulation of other people, undue invasions of other people's privacy, an anti-intellectual and amoral concern with the emotional aspects of human behavior? Would we all be better off if we cast aside these newfangled notions of "communication," "participation," "listening," "group dynamics," and "development of social skills" and returned to the fundamental emphasis on "the home," "the church," "the lessons of experience," "self-discipline," and "individual initiative and responsibility" of an earlier day?

Questions like these are being raised with increasing frequency. For example:

> Professor Malcolm P. McNair, in "Thinking Ahead: What Price Human Relations?" is skeptical about human relations training for younger men and believes that the very concept of "human relations skill" is a dangerous one.[1]

> Fortune Editor William H. Whyte, Jr., has written a best-selling book, *The Organization Man*, which argues that our present-day acceptance of "the social ethic" has disturbing implications for the future of our society.[2]

> Dr. Erich Fromm, the distinguished psychoanalyst, in an article, "Man Is Not A Thing," sees human relations leading to a distortion of the basic concepts and practice of democracy.[3]

> Peter F. Drucker, in *The Practice of Management*, argues that the insights of human relations have been essentially negative and discusses the inadequacies of the human relations approach for the job of managing an organization.[4]

What are we to conclude from the arguments of such responsible critics? Does it follow that the field of human relations is outliving its usefulness; that the interests, points of view, findings, and teach-

---

* From the *Harvard Business Review*, Vol. 35, No. 6 (November-December, 1957), pp. 41-47. Reprinted with permission.

[1] *Harvard Business Review* (March-April, 1957), p. 15.
[2] New York, Simon & Schuster, Inc., 1956.
[3] *The Saturday Review* (March 16, 1957), pp. 9-11.
[4] New York, Harper & Brothers, 1954.

ings of human relations specialists are at odds with the practical realities of effective business leadership; that the human relations approach is in conflict with our basic democratic ideals and our concepts of personal morality; that it is a mistake to try to teach executives and would-be executives human relations skills?

Drawing on my own experience—both practical and theoretical, in business and in education—I would like to try to put some of these issues in perspective. Let me tip my hand: my personal conviction is that the field of human relations has important relevance to executive action and business leadership, *provided* one recognizes that leadership, management, and business action involve more than just human relations. I find it hard to see where human relations and generally accepted moral and ethical codes are in conflict, *provided* one specifies what one means by human relations and does not ascribe to human relations itself a body of moral doctrine. I feel that human relations can and should be taught, *provided* one has a realistic understanding of how slow and difficult any real learning must be, and does not assume that human relations has a corner on wisdom.

While I am very definitely *pro* human relations, I am also *pro* "tough-mindedness," "making practical decisions," "self-discipline," "profit consciousness," "high standards of performance," "individual initiative," "creative imagination," "hiring able men," "firing misfits," and, above all, "getting results." What is more, I do not see any conflict between one and the other.

CENTRAL CONCEPTS

Probably one of the important sources of difficulty in talking about human relations is that the term now means so many different things to so many different people that one person's brand of human relations may differ in many respects from another's.

What I refer to here as human relations has its roots in the work done by Elton Mayo, Fritz Roethlisberger, and L. J. Henderson at Harvard University in the 1920's and 1930's. As conceived by this group, human relations is a field of research, teaching, and practice, just as is the field of medicine. While the professors at Harvard did not pretend to be businessmen, or even men of action, they felt that they and the businessman had a kindred interest and a kindred approach. Both theorist and practitioner were interested in the process of getting cooperative action in organized human activity.

Out of careful study of what goes on in actual, concrete situations where organized groups of poeple are trying to achieve a common goal, the human relations specialists felt they could identify *some* of the crucial determinants of effective collaboration, *some* of the reasons why attempts of people to work together end in chaos, confusion, unnecessary friction, and *some* of the roots of many of the disturbing and disruptive aspects of our modern industrial society.

Today interest in research, teaching, and practice in human relations has spread far beyond Harvard. Throughout the United States and the rest of the world, many other research workers, teachers, and people in business have picked up the threads of the work of the Mayo group.[5] While many of these people claim to have gone beyond the concepts and approaches of the original work in human relations, few deny their heritage from the Mayo group.

Executive effectiveness

There are two aspects of the original work in human relations which I think are at its core, so far as businessmen are concerned.

First, there is insistence that the traditional way organizational leaders have viewed their jobs, especially in industry, leaves out some of the major dimensions of the process of collaboration or cooperation. This does not mean that economic forces, technology, and logical action designed to achieve efficiency have little to do with shaping the destiny of an organization. Managers must of course plan, make decisions, apply analytical judgments, worry about costs, productivity, profits, competitive trends, and so forth, and typically are well aware of this fact. How well these jobs are done is what fundamentally determines whether or not a business is able to survive in a competitive economy.

At the same time, however, whether the process of cooperation itself is effective, whether individuals willingly and wholeheartedly work toward the common purposes of a group effort without loss of self-esteem and without giving up their individual identity and personal integrity, depends on much that the traditional ways of thinking about organizations will not explain.

To understand organizational behavior one must recognize that it is a product of human sentiments, nonlogical (but not necessarily illogical) behavior, personal hopes and aspirations, customs, traditions, and so forth. This is more than simply saying that the idiosyncrasies of individual human beings affect how they behave on the job. It is a contention of human relations that it is useful to view

---

[5] For a brief statement of current developments in human relations research, see William Foote Whyte, "Human Relations Theory—A Progress Report," *Harvard Business Review* (September-October, 1956), p. 125.

organizational effort *as a social or sociological process*, and that it is useful to view a group as having an organic structure of its own if one wants to understand why it behaves as it does.

The second fundamental tenet of human relations thinking is the conviction that both men of action and people interested in research in group behavior need to have a different method for observing, understanding, or working with the social process than is applicable to observing, understanding, and working with the technical, economic, or logical aspects of organization. This method the human relations people label "clinical," because it is analogous to the doctor's diagnosis of what happens in the human organism.

The clinical method helps the research student to obtain knowledge about group behavior, to develop simple generalizations to explain what happens, and to identify the kind of behavior which facilitates effective action. The clinical method helps the man of action become more effective. The specialists in human relations believe that if a person in a responsible position is able to supplement his ability to respond logically to the technical, economic, and purposive aspects of leadership with a clinical orientation toward the social process, certain results will occur:

(1) Within the group of which he is a part, cooperative action will be made easier, understanding between people will be improved, unnecessary conflict will be minimized, and useless frustration will be reduced. These of course are all relative matters; they are not keys to Utopia.

(2) The individuals within the group will be better able to serve the group's purposes without losing their personal identity, with a minimum of conflict between their own individual aspirations, goals, needs, or beliefs and the demands of the group itself. The hoped-for result is not conformity, but individual integrity—not happiness, but the right to work out one's own salvation.

These, I believe, are the essential elements of human relations: an insistence on the necessity for viewing concrete organizational situations not only in technical and economic but also in social terms, a conviction that you can understand the social process of group behavior only if you are committed to relating yourself to it with a clinical viewpoint, a fundamental belief that the person charged with the responsibility of getting action in group situations both facilitates cooperation and helps people maintain their own integrity if he is able to orient himself clinically to such situations.

Central to such a set of tenets, therefore, is the concept of a clinical orientation. Before we can ask, "Is all this valid, relevant, useful for the business leader?" we must explore further what is meant by the term "clinical."

CLINICAL APPROACH

Now, since what we will be talking about is a total, integrated, organic way of thinking, feeling, responding, and behaving, any attempts to describe or explain it, to reduce it to words, must of necessity be incomplete or fragmentary. Who is to say what makes up a doctor's skill? It is far easier to point to such an approach in concrete situations than to describe it. The danger in trying to reduce the concept of a clinical approach to words is that it is not something that can be inspected with a collection of "go-no go" gauges.

Despite the risks of oversimplification, however, I suggest that a leader has learned to approach concrete situations clinically if:

—An underlying element of his approach to other people is an attempt to understand them, which involves a high degree of acceptance of people as they are. This is a cornerstone of human relations in practice. It implies respect, tolerance, acceptance of human frailty, and recognition of the uniqueness of each human personality. Implied also is an ability to understand how other individuals see, feel, and think about themselves and their environment.

While I have said—and believe—that it is a mistake to view human relations as a code of ethics or series of moral absolutes, I do not believe it is possible for a person to respond clinically to concrete situations if he is incapable of accepting this one basic premise of our generally accepted traditions of civilization, morality, and religion.

This does not mean, however, that it is necessary for a leader to condone irresponsible action sloppy performance, or self-indulgent laziness. It is entirely possible for a good Marine sergeant to understand his recruits while a psychiatrist probing the innermost aspects of a patient's personality may not be capable of a clinical orientation if his actions are not based on respect.

—He has an awareness of and sensitivity to differences between his outlook and another man's, coupled with an ability to maintain his own individual point of view in the face of such differences. This is in a sense a corollary of the first point. A clinically oriented person takes it for granted that his values, aims, aspirations, and reactions are in some measure unique and does not expect other people to be exactly like himself. The sales manager who thinks all research scientists are simply "queer," the successful businessman who thinks all those who make less money than he does are therefore less able, the Republican who thinks all Democrats are stupid, the Anglo-Saxon Protestant who has no use for any Irish Catholics—these are all examples of the absence of a clinical orientation.

—He has an ability to respond to and understand not only the logical content of what other people say but also the feelings and sentiments implied in their words and their behavior. This particular aspect of the clinical approach and human relations, first articulated by the authors of the well-known study at Western Electric,[6] is the best known and most widely criticized.

Professor McNair in his recent HBR article points out that "sometimes people damn well mean what they are saying and will rightly regard anything less than a man-to-man recognition of that fact as derogatory to their dignity." [7] This is without a doubt true. At the same time, the emphasis on "listening" and on "reflecting feeling" has been put up by some human relations experts as an absolute precept: "The administrator must first and above all listen to other people." This is clearly nonsense.

But the fact remains that if you believe it appropriate to achieve some understanding or communication with a person who is angry, disturbed, or upset, an ability to go beyond the words he is using, to understand how he feels about something, will help you to get different results than if you simply respond to the logical content of his expression.

We do, after all, live in a world where it sometimes is necessary to try to understand or communicate with people who are not behaving as our own logic tells us they should. Sometimes it is desirable to understand why this is so. Sometimes it is useful to know that when a supervisor is criticizing the way another department is run, he is really asking for approval of what he himself is doing; or that when a group of people complain about the light in their office or the ventilation or the crowded facilities, they are prompted to do so by sentiments having more to do with pride than comfort.

The clinically oriented person is *able* to understand other people's feelings. Whether or not it is appropriate for him to manifest that understanding is an entirely different matter.

—He has some awareness of himself and of the impact of his behavior on other people. The qualifying word "some" is important, for this is a matter of degree, as are all aspects of the clinical orientation. Complete self-understanding is impossible. Undue preoccupation with self-analysis is unhealthy, as many critics of human relations have pointed out.

---

[6] See Elton Mayo, *The Social Problems of an Industrial Civilization* (Boston Division of Research, Harvard Business School, 1945), and F. J. Roethlisberger and W. J. Dickson, *Management and the Worker* (Cambridge, Harvard University Press, 1939).

[7] Malcolm P. McNair, op. cit., p. 28.

The executive who recognizes, however, that his own tensions may communicate themselves to his subordinates has a way of dealing with this problem. But the executive whose aggression, energy, and brilliance lead his subordinates to lean on him and who does not see that his own behavior has something to do with why "it's hard to delegate responsibility" may never understand what goes on around him. The one has self-awareness; the other has not.

Generally speaking, a distinguishing characteristic of the clinically oriented person is an intuitive understanding of himself and the way he acts which squares roughly with the way he looks to others.

—*He has an effective way of understanding the nature of the social structure or social system of which he is a part.* He has a feeling for the basic elements of social organization which human relations experts have identified: informal organization, status relationships, traditions or customs, and so forth.

It is beyond the scope of this article to try to explain in detail the concept of "social system," [8] or even to prove that organizations do in fact manifest regularities, uniformities, and characteristic ways of behaving which are a function of their prevailing social systems. At the same time, it is probably generally recognized that most companies have their office grapevines; that employees may establish "norms" limiting their output which have nothing to do with any rational concept of efficiency; that the factory worker will readily accept membership in a union while his blood brother making less pay in a white-collar job will have nothing to do with a union; that even though the president of a company boasts about his "open-door policy," few of the rank and file will visit him uninvited.

The point is not that any of these things are desirable or undesirable, but that they are part of the fabric of organizational behavior, factors which help to determine how effectively an organization will function. The clinically oriented person has some way of understanding this.

—*He is realistic about the existence of a hierarchy of authority, responsibility, status, and position in his particular organization and is alert to the way this hierarchy affects people's behavior, his own included.* That hierarchies do exist, that rank has its privileges, that people ordinarily do not act with their bosses the way they act with their equals, is probably generally accepted. Authority, rank, and status are special aspects of the basic concept of social struc-

---

[8] For a fuller discussion of this point, see Fritz Roethlisberger, *Management and Morale* (Cambridge: Harvard University Press, 1941), especially Chapter IV, "The Social Structure of Industry."

ture. But just how far relationships to persons of authority affect people's behavior is perhaps less well understood than the fact that the relationships do exist.

—*In taking action in an organizational situation, he is instinctively able to predict (within limits) how the organization will respond.* Again the qualifying "within limits" should be stressed. Human beings are not machines, and individual and organizational behavior is far too complex for anyone to be omniscient about it. What is important is that the clinically oriented person characteristically asks himself, "If I do this, what *will* happen?" instead of saying, "Since I believe that such and such *should* happen, other people *ought* to see it the same way and respond accordingly."

—*In taking action, he makes intuitive, judicious use of those generalizations about social phenomena which he has constructed and tested by his own experience, and at the same time he continually watches for the unique elements in every concrete situation.* It is axiomatic that experience is the best teacher, whether for the doctor, the scientist, the skilled mechanic, or the executive. What is not so well understood is that one important aspect of learning from experience is the assimilation of generalizations about the world around us. At a simple level, this is obvious: the child who avoids the stove after having been burned has learned, "If I put my hands on the fire, it will hurt."

One of the contributions of human relations research has been to point up some of the regularities in the way people respond to social situations, from one organization to the next, from one point in time to another. Without uniformities in human behavior, learning from experience would be impossible, and the idea of organization itself would be nonexistent.

The classic study at the Western Electric plant highlighted the fact that people respond in the form of higher productivity to a simple overt recognition of their importance. Since then a variety of experience has made it clear that people who are allowed to participate in the making of decisions will ordinarily be more effective in carrying out such decisions.

I also believe it is valid—despite the fuss and fury that surrounds this point—that on many occasions it is possible to understand another person's actions or statements by interpreting his behavior in a social context, by listening for what he feels rather than for the explicit meaning of his words. Once you have discovered for yourself the validity of some of these generalizations, in practice you do not need to start completely fresh in approaching every situation.

Again though, the qualifier "completely" is as important as the point itself. In some situations, stressing a recognition of people's importance may lead to less rather than to more productivity. If the fire chief allows participation in decision making, the house may burn down. Sometimes talking out in anger may lead to better communication than will listening.

TANGIBLE RESULTS

We come now to another question: Does the clinical approach, as just described, actually help an executive to develop cooperative action in a group while making it possible for the individual members of the group to maintain their personal integrity?

It would appear at first that all we need do to prove or disprove the basic propositions of human relations is test them. In an age where scientific inquiry is dominant, the accepted way to verify a basic hypothesis or assumption is to test it. In fact, over the last quarter of a century or so, much of the research work in human relations has been directed toward trying to demonstrate that a clinical orientation facilitates cooperative action and that the absence of such an approach leads to difficulty.

Nevertheless, it is not my purpose here either to try to review the results of such research or to prove the basic assumptions on which human relations rests. I believe that accepting these assumptions is as much an act of faith as an act of rational judgment. The world is too complicated a place, and human relations much too new (compare its 25 years as a field of systematic study with medicine's 2,500), to prove the implications of a clinical orientation in the same way that we can demonstrate the laws of gravity.

Once one has observed or taken part in situations where key participants have been able to bring to bear what I would describe as a clinical orientation, however, one is inclined to attribute what happens in part to the presence of such a point of view. What cannot be proved can often be illustrated. For this purpose let us take a few kinds of problems that must be faced in many business organizations. How does the kind of orientation I have been describing facilitate effective action in such situations?

Union negotiations

In labor problems disagreement, rather than agreement, is ordinarily the starting point. If the problem of reconciling this disagreement is treated simply as a conflict over dollars and cents or over basic management and union principles, the job of getting a contract is likely to be far more difficult, unproductive, and perhaps costly than if the negotiators recognize that bargaining is also a social process. The men at the machine do have different aims, aspirations, and sentiments from those of the management members or even the union brass. These often influence what happens just as much as differences over whether the contract should include a nickel or a dime per hour increase, or when seniority should prevail.

The management (or union) negotiator who starts with a recognition of this fact is more likely to keep the ball rolling than is the one who does not.

Interdepartmental disputes

It has surprised me on several occasions to find how much similarity there appears to be in widely differing organizations as to where points of friction occur among departments. Design engineers are often more likely to disagree with production superintendents than with other design engineers. A foreman is likely to find that his fellow foremen are extremely cooperative but that people in sales are usually very unreasonable. The sales manager cannot understand why he gets along so well with customers but has trouble with the controller.

In these situations, a problem may become insoluble if it is not understood. Here the clinical orientation on the part of one or more of the parties becomes a priceless ingredient in obtaining effective action.

Management meetings

There are probably few organizations in which the management has not wondered if too much time was being spent in meetings. Nonetheless, calling a group of people together to solve a problem or make a decision is one of the commonest activities in American business. No amount of awareness of social processes can make geniuses out of dullards. Yet it seems to me clear that the group that is fortunate in having a leader or participants who are alert to some of the dynamics of the group process, as well as the substance of what is being discussed, typically make more progress.

Reorganization

Someone has said that a tendency to change the organization structure is a peculiarly American characteristic. Be that as it may, it is frequently necessary for managers to reassign responsibilities, to bring in new people, to fire key subordinates, and to abolish groups performing a particular function.

Here, again, it seems to me that an ability to understand and predict what such steps will mean to an organization, and to sense when and how they can be handled with a minimum of disruption, involves a clinical orientation. And the gain in this case, as in the others just mentioned, is not only effective action. Personal integrity and independence, rather than conformity, should increase if the approach of responsible leaders is clinical. For the person who is concerned with understanding others and accepts differences as part of the scheme of things includes in his point of view a desire and willingness to respect and encourage others' attempts to be themselves.

The problem of conformity in an age of mass media, large organizations, and the common man cannot be assessed or dismissed lightly, but to ascribe to human relations the source of the problem seems by definition contradictory.

Aid to Leadership

Even if all that I have argued so far is true and the clinical approach is agreed to be valid, whether it is possible, appropriate, and desirable for the business executive remains to be shown. We may grant that such an orientation does facilitate cooperation, but is it the right approach for one who is or aspires to be a leader? This is a question which apparently has troubled some of the people who have been critical of the whole development called human relations.

It seems to me that the answer rests largely on what we mean by human relations. My understanding of human relations, spelled out earlier in this article, makes it hard for me to see why there need be any question of its relevance, appropriateness, and usefulness to executive action. But let me set some limits:

> Human relations and its point of view are *not* concerned with making everyone happy or sugar-coating harsh reality.
> Human relations, or the clinical orientation, is *not* and should not be equated in toto with the job of management or executive leadership.

So much, it seems to me, is obvious; but perhaps at times the more enthusiastic proponents of human relations in industry have tended to blur things. Running an industrial enterprise, or managing a part of it, requires a capacity to size up competitive trends, to understand the dynamics of cost and profit, to conceptualize a series of programs and objectives, to keep up with the technology of an industry, and to cope with a host of other things with which human relations as such is not directly concerned. Decisions, actions, plans, and day-to-day activities of businessmen must be carried out with reference to these things, as well as to the human aspects of cooperation.

If a person does not have the basic personal characteristics which make him an executive or potential executive, no amount of concern with human relations per se will make him one. Personal integrity, energy, intellectual capacity, moral courage, strength of purpose, and imagination, to mention a few, are the basic qualities of which successful organization effort is made. It is a mistake, as I see it, either to oppose these qualities to human relations or to ignore their importance. Many of them, however, coincide with the qualities demanded by the clinical approach.

The question of what makes a successful leader is probably an unanswerable one, if we are seeking to define one single road to glory. Being able to orient oneself clinically to social phenomena is probably *not* a necessary skill of *every* sucessful leader. Many people who possess an ability to facilitate cooperative effort in others lack other skills which are required for particular management jobs. It does seem to me, however, that every organization can increase its effectiveness if someone in a key position understands and has assimilated the characteristic approach to group activity I have attempted to describe. This may not be the top man, but a key subordinate.

I believe it is amply clear that the fundamental assumptions of human relations are valid and there is nothing inherent in human relations which conflicts with other management functions. Should we not continue our attempts, through research and teaching, to widen our understanding of human relations in American business?

QUESTIONS

1. Explain what Schoen means by his suggested clinical approach to human relations at work.
2. What are the central concepts of human relations that he presents?
3. What does Schoen claim executive effectiveness to rest upon?
4. Summarize Schoen's conclusions. Do you agree with them?
5. How does his clinical approach aid the leadership function?

HUMAN RELATIONS THEORY— A PROGRESS REPORT *

William Foote Whyte

As a field of research, teaching, and industrial training, human relations is still relatively new. But it has grown with exceptional rapidity, and the volume of current activity is enormous. Nevertheless, some critics still ask the disquieting question: Have we really learned anything since we started—or, to use a significant landmark, since 1933 when Elton Mayo's *Human Relations of an Industrial Civilization* [1] was published?

This article is intended as a progress report on the field of human relations. As I shall point out, advances have definitely been made; at the same time, much remains to be done in the interests of greater human satisfaction as well as greater industrial efficiency.

OUTLINE OF PROGRESS

In oversimplified form, the progress in human relations theory can be outlined in three stages:

1. *Staking out the claims*—This new field of study was opened up by the research that Elton Mayo and his associates in the Department of Industrial Research at the Harvard Business School, F. J. Roethlisberger and W. J. Dickson, carried on at the Western Electric Company. Through experimentation, observation, and interviewing, they demonstrated the fallaciousness of the old established theories of human behavior in industry.

2. *Following the leads*—For some years, we all followed Mayo's leads; we accepted and elaborated on his assumptions as we worked along the lines of our particular interests. But what we had learned from Mayo was, to a large extent, clarification of what was *not* true about behavior in industry rather than information as to what *was* true. So, while sometimes we came to fruitful conclusions, more and more we found ourselves going up blind alleys.

3. *Developing a new pattern*—Realizing we did not have all the answers, we were forced to rethink the work we had been doing. This led us toward a new pattern of theory and research. The pattern is not yet clear enough to provide many practical conclusions. It is emerging, nevertheless, and that emergence promises a brighter future both for the development of research and for its application to human problems in industry.

---

* From the *Harvard Business Review,* Vol. 34, No. 5 (September-October, 1956), pp. 125-132. Reprinted with permission.
[1] First published by The Macmillan Company; reprinted, Boston, Division of Research, Harvard Business School, 1946.

As I see it, we have now advanced beyond Mayo in several important ways, each of which deserves independent evaluation.

> We know how to use money more effectively as an incentive.
>
> We have gone beyond the simple "work group" concept to discover some of the different forms of group behavior actually to be found in industry.
>
> We are learning how the structure of the organization can affect morale and productivity.
>
> We have learned some of the limitations of human relations training—a necessary step in the development of more effective action.

OLD THEORIES DISCREDITED

Mayo attacked a theory of human behavior and a theory of organization.

According to the established management theory, the working man was thought to be an individual who responded to management's actions upon a completely individualistic basis. Money was thought to be the main, if not the only, incentive to which he responded.

On the organization side, the theories that went under the name of "scientific management" dominated the scene. Two points stood out—"functionalization" and the "span of control":

> (1) *Functional specialization* was equated with efficiency. The more specialization on the part of the worker or supervisor, the more effective he was supposed to be.
>
> (2) The concept of *span of control* involved an essentially mechanical theory of organization. It placed emphasis upon the formal structure and upon building control into the organization from the top down. It assumed that one man could supervise adequately only a small number of people. The theory recognized that the number should vary with the complexity of tasks assigned and with the extent of interdependence of tasks among those supervised. However, the emphasis was upon keeping down the number of men under a single supervisor, in order to maintain adequate control.

Of course, no experienced executive believed literally in the prevailing theories of individual and organizational behavior. Nevertheless, there was a tendency to reason toward conclusions as if the theories were true.

The challenge

It was Elton Mayo and his associates who made the first effective challenge to the prevailing theories of individual and organizational behavior. They did so by establishing the following propositions:

1. *The economic incentive is not the only motivating force to which the worker responds.* In fact, he often holds back his production to a point well below his physical capacity even when he is on piece rates and could make more money with more production. His production is importantly influenced by his relations with other workers and by his personal problems inside and outside the plant.

2. *The worker does not respond as an isolated individual.* He is a member of a work group, and the face-to-face relations he experiences have a great effect upon his behavior. Wherever men work togther, they tend to build up an informal organization which may not follow the lines of the formal organization as established by management.

3. *Extreme functional specialization does not necessarily create the most efficient organization.* Mayo and his associates did not give great attention to this point, but, in their study of the bank wiring room, they noted that the wiremen and soldermen frequently exchanged jobs, contrary to management's policy. These job exchanges had no adverse effects upon production and seemed to raise the morale of the entire work group.

Leads and blind alleys

We can accept Mayo's assumption regarding functional specialization without modification. A good deal of research and experience since Mayo's day leads us to believe that extreme functional specialization results in lower productivity and lower morale. In a number of cases it has been found that both morale and productivity have been raised by job enlargement (giving the worker more tasks to perform) and by allowing the worker to change jobs from time to time.

The Western Electric study focused attention on the effects of workers' personal problems on their morale and productivity. This suggested to the researchers the desirability of establishing a personnel counseling program. The counselor had no management authority, and his conversations with workers were kept confidential. His function was to provide workers opportunity to talk out their problems to a skillful listener.

All of us who have talked out some personal problem with a sympathetic listener can recognize the value of such an experience. This then seems to be a useful personnel technique. Unfortunately, however, this technique turned out to be the main practical outcome of the research program in the Western Electric Company. It is curious that this should have happened, for it violates one of the major findings of the research program: that changes in individual behavior and attitudes are effected primarily through changing human relations in the organization. The individual worker may be helped by counseling, but he (or even his foreman) is in a very nonstrategic position for changing human relations in the organization. Thus personnel counseling has proved to be a dead end so far as research is concerned.

New Approach to Incentives

Mayo and his associates performed an important service in demonstrating that the economic incentive is not all-important. But where do we go from there?

Money still vital

Some researchers in the field have gone on to assume that money—far from being all-important—is really not very important at all. This viewpoint is based on various questionnaire surveys which indicate that workers rank "good wages" seventh or eighth among the desirable conditions of work. Since items having to do with "fair treatment" by supervisors are consistently ranked higher, some people have come to think that workers are primarily concerned with human relations and do not worry very much about their take-home pay.

However, it has not been possible for us in human relations research to remove money from factory life. We have been forced to recognize that although workers may be thinking of other things too whenever they complain about wages, they are still most certainly concerned about money. Also, we have learned that the pattern of human relations in an organization can be such as to promote—or block—an enthusiastic response to an economic incentive.

It is futile to argue about the relative importance of money and human relations. We might just as well argue whether the engine or the gasoline is more important in making an automobile run. Our problem in research is to determine how the economic incentive and human relations fit together. More work has been done on this in recent years than can be summarized here, but I can point up two important areas of current research interest: the effect of incentives on intergroup relations and experimentation with new types of incentives.

Disrupting influences

Industry today is full of strife growing out of intergroup problems created by incentive systems. For instance, look at the now time-honored struggle between workers on incentive pay and those on hourly rates:

Take the skilled people in the maintenance department, who usually are more skilled than any other workers in the plant. Normally, they hold relatively high status or prestige in the plant community. But since their work is not directly measurable, they are not generally included in incentive plans. Yet a piece-rate system for production workers is likely to eliminate part or all of the differential in earnings between the two groups. In some cases, the production workers actually come out ahead in pay. This narrowing or reversal of the differential inevitably generates severe pressures within the union and from the union to management.

Even within production departments, incentives often give rise to intergroup problems. For example:

Suppose the production department consists of "grinders" and "polishers." The hourly rate for grinders is $1.90, that for polishers, $2.00. The polishing job is thought to require somewhat more skill and enjoy a higher status, and the promotional ladder calls for workers to move up from grinder to polisher.

Now suppose that incentives are introduced into the department. To make it easier for management, let us assume that the rates for grinders and polishers are set up at approximately the same time—a situation that is often *not* found in practice. Ideally, the incentive system will turn out so that the polishers maintain approximately the same earnings differential as they enjoyed on day rates. However, almost as often as not—and regardless of the rate-setting methods used—the incentive earnings will turn out something like this: polishers, $2.45; grinders, $2.65.

In other words, the incentive system has turned upside down the relative positions of the two jobs. What happens now is easy to predict. The polishers put pressure on union and management in order to get a loosening of the rate and re-establish the pre-existing differential. And the grinders become very reluctant indeed to "promote" into the polisher position.

Furthermore, there is no such thing as a once-and-for-all settlement of this problem, within the framework of piece rates. Even if the rates initially established should maintain the polishers in a superior earnings position, there will be changes in machine and work methods, and these will necessitate new time studies for setting new piece rates. Somewhere along the line the grinders are bound to turn up on top of the polishers, thus setting into motion the pressures described above.

How can management meet this type of intergroup problem? Men are concerned about their pay in *relative* as well as in absolute terms; the point is obvious to anyone with industrial experience, yet all too often we fail to draw the conclusions which logically follow. This means that, in planning the introduction of an incentive system, management cannot afford to concentrate its attention on the problem of motivating one particular group of workers alone. It must, at the same time, recognize the place these workers occupy in the status and pay system of the plant.

Management must anticipate the changes that incentives are likely to produce in the relative positions of work groups in the plant status system. It must be prepared to deal with the pressures that arise in response to such changes. On the basis of what we already know, there is no excuse for management to be taken by surprise by the intergroup problems that piece rates generate.

Plant-wide incentive

One way to by-pass the intergroup problems produced by piece rates is to abandon piece rates altogether. This does not necessarily mean giving up financial incentives. In recent years a few companies, following the lead of the late Joseph Scanlon, have been experimenting with incentives based on the performance of an entire plant. If the plant-wide formula does not eliminate whatever "inequities" workers may think exist, it at least has the merit of not introducing *new* inequities.

It is important to note that the plant-wide plan does not, in and of itself, produce results. Since the individual worker has so little direct effect on the payoff he receives, the success of a plant-wide formula depends on a new approach to motivation. Where the plan has been successful, it has been used as a symbol around which to reorganize human relations throughout the plant. The individual must feel that he is an important part of the organization, and he does not get this feeling simply by having management tell him how important he is. He feels appreciated only when he has an opportunity to contribute his ideas as well as his manual skills to the organization.

The plant-wide incentive program requires, therefore, a continuing program of discussion and action, whereby the individual can bring up ideas within his own department and whereby these ideas are carried for action to as high an organizational level as is necessary for decision making. This means stimulating workers to offer production ideas through the union channels. However, management people cannot just sit back and wait for union suggestions; they must also present production and cost problems to workers and union officers for discussion.

Without going into the mechanics of the system, some general comments can be made about its effectiveness. Under a successful plant-wide incentive, men will work more steadily, although it is not this harder work which accounts for most of the payoff. The successes have been achieved largely through a more effective mobilization of the knowledge and ideas of all members of the organization. In these cases, management and union have built a system in which workers gain feelings of pride and belonging through the contributions they make to the better functioning of their organization.

In the past, management has concentrated on setting up communication channels to *get the work done.* The new approach calls for setting up channels—from the bottom up as well as from the top down—through which *improvements in the organization of work* are constantly taking place. Here, the money offered by the plant-wide incentive is an important factor, but it does not motivate workers unless the social system of the plant is effectively organized.

Elton Mayo destroyed the orthodox economic theory of worker motivation. For a time we tried to develop a theory of motivation that would leave out money altogether. That too was found wanting, and we are now building a new theory that integrates economic incentives *and* human relations.[2]

ACCENT ON FACE-TO-FACE RELATIONS

Mayo and his associates showed that we cannot afford to think of an isolated individual employee. We must consider him as part of a work group. But where do we go from there?

Misleading conclusions

We have elaborated upon Mayo's assumption in ways that have led toward misleading conclusions. Let us examine the steps here.

At first, we took it for granted that in *every* factory department there was a work group, and furthermore that it had a well-organized structure that tended to have a good deal of stability. In this conclusion we were, of course, influenced by the classic Western Electric study of the bank wiring room, which did have a well-organized work group with a definite and stable structure. Neither Mayo nor any of his associates ever wrote that *all* factory departments must be organized in this pattern, but, when we had no comparable studies of other work groups, there was a natural tendency to assume that this was a universal pattern.

If there were such a work group structure, then it would follow that the foreman could supervise most effectively if he understood

---

[2] For more on this subject, see W. F. Whyte *et al., Money and Motivation* (New York: Harper & Brothers, 1955); also William Foote Whyte, "Economic Incentives and Human Relations," *Harvard Business Review* (March-April, 1952), p. 73.

the structure of the group and dealt with it through the informal leadership that had arisen. We therefore focused our attention on the relations between the foreman and the *informal organization* of his workers. Without being fully aware of what we were doing, we sought to discover the factors that would make for good relations between foremen and workers—regardless of the technology involved, the distribution of job skills, the over-all structure of the organization, and so on.

From this point of view, harmonious relations between supervisor and supervised and high morale among workers seemed to depend on the human relations skill and understanding of the supervisors. As we extended our studies to union-management relations, we looked to find ways in which local union leaders could affect the degree of harmony between workers and management and the degree of satisfaction experienced by workers. We recognized that the human relations skills of union leaders could have an important impact on the resulting relationships.

The assumption underlying all this work was that the nature of human relations in the plant was primarily determined by the human relations skills of the people in leadership positions. It followed that training efforts to improve the skill and understanding of these people would result in more harmonious relations.

This line of thinking has been severely jolted by three sets of studies.

More powerful forces

Clark Kerr and Abraham Siegel put to us the following embarrassing question: If cooperation in industry depends primarily on the skill and understanding of the key people involved, how do you explain the fact that there has been consistent conflict in the longshore industry in this country, and even internationally, while relations in the clothing industry have been reasonably peaceful?[3] Can it be that the key people in Industry A just happen to be skilled in human relations whereas their opposite numbers in Industry B are a bunch of bunglers?

This would be hard to believe, and as a matter of fact we do not believe it. We have had to recognize that there are certain forces operating that are more powerful than the human relations tech-

---

[3] "The Interindustry Propensity to Strike—An International Comparison," *Industrial Conflict*, edited by A. Kornhauser, R. Dubin, and A. M. Ross (New York: McGraw-Hill Book Company, Inc., 1954), p. 189.

niques of individual executives or union leaders. Along this line, Kerr and Siegel emphasize the homegeneity or heterogeneity of worker groups on the job or in the community:

> Strike-prone industries, they argue, are those in which most workers work in close proximity on the same or similar jobs, and in which they live in close association in communities where they are cut off from intimate contact with other types of workers or with management people.
>
> At the other extreme, heterogeneity leads to more peaceful union-management relations: workers who do a wide variety of jobs and are scattered through the community, among other types of people, are less likely to strike.

This is an oversimplification of the Kerr-Siegel argument, but, for our purposes, it need not be presented in detail. It is enough to note that they have drawn our attention to the powerful influence of job structure and community organization upon human relations on the job.

Multigroup relations

The work of Leonard Sayles and George Strauss has served to broaden our understanding of work groups.[4] A great variety of possible organizational patterns may be found among such groups. There are groups with stable organizations such as in the bank wiring room. There are also groups which may at times be so disorganized that it is hard even to speak of them as groups. Furthermore, we cannot think simply in terms of the supervisor in relation to *the* work group. In a department of any size, the supervisor must relate himself to *several* work groups. At any given time these groups may be in competition and conflict with each other, so the supervisor must deal in intergroup relations as well as in his own relations to each group.

Sayles is now pushing ahead in an effort to discover some of the laws of work group behavior. He has tentatively identified four types of work groups, in terms of their characteristic behavior patterns:

> (1) The *apathetic* group, whose members may be dissatisfied but are so divided against themselves they are unable to take concerted action.
>
> (2) The *erratic* group, which swings from passivity to outbursts of aggressive action—and often on issues that seem to management and union leaders too small to account for the emotional heat involved.

---

[4] *The Local Union* (New York, Harper & Brothers, 1953). See also their article, "Conflicts Within the Local Union," *Harvard Business Review* (November-December, 1952), p. 84.

(3) The *strategic* group, which constantly seeks to improve its position through carefully calculated, united action.

(4) The *conservative* group, whose members are capable of concerted action but who are generally satisfied enough so that they do not take the trouble to make themselves heard.[5]

Affixing a label has no value in itself, but Sayles is finding that the groups whose behavior fits a given label are reacting to very similar conditions of technology, level of skill, and arrangement of jobs. In other words, if we find groups in two different factories that fit the "erratic" behavioral description, we can expect to find them facing similar conditions in the social and technological work environment.

Study along this line is still in an early stage; within a few years we can expect to know a good deal more about work groups than we do today. Such knowledge can be invaluable in improving supervisory leadership and in increasing the effectiveness of local union leaders in their dealings with work groups. It will take us far beyond the simple work group concept.

The odds on training

The third force in upsetting our old conceptions of human relations has been provided by research evaluations of the impact of supervisory training programs.

In recent years, two solid pieces of research have been done along this line. In each case, the workers under the supervisors who were to be trained were given a questionnaire dealing with their relationship with the supervisors before the program began. The same questionnaire was administered some months after the conclusion of the program. The result? Disappointing, to say the least.

Edwin A. Fleishmann, Edwin F. Harris, and Harold E. Burtt at Ohio State found that the International Harvester Company program had effected no gain in these supervisor-worker relationships—and perhaps it had even resulted in a slight loss.[6] The University of Michigan Survey Research Center's study of a training program in two divisions of the Detroit Edison Company showed a small overall gain.[7] However, it was found that there had been a loss of ground

---

[5] Leonard Sayles, *Technology and Work Group Behavior* (Ann Arbor: University of Michigan, Bureau of Industrial Relations, scheduled for publication in late 1956).

[6] *Leadership and Supervision in Industry: An Evaluation of a Supervisory Training Program* (Columbus: Bureau of Educational Research, The Ohio State University, Monograph No. 33, 1955).

[7] See Norman A. Maier, *Principles of Human Relations* (New York: John Wiley & Sons, Inc., 1952), pp. 184-192.

in one division which was more than compensated for by a gain in the other.

How can we account for these results? Were the programs in themselves no good? No doubt better training can be given, but probably these courses were a good deal better than the average in industry today.

We find the best explanation by looking at the two divisions in the Detroit Edison study. The researchers found that in the division where progress had been made, the foremen were led by a higher management which supervised them very much in line with the principles developed in the course. On the other hand, in the division which lost ground the foremen were under superiors who directed them in a manner which was entirely out of harmony with the program.

These findings suggest that the effectiveness of a training program for lower-level supervisors depends in very large measure on the way that program is supported at higher levels in the organization. Nor can that support be simply verbal. Real success depends on the actions of top management in its day-to-day behavior.

What about training in human relations for the higher-ups?

Years ago management tended to make the foreman a sort of scapegoat for all human relations difficulties. It was assumed that if the foreman were only as good a leader of men as the president or vice-president of the company, then there would be no problem. Today few management people are that naive. They are ready to recognize that a change in behavior at higher levels may be necessary too, if the foreman is to do the skillful job of supervision expected of him. So it makes sense to direct training at these higher levels.

Nevertheless we are becoming increasingly doubtful whether training can do the job here. We often assume that people high up in management are free agents. If they put pressure on their subordinates in a way that hinders co-operation and lowers morale, we may assume that this is because they do not have the necessary human relations skills or because they have some personality difficulties. But the truth is that the big wheels are not free to do as they please. They too are under pressure.

The plant manager is in competition for advancement with other plant managers. He is struggling to meet a budget that is deliberately set tight so as to demand his best efforts. He works with accountants and cost control people who, as Chris Argyris has explained, gain their successes through discovering and reporting the failures of production people.[8] Faced with rising material costs and wages, the manager must spur his organization to greater efficiency, so that the plant produces in greater volume and still keeps prices down and profits up. He has design engineers, industrial engineers, personnel men, and other specialists to help him and his production men do this, and yet he finds much of his time and energy devoted to untangling the snarls that arise among the people who make up the complex and sensitive organism which he directs.

At still higher levels, the company executive may be under less direct pressure from above, but he generates his own pressure in response to his ideal of the successful American executive. That ideal demands that he not be content with today's achievement, that he be constantly pushing to improve or expand the organization. Progress may require him to gamble millions of dollars on projects whose payoff is years away. Responsibility is a heavy weight in itself.

Our problem involves certain things that are bigger than the individual and his social skills. What are these things? We are only beginning to understand them, but one of the important factors seems to be the formal structure of the organization.

RE-ENTER FORMAL ORGANIZATION

Stimulated by research that has come out of Sears, Roebuck and Co. under the leadership of James C. Worthy (later Assistant Secretary of Commerce and now back at Sears as Director of Public Relations), we are busy taking a new look at organization structure.

We find that the way you build your organization has a great influence on its pattern of human relations. If you follow the span of control theory, you will build a long, narrow hierarchy with many levels of authority from bottom to top. Since supervisors will have few people reporting to them, they will tend to supervise those people closely. Under such conditions, the subordinate will concentrate on pleasing the boss and will have little opportunity to display initiative and assume the responsibilities necessary to developing his capacities.

The span of control theory is irrefutable if you accept the assumption about behavior on which it is based: that men perform best when they are under close supervision. The fact is that research (especially at Rensis Likert's University of Michigan Institute for

---

[8] "Human Problems With Budgets," *Harvard Business Review* (January-February, 1953), p. 97.

Social Research) has been demonstrating the falsity of such an assumption. A number of studies have shown that both morale and productivity are higher under light, general supervision.

This means that the boss should delegate responsibility and authority to the men under him, giving them the chance to exercise their own capabilities. But can you get the boss to do this? Experience has shown that this is exceedingly difficult when the organization is based on the span of control concept and the boss has only a few people reporting to him. Despite training and management policy, he tends to keep close track (and control) of the work of his subordinates. It is easy for him to do so, and what else should he do with his time?

Flat structure

If we really want delegation of authority and the improved morale that seems to go with it, we might adopt the organization structure approach of giving the boss so many subordinates that he cannot possibly supervise them closely. Such a course means building a broad, flat structure with relatively few levels of authority from bottom to top. This management philosophy—the exact opposite of the span of control concept—is practiced by Sears and is becoming increasingly popular in American industry.

I am not suggesting that it is impossible to achieve a healthy degree of delegation of authority without changing the structure of the organization. And certainly not all companies would be able to model themselves after the Sears department store structure. The organizational pattern most appropriate for a particular business will depend on what it produces, its technology, the types of staff groups that must work with the line, and a number of other factors we are just beginning to investigate.

Nor am I trying to bury for all time the thinking that has gone into the span of control theory—which is still very much alive today, if we are to judge from the recent cogent statement of Lyndall Urwick.[9] My only claim is that we have come again to recognize the importance of formal structure—but now with a difference. Instead of theorizing in an *a priori* manner, we are beginning to carry on the empirical research that may some day enable us to plan the structure of the company so as to predetermine, in some degree, the nature of its human relations.

---

[9] "The Manager's Span of Control," *Harvard Business Review* (May-June, 1956), p. 39.

HUMAN RELATIONS IN PERSPECTIVE

In this article, I have pointed out the important influences upon human relations exercised by the pay system, the technology, the organization of work, and the formal structure. Does this mean that face-to-face relations are unimportant? Does this mean human skills and understandings do not really count for much?

The answer to both questions is *no*. However, research and experience have placed face-to-face relations in a new perspective. Both the morale and the productivity of an organization are tremendously influenced by the nature of face-to-face relations in that organization, but we have come to recognize that the relations we observe tend to be channeled within certain limits by the organization's structure, technology, and so on.

And yet these limits are not so narrow as to deprive the individual of any opportunity to influence the world around him. Man's behavior is not completely predetermined by these impersonal forces, for we have seen striking changes in human relations in some situations where there have been no substantial changes either in the form of organization or in the manner of performing the work.[10] Furthermore, organization structure and technology should not be considered as superhuman forces—they are determined by mere human decision.

In the past, management has characteristically thought only in terms of technical efficiency in planning structure and technology. Human relations entered into the picture only when disturbances arose out of technological and structural changes. Severe losses in efficiency as well as in morale have resulted from this mental separation of human relations from structure and work organization. Now that we recognize the intimate connection between the two, and as research begins to trace out the human relations patterns that go with different structural and technological arrangements, we can look for greater achievements through applying a human relations knowledge to industrial problems.

---

[10] William F. Whyte, *Pattern for Industrial Peace* (New York: Harper & Brothers, 1951).

QUESTIONS

1. What have been the principal advances in the area of human relations?
2. What are the new challenges to human relations according to Whyte?
3. How important are economic incentives to human relations?
4. How does job structure and community organization influence human relations on the job?
5. How does formal organization influence the pattern of human relations?

HUMAN RELATIONS IN INDUSTRY: RESEARCH AND CONCEPTS *

William H. Knowles

The causes of labor unrest and worker dissatisfaction in all their manifestations—from strikes and riots to passive insubordination—are a challenge to man's wit. Reformers of all kinds, revolutionaries, politicians, labor leaders, novelists, social scientists, and personnel managers have suggested ways to bring about labor peace and worker satisfaction. The problem has proved to be complex and stubborn. It remains with us, although it takes on changing forms.

The latest group to attack human problems in industry are specialists in "human relations," who approach industrial relations through the study of small-group behavior, and whom we shall call "human relationists" for want of a better term. They are sociologists, social psychologists, clinical psychologists, psychiatrists, social anthropologists, and, to a lesser extent, political scientists, who study small, informal groups.[1] Many human relationists have entered the field via schools of education, introducing into human relations the ideas of John Dewey and the concepts of progressive education. Only the economist and the historian have been left out of the interdisciplinary team.

A basic tenet of human-relations theory is that primary groups (the family, work crews, union committees, church and lodge groups, bowling clubs, etc.) are fundamental units of society, and that study of them yields a better understanding of the individual, the organization, and society as a whole. Specialists in *industrial* human relations are concerned with the behavior of informal groups at all levels of a business organization. In addition to research in industry, industrial human relationists apply research findings from the study

* Reproduced with permission from the *California Management Review*, Vol. 1, No. 1 (Fall, 1958), pp. 87-105. Copyright by the Regents of the University of California.

[1] For definitions of human relations see: A. Paul Hare, Edgar F. Borgatta, and Robert F. Bales (eds.), *Small Groups; Studies in Social Interaction* (New York: Knopf, 1955), pp. 1-9 for a historical view; Mark May, *Toward a Science of Human Behavior: A Survey of the Work of the Institute of Human Relations* (New Haven: Yale University Press, 1950), pp. 4-10 for a definition that places greater emphasis on the biological sciences; E. Wight Bakke and Chris Argyris, *Organizational Structure and Dynamics: A Framework for Theory* (New Haven: Yale Labor and Management Center, 1954), pp. 111-14; Keith Davis, *Human Relations in Business* (New York: McGraw-Hill, 1957), pp. 1-4; N. R. F. Maier, *Principles of Human Relations, Applications to Management* (New York: Wiley, 1952), preface.

of such diverse groups as ladies' sewing circles and army combat terms to work groups within the industrial setting.

EVOLUTION OF TRENDS

Human relations in industry began with the work of Elton Mayo and his associates, and developed from their classic studies at the Hawthorne Plant of the Western Electric Company.[2] Their findings about the informal organization, informal communication, and the informal work group have been reported interminably and their value judgments and philosophical framework have been the subject of a major debate in industrial-relations literature.[3] As the result of this debate, the propositions of the original Mayo group of human relationists at Harvard have been modified. Although individual human-relations specialists vary in their beliefs, in general it may be said that human-relations concepts since Mayo have been modified as follows:[4]

Human relationists no longer hold out the hope of developing an exact science of human behavior and social organization. In the tradition of the scientific managers, the industrial (behaviorist) psychologists and sociologists of the Durkheim positivist school, human-relations specialists in industry once hoped that laws of group behavior and industrial organization could be discovered, making prediction and control possible.[5] If anything, some human-relations specialists now tend to go to the other extreme and proclaim that true understanding of human behavior is subsconscious, subjective, and non-rational rather than intellectual. There tends to be an anti-intellectual, mystical element in present-day human relations.

---

[2] Elton Mayo, *The Social Problems of an Industrial Civilization* (Boston: Harvard University Graduate School of Business Administration, 1945) and *The Human Problems of an Industrial Civilization* (Boston: Harvard University Graduate School of Business Administration, 1946); F. J. Roethlisberger, *Management and Morale* (Cambridge: Harvard University Press, 1941); T. North Whitehead, *The Industrial Worker* (Cambridge: Harvard University Press, 1938).

[3] See William H. Knowles, *Personnel Management: A Human Relations Approach* (New York: American Book Company, 1955), pp. 74-118 for a review of this debate.

[4] Chris Argyris, *The Present State of Research in Human Relations in Industry* (New Haven: Yale Labor and Management Center, 1954); Mason Haire, "Group Dynamics in the Industrial Situation," in *Industrial Conflict*, Arthur Kornhauser, *et al.* (eds.) (New York: McGraw-Hill, 1954), pp. 373-385; William F. Whyte, "Human Relations Theory—A Progress Report," *Harvard Business Review*, Vol. XXXIV (September-October, 1956); Harold L. Wilensky, "Human Relations in the Workplace, An Appraisal of Some Recent Research," in *Research in Industrial Human Relations*, Conrad M. Arensberg, *et al.* (eds.) (New York: Harper, 1957), pp. 25-54.

[5] See Knowles (note 3), pp. 41-43, 61-62, 84, 102-103.

Although Mayo and his group tended to emphasize irrational motives as causes of industrial conflict, human relationists now recognize that such conflict may be a form of rational economic-behavior, and that economic incentives are often a strong motivating force.[6] On the other hand, economists must concede that there are other things in life besides money which men seek to maximize. The study of motivation has proved to be complicated and has yielded little of use to management and union leaders.

The discovery of the informal organization in industry (with its own communications net apparently independent of the formal one), which is sometimes the "real" organization for getting work done, at first led many human-relations experts to deprecate the importance of a conventionally drawn table of organization. They now recognize that the informal organization cannot always adjust itself to production and to the solution of the personal problems of the work force within the structure of the organization. The structure of the formal organization itself may be the actual cause of both production and personnel problems. Dissatisfied with traditional organization theory, specialists in human relations are seeking a reformulation of the principles of organization. Although they have made specific suggestions for the improvement of the formal organization, they have not yet produced a general theory of organization based upon human-relations principles.

Earlier human-relations specialists in industry tended to study the work environment as a closed social system and to ignore such external factors as economic conditions, the community, and the internal politics of the union.[7] Human relationists continue to emphasize the primary social group as fundamental to an understanding of both individuals and society, but they also recognize the importance of economic, political, and social factors. The earlier preoccupation with the work group was related to a philosophy which held that the external environment was essentially cold, hostile, and unfriendly and that the psychic needs of man could be best served in a kind of industrial monastery. Most human relationists today reject this romantic philosophy of "escape from freedom" and argue that the goal of human relations is to develop individuals who can be effective in many groups. Most of today's human relationists are proponents of the open society rather than of industrial feudalism.

---

[6] William F. Whyte, *Money and Motivation* (New York: Harper, 1955).

[7] Abraham J. Siegel, "The Economic Environment in Human Relations Research," in *Research in Industrial Human Relations*, Conrad M. Arensberg, *et al.*, (eds.), (see note 4), pp. 86-99.

Just as human-relations theorists now give greater weight to the formal organization and to the external environment, they also weight more heavily the importance of the individual—his values and his personality—in assessing the behavior of the group. Although psychologists may still be criticized for ignoring the influence of the group on the individual, psychologists-turned-human-relationists have tended to re-emphasize the importance of the individual in shaping the attitudes and values of the group. By placing stress on the social group, some human relationists have supported a philosophy of "togetherness" and the denial of individualism. Once again we are faced with the debate on human nature and the natural order of society. Recent human relationists have reasserted the importance of the individual by stressing the desirability of developing social groups that can be effective without infringing on the individual's right to privacy by tolerating a high degree of nonconformity.

In giving management the role of a benevolent, paternalistic, "natural elite," which understood the true needs of the worker better than the worker did himself, early human-relations literature (in the tradition of pre-World War II management-oriented labor-relations literature) seems basically authoritarian in philosophy.[8] Although this view still lingers, most human-relations specialists have become proponents of industrial democracy as a result of their more recent research in industry. The reasons for this, and the means by which democracy in industry is to be achieved, are a central theme in current industrial human relations and will be taken up later in this paper. Whereas pioneer human relationists were attacked as authoritarians and lackeys of management, the present stress on industrial democracy has caused criticism of another kind: that human relationists are "misty-eyed" idealists whose preoccupation with the rights and dignity of the individual causes them to lose sight of the need for efficiency and profits.

Early human-relations literature was notable for the absence of any extensive discussion of unions and for naiveté as to the unions' function and purpose. The authoritarian philosophical overtones of the Hawthorne studies were anti-union. Today's industrial human relationists understand unionism, recognize the unions' value in industrial relations, and study human-relations problems within the union itself and in union-management relations.[9] More sophisticated

---

[8] For review of authoritarian management philosophy see Knowles (note 3), pp. 149-165.

[9] See articles by Wilbert Moore, pp. 119-130; William F. Whyte, pp. 171-181; Mason Haire, pp. 182-191; and Solomon Barkin, pp. 192-213, all in *Research in Industrial Human Relations*, Arensberg *et al.*, (eds.), (see note 4).

human relationists have no plans for "taming the union," for making the union leaders a second-class nobility in the management elite, nor for establishing an era of unbroken union-management harmony. Just as there is no human-relations organization theory, the exact relationship between human-relations concepts and those of traditional unionism and collective bargaining has not been spelled out, though they do appear to supplement and complement one another.

Elton Mayo spoke of developing human-relations skills in management to resolve problems of industrial unrest, and was attacked for his manipulative approach to employee-employer relations. Present-day human relationists go to the other extreme of being anti-technique. "Manipulation" has become a dirty word. Today, human relationists hold that basic personality changes are necessary to "good human relations" and that simple techniques of getting people to do what they do not want to do are not only morally wrong but ineffective.[10] Manipulation as a continual one-way process may be generally impossible; it does not, however, seem reasonable to say that you cannot sometimes manipulate another person—that is, get him to do what you want him to do.

The Hawthorne and subsequent studies revealed the communications problem of modern industry, and stress was laid upon *channels* of communication, semantic problems, and frames of reference. The inference drawn from the studies was that if individuals could understand one another this would remove the *major cause* of industrial discontent. Latter-day human relationists realize that there are "real" causes for discontent, not arising from mere misunderstanding or lack of information, which are removed neither by channels of communication nor by catharsis. The communications problems raised by early human relationists are not dismissed, but are placed in their proper perspective. The present concern of human relationists in communications is with interpersonal, nonverbal communications invoking subconscious, vaguely-felt emotions.[11] Communications research is currently involved with the phenomena of perception, subception, and empathy in group interaction.

Pioneer human relationists appeared to be unaware that their conclusions from field research carried ethical inferences that did not inevitably follow from the studies. Critics pointed out that alter-

[10] William F. Whyte, (see note 4).
[11] S. I. Hayakawa, "Success and Failure in Communications," *Proceedings*, Sixth Western Regional Conference, American Society of Training Directors, San Francisco (October, 1957); Wendell Johnson, "The Fateful Process of Mr. A. Talking to Mr. B.," *Harvard Business Review*, XXXI, 1 (1953), 49-56.

native inferences from the same findings were possible. Human relationists are now more sophisticated and take care to distinguish
between findings of fact and value judgments. Initially, human relationists hoped to reduce ethics to a science, and in the process of
organizing a scientifically-constructed society, economy, and social
group, they expected that all interpersonal relations would be placed
on a scientifically ethical basis.

Although present-day human relationists have abandoned the
search for an exact science of society and human nature in the sense
of prediction and control (as noted previously in this section), the
quest for a scientific basis for an ethical society still goes on. Clinical
psychologists working with social anthropologists believe that some
societies, economies, organizations, and systems of values are conducive to mental illness and that others more in harmony with man's
nature produce satisfactory mental health. If mental health can be
equated with ethics, there is a scientific basis for recommending some
kinds of organizations, values, and leadership styles over others.[12]
While many may dispute this line of reasoning, it is refreshing that
human relationists are now concerned with the discovery of a suitable industrial environment for mankind rather than continuing the
pre-World War II emphasis on "adjusting men to machines."

Major Concepts in Human Relations

Interrelatedness of personality, primary group, organization, and culture [13]

These concepts are the building blocks of society, and all of them
are related to one another. An individual's personality, attitudes,
and values are to a large extent shaped by the primary groups to
which he belongs or has belonged; but, conversely, primary groups
are a reflection of the values, attitudes, and personalities of their
members. Most human-relations research has been an examination

---

[12] See Barbara Wooton, *Testament of the Social Sciences* (New York:
Norton, 1950); Erich Fromm, *Man For Himself* (New York: Rinehart, 1947).
For remarks relating the problem of mental health and culture directly to human
relations in industry see Michael Fogarty, *Personality and Group Relations in
Industry* (London: Longmans Green, 1956), pp. 23-40.

[13] S. H. Foulkes and E. J. Anthony, *Group Psychotherapy* (London: Pelican,
1957), pp. 40-47; Erich Fromm, *The Sane Society* (New York: Rinehart, 1955);
Frederick Herzberg, *et al.*, *Job Attitudes: Review of Research and Opinion*
(Pittsburgh, Psychological Service of Pittsburgh, 1957), pp. 19, 229-252; C. G.
Jung, *Modern Man in Search of a Soul* (New York: Harcourt Brace, 1933),
p. 61; Patrick Mullahy (ed.), *A Study of Interpersonal Relations* (New York:
Hermitage Press, 1949), especially articles by Ernest Beaglehole, Harry Stack
Sullivan, Talcott Parsons, and Harold Lasswell.

of the relationships between the individual and the group. Research has revealed, for instance, that personality change does take place as one changes membership in groups, that it is easier to change the attitude of the whole group than to change that of an individual member, that an individual gets more of his values from membership in primary groups than he does from the organizations to which these groups belong.

Similarly, the character of groups is in part shaped by the organization and the culture just as the organization is shaped by the culture and the groups. Culture, in turn, is the product of individuals, groups, and organizations. The complexity of these interrelationships explains the difficulty the political reformer has in attempting to bring about change from the top—the corporation president trying out a "new broom," the foreman seeking to change the habits of his crew, or the teacher trying to influence individual behavior.

The human-relations approach to the problems of industry is to assert that some combinations of personalities, groups, organizations, and cultures produce conflict, frustration, and mental illness and that other combinations produce harmony, satisfaction, and mental health. The more neurotic family is likely to produce neurotic children who may be well-adjusted to the neurotic groups and organizations they will join in their neurotic culture. Likewise, healthy individuals, groups, and organizations within healthy cultures interact so as to reinforce each other.

This framework of interrelationships is a very broad generalization. There can be frustrated, overly-aggressive groups and individuals within otherwise healthy organizations, and the opposite may also be true. Moreover, there are many kinds of personality types, groups, organizations, and cultures that are healthy and as many kinds that are unhealthy. Clearly, it is no simple this-or-that relationship. Human relationists have no vision of a static society of placid individuals in passive groups. Organizations, individuals, and groups are dynamic, the direction of their change is largely nonpredictable; but in the process of change the conditions for mental health can be preserved.

Personality problems

Psychologists continue to be perplexed by the infinite variety of personality traits (dimensions) and patterns (syndromes) which seem to defy analysis. Human-relations specialists in industry, however, single out two personality patterns as important to an understanding of the problems of industrial unrest. The first is the authoritarian personality, a personality which tends to be emotionally unstable, to repress facts which are contrary to belief, to be insensitive to the feelings of others, to wrongly estimate the goals of others, and to think of people and of problems in rigid stereotypes. Such a personality type has serious communication difficulties; he has no understanding of his own subconscious feelings, he has difficulty expressing his feelings and in understanding the feelings of others, he tends to judge too soon, and he does not know how to listen to others.[14] Nonauthoritarian, or democratic, personalities have the opposite tendencies.

Human-relations research indicates that the authoritarian personality is common in American industry and a basic cause of much conflict and misunderstanding. Economic issues and power struggles will always be present, but many conflicts which appear on the surface to be economic or to be power struggles are in reality the problems of sick individuals. The treatment of the authoritarian personality would eliminate a major source of industrial unrest and inefficiency. Conversely, no amount of smooth channels of communication or precision in the use of words will help the authoritarian who cannot listen and who thinks in stereotypes.

Another personality syndrome in industrial society that is stressed by human relationists is the *frustration-aggression pattern.*[15] Frustration arises out of the organization of modern industry and urban living in which individuals have casual relationships with many people but have few intimate friends. The result is a lack of "belongingness" to work groups, neighborhood, or even to family. Research indicates widespread frustration arising also from dull, monotonous jobs lacking in creativity and self-expression, from poor supervision, economic insecurity, and emphasis on economic incentives to the exclusion of nonmaterial incentives. The consequence of frustration is aggressive behavior, which only aggravates rather than solves frustration. Carriers of the mental disease of frustration can infect work groups and whole organizations in this manner.

Research suggests that no correlation exists between "normal personality" and work satisfaction or supervisory ability. A general

---

[14] T. W. Adorno, *et al., The Authoritarian Personality* (New York: Harper, 1950); J. A. C. Brown, *The Social Psychology of Industry* (London: Penguin, 1954), pp. 219-276.

[15] Maier (see note 1), pp. 34-36; Ross Stagner, *Psychology of Industrial Conflict* (New York: Wiley, 1956), pp. 155-196; Walter A. Weisskoff, "Industrial Institutions and Personality Structure," *Journal of Social Issues,* VII, 4 (1951), 1-6.

relationship seems to exist, however, between dissatisfaction on the job or lack of supervisory ability and (a) dissatisfaction with things in general, (b) lack of friendliness and identification with social groups, (c) emotional imbalance and lack of understanding of personal psychological needs, (d) poor interpersonal relationships, intolerance of the psychological needs of others, and insensitivity to the communication of those needs, (e) tendency to be unrealistic, arbitrary, and inflexible, and (f) an unhappy home in childhood, with a repetition of the pattern in adulthood.[16]

The work group

The social group is the center of focus of human relations studies in industry.[17] By measuring the roles and status of group members, human-relation specialists study the structure of work groups. By analyzing communication networks, they relate the formal and informal organization of the group to other groups and to the organization as a whole.

One important variable in the behavior of groups and their members is the degree of group cohesiveness, and human relationists are concerned with the causes and implications of cohesive work groups.[18] Another important variable is leadership, which the human relationists consider to be a function of group behavior rather than a characteristic of the individual in the leadership role. A leader can shape a cohesive group, enforce its norms, and change its norms only under certain conditions because he must first gain the acceptance of the group and meet its norms. Human relations, then, studies the nature of leadership and the relation of informal leaders, appointed outside leaders (foremen), elected leaders (shop stewards), multiple leadership, and shared leadership (leaderless groups) to the work group.

Emerging from a multitude of studies the following conclusions appear:

---

[16] Herzberg, et al., (see note 13), pp. 17-20.

[17] Since the group is the center of interest in human-relations studies, there is a vast body of literature on the subject. Some of the standard references are: R. F. Bales, *Interaction Process Analysis: A Method for the Study of Small Groups* (Cambridge: Addison-Wesley, 1950); Dorwin Cartwright and A. Zander (eds.), *Group Dynamics* (Evanston: Row, Peterson, 1953); Leon Festinger, Stanley Schachter, and Kurt Back, *Social Pressures in Informal Groups* (New York: Harper, 1950); Harold Guetzkow (ed.), *Groups, Leadership and Men* (Pittsburgh: Carnegie Press, 1951); George C. Homans, *The Human Group* (New York: Harcourt Brace, 1950); Muzafer Sherif and Carolyn W. Sherif, *Groups in Harmony and Tension* (New York: Harper, 1953); and Herbert Thelen, *Dynamics of Groups at Work* (Chicago: University of Chicago Press, 1954).

[18] Stanley E. Seashore, *Group Cohesiveness in the Industrial Work Group* (Ann Arbor: University of Michigan Survey Research Center, 1954).

1. Informal social groups exist in business and industry. The fact of their existence is important to both management and the worker.

2. Work is a social experience and most workers find satisfaction in membership in social groups. Accordingly, lack of a cohesive work group leads to low morale as expressed in absenteeism, turnover, and malingering.[19]

3. A work group may be cohesive in maintaining low production standards, resisting change, hostility towards supervision and/or other groups, denying membership to newcomers, and demanding strict conformity of its membership. On the other hand, a cohesive work group may have high work standards, accept technological change, be friendly to other groups, cooperate with supervision, and have minimum unwritten codes of conformity for membership.

4. Three factors seem to be important in securing the more desirable kind of cohesive group: leadership of a democratic style rather than an authoritarian or a laissez-faire style,[20] a climate which allows a high degree of participation on the part of the group in decisions affecting its work,[21] and—finally—a type of general organization which permits this kind of group, leadership, and participation in management.

The organization [22]

Not only do business enterprises tend to be dominated by authoritarian personalities, but the management hierarchy by its very nature

[19] Survey Research Center, *The Midwest Study, Report VI, Factors Related to Morale* (Ann Arbor: Michigan Institute for Social Research, 1951).

[20] Thomas Gordon, *Group-Centered Leadership* (Boston: Houghton Mifflin Co., 1955); Carroll L. Shartle, *Executive Performance and Leadership* (New York: Prentice-Hall, 1956); for documentation of research on leadership see Donald A. Laird and Eleanor C. Laird, *The New Psychology for Leadership* (New York: McGraw-Hill, 1956), pp. 22-60, 65-78, 87-94, 113-120, and 175-178.

[21] Brown (see note 14), pp. 186-211; Maier (see note 1), pp. 7-26, 46-49, 93-205; Sherif and Sherif (see note 17), pp. 204-218; Rudolf M. Wittenberg, *The Art of Group Discipline, A Mental Hygiene Approach to Leadership* (New York: Association Press, 1951), pp. 37-100. For documentation of research on democratic group decision-making see Laird and Laird (note 20), pp. 16-17, 83-86, 94-99, 103-108.

[22] Chris Argyris, *Personality and Orgnaization* (New York: Harper, 1957); E. Wight Bakke, *Bonds of Organization, An Appraisal of Corporate Human Relations* (New York: Harper, 1950); Eli Ginsberg and Ewing W. Reilly, *Effecting Change in Large Organizations* (New York: Columbia University Press, 1957); W. H. Scott, *Industrial Leadership and Joint Consultation* (Liverpool: University Press, 1952); Herbert Simon, *Administrative Behavior* (New York: Macmillan, 1957); Fogarty (see note 12), pp. 185-219.

For case studies of organization see Elliott Jaques, *The Changing Culture of a Factory* (New York: Dryden Press, 1952); F. L. W. Richardson, Jr., and Charles R. Walker, *Human Relations in an Expanding Company* (New Haven: Yale Labor and Management Center, 1948).

tends to be authoritarian and the traditional rules of organization contrary to democratic human-relations principles. Consequently, mature individuals with normal personalities are driven away or frustrated by the very character of the business organization. Research indicates that attempts to train supervisors in the democratic style of leadership in order to build effective work teams fails because such a primary group cannot survive in the authoritarian environment of the company as a whole.

The key to industrial peace lies not in "adjusting the worker," in the pre-World War II style, but in adjusting top management. The leadership criteria for good supervision should also be applied to top management, so that an organizational climate will be created in which effective work groups can operate. Corporate organizations following human-relations principles would be decentralized for wide participation in decision-making (because people resist goals that are imposed upon them but become committed to goals set by their group). Their structures would be viewed as interlocking, overlapping groups rather than as pyramids of superior-subordinate relationships between individuals. Accordingly, the traditional problem of delegating authority and responsibility (span of control) would be restated in terms of maintaining communications between groups. And, further, the supervisor's job would be changed from that of giving orders and maintaining quality and quantity standards to that of being spokesman for his group in its relations with other groups and maintaining an effective work team which sets its own goals, solves its own problems, and disciplines its own members.

The culture

Human-relations research reveals that these findings on personality, groups, and organizations are relevant mainly to the culture of the United States, and cannot be applied in wholesale fashion to other cultures. Those raised in authoritarian cultures, with authoritarian families and institutions, do not function effectively in a democratic climate. On the other hand, the United States has a long cultural tradition of democratic values.

Most American institutions, including the home and the public-school system, are democratic; in being authoritarian, business organizations are out of step with the cultural environment. In the past, industry could violate human-relations principles which are in harmony with American culture, so long as not many people were affected and so long as economic coercion was possible; but now, with the growth of industry, more people are affected and full employment and the spread of unionism make economic coercion less workable.[23] Moreover, as William H. Whyte correctly observes, human-relations principles gain much of their impetus from the growth of a middle-management class who are in revolt against the rugged individualists of top management. Finally, industry by its very success in creating wealth has caused men to turn from preoccupation with mere economic survival to a concern with a work environment and way of life which permits a greater degree of self-expression and creativity. (In this connection, human relationists refer to the demand for greater "self-realization.") In brief, our heritage is democratic and there is a general social movement for a more humane, dignified treatment of the individual, and industry is adjusting to this cultural demand.

Human-relations training

Training in human relations has become very popular. Many have relabeled their traditional training programs to capture the popularity of the term. Actually, human-relations training has its own body of theory and teaching method. At the outset, let it be noted that the goal of human-relations training is to bring about the changes in personality, groups, and organizations reviewed in the preceding sections.

Training theory and goals: [24] Training theory in human relations comes from four closely related sources: group dynamics, clinical psychology, progressive education, and the case method as practised by the Harvard Graduate School of Business Administration. A basic proposition is that most, if not all, learning situations take place on an emotional rather than an intellectual level. Accordingly books, lectures, and visual aids that appeal to conscious reason may bring intellectual understanding or even a change in attitude, but will not change *behavior*. Learning by doing means, then, having an emotional experience. From the viewpoint of the clinical psychologist

---

[23] Brown (see note 14), pp. 41-68; Ginsberg and Reilly (see note 22), pp. 18-39; David Riesman, Nathan Glazer, and Reuel Denny, *The Lonely Crowd* (Garden City: Doubleday Anchor, 1956), pp. 32-49, 151-166; Sherif and Sherif (see note 17), pp. 136-156, 159-188; Wittenberg (see note 21), pp. 108-111.

[24] Kenneth D. Benne and Bozidar Muntyah, *Human Relations in Curriculum Change* (New York: Dryden Press, 1951); Gordon (see note 20), pp. 13-45; Laird and Laird (see note 20), pp. 13-15; Maier (see note 1), especially pp. 3-17; Ashley Montagu, *Education and Human Relations* (New York: Grove Press, 1958); Sherif and Sherif (see note 17), pp. 219-229; Thelen (see note 17), pp. 34-91; Irving R. Weschler, Robert Tannenbaum, and John H. Zenger, *Yardsticks for Human Relations Training* (Los Angeles: Institute of Industrial Relations, 1957), pp. 5-11.

the major obstacle to learning is not lack of brain cells but emotional maladjustments which cause the individual to distort, or to close his mind to facts and reality. Accordingly, the learning theory and the theory of therapy for the emotionally disturbed parallel one another.

Although these theories may be challenged as being too inclusive, there is ample evidence that they do apply to problems in human relations. Personality problems prevent individuals from understanding their own difficulties and from being effective in interpersonal relations, and prevent their being sensitive to the needs of others. Lecturing, under these circumstances, increases resistance to change instead of bringing change about. It is no wonder that many executive-development, foreman-training, and salesmanship courses have had little success in actually changing leadership style or sales approach.

Some educational theorists believe that there are subject-matter areas that do not lend themselves to orderly analysis. Any principles that emerge from analytical study are so general as to be of little use to the practitioner in specific situations. Theory only causes the practitioner to be introspective when he should be acting, and a kit of how-to-do-it techniques may be clumsily applied to the specific case.

The goals of human-relationships training programs are:

(a) To gain a better understanding of one's self. To "know one's self" may range from resolving subconscious emotional conflicts to becoming aware of how others react to one's mannerisms.

(b) To broaden and sharpen sensitivity to the feelings of others.

(c) To develop respect for others and to accept individual differences. Reasonable as this may appear, human-relations trainers find that an underlying cause of industrial conflict, often not consciously stated, is conflict between age groups, between male and female, between ethnic groups, or between those with varying physical appearance.

(d) To establish the belief (rejected by authoritarians) that kindness is not a weakness.

(e) To treat all human-relations problems with a clinical approach—to be sympathetic and understanding as if seeking a cure for illness rather than to blame or make accusations as to motives.

From these goals follows a further goal of human-relations training: the overcoming of barriers to interpersonal communication in order to reduce conflict that arises from misunderstanding.

Training techniques: One important training technique in human relations is the unstructured (free-floating) discussion.[25] Group psychotherapists have learned that people with mild emotional difficulties can be helped through group discussion, which avoids the time and expense of psychoanalysis. Although this is not the place to review the theory of group psychotherapy, it should be noted that it has been successful in rehabilitating ex-prisoners of war, alcoholics, the physically handicapped, criminals, and juvenile delinquents. The same theory and techniques apply in sensitivity-training and leadership-development laboratories; group discussion of emotional problems has a therapeutic effect leading to a change in behavior. There is no denying emotional involvement in this learning situation.

A second training technique has resulted from the clinical psychologists' discovery that a patient gains relief, insight, and understanding if allowed to act out situations that seem emotionally disturbing. This therapeutic technique—called "psychodrama"—is applied to industrial situations under the name of role playing.[26] The student is confronted with a variety of typical industrial human-relations problems in which he can play different roles and practice different ways of dealing with the problem. Here again, the student learns no theory or technique, but he becomes more aware of his own style of behavior and its effect on others; he learns to understand others by playing their roles. He learns because he becomes emotionally involved.

Clinical psychologists have provided also a technique of counseling described as permissive, called "nondirective" counseling.[27] The counselor is a sympathetic and understanding listener who mirrors the feelings and thoughts of the patient and responds to his unstated emotions. The patient discovers that he must define his own problem in order to reach a solution by himself. The counselor only offers understanding and encouragement. Again, this is not the place to

---

[25] Warren Bennis and Herbert A. Shepard, "A Theory of Group Development," *Human Relations*, IX, 4 (1956), 415-435; S. H. Foulkes and E. J. Anthony (see note 13); Gordon (see note 20), pp. 112-272; Marvin A. Klemes and Verne J. Kallejian, "The Group Psychotherapist in Industry: A Preventive Approach," *The International Journal of Group Psychotherapy*, V, 1 (1955), 91-98; National Training Laboratory, *Explorations in Human Relations Training* (Washington, 1953), pp. 9-62; Robert Tannenbaum, Verne Kallejian, and Irving R. Weschler, "Training Managers for Leadership," *Personnel*, XXX (1954), 254-260.

[26] Chris Argyris, *Role Playing in Action* (Ithaca: New York State School of Industrial Relations), Bulletin No. 16 (1951); Davis (see note 1), pp. 210-226; Maier (see note 1), pp. 87-190.

[27] Carl R. Rogers, *Client-Centered Therapy* (Boston: Houghton-Mifflin Co., 1951); Davis (see note 1), pp. 383-402; Maier (see note 1), pp. 38-43; Norman R. F. Maier, Allen R. Solem, and Ayesha A. Maier, *Supervisory and Executive Development, A Manual for Role Playing* (New York: Wiley, 1957).

give a detailed account of the theory, but the technique is of therapeutic value.

Since many problems of employees are of the type that can be handled by counselors, human relationists have recommended that counseling be made a service of the personnel department. This recommendation has not taken hold. Some human relationists recommend also that everyone in the management hierarchy be trained in the techniques of nondirective guidance as a method of dealing with human-relations problems. If every supervisor practiced nondirective counseling, he could overcome subconscious resentment to him as an authority figure, improve communications, and deal with the subconscious personal problems underlying many production problems. In short, training in nondirective guidance is training in a leadership style desirable in democratic work-groups.

The study of cases is a fourth technique used in human-relations training.[28] As the Harvard Business School is deeply committed to the case-study approach for the teaching of skills in business administration, it is not surprising that their human-relations training program places emphasis upon case studies in human relations. Rather than to produce a therapeutic or cathartic effect, the Harvard Business School's objective in human-relations training is to sharpen understanding in an area where there are no general rules and no "right answers" by offering the students "concrete" situations which will permit them to develop a feel for human-relations problems.

CRITIQUE OF HUMAN RELATIONS RESEARCH IN INDUSTRY

Scientific validity

A fundamental objection to the conclusions derived from human-relations research is that they are not supported by adequate scientific evidence.[29] In spite of the bulk of the literature pertaining to human relations in industry, conclusions are based primarily upon four studies: the original Hawthorne study, the Harwood Manufacturing Company study, the Glacier Metal Company study (English), and the comparative studies of the University of Michigan Survey Research Center involving the Prudential Life Insurance Company, the Detroit Edison Company, the Baltimore and Ohio Railroad Com-

---

[28] Kenneth R. Andrews, *The Case Method of Teaching Human Relations and Administration* (Cambridge: Harvard University Press, 1953); Malcolm P. McNair (ed.), *The Case Method at the Harvard Business School* (New York: McGraw-Hill, 1954); F. J. Roethlisberger, *Training for Human Relations* (Cambridge: Harvard University Press, 1954).

[29] See Brown (note 14), pp. 83-95, 276-307.

pany, and the International Harvester Company. Except for the Survey Research Center's studies, the findings may be challenged on the grounds that the company environments selected for study are not typical of industry generally.[30] Human relationists have got a lot of mileage out of four studies. The human relationists deny this charge and point to a growing body of research involving a wide variety of industries and work groups. As classics in the human relations field, these four pioneering studies are most frequently cited, since subsequent studies seem to support the original findings.

Another argument to dispute the scientific validity of human-relations studies relates to the nature of their controlled experiments with small groups. First, the experiments involved school children, college psychology classes, and soldiers. The question may be raised (but not conclusively answered) whether work and management groups are comparable to the experimental groups. Second, do findings based upon temporary, *ad hoc* groups apply to groups that have a continuing relationship with one another? Third, it is pointed out that there is no power relationship in the experimental groups other than the "social power" of personalities, whereas economic power is a real factor in most relationships in industry. Fourth, there is a suspicion that experimental groups are so designed as to prove the hypothesis of the experimentor. (It would be interesting to design an experiment to test the hypothesis that autocratic leaders are more effective than democratic leaders, or that democratic, group decision-making will result in greater resistance to change.) In other words, experiments proving one set of propositions in human relations do not necessarily disprove other sets of apparently opposing propositions. To these criticisms human relationists reply that they do the best they can and will welcome suggestions for better ways of studying small-group behavior.

Finally, some critics question the scientific foundations of human relations on the grounds that much of its theoretical underpinning depends upon findings in clinical psychology, which is concerned primarily with treatment rather than scientific research. Thus its main conclusions are based upon "clinical insight" rather than upon controlled experiments.[31] Laymen are often amazed at the ingenuity of clinical psychologists in interpreting complicated, contradictory facts

---

[30] I am indebted to Daniel Bell for this observation.
[31] H. J. Eysenck, *Uses and Abuses of Psychology* (London: Pelican, 1953), pp. 1-18, 221-241; Foulkes and Anthony (see note 13), p. 196; Calvin S. Hall and Gardner Lindzey, *Theories of Personality* (New York: Wiley, 1957), pp. 1-6, 24-25; Homans (see note 17), pp. 15-46.

so as to create a unified picture and a reasonable, though long, chain of causal relationships. Others join the game by analyzing the psychologist rather than analyzing his analysis—which in turn permits the psychologist to analyze his critics rather than their analyses of his analysis. Clinical psychologists readily admit that they practice no exact science comparable to the physical sciences and charge that those who attempt to do this, like the experimental psychologists, are doomed to failure by the very nature of the problem. Rather than attempting to build an exact science, clinical psychologists try to be scientific in their attitude and in their insights. They are impressed by the consistency of patterns relating personality problems to childhood background, occupation, and group membership. Their accumulation of cases which indicate consistent patterns, while not conclusive, is impressive.

Emphasis on group

A second criticism of human-relations theories is the major theme of William H. Whyte's *The Organization Man*.[32] Human relationists are charged with denying individualism—which is part of our pioneer heritage, political liberties, and laissez-faire tradition—through human-relations training (collectivism in progressive education) and by seeking an environment which exalts the group. The discipline of the boss and of the organization, which can be resisted, is replaced by the discipline of the group which becomes internalized as self-discipline. As a consequence the individual loses his personality in stifling conformity to group norms. The point is well taken against those human relationists who claim that the group is more important than the individual, that the individual's values, attitudes, and personality are mere reflections of those of the group, and that his security, happiness, and status are dependent upon his membership in groups.[33] Such a conclusion from research in group behavior leads to the metaphysical proposition that the individual finds his true self and gains his liberty by completely losing himself in a group.

It is improper to describe the entire human-relations movement as anti-individualist, since other human relationists state the problem

---

[32] William H. Whyte, *The Organization Man* (Garden City: Doubleday Anchor, 1957), pp. 3-154.

[33] For development of the anti-conformity criticism see Clark Kerr and Lloyd Fisher, "Plant Sociology: The Elite and the Aborigines," in *Common Frontiers of the Social Sciences*, Mirra Komarovsky (ed.), (Glencoe, Illinois: Free Press, 1957), pp. 281-309; Riesman, *et al.* (see note 23), pp. 34-48, 161-163, 299-314; David Riesman, *Individualism Reconsidered* (Garden City: Doubleday Anchor, 1956), pp. 12-27. For a particularly bitter attack on anti-individualistic tendencies in human relations see Hans Illing, "C. G. Jung on Present Trends in Group Psychotherapy," *Human Relations*, X, 1 (1957), 77-83.

of group conformity in a different perspective. They point out that for most of human history man has been intimately tied to one single group—the family, which integrated economic, religious, social, political, educational, and recreational activity within a single group. (Social anthropologists observe that primitive peoples do not think of themselves as individuals but identify themselves completely with their group.) Modern society, however, permits membership in a great variety of groups having a variety of norms and values, and permitting a greater variety of personality types. Freedom to be an individual, to select or reject groups and their norms, and to belong to many different groups, is a relatively new experience that humans have yet to master. Instead of returning to primitive society, these human relationists favor the development of mature individuals who can take advantage of the freedom offered by industrial society to achieve self-realization.

To an increasing degree, however, work involves "dealing with people, not things," and decisions are made by committees rather than individuals. Liberal human relationists therefore seek to develop groups that are tolerant of a wide range of personalities and permit a large degree of nonconformity [34]—groups which can cooperate on common problems without first demanding proof of kinhip or loyalty oaths.

The nature of conflict

Another criticism, closely related to the conformity issue, is that many human relationists are too preoccupied with the building of group cohesion to reduce conflict and encourage harmony and cooperation.[35] Although it is true that some human relationists equate cooperation with goodness and consider conflict bad and, therefore, conclude that cohesive (harmonious) groups are the best,[36] others hold the more sensible view that only conflict arising from subconscious, nonrational motives and from failure in communications should or can be eliminated. There are enough real, substantive conflicts that groups must resolve. It is normal and healthy for indi-

---

[34] For viewpoints on human relations which respect the individual see Davis (note 1), pp. 57-67; Foulkes and Anthony (note 13), pp. 213-218; and Sherif and Sherif (note 17), p. 38.

[35] For criticism of the human-relations emphasis upon harmony, see Kerr and Fisher (note 33), pp. 300-302; Malcolmn McNair, "What Price Human Relations," *Harvard Business Review*, XXXV, 2 (1957), 20-25; William Gomberg, "The Use of Psychology in Industry," *Management Science*, III, 4 (1957), 358-370; Whyte (note 32), pp. 25-35.

[36] For a more balanced view see Sherif and Sherif (note 17), pp. 146-154; Stagner (note 15), pp. 449-514.

viduals and groups to be faced with a reasonable amount of tension from time to time. Life without conflict (challenge)—even if possible—would be intolerable.

The human relationists' emphasis upon harmony and nonlogical causes of conflict has led to the accusation that they ignore the economic, political, and ideological causes of conflict. They are charged with showing sloppy sentimentality when rigorous logic and analytical ability are required. It is said that human relationists, in both controlled experiments and field studies, have neglected the study of power. Sensitive to criticism, human relationists now are including the consideration of power and conflict in their research.[37]

Group decision-making

Human relationists are also criticized for maintaining the superiority of group decision over individual decision. Some critics contend that only individuals can be creative, that group decisions must necessarily be mediocre, that they are time-consuming, and that they are part of the buck-passing, responsibility-shirking trend of the new generation of managers (brought up on group projects in progressive schools). Experimental evidence on the speed and quality of group decisions and brain-storming is conflicting and inconclusive.[38]

There is of course a danger that groups become so imbued with the goal of cohesion and harmony that they hastily reach an agreement without careful examination of facts, alternatives, or consequences. On the other hand, an increasing number of business decisions must be made in committee. Human relationists state that the curse is not the committee system but the inability of people to conduct themselves in committees so as to reach efficient, high-quality decisions. Human-relations research has yielded many practical suggestions for more effective committee operation.[39]

Although some day it may be proved that individual decision is superior to group decision, it has been established that decisions made by the group are more acceptable to the membership.[40] Subordinates resist decisions handed down by superiors simply because they resent authority. People come to understand a problem better if they have a hand in solving it. They become aware of their sub-

---

[37] For criticisms of group decision-making see Whyte (note 32), pp. 63-65.

[38] For a discussion of research on decision-making see Maier (note 1), pp. 254-377; Warren H. Schmidt and Paul C. Buchanan, *Techniques that Produce Teamwork* (New London: Croft, 1954).

[39] For practical suggestions for effective committee operation see Thelen (note 17), pp. 3-33, 284-297; Schmidt and Buchanan (note 38), especially pp. 26-38.

[40] Davis (see note 1), pp. 270-307; Thelen (see note 17), pp. 245-275.

conscious feelings about the problem in the course of discussion. People are more apt to carry out a decision they have participated in making. The group tends to enforce the carrying out of the decision. There are instances where the acceptance of a decision (as in production standards) is more important than the quality of the decision.

The meaning of democracy

Human relationists are criticized for their loose use of the term "democracy" and their tendency to equate nondirective, permissive leadership with democracy.[41] Just as there are times when our national government requires firm, directive leadership, so too in industry. While the emotionally-disturbed patient may need and appreciate nondirective guidance, it does not necessarily follow that normal well-adjusted students, offspring, spouses, or employees will respond enthusiastically to the teacher, parent, husband, or supervisor who serves only as a sounding board for thoughts and feelings. Child psychologists have learned that children worry over the abnormal eunuch-like behavior of parents who conform to the text book ideal of understanding parents. It would seem that supervisors under appropriate conditions may accurately communicate feelings of righteous indignation to enforce the intellectual content of their message. When to express true feelings of emotion and when to bide one's time is a human-relations problem, but has nothing to do with democracy. Some human relationists have equated democracy with "leaderless groups" where rank disappears and all are equal, while others have held that democracy pertains to political democracy (intergroup relations) and is not relevant to small groups. A middle ground would be that collective bargaining and grievance procedure, supplemented by decentralized management down to the work-group level, increases the degree of industrial democracy.[42]

Mysticism

Some human-relations specialists have, in my opinion, a mystical, anti-intellectual bias in their writing that is not supported by research evidence and which detracts from the positive contributions of the

---

[41] Whyte (see note 32), pp. 25-35, 59-61. For an overall discussion of human relations and democracy see F. K. Berrien and Wendell H. Bash, *Human Relations: Comments and Cases* (New York: Harper, 1957), pp. 214-253.

[42] For a balanced view on industrial democracy see Fred H. Blum, *Toward a Democratic Work Process* (New York: Harper, 1953); Maier (note 1), pp. 204-205, 254-301. For a view rejecting democracy in small groups, see Homans (note 17), pp. 419-422, 432-433, 464-467.

movement.[43] Just as clinical and Gestalt psychologists stress the total personality and total environment—saying that the whole cannot be understood by the analysis of component parts—human relationists speak of "the personality of the group" and "the totality of the group situation." Such a view is supported by some experimental evidence, but it does not follow that the group as a mystical body (Herder's romantic *herrenvolk*) is of greater value than the individual members. A group may be something more than the sum of its individual members, but this does not detract from the worth of the individual, nor imply that life is meaningful only through complete identity with a group.[44]

Similarly, some human relationists speak of the "wisdom of the group" not in the sense that two heads are better than one, but in the sense that the group, as an entity, is the carrier of a primordial wisdom more trustworthy than the intelligence of individuals.[45] The wisdom of the group is sometimes compared to the "wisdom" of the human body in healing itself without conscious effort and to the "wisdom of nature" which operates best when not thrown into disequilibrium by the purposeful activity of man.[46] The group subconscious is held to be the repository of ancestral wisdom.[47] Some human relationists argue that the "logic of feelings" is greater than the "logic of thought"; that "Seeing is believing, but feelings are the truth." [48] The implication is that conscious, intellectual analysis is "obsessive" and will not lead to right answers and that the subconscious, non-rational, emotional aspects of man should be sharpened and given free rein for creative thought.[49]

---

[43] For a reveiw of the mystical approach which is applicable to mysticism in human relations, see Bertrand Russell, *Mysticism and Logic* (Garden City: Doubleday Anchor, 1957), pp. 1-31. The term "mysticism" is used in this article in the sense used by Russell: 1. The belief in a way of wisdom, sudden, penetrating, coercive, which is contrasted with the slow and fallible study by science. 2. The belief in unity and the refusal to admit opposition or division anywhere. 3. The belief that evil is illusory and all reality is good. Mystics among the human relationists do not seem to follow Russell's other characteristic of mysticism: denial of the reality of time.

[44] For criticisms of mysticism in human relations see David Stafford-Clark, *Psychiatry Today* (London: Penguin, 1953), pp. 134-136, 150-154; Eysenck (note 31), pp. 226-227, 233; Foulkes and Anthony (note 13), pp. 39, 196, 235-255; Clara Thompson, "Anti-Intellectualism and the Individual," *Journal of Social Issues*, XI, 3 (1955), 48-50; Rollo May, "A Psychological Approach to Anti-Intellectualism," *Journal of Social Issues*, XI, 3 (1955), 41-47; Wittenberg (note 21), pp. 5-10.

[45] Abraham Zaleznik, *Worker Satisfaction and Development* (Boston: Harvard University Graduate School of Business Administration, 1956), pp. 130-136.

[46] Homans (see note 17), p. 87.

[47] On the concept of the collective subconscious which has influenced some human relationists, see C. G. Jung, *Two Essays on Analytical Psychology* (New York: Meridian, 1956).

[48] Maier (see note 1), preface and p. 17.

[49] Berrien and Bash (see note 41), pp. 54-69.

In contrast, then, to early human relationists who sought an exact science, some human relationists today would argue that scientific attempts to understand interpersonal relations must fail because the impartial observer cannot become emotionally involved. The emotionally-involved participant, however, has subconscious understanding that he cannot explain because he is too involved to be an analytical observer. The implication is that the development of conscious-level, intellectual ability destroys the more primitive, intuitive powers which are actually a more useful means of reaching decisions on interpersonal relations. Although some human relationists seek to eliminate the "hidden agenda" of emotional undercurrents which obstruct task-oriented group activities, others prefer to trust emotional expression, insights, and feelings as the higher level of reality. The study of group behavior necessarily leads to concern with problems of unspoken communications, the main springs of creativity, and suppressed emotions. Human relationists must deal with these problems, and one can, after all, assert that these forces within groups do not lend themselves to scientific analysis without becoming a mystic.

Evangelism

Those human relationists who are closely allied to the mystics see human relations as a revolutionary movement to save Western civilization from impending doom.[50] The doom theme is an old one, going back to the reaction of the Romantic philosophers to the Industrial Revolution. Durkheim, Mayo, Fromm, and Toynbee further developed the imminent doom thesis. To summarize briefly, the doom thesis holds that modern industrial society is out of tune with the basic needs of human beings. The impersonal, market-oriented economy causes mental illness, creating a market-oriented personality type which, in turn, reinforces both the market orientation and the illness. The tyranny of the impersonal forces of an atomistic free market is more devastating to the individual than the tyranny of the group.

The process through which this occurs is circular: individual freedom leads to competition which in turn leads through rapid technological change to job specialization. Job specialization means the

---

[50] For development of the doom thesis and social neurosis see Berrien and Bash (note 41), pp. 3-21, 254-273; Foulkes and Anthony (note 13), pp. 41-44, 253-254; Homans (note 17), pp. 271, 313-368, 454-468; Jung (note 13), pp. 196-244; Karl Menninger, *Man Against Himself* (New York: Harcourt Brace, 1938); Montagu (see note 24), pp. 26-27, 84-85, 90-96, 122-146; J. L. Moreno, *Sociometry, Experimental Method and the Science of Society* (New York: Beacon House, 1951).

loss of meaningful work—which, because life is no longer meaningful, causes abnormal acquisitiveness of material things. This emphasis on the high standard of living leads ultimately to more competition. Modern industry and urban living destroy primary groups, create uncertainty as to status, and cause psychological insecurity. Proof of this condition is found in the rise in suicides, divorce, alcoholism, mental illness, functionless families, functionless older people, and juvenile delinquents, and in the decline in worker membership in community organizations.

For some human relationists, the solution to this state of affairs lies in human-relations metaphysics. It offers a philosophy which will give meaning to life and to work and will end the evils of acquisitiveness and rootlessness by teaching man how to love his fellow man again. This way of life is that of the cohesive social group, which offers love, security, and purposefulness for the individual. Human relations, in this sense, becomes a revolutionary, evangelical sect whose goal is to remake individuals, groups, organizations, and cultures. Those human relationists who reject the emphasis upon harmony, cohesiveness, and belongingness also reject the doom thesis and feel no need to save the world. While not all human relationists have a revolutionary mission to save the world, few of them deny that there appears to be an interrelationship between labor unrest, social disorganization, modern technology, industrial organization and a highly competitive, materialistic market-oriented economy. Human relationists who are concerned with these variables are not necessarily either romanticists or utopians.

Training

Finally, human-relations training is the subject of much criticism. First, it is said that the training cannot be proved to be of value.[51] This is a difficult objection to cope with, for scientific evaluation is hard and the findings are inconclusive. Some studies suggest that human-relations training has no effect or has negative results, and others indicate that human-relations training yields positive results. However, since no one has demanded a scientific evaluation of the effectiveness of liberal-arts and business-administration curricula, it is not reasonable to ask it of the human-relations curriculum.

---

[51] For discussion of the evaluation of human-relations training see Kenneth Andrews, "Is Management Training Effective?" Part I, *Harvard Business Review*, XXXV (1957), No. 1, pp. 85-94 and No. 2, pp. 63-72; Gordon (note 20), pp. 273-302; Floyd C. Mann, "Studying and Creating: A Means to Understanding Social Organization," in *Research in Industrial Human Relations* (note 4), pp. 146-157; Weschler, *et al.*, (see note 24).

The second criticism of human-relations training parallels the current attack on progressive education's life-adjustment courses.[52] It may be true that the businessman's biggest problems both quantitatively and qualitatively are human-relations problems, but somewhere, someone must have some technical competence. It may be true that administrators must be "specialists in the general," get the "big picture," and must "like people," but the details of running the enterprise cannot be left entirely to the engineers, accountants, and lawyers. Instead of skills in group decision-making, which critics call shirking responsibility, it is suggested that skill in individual judgment and self confidence be taught. Rather than developing listening ability, critics urge that future executives learn how to present ideas effectively. Human-relations training, which necessarily stresses insight, sensitivity, a feeling for the situation, and the premise that "there are no *right* answers," cannot evaluate student performance. It may be that education is not meant to be painless or to be fun, but to be hard, rigorous work. As in progressive education, perhaps there should be a balance between what are called "hard" content-oriented courses and "soft" human-relations training courses.

The third criticism of human-relations training relates to the mystical and revolutionary evangelism of human relations.[53] It is doubtful whether one should be taught to trust his hunches rather than logical analysis. Individuals and groups may suffer from Calvinistic inhibitions, but it is questionable whether the free reign of feelings in a revival-camp meeting atmosphere is the solution to the problem. When sensitivity becomes sentimentality and self-awareness becomes self-pity, training in human relations is not developing mature individuals. There is a fine line between being conscious of one's motives and reactions, and being so preoccupied with one's self as to become ineffectively self-conscious. Although the revolutionist stresses belongingness as a virtue to be learned in training laboratories, group therapists consider this to be the adolescent stage in group development in which individuals use the group as an emotional crutch. Instead of encouraging this development, some human relationists work toward "group maturity" in which individuals can

---

[52] For points of view on "life adjustment" versus "narrow specialism," see Robert Browne, "Winds of Doctrine," *Adult Education*, III, 2 (1958); McNair (note 28), pp. 25-28; Montagu (note 24), pp. 9-12; Riesman, *Lonely Crowd* (see note 23), pp. 162, 275-336.

[53] For criticisms of the anti-intellectual element in human relations training see Theodore Brumeld, "Anti-Intellectualism in Education," *Journal of Social Issues*, II, 3 (1955), 36-40; Riesman (see note 23), 224-236; Whyte (see note 32), pp. 56, 86-110.

preserve "self" while effectively participating in groups from which they can withdraw to be emotionally independent.[54]

Finally, some critics, raising the question of whether human relations can be or should be taught, argue that the seriously maladjusted need clinical treatment which should not be financed by industry or schools of business administration. For those who would benefit from human-relations training, on the other hand, it is claimed that the course is too brief, that personality change cannot be brought about by a one-semester course or a two-week seminar. To put it briefly, good interpersonal relations are a way of life in which a person must be reared.[55]

In response to these criticisms, human relationists reply that training programs are for normal individuals and that there is experimental evidence that the training, admittedly brief, does improve both on-the-job and marital relations. Human-relations training supplements content-oriented courses and is not intended to replace the established curriculum. Industry and the professional schools in universities include human-relations training as part of the general training program because it is a valuable part of the overall education of the executive, supervisor, administrator, educator, and social worker. Finally, critics of human-relations training cannot escape the fact that traditional teaching methods are not highly effective. Human relationists argue that teachers of subject matter courses will borrow human-relations training methods, as is now being done in business conferences and conventions, to improve the learning process.

EVALUATION

Industrial human relations has two main trends that are so interwoven as to cause confusion and controversy. The first is an evangelical, missionary framework of thinking. Essentially, this is a revolutionary view which sees civilization as on the brink of destruction; those who hold this view believe it to be their duty to save the world. Just as scientific management elevated a few techniques of industrial engineering into a movement aimed at revolutionizing the structure of society, some human relationists have raised the study of primary groups to the level of a utopian ideology. In the scientific-management movement the perfection of tools of measurement yielded natural laws of cooperation which, in turn, led to a technocrat's

---

[54] Foulkes and Anthony (see note 13), pp. 205-210, 227, 242-249.
[55] Gomberg (see note 35), pp. 362-363; McNair (see note 28), pp. 18, 30.

utopia. Human-relations cultists seek cooperation through therapy, "revolution by infiltration" into industry and government via human-relations training courses, and believe that the "withering away" of the state will follow from the decentralizing of authority to leader-less groups.

The cult of human relations, however, is not as modest as psychiatry, whose practitioners admit that the answers to philosophical questions regarding the meaning of life cannot be found in psychiatry. Beyond the treatment of emotional difficulties, the evangelists among the human relationists offer a philosophy of life in mystical union with the group. Where the psychiatrist expects to find a degree of self-sufficiency, tension, conflict, and loneliness in the life of a normal individual, the cultist sees these as defects which create mental illness. From the psychiatric point of view, human-relations training by the cultists may hurt rather than help emotional cripples. It may even be that enthusiastic participation in human-relations alumni clubs is a sign of immaturity rather than a vision of a new era of peace and love—an indication of retarded development rather than of rebirth.

The mystical human relationists draw anti-intellectual conclusions from their interpretation of psychoanalysis. They emphasize the subconscious, the nonrational, the instinctive, and distrust conscious, rational, analytical processes. Moreover, it is the *collective* subconscious that is the source of wisdom, superior decisions, truth, and reality. Science is too objective to discover the truth. Reality is an emotional experience that can be felt but cannot be understood. According to the mystics, rational compartmentalization of knowledge obscures the truth whereas the Gestalt of the group unconscious will discover truth.

The second major trend in the movement puts human relations in its proper perspective. This is the application to industry of concepts and research in the social sciences. In this respect, human relations has made a contribution in providing a general framework for the analysis of industrial relations.

Human relations research has provided us with valuable information about informal groups, organization, leadership, and training. Along with time-and-motion study, this body of information is being applied to the problems of the business enterprise. Human relations has made a contribution by increasing our awareness of the emotional, nonrational, subconscious aspects of interpersonal relations.

These unconscious forces are not limited to those in mental institutions but constitute problems with which all must deal. Furthermore, human-relations studies have made clear that these difficulties are not entirely the consequences of the birth trauma or of rejecting mothers. The nature of the business organization, its leadership, or groups within industry may themselves cause emotional disturbances which are harmful to business as well as to individuals. Finally, the human-relations approach raises questions concerning our industrial, urban culture as a cause of individual, group, and organizational maladjustments. Although mental health is not an exclusive measure of the worth of a culture, it is a fruitful one worthy of further exploration. Followers of this trend within the human-relations movement, instead of wallowing in the nonlogical, would raise subconscious motivation to the conscious level so that irrational conflicts could be eliminated.

As indicated in the first section of this paper, the approach of early human relationists had a management-oriented flavor which was opposed by those labor-relations specialists who saw in collective bargaining a democratic industrial government that both preserved the dignity of the individual and made large-scale business enterprise workable in a political democracy. These same specialists attack as incompatible with individual freedom, collective bargaining, and democracy, that part of the present-day human-relations movement which stresses harmony through conformity.

The other major trend in human relations, however, complements the concept of mature, democratic industrial government. Research evidence supporting greater participation in decision-making by all employees, and favoring a less authoritarian organizational structure and style of supervision, is encouraging to those with a democratic philosophy.

Human relations in industry brings into sharper focus but does not give final answers to questions of industrial democracy, power relationships, conformity, and efficiency. Unless human-relations research comes up with new experiments and fresh ideas there will be no general theory of human relations. As indicated elsewhere in this paper there are gaps in the general theory, which is suggestive rather than conclusive. Current research supports ideas already developed and as such tends to be repetitious. Unless major developments take place, human relations, like scientific management, may be reaching a dead end. In brief, there is one trend in the human-relations movement that, in its extreme form, is a mystical revolutionary cult and may be harmful to both individuals and organizations. Another offers a better understanding of groups and organizations, and, although its framework appears to be limited, it supports viewpoints found in the concept of mature industrial government.

Questions

1. Summarize the major concepts that Knowles presents as vital to human relations.
2. List and explain the criticisms he makes of human relations.
3. What does Knowles feel the future of industrial human relations to be?
4. What trends have led to the development of human relations theory and practice as we know it today?
5. What were Elton Mayo's contributions to this movement?

IS HUMAN RELATIONS OBSOLETE? *

William V. Machaver

In recent years, a new call to arms has been sounded, heralding a crusade dedicated to debunking and belittling the human relations philosophy in industry. The crusaders, men of unquestioned reputation and integrity, have voiced their objections in such well-known periodicals as the *Harvard Business Review* and *Fortune* magazine, and in such widely read books as *The Organization Man*.

As I understand it, the human relations philosophy has been attacked on three fronts. The critics of human relations claim (1) that little or nothing has been accomplished by the adherents of this philosophy; (2) that the human relations philosophy has been supported by simpletons, incompetents, or, even worse, manipulative charlatans; and (3) that the proponents of human relations throttle individuality and encourage blind conformity by worshipping at the altar of organization.

It has always been my understanding (supported, I believe, by reputable industrialists, scholars, and leaders in general) that the antithesis of organization is anarchy, and that in any society people require a set of values or mores—laws and principles of conduct—in order to live together in harmony, with mutual respect and understanding. I now discover that what our industrial society *really* needs is more rugged individualism; that organizational concepts are stifling; and that it is necessary for the survival and growth of American industry to insure each individual the freedom to fulfill his own desires, needs, and ambitious, *regardless* of the impact of his efforts toward such fulfillment upon the organization.

Teamwork or tooth-and-claw?

To evaluate these criticisms intelligently, let us review some of the basic human relations concepts as they have been developed and practiced in industry. I have always thought that the major responsibilities of any manager are to lead and direct people, to encourage cooperative effort and high levels of productivity, to inspire respect for and confidence in the company, and to provide satisfaction for individual employees. Toward the attainment of these objectives,

---

* From *Problems and Practices in Industrial Relations*, American Management Association Report No. 16, 1958, pp. 7-13. Copyright, 1958, by the American Management Association. Reprinted by permission of the American Management Association.

managers have been encouraged to meet together in order to discuss problems of organization, economics, leadership, and other related subjects. In such training conferences, a body of information based on the experience of successful executives and the findings of scholars in psychology, sociology, and economics is presented for comment and discussion by the group. In addition, the managers participating analyze their own problems, exchange ideas, and search for more effective ways of motivating and supervising their people. It has been my experience that, through such conferences, each manager develops a greater body of knowledge and skill upon which he may draw in discharging his daily responsibilities; that each selects for use those ideas and tools which he finds most effective; that each applies what he has learned in a manner shaped largely by his own personality and his own needs; and, finally, that the organization as a whole profits.

But now I realize how "misguided" I have been. According to our critics, such meetings have stifled creativity and initiative, and encouraged men to become robots and conformists, stripped of courage and individuality. Yet, if these are truly the effects of group education and group discussion, how can we justify the existence of our colleges, our universities, or, in fact, our entire public school system?

Another fundamental concept to which many of us have subscribed over the years is that broader participation in developing policies and making decisions instills in people a feeling of belonging—of mutual confidence and understanding. Our acceptance of this concept is based on the belief that when people are well informed—when they understand the objectives and plans of the business—they are more likely to apply themselves willingly and enthusiastically to their jobs. We have also encouraged managers and supervisors to work together in committees and project groups, believing that such face-to-face contact permits them to achieve a better insight into one another's problems and, through moderation and compromise, to arrive at decisions which meet the company's need for efficient operation.

I now discover that we have been badly "mistaken" in these beliefs; apparently we have succeeded only in destroying independence and initiative. According to the new crusaders, it is healthy to have department heads and executives fight it out. This develops character; it gives men a sense of pride and accomplishment. The fact that this inter-departmental strife causes some unhappiness, friction, and dissatisfaction is relatively unimportant. The fact that the operations and processes of the company are bogged down while rugged individualists wear each other out is likewise not significant. The only really significant thing is the need to encourage individualism.

Let me quote some passages from *The Organization Man*, by William H. Whyte, Jr., one of the most articulate of the new crusaders. At one point, Mr. Whyte describes a sales training program (specifically, the Vick Chemical Company's School of Applied Merchandising) in which he participated in the late 1930's, and which he apparently feels is vastly superior to the modern training program predicated upon the human relations concept:

> The company sent its head training supervisor to see if anything could be salvaged. After several days with me, this old veteran of the road told me he knew what was the matter. It wasn't so much my routine, wretched as this was. It was my state of mind. "Fella," he told me, "You will never sell anybody anything until you learn one simple thing. The man on the other side of the counter is the *enemy*."
>
> It was a gladiators' school we were in. Selling may be no less competitive now, but in the Vick program, strife was honored far more openly than today's climate would permit. Combat was the ideal—combat with the dealer, combat with the "chiseling competitors," and combat with each other. There was some talk about "the team," but it was highly abstract. Our success depended entirely on beating our fellow students, and while we got along when we met for occasional sales meetings the camaraderie was quite extracurricular.[1]

And here is another illuminating passage describing the motivation and thinking of our top executives today:

> Fundamentally, however, they [modern business executives] are motivated by the Protestant Ethic. In the sense that younger men conceive the quality, they are not well rounded for the simple reason that, if they had been well rounded, they wouldn't have gotten to be executives in the first place. Officially, the organizations they run deify cooperation; in actuality, they remain places where success still comes to those motivated essentially by the old individualistic, competitive drives.[2]

Leadership or management by consent?

Many successful executives have come to feel that it is necessary and wise to review the work of their subordinates periodically in order to obtain an objective and comprehensive appraisal of their performance and abilities. This need has been accepted on the basis of three major assumptions: (1) that men work better when they know where they stand; (2) that the organization will operate more effectively if a man and his boss have a common understanding of his

---

[1] William H. Whyte, Jr., *The Organization Man* (New York: Simon and Schuster, 1956), p. 117.
[2] *Ibid.*, p. 141.

rseponsibilities and the standard of performance he is expected to achieve; and (3) that, in this way, men can be helped to make their maximum contribution to the company and to make the fullest use of their abilities and skills. Successful executives have said that such periodic review and appraisal stimulates and encourages subordinates to realize their full potentials, and thus results in increased work satisfaction and morale.

But here again, it seems, we have "blundered." We are being autocratic, telling subordinates what is expected of them. We are frustrating our management and supervisory people, destroying their creativity, confining them within narrow limits. Apparently, each manager or supervisor should encourage his subordinates to decide what must be done and how well, so that each individual can set his own goals with a minimum of restriction. Consider the following brief quotation from an article appearing in the *Harvard Business Review*:

> I have sought to show that the conventional approach to perform-
> ance appraisal stands condemned as a personnel method. It places the
> manager in the untenable position of judging the personal worth of
> his subordinates and of acting on these judgments. No manager pos-
> sesses, nor could he acquire, the skill necessary to carry out this respon-
> sibility effectively. Few would even be willing to accept it if they were
> fully aware of the implications involved. . . . A sounder approach, which
> places the major responsibility on the subordinate for establishing per-
> formance goals and appraising progress toward them, avoids the major
> weakness of the old plan and benefits the organization by stimulating
> the development of the subordinate.[3]

I used to think that leaders were supposed to lead. Apparently the function of the modern manager is to consult and consent.

In this regard, let me mention another "grave error" that we have committed. Many of us have devoted a large part of our careers to studying the problems of organization and human relationships. We have tried to help managers develop more effective skills in directing and leading their people. Just as the line executive depends upon specialists to advise and assist him on problems relating to finance, costs, engineering, research, purchasing, and the like, it appeared logical that he should turn to men qualified in the personnel profession for assistance in handling his human responsibilities. Again, however, we have been mistaken. Another crusader, again in the *Harvard Business Review*, has enlightened us on this point as follows:

---

[3] Douglas McGregor, "An Uneasy Look at Performance Appraisal," *Harvard Business Review*, Vol. 35, No. 3 (May-June, 1957), p. 94.

As soon as a man consciously undertakes to practice human relations, one of several bad consequences is almost inevitable. Consciously trying to practice human relations is like consciously trying to be a gentleman. If you have to think about it, insincerity creeps in and personal integrity moves out. With some this leads by a short step to the somewhat cynical point of view which students in Administrative Practices courses have described by coining the verb "ad prac," meaning "to manipulate people for one's own ends." A less deliberate but perhaps even more dangerous consequence may be the development of a yen for managing other people's lives, always, of course, with the most excellent intentions. . . . Hence I am disturbed about the consequences to business management of human relations blown up into pseudoscience—with a special vocabulary and with special practitioners and experts. In fact, to my mind there is something almost sinister about the very term "human relations practitioner" though I am sure that all sincere devotees of human relations would vigorously disclaim any such imputation.[4]

Thus the new crusader regards the professional personnel man.

"Rugged individualism" reconsidered

Such statements as those we have considered above raise some interesting questions. If an executive with no special training and no professional assistance undertakes the development of his people, to what degree will he unconsciously force them to be so many carbon copies of himself? We know that helping people to improve and grow is a very delicate problem, requiring a great deal of knowledge and skill. Is it not possible that an untrained executive with the best of intentions can do a great deal of harm unwittingly?

Critics talk about "ineffective training," "conformity," "superficiality," and "manipulation." Exactly what practices, policies, activities, and programs are they criticizing? If I were to describe the work being done by many of my colleagues, I should say that they were assisting managers to guide and train their subordinates to help each individual employee perform at his maximum capacity and attain his full potential growth, in order that he may make his maximum contribution to the success of the enterprise. Further, I should say that we are trying to develop an approach by which men and women in industry may work together in harmony to achieve the goals of the organization in such a way as to provide for the fullest possible job satisfaction on the part of every member of the organization.

These, of course, are merely words. If we are to evaluate and criticize intelligently, we must be specific and concrete. Constructive

---

[4] Malcolm P. McNair, "What Price Human Relations " *Harvard Business Review*, Vol. 35, No. 2 (March-April, 1957), p. 28.

criticism is not only desirable but necessary for progress. Negative, sarcastic criticism creates confusion and doubt, and does immeasurable harm to the vast majority of constructive, valuable human relations activities that have been of great benefit to all in our industrial society, employees and managers alike.

In many of the recent attacks on human relations, I seem to detect a plaintive cry for a return to the ruthless "rugged individualism" of the past. It is true that the rugged individualist has made some great contributions to industry and to society in general; yet the industrial history of the past quarter of a century vividly reveals the shortcomings of rugged individualism as a general business philosophy.

I have quoted at some length from the new crusaders; for a brief glance at the other side of the coin, I should like to quote a passage from the book *But*, written by one of our great business leaders, Robert W. Johnson, chairman of the board of Johnson & Johnson:

> It is important to note that for many years we have chosen our management from men who have been educated as technicians and specialists. Unfortunately, the graduates of our great engineering schools and the products of our American universities were not equally well educated in the great science of human engineering. Recently it has become apparent that the greatest technical skill is worth little unless men and women can be persuaded to carry out the decisions essential to making that skill effective. We are now discovering that a scientific and technological understanding of a subject does not of itself develop or produce ability to lead large groups of people into enthusiastic day-in and day-out response. This means that we must have new managers—managers not only skilled in the techniques but equally well grounded in the field of human relations.[5]

Some fundamental concepts

In order to view human relations in its proper perspective and to recognize its contribution to successful business operation, it is necessary to understand some fundamental concepts:

> An understanding of human relations provides an atmosphere in which each individual is encouraged to express himself freely and forthrightly.
> Human relations does not mean mollycoddling, paternalism, or universal happiness. It means that the business executive must understand human behavior and human motivation in order to provide the leadership necessary to achieve the goals of the enterprise.
> Human relations is not the whole management job. Every executive must be concerned with markets, competition, costs, technology, and a

5 Robert W. Johnson, *But* (Princeton, N. J.: Princeton University Press, 1945).

host of other vital factors. Human relations, however, is a necessary and critical responsibility of the business leader.

There is no essential conflict between an acceptance of human relations and the need to be firm, to maintain the highest standards of work performance, and to make realistic practical decisions.

Men who are truly concerned with understanding human relations inspire creative thinking, encourage difference of opinion and independence of thought, and by this very process discourage conformity.

It is my firm belief that the survival of our entire economic system, our whole way of life, depends largely upon the leadership provided by American management, now and in the future. Sixty-five million Americans demand a measure of dignity and satisfaction in their daily work. They want to live in an organization where there is goodwill and teamwork, mutual respect and understanding; and they look to their management, their leadership, to provide this atmosphere.

To reply quite briefly to those who decry conformity in organization and yearn longingly for unfettered, unrestricted individualism, I would simply answer the question posed long ago by Cain: *Yes, I am my brother's keeper.*

QUESTIONS

1. Why are some people today being overly critical of human relations philosophy?
2. What is "management by consent"?
3. How can individualism and conformity be reconciled in the business firm of today?
4. State the fundamental concepts of human relations listed in this article.
5. Contrast this article with Schoen's. In what ways are they alike? How do they differ?

GENERAL QUESTIONS ON PART 10

1. List and evaluate the many criticisms of human relations principles presented in this chapter.
2. What are the major strong points of these principles?
3. How does the practice of human relations relate itself to executive success?
4. Compare McNair's article with Schoen's. In what ways do they agree? How do they differ?
5. What do you think the future is for industrial human relations?
6. Why do you think the human relations movement in industry has become so important in today's economy?
7. What attitudes toward human relations should an executive adopt?

8. Of what importance is the group in human relations theory?
9. Do you feel that human relations will ever become an exact science? Why or why not?
10. What were some of the historical landmarks in the growth of human relations in industry?

BIBLIOGRAPHY FOR PART 10

Articles

CALHOON, R. P. "Personnel Administration and Human Relations: Which One, or Both?", *Office Executive*, Vol. 34. No, 6 (June, 1959), pp. 47-48.

COLLIER, ABRAM T. "Dilemma in Human Relations," *Harvard Business Review* (September-October, 1955), pp. 59-67.

GORDON, R. M. "Management or Human Relations," *Personnel*, Vol. 34, No. 3 (November-December, 1957), pp. 51-54.

HOPPER, J. R. "Some Critical Reflections on the New Paternalism," *Personnel*, Vol. 34, No. 3 (November-December, 1957), pp. 31-34.

McGREGOR, DOUGLAS. "Changing Patterns in Human Relations," *Management Record* (September, 1950), pp. 322-323, 366-368.

ODIORNE, G. A. "The Status of Human Relations in Industry," *Personnel Administration* (September, 1954), pp. 20-24.

SCHOENFELD, ERWIN. "Authoritarian Management: A Reviving Concept?", *Personnel*, Vol. 36, No. 1 (January-February, 1959), pp. 21-24.

SPATES, THOMAS G., PETER F. DRUCKER and CHRIS ARGYRIS. "Human Relations: Where Do We Stand Today?", *Management Record*, Vol. 21, No. 3 (March, 1959), pp. 78-84.

Books

ARGYRIS, C. *Personality and Organization*. New York: Harper and Brothers, 1957.

The Executive Life. Garden city, N. Y.: Doubleday and Company, Inc., 1956.

BARNARD, C. *The Functions of the Executive*. Cambridge, Mass.: Harvard University Press, 1938.

DRUCKER, P. *The Practice of Management*. New York: Harper and Brothers, 1954.

McFARLAND, D. *Management: Principles and Practices*. New York: The Macmillan Company, 1958.

INDEX